C0-ALB-079

Peace Education Evaluation: Learning from Experience and Exploring Prospects

A Volume in:
Peace Education

Series Editors
Jing Lin, Edward Brantmeier, and Ian Harris

Peace Education

Series Editors:

Dr. Jing Lin
University of Maryland, College of Education

Dr. Edward Brantmeier
James Madison University

Dr. Ian Harris
University of Wisconsin—Milwaukee

Peace Education Evaluation: Learning from Experience and Exploring Prospects

Edited by

Celina Del Felice
Aaron Karako
Andria Wisler

INFORMATION AGE PUBLISHING, INC.
Charlotte, NC • www.infoagepub.com

Library of Congress Cataloging-in-Publication Data

Peace education evaluation : learning from experience and exploring prospects / edited by Celina Del Felice, Aaron Karako, Andria Wisler.
    pages cm. -- (Peace education)
    ISBN 978-1-62396-973-8 (pbk.) -- ISBN 978-1-62396-974-5 (hardcover) -- ISBN 978-1-62396-975-2 (ebook) 1. Peace--Study and teaching--Evaluation. 2. Peace--Study and teaching--Methodology. I. Del Felice, Celina, editor of compilation. II. Karako, Aaron, editor of compilation. III. Wisler, Andria, editor of compilation.
    JZ5534.P4272 2015
    303.6'6071--dc23
                                        2014050216

Copyright © 2015 Information Age Publishing Inc.

All rights reserved. No part of this publication may be reproduced, stored in a retrieval system, or transmitted, in any form or by any means, electronic, mechanical, photo-copying, microfilming, recording or otherwise, without written permission from the publisher.

Printed in the United States of America

CONTENTS

v

PART 3

IDEAS FOR EXPERIMENTATION AND "NEXT MOVES"

ACKNOWLEDGEMENTS

Our acknowledgements are many and thus we upfront offer our apologies to anyone we may have forgotten from this list. This volume has witnessed two marriages (Andria, Aaron) three pregnancies and births (Andria's son, Jackson and Celina's daughters, Isabel and Silvia), an MA (Aaron in Conflict Resolution from Georgetown University), a PhD (Celina in Development Studies from Radboud University), transcontinental moves (Celina), new jobs (all three of us) and countless late nights and early mornings. Thus, we are thankful for our partners, children, families, co-workers, students and professors, for their interest in this volume and support of its success but more so for their faith in us to complete the task. Celina offers her appreciation for her husband, Pablo and parents, Nora and Héctor, whose support, trust and sharing of reproductive tasks makes her work outside home possible. Aaron's gratitude is extended especially to his wife Emma. Andria thanks her team at the Center for Social Justice at Georgetown University for giving her time, just interrupted enough, to make the final preparations of the volume for publication, and her husband, Bill. Andria and Celina offer thanks to the extremely special village of Stadt Schlaining, Austria and the European Peace University for first bringing them together in 2005. Andria would also like to thank the Masters in Conflict Resolution program at Georgetown University for providing her with Aaron as a research assistant in 2011.

Peace Education Evaluation: Learning from Experience and Exploring Prospects,
pages ix–x.
Copyright © 2015 by Information Age Publishing
All rights of reproduction in any form reserved.

Our appreciation for the authors of these twenty chapters is deep. They all worked through draft after draft with us but more important have committed fully to peace education in diverse corners of the world in numerous inspiring ways. We have learned so much more than we ever imagined by delving with them into their new concepts, data, and challenges as they do this challenging and significant work for peace education. Their patience as we completed the volume was a gift and we look forward to working with them all in the future in this field.

We would also like to thank the visionaries of this Peace Education series with Information Age Publishing—Ian Harris, Jing Lin, and Edward Brantmeier. These three advocates and leaders of peace education have created this necessary outlet for peace educators, evaluators and researchers to publish on the field, practice and philosophy about which they care so deeply.

The three of us have all been blessed to be teachers and have had amazing, challenging, and risk-taking students who have pushed us further in our thinking, practice, and everything in between when it comes to education. Moreover, we have had the gift of exceptional teachers who have molded us into the peace educators we are today and whom we strive to become. Celina is deeply thankful to Ma. Esther Rodriguez de Bianchini, Alicia Cabezudo, Maria Kooijman, Nikolai Firjubin, Augustin Rusekampunzi, Marks and Margaret McAvity. Andria's profound gratitude is extended to educators Connie Bush, Mary Claire Ryan, Fran Vavrus, Betty Reardon, and Kathleen Maas Weigert. Aaron offers his sincere thanks to Craig Zelizer, Adina Friedman, Nevzer Stacey, and innumerable informal educators fostering a more peaceable world.

PEACE EDUCATION EVALUATION

Learning from Experience and Exploring Prospects

Federico Mayor Zaragoza

For thoughts to change the world
the life of their author must first change.
He must become an example."

—Albert Camus in Carnets

A system for evaluating education is appropriate to the extent that it reflects changes brought forth in participants' daily conduct and lives. It is the degree of "integration" of knowledge so that learning can be as relevant as possible. Approaching education evaluation from this perspective emerges from Paulo Freire's contributions: permanent education for peace for all, formal and informal, for our whole lives.

Few authors have addressed the challenges of evaluation of such an encompassing peace education approach. Monclús and Sabán (1999) are among those few who analyze education for peace from psychological and socio-cultural per-

Peace Education Evaluation: Learning from Experience and Exploring Prospects,
pages xi–xiv.
Copyright © 2015 by Information Age Publishing
All rights of reproduction in any form reserved. **xi**

spectives and offer useful reflections and tools on evaluation. For example, elements for planning peace education, defining objectives in relation to the objectives of the "Declaration on Education for Peace, Human Rights and Democracy" (1995), and defining indicators, such as tolerance indicators.

Planning and evaluation tools are necessary to reflect on progress made toward achieving ambitious but vital goals–fundamentally changing education to achieve sustainable peace. The Hague Appeal for Peace[1] is the framework from which the Global Campaign for Peace Education emerges and a deep shared awareness of this task is evident in the text of the appeal: "It is time to create the conditions in which the primary aim of the United Nations, 'to save succeeding generations from the scourge of war', can be realized". It is necessary to provide the radically different education that those being educated for "peace, nonviolence and international cooperation" deserve.

As indicated in the basic Campaign Statement, educators agreed that "a culture of peace will be achieved when citizens of the world understand global problems; have the skills to resolve conflict constructively; know and live by international standards of human rights, gender and racial equality; appreciate cultural diversity; and respect the integrity of the Earth. Such learning cannot be achieved without international, sustainable and systematic education for peace".

Any evaluation approach necessarily will strive to understand how values are shaped among participants. Betty Reardon identifies the core and other overarching peace values to be cultivated by education for a culture of peace. The values and the corresponding capacities are: environmental sustainability, ecological awareness, cultural integrity, diversity, cultural proficiency, human solidarity, global citizenship, social responsibility, conflict competency, gender equality and gender sensitivity, reconciliation, peace-keeping and disarmament. These values and capacities are attainable with civil society awareness, commitment and involvement.

Learning from experience! I would like to underscore this subtitle, because experience–particularly as longevity increases–provides the best source of knowledge and practice, but is unfortunately the least-explored "road map". Of particular interest are "students' *transformative* learning" and "tools and lessons learned in measuring *attitudinal and behavior change*".

In the early 1990s I invited the then President of the European Commission, Jacques Delors, to preside over a world commission of educators, teacher trainers and philosophers aiming to illuminate roads to the future. The result of their report on education for the 21st century was published under the title "Learning: The Treasure Within,"[2] and outlines the four common pillars that sustain all "free and responsible" educated people: learning to know; learning to do; learning to be; and learning to live together. I added "learning to endeavor," because just as important as "daring to know" (*sapere aude*) is to know when to risk expressing one's own thoughts, ideas, discoveries and inventions.

A very significant aspect of the success of any educational process is ongoing teacher training so that both teachers and their students can make appropriate use of new educational tools, while at the same time ensuring that mind prevails over method.

In effect, it is necessary to underscore that the quality of education must be judged in terms of learning. "If education doesn't prepare us for something specific, it is merely mechanically 'going through the motions'... Without peace education,"quoting María Zambrano,[3] "there can be no peace. If leaders can make peace, only education can ensure that peace endures... Peace must arise in the hearts of men, where education finds fertile terrain, its most specific action. Without peace education there can be no lasting peace. Once more, it is our teachers who are responsible, although not they alone, for the world's future."

Since the beginning of time, human beings have been invisible, anonymous, unmoving and fearful spectators. Subjected, accepting their destinies as inevitable, enduring–as they still do today–the most bitter and tragic circumstances to the point of, at the height of social injustice, having to see each day how thousands die of hunger, many of them children under five years old, as if they were the "collateral effects" of the well-being of just a few. Then as now they choose to look the other way, while at the same time allowing security to prevail over peace, and enormous outlays in weapons and military spending. "If you want peace, prepare for war" was the perverse principle that has been put into practice, practically without exception, by the few men who have exercised absolute power throughout history.

But at present, at last, we can now express ourselves. For the last two or three decades, changes have been taking place that are progressively opening our perspectives to light and hope. Today, thanks to modern communications and information technology, people are no longer invisible and can convey their thoughts and opinions. This capacity for citizen participation is extraordinarily relevant for strengthening both democracy and peace. Today we are acquiring a global conscience after centuries of intellectual and territorial confinement. Citizens today are already acquainted with the world in general and are able to appreciate what they have and learn first-hand about the needs of others. Brotherhood is becoming an ethical requirement. Moreover, for the first time in history, women are finding themselves on the threshold of power; power that they exercise not mimetically, but rather with their inherently distinctive traits.

The great transitions, so long dreamed of, are now possible:

- Transition from an economy of speculation, delocalized production and war to an economy of sustainable global human development.
- From a culture of imposition, domination and violence to a culture of dialogue, conciliation, alliance and peace.
- In essence, from force to words; the great historical turning point is awaiting on the horizon.

Thanks to the popular outcry that is now feasible, in a few years the mobilization of society will radically change our priorities for action worldwide: food, clean water, health services, environmental protection, education, justice and peace. This historic new beginning is led by the educational, scientific and artistic communities–by intellectuals. Juan José Tamayo[4] wrote that "Intellectuals destabilize the established order, awaken lethargic consciences and revolutionize unquestioning minds." It is essential to underscore this because the immense power of the media seeks to neutralize the social expectations and demands of many of our youth, converting them into indifferent witnesses rather than participants. Jesús Massip warned us of the danger of becoming distracted, downtrodden and indistinguishable: "Time will return / to find us / mindless and docile."

In promoting the evaluation of education for peace, the contribution of the authors and editors of this volume is essential so that this current era of change may become the change of era that the majority of the inhabitants of the earth so desire. Human rights can never be fully exercised except in a genuinely democratic context. Democracy is the source of justice. And justice is the source of peace.

I am sure that the efforts of the authors and editors will receive all of the compensation they deserve.

NOTES

1.   Reardon, B. A., & Cabezudo, A. (2002). *Learning to abolish war: Teaching toward a culture of peace. book 1. Rationale for and approaches to peace education.* New York, USA: The Hague Appeal for Peace.

2.   Delors, J. (1996). *La educación encierra un tesoro.* Madrid, Spain: UNESCO.

3.   Zambrano, M. (1996). La educación para la paz. *Revista Educación, 309,* 151–159.

4.   Tamayo, J. J. (2013). *Cincuenta intelectuales para una conciencia crítica.* Barcelona, Spain: Fragmenta Editorial.

INTRODUCTION

Practice and research of peace education has grown in the recent years as shown by a steadily increasing number of publications, programs, events, and funding mechanisms filling the field. The oft cited central point of departure for the peace education community is the belief in education as a valuable tool for decreasing the use of violence in conflict and building cultures of positive peace hallmarked by the presence of just and equitable structures. As described in a report for the United Nations sponsored Decade for a Culture of Peace for the Children of the World which gathered information on the peace education programming of more than 1,000 organizations, the experiences of peace education participants, researchers, and practitioners are numerous and varied, and showcase a wide spectrum of creativity, concerns, and actions.

Educators and organizations implementing and executing peace education activities, however, often lack the appropriate tools and capacities for evaluation and thus pay scant regard to this necessary step in successful program management. Reasons for this inattention are related to the perceived urgency to prioritize new and more action in the context of scarce financial and human resources, notwithstanding violence or conflict; the lack of skills and time to indulge in a thorough evaluative strategy; and the absence of institutional incentives and support. Overall, evaluation seems currently demand-driven by donors who emphasize accounting and does not result from the internal insistence for learning from

Peace Education Evaluation: Learning from Experience and Exploring Prospects,
pages xv–xvi.
Copyright © 2015 by Information Age Publishing
All rights of reproduction in any form reserved.   **xv**

experience and past programming, though in this volume we find evidence that this may be changing.

Program evaluation is often considered an added burden to already over-tasked educators and programmers who are unaware of the incentives and added value of successful assessment techniques. Further, peace education practitioners are typically faced with forcing evaluation frameworks, techniques, and norms that are standardized for traditional education programs and venues. Together, these conditions create an unfavorable environment in which evaluation becomes under-valued, de-prioritized, and mythologized for its laboriousness and drudgery.

After working in difficult contexts, including societies in and after violent conflict, peace education practitioners too easily question their own "results." Simultaneously, given the current context of international development assistance and budget cuts, organizations are pressed to show outcomes of their activities. A cost-benefit analysis has become an important feature of the traditional education assessment as budget reductions are accompanied with increased expectations (e.g. McDonnell et al., 2003, p. 18). The obligation to show results presents a plethora of challenges as observed by Bourn (2010):

> One reason often given is the lack of evidence that it is having an impact.... [A] strong political and ideological agenda often creates the problem that evaluation, and sometimes even research, is being looked at through the lens of development and not in terms of learning outcomes and educational criteria.... Development Education evaluation is framed within models of measuring progress in terms of changes in behaviour, action taken, numbers of people attending events, or sales of materials. Whilst these are important surely a more appropriate approach would be to build into any programme ways to capture and assess what the participants have learnt, and how to continuously reflect upon this learning.

Bourn's analysis of the difficulties of assessment confronting the field of development education can be easily transferred to peace education and composed the grounding reasons for this edited volume project.

SURVEYING THE LANDSCAPE OF EVALUATION IN PEACE EDUCATION

We felt it was necessary to survey the field and examine the existing evaluation practices of peace educators in order to identify needs and respond to gaps. Our literature review revealed three noteworthy points supporting the publication of an edited volume on the proposed inquiry: the dearth of examples and models of educational evaluation in peace education; the set of common challenges facing peace educators and evaluators despite the wide spectrum of peace education programs and contexts; and the need for peace education specific evaluation frameworks and tools. Ian Harris' (2003) presentation at the American Education Research Association (AERA) conference offered the original inspiration for this project when we—Celina and Andria—first met and discussed such a project in

2006. In response to the question, "What can and can't be provided from peace education evaluations," Harris describes in part the need for evaluation so that educators can have a real sense of what their efforts might achieve. This information can contribute to curbing the sense of pessimism, frustration, and burnout that can plague peace educators from sustaining their commitment. This project arises in response to Harris' call for peace educators to be aware of the limitations of their work, not to expect structural change to occur instantly, and to relish in the possibility of a slow, ripple effect change that is not easy, but certainly necessary.

First, there are few well-documented cases of a thorough evaluation of a peace education program and, similarly, only one well-known existing meta-evaluation of assessment practices currently comprising the field. A meta-evaluation is designated as a way to "build an evaluation framework that is broad, flexible, rigorous, and theoretically sound" (Ashton, 2004). Of the programs and curricula that have been evaluated (typically school-based conflict resolution education and social-psychological research on contact hypothesis), few assessments were conducted in ways that identified reasons for success or that were conducive for the transfer of good practices (Ashton, 2004). Ashton (2007) recognizes that less work has been done on evaluating peace education programs than on researching what constitutes peace education, and evaluations that have been completed lack consistency.

Second, the literature revealed a widely agreed upon set of common challenges facing peace educators and evaluators in terms of the tools available for program assessment. For example, peace education programs often assert the promise of both short-term and long-term impact, the latter being incredibly difficult to predict, gauge, or follow in practical terms (Ashton, 2004). Salomon (2006) writes about the changes to the periphery and core of a person's or group's behaviors and attitudes, with observable changes made to the periphery but more important lifelong transformation occurring at the core. Evaluation is often considered elusive for peace education, given the ephemeral nature of transformation: is it enough for a participant to undergo the process and "transform," or must one transform to a predetermined endpoint?

Finally, there is need for specific tools and approaches for evaluation that take into genuine consideration the objectives and formats of peace education programs. Salomon (2004) reminds us that not all conflicts are alike, and not all peace education efforts have the same objective; it is important to note the various contexts and goals of peace education, which he delineates as focusing on inter-group relations, in opposition to conflict resolution education, which pertains to interpersonal relations (Salomon, 2004). Although many participants and peace educators offer a qualified "yes" to whether their attitudes and mindsets have changed post-program, there is concern about the unknown effects of peace programs on actions and behaviors, as much of what peace education programs hope to accomplish over time and through sustained effort can be "undone" in an instant, given the volatile nature of politics, relationships, and structural realities.

The results of a program are highly dependent on the individual and often merely reinforce existing attitudes.

OBJECTIVES OF THE VOLUME

The literature review upheld our contention that tools must be developed to address the existing lacuna, and that the literature and experience of related fields, such as development education, civic education, and comparative and international education, must be utilized for comparison, adaptation, and inspiration. Assessing outcomes of peace education requires specific redesign of existing evaluation tools applied in the social sciences and in the fields of management, public policy, educational evaluation, and development cooperation, to name a few. Outcomes should be examined from the perspectives of:

- Education: How and to what extent do participants learn skills, change their attitudes and acquire knowledge?
- Efficacy: How does learning contribute to social change? What action do participants take due to their new learning and experiences?
- Pedagogy: How does learning and evaluation adopt principles of peace education?

This volume has three inter-related objectives that correspond with the triadic structure of the volume. The first objective is to offer a critical reflection on theoretical and methodological issues regarding evaluation applied to peace educational interventions and programming. The overarching questions of the nature of peace and the principles guiding peace education, as well as governing theories and assumptions of change, transformation, and complexity are explored.

The second objective is to study and reflect on existing evaluation practices of peace educators to identify what needs related to evaluation persist among practitioners. Promising practices are presented from peace education programming in different settings (formal and non-formal education), within various groups (e.g. children, youth, teachers) and among diverse cultural contexts.

The third objective is to propose ideas of evaluation, novel techniques for experimentation, and creative adaptation of tools from related fields. This section offers both pragmatic and philosophical substance to peace educators' "next moves" and inspires the agenda for continued exploration and innovation.

Overall, the volume aspires to bring evaluation to the minds, budgets, and action plans of peace educators, schools, and organizations around the world. We purport that evaluation, similar to peace pedagogy and peace research methodologies, provides another constructive venue through which peace educators can model the spirit and action of collaboration, democratic transparency, and nonviolent means that guide the field. Even as peace education becomes increasingly more vital around the world, it simultaneously needs a stronger case to assure its implementation and sustainability; the active pursuit of data and commitment to shared evaluation resources will strengthen the quality of future peace education programming as well as build a wider net of support for the field.

AUDIENCE AND CONTRIBUTIONS

The audience for this edited volume encompasses the many varied actors in the field of peace education. Teachers and practitioners of peace education will learn from peers from around the world and find practical tools that they can adapt and incorporate to their work. Non-formal educators working for development non-governmental organizations (NGOs), youth organizations, and international organizations with peace education programming will find the volume a source of reflection on their own often implicit theoretical assumptions of change. In this way, they can reflect on what "success" means for them and the people with and for whom they work. The volume will also resonate with grant foundation administrators and funding managers who support peace education efforts; they will find a plethora of examples that demonstrate the potential and legitimacy of non-traditional assessment tools. Policy makers considering peace education programs in their districts or countries will find that the volume offers a more thorough understanding of the kind of results that can be expected from peace education. They will be able to reflect on the kind of demands that they place on actors and analyse the best ways to support peace education programs. The text will enrich the work of researchers on educational policy and peacebuilding who strive to document the diversity of conflict transformation strategies available for a spectrum of environments. Lastly, students of peace and conflict studies, international educational development, comparative and international education, social work, and research methods among other fields will be attracted by up-to-date evidence that problematizes what "works" in different contexts and forms of peace education as well as novel formulas and transformative solutions.

Although information on good practices and tools are offered, emphasis has been placed on the need for each organization and group to define its own evaluation practice and tools, respond to external demands, and be prepared to engage in constructive in-depth dialogue about various visions of "success." Overall, the volume aspires to be a communal source of reflection, inspiration, and action for those active in peace education to innovate and incorporate evaluation into daily practice and future plans.

STRUCTURE OF THE BOOK

Following these three objectives, this volume is organised in three parts. The first section, "Critical Reflections," is composed of five chapters, all of which stress the need for evaluation frameworks and methodologies to reflect the principles of peace education, namely dialogue, participation and empowerment. In the first chapter, Hakim Williams warns about the incongruence of some evaluation approaches with the epistemological logic and ethics of peace education. He proposes the concept of peaceableness as a potential way for improving peace education's evaluability and argues for its potential through a compelling example of a youth participatory evaluation. Williams' chapter is followed by a chapter by Werner Wintersteiner, who argues for a more complex conceptual understanding of peace education, to include creating and practicing a culture of peace. Education, and its evaluation, should emphasize the capacities of learners. Rather than controlling evaluation, Wintersteiner forwards a notion of empowering evaluation, and writes: "we need to develop genuine ways of evaluation for such a special field as peace education, based on ethical principles." He offers by example an evaluation experience of a peace education teacher training programme in Europe utilizing Bourdieu's concept of "habitus" and on the practice of action research in which there are different moments of data gathering, reflection and action. His chapter inspires a culture of feedback and evaluation in which the learners become active participants and not objects of control.

Following in the third chapter, Helga Stokes and Rodney Hopson examine the importance of adopting a cultural lens in peace education evaluation. Evaluation is not value neutral, thus evaluators need to be aware of power differentials and cultural diversity in their methodological choices, and in the design and implementation of the evaluation activities in general. In the final chapter of this first section, Cheryl Woelk argues that language must be given attention in the evaluation of peace education. She supports her argumentation with an analysis of how language is inextricably linked to power and how attitudes are shaped and ultimately, human action is given meaning through language. Her contribution is important given the fact that many international peace education programs use a foreign language for most participants, most commonly English, which in turn has important implications for defining concepts and identities. Based on research and educational experiences, she proposes detailed methods to take into account language in peace education evaluation practice.

The second section, under the heading "Taking Stock and Learning from Experiences," is the most voluminous with a total of eleven chapters covering evaluation experiences taking place in the contexts of primary and secondary schools (2), universities (3), civil society organisations (5) and donors (1). The section begins with chapter five by Erin Dunlevy and Christina Procter, teachers at the High School for Arts, Imagination and Inquiry, a public school in New York City where staff have committed to peace education as an active, pedagogical framework, specifically through the use of restorative practices. Their chapter sheds light on the understanding of schools as systems of groups, thus transcending current modes of school-based evaluation. In chapter six, Roberta and Warren Heydenberk attend to bullying and its consequences in order to enable practitioners to design relevant evaluation strategies and valid measures to assess anti-bullying program effectiveness. Next, in chapter seven, Antonia Mandry moves the discussion towards higher education in Turkey, and identifies three peace education approaches since the founding of the Turkish republic: citizenship education, human rights education and social responsibility education. She tells a rich story about a Sabanci University course called the Civic Involvement Project (CIP), and the formal and informal methods to evaluate its impacts. In chapter eight, Rajashree Srinivasan keeps this focus on tertiary education and highlights the reflective evaluation work of an elementary teacher education program in India. Following in chapter nine, Zulfiya Tursunova offers a descriptive analysis of an evaluation utilizing personal narrative in its methodology of a European graduate peace and conflict studies program. H.B. Danesh broadens the evaluative scope from one school to a country-wide system of education in chapter ten, in which he describes the conceptual framework and activities of the *Education for Peace* program in Bosnia-Herzegovina as well as the evaluation plan and outcomes of its implementation in schools thus far.

With chapter eleven, Ned Lazarus shifts section two's focus to civil society organizations and non-formal education programs, with key findings from his evaluation of the prominent peace education Seeds of Peace (SOP) program. Lazarus moves beyond conceptualizing impact in terms of short-term attitudinal changes among peace education participants, to tracing what he understands as *peacebuilding activity* among SOP graduates over a period of 8-15 years, in order to measure the endurance of the program's impacts. In the following chapter, authors Daniel Wehrenfennig, Daniel Brunstetter, and Johanna Solomon examine the Olive Tree Initiative at the University of California, Irvine, a diverse student, faculty and community program promoting dialogue and understanding about the Israeli-Palestinian conflict through experiential learning. This chapter sheds light on some of the challenges that the program's directors faced as they sought to evaluate the program in varied qualitative and quantitative ways.

The next two chapters attend to evaluations of peace education programs of and for youth. In chapter thirteen, Lillian Solheim, Imke van der Velde, Meghann Villanueva, Eefje van Esch—all from the United Network of Young Peacebuilders (UNOY) in the Netherlands—attend to the reputation that evaluation has as difficult and time-consuming for youth workers in peace education. The authors reflect on the evaluation practices of non-formal peace education initiatives for youth, in order to show that evaluation can result in opportunities for learning and further development. Susan Armitage's chapter on IREX's Youth Theater for Peace programs in Central Asia showcases the quantifiable effects of potentially transformative experiences for youth in this peace education program. Finally, chapter fifteen prioritizes the role of the donors in post-conflict reconciliation processes; utilizing a comparison of two evaluation studies in Southern Sudan and Rwanda, Ruerd Ruben offers implications for program design and policy evaluation.

The third section of the volume, "Ideas for Experimentation and Next Moves," consists of four chapters. The first, chapter sixteen by Cécile Barbeito and Johanna Ospina, focuses on evaluation of peace education initiatives at a structural level, through tackling some of the methodological challenges of creating and using national indicators of peace education. Following this chapter, Karen Ross proposes the use of a social movement lens to assess peace education; she presents alternative approaches to expand what success looks like in peace education, as well as to broaden the conception of the term *impact*. The eighteenth chapter by Nagmeh Yazdanpanah proposes the idea that peace education is inherently evaluative. Based on an analysis of the writings of Paulo Freire, Mikhail Bakhtin and Mahatma Ghandi, she offers the concept of a pedagogy of addressivity. Chapter nineteen by Thomas de Hoop and Annette Brown explores the use of counterfactual analyses in the evaluation of peace education programs. And, in the penultimate chapter, Maria Lucía Uribe Torres emphasizes the potential of teachers as role-models and key actors of evaluation.

The book concludes with a short synthesis indicating the main ideas emerging from the volume, pointing to a clear convergence towards common points for further reflection and future action.

Overall, the insights generated in this volume deepen and widen our understanding of the imperative for thoughtful, sustained and creative peace education evaluation and point to the wealth of human energy dedicated to this endeavor in the pursuit of a more just and peaceful world. By using a transdisciplinary lens and scope of voice, we hope that these chapters speak to the numerous actors significantly engaged in the success of this necessary venture—from policy makers to practitioners to participants. Taken together, the chapters provide compelling insights and helpful information for a diverse readership who is concerned with the state of our world, committed to the power of education to promote a culture of peace, and interested in tools for self-reflective practice and evaluation.

WORKS CITED

Ashton, C. (2004, March). *The case for peace education evaluation as a strategy for supporting sustainability.* Paper presented at the Annual Meeting of the International Studies Association in Montreal, Canada.

Ashton, C. (2007, Fall). Using theory of change to enhance peace education evaluation." *Conflict Resolution Quarterly 25(1):* 39–53.

Bourn, D. (2010, January). "Moving From Evaluation to Research in Development Education." *Irish Newsletter for Development,* Issue 25. Accessed 15 February 2011 at: http://comhlamh.org/assets/files/pdfs/compass/index25WEB(1).pdf.

Harris, I. (2003, April). "Peace education evaluation." Paper presented at the Annual Meeting of the American Educational Research Association in Chicago, Illinois.

McDonnell, I., Lecomte, H.-B. S., & Wegimont, L. (2003). *Public opinion research, global education and development co-operation reform: In search of a virtuous circle,* Working Paper No. 222, OECD.

Salomon, G. (2004). Does peace education make a difference in the context of an intractable conflict? *Peace and Conflict: Journal of Peace Psychology 10*(3), 257–274.

Salomon, G. (2006). Does peace education *really* make a difference? *Peace and Conflict: Journal of Peace Psychology 12*(1), 37–48.

PART 1
CRITICAL REFLECTIONS

CHAPTER 1

PEACEABLENESS AS RAISON D'ÊTRE, PROCESS, AND EVALUATION

Hakim Mohandas Amani Williams

INTRODUCTION

Pressure emanates from many constituent groups interested in increased accountability for peace education activities; they want to know if peace education is indeed accomplishing what it purports (Harris, 2003). Within donor countries there are mounting calls for increased accountability of investments made for peacebuilding efforts in other countries (Stave, 2011). While most stakeholders would acknowledge the utility of peace education evaluations, there is a concern that pressure from donors and policymakers may foster exaggerated expectations of evaluations, thereby impelling the measurement of more short-term results of peace efforts to the exclusion of a focus on more longer-term processes (Fischer, 2009). Since peace education is concerned with negative and, especially with, positive peace (Reardon, 1988), "drive-by," donor-driven evaluations could engender some not insignificant issues, the least of which is the reductionist risk

Peace Education Evaluation: Learning from Experience and Exploring Prospects, pages 3–18.
Copyright © 2015 by Information Age Publishing
All rights of reproduction in any form reserved.

of hyper-instrumentalizing peace education efforts, thereby diminishing the panoramic reach of peace education itself.

This chapter intends to shed light on the incongruence of positivist evaluation with the epistemological and ontological logics of peace education. To provide sufficient, solution-oriented contrast, the latter part of the chapter will then present the case for the types of evaluation methodologies commensurate with critical peace education. The chapter is organized into various subgroups, which are tagged by several subheadings. I discuss how the lofty vision of peace education is its inspiration and its curse, as well as its potential incongruence with the logic of positivist evaluation. I also address the challenges that the discipline of evaluation itself faces and present the concept of peaceableness as a potential way for augmenting peace education's evaluability. I conclude with participative evaluative methodologies as well as a brief example from personal research experience to highlight the need for such methodologies, especially when working with less empowered and marginalized communities.

DEFINITION

Peace education unabashedly posits rather lofty objectives. It is concerned not only with the cessation of violence, otherwise called negative peace, but is transfixed on positive peace, the dismantling of structural violence. Peace education "is generally defined as educational policy, planning, pedagogy, and practice that can provide learners—in any setting—with the skills and values to work towards comprehensive peace" (Bajaj, 2008, p. 1), and it often includes "the areas of human rights education, development education, environmental education, disarmament education and conflict resolution education" (p. 2). In sum, peace education's raison d'être is the rebuke of the current global culture of war and violence, and the germination and sustainable flourishing of a global culture of peace (Reardon, 1988).

ADMITTED PAUCITY OF EVALUATION

There are obviously several perspectives on how to engender and sustain a global culture of peace; some of these perspectives are not without their discontents. Defining peace in itself is quite contentious; ergo, its operationalization and measurement will perhaps be as doubly controversial. Because peace efforts are often neither linear nor fully predictable (Stave, 2011), measuring long-term effects becomes extremely complicated (Harris, 2003). While the moral imperative of peace education's necessity seems apparent, the "peace research community is also interested in peace education evaluation to understand how educational efforts contribute to reducing violence and building peaceful societies" (Harris, 2003, p. 6). There has been quite a bit of work done in demarcating the definitional and descriptive parameters of peace education, but "less work has been done on evaluating its [peace education's] effectiveness" (Ashton, 2007, p. 41). Research by Nevo & Brem (2002) support this claim; they analyzed about three hundred peace education related items over a 1981–2000 literature span and found that approximately only a third featured "elements of effectiveness evaluation," prompting them to infer that

> [t]his figure by itself is a testimony to the relative scarcity of evaluation studies in [Peace Education]. It is quite clear that hundreds of programs are initiated and operated around the globe, at any particular period, without being subjected to any act of empirical validation (p. 275).

Indeed, the moral heft of peace education seems inadequate in satiating the clamoring calls from the donor community for more accountability of peace efforts. These calls for increased accountability are not exclusive to peace education, but to many neighboring fields and efforts: peacebuilding, development work, aid assistance, peace mediation, and conflict resolution. Peace education can learn much from the evaluation challenges and growth that have taken place in the field of peacebuilding, just as peacebuilding has been encouraged to learn from international development (Blum, 2011). For example, within peacebuilding, the Local Capacities for Peace Project brought together varied development NGOs working in conflict areas to determine the effect of aid. Simultaneously, the International Development Research Centre developed the Peace and Conflict Impact Assessment (PCIA) methodology, which "focused on assessing the actual impact of a particular project in a conflict context before, during and after its implementation" (Lanz et al., 2008, p. 8). However, these efforts have been subsequently critiqued for being too linear in measuring complex, non-linear real life processes. Peace mediation provides yet another example of this challenge; peace mediators have said that "the process of mediation is often more important than its measurable outcomes and a linear evaluation framework does not sufficiently capture these dynamics" (Lanz et al., 2008, p. 11). In part, this applies to peace education as well, although the capacity to measure gains in knowledge, skills, and attitudes does exist. Peace education thus represents a good place to combine both process-oriented and outcome-oriented approaches (Nevo & Brem, 2002).

Accountability, per se, is not necessarily the issue at hand, for peace efforts stand to gain through increased accountability. Peace efforts, including those of peace education, are often in avid pursuit of sustainable peace or peace writ large—a peace that is lasting and stable. The enterprise of engendering sustainable peace, however, takes years, even decades, with regressions and digressions along the way. It is this non-linearity and long-term aspect that excessively and frustratingly complicates the evaluability of some peace efforts. This commingling of increased pressure for evaluations with the pursuits of a rather amorphous phenomenon called peace highlights the evaluative challenges that peace education faces.

LOFTY VISION: INSPIRATION *AND* CURSE

Because peace education is centered on comprehensive peace (Reardon, 1988)—that is, it is not only concerned with the cessation of violence (negative peace), but also the dismantling of structural violence—peace educators aspire to transcend the educating-about-peace paradigm, and to embrace the educating-*for*-peace paradigm (Reardon, 1997). This is an educative venture that involves the dispensation of knowledges and skills, and the consequent fostering of attitudinal and behavioral changes: a panoramic vision indeed. But peace education's lofty reach is also its challenge: "debates continue on the undefined boundaries of the field, its shifting terminology and focuses, and the varied philosophies it exhibits" (Fitzduff & Jean, 2011, p. 8). As regards evaluating knowledges and skills, one can conduct pre—and post-intervention comparisons, but what is far more complicated is evaluating "the affective, dispositional, and behavioral outcomes" (Harris, 2003, p. 16). While the need for peace education programs has been demonstrated by large organizations such as UNICEF, UNESCO, the Soros Foundation, and the Ford Foundation, there does not exist a persuasive body of evidentiary support for the impact or effectiveness of said programs (Ashton, 2007). Additionally, longitudinal studies, necessitated by an educative project that has long-term goals, are sorely lacking (Harris, 2003). The prospect of many longitudinal studies seems dim in light of the fact of stringent resources. There are risks to simply applying generalized evaluative norms to peace education without a critical interrogation of the potential problems.

INCONGRUENCE WITH THE LOGIC
OF POSITIVIST EVALUATION

The discipline of evaluation has indeed come a long way; the interpretive and postmodern paradigms have left their indelible intellectual footprints. However, the ensuing upheaval is anything but settled; there are still ongoing and rigorous debates within the discipline of evaluation among the adherents of the positivist and of the postmodernist approaches, and those in between.

The positivist camp asserts that the evaluator's credibility rests on her professional distance from the evaluand, and that her independence is vital for procuring any credence for the evaluation that she will eventually produce. That some evaluations can engender policy shifts is testimony to the caliber of the evaluations themselves and augments the overall professionalization of the field of evaluation. The positivist approach is undergirded by certain beliefs and assumptions that are differentiated from those of the interpretive approach. The former views reality as single; that the "knower and known are independent"; that "generalizations are possible, and are time—and context-free"; that "there are real causes, that precede or are simultaneous with their effects"; that "inquiry is value-free"; and that predicting phenomena is possible by objectively investigating them (Adapted from Lincoln & Guba, 1985, as cited in Neufeldt, 2007, p. 7). Conversely, those within the interpretivist camp believe that "realities are socially constructed"; that "there can be multiple constructions and realities"; that "knower and known are interactive and inseparable"; that "only time—and context-bound working hypotheses are possible"; that "all entities are in a state of mutual simultaneous shaping, so that it is impossible to distinguish causes from effects"; that "inquiry is value-bound"; that "research is a type of practice that affects the context and can be a deliberate intervention strategy", and that this approach can offer penetratingly deep understandings of phenomena (Adapted from Lincoln & Guba, 1985, as cited in Neufeldt, 2007, p. 7). These distinctions emanate from starkly different epistemological orientations and thus, depending on which is employed, can engender wide-ranging ontological ramifications. The choice of approach can profoundly influence the design of the evaluation, the methodologies that are utilized, the types of data sought and subsequently collected, what the final products are, and how they are presented and ultimately used.

> Nevertheless, it is without a doubt that evaluations are essential: In terms of the evolution of the human race, evaluation is possibly the most important activity that has allowed us to evolve, develop, improve things, and survive in an ever-changing environment. Every time we try something new—a farming method, a manufacturing process, a medical treatment, a social change program, a new management team, a policy or strategy, or a new information system—it is important to consider its value. Is it better than what we had before? Is it better than the other options we might have chosen? How else might it be improved to push it to the next level? What did we learn from trying it out? (Davidson, 2005, p. 1)

Despite the potentially noteworthy benefits derived from evaluations, for many persons and organizations, evaluation connotes "judgment": "the systematic determination of the quality or value of something" (Scriven, 1991, as cited in Davidson, 2005, p. 1). Here, the 'systematic' aspect is not the source of consternation for many program implementers, but rather the adjudicative component: ascertaining the "merit" or "worth." However, through the positivist lens, and for the sake of 'objective' distance between the evaluator and the evaluand, there exists an attendant risk of over-objectifying the evaluand. This objectivist arrangement between the evaluator and evaluand features a form of power disequilibrium that is incongruent with the elemental postulates of peace education. It is not dissimilar from the traditionalist teacher/student dyad, upon which Freire (2003) rendered a stinging critique because of the power imbalance therein, whereby the student is objectified in this intensely hierarchized relationship:

> [T]he methods for evaluating "knowledge", the distance between the teacher and the taught...everything in this ready-to-wear approach serves to obviate thinking. ...Based on a mechanistic, static, naturalized, spatialized view of consciousness, it transforms students into receiving objects. It attempts to control thinking and action, leads women and men to adjust to the world....(Freire, 2003, pp. 76–77).

This hierarchical relationship between evaluator and evaluand is exacerbated by the ever-increasing pressures for accountability from donors. Donors (including agencies, governments, policy makers, and tax payers, especially in this era of global fiscal austerity), lobby for reliable evaluations (Fischer, 2009). Although these robust calls for accountability are a "relatively recent development," such as in the field of peacebuilding, (Kawano-Chiu, 2011, p. 7), large government aid agencies are quite explicit in seeking to "obtain maximum value for money in [their] development assistance" (DANIDA, 2005, p. 3). As a result, evaluations can be quite high stakes for many implementers, with the risk of losing funding altogether (Kawano-Chiu, 2011). These top-down pressures, coupled, with the objectifyingly surveilling gaze of the evaluator upon the evaluand, may not be empowering in the sense that peace education promulgates, essentially representing a dissonance between some aspects of the logic of evaluation and aid agencies and that of peace education.

Evaluation and Its Own Discontents

In a world where donors want programs to demonstrate quick, measurable results, evaluations are increasingly being fashioned by a business ethic (Church, 2011). This business ethic has helped usher in an era of "managing for results" into the discipline of evaluation. No longer is the focus merely on deliverables but now on impact assessment (Conlin & Stirrat, 2008). In international development, agencies aim to boost donor aid coordination, (DANIDA, 2005; Lawson, 2010), with specific interest in the alignment and harmonization of aid objectives. However, harmonization among the "often contrasting systems of evaluation employed by donors and partner countries" has remained a problem (Conlin & Stirrat, 2008, p. 196; Lawson, 2010). This harmonization has witnessed a corollary focus on sector wide approaches (SWAPs), and a concomitant diminution of interest in disparate projects. While, many laud SWAPs, it ought to be noted that their use has made the task of evaluators more difficult:

> The sector approach addresses a wide range of activities—from reforming the regulations in the sector to improving physical infrastructure and supporting training and capacity development. ...increasingly donor assistance takes the form of pooled support of both financial and technical assistance. Thus the role of individual donors becomes much less clear and the evaluator's task much more complex. But this is not the only problem facing today's evaluators. The shift to SWAPs has only exacerbated the problem of attribution in that it is increasingly difficult to disentangle the results of donor assistance from the overall processes at work in any particular sector. ...As far as the evaluator is concerned, the challenge of reaching firm conclusions as to attribution of results to inputs and the chain of causation becomes more and more difficult (Conlin & Stirrat, 2008, p. 196).

This issue of causal attribution is especially pertinent to peace education since peace education programs are usually focused on long-term and macro effects. At the macro level, some studies have indicated that quantifiably discerning impacts of individual interventions is near impossible (Fischer, 2009):

> Evaluations which combine qualitative and quantitative procedures for data collection can offer important entry points, but generally only identify impacts achieved in the immediate project context. The expectation that beyond this evaluations can draw well-found conclusions about the benefits and impact of individual measures on the bigger picture, i.e. peace writ large, in a crisis region is not just overly ambitious (given that evaluations are usually limited in resources and timeframes): it is also questionable from a (funding) policy perspective. Peace actors engaging in overzealous debate about this issue should be clear that they are thus raising excessive and unrealistic expectations among donors about the demonstrability of impacts—expectations which can never be fulfilled, at least not within the framework of the short term evaluations that the donors usually fund (p. 91).

Difficulties in gauging causal linkages between interventions and outcomes therefore present the field of peace education with a challenge that cannot go unaddressed: evaluability.

EVALUABILITY: A CORE CHALLENGE

Apart from having insufficient evaluations conducted within the field of peace education, a related issue thus becomes evaluability. If the goals and objectives of a peace education program are so extravagant or unclear and not matched to impact, then the program can be deemed un-evaluable. Since the moral imperative of peace efforts offers an insufficient buffer against calls for increased evaluation of peace education programs, un-evaluability of peace programs only exacerbates the challenges that this field faces. It is vital that peace education learn from neighboring fields, such as peacebuilding, international development, peace mediation, and conflict resolution, to ascertain potential ways forward, as those fields are also subject to the challenges of overclaiming and evaluability (Kawano-Chiu, 2011). A starting point, as proffered by noted peace educator Ian Harris (2003), is for peace education to avoid overclaiming:

> Bringing peace to this world is a complex activity that ranges in scope from political leaders negotiating arms agreements to lovers amicably settling disputes. Influencing community and school-based politics seems outside the classroom realm. Peace educators have certain cognitive and affective goals for their students, but they should avoid extravagant claims that their efforts will stop violence. Teachers many want their students to become aware of the role of violence in their lives, but awareness does not necessarily lead to action. What happens as a result of a particular instructional act is quite outside a teacher's control. The activities of educators do not seem so much to be changing political structures as creating both a belief system and a way of life that embraces peace. Building such beliefs and skills may be a necessary condition for building a culture of peace (p. 24).

An evaluable direction for peace education would seem to be more realistic goal-setting, with more measureable discrete objectives. There is a risk to these efforts to 'downsize' lofty aims and goals, as has been witnessed in peacebuilding efforts. As a result of the efforts to not overclaim the expectations with evaluations, there is "a clear danger now that evaluations are mainly targeted at 'measuring' short-term results of peace activities and thus tend to ignore longer-term processes, changes in the political context and consequently the needs for the change of strategies" (Fischer, 2009, p. 90). The emergent critique is that these short-term foci are tantamount to "technical peacemaking rather than conflict transformation…which are not robust or sustained enough to address major problems of structural inequalities" (Fitzduff & Jean, 2011, p. 21). Additionally, research has shown that discrete, measureable interventions may have limited long-lasting effects; for example, "in diversity workshops, new perceptions of and more positive attitudes toward the outgroup may have little or no effect on intergroup behavior because of countervailing pressures from other determinants of behavior" (McCauley, 2002, p. 252). This presents an obvious conundrum for peace education: its concern for structural violence complicates its evaluability, and in attempts to become more evaluable, it may end up reductionistically aiming for short-term interventions that may not contribute to a sustainable peace.

AUGMENTING EVALUABILITY

A balance is needed, one that simultaneously upholds the principles of peace education and allows the field to gain increased legitimacy. Part of this augmented legitimacy is indeed evaluability. What may boost the evaluability of some peace education programs is not aiming to create a culture of peace, but perhaps aiming to foster more peaceableness in human beings. As Harris (2003) notes, "peace educators may not be changing the social structures that support violence, but they are attempting to build a peace consciousness that is a necessary condition for creating a more peaceful world", and "in teaching about peace and violence they (teachers) take one small step towards creating a less violent world, and they should appreciate the importance of that step" (p. 20). As opposed to a culture of peace, it is perhaps more evaluable to measure a posture of peaceableness in students:

> Teachers can control both the information given students and the manner in which it is presented, peace educators can evaluate at the end of educational programs whether students have acquired knowledge about the roots of violence and strategies for peace. The effectiveness of peace education, therefore, cannot be judged by whether it brings peace to the world, but rather by the effects it has upon students' thought patterns, attitudes, behaviors, values, and knowledge stock (Harris, 2003, p. 19).

Measuring peaceableness may sound especially unquantifable to a positivist evaluator, but, much to the benefit of peace education, the discipline of evaluation has undergone, and continues to endure, major epistemological renovations, with far-ranging theoretical and methodological implications. Additionally, the global atmosphere around peacebuilding and international development seems to be embracing an ethic of mutual transparency and partnership. These changes bode well for enlarged spaces in which peace efforts can enjoy increasingly differentiated ways of being.

SHIFTS IN DONOR LOGIC

These enlarged spaces, in which peace efforts may not have to monolithically follow a narrow trajectory, are occurring because of shifts within donor agencies in terms of their thinking about their relationship with aid recipients and program/ project implementers. Large donor agencies are recognizing the necessity of conceptualizing the efficacy of aid within a framework of 'mutually committing' partnerships (DANIDA, 2005; OECD, 2011). Funders are being taken to task for fostering reciprocal transparency. For example, one report offers funders this advice:

As you ask for transparency from your implementing partners, it is important that transparency is reciprocated. An evaluation with an end goal of solely accountability which can have consequences on future funding, is different in scope and nature from an evaluation with an end goal of learning, which can allow an implementer to try newer program designs. It is important to clearly communicate your goals and consequences of an evaluation (Kawano-Chiu, 2011, p. 15).

Here, there is vital space and need for implementers to manage up, a scenario in which implementers actively educate their donors about their own context-specific strengths, values, and limitations, so that donors come to understand how "well-designed, focused programs can contribute to peace writ large with sustained investment over time" (Kawano-Chiu, 2011, p. 21). A win-win situation is therefore the goal.

The notions of top-down accountability have also morphed into mutual accountability (Conlin & Stirrat, 2008) to match this emerging partnership framework. It is not only a matter of funders' accountability to implementers and vice versa, but also implementers' accountability to those they serve; a veritable constitution of top-down, bottom-up, and middle-out processes (Lederach, 1997, as cited in Fischer, 2006). Evaluations have thus evolved beyond merely aiming for accountability but are heavily tasked with learning. Funders are increasingly pressing for the inclusion of feedback mechanisms in evaluations and programming, and more encouragingly for the field of peace education, donors are registering genuine interest in "exploring a range of evaluation methods, including empowerment evaluation, action evaluation, [and] developmental evaluation" (Kawano-Chiu, 2011, p. 35). It is these types of evaluations that seem best suited for a field as varied as peace education, and a goal as complex as peaceableness.

IMMERSION IN PEACE EDUCATION PHILOSOPHY

The starting point for any peace education evaluator has to be an educative engagement with the main guiding principles of the field. The concept of *conscientizaçao*, or conscientization (consciousness-raising), posited by the Brazilian educator Paulo Freire (2003), is central to peace education. Seminal to conscientization is another Freireian notion, that of praxis, constituted by the confluence of reflection *and* action aimed at ultimately fostering transformation (Bartlett, 2008). In light of this, a definition of peace education, as used by UNICEF, is enlivened:

> The process of promoting the knowledge, skills, attitudes, and values needed to bring about behavior changes that will enable children, youth, and adults to prevent conflict and violence, both overt and structural; to resolve conflict peacefully; and to create the conditions conducive to peace, whether at an intrapersonal, interpersonal, intergroup national or international level (Fountain, 1999, p. 1).

Peace knowledges, skills, values, and attitudes are meant to energize a social imagination towards sustained and impactful action. But all of this is not possible in an environment where traditional hierarchies and false binaries are maintained. In the peace educative milieu, knowledge is co-constructed with the teacher viewing herself also as a student and truly respecting that students are teachers as well (Bartlett, 2008).

Beyond content issues, peace educators are also equally concerned with form. Noted peace theorist Johan Galtung (2008), lays out the argument most lucidly:

> First, the form of peace education has to be compatible with the idea of peace, that is, it has to exclude not only direct violence, but also structural violence. This is important because schools and universities are still important means of education and in the structure is the message. ...But structural violence remains and takes the usual forms: a highly vertical division of labor manifesting itself in one-way communication; the fragmentation of those on the receiving end preventing them from developing horizontal interaction that will allow them to organize and eventually turn the communication flow the other way (p. 51).

If a critical pedagogue fails to employ critical methods then the message s/he is attempting to impart is diminished, as modeling is another key component of peace education. With that said, one understands why any evaluation will not do. In peace education, everyone is responsible for this sought-after culture of peace, and for this, dialogic relationships are imperative. Ergo, evaluative methodologies employed in the field of peace education must be those that can competently and genuinely imbue, appraise, and foster this participative ethic. Since, peace education's content and form must be conscientizational (i.e. engendering conscientization), then so too must its evaluation. Perhaps it is a serendipitous gift, that as the calls for evaluation of peace education programs have been increasing, the discipline of evaluation itself has been affected most deeply by the epistemological interpretive turn. Therefore, there are now types of evaluative methodologies whose core objectives are compatible with those of peace education: bolstering participation and fostering empowerment.

In peace education's struggles to mainstream, increased rigorous evaluations that indicate what works and what does not can assist with this challenge. Despite this aspiration by some peace educators, there are others who fervently denounce any attempts to "promote regulation, universalization, and development of rigid normative standards for what peace education ought to be" (Bajaj & Brantmeier, 2011, p. 221). These two camps are not necessarily mutually exclusive, so long as the focus remains on activating "transformative agency" (Bajaj, 2009), a concept that is elemental to critical peace education (Bajaj, 2008). It is apparent that "peace education requires continued reinforcement" so that, as it is elevated to more mainstream heights, it maintains its core and distinguishing features (Brahm, 2006, p. 1).

This tension is demonstrated in the raging debate within the discipline of evaluation about a distinguishing feature of peace education: its focus on fostering a shift in values. Those evaluators on the positivist end of the spectrum aim for value-free scientific inquiry, yet there are others who say that no evaluation is void of values (Davidson, 2005). Others view this dichotomization of objectivism and subjectivism as a false argument (Freire, 2003). This author takes the position that it is preferable to explicitly declare, in a transparent manner, the values that inhere to one's e(value)ative choices. Action evaluation, fourth generation evaluation, empowerment evaluation, inclusive evaluation, and youth participatory evaluation, in some form or the other, all ally themselves with the values of social justice. They represent a postmodern semi-collapse of panoptical surveillance—semi-collapse because even if one evaluation is in the interpretivist tradition, it may be meta-evaluated through a positivist evaluative lens to facilitate, for example, comparisons. Positivist evaluation, with its objectivist distance from the evaluand, runs the risk of docilizing evaluated subjects into objects (Foucault, 1995). The interpretive turn in evaluation is a reflexive interrogation of the role of power; which, in *form*, is an affirming reflection and reification of peaceableness and transformative agency.

PARTICIPATIVE EVALUATIVE METHODOLOGIES

Peace education has been characterized as empowerment education, one that reinforces diverse participation (Harris & Morrison, 2003), and the evaluative methodologies that focus on participation can help to facilitate this empowerment. They fully embrace the participation hypothesis which posits that with increased participation comes increased commitment (Ross, 2001).

One such methodology is action evaluation, in which goal setting, monitoring, and evaluation are rolled into one, instead of viewed as distinct components. In this manner, implementers become more self-aware of their own goal setting and of the iterative and incremental nature of such an endeavor (Ross, 2001). This aims to build capacity among implementers and, in so doing, becomes a "means of intervention itself" (Eliott, d'Estrée & Kaufman, 2003, p. 4).

There is also empowerment evaluation, popularized by David Fetterman (2003), in which

> [evaluation] concepts, techniques and findings [are used] to foster improvement and self-determination....It is designed to help people help themselves and improve their programs using a form of self-evaluation and reflection. Program participants—including clients, consumers, and staff members—conduct their own evaluations; an outside evaluator often serves as a coach or additional facilitator depending on internal program capabilities. By internalizing and institutionalizing self-evaluation processes and practices, a dynamic and responsive approach to evaluation can be developed (p. 64).

This type of evaluation commences with the implementers self-defining their mission, then taking inventory of the elements key to their program, followed by goal setting and strategizing about attaining these goals.

Fourth generation evaluation explicitly rebukes positivist evaluation's lock on truth, and is akin to inclusive evaluation (Lincoln, 2003). In inclusive evaluation, the evaluator, who believes in social transformation, is willing to challenge the status quo. Donna Mertens (2003) offers this exhortation: that "the principle of objectivity need not find itself on the opposite side of the fence from addressing the needs of marginalized and less empowered groups" (p. 96). It is a type of evaluation that may use quantitative, qualitative, or mixed methods, but the key is having members of the evaluated community be a part of the decision-making around the design of the study. The evaluator here must be sensitive about diversity, even within subgroups of seeming homogeneity, must remain critical about his own values and about the penetrating questions that must be asked, while striving to blunt the potency of power imbalances in distorting the study's findings (Mertens, 2003).

Yet another evaluation that is being utilized is youth participatory evaluation (YPE). It entails the recruitment of youth, within the evaluated community, to be a part of developing an evaluative agenda; youth are trained how to conduct interviews, surveys, and focus groups, and do journaling and report writing (Flores, 2008). YPE offers an opportunity for youth to be self-reflective about their own personal and inner-growth, in essence, a reflexivity about their own peaceableness—certainly a key trigger for transformative agency. In being explicit about their social change directionality, YPE and the other afore-mentioned evaluative types constitute peace action, an integral component of peace education. By imbuing praxis—reflection and action—they demonstrate the necessity and potency of conscientizational evaluations.

PERSONAL RESEARCH EXPERIENCE

Participative evaluations do indeed require a certain posture; as regards critical peace education, evaluations should be inclined towards inclusion of less empowered and marginalized groups. From November 2009 to June 2010, I spent seven months conducting a case study at a secondary school in Trinidad and Tobago (in the Caribbean). I was interested in how constituents conceptualize school violence, its influences, and interventions. This was a school (Survivors Secondary School, or SSS) where many, if not most, of the students came from economically depressed communities. SSS was deemed by the Ministry of Education as a high-risk school in terms of youth violence; it was subsequently selected as part of a violence-prevention project called the Violence Prevention Academy (VPA), conducted by an American criminologist. The VPA was a pilot study of twenty-five schools where data were collected and a school-specific plan was crafted to deal with one selected form of violence at the respective schools. At SSS, school personnel selected gambling as its biggest issue related to violence. After a year and a half of the pilot project, the VPA final report indicated that gambling at SSS had decreased exponentially. As part of a VPA-conducted evaluation of its project, questionnaires were filled out by students and teachers and other school personnel. Despite these efforts, the majority of the teacher respondents could not articulate the aims and findings of the VPA; student respondents did not fare any better in their knowledge of the VPA. The design of this project did not directly involve student input nor did the evaluative components. Although the VPA final report indicated that gambling had decreased at SSS, conversations with respondents revealed that perhaps gambling was more a symptom of deeper issues, such as students resorting to gambling because of a lack of money to facilitate their return trips home after school or to purchase lunch. These were not the sole reasons for gambling, for it is possible that some students were simply gambling for the sake of it. However, an entire project created to assist schools with violence prevention omitted the supposed beneficiaries of this project (i.e. students) from the design of both the project and its evaluation. While students did fill out questionnaires about the impact of the project, none of the eighty-four student respondents could articulate the VPA's aims and impact, perhaps indicating that they were merely objects of the project and its subsequent evaluation. Tackling gambling as an issue ignored the deeper issues at play and the more structural factors that contributed to violence at SSS. The VPA strategies seemed to have been of a negative peace orientation, ones merely centered on a cessation of violence, and not focused on, as positive peace postulates, empowerment and genuine transformation of structural violence. Although the VPA was not explicitly self-framed as peace education, its design, and implementation were of a negative peace orientation; a vital, but insufficient posture, which may sometimes reinforce the status quo instead of exposing and upending societal inequities that may undergird manifestations of youth violence.

CONCLUSION

While participative evaluations are lauded for their potential to empower, we are reminded that participation does exist along a continuum and that there may be some types of participatory evaluations that veer towards the lower end of participation because of power differentials, stemming from the professional expertise of the evaluator, or because of resistances among subgroups in the evaluated community. Those in the field of evaluation have noted a dearth of how-to information on successfully carrying out participatory evaluations (Gregory, 2000). However, the interpretive turn in evaluation is a step in the right direction. It is a clarion call to reject neither accountability nor participation; both can co-exist (Fetterman & Wandersman, 2007). Both peace education and the discipline of evaluation must remain flexible in recognizing that there is not any one-size-fits-all approach. In fact, the evaluative approach shall depend on the context and what is to be evaluated (Bledsoe & Graham, 2005).

Peace education's legitimacy crisis is understandable. It has lofty goals but wishes to be taken seriously. Intellectual rigor is indeed the order of the day. In the rush to procure legitimacy, peace education must ardently stay true to its principles. Peace educators must remind ourselves, funders, and the wider society that sustainable peace requires time, effort, and patience. Inculcating peaceableness and the transformative agency necessary to envision and actuate a different world where a culture of peace is a naturalized existential ethic will not occur overnight. We may need to embrace the notion of success as a continuum with setbacks and triumphs, celebrate the incremental breakthroughs, and utilize multiple measures of success (Ross, 2000)—successes that need to be centered on peaceableness as raison d'être, as process, and as evaluation.

REFERENCES

Ashton, C. V. (2007). Using theory of change to enhance Peace Education evaluation. *Conflict Resolution Quarterly, 25*(1), 39–53.

Bajaj, M. (2009). 'I have big things planned for my future': the limits and possibilities of transformative agency in Zambian schools. *Compare, 39*(4), 551–568.

Bajaj, M. (2008). Introduction. In M. Bajaj (Ed.), *Encyclopedia of peace education.* North Carolina: Information Age Publishing, Inc. 1–11.

Bajaj, M., & Brantmeier, E. J. (2011). The politics, praxis, and possibilities of critical peace education. *Journal of Peace Education, 8*(3), 221–224.

Bartlett, L. (2008). Paulo Freire and peace education. In M. Bajaj (Ed.), *Encyclopedia of peace education* (pp. 39–46). North Carolina: Information Age Publishing, Inc.

Bledsoe, K., & Graham, J. (2005). The use of multiple evaluation approaches in program evaluation. *American Journal of Evaluation, 26,* 302–319.

Blum, A. (2011). *Improving peacebuilding evaluation: A whole-of-field approach.* Washington, DC: USIP. Retrieved November 1, 2011from http://www.usip.org/files/resources/Improving_Peacebuilding_Evaluation.pdf.

Brahm, E. (2006). *Peace education. Beyond intractability* (G. Burgess & H. Burgess, Eds.). Boulder: University of Colorado. Retrieved October 15, 2011 from http://www.beyondintractability.org/bi-essay/peace-education .

Church, C. S. (2011). *The use of reflecting on peace practice (RPP) in peacebuilding evaluation.* Colloborative Learning Projects (CDA). Retrieved November 1, 2011 from http://www.cdainc.com/cdawww/pdf/other/rpp_use_in_evaluation_scharbatke_church_05232011_Pdf.pdf.

Conlin, S., & Stirrat, R. (2008). Current challenges in development evaluation. *Evaluation, 14*(2), 193–208.

DANIDA. (2005). *Globalisation—Progress through partnership: Priorities of the Danish government for Danish development assistance 2006–2010.* Denmark: Ministry of Foreign Affairs of Denmark. Retrieved October 15, 2011 from http://www.amg.um.dk/NR/rdonlyres/BD805561-B40B-462D-BC2F-C541823EFB29/0/GlobalisationProgressThroughPartnership.pdf.

Davidson, E. J. (2005). *Evaluation Methodology Basics: The nuts and bolts of sound evaluation.* London & New Delhi: SAGE Publications.

Elliott, M., d'Estrée, T., & Kaufman, S. (2003). *Evaluation as a tool for reflection.* Retrieved October 15, 2011 from http://www.beyondintractability.org/bi-essay/evaluation-reflection.

Fetterman, D. (2003). *Empowerment Evaluation Strikes a Responsive Cord.* In S. I. Donaldson & M. Scriven (Eds.), *Evaluating social programs and problems: Visions for the new millennium* (pp. 63–76). New Jersey: Lawrence Erlbaum Associates.

Fetterman, D., & Wandersman, A. (2007). Empowerment evaluation: Yesterday, today, and tomorrow. *American Journal of Evaluation, 28,* 179–198.

Fischer, M. (2006). *Civil society in conflict transformation: Ambivalence, potentials and challenges.* Retrieved October, 1, 2011 from http://www.berghof-handbook.net/documents/publications/fischer_cso_handbook.pdf.

Fischer, M. (2009). *Participatory evaluation and critical peace research: A precondition for peacebuilding.* Retrieved October 15, 2011 from http://www.berghof-handbook.net/documents/publications/dialogue7_fischer_comm.pdf.

Fitzduff, M., & Jean, I. (2011). *Peace education: State of the field and lessons learned from USIP Grantmaking. No. 74.* Washington, DC: USIP. Retrieved November 1, 2011 from http://www.usip.org/files/resources/PW74.pdf.

Flores, K. S. (2008). *Youth participatory evaluation: Strategies for engaging young people.* California: Jossey-Bass.

Foucault, M. (1995). *Discipline and punish: The birth of the prison.* New York: Vintage Books. (Original work published in France in 1975).

Fountain, S. (1999). *Peace education in UNICEF.* New York: UNICEF. Retrieved October 1, 2011 from http://www.unicef.org/education/files/PeaceEducation.pdf.

Freire, P. (2003). *Pedagogy of the oppressed.* New York: Continuum Press. (Original work published in 1970).

Galtung, J. (2008). Form and Content of Peace Education. In M. Bajaj (Ed.), *Encyclopedia of peace Education* (pp. 49–58). North Carolina: Information Age Publishing, Inc.

Gregory, A. (2000). Problematizing participation: A critical review of approaches to participation in evaluation theory. *Evaluation, 6,* 179–198.

Harris, I. (2003). *Peace education evaluation.* Retrieved July 15, 2011 from http://www.eric.ed.gov/PDFS/ED480127.pdf.

Harris, I., & Morrison, M. L. (2003). *Peace education.* North Carolina & London: McFarland & Company, Inc.

Kawano-Chiu, M. (2011). *Starting on the same page: A lessons report from the Peacebuilding Evaluation Project.* Washington, DC: Alliance for Peacebuilding. Retrieved October 15, 2011 from http://www.allianceforpeacebuilding.org/resource/collection/9DFBB4C8-CABB-4A5B-8460-0310C54FB3D9/Alliance_for_Peacebuilding_Peacebuilding_Evaluation_Project_Lessons_Report_June2011_FINAL.pdf.

Lanz, D., Wählisch, M., Kirchhoff, L., & Siegfried, M. (2008). *Evaluating Peace Mediation. Brussels: Initiative for Peacebuilding.* Retrieved October 15, 2011 from http://id.cdint.org/content/documents/Evaluating_Peace_Mediation.pdf.

Lawson, M. L. (2010). *Foreign aid: International donor coordination of development assistance.* DC: Congressional Research Service. Retrieved January 30, 2012 from fpc.state.gov/documents/organization/142758.pdf.

Lincoln, Y. S. (2003). Fourth generation evaluation in the new millennium. In S. I. Donaldson & M. Scriven (Eds.), *Evaluating social programs and problems: Visions for the new millennium* (pp. 77–90). New Jersey: Lawrence Erlbaum Associates.

McCauley, C. (2002). Head first versus feet first in peace education. In G. Salomon & B. Nevo (Eds.), *Peace education: The concept, principles, and practices around the world* (pp. 247–258). New Jersey: Lawrence Erlbaum Associates.

Mertens, D. M. (2003). The inclusive view of evaluation: Visions for the new millennium. In S. I. Donaldson & M. Scriven (Eds.), *Evaluating social programs and problems: visions for the new millennium* (pp. 91–107). New Jersey: Lawrence Erlbaum Associates.

Neufeldt, R. (2007). *"Frameworkers" and "Circlers"—Exploring assumptions in peace and conflict impact assessment.* Retrieved October 15, 2011 from http://www.berghof-handbook.net/documents/publications/neufeldt_handbook.pdf.

Nevo, B., & Brem, I. (2002). Peace education programs and the evaluation of their effectiveness. In G. Salomon & B. Nevo (Eds.), *Peace education: The concept, principles, and practices around the world* (pp. 271–282). New Jersey: Lawrence Erlbaum Associates.

OECD (2011). *DAC Global Relations Strategy.* Organisation de Coopération et de Développement Économiques. Retrieved from http://www.oecd.org/dac/49102914.pdf

Reardon, B. (1988). *Comprehensive peace education.* New York: Teachers College Press.

Reardon, B. (1997). Human rights education as education for peace. In G. J. Andreopoulous & R. P. Claude (Eds.), *Human rights education for the twenty-first century* (pp. 21–34). Philadelphia: University of Pennsylvania Press..

Ross, M. H. (2001). Action *Evaluation in the Theory and Practice of Conflict Re*solution. *Peace and Conflict Studies, 8*(17), 2–47.

Ross, M. H. (2000). "Good-enough" Isn't so bad: Thinking about success and failure in ethnic conflict management. *Peace and Conflict Studies, 6*(1), 27–47.

Stave, S. E. (2011). *Measuring peacebuilding: Challenges, tools, actions.* Norway: The Norwegian Peacebuilding Resource Centre (NOREF). Retrieved October 15, 2011 from http://www.peacebuilding.no/var/ezflow_site/storage/original/application/906762cb32e2eed5dc810bafa139f4ce.pdf.

CHAPTER 2

TOWARDS A MORE COMPLEX EVALUATION OF PEACE EDUCATION

Peace Education, the Evaluation Business, and the Need for Empowering Evaluation[1]

Werner Wintersteiner

INTRODUCTION

Peace education is a field of the theory and practice of education related to the idea of promoting knowledge, values, attitudes, and skills conducive to peace and non-violence, and to an active commitment to the building of a co-operative and caring democratic society. It is targeted towards the empowerment of an individual and the promotion of social well-being through the protection of human dignity for all, the promotion of social justice, equality, civil responsibility and solidarity, and the ac-

---

[1] My sincere thanks to Professor Gavriel Salomon and to Wilfried Graf for their critical remarks on an earlier version of this chapter.

Peace Education Evaluation: Learning from Experience and Exploring Prospects, pages 19–37.
Copyright © 2015 by Information Age Publishing
All rights of reproduction in any form reserved.

19

cepting of a dynamic global perspective, by utilising the concepts and practices of peaceful conflict-resolution and non-violence. (EURED, 2002, p. 10)

Even this relatively simple definition of peace education, elaborated by a group of European peace educators and which focuses strongly on the inputs and neglects the needs, expectations, experiences, and resistance of the learners, provides an idea of the complexity of peace education. It is legitimate to ask: how, and in which ways, can peace education best contribute to making societies more peaceful? For a long time, however, this was not considered an empirical question. Instead, ideological discussions on the function of peace education, compared to peace research and peace movements, were debated. Some discussants denied that peace education—as restricted to the field of education—could have any impact on political questions like war and peace (cf. Wintersteiner, 2010, p. 50). As with all ideological debates, the arguments were too general to find a satisfying answer. At least, these debates helped understanding that, as long as peace remains defined as a strictly political issue, education has indeed no role to play in the game. If we conceive of peace in the wider context of a culture of peace, however, education becomes a fundamental cornerstone.

A preliminary statement can be made that when evaluating peace education, generally speaking the focus is on the contribution of peace education to a culture of peace. According to a commonly shared definition by the United Nations, "the Culture of Peace is a set of values, attitudes, modes of behaviour and ways of life that reject violence and prevent conflicts by tackling their root causes to solve problems through dialogue and negotiation among individuals, groups and nations" (UN Resolutions A/RES/52/13). Culture is described as an activity, a daily practice. This concept assigns education a crucial task in developing the values, attitudes, modes of behavior, and ways of life necessary for a culture of peace. Thus, a second assertion is that evaluating peace education means to evaluate how (much) it enables the learners to establish and to practice a culture of peace. The question pertains to the capacities of the learners, not to unrealistic expectations of achievements in building peace in general, which depend on many opportunities that are out of control of any educational process and are instead due to (political) circumstances.[2] This coincides with Ian Harris' criticism of inadequate expectations for peace education evaluation: "The effectiveness of peace education cannot be judged by whether it brings peace to the world, but rather by the effect it has upon students' thought patterns, attitudes, behaviors, values, and knowledge stock" (Harris, 2003, p. 3, see also Fischer, 2008).

Peace education is *transformative* rather than *formative*; it aims to overcome ideologies, cultural patterns, and social structures that reproduce a culture of war and violence, including such structures in the educational system itself. An anti-pedagogic current in peace education has overworked this argument and drawn a radical, if not misguided, conclusion that peace education should refuse any

---

[2] This was, for a moment, postulated by some too-enthusiastic peace educators (cf. Harris, 2003).

integration into the (state) school system. The noble aims of peace education, it is perceived, will be necessarily corrupted as soon as it enters the repressive school structures. The structural and cultural violence of school is an obstacle to any kind of alternative education, including peace education. Robin Burns calls this the "the kiss of death" argument: if peace education is mainstreamed, its very concerns are killed (Burns, 1996, p. 121).This argument explains in part why especially the older generation of peace educators has maintained resistance against evaluation, which was considered an obligation of "the system" and in direct opposition to the aims of peace education as transformative education.

The main thesis of this chapter is to distinguish between a *controlling* and an *empowering* evaluation. On the one hand, we must not ignore the ideological and political context of the evaluation discourse if it comes to apply evaluation to peace education programs and interventions. I will give some good reasons for the resistance against evaluation. On the other hand, I argue, we should not neglect the opportunities that evaluation offers to the further development of peace education. Thus, I plead for working on alternative ways of evaluation. With this objective, I discuss the question of evaluation in peace education from three angles and at three levels of abstraction respectively concreteness:

1. a critique of the rise of the evaluation business in education;
2. a reflection on the difficulties of peace education evaluation; and
3. a discussion of a concrete example: the evaluation of a peace education in-service teacher training curriculum.

I try to avoid two extreme positions—the blind belief in evaluation which too often turns out to be part of a system of control instead of a self-determined process, on the one hand, and the equally blind refusal of evaluation, arguing that peace education is something "totally different" from any other education, on the other hand.

EVALUATION AS A BUSINESS AND A SYSTEM OF CONTROL

Evaluation is far from being an innocent technical term, a special field of education. Of course, to examine the outcome of any educational endeavor is an integral part of the theory and practice of teaching and learning. However, the reason for the rise of evaluation as a key word in education—and beyond, in other social fields—lies not in the inner development of the pedagogical discipline, but comes from the outside. It is a consequence of the ongoing "commercialization" of education. The current esteem or even excitement for evaluation does not, or not primarily, arise from the need to ensure the effectiveness of education, but more often than not from the need to satisfy a sponsor, of proving that the investment was used in a meaningful way, or, in the educational system, to meet the need for monitoring and control.

In Europe generally, and in the German-speaking countries in particular, there was no "evaluation culture" in education twenty years ago. More precisely, the evaluation business did not yet invade autonomous academic work. Meanwhile, neoliberalism and the market system have made a strong impact on schools and universities which are still, to a large degree, run by the state. Evaluation, in this context, is a key instrument of power politics, not only in education, but also in other social fields, including the health care system and the judicial system. Since in continental Europe, in comparison to the US and the UK, the grasp of big business on education is a relatively new fact, the sensitivity and also the resistance are more obvious (see Laval, 2010; Liessmann, 2006; Münch, 2009, or Milner, 2011). Namely, in Germany and in France, there is a severe criticism of evaluation as a new element of control and of "economization" of education. As some authors point out, the language of evaluation derives from a police vocabulary, with revealing key words including *autopsy, evidence,* and *proof.* (Milner, 2011, p. 23). Evaluation, in this context, is considered a "Trojan horse": without an overt discussion of the aims of education, the traditional ethics and emancipatory concepts of education are subverted by a practice of evaluation whose criteria come from a market orientation. The learners are no longer considered citizens but rather consumers.

Christian Laval (2010) denounces the false promises and erroneous beliefs of what he calls the "cult of efficiency" and evaluation as its most important ritual (p. 222). The silent basic assumptions of evaluation follow:

- Educational processes are basically not specific, according to the target group, the teacher, the given situation, but "good methods" can be applied in or at least adapted to any educational situation.
- The quality of an educational process can always be measured by its outcome, as long as suitable measurement instruments are available.
- The evaluation process is something objective and neutral; the measurement instruments do not affect the measured object.

In fact, education is a complex and open-ended process. The "good method" is only one among the many factors which decide whether the process is successful or not. There is a clear limit to the transferability of methods into another context—a fact that should also be taken into account by the evaluation. The "outcome," the acquired knowledge, is a strong indicator of the quality of education, but we have to distinguish between short term effects (measured) and long-term effects (not measured). Further, knowledge is not the only factor. Changes of attitudes can be as important as the gain of knowledge. Moreover, the evaluation itself is far from neutral; it is a special view on the process, and while shedding light on some aspects, it unavoidably also has blind spots. This is not an argument against evaluation but rather a warning not to trust an evaluation that reduces the complexity of education to a small list of parameters and numbers. To summarize, the "cult of evaluation" sets exaggerated expectations not only for evaluation, but also for education itself, or for social change in general, because it is based on simplified models of educa-

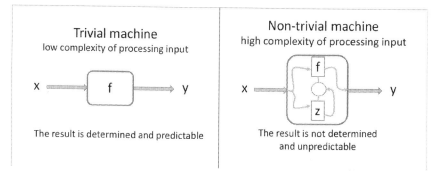

Trivial machine	Non-trivial machine
low complexity of processing input	high complexity of processing input

The result is determined and predictable

The result is not determined and unpredictable

FIGURE 2.1. Trivial and Non-trivial Machine, According to von Foerster

tion, considering the learners "trivial machines" (Heinz von Foerster, according to Riegler, 2011)[3]. This means that there is an expectation that the educational process is determined, and that its results are predictable and thus easily measurable. A trivial machine has a clear logic: the output always corresponds directly to the input. A famous example, given by von Foerster himself, is the chewing gum machine: When you insert a coin you always get a chewing gum, and nothing else. In contrast, with a non-trivial machine, you never know exactly what the outcome will be because the system "digests" the input in an autonomous way. While the trivial machine model applies only for some very limited parts of the learning process, the non-trivial machine model can be applied to the educational process as a whole. The learners deal with the inputs they receive in many different manners, according to their capacities, knowledge, disposition, or character. Thus, a strict evaluation of the input-output process in education according to the trivial machine model can necessarily only focus on the *intended* output, and even more, only on *some aspects* of the intended output—basically short-term acquired knowledge or skills that are easily measurable. This is not negligible and remains important, but it is definitely not the whole result nor all the consequences of the educational process.

For instance, a peace education program may have a couple of intended short-term results—knowledge of reasons of violence that can be reproduced in a test. This corresponds more or less to the way a trivial machine works. However, what really count are results such as the capacity to analyze new situations using the knowledge of violence. Such an analysis has not one but many possible solutions, corresponding to the complexity of any social situation, and demands complex thinking as an answer. This cannot be measured, at least not with "industrialized" tools of evaluation. It can only be "interpreted" (like a poem or a film) which means that the evaluation may be reasonable but not "objective" like the results of natural science research.

---

[3] http://www.univie.ac.at/constructivism/HvF.htm (January 3, 2012)

Laval (2010) shows that mainstream evaluation follows the rules of the market—in fetishizing the "number" which is, according to him, typical particularly in the Anglo-Saxon context. This kind of evaluation is inspired by the trivial machine model and leads to a "normalization," a standardization of education, following the industrial model of production of goods. Evaluation thus reflects that education increasingly becomes merchandise. As a result, the aims of education are pushed from sight. In a sort of hybridization of market liberalism and the logics of bureaucracy, evaluation serves two aims—the wish to make profit or to reduce the costs of education, and the wish to control (cf. Laval, 2010, p. 239).[4]

What makes this kind of evaluation so powerful? It is more or less directly linked to the allocation of financial means. As a matter of fact, the state is increasingly cutting funding to educational institutions, especially universities, urging them to look for needed resources from the "free market." Thus, more and more research projects are chosen, financed, and realized that are compatible with the profit-oriented market system. More often than not, this turn is experienced as a liberation, including by peace educators, who were in the past often unable to convince the state educational bureaucracy to sponsor projects related to peace and human rights. However, this new freedom has its limits, clearly exemplified by evaluation which has become a lucrative business, evidenced by the establishment of specialized agencies that continue to gain power. The evaluation business makes good money nibbling, one more time, on the modest allocations the state provides to its universities and to the higher education system. Universities are forced to spend a growing part of their small means on evaluation and accreditation agencies in order to run their programs.

How can we react to this situation? We can identify two positions. First, some peace educators criticize "evaluation and quality standards" as a capitalistic approach that has nothing to do with the real problems of peace education. They blame their fellow educators for being naïve to accept even their discussion. Occupying the second position, they are themselves criticized by others for their "blindness" and dogmatism that potentially hinders further development of peace education. In my view, a position that accepts the arguments of the critics but without "throwing out the baby with the bath water" is needed. While we have to reject standardized evaluation criteria and methods coming from outside, we need to develop genuine ways of evaluation for such a special field as peace education, based on ethical principles.

This effort is even more important since peace education rarely had the chance to develop as an academic discipline with its own standards and traditions of self-evaluation. More often than not, the lack of willingness to fund peace projects hinders the development of a genuine peace education culture. Thus, peace educators content themselves often with proclaiming principles instead of carrying out projects. Or, if they carry out projects, they "forget" to verify if the results meet

---

[4] I refer here and in the following mainly to higher education.

the proclaimed aims. Another problem is the "evaluation" of programs that is done only to satisfy the donors. This kind of evaluation does not show the weak points of an approach nor the program's obstacles, but rather is only completed to convince the donor that he or she has invested his or her money in the right "business." It has no scientific value.

Laval (2010) himself distinguishes an authentic scientific approach to evaluation from the evaluation business. Without rejecting the need for data on the efficiency of educational activities, he clearly insists on the limits of such procedures. In order to be at the level of the complexity of the educational process, which is always "uncertain" and open, evaluation methods as well have to be complex and include all stakeholders, not just evaluation experts, he argues. Laval resumes: "A different evaluation is surely possible and desirable because it would be more 'efficient', but it must come from the reflection and the collective deliberations of the teachers and not from the power of experts and administrators" (Laval, 2010, p. 231, author's translation). Evaluation has to play a role as a tool for improving specific ways of peace education, instead of being a tool for standardizing peace education according to criteria coming from outside—the education and evaluation business. In the following sections, I discuss pros and cons of evaluation approaches and conclude by developing my own perspective.

MYTHS AND REALITY OF PEACE EDUCATION EVALUATION

For the reasons discussed above, evaluation is often regarded as a weak point of peace education. Many authors deplore that little research on the effects of peace education has been conducted (cf. Harris 2003, p. 7). A survey of around 300 articles on peace education programs (from the period between 1981 and 2000), carried out by Baruch Nevo and Iris Brem (2002), showed that only one-third had elements of evaluation of the program's effectiveness. The authors conclude: "This figure by itself is a testimony to the relative scarcity of evaluation studies in PE" (p. 275). What has changed in the ten years since the publication of this study? An overview of eight years of *Journal of Peace Education* (2004–2011) shows that 16 out of a total of 107 articles deal with the efficiency of peace education programs—nearly one article in every issue. Given the wide range of articles, including theoretical contributions, textbook analyses, and historical articles, a total of about 15% for evaluation of peace education programs is relatively high.[5] Another indicator would be the many achievements of peace education institutes focusing on evaluation in the last decade, namely the Center for Research on Peace Education (CERPE) at Haifa University (see Salomon, 2009). It seems that

---

[5] Of course, this short look does not include any judgment of the quality of the respective evaluation reports.

peace educators are more aware of the need for peace education evaluation and able to cope with it.[6]

Objections

It is necessary to discuss the objections against peace education evaluation (or the way evaluation is usually carried out) as they make us aware of the weak points of evaluation to overcome in order to develop a state-of-the-art peace education evaluation. First, some authors deny that peace education evaluation makes sense at all. Their argument is that what is currently propagated as evaluation is actually monitoring—a control of the actors. It is more alienating than helpful and empowering, meeting the needs of the "system" rather than the needs of the teachers and learners. This is, as shown above, partially true. Thus, without accepting the paradigm of this kind of evaluation, we must not deny the idea of evaluation itself. It depends on *how* it is carried out.

Second, usual forms of tests are unsuitable for peace education because they evaluate the acquired knowledge, instead of "a state of mind" (Bar-Tal, 2002, p. 34). This objection also holds partial truth, although it is unconvincing. A focus only on the acquired knowledge *about* peace is too narrow of a concept to evaluate the results of peace education. Knowledge-centered evaluation methods (such as tests) do not fit peace education. But knowledge is an important component of any peace education; it is not only about values, attitudes, or a "state of mind." The aim of peace education is not simply to educate people to have peaceful minds in a violent world but to enable them to work in order to make the world less violent. Therefore peace education (like any civic education) works on the triad of knowledge, skills, and attitudes, including emotional and motivational aspects.

Third, peace education is a long-term process, and thus its results cannot be measured by usual short-term means. "With peace education, it's difficult to demonstrate the instrumentality of a particular act of instruction, e. g. does that educational activity contribute to 'peace writ large'?" (Harris, 2003, p. 12). This is true, and not only for peace education but for any substantial educational process. This means that the question of "efficiency" of certain methods will hardly lead to convincing results. It makes more sense to focus on a "thick description" (Geertz, 1973) of the educational project, using different forms of data, including the opinions of the involved people. As already mentioned, we have to be aware that in any meaningful educational process we do not "measure" or "weigh" the outcome, but rather *interpret* it. In this sense, evaluation is not so much about certainty of the facts, but about the plausibility of the arguments.

Put this way, evaluation has some positive effects even before beginning it. To know that at the end of a program or a curriculum there will be an evaluation obliges clearly defined intentions and aims. Thus, the fact that an evaluation is in-

---

[6] This is also true for German-speaking countries; see for instance Frieters-Reermann, 2009, Lenhart et al., 2010, and Lenhart et al., 2011.

TABLE 2.1 Culture of Reflection and Assessment of (Pedagogical) Activities

Feedback	Evaluation	(Evaluation) Research
Given by the learners	Done by the teachers	Done by researchers
Aim: to tell feelings and judgments in or after an educational activity	Aim: to improve ongoing or coming educational activity	Long term aims, directly or indirectly linked to the educational activity

cluded improves the program because it shapes its profile. This can also be turned the other way around. As a rule we can state: the more a curriculum is reflected upon, structured and well-planned, the easier is it to evaluate it. In other words: half of the evaluation job is complete once a clear concept of the aims of a given course or program are expressed. As Angelika Spelten (2006) states: "Reflecting about how to verify the effects already has effects" (p. 147, author's translation).

In this context, it seems useful to place evaluation (in a narrow sense) in the midway between simple feedback on the one hand and elaborate empirical research on the other hand. Table 2.1 elaborates on these categories. While feedback is given spontaneously or on request by learners, evaluation is a planned and systematic activity of the teacher or somebody assigned by the teacher. Empirical research instead is often more sophisticated in its methods and independent from the aims of the teacher, following its own independent research agenda. Evaluation (in a narrow sense), in turn, is—in my definition—always driven by the actors of a pedagogical intervention, in order to improve their action and, of course, to legitimate it in the eyes of sponsors or the authorities. Concluding from this, we can identify two criteria for an authentic evaluation of educational interventions that empowers the actors:

1. The criteria of the evaluation correspond to the intentions of the educational intervention; and
2. The methods of the evaluation correspond to the intentions of the evaluation.

Thus, the goal-oriented question "Did we reach our aims?" is the main evaluation question which always has to be differentiated and concretized according to the particular program, activity, or intervention. In this respect, peace education is no exception.

SOME CRITERIA FOR PEACE EDUCATION EVALUATION

When choosing among the many forms, aims, and philosophies of evaluation (cf. Boulmetis & Dutwin, 1998, p. 79), we have to keep in mind the aims of peace education—to enable the learners to create a culture of peace, which includes the struggle against any structure and power system which hinders a peaceful coexistence of people. As mentioned before, this has at least three dimensions: it teaches knowledge, develops skills, and changes (or refines) attitudes. The challenge is that the evaluation method has to correspond to the complexity of the peace education process. Quite often in evaluation what is measured is not what is intended to teach but what is easy to measure. Thus, evaluation risks limiting the perspective of peace educators, first by restricting their evaluation focus, and second by affecting their focus of teaching, as well, because evaluation quite often has a strong backwash-effect on the teaching. What is not evaluated has less value and thus is less taught in the long run.

Many evaluation approaches range between the focus on the change of attitudes and on the increase of knowledge—definitely two important factors, but in isolation they are insufficient. The question is how attitudes, knowledge, and skills work together. What makes somebody able to use his/her knowledge in a given situation? How are the (changed) attitudes transferred into concrete acts? One step forward is the theory of competencies, now popular in (psychometric) evaluation: "Competence indicates sufficiency of knowledge and skills that enable someone to act in a wide variety of situations"[7] (according to the Business-Dictionary.com definition, n, n. d.) This aspect is very important. Competencies are much more than just (reproduced) knowledge. Competencies are the capacity to master unattended and new situations as well. Thus competencies are not "real" qualities of people that one can directly observe, but rather mental constructions which help better explain why and how people are able to deal with unexpected situations. The proof of the competencies is their use in a given situation. For instance, a reading competence has to be proved by reading and explaining a text of a certain difficulty. This is the way "output control" in education works. The students do not simply show what they have learned, reproducing the input of their teacher. Rather they have to pass sophisticated tests, constructed to give them a chance to demonstrate their competencies.

Despite this progress (compared to earlier ways of testing), even the notion of competencies is too oriented on cognitive skills and neglects attitudes, values, and ethics. Therefore, I would like to propose a slightly different approach that better takes into account the complexity of peace education. I propose as the element that links knowledge, skills, and attitudes the *habitus*. By habitus I mean, borrowing from Bourdieu (1980, 1982; see also Bohn, 1991), *the matrix of perceptions, actions, and thoughts* that actors use to delimit a field of action within which they have unconstrained scope for action. The habitus is the internalized basic attitude that provides orientation in unforeseen situations never previously encountered. This is true for any peace education, but it is maybe even more relevant for peace education teacher training since peace education requires a special habitus of teachers. I apply these general considerations of peace education evaluation to the field of in-service teacher training.

---

[7] http://www.businessdictionary.com/definition/competence.html#ixzz1jba1Q0Rf (January, 15, 2012)

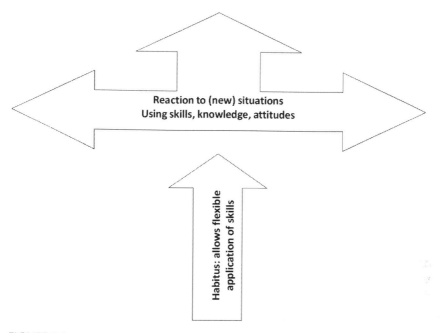

FIGURE 2.2.

The habitus of the teacher is not restricted to individual pedagogical skills, but is rather the underlying general attitude that permits the flexible application of these skills in changing conditions and situations. The habitus must not be regarded as a restricted specification of rules but rather as a framework within which the teacher's own style of pedagogical action can develop. However, the framework also represents a limit that is difficult to perceive as such and to surpass. Thus, it permits variety within homogeneity. The pedagogical habitus refers on the one hand to the professional field, i.e. the interpretation of what school and education serve generally, and, on the other hand, to the professional image itself, i.e. what the functions of the teacher are in order to implement the underlying educational objectives. The habitus is implicit; it is not taught, but acquired in the course of teacher training and in professional life. It becomes, as it were, subcutaneous, communicated together with the specific skills that teachers acquire for their profession. This is not to say that the habitus cannot be modified and changed. The more somebody becomes aware of his/her own habitus, the more this person is able to refine it or redirect it (Figure 2.2).[8]

The habitus concept allows for a clearer picture of what peace education can and cannot aim towards. It does not make the job of evaluating easier, but rather it helps to take the complexity of peace education into consideration.

---

[8] This paragraph is borrowed from EURED, 2002, p. 22.

The EURED Course Evaluation as an Example

The following example shows how the evaluation of a peace education teacher training, when referring to the habitus concept, was carried out. The course was evaluated as very successful both by participants and trainers. For the aims of this chapter, however, the focus is not whether the course was successful, but whether the evaluation of the course was appropriate. What is interesting in this context, is in fact not the outcome of the evaluation, but its methodology.

Philosophy and Structure of the EURED Course

EURED ("European Education as Peace Education") was an in-service teacher training course in Peace and Human Rights Education, held under the auspices of UNESCO and the Austrian National Commission of UNESCO, in the form of a "university course" (under the author's direction) at the University of Klagenfurt/ Austria from 2004 to 2006, open to teachers and teacher trainers in Europe, inside and outside of the EU. Its aim was to act on the habitus of the teachers through the choice of contents and training methods. An important factor was sufficient time for the self-determined learning process. The curriculum, a forty-page handbook, followed a *holistic and dynamic approach*, in contrast to two simpler models of teacher training, i.e. seminars with an *information focus* and seminars concentrating on *methodology*. The holistic approach provided information as well as methodological skills, but its aims were much higher, namely to work on the teachers' fundamental attitudes as well as on their personal styles of teaching. The aim was to create an awareness of each teacher's own pedagogical habitus.

Working on one's own attitude can only be an autonomous self-determined process. It must be based on voluntariness and insight. In-service training can provide both the framework for this process as well as inputs to move the process forward. The framework was a series of five seminars over two years, with inputs and phases of reflection, tasks to fulfil and opportunities of exchange among peers, classroom learning and excursions for field studies. Basically, there was a triple structure:

1. Inputs (lessons, excursions, reading of texts, movies);
2. Reflection (of their own practice, of traditional concepts); and
3. Practice (reports and exercises, drawing from the practical experience of the participants).

Table 2.2 shows the structure of this course.

The EURED Evaluation Approach

The evaluation was, as an integral part, included into the curriculum and refined during the preparation of the course and each single seminar. How could we evaluate the results of this course? When peace education is considered a long-

TABLE 2.2.   The Structure of the EURED Course

Time	Activities	Venue
Summer 04 SEMINAR I	Human rights, peace, peace education and culture of peace: Basic knowledge	Gernika, Spain
Winter 4/05 NETWORKING, E-LEARNING, PRACTICE ASSIGNMENT I		
Spring 05 SEMINAR II	Human rights and peace education: Theory, policy and practice	Magdeburg, Germany
Spring 05 NETWORKING, E-LEARNING, PRACTICE ASSIGNMENT II		
Summer 05 SEMINAR III	Human rights and peace education: Methodology of teaching and specialisation	Budapest, Hungary
Winter 05/06 NETWORKING , E-LEARNING, SPECIALISED STUDY		
Spring 06 SEMINAR IV	Specialisation—selected topics	Brixen/Bressanone, Italy
Spring 06 NETWORKING , E-LEARNING , SPECIALISED STUDY		
Summer 06 SEMINAR V	Approaching human rights and peace education in Europe	Stadtschlaining, Austria

term transformation of the habitus and a never-ending development of knowledge and skills, it is difficult to differentiate the impact of a single course, even a two-year-program. Thus, we used indicators which seemed appropriate for our aims. Since the concept of "hard facts" did not apply to our case, a main resource was the wisdom of the "experts" involved in the process. In our opinion, these experts were not only the trainers, but all participants of the seminars. They had impressive professional qualities, high levels of commitment (they were not forced to do the training course and contribute financially for it), and had not only "experienced" the seminars, but enriched them through their active participation and their feedback.

It was, according to the categories of Boulmetis and Dutwin (1998, p. 76), a goal-based evaluation. The success criteria were two-fold: the quality of the learning process of each participant as well as the quality of the course program as such. Due to the lack of means, we had no separate staff members dedicated to evaluation tasks, and thus rather opted for self-evaluation, including that of the whole staff and involving all participants. One member was responsible for documentation and feedback when evaluation was prepared and discussed by the whole staff. But this was no handicap. On the contrary, internal evaluators are advantaged by better overall understanding of the program and possess informal knowledge of the program. What is essential is the *triangulation* or the cross-checking of data through the use of more than one source and the acceptance of more than one perspective. Thus triangulation is an "attempt to map out, or explain more fully, the richness and complexity of human behavior by studying it from more than one standpoint" (Cohen & Manion, 2000, p. 254).

This kind of complex evaluation comes very closely to the principles of action research, which were explicitly mentioned in the EURED curriculum. The action research approach has repeatedly proven its value as an evaluation model, in particular as a tool for self-evaluation. The evaluation of EURED was a form of self-reflective academic examination undertaken in order to better understand the causes of our own actions, to arrange future actions more reasonably, and to consolidate understanding of pedagogical interaction (cf. Altrichter, Feldman, Posch & Somekh, 2008). This is similar to the approach proposed by Christian Laval (2010), cited at the end of section 1 (p. 231).

Evaluation theory distinguishes summative from formative evaluation, even if some authors are skeptical about the possibilities to differentiate between these two dimensions (cf. Alkin, 2011). The EURED evaluation was "formative" and "summative" at the same time. The evaluation of each single seminar was implemented in order to improve the following seminars (thus formative) but they also contributed to the overall evaluation at the end of the whole course (summative). This overall evaluation, again, was formative in that it helped us to garner new insights to improve the course concept for a possible second cycle.

The course curriculum itself demanded regular feedback and, in general, active cooperation of the participants by not planning all seminar days in detail, but allowing space according to the wishes of the participants. This open planning process was also helpful for evaluation because a culture of critical reflection was established for both the course facilitators and the participants.

The Evaluation Structure

The reflection and transformation of the habitus of the participants was broken down to two main questions:

- When completing a task, which capacity did participants show? (instead of measuring their knowledge)
- Which attitudes are expressed by their activities? (instead of scanning their attitudes)

These preliminary considerations led to the following evaluation structure (Table 2.3).

At the end of each seminar, there was oral and written feedback by the course participants and reflection by the course directors. A special focus was on seminar I since it was the first one, in order to get a better orientation on how to continue

TABLE 2.3.

During each seminar	Feedback
At the end of each seminar	Evaluation of the seminar
At the end of the course	Overall evaluation

with the course. In seminar *V*, there was not only an evaluation of the last seminar, but also one related to the course in its entirety.

The evaluation of each seminar was based on the comparison and judgment of several different data:

1. An open group evaluation (different techniques at different seminars), for example: participants put a mark in a circle with six segments: *content, structure, trainers, working facilities, cultural events, group atmosphere.* The placement of the mark closer to the center of the circle correlated with the participant's positive impression.
2. Written individual anonymous feedback (questionnaire) by the participants.
3. An evaluation by the course directors, based on their own observations and discussions with the whole staff.

The 16-item questionnaire concerned the topics, the structure of the seminar, trainers, material, venue, as well personal development and the perception of the field. After each seminar, the course directors wrote an analysis of the results of the questionnaire, which was, with their own observations, then subject to discussion in the staff meetings. The analysis helped to refine and even to modify the program of the following seminar.

The overall course evaluation was similar to the individual seminar evaluation, but more complex and used new kinds of data collection for a richer triangulation. A model for us was Phil Cohen (1994) whose research on violence in British schoolyards used a multifaceted approach—different data and interpretations around one single event. First, the researchers filmed scenes with pupils in the schoolyard during a break. Second, they asked different groups to interpret these scenes, including pupils, teachers, and supervisors. Finally, the researchers themselves reinterpreted the results.

Thus, we used four approaches:

1. Self-evaluation of the participants (questionnaire and oral statements)
2. Interpretation of outcome of the participants' final papers
3. Other achievements of the participants
4. Overall interpretation of all these data

(1) Self-evaluation of participants

The participants were asked about the impact of the course on their experiences, attitudes, and behaviors. These questions had two intentions—personal transformation and professional application: "What did you learn, or how did you change? Where and how are you going to use this?" (see Box 2.1.)

Of course, this evaluation method is not neutral. When using it, we obtained information from the participants, and our questions were a sort of "last input" by

---

Box 2.1

Extract of the EURED evaluation questionnaire

There were five main points:

1. Personal transformation

2. Change of (professional) habitus

3. Conception of peace education through several approaches

4. Learning about Europe

5. Suggestions for a new course

For any point, there were two questions:

- What did you learn, or how did you change?

- Where and how are you going to use this?

---

the trainers. The questionnaire inspired the participants to reflect, again, on their accomplishments. Such reflection may not have happened without the questionnaire.

(2) Outcome of the Course (Papers of Participants)

For their final papers, the participants had to both research the theoretical backgrounds of their selected topic as well as conduct empirical research. That the papers were to be written in English (not the mother tongue of most participants) provided an even greater challenge. The papers, documents of the participants' personal achievements, were also an indicator of the success respective to failure of the whole course. The quality of the papers was discussed in the evaluation meetings of the course directors and staff.

Some participants co-wrote their papers, such as two participants from Spain on cooperative games. Others worked alone, such as a teacher form Greece who wrote on intercultural education and human rights education in the classroom. Some focused on classroom experiences while others focused on educational issues ("Being a girl, being a boy. Exploring gender bias and behaviour") or on methods ("Using a Memorial Place to Educate for Peace, Freedom, Democracy and Human Dignity"). Others gave an overview of the situation of peace education in their country ("Peace Education in Italy") or reported on their experiences with NGOs ("Peer-To-Peer Education in Armenia").

(3) Other Achievements of Participants

Fortunately, in this course, there were outstanding participants with amazing achievements in human rights and peace education. Although these achievements were obviously not the direct result of the course, the participants felt encouraged and supported by the course on their way. These data entered also into the overall evaluation. Here are some examples:

- Two Armenian teachers have managed to make a contract with their Ministry of Education that authorised their NGO to give teacher training in conflict resolution throughout their whole province.
- A German participant founded a faith-based private school with peace education as its principal foundation.
- An Italian participant succeeded in creating a center for peace research at his university.

(4) Statements of the Final Staff Meeting

The observations and statements of the staff of the course were confronted with the evaluation of the three former points. For the final assessment of the course we also included the evaluation of all single seminars. The most important data were published in a brochure (Wintersteiner, 2007). The evaluation report was not publicly published but rather served the staff to better understand the strong and the weak points of its work.

In summary, the strengths of this evaluation approach included: (a) a focus on the habitus and the evaluation of the activities, not only attitudes, of participants as an indicator; (b) the use of different kinds of data for interpretation, grounded in the belief that changes of the habitus cannot be "objectively" measured; and (c) the integration of evaluation into the course program, and thus the creation of a culture of feedback and evaluation. The weak points, on the other hand, were: (a) we could not exclude that the subjectivity of participants and staff played a large role in the evaluation and (b) we did not apply this action research method fully on ourselves, as staff members.

Despite these self-criticisms, the use of different data and perspectives remains an example of a sound and well-done evaluation immediately after the course. What lacked in this evaluation was a long-term perspective in order to find out if the positive effects of the course were sustainable over time. For this there are only a few non-reliable indicators, not enough for a scientific evaluation. The fact that—several years after the course—many of the former participants are still working in the field of peace education, have made new professional achievements, and are in regular contact with each other are all indicators of longer-term success.

Conclusion and Outlook

Peace educators must make a basic distinction between *controlling* and *empowering* evaluation. Empowering evaluation should not be limited to the "effects" of peace education but should rather enable the actors to do what they are doing in more reflective ways. This needs complex methods which consider the learners active participants, not objects of the research. This kind of evaluation needs to become an integrated part of any peace education program. Moreover, it should become an integrated part of any peace education course to train future peace educators. In other words, peace education should be approached with the professional standards of education in general. The argument that the aims and methods of peace education are too special or different must no longer be used as a pretext to avoid the delicate question of evaluation. Instead, specific ways of evaluating peace education programs must be developed. As shown in this chapter, the most important challenge is to find methods compatible with the complexities of peace educational processes. As always when it comes to empirical work, this requires first and foremost increased theoretical efforts.

REFERENCES

Alkin, M. C. (2011). *Evaluation essentials. From A to Z.* New York & London: The Guilford Press.

Altrichter, H., Feldman, A., Posch, P. & Somekh, B. (2008). *Teachers investigate their work; An introduction to action research across the professions* (2nd ed.). Milton Park: Routledge. .

Bar-Tal, D. (2002). The elusive nature of peace education. In G. Salomon & B. Nevo (Eds.), *Peace education: The concept, principles, and practices around the world* (pp. 27–36). Mahwah, NJ: Lawrence Earlbaum.

Bohn, C. (1991). *Habitus und Kontext. Ein kritischer Beitrag zur Sozialtheorie Bourdieus.* Opladen: Westdeutscher Verlag.

Boulmetis, J. & Dutwin, Ph. (1998). *The ABCs of evaluation. Timeless techniques for program and project managers.* San Francisco: Jossey-Bass Publishers.

Bourdieu, P. (1980). *Le sens pratique.* Paris: Éditions de Minuit.

Bourdieu, P. (1982). *Leçon sur la leçon.* Paris: Éditions de Minuit.

Burns, R. J. (1996). Problems of legitimation of peace education. In: R. J. Burns & R. Aspeslagh (Eds.). *Three decades of peace education around the world. An anthology* (pp. 113–128). New York/London: Garland.

Cohen, L., & Manion, L. (2000). *Research methods in education* (5th ed.). Milton Park: Routledge.

Cohen, P. (1994). *Verbotene Spiele. Theorie und Praxis antirassistischer Erziehung.* Hamburg: Argument-Verlag.

Competence (n. d.) BusinessDictionary.com. Retrieved from http://www.businessdictionary.com/definition/competence.html

EURED. (2002). *The EURED teacher training programme. Curriculum of a European peace education course.* Klagenfurt.

Fischer, M. (2008). Friedenswissenschaftliche Evaluierungs—und Aktionsforschung. *Wissenschaft & Frieden 4,* 36–38.

Frieters-Reermann, N. (2009): *Frieden lernen. Friedens—und Konfliktpädagogik aus systemisch-konstruktivistischer Perspektive.* Duisburg-Köln: Wiku.

Geertz, C. (1973). *The interpretation of cultures: Selected essays.* New York: BasicBooks.

Harris, I. M. (2003). *Peace education evaluation.* Paper presented at the Annual Meeting of the American Educational Research Association. Chicago, IL, April 21–25, 2003.

Laval, C. (2010). *L'école n'est pas une enterprise. Le néo-libéralisme à l'assaut de l'enseignement public.* Paris: La découverte.

Lenhart, V. & A. Karimi &T. Schäfer (2011). *Feldevaluation friedensbauender Bildungsprojekte.* Osnabrück: Deutsche Stiftung Friedensforschung.

Lenhart, V. & Mitschke, R. & Braun, S. (2010). *Friedensbauende Bildungsmaßnahmen bei bewaffneten Konflikten.* Frankfurt: Peter Lang.

Liessmann, K. P. (2006). *Theorie der Unbildung.* Wien: Zsolnay.

Münch, R. (2009): *Globale Eliten, lokale Autoritäten. Bildung und Wissenschaft unter dem Regime von PISA, McKinsey & Co.* Frankfurt: Suhrkamp.

Milner, J.-C. (2011). *La politique des choses.* Court traité politique I. Lagrasse: Verdier.

Nevo, B., & Brem, I. (2002). Peace education programs and the evaluation of their effectiveness. In G. Salomon & B. Nevo (Eds.), *Peace education: The concept, principles, and practices around the world* (pp. 271–283). Mahwah, NJ: Lawrence Earlbaum.

Riegler, A. (2011). The Heinz von Foerster page. Retrieved from http://www.univie.ac.at/constructivism/HvF.htm.

Salomon G. (2009). *Recent research findings by the center for research on peace education.* Retrieved January 13, 2012 from http://cerpe.haifa.ac.il.

Spelten, A. (2006). Schon das Nachdenken über Wirkungsnachweis zeigt Wirkung, In: J. Calließ (Ed.), *Tun wir das, was wir tun, richtig? Tun wir das Richtige? Evaluation in der zivilen Konfliktbearbeitung* (pp. 147–154). Loccumer Protokolle 14/05. Rehburg Loccum.

UN Resolution A/RES/52/13, *Culture of peace.* Retreived January, 6, 2012 from http://www3.unesco.org/iycp/kits/res52-13_en.htm.

Wintersteiner, W. (2007). *Overall evaluation EURED course "human rights and peace education in europe".* (ULG Alpen-Adria-University Klagenfurt 2004–2006). Unpublished manuscript.

Wintersteiner, W. (2010). Educational Sciences and Peace Education: Mainstreaming Peace education Into (Western) Academia? In G. Salomon & E. Cairns (Eds.). *Handbook on Peace Education* (pp. 45–59). New York: Psychology Press.

CHAPTER 3

INFUSING CULTURAL RESPONSIVENESS INTO THE EVALUATION OF PEACE EDUCATION PROGRAMS

Rodney K. Hopson and Helga Stokes

INTRODUCTION

The notion that evaluation is an added burden to the design and delivery of peace education programs should be rethought in light of the benefits of participatory and culturally responsive evaluation practice. Such an evaluation practice can enhance program outcomes and lead to sustainability because program beneficiaries are key voices in the evaluation process.

An evaluation that seeks to ascertain the effectiveness of a peace education program, and which addresses personal growth issues in the domain of value formation, identity, and peaceful conflict resolution, has to look beyond measurable manifestations of certain behaviors. Deep-rooted convictions need to be explored in the context of the larger community and culture. Cultural responsiveness becomes a necessity.

Peace Education Evaluation: Learning from Experience and Exploring Prospects,
pages 39–52.
Copyright © 2015 by Information Age Publishing
All rights of reproduction in any form reserved.

Evaluation that is culturally responsive takes into the program culture and program beneficiaries in robust ways (Frierson, et al., 2010), while recognizing the importance and value of lived experiences, especially in communities of color or indigenous groups (Hopson, 2009). Peace education addresses highly relational issues in human behavior (Feuerverger, 2008). Therefore, the culture of those participating in a peace education program is a vital element in program design as well as in the understanding of its impact. Close collaboration with program beneficiaries and a search for deep understanding of the program context could potentially strain the evaluation endeavor. However, if all stakeholders understand that the evaluation serves not just funding agencies or remote program designers, but is also a tool for better understanding their own problems—and if they work locally towards sustainable solutions—the evaluation becomes an integral program support tool.

The chapter analyzes the evaluation process when infused with culturally responsive evaluation (Hopson, 2003) in relation to peace education programs and offers practical experiences to illustrate the application of such an evaluation. More specifically, this chapter is a critical reflection on methodological and theoretical issues in evaluation with respect to peace education programs. The methodological discussion is illustrated with experiences gained during the evaluation of a culturally responsive arts education program that aims to educate stakeholders in an urban school district in Southwestern Pennsylvania about racism and racial upliftment by integrating culturally responsive arts across the curriculum. The theoretical discussion builds upon literature in the evaluation and peace education fields with intentions to think more critically about infusing cultural responsiveness into the evaluation of peace education programs. The program of study, which will serve as the case example in this chapter, was conceived in order to overcome long-standing educational inequities, racial tensions, discrimination, and marginalization of African Americans in the school district and the community at large (Trotter, 2010). The program seeks to build resilience and positive racial identity among upper elementary school children of largely African American background with a smaller percentage of European American children. Education about the arts of Africa and the African diaspora infused across the curriculum is intended to lead to better cross-cultural understanding for European American children and a more positive notion of their own heritage and contributions to societal development for the African American children. One key goal is to develop more caring, peaceful, and understanding relationships among students, teachers, and parents through a better understanding of each others' and one's own lived experiences, using the arts as an expressive tool and as a source for learning about culture (CRAE, 2009).

PEACE EDUCATION AND EVALUATION

Lin, Brantmeier, and Bruhn (2008) describe a new peace education paradigm that addresses various assumptions and values such as the attainability of a culture of peace, the existence of universal values underlying peace education efforts, the interdependence of inner and outer peace and the affirmation of diversity, and the building of common understanding. They state that:

> Education for peace should both affirm diversity and build common understanding... Peace education efforts need to be linked to social justice. Examining power, oppression, privilege, and social stratification in relation to gender, class, race, dis/ ability, sexual orientation, religion, national origin, and language are essential to peace education efforts. A critical peace education should guide peace education efforts (p. xv).

Peace education projects take on many different forms. There is education about peace and about conflict, its causes, and resolutions. There are skill-building efforts for conflict resolution, educational efforts aimed at changing attitudes and perceptions of the "other" and oneself (Feuerverger, 2008). Anti-oppressive education and education for social justice (Kumashiro, 2009) serve the goals of peace education by allowing learners to comprehend inequities and power imbalances and address those constructively, thus, eventually achieving a culture of healing (Danesh, 2008).

Evaluating such programs and assessing the impact on learners has proven to be difficult (Harris, 2008). Even if students might know about ways to resolve conflicts, understanding their origins on a large or small scale and pathways to resolve them, will they be able to actually act upon this knowledge? Will there be long-term effects that lead to more peaceful relationships as a result of an intervention? Harris (2008) points to the many violence prevention and peace building efforts in schools and the challenges for evaluators to prove that these efforts are furnishing results. Outcomes-based evaluation with pre- and post-tests or the use of control groups is made difficult by fluid and changing environments, confounding variables, hard to quantify outcomes, and often subtle changes that are unique for individual participants. Formative and summative evaluation might shed some light on program implementation, but it would be beneficial if such evaluations go together with an understanding of a larger context and the lived experience of participant and demonstrate cultural responsiveness (Hopson, 2003, 2009).

CULTURAL RESPONSIVENESS AND COMPETENCE IN EVALUATION

Cultural responsiveness and competence in evaluation is but one of diverse evaluation positions that seeks to overcome the notion that evaluation is value neutral and can look at isolated phenomena while taking the larger context of a program or project into account. Being culturally responsive challenges the evaluators to gain a deep understanding of the people participating in any given program or project, to learn their histories, perceptions, notions of identity, ways to communicate, power relationships, and everyday lived experiences. This attitude is not an additional evaluation method, but rather an informed understanding of the context surrounding an evaluation task (AEA, 2011). Achieving cultural responsiveness is ongoing learning, reflection, and action by the evaluators on their personal lenses and the evaluation design. Cultural responsiveness requires humility (Morris et al., 2005) on the part of the evaluators, which would translate into valuing all stakeholders as empowered decision makers in the evaluation process (Fetterman & Wandersman, 2005). This understanding in turn informs all aspects of an evaluation cycle. It shapes how evaluators would endeavor to integrate program/project participants in the design, implementation, analysis, and use of an evaluation. It shapes the choice of methods, the recruitment of participants, design of data collection instruments, analysis, reporting, and recommendations. It shapes the intended use and expectations for the long-term desired effect of an evaluation. Will the evaluation simply be a verdict about whether or not an intervention works, or does evaluation serve value-laden purposes with long-term effect on social justice?

In a public statement on cultural competence in evaluation commissioned by the American Evaluation Association, it is stated that

> Cultural competence is a stance taken toward culture, not a discrete status or simple mastery of particular knowledge and skills. A culturally competent evaluator is prepared to engage with diverse segments of communities to include cultural and contextual dimensions important to the evaluation. Culturally competent evaluators respect the cultures represented in the evaluation (AEA, 2011, p. 1).

The statement defines culture as the shared experience by population groups. Population groups can have commonalities beyond the typical classifiers of race/ethnicity, religion, nationality, gender, or social class and include a variety of traits that are changing and evolving. Broad descriptors frequently continue stereotyping and overlook differentiations within cultural groups. People belong to a variety of groups and have a diversity of life experiences. Individuals draw on many different identifiers for defining themselves. An evaluation that does not take into account these different experiences would, according to Karen Kirkhart (2005), be at threat for better understanding the relational and experiential justifications of multicultural validity.

An evaluator will need to understand the diverse experiences and contrast and compare them to his/her own experience to gain a deep understanding of the population group. But it is not sufficient to understand a group as a stand-alone entity. The relationships among groups are essential because belonging to a group is linked to access to goods and services, to being able to collaborate in decision-making, and to assume certain professional or political positions. The power differentials based on assumed or inherited identity are the sources of conflicts, not the identity in itself (Maalouf, 2000). When conducting an evaluation of a peace education program, the evaluator needs to understand these power differentials, recognize the benefit of being informed by a cultural lens, and consistently build program understanding through the vigilant understanding of cultural differences in the entire practice.

PEACE EDUCATION PROGRAMS AND CULTURAL RESPONSIVENESS AND COMPETENCE

Peace education programs or projects intend to raise awareness about and remedy historical and current power imbalances in societies, address injustices, and overcome oppression. Essential for peace education programs is the recognition that

> Cultural groupings are ascribed differential status and power, with some holding privilege that they may not be aware of and some being relegated to the status of "other." For example, language dialect and accent can be used to determine the status, privilege, and access to resources of groups. Similarly, in some contexts, racialized "others" are framed against the implicit standard of "whiteness" and can become marginalized even when they are the numerical majority. Cultural privilege can create and perpetuate inequities in power and foster disparate treatment in resource distribution and access (AEA, 2011, p. 7).

Peace education programs help conflicting parties to establish a dynamic peace in which conflicts lead to deeper understanding the design of innovative new systems in order to replace or reshape defunct systems in societies. Diverse perspectives and divergent understandings are brought together in order to gain a more comprehensive understanding of an issue, which in turn would allow conflicting parties to explore mutually beneficial solutions (Banathy & Jenlink, 2005). Peace education programs seek to shape very personal beliefs and identities. They challenge participants to engage in critical reflections about their values and attitudes, their understanding and interpretation of occurrences in a society, and the factual learning that shaped values, attitudes, understanding, and interpretation (Feuerverger, 2008). Any evaluation would be intertwined in such processes and needs to seek a deep understanding of the occurring processes along with measurable outcomes.

Evaluators need to understand the power differentials and inevitable conflicting parties and be sensitive to them, while looking for opportunities to acknowledge stakeholder views, interests, and value judgments (Yarbrough, et al., 2011). That translates into careful crafting of language to eliminate bias and challenge stereotyping and marginalization. It means using a language understood and preferred by program participants and having communication pathways that are horizontal and include all voices (AEA, 2011, Figueroa et al., 2002)

SEEKING CULTURALLY RESPONSIVE EVALUATION OF AN EDUCATION PROGRAM AIMED AT OVERCOMING RACE-BASED INJUSTICES

It is well documented that assimilation policies and an educational setting shaped by a dominant white European culture disadvantages students from diverse minority backgrounds (Ladson-Billings, 2009; Lucas, 2008; Nieto, 2010; Pollok, 2008). The program used here to illustrate and reflect on cultural responsiveness in peace education intends to overcome the persistent achievement gap for African American children by rebuilding a shattered racial identity. The premise is that the dominant curriculum and school structures do not allow African American children to build on the strength of their cultural heritage. Instead they continue to be labeled as deficient and are encouraged to overcome the lack of achievement by assimilating into a dominant mainstream. Hanley and Noblit (2009) describe how, even in the context of desegregation, assimilation goals remained strong to the detriment of cultural uplift

> ...school desegregation meant that African Americans were now subject to a key historical logic of public education in the United States—an assimilation logic. This logic was developed early in the history of public schooling to deal with immigration from Europe, and was intended to "Americanize" the waves of European immigrants in the 19th and early 20th centuries. The logic argued that by rejecting one's heritage and mimicking the cultural beliefs and practices of the dominant Anglocentric group, one would gain access to benefits of American society (p. 16).

This continued denial of bringing one's roots and experiences into the academic formation is seen as a major detriment to achievement. Based on these insights, an urban school district with support of a local and regional foundation piloted a culturally responsive arts education program.

The Culturally Responsive Arts Education (CRAE) Program

The mission and vision of the Culturally Responsive Arts Education (CRAE) program is to integrate African and African diaspora art into the curriculum in order to help participating children improve their artistic and academic skills, develop a positive racial identity, build resilience when encountering manifestations of racism and oppression, demonstrate leadership and positive behavior, and foster supportive relationships with the community and among artists and teachers. It is hoped that upliftment of a marginalized group, together with a better understanding of the group by others, leads to more caring and peaceful relationships with benefits for all.

The arts of Africa and the African diaspora and learning about the origin and intent of the various art forms were to be employed and infused throughout the curriculum with the above stated goal in mind (PPS CRAE). Schools were invited to submit proposals for designing a culturally responsive arts education program at their school. From among the applicants, three K-8 schools were chosen. The schools are all located in a predominantly African American and economically distressed urban area in the northeastern United States. The students are mostly African American while the majority of the teachers are of white European background.

Each school developed different plans around the general goal of the program. Local artists of African and African American background were recruited to work with art and core subject matter teachers. The artists taught their respective disciplines and infused the teaching of the arts with background knowledge about the culture, history, and values. They co-taught with visual arts and music teachers for several hours each week during the school day and in one school during after-school hours. The teachers of core subject matters were also asked to collaborate and infuse the arts and culture of Africa and the African diaspora into the general curriculum, where possible. Each school selected a certain grade level for participation, mostly fifth to eighth graders. Approximately 50 students at each school participated.

This pilot program was to inform a larger effort by the school district towards culturally responsive education. The program itself was funded for four years, one year of planning and three years of implementation. The evaluation began towards the end of the first year of implementation.

Evaluating Perceptions of Racial Identity and Resilience towards Discrimination, Racism, and Oppression

This culturally responsive arts education program seeks to frame culture and racial identity as an asset and intends to help students develop caring relationships. The evaluators are challenged to find out if a positive perception of racial identity occurred among the largely African American students and if caring relationships are emerging. They need to document the subtleties of such shifts in perception and behavior, how the children and other key stakeholders like teachers, teaching artists, building administrators and others understand the extent to which the themes of the program were realized. To achieve this, cultural responsiveness needed to be infused into all stages of the evaluation. Evaluators needed to diffuse initial anxieties on the part of teachers who see evaluation as a critique of their classroom practices and yet another imposition on their already heavy workload. They also needed to become an accepted presence in the classroom so the children would feel comfortable voicing their thoughts and feelings.

Evaluating an education project that addresses racial identity issues and wants to foster a positive racial identity is a delicate matter in the context of U.S. schools. Evaluators need to know the circumstances that shaped a largely discouraging and disempowering racial identity and understand how such a perception of oneself can lead to low school achievement and high dropout rates. Evaluators are also trying to unearth very private feelings and determine if these have changed based on a program intervention.

Gaining Trust

The evaluation process can become a contributing or distracting factor. It can help the program achieve its goals or be an obstacle. The way questions are asked, evaluation instruments designed, and field observations noted down will add a layer of interpretation. How evaluators interact with program participants can build trust or close down sharing of personal perceptions, especially when trying to explore these very sensitive feelings around race and identity. In addition the majority of the program participants and those interviewed and observed were children from around ten to thirteen years of age. These children are just learning the language around identity and race and the complex American and African diaspora history involved.

Cultural responsiveness begins with the formation of an evaluation team. Whether or not individual evaluators are from the same racial, ethnic, or socio-economic background, they should make an effort to become very familiar with the program setting and approach program participants as collaborators (Millet, 2002). This necessitates that the flow of communication is horizontal, rather than vertical or top-down. Open communication is essential but, in reality, not always easy to achieve, especially if evaluators work within the confines of a still very hierarchical education system setting.

In the case of the CRAE program evaluation, the team includes some evaluators intimately familiar with the struggle around racial discrimination and with public school settings. They personally know the neighborhoods and schools, having taught or hired in them within the larger school district. In addition, the team made a conscious effort to become familiar with the history and current circumstances of the neighborhoods and school district

Program participants—here mostly the teachers and teaching artists—shared information about the neighborhood, the children's lived experiences, and the schools' circumstances. Program participants are not simply to be evaluated, but their expressed views and requests ought to shape the evaluation design. The children themselves need to see the evaluators as trustworthy and remain assured that what they say and do does not reflect negatively on them. All should see a benefit in the evaluation and be confident that the outcomes, even the less favorable ones, inform program improvement and learning and do not reflect negatively on their work performance. Ideally, the program participants themselves should be the ones requesting help of evaluators and using the data gathered to inform their program implementation, but in the case of the CRAE program the funders required the evaluation, which meant that the evaluators had to overcome some initial mistrust. Teachers were rightfully skeptical that the program evaluation could impact their official work performance evaluation.

Developing the Evaluation Design

As mentioned, cultural responsive evaluation is not a new method added to the toolbox of evaluation methodologies; rather, it means that evaluators include cultural context and participants' values and expectations at all stages of an evaluation process. While the evaluation itself might well follow the customary steps of an evaluation, the various activities carried out during an evaluation are infused with knowledge about the context, understanding of local perceptions, establishing the purpose of the evaluation, seeing a greater good in the evaluation, and ongoing open communication.

The ongoing open communication is a process issue and a skill, which is not necessarily thought about when figuring out the technical aspects of an evaluation design. It is crucial, however, to pay attention to it because the flow of communication is an indicator of power structures, and when practicing culturally responsive evaluation, communication ought to be authentic and democratizing (Jenlink, 2004). Instead of preconceived agendas and using power relationships to influence outcomes there ought to be an open exchange of observations around the program implementation, its successes, and its challenges. Voicing critical observations needs to be acceptable and not have any detrimental consequences for those who are stating them. This, then, will help to uphold the level of trust needed to carry out an honest evaluation. After the first year of the evaluation, evaluation questions were overhauled and re-established after a series of meetings between the evaluation team and the school district deputy superintendent and key staff based on the results of the Y1 evaluation. In this case, as a result of critical and reflective results of the program and the evaluation, including key program staff changes, a revised evaluation design was developed which better capture the dynamic program time elements, better reflected the school district's needs of the program, and more aptly reflected how the program impact was to be understood.

While the evaluators intended to have open and free flowing communication, time constraints and the hierarchical nature of schooling, along with the fact that the evaluation was a requirement by funders and not requested by the program participants, limited the flow to some degree. The evaluation design itself, though, was vetted with program designers and received feedback from teachers and artists during and after the first full year of evaluation work.

Evaluation Methods

In order to capture the subtleties of identity formation and attitudes about race and race-based injustices, the evaluation methods included an ongoing presence of the evaluators in the field. Through observations and conversational interviews, these issues were explored. The evaluators documented gains in academic and artistic achievement, which called for a more quantitative approach. Mixed methods were used and each theme was researched using a variety of tools; they included:

- Classroom observation of CRAE classes
- Surveys of teachers involved in CRAE, teachers and learning support personnel in general at each school, school administrators, teaching artists, parents, and students.
- Conversational interviews with CRAE teachers, teaching artists, school administrators, and students
- Secondary data: Grade averages, disciplinary records, absences (available through PPS office of research); Selected student artistic and performative work; Art rubric applied to selected student work (developed by PPS CRAE teachers and teaching artists).

Table 3.1 summarizes which of the instruments addresses each theme (Stokes, et al., 2011). The table illustrates that to capture racial identity and resilience to-

TABLE 3.1.

INSTRU-MENT	Arts Learning	Academic Learning	Racial Identity & Resilience	Leader-ship	Collabo-ration	Engage-ment	Cultural Exposure	Profes-sional Growth
Observa-tions	√	√	√	√	√	√	√	
Parent Survey	√		√	√	√	√	√	
Child Sur-vey	√		√	√		√	√	
Teacher/TA/Admin Survey	√		√	√	√	√	√	
Staff Inter-views	√	√	√	√	√	√	√	√
Parent Interview	√	√	√	√	√	√		
Student Interview	√		√	√	√	√		
Arts Ru-bric	√							

wards racial oppression, several tools were used. The students themselves were asked about their perceptions during a conversational interview and with surveys. Questions asked to what degree respondents agreed with the following:

- I am proud of my racial background and heritage.
- I am learning more about my racial background and heritage.
- I say positive things about myself.
- I say positive things about my racial group.
- I hear positive things about myself at school.
- I hear positive things about my racial group at school.
- I have positive role models at the school.
- I am aware of positive contributions African Americans have made.

Teachers, artists and parents were asked similar questions asking about their observations of the students' attitudes, knowledge, and behavior. Triangulation of answers from various sources led to a more complete picture of student perceptions and attitudes. Anecdotes offered by teachers and artists helped to illustrate shifts in student attitudes, such as this one told by one of the teaching artists:

> So you know I think in terms of having high regard for who you are and where you come from is one of the things that we've been able to instill in the kids, to be proud of Africa. When we started last year, in particular [a student] he said, 'I am not Afri-

can. I don't know what you're talking about. I am not black. I'm this. I'm that.' I'm like, 'That's okay.' Now he's like, 'You know what? It's cool. I like Africa. I like African Americans' (Stokes, et al., 2011, p. 37).

The surveys and interviews occurred at the end of year one, two and three of the program implementation. This allows evaluators to see long-term changes. Observations too are done on a regular monthly basis in each classroom and efforts are made to observe each artist and participating teacher with each of their classes at a minimum of once per month throughout the school year. Participation in CRAE team meetings and attendance of special events such as student performances or exhibitions of artwork allow evaluators to be immersed in the program's larger context.

The combination of approaches was chosen to gain insights into very personal attitude changes and also to track whole-group shifts in perceptions of racial identity and resilience. The survey analysis used descriptive statistics to summarize agreement or disagreement with statements such as the ones listed above. Open ended survey questions, conversational interviews, and observations allowed for a more in-depth focus on the individual. Together, these mixed methods aim for a comprehensive picture.

Critical Reflection on the Theoretical Issues Underlying the Choice of Methods

The evaluators embarked on the evaluation with personal goals of aiding the education of a group of students disadvantaged by an assimilationist agenda of an education system (Hanley & Noblit, 2009). The realities of implementing a culturally responsive education program into a rigid school setting, where subjects are taught in discrete blocks and forty-five minute periods, uncovered the power structures inherent in current education practices. Teachers were often handicapped by time constraints, mandated curricula, time consuming standardized testing requirements, or lack of preparation in doing what they wanted to do with the program. Teachers have to conform their teaching styles and content to mandates handed to them in the form of standards, mandated curricula, and prescribed textbooks. Teacher-centered classroom practices are still ingrained in the daily teaching routines, and teachers as well as students needed to get used to more constructivist teaching practices, which are a logical requirement for culturally responsive teaching. As the evaluation proceeds, evaluators are challenged to point out these larger inequities and development needs that influence program implementation. The evaluation might well show that issues of inequity and cultural oppression within the education system at large can seriously handicap well meant but small-scale programs. The evaluation itself is then propelled into a larger context and begins to serve educational change issues beyond mere program evaluation.

Veronica Thomas and Brook McKie (2006), in their article on collecting and utilizing evaluation research for public good on behalf of African American children, point out that a culturally and contextually responsive evaluation can furnish data to inform a more equitable school reform (p. 341). The authors conclude that evaluations are

> ... not done *to* the students, the school context, and educational projects; but, instead are done *for* the students, the school and the educational effort under study. ... Educational evaluators working in this area should seek to make a positive difference in the lives of African American students and the settings where evaluators work, changing them in some important and constructive ways through data that are collected and the utility of the findings that are reported (p. 349).

The evaluator thus takes on an advocacy role, one that should not prevent a critical and objective collection and analysis of data in favor of steering the reporting more heavily towards positive outcomes. Only a balanced reporting will allow the pinpointing of areas in need of improvement and larger contextual issues that might impede program development. Here again trust and open communication will weigh in (Stokes, 2008). The choice of methods should always follow the recommended standards for good evaluation design (Yarbrough et al., 2011). But the interactions among evaluators, program participants, and other beneficiaries of the evaluation shape the evaluation processes. If trust is established through open communication and cultural responsiveness, the necessary honesty to address shortcomings constructively is possible.

CONCLUSION

The evaluation of peace education programs is challenging because of the complexity and open-endedness of peace education programs. Peace education programs reach beyond the acquisition of facts and skills and want to change ingrained attitudes and identities. Hard to quantify outcomes might frustrate the efforts of program designers to clearly communicate the benefits of a program. For evaluators it is a prerequisite to gain a deep understanding of the context of the program to be evaluated, become culturally competent, and employ methods that are culturally responsive. It needs to be recognized that evaluation cannot be culture-free. Evaluators need the humility to acknowledge that they always learn from program participants and the setting and should not assume that cultural competence is a static skill. Trust among all participants is essential for achieving valid evaluation results. If program participants realize that the evaluation helps them to better understand the program impact and resulting changes in their own perceptions and identities, they can take more ownership of the evaluation and become reliable generators of evaluation data. Program participants themselves need to deeply understand the aims of the program so they can reflect accurately on their learning gains and attitude shifts and communicate those to evaluators. Cultural relevance and competence, along with an understanding of power dynamics, are thus key to achieve and maintain trusting relationships and open communication.

REFERENCES

American Evaluation Association (2011). *Public statement on cultural competence in evaluation.* Retrieved on Nov 1, 2011 from http://www.eval.org/ccstatement.asp.

Banathy, B. H., & Jenlink, P. M. (Eds.). (2005). *Dialogue as a means of collective communication.* London: Kluwer Academic/Plenum Publishers.

CRAE Advisory Committee (2009). *Culturally responsive arts education core themes.* Pittsburgh Public Schools, Request for Proposals (Unpublished).

Danesh, H. B. (2008). Creating a culture of healing in multiethnic communities: An integrative approach to prevention and amelioration of violence-induced conditions. *Journal of Community Psychology, 36*(6), 814–832.

Fetterman, D. M., & Wandersman, A. (2005). *Empowerment evaluation principles in practice.* New York: Guilford Publications.

Feuerverger, G. (2008). Teaching about peaceful coexistence. In J. Lin, E. J. Brantmeier, & I. Harris (Eds.), *Transforming education for peace* (pp. 129–142). Charlotte, NC: IAP- Information Age Publishing.

Figueroa, M. E. D., Kincaid, L., Rani, M., & Lewis, G. (2002). *Communication for social change: An integrated model for measuring the process and its outcomes.* New York: The Rockefeller Foundation.

Frierson, H. T., Hood, S., Hughes, G. B., & Thomas, V. G. (2010). A guide to conducting culturally-responsive evaluations. In J. Frechtling (Ed.), *The 2010 user-friendly handbook for project evaluation* (pp. 75–96). Arlington, VA: National Science Foundation.

Hanley, M. S., & Noblit, G. W. (2009). *Cultural responsiveness, racial identity, and academic success: A review of literature.* Paper prepared for the Heinz Endowments.

Harris, I. (2008). The promise and pitfalls of peace education evaluation. In J. Lin, E. J. Brantmeier, I. Harris (Eds.), *Transforming education for peace.* Charlotte, NC: Information Age Publishing. 245–263.

Hopson, R. K. (2009). Reclaiming knowledge at the margins: Culturally responsive evaluation in the current evaluation moment. In K. E. Ryan & J. B. Cousins (Eds.), *The Sage international handbook of educational evaluation* (pp. 429–446). Sage: Los Angeles.

Hopson, R. K. (2003). *Overview of multicultural and culturally competent program evaluation issues, challenges and opportunities.* Woodland Hills, CA: The California Endowment.

Jenlink, P. M. (2004). Discourse ethics in the design of educational systems: Consideration for design praxis. *Systems Research and Behavioral Science 21(3).* 237–249.

Kirkhart, K. E. (2005). Through a cultural lens: Reflections on validity and theory in evaluation. In S. Hood, R. K. Hopson, & H. T. Frierson (Eds.), *The role of culture and cultural context: A mandate for inclusion, the discovery of truth, and understanding in evaluative theory and practice* (pp. 21–39). Greenwich, CT: Information Age Publishing, Inc.

Kumashiro, K. K. (2009). *Against common sense: Teaching and learning towards social justice.* New York: Taylor and Francis.

Ladson-Billings, G. (2009). *The dream-keepers: Successful teachers of African American children.* San Francisco: Jossey-Bass.

Lin, J., Brantmeier, E. J., & Bruhn, C. (Eds.). (2008). *Transforming education for peace.* Charlotte, NC: Information Age Publishing.

Lucas, S.R. (2008). Constructing colorblind classrooms. In M. Pollock (Ed.) *Everyday anti racism: Getting real about race in school* (pp. 62–66)a. New York: The New Press.

Maalouf, A. (2000). *In the name of identity: Violence and the need to belong.* New York: Arcade Publishing.

Millett, R. A. (2002). Missing voices: A personal perspective on diversity in program evaluation. *American Journal of Evaluation, 20,* 1–14.

Morris, J. A., Brotheridge, C. M., & Urbanski, J. C. (2005). Bringing humility to leadership: Antecedents and consequences of leader humility. *Human Relations, 58*(10), 1323–1350. Retrieved from http://hum.sagepub.com/content/58/10/1323.full.pdf.

Nieto, S. (2010). *The light in their eyes: Creating multicultural learning communities.* New York: Teachers College Press.

Pollok, M. (2008) (Ed.). *Everyday antiracism. Getting real about race in schools.* New York: The New Press.

Stokes, H., Hopson, R., Generett, G., Good, T., Allie, A., McGuirk, L., & Bantum, K. (2011). *Annual evaluation report of the Culturally Responsive Arts Education Program (CRAE), School year 2010–2011.* Prepared for Pittsburgh Public Schools. Unpublished.

Stokes, H. (2008). Design conversation, an instrument for peace education. In J. Lin, E. J. Brantmeier, & C. Bruhn (Eds.), *Transforming education for peace* (pp. 163–184). Charlotte, NC: Information Age Publishing.

Thomas, V. G., & McKie, B. K. (2006). Collecting and utilizing evaluation research for public good and on behalf of African American children. *The Journal of Negro Education, 75*(3 Summer).

Trotter, J. & Day, J. (2010). *Race and renaissance: African Americans in Pittsburgh since World War II.* Pittsburgh: University of Pittsburgh Press.

Yarbrough, D. B., Shulha, L. M., Hopson, R. K., & Caruthers, F. A. (2011). *The program evaluation standards: A guide for evaluators and evaluation users.* Los Angeles, CA: Sr.

CHAPTER 4

NAMING THE SPACE

Evaluating Language in Peace Education through Reflective Practice

Cheryl Woelk

INTRODUCTION

"You know when you want to express something, but you can't express it. It's very painful in your heart." "Sometimes I feel the pressure to kind of conform to this kind of language, their kind of language." "At times it feels like it is a kind of imperialism, like you have to export the terms." "It's not just the translation of words and ideas that need to shift, but it almost feels like you're shifting your whole person into a new space." "I'm still learning about English. English is not even my second language. It's my third language."

These are words of adult learners reflecting on their experience of language and peacebuilding in education. They came from a study at a graduate program and language institute in a small university in the eastern U.S. designed to identify the ways that educators who use the values and approaches of peace education respond to dynamics of language in the classroom (Woelk, 2011). As an international graduate student, language learner, and peace educator, I had watched interactions in the classrooms around me and began to notice that language played a major role in the direction of class discussion, the level of participation by learn-

Peace Education Evaluation: Learning from Experience and Exploring Prospects,
pages 53–66.
Copyright © 2015 by Information Age Publishing
All rights of reproduction in any form reserved.

ers, and the attention of the instructor. Wanting to explore these observations further, I decided to research how peace educators create space for language in the classroom. The resulting observations, discoveries, and questions led me to believe that language is even more important in peacebuilding and education than I had realized. I have come to believe that language must be given attention in the evaluation of peace education and also that educators can conduct such evaluation through methods of individual and collective reflective practice.

While there seems to be a growing number of resources on peace education, not many deliberately connect peace, education, and language. The few articles that do connect these fields also note the absence of research and call for more (Friedrich, 2007; Mirici, 2008; Morgan & Vandrick, 2009; Wenden, 2003). These articles come from several fields, including peace studies, education, and linguistics. Reports of peace education practice, however, draw from a variety of settings. Public schools, private schools, after-school programs, summer camps, workshops, training sessions, higher education, and religious training for a range of ages and contexts have been documented (Harris & Morrison, 2003; Salomon, 2002). Many of these programs take place in multilingual contexts, or even seek to build intercultural understanding between two or more groups (Ardizzone, 2002). In some settings, such as recent peace camps in northeast Asia (Eberly & Espenshade, 2009), English acts as a common language among participants. In any of these multicultural and multilingual settings, language cannot be ignored. Naming language as an aspect of peace education evaluation is necessary due to the connection of multiple dimensions of language to essential issues in peace education in terms of narratives or meaning-making; power and domination; and transformation of knowledge, attitudes, and behaviours.

WHAT DOES *LANGUAGE* MEAN?

The language that must be evaluated in peace education is a complex system of creating and communicating meaning. As Halliday and Webster (2006) aptly describe, "…language is at the same time part of reality, a shaper of reality, and a metaphor for reality." Language exists concurrently on multiple levels of human experience, thus making it complicated to analyze. From the study, however, I was able to articulate several aspects of language that educators identified as relating in some manner to peace education. These aspects are depicted visually in Figure 4.1. Each of these language dimensions, and possibly more, needs to be a part of the evaluation process.

There are five interconnected levels described in the diagram that need to be a part of peace education evaluation. The most apparent is the language system, for which names such as English, Korean, or French are given. Those who need not spend energy to focus on the system of language in a context have linguistic privilege (Rauf & Iqbal, 2008) and can instead focus on the other levels of language in the diagram. At the discourse level, peace educators need to pay attention to how content is communicated, including the use of what educators in the study

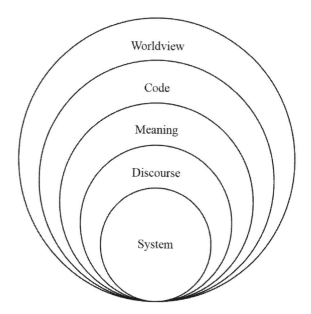

FIGURE 4.1. Levels of Language as Referred to in Study, Arranged by Ease of Perception.

called "good communication skills." Next is the level of meaning, which includes both the denotations and connotations of concepts. Even if a word has a translation from one language system to another, understandings, nuances, and feelings associated with the concept may vary. The fourth dimension in the diagram could be defined as the code and refers to the larger cultural context of communication, including the distinctions as academic or conversational language (Cummins, 2000). The code often carries unarticulated expectations that accompany interaction within a certain context. On the outer level of the diagram are narrative and worldview, which are embedded within the language to the extent that speakers often cannot articulate their worldview until it comes into contrast with another.

In considering evaluation of peace education programs, each dimension of language, those I have called the language system, discourse, meaning, code, and worldview, must be addressed. Participants in peace education programs must have the opportunity to experience and learn about peace in each of these areas of language use and reflection.

THE ROLE OF NARRATIVE

Language on each of these levels is inherently connected to the ways in which individual and collective stories of peace and conflict are told. Essentially, language is used to make meaning of human experiences by connecting them in stories (Bruner, 1990). These narratives shape who we are and how we see ourselves in relation to others. Understanding dynamics of individual and collective identity and narrative is a key aspect of building peace. As one educator in the study put it, "[If] you don't start with the assumption that we share a worldview and we share a sense of reality... then language becomes everything."

Narrative theory helps to make sense of the multiple dimensions of language and their impact on human identity. From a narrative perspective, the manner in which people talk about themselves and the world around them constructs their identities as they choose how to interact with others (Crossley, 2000; Madigan, 2011; Ochs & Capps, 1996; Winslade & Monk, 2000). Choice of language on any level identifies a social in-group or the sense of "we" that Wenden (2003) calls a "scope of identification," also delineating who is excluded, drawing boundaries between us and them (Nan, 2008). Thus each dimension of language, as described above, is involved in the construction of narratives that shape individual and collective identity. People tell stories within a linguistic system, using certain styles of discourse in particular settings depending on who is present, utilizing multiple levels of meaning connected with cultural understandings, articulated in a code, and set in a larger worldview influenced by the culture and also unique to each individual.

If narratives have such great importance for constructing human identity and perception of reality, then stories must also be integral to ethics, morality, and understandings of peace. As Crossley (2000) articulates, "Human beings think, perceive, imagine, interact and make moral choices according to narrative structures," and these structures become our reality. Human concepts of what is good, how we fit into those concepts, and what we need to do to create peace are transferred and constructed through stories that are told in our communities and cultures. Bradshaw (2002) suggests that the exact function of narratives in our societies is that they provide legitimacy for human action, construct individual and collective identities, give people agency in shaping their histories, create customs and traditions, articulate the values and concept of morality of a community, and continue the story in a "vision for the future" (p. 30). Through rituals and language, people in a particular culture create their perception of "the good" (Crossley, 2000). Members of that cultural group shape their attitudes and behaviours in reference to these common understandings of ethics. Change within a culture, then, will also include "a moral aspect and is intimately related to cultural narratives, which contain the values that shape human character and govern ethical action" (Bradshaw, 2002, p. 17).

Within peace education and peacebuilding fields an understanding of narrative is already being applied, which recognizes in practice the importance of language. Understanding narratives about conflict and finding ways to create new narratives can help to manage and resolve conflict situations in a variety of settings (Kellett & Dalton, 2001). Narrative approaches developed by White and Epston (1990) are being used in dealing with trauma healing and therapy (Crossley, 2000; Madigan, 2011). Mediation techniques that rely on narrative understanding to re-shape conflict narratives have been developed and documented by Winslade and Monk (2000, 2008). Restorative justice approaches in schools and health care have been influenced by narrative understanding (Winslade & Monk, 2008). Fields such as conflict coaching (Jones & Brinkert, 2007) and alternative dispute resolution (Stewart & Maxwell, 2010) also rely heavily on concepts of narrative and story-telling. In all of these peace-related fields, narrative theory provides a means for peacebuilding through and in reference to language.

Because human narratives influence our identities and experiences of reality in and through language, evaluation of peace education programs must take the role of narrative and language into account. Creating lasting cultural change for peace requires changing individual and collective narratives. As the thirteenth century Persian poet Rumi says, "Speak a new language so that the world will be a new world."

LANGUAGE AND POWER DYNAMICS

Another reason why language must be part of peace education evaluation is the link between language and power, which is an essential dynamic to address in seeking to build peace in educational settings and society. Power issues related to language arise on both the micro level in the peace education context, such as classrooms and other educational settings, and on the larger macro level of the society and global context of the program.

One aspect of language and power in peace education on a micro level is the ability to participate fully in the language system that is the medium of instruction. Rauf and Iqbal (2008) use the term "linguistic privilege," which is "the privilege of being proficient in the language of instruction, the language of the text taught, content delivered, and the language of the communication in the discourse of teaching and learning" (p. 46). Those with linguistic privilege do not need to give effort to thinking about language form and meaning and can concentrate on the content. Those without linguistic privilege have fewer chances to share their ideas; thus they are relegated to a lower position of status (Rauf & Iqbal, 2008). Buzzelli and Johnston (2002) also claim that social roles and norms that form within a group are assigned through language, resulting in "the relative distribution of power and status among participants" (p. 28). Language, then, affects a student's status in the group, influencing levels of participation and learning in peace education.

Another aspect of power and language in peace education relates to dominant narratives and the control of narrative. Who speaks in the classroom? Who does not? What kind of communication is used or preferred? Whose knowledge or stories are valued? These ethical connotations of language power and privilege arise within classroom interaction. As Crossley (2000) points out, "The choice of one narrative over another often has serious implications for the construction of images of self, responsibility, blame and morality" (p. 21). Power is linked to the stories we tell. Buzzelli and Johnston (2002) explain that the social interaction of language is a moral meaning-making activity. Any language contains both content and a hidden message of ideologies supporting the content and shaping the interaction (Buzzelli & Johnston, 2002; Wenden, 2003). Participants may not be aware of the ways in which language "is being used to shape their understanding and to communicate beliefs and values, such as an ideology, that justifies and legitimates what is understood" (Wenden, 2003, p. 186). The narratives chosen and stories told in peace education programs can unknowingly empower or disempower participants.

On the macro level, power dynamics among language groups also have major implications for peace education programs. This is particularly true in regard to the power of English as a dominant global language. A "critical / transformative" (Tsuda, 2008, p. 47) perspective on English draws attention to the "global disparity and discommunication" (Pennycook, 2003, p. 6) that the use of English creates between speakers of English and those who do not speak English. The loss of indigenous languages as people shift their primary languages to English happens at a faster rate when dealing with the social, political, and economic power of an "empire" (Wong & Motha, 2007). The sociopolitical power of English pushes people to learn and apply the language in order to function in a globalized society (Tsuda, 2008). As a result, many people choose to teach the dominant language rather than heritage languages to the next generation, which affects identity of self and group (Epstein, 1999; Wong & Motha, 2007). Epstein (1999) asserts that everyone is affected by the power of English. Whether as a native speaker, learner, or someone who has no knowledge of it, the dominance of English in a globalized context affects all humanity.

Also, the issue of linguistic discrimination greatly influences peace education programs conducted in any language. Linguistic prejudice, or "linguicism" (Phillipson, 1992; Zuidema, 2005), occurs whereby people who speak primarily the dominant language "dare to ignore or dismiss entire groups of people because of what [they] assume their linguistic habits reveal about them" (Zuidema, 2005, p. 666). Linguistic prejudice can lead to discrimination in institutions and support for unfair and discriminatory policies (Cummins, 2000; Friedrich, 2007; Zuidema, 2005). In addition, a general lack of sensitivity to the needs of minority multilingual speakers is often present where monolingual speakers of the dominant language are majority (Friedrich, 2007). Thus, language connects intimately with identity, status, dominion, and oppression (Phillipson, 1992), which are all issues in building peace.

In addition, the experience of imbalanced power dynamics arises for participants within peace education settings. In the study I conducted, students expressed frustration with learning about peace through English. As one student communicated, "At times it feels like it is a kind of imperialism, like you have to export the terms." The language of peace becomes another form of domination, which becomes more apparent when trying to translate expressions into the student's home context. Another student described this complexity of studying peace in English by referring to a line quoted by Hooks (1995) "this is the oppressor's language / yet I need it to talk to you." Furthermore, the availability of peace-related resources in English in publications and the internet means that access to English is access to peace studies fields. Even the development of peace education materials, research, and evaluation are dominated by English despite the fact that peace education practice occurs in various linguistic settings.

EFFECTIVENESS OF PEACE EDUCATION

Attention to language influences the effectiveness of peace education or the transformation of knowledge, attitudes, and behaviours to make for more peaceful societies and relationships in that the concept of effectiveness is embedded in language and narratives; transformation of individuals, relationships, and societies is only understood and expressed through language; and experiences of peace connect with experiences of language dynamics.

The question of effectiveness in evaluating peace education is one that greatly depends on the language used in a particular context. It must be acknowledged that effectiveness of a peace education program is not necessarily linear in a Euro-American narrative of time and progression. If the goals of peace education are generally to effect change in attitudes, behaviours, and skills of program participants and in their contexts (Salomon, 2002), effectiveness will be a complicated change process which could use multiple narratives to shape its meaning. Change takes place in the complex sense of a "multidimensional" and "polychronistic" (Lederach, 2010, p. 137) concept of time. That is, change for peace does not necessarily begin now and continue forward in a sequential progression. This narrative of forward progression is only one way of thinking of effectiveness. Peacebuilding, like any kind of transformation or healing, is a multistoried process (Madigan, 2011), reaching to "the past we see before us" and "backward into the future" (Lederach, 2010, p. 136), and rooted in individual stories of events, communal interactions, personal and collective identities, and history.

Even if effectiveness is defined as the transformation of knowledge, attitudes and behaviours, this change can only be expressed and understood through multiple dimensions of language. Peace education program evaluations attempting to measure change in traditional linear methods have shown that evaluation cannot prove a direct correlation between peace education programs and increased peace in societies (Harris, 2003; Nevo & Brem, 2002). However, there is much research and personal experience to show that peace education can contribute to significant and lasting change in a community or society (Ardizzone, 2002; Salomon & Nevo, 2002). The type of qualitative research used to gather this information about peace education programs includes surveys, interviews, writing, focus groups, and other language-rich methods. Because language relates to the process of reflexivity and thinking about ourselves and our actions (Crossley, 2000), language must be used in trying to identify ways that peace is present through careful communication and a deep understanding of cultural context and nuances of language in order to perceive the connections between peace education and its influence on individuals and societies.

Also, participants' experience of language must contribute to their experience of peace for a peace education program to be evaluated as effective. If participants learn about peace issues in the world, conflict transformation skills, and even healthy communication patterns—but experience the silencing of their voice in a training context—the peace education program cannot be classified as effective. An example is a discussion by educators in the study questioning the values-centered approach of peace education and the related assumptions about evaluation. Peace education assumes change in the participants' attitudes, knowledge, and behaviours and thus, to some extent, identity. In most situations, these changes are also assumed to be positive changes. Yet, the educators asked, what if the participants are being encouraged to change in unwanted ways that their experience, personal values, or culture resists? For peace education occurring in English with participants of multilingual and multicultural backgrounds, thought patterns and paradigms are embedded in language and language structures. By learning about peace in a specific language, are there unintentional consequences of cultural domination taking place where one way of thinking overshadows another, even across languages? These questions must be asked in any evaluation of peace education programs.

A Suggestion for Evaluating Language in Peace Education

The research approach of reflective practice, used in assessing the peace education contexts in which I participated, can be one method for peace educators to evaluate language in peace education. As the literature suggests, reflective practice is a fundamental process for gaining knowledge and for articulating tacit knowledge, tying together the work of theory and practice (Schön, 1983; Smith, 2001). Thus, in my research, I began with self as part of practice; not separating theory and practice, but developing theories from practice and using theory to inform practice. A significant result of the study was its influence on my tacit and explicit knowledge through the articulation of my assumptions and perspectives by means of reflective journals and document analysis. Previously, I had not been able to verbalize explicitly my tacit knowledge of perspectives on language and peacebuilding in curriculum and instruction. This change occurred because of the research process. I began to apply the findings in each cycle of data collection as I analyzed the data. In addition, I observed in the reflective journals that I had become more intentional about my practice as I wrote regularly. Due to my commitment to writing regularly, and thus knowing that all would be recorded, I began to focus on my actions and responses to students during the class period. My ongoing reflective practice skills became stronger because of the intentional reflective research process.

However, the reflective practice did not end with me. I developed methods to engage colleagues in collective reflective practice rooted in three main theories of appreciative inquiry, organizational knowledge creation, and grounded theory. Through journals, questionnaires, interviews, observations, and focus groups, I and the other participants articulated our knowledge about peacebuilding and language and common key themes emerged as essential to engaging language in curriculum and instructional strategies. Because the apparatus I used continued to emerge over the course of the study based on feedback from the participants and data, and only developed more fully as knowledge was articulated, the research itself empowered participants to reflect and apply their insights. As a result, both I and the other participants in the study could learn from the data analyzed to work for positive change in peacebuilding and language education both during and beyond the course of the research.

The first theory that I used in the study was appreciative inquiry, which attempts to identify successful functioning and build on strengths (Cooperrider & Whitney, 2005). This means finding constructive ways to elicit self-reflection and evaluation from a group of people, which is generally more effective than a critical approach. Looking for aspects already being implemented that worked well and for aspects that I and my colleagues recognized as weak or missing was easier to initiate than critiquing negative aspects of our practice. The interviews that I conducted with colleagues used the appreciative approach. Asking "how do you engage language in the classroom from a peacebuilding perspective" prompted stories of language that contributed to experiences of peace in and beyond the classroom. When difficult stories arose, I was able to ask how those situations might have been different or what was learned from the situation. The appreciative approach allowed educators, and allowed me, to open up in reflection more freely than a critical approach.

Organizational knowledge creation theories, which are designed to move tacit knowledge to explicit knowledge (DeLong, 2004; Nonaka & Takeuchi, 1995) and compare theories-in-action to espoused theories (Argyris, 1991) also informed the study. Organizational knowledge creation theories see peace educators as co-creators and selectors of knowledge, not simply subjects to be evaluated. These theories seek to find ways to move tacit knowledge to explicit knowledge that can be shared with other educators and contexts. This is a circular process that involves "externalization" or reflecting on knowledge and trying to articulate it, "combination" of ideas from different individuals, "internalization" of the collective knowledge, and "socialization" of the knowledge into the culture and tacit knowledge of the people in the organization (Nonaka & Takeuchi, 1995). The study focused particularly on the "externalization" and "combination" phases of the cycle, but in effect led to some "internalization" of the knowledge for me as I reflected, compiled, and analyzed data.

The third theory influencing the study was grounded theory, which explains a phenomenon based on information gathered from those who have experienced the phenomenon (Corbin & Strauss, 2008). Grounded theory looks at what exists and finds learning from the situation, then builds theories based on practice more than observing. This approach helped nurture the development of a theory of engaging language in curriculum and instruction in higher education from a peacebuilding perspective based on the data collected from participants during this research. In my study, the theory of multiple dimensions of language in Figure 4.1 came out of my practice and the reflection of other educators on their experiences. Theories that emerge from research can be used as models for further evaluation. For example, another theory that emerged from my study is that there are at least seven specific areas that educators work at to create a *space* for peace and language in the classroom, including knowledge and experience; empowerment and participation; community and relationships; identity and culture; narrative and values; transformation and change; and emotions and spirituality. Reflective research conducted in other peace education programs may elicit similar themes, but grounded theory would allow practitioners and educators to articulate theories for use in their contexts.

There are limitations, however, with the methods used in the study as a way of evaluating language in peace education. One limitation is that it needs to be ongoing. Just as effectiveness is not about getting from point A to point B in peace education, evaluation is a continuous process of reflection, articulation, sharing ideas, and then bringing those ideas back into practice. The "internalization" and "socialization" (Nonaka & Takeuchi, 1995) phases of the organizational knowledge creation only begin with the conclusion of a study. Perhaps educators could take turns engaging in intensive reflective studies on their practice in their peace education programs, or perhaps a less intensive approach could be more ongoing. There is also a need for a critical approach, particularly in research and theory. Appreciative inquiry may tend to overlook missing elements or aspects that should be reconsidered in education. Finally, a major problem with this study is that the evaluation itself must occur in all the languages being used, not only in the dominant one—especially if it is English. If the program is a bilingual or multilingual peace education program, it would be even more important to include data, analysis, discussion, and sharing of the results in multiple languages.

Nonetheless, language is a necessary element to consider in peace education and peace education evaluation. The approach described above could be one way to evaluate, yet this type of reflective practice would look different in each setting. Based on results and further reflections on the study I conducted, the following suggested questions may assist in creating a similar evaluation on language and peace education.

Language in Peace Education

- What language systems are present in the classroom?
- What codes and worldviews are present?

- How does each dimension of language interact with the peace education curriculum and instruction?

Narrative and Language in Peace Education

- What stories are spoken in the classroom?
- How is meaning explored and defined?
- What space is there to ask, "What do you mean by ____?" when unusual or unfamiliar—language arises in the classroom?
- How does the educator problematize or unpack concepts and terms to explore deeper meaning?
- How are multiple meanings negotiated, validated, and valued?
- How are hidden or tacit narratives articulated and explored?
- What framing is used to present peace concepts? How is this framing discussed for other contexts?

Power and Language in Peace Education

- What level of agency do participants have? How is this agency articulated or expressed?
- What privileged languages, narratives, and knowledge exist in the classroom? How do they influence participants?
- How do educators address issues of status in the classroom?
- Who speaks and who listens? Who doesn't speak?
- How are critical thinking and creative thinking used to empower participants?
- How do macro levels of language dominance influence participants? In what ways do educators address these power dynamics?
- In what ways does the peace education program contribute to or work to deconstruct imbalances of power in language?

Effectiveness and Language in Peace Education

- Does evaluation of the effectiveness of the peace education program take language into account?
- How is language on multiple dimensions engaged during reflection on experiences of peace and influences of the peace education program?
- How and with what kinds of language are evaluations of the peace education program conducted?
- How do the participants' experiences of language in the educational setting contribute to their understanding of peace?
- How might language be perpetuating certain cultural or epistemological expectations in evaluation of peace education programs?

While these questions are not exhaustive, they begin to reach some of the concerns and feelings of frustration about the lack of awareness of language that the student voices in my study expressed. Indeed, for most of the participants, the research was the first time they had intentionally reflected on language dynamics within peace education approaches. Although some educators had thought of language from time to time, the general lack of awareness seemed to stem from few opportunities to articulate and discuss the issues. For my practice as well, the study increased my awareness and I began to have the *language* to talk about language in peace education with others. The power of naming the issues that I observed in the classroom led to the transformation of my practice, and I began to reflect more critically on my use of and response to language in the classroom from a peace education perspective. Perhaps other well-intentioned and successful education programs for peacebuilding may be overlooking ways for intentionally creating space for peace within their classroom through and for language. More research and attention to language within peace education programs is required. However, significant opportunities for change can begin with naming the space for language within evaluation through reflective practice.

REFERENCES

Ardizzone, L. (2002). Towards global understanding: The transformative role of peace education. *Current Issues in Comparative Education, 4*(2), 16–25.

Argyris, C. (1991). Teaching smart people how to learn. *Harvard Business Review, 69*(3), 99–109.

Bradshaw, B. (2002). *Change across cultures: A narrative approach to social transformation.* Grand Rapids, MI: Baker Academic.

Bruner, J. (1990). *Acts of meaning.* Cambridge, MA: Harvard University Press.

Buzzelli, C. A., & Johnston, B. (2002). *The moral dimensions of teaching: Language, power, and culture in classroom interaction.* Retrieved from http://books.google.com.

Cooperrider, D. L., & Whitney, D. (2005). *Appreciative inquiry: A positive revolution in change.* San Francisco, CA: Berrett-Koehler Publishers.

Corbin, J. M., & Strauss, A. L. (2008). *Basics of qualitative research: Techniques and procedures for developing grounded theory.* California: Sage Publications, Inc.

Crossley, M. L. (2000). *Introducing narrative psychology: Self, trauma and the construction of meaning.* Philadelphia, PA: Open University Press.

Cummins, J. (2000). *Language, power, and pedagogy: Bilingual children in the crossfire.* Clevedon, UK: Multilingual Matters.

DeLong, D. W. (2004). *Lost knowledge: Confronting the threat of an aging workforce.* Oxford: Oxford University Press.

Eberly, E., & Espenshade, L. (2009, Oct 29, 2009). *Northeast Asian camp brings teens together to discuss prejudices.* Retrieved Nov 9, 2011, from http://www.mcc.org/stories/news/northeast-asian-camp-brings-teens-together-discuss-prejudices.

Epstein, R. (1999). *Taming the cobra: English, multilingualism, and language education in South Africa.* University of Saskatchewan.

Friedrich, P. (2007). English for peace: Toward a framework of Peace Sociolinguistics. *World Englishes, 26*(1), 72–83.

Halliday, M. A. K., & Webster, J. (2006). *On language and linguistics*. New York: Continuum.

Harris, I. (2003). *Peace education evaluation*. Chicago, IL: Paper presented at the Annual Meeting of the American Educational Research Association.

Harris, I., & Morrison, M. L. (2003). *Peace education* (2nd ed.). Jefferson, NC: McFarland.

Hooks, b. (1995). "This is the oppressor's language / yet I need it to talk to you": Language, a place of struggle. In A. Dingwaney & C. Maier (Eds.), *Between languages and cultures: Translation and cross-cultural texts* (pp. 295–302). Pittsburgh, PA: University of Pittsburgh Press.

Jones, T. S., & Brinkert, R. (2007). *Conflict coaching: Conflict management strategies and skills for the individual*. Sage Publications.

Kellett, P. M., & Dalton, D. G. (2001). *Managing conflict in a negotiated world: A narrative approach to achieving dialogue and change*. Sage Publications.

Lederach, J. P. (2010). *The moral imagination: The art and soul of building peace*: Oxford University Press.

Madigan, S. (2011). *Narrative therapy*. Washington, DC: American Psychological Association.

Mirici, I. H. (2008). Training EFL/ESL Teachers for a Peaceful Asia-Pacific Region. *Asia Pacific Education Review, 9*(3), 344–354.

Morgan, B., & Vandrick, S. (2009). Imagining a peace curriculum: What second-language education brings to the table. *Peace & Change, 34*(4), 510–532.

Nan, S. A. (2008). Social capital in exclusive and inclusive networks: Satisfying human needs through conflict and conflict resolution. In M. Cox (Ed.), *Social capital and peacebuilding: Creating and resolving conflict with trust and social networks*. London, UK: Routledge.

Nevo, B., & Brem, I. (2002). Peace education programs and the evaluation of their effectiveness. In G. Salomon & B. Nevo (Eds.), *Peace education: The concept, principles, and practices around the world* (pp. 271–282). Mahwah, NJ: Lawrence Erlbaum Associates.

Nonaka, I., & Takeuchi, H. (1995). *The knowledge-creating company: How Japanese companies create the dynamics of innovation*. Retrieved from www.books.google.com.

Ochs, E., & Capps, L. (1996). Narrating the self. *Annual Review of Anthropology, 25,* 19–43.

Pennycook, A. (2003). Beyond homogeny and heterogeny: English as a global and worldly language. In C. Mair (Ed.), *The politics of English as a world language: New horizons in postcolonial cultural studies* (pp. 3–18). Amsterdam: Rodopi.

Phillipson, R. (1992). *Linguistic imperialism*. Oxford: Oxford University Press.

Rauf, S., & Iqbal, H. M. (2008). Power of linguistic privilege: Critical discourse analysis of the narratives of Pakistani immigrant students in American schools. *Bulletin of Education & Research, 30*(2), 45–60.

Salomon, G. (2002). The nature of peace education: Not all programs are created equal. In G. Salomon & B. Nevo (Eds.), *Peace education: The concept, principles, and practices around the world.* (pp. 3–14). Mahwah, NJ: Lawrence Erlbaum Associates.

Salomon, G., & Nevo, B. (Eds.). (2002). *Peace education: The concept, principles, and practices around the world.* Mahwah, NJ: Lawrence Erlbaum Associates.

Schön, D. A. (1983). *The reflective practitioner: How professionals think in action*. Retrieved from http://books.google.com.

Smith, M. K. (2001). Chris Argyris: Theories of action, double-loop learning and organizational learning. In *The Encyclopedia of Informal Education* (website): www.infed.org/thinkers/argyris.htm.

Stewart, K. A., & Maxwell, M. M. (2010). *Storied conflict talk: Narrative construction in mediation.* John Benjamins Pub. Co.

Tsuda, Y. (2008). English hegemony and English divide. *China Media Research, 4*(1), 47–55.

Wenden, A. L. (2003). Achieving a comprehensive peace: The linguistic factor. *Peace & Change, 28*(2), 169–201.

White, M., & Epston, D. (1990). *Narrative means to therapeutic ends*: Norton.

Winslade, J., & Monk, G. (2000). *Narrative mediation: A new approach to conflict resolution.* San Francisco, CA: Jossey-Bass.

Winslade, J., & Monk, G. (2008). *Practicing narrative mediation: Loosening the grip of conflict.* San Francisco, CA: Jossey-Bass.

Woelk, C. (2011). *Where humanities touch: Peacebuilding and language in curriculum and instructional strategies.* Unpublished manuscript, Department of Education, Eastern Mennonite University, Harrisonburg, VA.

Wong, S., & Motha, S. (2007). Multilingualism in post-9/11 U.S. schools: Implications for engaging empire. *Peace & Change, 32*(1), 62–77.

Zuidema, L. A. (2005). Myth education: Rationale and strategies for teaching against linguistic prejudice. *Journal of Adolescent & Adult Literacy, 48*(8), 666–675.

CHAPTER 5

BRIDGING RESTORATIVE PRACTICES AND GROUP THERAPY

New Evaluative Measures for School Groups

Christina Procter and Erin Dunlevy

INTRODUCTION

This chapter adds to an international conversation about restorative practices by suggesting new ways to assess the efficacy of culture-building, peace-keeping, and conflict resolution Circles in schools. Our research stems from the limitations we experienced while trying to evaluate the success of a multi-year implementation of restorative practices at the High School for Arts, Imagination and Inquiry, a public school in New York City, New York (HSAII). The implementation, which is now in its fourth year, has focused on training staff and students in the facilitation of peacemaking Circles that are used both proactively (community building) and reactively (for peacemaking, problem solving, or in response to conflict). As such, we define Circle as the structured meeting of groups to build community and cohesiveness, address relevant group issues, and respond to conflict. Additionally,

Peace Education Evaluation: Learning from Experience and Exploring Prospects,
pages 67–82.
Copyright © 2015 by Information Age Publishing
All rights of reproduction in any form reserved.

we presuppose in this chapter that Circle, though not exclusive to the practice of *restorative justice*, is a fundamental aspect of that model. Our research addresses the challenges we have experienced when evaluating restorative practices in our school setting, specifically by acknowledging the limitations of analyzing incident data as a main indicator of success. With these challenges in mind, we propose that in order to accurately quantify the efficacy of school-based restorative peacemaking practices, we must first understand schools as intricate systems of groups that, when cohesive, facilitate the development of academic skills and socialization. Therefore, we draw from the vast data that already exists on the management of groups and their dynamics in order to better understand and evaluate the impact of a restorative school.

Our work with restorative practices in schools reflects a commitment on the part of the HSAII staff to peace education as an active, pedagogical framework. Restorative practices are a vehicle for the mission of peace education, which Ian Harris and Mary Lee Morrison (2003) posit is to reveal and tap into those energies that make possible the full human enjoyment of a meaningful and productive existence (p. 5). A restorative relationship among all parties in the micro-society of a school can establish patterns of behavior that are necessary to promote peace in an increasingly volatile world: "as modern nations produce weapons systems that can annihilate human existence, this may portend the altering of the structure of human consciousness, which will in turn affect the pedagogical relationships between teachers and students" (p. 5).

Our approach to the work of peacemaking in schools is integral to our roles as educators, and our interest in exploring new evaluative measures stems from a lack of a concrete vocabulary that can be applied to evaluate a school that has established peacemaking as an essential component for academic and social success. Therefore, our exploration of this topic is personal and ongoing. We are an English teacher (Procter) and a Spanish Native Language Arts teacher (Dunlevy). Additionally, we were responsible for writing the 10th and 12th grade portions of a comprehensive four-year Advisory program for HSAII, which we did within the framework of restorative practices. These Advisory classes, and our decision as a school to conduct staff meetings and disciplinary procedures in Circles, are the practices that led us to further explore evaluative measures for restorative practices in school settings. Our work is ongoing, and it is our understanding that despite the academic challenges to defining restorative justice in school settings (Morrison, 2007), we can establish one unifying factor in all definitions: restorative justice in all its manifestations attempts to engage whole groups (communities) in both the prevention of and response to harm. Our work led us to question what we as educators and evaluators should be looking for when assessing a school. It has become clear that standard indicators like incident data, test scores, and student and teacher attendance data are subject to too many variables to be considered reliable. The peacemaking successes we experienced at HSAII seemed to us much more intimately connected to the intricate dynamics of the various groups functioning within the school. This led us to believe that current evaluation methods have focused on the wrong information. We find that schools function as a complex system of groups and, for this reason, practitioners can enhance and evaluate restorative methodologies through adapted use of the criteria already established in the field of group therapy. Consequently, after the first three years of experimentation, it has become our belief that a school implementing restorative practices as a model for socialization and peace-building will exhibit the eleven interrelated therapeutic factors evident in high-functioning groups, as defined by Yalom and Leszcz (2005). These indicators offer a much-needed structure and vocabulary for the implementation and evaluation of restorative practices in schools.

In contrast to these criteria, schools labeled "restorative" are often critiqued as such through frameworks largely devised within the academic field of restorative justice. While this may serve to further important research and provide schools with crucial feedback, it falls short as a system for determining the potency of restorative practices in schools with wider needs. If we view schools as systems of groups, we can apply group therapy practices that transcend current modes of school evaluation. To this end, we offer a brief rationale for restorative practices in school settings, review current evaluation trends and their findings, and reframe schools as dynamic systems of groups. We establish a framework and vocabulary to develop group functioning according to the work of Irvin D. Yalom and Molyn Leszcz (2005) and explore new intersections for the evaluation of school groups. Finally, we discuss our plans to develop a School Group Survey (SGS) to measure the impact of Circle and group therapy techniques in school communities. In this way, our work sets the foundation for merging restorative practices with group psychotherapy methodology and evaluation in school settings.

A Rationale for Restorative Justice in Schools

Restorative justice as a philosophical framework for school management is a comprehensive approach to the well-documented decline of moral authority within school systems (Arum, 2003). While statistical data documenting suspension reduction and the inherent community-based nature of a restorative approach to school management are convincing selling points for implementation, there has not been sufficient cohesion between research about the impetus for restorative practices as a management framework and the shifts in the perception of school authority by students that have taken place during the last 30 years. As a result, the evaluation of school-based restorative practices has not consistently reflected the recent litigious history of schools.

The work of Richard Arum (2003) and his comprehensive investigation of the crisis of moral authority in schools is a complement parallel to current studies on restorative justice. Court rulings in favor of students during the 1960s and 1970s significantly increased student rights and heralded the rise of due process for students in U.S. public schools (Arum, 2003). These rulings consequently weakened the *in loco parentis* moral authority of teachers and school staff. In spite of these changes, Arum reinforces the Durkheimian theory that socialization remains as important as content acquisition for children within school systems, and moral authority is central to the socialization of students. He states, "The moral authority of school discipline is critical in fostering students' ability to be individuals and productive citizens" (p. 186). Arum's work challenges the perception that the role of education is solely to impart knowledge and cognitive skills, and instead frames the school as a microcosm of society within which students must be able to transition to adulthood with a strong foundation for empathy, agency, and citizenship. Arum also suggests that fostering cohesiveness and attachment to the school community through relationship building can directly result in reduced violence:

> We have hypothesized here and elsewhere that schools can enhance student 'attachment, involvement and commitment'[1] by making educational experiences more intimate (smaller schools and classrooms), as well as more relevant (curriculum differentiation). ...As Harvard educational researcher and sociologist Pedro Noguera noted, 'anonymity increases the vulnerability of schools to outbreaks of violence because it limits the possibility that a responsible adult will know when a student is in distress and in need of help' (p. 196).[2]

Similarly, Arum contends that students are far more likely to comply with school policies if they perceive them to be fair and legitimate. Fairness committees, responsive in-class Circles, pre- and post-suspension Circles, and staff Circles are tremendous tools for creating more peaceful, productive school communities within which students are held to high standards of behavior that are morally authentic and empathy-based rather than authoritarian.

The implications of restorative practices in schools will correlate with the desired outcomes. It is insufficient to justify school-wide implementation simply for the improvement of social climate. As previously stated, if the purpose of schools is to create active, empathic citizens, we must acknowledge that we are working within a system to prepare students to function in greater social, academic, and professional systems. There is a widely untreated disconnect between a more Freirean style of pedagogy that intends to dismantle oppressive systems and a philosophy like restorative justice, that while aiming in many ways to circumvent certain traditional systematic responses to harm, does, in essence, seek to normalize behavior so that people can coexist with increased social and emotional stability. In this way, our purpose in exploring restorative practices has not only been to foster a more peaceful school community, but also to provide students with sufficient social capital to access power. For this reason we rarely, if ever, describe our restorative Circles as democratic in nature, because we do not inherently disagree with the idea of centralized authority within school groups. It is unwise to assume that the onus of defining and realizing morality and citizenship should fall princi-

---

[1] See Arum & Beattie, 1999.
[2] See Noguera, 2001.

pally on our students. To the contrary, students rely on strong moral authority in order to imitate or "try on" the role of a morally responsible adult.

Restorative Circles in our school have had a significant impact on the reduction of violence precisely because they contribute to increased empathy, cohesiveness, and accountability within and between the school's many groups. The nature of the restorative Circle, either within a classroom, as a format for teacher meetings, or as a responsive measure, is to transform the community into a system of mutually dependent, self-analytic groups. These groups create the environment that Arum (2003) and Noguera (2001) describe as essential to increased socialization and decreased violence. The Circle process reinforces moral authority by providing a venue for the active engagement of all community members in maintaining peace. With this in mind, we are not alone in our observation that there is a disconnect between this research and the general perception that schools exist primarily to develop academic skills. State-led assessment models rarely address the fact that school management, classroom practices, and approaches to discipline must be dramatically rethought because schools no longer function with autonomous moral authority.

This is where restorative justice presents as a model that meets the new needs of the modern school. To date, school institutions tend not to prioritize socialization. The New York Civil Liberties Union (NYCLU) recently issued a report titled "Safety with dignity: Alternatives to the over-policing of schools" (Ofer, Jones, & Miller, 2009). One of the key characteristics of a "successful school" is the presence of an approach to conflict resolution, yet Elayna Konstan, CEO of the Office of School and Youth Development at the Department of Education (DOE), testified in 2007 that only 800 of New York City's teachers have been trained on conflict resolution programs—that is less than 1% of the approximately 83,000 teachers in the system (p. 19). We must empower school practitioners as primary agents in facilitating the socialization of responsible citizens, and assess schools accordingly. It is to this end that we seek to draw a previously un-established bridge between classroom pedagogy, school management, and group therapy; at the crux of these fields, the restorative Circle is a vehicle for radical change in school communities.

New Directions for the Evaluation of Restorative Justice in Schools

Although multiple comprehensive studies on restorative justice in schools yield promising results,[3] findings are also mixed and often contradictory[4] (Mor-

---

[3] The Minnesota Department of Children, Family, and Learning (MDCFL 2002) found that restorative practices resulted in a marked decrease in suspensions and discipline referrals. This data has been replicated by the International Institute for Restorative Practices in the United Kingdom (UK), Pennsylvania, and Canada (Lewis, 2009).

[4] In the UK, the Youth Justice Board for England (YJB) conducted a wide-scale study and found that compared to "non-programme" schools, "programme" schools did decrease expulsion rates, but it was difficult to prove the correlation with restorative practices, in part due to varying interpretations

rison, 2007). While the adoption of restorative practices often correlates with an initial decrease in student violence and recidivism, this occurrence typically wanes as schools struggle with long-term implementation. In our school, the practice of Circles correlated with an 82% reduction of suspensions after the first fifteen months of teacher-led implementation. These numbers continued to drop as HSAII formalized the practice: from September to February in 2009–2010, the school suspended 72 students, while in the same months of the subsequent school year, only 43 were suspended (Online Occurrence Reporting System, OORS). Student and teacher feedback on questionnaires administered in 2009–2010 indicated an increased sense of safety, empathy, and belonging within the community. One teacher stated, "Since restorative justice has been fully integrated into our school there has been a dramatically positive change in our school culture. There's no longer a need to constantly be on guard walking the halls wondering where the next fight is going to break out." Demonstrative student responses include:

It... helps the students realize that they are not alone. It helps them realize that they have someone else in the group who feels the same way. It also helps our community see that not all problems have to be solved with violent actions. We can solve problems by sitting side by side and talking about them;

The outcome of Circle is that teachers and students get to know each other better and it's a great way to let out your feelings and everybody is calmer. It is just a better atmosphere;

I got a 55 in English class first and second marking period. This past marking period I got a 95. Circle made me care about school. It also taught me that I have a voice.

Sustained, whole-school implementation, however, has been challenging. Although the entire staff was trained in restorative practices, HSAII never achieved full staff buy-in, leading to inconsistency in implementation from classroom to classroom.

Based on our own experiences and the data provided by current international research, it is our belief that well-executed restorative practices work, but the complications of successful long-term implementation are manifold. Morrison (2007) summarizes that "the practice of restorative justice must ground a whole-school framework for thinking about how behaviour and relationships are managed in schools" (p. 339). We therefore contend that new measures must evaluate: 1) methods of implementation; and 2) how effective restorative practices are in

---

of discipline codes from school to school. The evaluation also revealed, through qualitative surveys, that even in "programme" schools demonstrating successful data, 43% of the teachers knew nothing or very little about restorative principles and many of the remaining 57% conveyed serious misconceptions about them. The Youth Justice Board concludes: "Restorative justice is not a panacea for problems in schools but, if implemented correctly, it can improve the school environment, enhance learning, and encourage young people to become more responsible and empathetic" (as cited in Morrison, 2007, p. 343).

managing behavior and relationships within the school community. This second evaluation objective is our focus, and it necessitates the aforementioned attitudinal shift in understanding school as a mechanism of socialization (Arum, 2003), which we propose is most powerfully facilitated by a dynamic system of cohesive groups within the school community.

Redefining Schools as Systems of Groups in Need of Cohesiveness

If each classroom is redefined as a working group of students, individuals will become entrenched in the practices that make any group productive, thus effecting socialization processes that help students navigate conflict and other detriments to learning. If we understand classes as groups with potential for self-management, we can draw from the field of group therapy to reliably measure what makes a group high-functioning.

Schools are already systems of groups; the challenge for school leaders is to establish a unifying framework to maximize their potential functioning. Any given group of students is embedded in an open, dynamic system of other groups and structures in the school environment. Thus, the sporadic efficacy of Circles in some classrooms is not enough to effect school-wide change. The concept of *holon* in general systems theory understands that any entity—in this case any group—is simultaneously both part and whole (Bowen, 2006). Bowen explains, "A single classroom may also be studied as a social system. Its inputs and processes, however, are tied to the operating processes of the entire school" (p. 64). We believe that the most effective way to strengthen a complex system of interacting groups is to increase the strength of micro—and macro-level overlapping relationships (student-student, student-teacher, student-administrator, student-school as a whole, teacher-school as a whole, and so forth). Bowen (2006) defines social organization as "networks of relationships among people, their patterns of exchange and levels of reciprocity, and the degree to which they provide instrumental and expressive support to one another in achieving their individual and collective goals" (p. 67). O'Day (2002) understands the subgroups of a school as complex adaptive systems with a synergic relationship of layered interaction. She contends, "The more frequent and powerful those interactions are, the more influence they are likely to have on the behavior of individual actors" (p. 439). The aim is to implement restorative practices as a means to strengthen group relationships and revamp methods of restorative school evaluation to acknowledge these relationships as the necessary condition for a successful academic community.

A perhaps intuitive but essential caveat must be made: school relationships alone cannot transform a school. Without what Shouse (1997) calls "academic press," an overemphasis on community building can actually be detrimental to high-need schools in particular. Social organization researchers identify two primary indicators of school success: academic press (rigor, variety, and innovation of instruction) and sense of community. Interestingly, Shouse's (1997) study on the impact of academic press and sense of community revealed that in mathematics test scores of a national sample of students, academic press had a positive and significant impact, while sense of community had little impact. Shouse then examined the impact of these indicators on populations of low socioeconomic status (SES). He found that in low-SES schools, sense of community did enhance student achievement, but only when academic press was high. Importantly, at low-SES schools with a low level of academic press, higher levels of sense of community actually lowered student achievement on mathematics tests. Shouse (1997) warned that these schools may become "socially therapeutic" without being "academically challenging" (as cited in Bowen, 2006, p. 70). It would be interesting to replicate this study with humanities-based achievement measures, as well as to examine the impact of sense of community on attendance and discipline rates, but the warning remains important.

The new direction for restorative school evaluation, then, is to focus on group functioning and relationships. The field of psychology has abandoned the "specificity myth" of its varying pedagogical approaches by acknowledging that the common factor of success in any sort of therapy is the relationship between therapist and client (Bozarth, 2000). Meta-analytical reports on psychotherapy that span the 1980s and 1990s are best summarized by Sexton and Whiston (1994): "It is only the *counseling relationship* that has consistently been found to contribute to the success of the therapeutic process" (as cited in Bozarth, 2000, para. 3). Yalom and Leszcz (2005) further define this relationship: "Successful therapy... is mediated by a relationship between therapist and client that is characterized by trust, warmth, empathic understanding, and acceptance" (p. 54). The National Research Council and the Institute of Medicine also cited "supportive relationships" as a key focus of social intervention in effective youth development programs (as cited in Bowen, 2006, p. 75).

We propose that the same common denominator can hold true for successful classrooms, wherein educators must not only forge a strong relationship with individual students and the group as a whole, but also facilitate relationships within and between subgroups of students. The same holds true for relationships among staff and administrators. The quality of these intersecting relationships determines a group's level of cohesiveness. Yalom and Leszcz (2005) posit cohesiveness as the therapeutic factor at the core of all group functioning and describe it as follows:

> Groups differ from one another in the amount of 'groupness' present. Those with a greater sense of solidarity, or 'we-ness,' value the group more highly and will defend it against internal and external threats. Such groups have a higher rate of attendance, participation, and mutual support. (p. 55)

Although many effective educators instinctively foster cohesiveness in their classes, educational pedagogy has yet to recognize the potential of the classroom as a "group" of people. Rather, it is often conceptualized as an academic situation with teacher and students in a dyad relationship. If we borrow from the wealth of research in group psychology, we can establish entirely new possibilities for the effective socialization of school communities. With greater attention to the management of group dynamics, each classroom is a possible metonym for a new vision of society where authority and justice are decentralized through the inherently inclusive process of Circle. This not only transforms the classroom and school at large, but also sets the foundation for subsequent generations of citizens who feel more connected and responsible to communities.

Developing High-Functioning Groups in Schools: The Therapeutic Factors

One of the greatest benefits of group therapy is its impact on an individual's self-awareness of his or her functioning within a group. Adolescents in particular tend to prioritize peer opinions in the construction of their identity and self-esteem, and educators can constructively channel this dynamic by facilitating cohesive, empathic groups in school communities. Morrison (2007) cites National Research Council findings on the vital importance of social standing for adolescents, something that many young people will resort to violence in order to defend:

> In this context, social and emotional skills are the core element for the health, well-being and safety of the school community. When a member of the school community is harmed, or has harmed, the intensity and collateral effect can be deeper and more extensive in these tightly woven, face-to-face communities (p. 324).

Restorative practices focus on the effect of behaviors on the community and this is precisely the aim of the group therapist, to help make evident interpersonal dynamics that may be causing a client pain. Because an individual's personal pathologies will inevitably emerge in the social microcosm of the group (Yalom & Leszcz, 2005), a high-functioning group can analyze the emergent behavior and its impact, thus helping individual members acknowledge and address harmful habits. If a group becomes versed in the process of open discussion and feedback, as facilitated by the Circle process, individuals can be made aware of behaviors detrimental to learning, such as the tendency to give up, shut down, lash out, or any other array of behaviors that frequent the life of the classroom. If such behaviors are left unacknowledged, they can cause serious damage to individual and group progress. Conversely, a high-functioning group can make great use of these behaviors, thus maximizing the socialization that is essential to youth development.

In 2010–2011, we began the work of merging Circle with the techniques of group therapy at our school. This is happening most explicitly in Advisory, a social-emotional and academic support class that employs Circle practice by curricular design. We have found that an effective group will increasingly exhibit the following eleven interrelated therapeutic factors outlined by Yalom and Leszcz (2005): *instillation of hope, universality, imparting information, altruism, the corrective recapitulation of the primary family group, development of socializing techniques, imitative behavior, interpersonal learning, group cohesiveness, catharsis, and existential factors.* While these are widely accepted by the field of psychology to constitute a high-functioning group, these indicators—largely ignored by classroom pedagogy and assessment—provide a much-needed vocabulary to define and quantify the impact of the restorative Circle. A brief illustration, supported by student testimonials, illuminates the potency of these therapeutic factors at play in school groups. Although these factors may be "therapeutic" in nature, they have implications not only for the socialization of groups, but also for the academic progress of students.

The *instillation of hope* is already common practice in educational pedagogy—students must believe that they can change, progress, and achieve despite challenges. *Universality* is the realization that one is not alone in his or her experience of life, particularly in suffering. Too often, individuals feel isolated in their intrapsychic pain and operate under the illusion that no one else is experiencing similar difficulties. This perception may be particularly exacerbated for developing adolescents. The simple power of hearing a peer's anxiety or struggle can have a profound impact on a person's ability to cope and persevere. We find evidence of *universality* in excerpts from student reflections on their Advisory classes. One student wrote, "Just hearing different types of problems people goes [sic] through makes me feel like I'm not the only one with problems in life." Another expressed, "When you are depressed are you able to talk to someone or able to have someone to empathize with or listen to you? In my school we have Advisory and I have been feeling better." Yalom and Leszcz (2005) posit that the members of any given group fall on a coping-collapse continuum; the same can be true for all groups of students, both in an academic and personal regard. For instance, students might be asked to analyze and assess the behaviors they are displaying in response to a challenging task, as well as to articulate how they feel over the course of its completion. This is powerfully enacted in a full-class Circle, but can also be facilitated by small groups of students that then report back, creating a nested system of working groups within a class community. We find that self-reflexive, analytic methods such as these provide support structures for students who might otherwise opt out of a daunting assignment. A cohesive group will become adept at identifying and giving feedback about patterns of detrimental attitudes or behaviors recurrent in its individual members.

This process creates opportunities for *altruism*, wherein students feel empowered by the act of providing support or comfort to their peers. Yalom and Lesczc (2005) describe:

> Many psychiatric patients beginning therapy are demoralized and possess a deep sense of having nothing of value to offer others. They have long considered themselves as burdens, and the experience of finding that they can be of importance to others is refreshing and boosts self-esteem. (p. 13)

The same is particularly true for at-risk students who too often experience failure and demoralization in schools. Student reflections allude to the experience of *altruism*: "Over the past few weeks my classmate has been feeling very stressed out, and I know it is not easy. Like I tell my close ones, if you try and keep trying that's mostly what counts". Another student describes how it feels to give another group member feedback:

> One reason why I feel Circle is beneficial is because of the fact of getting to know each other we are able to help one another. An example of this is J would say something like 'I'm very tired' and she would then pass the talking piece because she is shy, put on the spot. S would receive the talking piece and is aware that J was put on the spot and would say 'I agree with J I am very tired also because...' Just from this I learned that if my peer is stuck or needs my help that I will offer a helping hand. This changed me. The old me wouldn't say anything at all and the person would be left feeling sad.

This student articulates a shift in behavior and a stronger sense of self after experiencing the altruism involved in the work of the group. These same students engaged in a challenging math problem, for example, will have a new level of empathic interaction—a skill essential to the classroom, workplace, and society.

As we train students to engage in analytic group discussion, we must also remember that they exist in multiple groups outside of the school community. Individuals tend to reenact ways of being in their primary family group as part of their identity in other groups (Yalom & Leszcz, 2005). While we have no control over what happens in the primary group, we can capitalize on opportunities to heal harm and reshape behaviors in the context of an individual's secondary group—the classroom. Student responses to authority are behaviors of particular interest in this regard and the classroom provides a unique opportunity to correct these behaviors before they become more permanent patterns of character. *The corrective recapitulation of the primary family group* allows for students to exhibit, analyze, and work to correctively redirect behaviors that may otherwise impede their progress.

As students begin to understand their roles within groups, they may also exhibit *imitative behavior*, which refers to the process of trying on and shedding qualities exhibited by the group facilitator, in this case the teacher. It is vital that the facilitator model communicational patterns conducive to group cohesiveness, such as analytic, non-judgmental responses to others, and a willingness to disclose personal experiences where appropriate (Yalom & Leszcz, 2005). As students experiment with new behaviors, the imitative process provides opportunities to try out alternate ways of being.

Interpersonal learning is that which occurs within a matrix of interpersonal relationships (Yalom & Leszcz, 2005). We believe that a nested-group approach will strengthen the quality of these relationships, with subgroups of students facilitating frequent mini-Circles as a regular feature of instruction. This may take the form of a quick go-around check-in at the start or close of class (what is one word to describe how you are doing today? Choose one person in group and describe a positive contribution s/he made to the work in class today), or a deeper discussion (how is everyone in group coping with the homework assignments lately? Does anyone have anything on their mind preventing them from being fully present for the project we are about to start?). Once students master the practice of full-class Circles, their ownership over the process will create profound opportunities for interpersonal learning in smaller groups.

The remaining therapeutic factors require a brief explanation. *Imparting of information* is redundant to the classroom experience; it refers to the didactic instruction provided in some group therapy sessions. *Catharsis* is the relief experienced after open and honest expression of emotion.[5] Finally, working through *existential factors* involves recognizing the existential qualities of life, such as accepting that it is frequently unfair, that at times there is no escape from pain, and that feeling isolated is part of the human condition (Yalom & Leszcz, 2005).

As students become entrenched in the practices of a critical, yet supportive working group, they develop strategies to cope with conflict when it arises. Yalom and Leszcz (2005) emphasize that a high-functioning group is not conflict-free; rather, conflict is an essential part of the group's life-force, and when dealt with constructively, can deepen relationships and increase socialization. An example of this is perhaps best told by a student who shared her experience during an Advisory class Circle:

> We had a time where a student had mentioned that he didn't like a certain racial group of people. I know he meant it in a different way but it came out wrong… I thought that certain people that were related to that group of people were going to jump him, and I saw some people at the edge of their seats, but surprisingly they were able to react in a positive way that didn't use any violence, just re-wording. Everyone got to say how they felt in that moment and we helped that student think about things in new ways.

As the example demonstrates, restorative practices have the long-term capacity to develop strong, working groups of people who are able to navigate conflict and hold each other accountable to community values that prioritize inclusion, self-monitoring, and reparation of harm.

A few important distinctions must be made between the encounter of a therapy group and a classroom group. First, high-functioning therapy groups require a

---

[5] Catharsis is an important element of Circle and group therapy sessions. This is reflected in student testimonials. One student describes, "When I had the talking piece I felt very nervous, I felt I had something behind my back that burned a lot and started getting red. But after all I spoke to the whole class about something very awful that happened in my personal life. After I told them, I wasn't nervous anymore instead I stood up and wanted to keep on going. I was very shocked at myself because I'm one of those kids who barely talks a lot." Another student stated simply, "Circle is like a release towards your chest."

focus on the here-and-now (this means avoiding recounting stories of the past, but rather analyzing patterns of interaction as they emerge for an individual in the moment and in the context of the group). While this may be useful in the analysis of individual behaviors as they emerge, a consistent here-and-now focus is not the primary aim of classroom Circles. Second, therapy groups prioritize disclosure and spontaneous discussion usually unfettered by prompts or a sequential method of discussion. Classroom Circles are not opportunities for free and open disclosure, but are structured around an outcome that is ultimately academic in nature. Also, while some Circles are run non-sequentially, the standard method is to pass around a tangible or metaphorical "talking piece". These distinctions aside, the therapeutic factors offer a new framework and vocabulary for the facilitation of high-functioning groups within restorative school communities.

Evaluating School Groups

We propose that an effective evaluation of a school that has implemented restorative justice as a management model will in part assess the strength of its many groups. We aim to use measurements employed by group therapists to first evaluate group functioning and then examine correlations with the academic performance (transcripts, state, and national assessments) and personal well-being (disciplinary and attendance data as well as self-report surveys) of individuals within those groups. We propose the development of a School Group Survey (SGS) and recommend a similar design model that JuliAnne Krogel (2008) used to create the Group Questionnaire (GQ). The SGS can be used for formative classroom and internal school assessment, with the hope that such a measurement— subsequent to reliability and validity testing—would become a significant aspect of restorative practice evaluation in school settings.

Johnson, Burlingame, Davies, and Gleave (2005) conducted a large-scale study to conceptualize the therapeutic relationship within groups, and used four group therapy measurements to establish a three-factor model. Johnson et al. collected data from 662 participants from 11 different counseling centers and institute groups at the American Group Psychotherapy Association (AGPA) and concluded that a therapeutic relationship is characterized by: *Positive Bonding* (cohesiveness), *Positive Working* (patterns of group functioning) and *Negative Relationship* (how the group constructively works through conflict) (as cited in Krogel, 2008). In her dissertation, Krogel uses this unified theory as a base for creating the Group Questionnaire (GQ).

Two of the original group therapy assessments used by Johnson et al. (2005) test member to group relationships. MacKenzie's Group Climate Questionnaire-Short (GCQ-S) measures members' perception of *the importance of cohesion* (Engagement), their *reluctance to take responsibility for change* (Avoidance), and *interpersonal friction and distrust* (Conflict) (as cited in DeLucia-Waack & Brimbord, 2000). MacKenzie (1990) shortened his original 32-item, eight subscale measurement to a survey of 12 items with the three aforementioned subscales.

Each item is rated by self-report on a Likert scale of helpfulness, from 1 (*not at all*) to 6 (*extremely*). This shortened version allows for more frequent data on individual perceptions of the group and might be used weekly by classroom teachers implementing the practice of Circle. Additionally, the Therapeutic Factors Inventory (TFI; Lese & MacNair-Semands, 2000) includes a subscale for cohesion that is comprised of 12 items on a seven-point Likert scale. This survey measures the extent to which individual members feel accepted and part of the group, as well as how secure, caring, trusting, and able to work together that group is perceived to be.

The next two assessments measure member to leader relationships. The Empathy Scale (ES) (as described by Burns in Krogel (2008)) includes 10 items that examine clients' perception of the therapist's warmth, genuineness, and empathy; also a Likert scale of self-report, it is probably the most commonly used measure for empathy (Krogel, 2008, p. 10). Finally, the Working Alliance Inventory (WAI; Horvath & Greenburg, 1989) includes 36 items with three subscales that measure varying aspects of the client-therapist bond, which would be adapted to measure student-teacher, teacher-administrator, and student-administrator relationships in schools practicing restorative methods.

We assess that Krogel's (2008) 30-item Group Questionnaire (GQ), based on Johnson's three-scale model of the therapeutic relationship, synthesizes the four discussed group therapy assessments in a succinct, easy-to-administer measurement that is most current with what we know about group functioning and its impact on academics and socialization. We aim to employ Krogel's design methodology to also address Johnson's three-scale model as subscales for a School Group Survey (SGS) that would evaluate groups practicing restorative Circles. This should employ language from the field of restorative justice and address the strength of therapeutic factors in different school groups. For instance, an item addressing the subscale "Negative Relationships" might read: *When someone has caused harm to this class community, we listen to his/her side of the story.* Students would rate items on a Likert scale of: 1 (Strongly) disagree, 2 (Disagree), 3 (Neither agree nor disagree), 4 (Agree), and 5 (Strongly agree). Similarly, to examine the therapeutic factor of *universality* as part of the "Positive Working" subscale, an item might read: *I feel like my classmates have been through emotions and experiences similar to my own.* Another item might read: *I feel like very few people in this class understand me.* A similar survey would be adapted to evaluate inter-staff relationships. Subsequent to reliability and validity testing, this 30-item self-report measure with 10 items for each subscale would assess the functioning of restorative school groups. In essence, the development of a School Group Survey (SGS) could mark a departure from current evaluations of restorative schools by borrowing from the field of group therapy to better assess what is happening in school groups.

CONCLUSION

Schools are complex systems of porous groups, and the cohesiveness with which these groups interact will be a defining factor in the school's success. Yalom (2002) refers to the "occupational hazards" experienced by therapists—the most acute, he claims, is a sense of isolation, despite the extremely social nature of the job. Such is often the experience of administrators and educators who may experience a sense of aloneness or hopelessness in facing the enormous task of educating and socializing youth, particularly in high-need schools. This experience can be exacerbated by the significant reduction of the *in loco parentis* moral authority that has taken place in schools during the last 30 years (Arum, 2003). As the needs of students change, so do the needs of school personnel. It is imperative that schools reexamine approaches to managing student behavior while simultaneously establishing the authentic relationships that yield both academic and social development.

Restorative justice, based in community building and group problem solving, is a logical group management model for addressing these needs. However, schools must have evaluation methods for assessing the efficacy of the restorative model that go beyond isolated studies within the field itself. If, in fact, restorative practices address the needs of groups, it is essential that we consult and implement the vast research already available on the qualities of high functioning groups. The development of a School Group Survey (SGS), based on current, ongoing research in the field of group therapy, could synthesize group therapy assessments in a succinct, easy-to-administer measurement that is most current with what we know about group functioning. The creation and implementation of this kind of survey could offer a dramatically improved picture of the efficacy of a restorative school.

REFERENCES

Arum, R. (2002). Education and crime. In J. Dressler (Ed.), *Encyclopedia of crime and justice* (p. 607–613). New York: Macmillan.

Arum, R. (2003). *Judging school discipline: The crisis of moral authority.* Cambridge: Harvard University Press.

Arum, R., & Beattie, I. (1999). High School Experience and the Risk of Incarceration. *Criminology, 37*, 515–539.

Bowen, G. L. (2006). In P. Allen-Meares, (Ed.), *Social work services in schools* (5th ed., pp. 53–70). Boston: Pearson.

Bozarth, J. (2000). *The specificity myth: The fallacious premise of mental health treatment.* Retrieved from http://personcentered.com/specificity.html.

DeLucia-Waack, J., & Bridbord, K. (2004). Measures of group process, dynamics, climate, leadership behaviors, and therapeutic factors. In J. DeLucia-Waack, D. Gerrity, CynthiaKalodner, & M. Riva (Eds.), *Handbook of group counseling and psychotherapy* (pp. 120–131). Thousand Oaks: Sage Publications.

Harris, I. & Morrison, M., (Eds). (2003). *Peace Education* (2nd ed.). Jefferson, NC: McFarland & Company, Inc., Publishers.

Horvath, A. O., & Greenberg, L. S. (1989). Development and validation of the Working Alliance Inventory. *Journal of Counseling Psychology, 36*, 223-233.

Johnson, J. E., Burlingame, G. M., Olsen, J. A., Davies, D. R., & Gleave, R. L. (2005). Group climate, cohesion, alliance, and empathy in group psychotherapy: Multilevel structural equation models. *Journal of Counseling Psychology, 52*, 310–321.

Krogel, J. (2008). *The group questionnaire: A new measure of the group relationship.* (Doctoral dissertation). Retrieved from http://contentdm.lib.byu.edu/ETD/image/etd2553.pdf.

Lese, K. P., & MacNair- Semands, R. R. (2000). The Therapeutic Factors Inventory: Development of a scale. *Group, 24*(4), 303–317.

Lewis, S. (2009). Improving school climate: Findings from schools implementing restorative practices. *International Institute for Restorative Practices* (IIRP). Retrieved from http://www.iirp.edu/iirpWebsites/web/uploads/article_pdfs/92115_IIRP-Improving-School-Climate.pdf.

MacKenzie, K. R. (1990). *Introduction to time-limited group psychotherapy.* Washington, DC: American Psychiatric Press.

Morrison, B. (2007). Schools and restorative justice. In G. Johnstone & D. W. Van Ness (Eds.), *The handbook of restorative justice* (pp. 325–350). Cullompton, Devon: Willan Publishing.

Noguera, P. (2001). Finding safety where we least expect it: The role of social capital in preventing school violence. In W. Ayers, B. Dorhn & R. Ayers (Eds.), *Zero tolerance: Resisting the drive for punishment in our schools.* New York: New York Press.

O'Day, J. (2002). *Complexity, accountability, and school improvement.* Retrieved from www.politicalscience.uncc.edu/.../Oday%20Accountability%20and%20Testing.pdf.

Ofer, U., Jones, A., & Miller, J. (2009). Safety with dignity: Alternatives to the over-policing of schools. *The New York Civil Liberties Union.* Retrieved from http://www.nyclu.org/content/safety-with-dignity-alternatives-over-policing-of-schools.

Sexton, T. L., & Whiston, S. C. (1994). The status of the counseling relationship: An empirical review, theoretical implications, and research directions. *The Counseling Psychologist, 22*(1), 6–78.

Shouse, R. D. (1997). Academic press, sense of community, and student achievement. In J. S. Coleman, B. Schneider, S. Plank, K. S. Schiller, R. Shouse, & H. Wang, *Redesigning American education* (pp. 60-86). Boulder, CO: Westview Press.

The Online Occurrence Reporting System. (2011). *The department of education.* Retrieved from http://schools.nyc.gov/RulesPolicies/RespectforAll/OORS0809.

Yalom, I. D. (2002). *The gift of therapy: An open letter to a new generation of therapists and their patients.* New York: HarperCollins Publishers.

Yalom, I. D., & Leszcz, M. (2005). *The theory and practice of group psychotherapy.* New York: Perseus Books Group.

PART 2

TAKING STOCK AND LEARNING FROM EXPERIENCES

CHAPTER 6

FROM RISK TO RESILIENCE

Understanding and Preventing Bullying and Bias

Roberta A. Heydenberk and Warren R. Heydenberk

INTRODUCTION

The United Nations Children's Fund (UNICEF) contends that peace education is "an essential component of quality basic education" and "has a place in all societies—not only in countries undergoing armed conflict and emergencies" (Fountain, 1999, p. 1). Schools should function as "zones of peace—where children are safe from conflict" (p. 5). These "zones" should be achieved by developing a positive school climate, teaching conflict resolution and "teaching methods that promote participation, cooperation, problem-solving and respect for differences" (p. 6). In a similar vein, the United Nations (UN) Convention on the Rights of the Child (CRC) states that education should include "preparation of the child for a responsible life in a free society—in the spirit of understanding, peace, tolerance, equality of sexes, and friendship among peoples" (Article 29 of the UN General Assembly, 1989).

To these ends as described by the UN, conflict resolution and mediation programs offer powerful strategies to achieve goals of developing safe zones charac-

Peace Education Evaluation: Learning from Experience and Exploring Prospects,
pages 85–101.
Copyright © 2015 by Information Age Publishing
All rights of reproduction in any form reserved.

terized by a positive school climate for the all students. Conflict resolution training improves school climate, and enhances empathy, reflection, understanding of differences, cooperative interaction, and higher level moral reasoning (Heydenberk, Heydenberk & Bailey, 2003; Heydenberk & Heydenberk, 2007).

Students who are confident in their ability to resolve conflict are more likely to stand up for the rights of others-even those with whom they disagree (Heydenberk, Heydenberk, & Bailey, 2003). Although a traditional education is essential to peaceful, democratic societies (Glaeser, Ponzetto & Shleifer, 2007), it is not always sufficient to sustain peaceful societies. For instance, well educated citizens were compliant and often willing participants in the genocides in World War II (Oliner & Oliner, 1992), Rwanda (Cose, 2008), and murders and genocide in other parts of the world. However, we know that those who rescued intended victims of genocide at great personal risk often explained their reasons for helping others by describing a sense of human rights developed in childhood (Oliner & Oliner, 1992). At a young age, rescuers developed a moral literacy and a sense of autonomy (vs. blind obedience to authority) that inspired them to do the right thing despite the danger. When we expand our definition of education to include peace education, conflict resolution, and bullying prevention, we move beyond superficial academic achievement to create competent thinkers in a compassionate society.

From schools to our streets, however, bullying poses a unique and complex challenge that is not easily resolved with traditionally taught conflict resolution and mediation methods (Ttofi & Farrington, 2010). Commenting on the "evolving awareness about the morbidity and mortality associated with bullying," the World Health Organization (WHO) characterizes bullying as "a major public health problem that demands the concerted and coordinated time and attention" (Srabstein & Leventhal, 2010, p. 403) of policy makers, among other stakeholders. This chapter begins by providing a brief overview of the prevalence of bullying, types of bullying, and the consequences of bullying across cultures-from schools to the workplace. Understanding bullying and the consequences of bullying enables researchers to design relevant evaluation strategies with high construct validity. Following the overview, promising practices for reducing bullying and bias are presented with a discussion about developing valid measures to assess program effectiveness.

LITERATURE REVIEW: BULLYING AND RELATED CONSEQUENCES ACROSS CULTURES

Across cultures, the research on bullying paints a compelling picture of this pervasive problem. Extensive research of youth bullying in 40 countries reveals that "bullying and victimization is a universal public health problem and impacts large numbers of adolescents...[with] 26% of participating adolescents" reporting direct involvement with bullying (Craig et al., 2009). Another international study that included bullies and victims from 28 countries found that victims' psychological and physical symptoms were strongly correlated with bullying abuse in each of the countries (Due et al., 2005). Victim's symptoms typically included headache, stomach ache, dizziness, backache, depression, insomnia, a sense of alienation, and helplessness. Although bullying rates vary between countries, "there was a consistent, strong association between bullying and each of 12 physical and psychological symptoms among adolescents in all 28 countries." Lower academic achievement is a "direct consequence" of victimization (Card & Hodges, 2008, p. 454). Students who are victimized are less interested in school and have negative changes in brain function which impair the ability to focus and learn (Card & Hodges, 2008; Harris, 2009). The consequences of bias and bullying in schools or the workplace include serious, long-term psychological damage to all involved—bullies, bystanders, and victims (Due et al., 2005; Einarsen, Hoel, Zapf & Cooper, 2011).

From schoolyards to boardrooms, the majority of bullies engages in a "shopping process" to identify victims who passively avoid conflict or retaliation (Fried & Sosland, 2009, p. 29). Although the characteristics of victims change, there are certain traits and social dynamics that create vulnerable individuals in any environment. In order to assess bullying rates, it is helpful understand which individuals and groups are at a higher risk of being bullied. First, bullies often chose passive victims and victims who are different from the group/majority culture in any way. This risk-factor for bias and bullying is called *person-group dissimilarity* and it predicts who will become a victim across cultures (Juvonen & Galvan, 2009, p. 300).

A dissimilarity such as an accent, a different dialect, different hairstyle or clothing items, different educational needs (gifted or special education status), non-majority sexual orientation or simply being new in a community, will increase the risk of bias and victimization (Janssen, Craig, Boyce, & Pickett, 2004; Twyman, Saylor, Saia, Maclas, Taylor & Spratt, 2010). In some workplace settings, minorities are subjected to a bullying rate that is several times higher than their peers (Lewis, Giga, & Hoel, 2011). Research has shown that gifted students are more likely to be bullied in schools (Peterson & Ray, 2006) as are the hardest workers or more competent achievers in many workplace settings (Lewis et al., 2011).

People who are gay, lesbian, questioning or bisexual are also more likely to be targeted for bullying and bias in schools (Wormer & McKinney, 2003) and the workplace (Lewis, et al., 2011). Although both men and women are more likely to bully within their gender, when bullying crosses gender lines it is almost exclusively males bullying females (Lewis et al., 2011). Finally, those who are economically disadvantaged are also more likely to become targets of bullying and bias. A study of 5,998 students in 36 countries found that the poorest students in areas with wide economic irregularities are more likely to become victims of bullying (Michaud, 2009). It is not the country's wealth that predicts bullying, but instead it is the *relative* poverty that increases the risk of victimization in the diverse countries studied (Michaud, 2009). Bullying is about power, oppression, ostracism, and alienation.

Physical bullying causes physical harm and often involves pushing, punching, kicking, choking, poking, groping or tripping a victim. This overt and easily observable type of bullying is the most easily identified reported form of bullying by both youth and adults, although it is not necessarily the most common or damaging type of bullying. Indirect bullying and relational aggression (RA) are forms of bullying intended to control and damage the victim's relationships (Swearer, Espelage, & Napolitano, 2009). Relational aggression employs rumors, slander, prejudice, and lies with the intent to socially ostracize, shun or isolate a victim. Indirect bullying may also involve cyber bullying, which may include spreading rumors, blocking online friendships, or posting photos which are altered or unflattering.

Research that included over 1,500 children and adults revealed that, after the age of nine, over 95% of those interviewed would rather endure a punch, kick, or slap (physical pain) than be subjected to relational aggression such as public slander, insults, or rumors (Heydenberk & Heydenberk, 2011). During interviews, the majority of research participants explained their preference for physical pain by explaining that physical pain "goes away" or is forgettable. In contrast, the majority of subjects felt that the pain of relational aggression (social pain) had long-lasting impacts–ranging from damaged relationships, insomnia and depression to avoiding school or work. Subjects exposed to prolonged relational aggression reported changing schools, colleges, jobs, and moving to avoid further exposure. No one in the sample of over 1,500 people changed a job, school, or living arrangement to avoid a physical bullying incident (Heydenberk & Heydenberk, 2011).

SOCIAL BEINGS: THE CONSEQUENCES OF BULLYING, BIAS, AND OSTRACISM

We are social beings; "recent research has suggested that the need to belong is so fundamental that a lack of social connection, like a lack of other basic needs (e.g., food, water), can feel painful" (Masten & Eisenberger, 2009). Beyond the consequences of physical pain, social isolation and ostracization eventually causes adverse psychological and physical changes to victims (Harris, 2009). The need to belong is not a cultural artifact. A sense of belonging is "universal across civilizations and time" (Crescioni & Baumeister, 2009, p. 252). Social ostracism by a bully causes a set of cognitive changes called cognitive deconstruction, characterized by an absence of emotion or flattening of emotion, lethargy (inability to feel), an altered sense of time, and inability to focus on a meaningful thought (Crescioni & Baumeister, 2009). Laboratory research that exposes participants to social exclusion causes the excluded "people to perform worse on IQ tests, logical reasoning activities, and reading comprehension tasks…[and] social exclusion causes widespread impairment in how the brain processes….[causing] deficits on both rote memorization and logical reasoning tasks" (DeWall, 2009, p. 203). Bullying of young people has increased developmental impacts, such as "weakened development of social competencies which may harm future social and work prospects" as well as the devastating "health effects of negative social interaction" (Due et al., 2005, p. 130).

Studies of adults who were bullied in their youth reveal long term consequences and including shame, anxiety and difficulty in relationships (Carlisle & Rofes, 2007). A study of thousands of grown men (n=6094) revealed that "those exposed to bullying in school were at a significantly increased risk of having been diagnosed with depression between the ages of 31–51 years (Lund et al., 2009). Longer duration and higher intensity of bullying predicted depression later in life (Lund et al., 2009). Furthermore, when the former victims have their own children, they often become over protective and sheltering, which "may inhibit the development of conflict resolution skills and social skills in their children—placing the children at heightened risk of becoming the next generation of victims" (Smokowski & Kopasz, 2005, p. 105). The repetitive oppression, humiliation, and ostracism at the hands of a bully have the potential to permanently change the trajectory of life and may impact the next generation.

However, victims are not the only individuals harmed by bullying. Bullies and bystanders also endure negative consequences. Bullies experience "long-term effects and consequences as a result of their bullying" including underachievement or failure in school and the workplace (Smokowski & Kopasz, 2005, p. 103). Bullies are much more likely to have criminal convictions by age 24 as compared to non-bullies, and 40% of bullies may have three or more criminal convictions as young adults (Smokowski & Kopasz, 2005). Research shows that frequent bullies (8.8% of 2551 boys in one study) were found to be responsible for a disproportionate 33% of crimes in a four year study period (Sourander et al., 2006). Bullies are at higher risk for drug abuse, setting fires, self-injury and carrying weapons (Srabstein & Piazza, 2008) and bullies are more likely than uninvolved peers to suffer from depression and suicidal ideation (Klomek, et al., 2008). Involvement in bullying as a bully, or as a victim places the individual in "peril of dying of any of three main causes of mortality among young people—suicide, homicide, or accidents" (Srabstein & Piazza, 2008, p. 229). Both "bullying and victimization are associated with later suicide attempts and completed suicides" (Sourander et al., 2009, p. 254).

Bystanders' experiences should be considered when evaluating the impact of a anti-bullying, anti-bias program. Bystanders are not immune to the toxic effects of bullying. Numerous studies have revealed negative impacts of witnessing bullying on bystanders, including fear, guilt, and depression (Janson et al., 2009). Researchers studying bystanders in 14 public schools found that witnessing bullying was associated with bystanders' greater use of alcohol and drugs as well as bystander trauma and anxiety (Rivers, Poteat, Noret, & Ashurst, 2009). Bystanders' level of trauma has been confirmed in laboratory research. When researchers asked bystanders to recall witnessing abuse, bystanders' levels of "psychological distress were unexpectedly high and were comparable to levels of distress experienced by combat veterans diagnosed with posttraumatic stress disorder" (Janson & Hazler, 2004, p. 239). School bullying negatively impacts bullies, victims and bystanders–approximately 85% to 90% of a typical student population. Fortunately, interventions that reduce bullying and bias often have a significant positive impact on bystanders–increasing their sense of well-being and transforming the bystanders' ability to learn or function in a previously hostile environment (Heydenberk & Heydenberk, 2011). The consequences of bullying may negatively impact everyone in a community. A comprehensive, ecological approach empowers bystanders to become upstanders who work together to end bullying, bias and aggression–transforming social norms and creating safe, productive communities.

ADULT AND WORKPLACE BULLYING

Left unchecked, do bullies take their aggression to the workplace? Reviewing prevalence of workplace bullying in the U.S., researchers conclude that "adult bullying at work is shockingly common and enormously destructive" (Lutgen-Sandvik & Sypher, 2009). Comprehensive international research of workplace bullying reveals that 48% of those in the workforce are negatively impacted by bullying worldwide, either as a victim or a bystander (Lutgen-Sandvik & Sypher, 2009). Adult victims of workplace bullying suffer from an inability to concentrate, insomnia, mood swings, anxiety, depression and physical symptoms which eventually cause impairment at work and increased rates of absenteeism or presenteeism (being present at work but unable to function optimally) and the majority (84%) of adult victims of chronic workplace bullying show symptoms of post traumatic stress disorder (Einarsen et al., 2011; Hogh et al., 2011). Comprehensive evaluation should assess absenteeism rates and presenteeism (through fluctuations in productivity) when possible.

Although the financial costs of bullying in the workplace are difficult to quantify, the estimates indicate that the direct costs of bullying are in the range of billions of dollars annually (Hoel et al., 2011) in developed countries. Victims of bullying are significantly more likely to suffer illness and miss work (Einarsen et al., 2011; Namie et al., 2009) and they are likely to leave a job as a result of bullying. One quarter of the bystanders who witness bullying will leave their job due to the stress of witnessing abuse and bias. Bullying incurs expenses from sickness, absenteeism, loss of talent, recruiting, and training new employees. However, these expenses are less than the estimated costs of presenteeism–reduced cognitive effectiveness and reduced productivity in the workplace–which is estimated to "outstrip the cost of absenteeism" (Hoel et al., 2011).

PROMISING PRACTICES: THE A-B-CS OF PREVENTION, INTERVENTION, AND ASSESSMENT

A: Awareness, Assessment, and Autonomy

Because it differs from routine conflict, bullying must be clearly described before pretesting. Defining both physical and relational aggression and distinguishing bullying from healthy conflict by using examples creates awareness. Simply increasing *awareness* of bullying by defining and discussing bullying may have a positive and protective effect—lower bullying rates and helping victims feel less alienated, even before new program policies are in place (Sainio, Veenstra, Huitsing, & Salmivalli, 2010). A longitudinal study of a bullying program found that bullying decreased as a result of defining and discussing bullying during pre-testing. Although more significant decreases in bullying were found after program implementation, bullies were essentially exposed during pre-test discussions and definitions of bullying tactics; bystanders were sensitized to the issues and victims felt hopeful as a result of the increased awareness that pre-testing created (Heydenberk & Heydenberk, 2011).

However, increasing awareness of bullying and bias may have an unexpected impact on *assessment* efforts. Research shows that many effective bullying programs appear to fail because people/participants become increasingly aware of bullying incidents during the program, particularly indirect bullying and relational aggression, which is often under-reported in early assessments. Because of their increased sensitivity and awareness about bullying following pre-testing (Campbell & Stanley, 1963), research participants notice incidents of bullying and bias that they did not notic prior to testing. The majority of research participants interviewed in one six-year study acknowledged this *awareness effect*, which makes post-test prevalence/bullying rates appear as almost as high as pre-test rates (Heydenberk & Heydenberk, 2011). For this reason, clear definitions and awareness are essential prior to pretesting. As well, including *post-test only questions* such as, "*Has bullying decreased?*" and "*If so, by what estimated %?*" helps researchers identify any awareness/sensitivity testing effect and diminish this threat to validity (Heydenberk & Heydenberk, 2011). After defining bullying, an anonymous assessment of bullying including observations, anonymous surveys, and a review of disciplinary actions provide the most accurate results.

Autonomy and a sense of self efficacy are essential aspects of creating a safe, peaceful community. Members of a school or workplace community must understand that their choices impact others and they must have the skills to resolve conflicts and peacefully defend their values. Conflict competence and social skills provide a foundation for an authentic sense of self-efficacy and autonomy. Simple, empty affirmations and praise without reason or prosocial behavior may lead to increased aggression, and self-aggrandizement (Baumeister, 2001). In fact, studies show that violent offenders have higher mean scores than any other group on narcissistic self esteem measures (Baumeister, 2001). The essential difference between healthy and unhealthy self esteem is that positive assessment of self efficacy and a sense of autonomy must be earned--not entitled. As Davis (2005) explains, "earned self statements help [people] persist and overcome obstacles. Unearned or unrealistic positive self statements can lead instead to complacency and a sense of entitlement" (Davis, 2005, p. 51). When evaluating the effectiveness of an anti-bullying/bias education program, measures of self-efficacy are more relevant than measures of self-esteem.

In contrast, an earned sense of self-efficacy and autonomy lead to higher levels of moral reasoning and moral choice (Heydenberk, Heydenberk, & Bailey, 2003). Members of peaceful communities must be autonomous, empowered with conflict resolution skills and they must have opportunities to make positive, prosocial choices. Unfortunately, people who are not empowered to make choices based on their own humanitarian values may mindlessly follow a charismatic leader—even if the leader is a bully or a tyrant. Learning to ask questions or to reflect increases autonomy by developing self-awareness and self regulation. This metacognitive reflection is a strong predictor of success throughout life (Goleman, 2006). Survey/self report measures may include questions such as "I sometimes go along with my friends/colleagues even though I know what they are doing is wrong" and "I can stand up for what I believe is right." to assess changes in autonomy and use of related prosocial skills.

B: Bullying Policies and Bullying Education Programs

After clearly defining bullying, it is possible to design policies that prohibit bullying. Establish methods to make it easy for students, parents, and staff to report bullying incidents and require teachers and school staff to report bullying incidents that they observe. Because teacher attachment (a positive, caring, and nurturing connection between teachers and students) is the "strongest predictor of lower levels of bullying," teacher education and empowerment is an important part of any school program design (Swearer, Espelage, & Napolitano, 2009, p. 20). Parents and bystanders are also essential partners in creating safe school environments. Although it is unacceptable and unsafe to make student bystanders/peers responsible for the behaviors of bullies or the defense of victims in school (Ttofi & Farrington, 2010), it is helpful for bystanders to know that they have the ability to report (anonymously if they prefer) bullying incidents. Educating staff and students about bullying and providing students with affective, pro-social communication and conflict resolution skills, allows empowered bystanders to assert themselves and to resist becoming the unwilling accomplices to a bully's struggle for power (Heydenberk et al., 2003; Heydenberk & Heydenberk, 2005), however traditional conflict resolution and peer mediation are usually not recommended for bullies and victim dyads after bullying has occurred (Ttofi & Farrington, 2010). Successful mediation requires that both parties wish to engage in problem-solving and creative brainstorming in order to work toward a win-win/integrative solution. This requirement is often not satisfied in the case of bully/oppressor and victim dyads.

As in the case of school anti-bullying policies, workplace, anti bullying policies must be clear and supported by the entire workplace community. Developing strong anti-bullying policies and educating employees at all levels of employment increases the effectiveness of bullying reduction programs. Although support at the administrative level in a workplace is an essential first step toward transforming a toxic workplace culture, developing teams to support a positive climate and support the policy ensures success of anti-bullying and anti-bias efforts (Eddy, 2008). Staff training designed to help employees recognize bullying and confidential reporting systems work together to improve workplace environments (Eddy, 2008) and improve productivity, and employees' mental and physical health (Einarsen et al., 2011).

Instead of creating employee teams that look for problems among their peers, it is more effective to envision a bully free environment by defining supportive and respectful workplace behaviors. For instance, designing a "dignity at work" policy (Rayner & Lewis, 2011, p. 331) or a climate of respect policy enables employees to create a safe, bully-free environment. When problems with a lack of respect are identified, restoring respect without stigmatization allows for moral growth rather than creating conflict and inspiring a defensive posture. Support, education and training are critical to policy success; writing a policy and enforcing it without sufficient training of staff "may actually be counterproductive" (Rayner & Lewis, 2011, p. 37). Communication, support, and team meetings ensure success.

C: Community: Creating Connections

Community building, conflict competence, social skills and a sense of self-efficacy are protective factors enhancing resilience in diverse, challenging environments (Baskin et al., 2010; DePanfilis, 2006; Guerra & Bradshaw, 2008). Community connectedness requires "both opportunities and skills" (Guerra & Bradshaw, 2008, p. 3). Although it is complex, this sense of "connectedness across multiple domains is a primary deterrent of negative outcomes and aggression" (Guerra & Bradshaw, 2008, p. 12). Humans are "genetically prewired to develop social attachments" (Guerra & Bradshaw, 2008, p. 12). Failure to develop positive attachments has serious consequences ranging from alienation, academic failure, criminal behavior, self-injury, and risk taking to aggression and worse.

Core competencies, including social skills, self-efficacy, self control and moral reasoning can be developed, nurtured and significantly enhanced in a conflict positive environment (Heydenberk & Heydenberk, 2000). Connectedness or a sense of belonging is not just protective, but it also increases cognition and creativity (Heydenberk & Heydenberk, 2007). Decades of research have shown that core team meetings in the workplace and class meetings in schools are the most effective strategies for fostering connections among group members. Meetings with a positive focus, even when problem solving (e.g., solution focused rather than blame-focused), and a personally supportive focus create a sense of community Furthermore, using meetings to focus on team or class priorities and progress improves connectedness, resilience, and productivity in diverse communities (Landau & Gathercoal, 2000).

Although the majority of people in a school or workplace do not bully others or endorse mindless aggression, a bully can quickly intimidate bystanders and redefine the culture of a school or workplace. A bully commands all attention, dominates the culture and creates the false impression that his/her tactics are endorsed by the majority. Increased awareness of the fact that the majority of the population is comprised of people who do not engage in bullying is the first step for a positive climate change. This approach is called social norming (Fried & Sosland, 2010). Social norming strategies are successful in creating positive change in communities. Higher levels of victimization and bullying are more likely in environments where group norms support aggression (Vernberg & Bigg, 2010). Changing social norms by establishing pro-social climate with clear anti-bullying policies, team meetings, and positive methods of resolving conflict significantly reduces bullying and bias (Heydenberk & Heydenberk, 2000, 2007).

Cultural differences impact how aggressively people respond to negative or benign interactions and events. When comparing communities and cultures with higher levels of violence and aggression to those with lower levels of aggression, the research reveals that in a culture that places an unusually high value on defending personal honor and respect, individuals are more easily moved to violence in defense of that perception regarding respect. In other words, perceived disrespect is more likely to evoke a violent response in some cultures (Dodge, 2006). A bump in passing in a crowded hallway, a roll of the eyes, or a sarcastic comment that would not even garner attention in many cultures can lead to violence in others. The bump or any other perceived sign of disrespect may be accidental and therefore ignored by a less aggressive, less defensive individual. A sarcastic comment may be perceived as friendly humor in one culture but perceived as a hostile threat to personal honor by an individual in another culture.

A common understanding of respect develops through discussions about how others perceive respect, how they show respect, and their cultural rituals related to respect. Understanding cultural differences creates common ground on this universal issue. It is not necessary for everyone in a community to embrace the same cultural traditions or values; understanding others and respecting their traditions and rituals, however, may prevent violence, bullying and stereotyping.

Conducting core team meetings to share ideas about creating a respectful workplace or learning environment can be a positive, informative, and enjoyable method of reducing bullying and the objectification of others in the schools or the workplace. Positive, respectful, democratic meetings nurture relationships. Objectification of others is less likely when people begin to understand others in their communities (Landua & Gathercoal, 2000).

Respect and appreciation create positive emotions in schools and in the workplace. These "positive emotions foster transformative cooperation by building relationship strength [connectedness/bonding] thereby expanding capacity at both the individual and organizational levels" (Sekerka & Fredrickson, 2008, p. 2). Respect, positive emotions and a positive organizational climate build capacity, increase bonding and commitment, and enhance cognition, health and productivity (Sekerka & Fredrickson, 2008).

INDIVIDUAL INTERVENTIONS FOR VICTIMS

Passive victims are easier targets because they tend to feel inadequate and blame themselves for their abuse (Ross, 2002). Passive victims often lack effective, assertive social skills, and a related sense of self-efficacy (Hunter et al., 2004), and exhibit lower self esteem (Seals & Young, 2003). Social skills and opportunities for positive social interaction (e.g., team/class meetings) may provide protection against future incidents (Vernberg & Biggs, 2010), and social skills help victims create protective friendships (Flanagan & Battaglia, 2010).

Victims often suffer from Post Traumatic Stress Syndrome (PTSD), including intrusive thoughts of the bullying attacks, reliving the bullying events, or avoiding situations that remind the victim of the events—manifesting as increased work or school absences, or avoiding areas that remind the victim of the bullying incident as well as numbing of emotions or sleep disturbances. Cognitive behavioral therapy has received extensive empirical support as an effective PTSD treatment (Copeland-Linder, & Serwint, 2010; Foa et al., 2009) and has brought about significant improvements even severely traumatized cases. Cognitive Behavior Therapy helps victims identify, challenge and transform automatic, intrusive negative thoughts and plan more positive responses to the challenges they face. Counselors may assess individual victims' sense of self-efficacy including the use of assertive responses to bullying or bias as well as changes in victims' levels of depression, suicidal ideation, academic achievement or workplace productivity.

INDIVIDUAL INTERVENTIONS FOR BULLIES

Whenever possible, consequences for bullying behavior should be constructive, leading to an understanding and developing alternative responses with a new set of pro-social choices. Counseling may be indicated for serious and serial bullies (e.g., bullies who display anti-social personality disorder, narcissistic personality disorder, attention and impulse disorders, paranoid disorder).

The characteristics of bullies differ as do the characteristics of victims and bystanders. When working with bullies it is helpful to ask a series of questions about how the bullying occurs (Orpinas & Horne, 2006). For example, does the bullying maintain the bully's self esteem? Is the bullying a response to perceived threats or perceived hostile intent indicating hostile attributional bias? Is the bullying instrumental (e.g., used to social or economic power)? Does the bullying reflect low impulse control, indicated by angry outbursts followed by regret or attacks and outbursts under stress?

Bullying intervention is most effective when it targets a bully's specific intentions (e.g., power, self esteem), needs and personal characteristics such as low impulse control, hostile attributional bias, social skills deficits, or problem-solving deficits. Solution focused approaches can be designed to specifically target cognitive disorders or impulse control issues following evaluation (Orpinas & Horne, 2006). For example, a problem-focused question: "What is wrong with the bully?" becomes solution focused: "How can we solve this problem and what skills can we develop?" Why is the bully aggressive and angry?" becomes "How can I help this person control his/her anger and develop less aggressive behaviors." Building a repertoire of pro-social skills and challenging hostile attributions in multi dimensional interventions may be the most promising approach for helping bullies. CBT helps bullies challenge the biased and aggressive thoughts that cause a misperception of social clues.

Many bullies show signs of moral disengagement (Grills et al., 2010; Fried & Sosland, 2009). Moral disengagement depends on justifications, rationalizations, ignoring consequences, and dehumanizing victims. In fact, the most significant predictor of moral disengagement is a "readiness to provide moral justification for detrimental conduct" (Bandura, Barbaranelli, Caprara, & Pastorelli, 1996, p. 268). Assessment of individual interventions for bullies may include measuring changes in moral disengagement (e.g., taking responsibility for actions rather than rationalizing aggression), empathy, perspective-taking, and impulse control.

Assessment at the group level may include scales to measure exposure to violence, violent behavior checklists, and aggression scales (Hamburger et al., 2011), measures of productivity, academic achievement, absenteeism, and disciplinary reports. Positive changes may be assessed, such as changes in school attachment, workplace commitment, and feedback on the productivity of team/classroom meetings. After implementing an educational program or intervention to reduce bullying and bias and asking relevant questions with high construct and content validity, it is helpful to review assessment efforts through a framework of questions intended to strengthen internal and external validity (Campbell & Stanley, 1963). For example, the following questions identify confounding variables that may pose a threat to internal or external validity.

History: Consider any specific events that would impact outcomes that have occurred between pre and posttests. For instance, has a new disciplinary policy been put in place? Has an administrator left the work/school environment? Has a bully been fired or has he changed schools? Knowing program participants and the history impacting the community helps researchers identify and evaluate this threat.

Maturation: Maturation is a particularly relevant threat to internal validity in an educational setting. Comparison or control groups are the ideal way to assess this threat. However, if comparison groups are not available it is important to understand how patterns of bullying are related to age of the participants in the program. Assessing trajectories toward peak bullying ages may help ameliorate this threat. If peak bullying rates occur between ages eight and nine, any decrease in bullying in this age group may be a more significant gain than scores indicate when compared to population patterns for this age group. For example, a 30% reduction in bullying behaviors among 9 year old students is a more significant outcome when the general population in this age group experiences a 25% increase in bullying rates during the same time.

Statistical Regression: Statistical regression is often a threat to the internal validity of anti-bullying/anti-bias programs. Programs may be initiated during a time of unusually high bullying rates (extreme scores). Statistically, extreme scores (e.g., unusually high levels of bullying) tend to return to the mean. Therefore, any apparent reduction in bullying following an intervention may simply be a regression to the mean—a change that would have occurred without an educational intervention. It is helpful to broaden pretest baseline data by examining disciplinary records of bullying for an extended period of time prior to the pretest. Gathering baseline data on bullying means from previous years will help an evaluator attain a more accurate mean.

Testing Threats: As mentioned earlier, testing may increase participants' awareness and sensitivity to variables which may make a program appear to be ineffective or less effective at the time of the post-test. After a bullying pretest increases awareness and sensitizes participants' to the issue of bullying, the participants are more likely to notice bullying. Strategies for reducing this threat may include pre-sensitizing participants a week prior to pretesting or unobtrusive observations (e.g. parking lots, playgrounds, hallways) prior to pretesting and prior to post-testing. Reactive or interactive testing effects pose a threat to external validity if the testing process increases awareness and sensitivity to the issues of bullying and bias. Untested populations may not respond to the intervention to the same extent without the testing sensitivity effect.

Other threats to external validity: The ability to generalize to a larger population—should be considered. Questions about the representativeness of program participants are helpful when assessing external validity. For instance, is this population significantly different from other groups who might hope to benefit from this program? Are there significant differences in socioeconomic status, gender, culture, age, intelligence, religion…that may skew the outcome?

Finally, researchers should consider moving beyond the program setting and time limits by measuring transfer of cognitive dispositions and attendant skills in non school or workplace settings. Often the most meaningful changes appear in participants' use of new strategies in home and community settings long after an anti-bullying program posttest. These longitudinal measures reveal the internalization of skills and processes which transform participants' lives.

REFERENCES

Bandura, A., Barbaranelli, C., Caprara, G.V., & Pastorelli, C. (1996). Mechanisms of moral disengagement in the exercise of moral agency. *Journal of Personality and Social Psychology, 71*(2), 364–374.

Baskin, T., Wampold, B., Quintana, S., & Enright, R. (2010). Belongingness as a protective factor against loneliness and potential depression in a multicultural middle school. *The Counseling Psychologist, 38*(5), 626–651.

Baumeister, R. (2001). Violent pride: Do people turn violent because of self-hate or self love? *Scientific American, 284*(4), 96–101.

Campbell, D.T., & Stanley, J.C. (1963). *Experimental and quasi-experimental designs for research.* College Pub. Co., Chicago, Ill.

Card, N., & Hodges, E. (2008). Peer victimization among school children: Correlations, causes, consequences, and considerations in assessment and intervention. *School Psychology Quarterly, 23,* 451–461.

Carlisle, N., & Rofes, E. (2007). School bullying: Do adult survivors perceive long-term effects? *Traumatology, 18*(1), 16–26.

Copeland-Linder, N., & Serwint, J. (2010). Posttraumatic stress disorder. *American Academy of Pediatrics, 29,* 103–104.

Cose, E. (2008, April 21). The lessons of Rwanda. *Newsweek,* April 21, 2008.

Craig, W., Harel-Fisch, Y., Fogel-Grinvald, H., Dostaler, S., Hetland, J., Simon-Morton,B., Molcho, M ., de Mato, M ., Overpeck, M., Due, P., Pickett, W., & HBSC Writing Group (2009). A cross national profile of bullying and victimization among adolescence in 40 countries. *International Journal of Public Health, 54*(2), 216–224.

Crescioni, A., & Baumeister, R. (2009). Alone and aggressive: Social exclusion impairs self-control and empathy and increases hostile cognition and aggression. In M. Harris, (Ed), *Bullying, rejection and peer victimization: A social cognitive neuroscience perspective* (pp. 251–278).. New York: Springer Publishing.

Davis, S. (2005). *Schools where everyone belongs: Practical strategies for reducing bullying.* Champaign, IL: Research Press.

DePanfilis, D. (2006). *Child neglect: A guide for prevention, assessment and intervention.* US Dept. of Health and Human Service, Adm. for Children and Families, Children's Bureau, Washington, D.C.

DeWall, N. (2009). The pain of exclusion: Using insights from neuroscience to understand emotional and behavioral responses to social exclusion. In M. Harris, (Ed.), *Bullying, rejection and peer victimization: A social cognitive neuroscience perspective* (pp. 201–224). New York: Springer Publishing.

Dodge, K., (2006). Transactional science in action: Hostile attributional style and the development of aggressive behavior problems. *Development and Psychopathology, 18,* 791–814.

Due, P., Holstein, B., Lynch, J., Diderichsen, F., Gabhain, S., Scheidt,P. & Currie, C. (2005). The health behavior in school-aged children. *European Journal of Public Health, 15*(2), 128–132.

Eddy, B. (2008). *Bullies at work.* Mediate.com. Retrieved on Febuary 9th,2011 from www.mediate.com/articles/eddyBl.cfm.

Einarsen, S., Hoel, H., Zapf, D., & Cooper, G. (2011). The concept of bullying and harassment at work: The European tradition. In S. Einarsen, H. Hoel, D. Zapf, & C. Cooper. (Eds.), *Bullying and harassment in the workplace: Developments in theory, research and practice* (pp. 3–40). Boca Raton, FL: CRC Press.

Flanagan, K., & Battaglia, K. (2010). Selected group interventions for children who exhibit significant involvement in bullying. In E. Vernberg & B. Biggs (Eds.) *Preventing and treating Bullying and Victimization* (pp. 187–214). Oxford, New York: Oxford University Press.

Fountain, S. (1999). *Peace education in UNICEF.* UNICEF Staff Working Papers. New York: UNICEF.

Foa, E., Keane, T., Friedman, M., & Cohen, J. (2009). *Effective treatment for PTSD: Practice guidelines from the International Society of Traumatic Stress Studies.* NY: Guilford Press.

Fried, S., & Sosland, B. (2009). *Banishing bullying behavior: Transforming the culture of pain, rage and revenge.* Lanham, NY: Rowan & Littlefield Pub. Inc.

Glaeser, E., Ponzetto, G., & Shleifer, A. (2007). Why does democracy need education? *Journal of Economic Growth, Springer, 12*(2), 77–99.

Goleman, D. (2006). *Emotional intelligence (10th anniversary edition): Why it can matter more than IQ.* New York: Bantam Pub.

Grills-Taquechel, A., Polifroni, R., & Pane, H. (2010). Methods for assessing and treating bully-victim problems for individual children and adolescents. In E. Verhberg & B. Biggs (Eds). *Preventing and treating bullying and victimization* (pp. 135–160). Oxford, New York: Oxford University Press.

Guerra, N., & Bradshaw, C. (2008). *Core competencies to prevent problem behaviors and promote positive youth development: New directions for child and adolescent development.* Jossey-Bass.

Hamburger, M., Basile, K., Vivolo, A. (2011). *Measuring bullying victimization, perpetration, and bystanders experiences: A compendium of Assessment Tools.* Centers for Disease Control/National Center for Injury Prevention and Control, Atlanta, GA.

Harris, M. (2009). *Bullying, rejection and peer victimization: A social cognitive neuroscience perspective.* New York: Springer Pub.

Heydenberk, W., & Heydenberk, R. (2000). *A powerful peace: The integrative thinking classroom.* Needham, MA: Allyn and Bacon Pub.

Heydenberk, W., Heydenberk, R., & Bailey, S. (2003). Conflict resolution and moral reasoning. *Conflict Resolution Quarterly, 21*(1), 27–45.

Heydenberk, R., & Heydenberk W. (2005). Increasing metacognitive competence through conflict resolution. *Education and Urban Society, 37,* 431–457.

Heydenberk, R., & Heydenberk, W. (2007). The conflict resolution connection: Increasing school attachments in cooperative classroom communities. *Reclaiming Children and Youth, 16*(3), 18–22.

Heydenberk, R., & Heydenberk, W. (2011). The *Peace Center program evaluations, 2000–2010.* Unpublished manuscript.

Hoel, H., Sheehan, M., Cooper, C. & Einarsen, S. (2011). Organizational effects of workplace bullying. In S. Einarsen, Hoel, H., D. Zapf & C. Cooper (Eds.), *Bullying and harassment in the workplace: Developments in theory, research and practice.* Boca Raton, FL: CRC Press.

Hogh, A., Gemzoe, E., Mikkelsen, E.G., & Hansen, A.M. (2011). Individual consequences of workplace bullying/mobbing. In S. Einarsen, H., Hoel, D. Zapf & C. Cooper (Eds.), *Bullying and harassment in the workplace: Developments in theory, research and practice* (107–128). Boca Raton, FL: CRC Press.

Hunter, S., Boyle, J., & Warden. (2004). Help seeking amongst child and adolescent victims of peer-aggression and bullying: The influence of school-stage, gender, victimization, appraisal, and emotion. *British Journal of Educational Psychology, 74*(3), 375–90.

Janson, G. R., Carney, J. V., Hazler R. J., & Oh, I. (2009). Bystanders' reactions to witnessing repetitive abuse experiences. *Journal of Counseling & Development, 87*(3), 319–326.

Janson, G.,& Hazler, R. (2004). Trauma reactions of bystanders and victims to repetitive abuse experiences. *Violence and Victims*, *19*(2), 239–255.

Janssen, I., Craig, W., Boyce, W., & Pickett, W. (2004). Associations between overweight and obesity with bullying behaviors in school-aged children, *Pediatrics*, *113*(5), 1187–1194.

Juvonen, J., & Galvan, A. (2009). Bullying as a means to foster compliance. In M. Harris, (Ed), *Bullying, rejection and peer victimization: A social cognitive neuroscience perspective* (pp. 299–318) New York: Springer Publishing.

Klomek, A., Soourander, A., Kumpulainen, K., Piha, J., Tamminen, T., Moilaner, I., Almqvist, F., & Gould, M. (2008). Childhood bullying as a risk for later depression and suicidal ideatuion among Finnish males. *Journal of Affective Disorders*, *109*(1), 47–55.

Landau, B. M., & Gathercoal, P. (2000). Creating peaceful classrooms: Judicious Discipline and class meetings. *Phi Delta Kappan*, *86*(6), 450–454.

Lewis, D., Giga, S., & Hoel, H. (2011). Discrimination and bullying. In S. Einarsen, H. Hoel, D. Zapf, & C. Cooper (Eds.), *Bullying and harassment in the workplace: Developments in theory, research and practice* (pp. 267–282). Boca Raton, FL: CRC Press.

Lund, R., Nielsen, K., Hansen, D., Kriegbaum, M., Molbo, D., & Christensen, C. (2009). Exposure to bullying at school and depression in adulthood: A study of Danish men born in 1953. *European Journal of Public Health*, *19*(1), 111–116.

Lutgen-Sandvik, P. & Sypher, B. (2009). *Destructive organizational communication*. New York: Routledge Press.

Masten, C., & Eisenberger, N. (2009). Exploring the experience of social rejection in adults and adolescents: A social cognitive neuroscience perspective. In M. Harris (Ed.). *Bullying, rejection, and peer victimization: A social cognitive neuroscience perspective* (pp. 53–78) New York: Springer Publishing.

Michaud, P. (2009). Bullying: We need to increase our efforts and broaden our focus. *Journal of Adolescent Health*, *4*, 323–25.

Namie, G., Namie, R., & Lutgen-Sanduik, R. (2009). Workplace bullying: Causes, consequences, and corrections. In Lutgen-Sanduik, R. & Sypher, B. (Eds.), *Destructive organizational communication*. New York, NY. Routledge Press.

Oliner, S., & Oliner, P. (1992). *The altruistic personality: Rescuers of Jews in Nazi Europe*, New York: McMillian/Free Press.

Orpinas, P. & Horne, A. (2006). *Bullying prevention: Creating a positive school climate and developing social competence*. Washington, D.C.: American Psychological Association.

Peterson J., & Ray K. (2006). Bullying and the gifted: Victims, perpetrators, prevalence, and effects. *Gifted Child Quarterly*, *50*,148–168.

Rayner, C., & Lewis, D. (2011).Managing workplace bullying: The role policies. In S. Einarsen, H., Hoel, D., Zapf., & C. Cooper (Eds.), *Bullying and harassment in the workplace: Developments in theory, research and practice*. Boca Raton, FL: CRC Press.

Rivers, I., Poteat, V., Noret, N., & Ashurst, N. (2009). Observing bullying at school: The mental health implications of witness status. *School Psychology Quarterly*, *24*(4), 211–223.

Ross, D. (2002). Bullying. In J. Sandoval (Ed.), *Handbook of crisis counseling, intervention and prevention in schools* (pp. 105–136).NJ, London, England: Lawrence Erlbaum Associates, Publishers.

Sainio, M., Veenstra, R., Huitsing, G., & Salmivalli, C. (2010). Victims and their defenders: A dyadic approach. *International Journal of Behavioral Development, 35,* 144–151.

Seals, D. & Young, J. (2003). Bullying and victimization: Prevalence and relationship to gender, grade level, ethnicity, self-esteem, and depression. *Adolescence, 38,* 735–747.

Sekerka, L, & Fredrickson, B. (2008). Establishing positive emotional climates to advance organizational transformation. In N. Ashkanasy & C. Cooper (Eds.), *Research companion to emotion in organizations.* (pp. 531–544) Cheltenham, UK.: Edagar Elgar Publishing.

Smokowski, P., & Kopasz, K. (2005). Bullying in school: An overview of types, effects, family characteristics, and intervention strategies. *Children and Schools, 27*(2), 101–110.

Sourander, A., Klomek, A., Niemela, S., Haauisto, A., Gyllenberg, D., Helenius, H., Sillanmaki, L, ristkari, T., Kumpulainen, K., Tammineu, T., Moilanen, I., Piha, J., Stein, J., Dukes, R., & Warren, J. (2006). Adolescent male bullies, victims, and bully victims: A comparison of psychological and behavioral characteristics. *Journal of Pediatric Psychology. 32*(3), 273–282.

Srabstein, J., & Leventhal, B. (2010). Prevention of bullying-related morbidity and mortality: A call for public health policies. *Bulletin of the World Health Organization, 88*(6, June), 401–480.

Srabstein, J., & Piazza, T. (2008). Public health, safety and educational risks associated with bullying behaviors in American adolescents. *International Journal of Adolescent Medical Health, 20*(2), 223–33.

Swearer, S., Espelage, D., & Napolitano, S. (2009). *Bullying prevention and intervention: Realistic strategies for schools.* NY: Guilford Press.

Ttofi, M. M., & Farrington, D. P. (2010). Effectiveness of school based programs to reduce bullying: A systematic and meta-analytic review. *Journal of Experimental Criminology, 7,* 27–56. Retrieved on January 13, 2011 from http://link.springer.com/article/10.1007%2Fs11292-010-9109-1#page-1.

Twyman, K, Saylor, C., Saia, D., Maclas, M., Taylor, L., & Spratt, E. (2010). Bullying and ostracism: Experiences in children with special health care needs. *Journal of Developmental and Behavioral Pediatrics, 31,* 1–8.

UN General Assembly. (1989). *Convention on the Rights of the Child, United Nations Treaty Series* (vol. 1577, p. 3).

Vernberg, E. & Biggs, B. (2010). *Preventing and treating bullying and victimization.* Oxford, NY: Oxford University Press.

Wormer, K., & McKinney, R. (2003). What schools can do to help gay, lesbian, bisexual youth: A harm reduction approach. *Adolescence, 38*(151), 409–420.

CHAPTER 7

EVALUATING A PROJECT-BASED PEACE EDUCATION COURSE IN TURKEY

The Civic Involvement Projects

Antonia Mandry

INTRODUCTION

Peace, human rights, and social justice have increasingly become subject to pedagogical attempts to incorporate them into educational systems that can be inimical or even hostile to peace pedagogy. Nevertheless, since the 1980s, the world has seen an increase in human rights education (Ramirez et al., 2006) as well as in the dissemination of related pedagogies into formal education curricula. The evaluation of such programs is a key component of their development and improvement.

In Turkey, three approaches have emerged in the education sector since the foundation of the Turkish Republic that aim to educate the individual in its role in society.[1] These three paradigms are citizenship education, human rights educa-

---

[1] The Republic of Turkey was founded in 1923 after the Ottoman Empire was defeated in World War I and lost much of its imperial territory.

Peace Education Evaluation: Learning from Experience and Exploring Prospects,
pages 103–115.
Copyright © 2015 by Information Age Publishing
All rights of reproduction in any form reserved.

tion, and social responsibility education.[2] Although introduced sequentially, the associated courses and components continue to coexist, serve similar roles but with different purposes, and encompass issues of national identity, democracy, human rights, and social justice. Traditional citizenship education courses, which have been in place since the 1920s, aim to inculcate values of citizenship that are desirable to the nation-state: in this case, democratic principles and respect for the military as the guardians of secularism (Altınay, 2004). The newer human rights education courses (implemented in 1998) in Turkey sought to teach the human rights and responsibilities of an individual regardless of citizenship.[3] Following the education reforms of 2005, these courses were abolished and integrated throughout the curriculum. Finally, the emerging social responsibility courses offer practical opportunities for students to contribute directly to their community, while drawing on multiple frameworks including social justice, peace education, and human rights (Çetindamar & Hopkins, 2008).[4]

A significant component when introducing new curricular approaches is evaluation. For peace education and similar courses, the challenges of evaluation become greater in that:

> it is difficult to evaluate the achievements of peace education, because its objectives pertain mainly to the internalization of values, attitudes, skills and patterns of behaviors. The texts and exams normally used in schools are unsuitable...because they do not usually evaluate a state of mind but rather the level of acquired knowledge. The evaluation...requires special techniques adapted to...a different kind of outcome. (Bar-Tal, 2002, p. 34)

In some courses, exams themselves are irrelevant. Thus, in any fruitful evaluation of a course, the objectives, the standards, and the reception of the course are central features. Evaluations must adapt the differing approaches to a pedagogy of peace at the different levels of education.

While the introduction of social responsibility courses at the primary and secondary education levels in Turkey is also worthy of study, it is at the tertiary level where peace pedagogy is of particular interest to this study and to educators who are searching for ways to approach perceived gaps in Turkish education. At Sabancı University in Istanbul, one course in particular is regularly featured in national newspapers, has been exported to other universities under a Soros grant, and has even been the inspiration for similar courses introduced at the secondary level. This chapter chooses to focus on that course, namely the Civic Involvement Projects (CIP).

---

[2] Loosely grouped under the term "Social Responsibility," the courses and their components are also called Civic Involvement, Community Involvement, or Community Service.

[3] For more information, see Çayır and Bağlı (2011).

[4] While many primary and secondary schools had elective or club activities that focused on community service, in 2005 the Ministry of National Education (MEB) mandated that all students must participate in social service (MEB, 2005).

In this chapter, I aim to explore the story of CIP, focusing on: educators' aims; students' perceptions of these aims; methods of evaluation; educators' concerns regarding evaluation techniques; and students' reactions and opinions of these courses. This chapter tells part of a richer story that constitutes a larger study (Mandry, 2012) on one academic community's perceptions of human rights concepts; thus, much is omitted in order to focus only on the data that informs this particular publication. The study took place from September 2010 to January 2011 and data was collected from 150 questionnaires, 50 interviews, and observations of 9 total projects.[5,6]

First, I provide an overview of peace education and evaluation that highlights both recent scholarship on evaluation and the challenges presented by evaluating peace education specifically relevant to CIP. Next, I draw a detailed picture of the context of the study, both the Turkish university system and CIP in order to clarify how the course works. The following sections delve deep into the goals of the educators, examining the impetus toward creating a culture of volunteerism and mandating that volunteerism. This section investigates how the students perceive these goals as well as the program overall. These elements are reflected in the types of evaluation of CIP carried out. Thus, a major component of the chapter looks at the formal and informal methods to evaluate the impact of the course and the educators' opinions of these techniques as related specifically to the previous sections on aims and the mandatory nature of the program.

EVALUATING PEACE EDUCATION PROGRAMS

Peace education remains a difficult field in which to conduct rigorous and robust evaluation due to the diversity in aims of practitioners and curricula, but also, "because its objectives pertain mainly to the internalization of values, attitudes, skills, and patterns of behaviors" (Bar-Tal, 2002, p. 34; Harris & Morrison, 2003). In addition to these challenges, peace education programs have historically engaged in weak evaluation, if any. The minority that do conduct evaluations use methods such as self-reporting surveys and behaviors, observations, essay analysis, tests, and structured interviews (Nevo & Brem, 2002). Nevo and Brem, in their study on 20 years of evaluation research on peace education program effectiveness, report that while the minority of the programs they looked at did not engage in effectiveness evaluation, most of those that did were found to be highly effective. They also created a rubric by which to understand the evaluation research, which included program purpose, participant age, pedagogical approach, length of program, and evaluation methods. Harris and Morrison (2003) also stress that timing of program evaluation is critical, including three discrete stages of evaluation: be-

---

[5] The questionnaires used the imaginary island scenario based on Kolouh-Westin, 2004.

[6] Seven academic year projects were observed during the fall 2010 semester. In addition, two voluntary projects were observed during summer 2010 and winter 2011 on site in rural, impoverished areas of eastern Turkey.

fore, during, and after. This process aids in the successive improvement of courses and stresses the iterative nature of curricular development in such a challenging field. A brief overview of peace education evaluation, its challenges, and its past uses, is critical to understanding the program that is the focus of this chapter, the Civic Involvement Projects at Sabancı University in Istanbul.

SOCIAL RESPONSIBILITY COURSES IN UNIVERSITIES AND THE CIVIC INVOLVEMENT PROJECTS

The term *social responsibility* allows institutions of higher learning broad discretion on what kind of peace pedagogy they introduce into the university classroom. Due to loose restrictions from the Higher Education Council (YÖK), many universities contribute to a pedagogy of peace by creating related courses, associating with human rights institutes, or opening peace and conflict studies departments.[7] These courses range from elective to mandatory, undergraduate to graduate, and core courses to major-specific courses.

Universities such as İstanbul Bilgi University offer social responsibility courses as electives. The first semester of the course is mainly discussion-based while the second aims for the planning and production of a civil society-based project. Ankara University offers, in contrast, a human rights education course for undergraduate students training to be teachers that is centered on information and emphasizes knowledge rather than process-based learning. Other universities, such as Akdeniz University in Antalya, promote social responsibility or community service work through student clubs. Within the educational community of higher education in Turkey, Sabancı University, a private institution founded in 1996, stands out as a leader in peace and human rights-oriented content. In keeping with Sabancı University's broader philosophy to develop an academic community with "the ability to reflect critically and independently, combined with a strong sense of social responsibility" (Sabancı University, 2009), this university established CIP in 1999. By special arrangement with YÖK, regulations for universities were circumvented to enable the implementation of the university mission, making way for core courses like CIP.[8] This mandatory course for undergraduate students aims to enhance students' understanding of participatory citizenship and engage students in projects concerning issues such as human rights and refugees. It is an experiential course that is both student-led and project-based, and offers opportunities for critical discussion and transformative action. Although CIP I is a core course, students who express interest may subsequently take the optional electives CIP II through CIP VI.

Despite the mandatory nature of the course, CIP I does allow for some flexibility as to how the project is carried out. Students form project teams with a par-

---

[7] YÖK, founded in 1981, is an independent council responsible for the supervision of universities in Turkey.

[8] Such regulations include the declaration of the major course of study upon entry into university.

TABLE 7.1. Project Selections for Academic Year 2010–2011 CIP (Number of Sections)

Cezaevi Projesi (1) (Prison Project)	Bilişimde Genç Hareket (1) (IT Youth Movement)	Mülteciler (1) (Refugees)
Engelsiz Engelli Küreği (1) (Abled Disabled Rowing)	İnsan Hakları (2) (Human Rights)	Bir Dilek Tut (1) (Make a Wish)
Çöp(m)adam (1) (Garbage Ladies)	Bağımlılık (1) (Addiction)	Deprem Eğitimi (1) (Earthquake Education)
Kurum çocuk (5) (Orphanage)	Kültürel Miras (1) (Cultural Heritage)	Cinsel Sorumluluk (2) (Sexual Responsibility)
Okul çocuk (32) (Schoolchildren)	Çevre Projeleri (5) (Environment Projects)	Hayvan hakları (2) (Animal Rights) Engelli (5)
(Disabled Projects)	Yaşlı Proje (5) (Elderly Projects)	Toplumsal Cinsiyet (2) (Gender Project)
	Total:	69 (683 students)

ticular focus, which can be very diverse. For example, out of the 69 projects that took place during the 2010–2011 academic year, topics ranged from animal rights to Make a Wish projects (see Table 7.1 for a complete list). The students must design and implement a project that contributes to society. The team members work directly with CIP supervisors, students who have applied for the positions after having previously completed CIP I (Çetindamar and Hopkins, 2008). In addition, advanced students offer further support to the supervisors in the role of advisors. The project structure is highly collaborative and encourages agency and responsibility among the students. Meetings where teams with different projects can brainstorm and share progress as well as information on implemented activities are held weekly. Throughout this process, the permanent staff of educators serves in an advisory and facilitative capacity.

UNDERSTANDING THE GOALS OF THE COURSE

The overarching goal of the CIP is "to give students an understanding that every individual not only can, but also has a responsibility to contribute positively to society" (Sabancı University, 2005). This understanding takes the form of raising the awareness of students about the world around them—an understanding the students lack because, as one educator noted, "they live in this bubble" (Feride, interview, November 26, 2010). Feride sees this bubble as being created by the wealth of many of the students, and reinforced by many private universities in Istanbul, which are often located in the midst of impoverished areas. These universities thus become wealthy gated academic communities within poverty, which "is very threatening to them actually" (Bahar, interview, June 8, 2010). İstanbul Bilgi University has one of three campuses located in Dolapdere, a run-down area of Istanbul. Sabancı University is located near the industrial, poor and conservative town of Tuzla. Thus, educators are concerned about the unrealistic "bubble" that their students live in and want to "build awareness in…students" (Ozlem, April 8, 2010), "create awareness" (Emre, interview, January 21, 2011) and "open their awareness" (Işıl, interview, December 10, 2010). This is done "indirectly" (Feride, interview, November 26, 2010) by giving the students "the chance to take a step out of their very small circle they live in and interact with society…[and] a different perspective on how to do something good in society" (Deniz, interview, January 14, 2011). This is clearly a major goal of the CIP course: to raise awareness of the "realities of life and learning to play an active part in understanding these" (Çetindamar & Hopkins, 2008, p. 405). The second goal is clearly to inculcate in students the ability and sense of responsibility to act on their raised awareness. Here, the educators are pursuing their objective to create a culture of volunteerism and impact society beyond these students and their time at Sabancı.

CREATING A CULTURE OF VOLUNTEERISM

One of the educators' main objectives for creating the Civic Involvement Projects course was the development of a new generation that was committed to the notion of volunteerism. In creating a culture of volunteerism, it was perceived by staff members that these students would learn to address and act on issues of social justice. Generationally, then, the cumulative effect would build and grow a culture of volunteerism.

To grow such a culture required a deep understanding of the landscape of voluntary work in Turkey as well as local and cultural challenges. One of the primary obstacles was the standard of volunteerism in the country; the majority of the individuals who engaged in such work were professionals. Unpaid volunteers were rare and perceived as untrustworthy. In fact, the relationship between civil society organizations and external volunteers, or the lack of such a relationship, deeply influenced the creation of CIP. According to two CIP educators:

Seeing Civil Society Organizations [CSO]—seeing so many organizations that are professionals that don't know what to do with volunteers. Organizations need to know they will come again. Maybe under duress. (Ella, interview, September 6, 2010);

After the coup, people started to hate civil society…always blaming NGOs and civil society for everything…by the 90s, the views changed a little bit…Mostly by [1999], most [NGOs] did not know what they were doing…They had no aims, just a bunch of people who agreed on one point on one topic…[and] they were very territorial… No understanding of volunteerism…The first 3 years of CIP—we could not explain to them why they would need volunteers. [Somehow they thought we] do not want them...(Deniz, interview, January 14, 2011)[9]

Ella's and Deniz's comments underscore the fundamental distrust that can exist between organizations and individuals in Turkish society. Furthermore, even when the will exists, there may be a lack of understanding in how best to use a volunteer base. Thus, an unspoken component of CIP is not just educating students to value social responsibility and a culture of volunteerism, but also to educate organizations about the possibility of drawing on a student body experienced with volunteerism.

COMPULSORY VOLUNTEERISM AND CONCEPTUAL CHALLENGES

Despite my use of the term volunteerism in the previous section, the educators struggle with this word throughout their experience of designing, implementing, and revising the program. CIP is a mandatory course that all undergraduate students must take in their first year. For many educators, "mandatory doesn't sound to me very friendly" (Bahar, interview, June 8, 2010). Nevertheless, two conceptual issues emerge when analyzing the interviews with the educators. First, the linguistic and conceptual challenges when dealing with the term volunteerism in Turkey, and second, the local realities and history of the context that complicate the creation of a culture of volunteerism.

In Turkish, the word for volunteer is *gönüllü*, which means "with heart" and "from the heart" (Deniz, January 14, 2011).[10] For educators like Bahar, the word *gönüllü* carries a problematic connotation.

[It's about] to give something, to give with your heart...So for some other people, you have the source is and you're a good person and you shared this opportunity... the helper is very honorful [and]...is [in] a very high position, has money, is educated, is a good person. (Bahar, June 8, 2010)

Other educators like Deniz also find the word troubling, but primarily how it impacts students and society's perception of action and responsibility.

[The word] really messed things up...because the understanding is that...if I want do it, I will, if I don't, I won't...Ok, and that doesn't go like that, even if you are a volunteer you need to be there. Each week, each month...It's not like if your heart wishes. So the words gönüllü in Turkish used to be and still is very empty of a term. People didn't understand that they need to be committed...when you volunteer for something. (Deniz, January 14, 2011)

---

[9] After fighting between ultra nationalists and communists intensified in the late 1970s, the military took control of the government in a coup and implemented martial law and drafted a new constitution that restricted civil liberties.

[10] In English, the word volunteer has a Latin root, *voluntas*, which means free will or want.

Deniz explained that in her idea *gönüllü* should be about responsibility rather than volunteerism and thus obligatory. While some CIP educators admitted that the mandatory nature did not necessarily fit with the personal belief of social justice on which their choice of careers was based, they acknowledged that the local Turkish reality required such an obligation.

> Given the realities of Turkey right now, the education system, the lack of direct involvement, lack of responsibility, I still think it's ok. I think eventually it shouldn't be mandatory and I like to think it can be an elective ——more academic, more theoretical. More like some of the service learning programs in the United States but NOT taught by other instructors because other instructors have too much to do already. Eventually it can reach that level, but not yet. It would have to take a rehaul of the educational system. (Ella, interview, September 6, 2010)

Deniz partially agrees, but points out that changing the course to an elective will not happen in her lifetime.

> I don't think we will see the day where everybody from high school they would know the need and how...to get involved in societies; and secondly it is very good to have this as a mandatory course. I always say that when you graduate from university it's like a package. And in that package you get math, science...and with that package you move on to your next stage of life. That package needs to include social responsibility. (Deniz, interview, January 14, 2011)

The concerns of the educators greatly influenced the creation of CIP as well as factored into the approaches for its evaluation.

EVALUATING CIP: PURPOSE, METHODS, STRENGTHS, AND CHALLENGES

The question with any project that engages with social justice, human rights, or peace education is how effective it is and how this efficacy is measured. Peace education has historically been extremely weak in evaluation techniques (Harris & Morrison, 2003; Nevo & Brem, 2002) due to an emphasis on transformational processes rather than establishing standards and measures. In the case of the Civic Involvement Projects, evaluation was also a secondary issue. The educators of CIP placed more importance on the process that students experienced while carrying out the projects. It was deemed more important to teach students "why they need to be responsible, how they can be responsible, and how they can take action" (Deniz, January 14, 2011). This was done primarily through student-led, project-based experiential learning. Evaluating such a program requires a variety of methods, including questionnaires, observations, and anecdotal evidence.

The CIP staff ended the academic year by distributing questionnaires to all CIP students to evaluate the students' responses to the program. The 2010–2011 questionnaire, for example, asked about: students' previous knowledge of CIP; previous volunteer work; what students learned from the CIP experience; how the students or those with whom they worked benefited; whether CIP should be mandatory; whether they would like to participate in CIP again; what they thought of their supervisor; whether they interacted with the project advisor; and if there was a need for such interaction.

The questionnaire offered special insight into the concerns of the educators and adhered closely to the program's goals. For example, the compulsory nature of the course, while in the end deemed a necessity, remained a problematic issue— one that is wrestled with by the educators and one that they must address often. Nevertheless, the educators continue to inquire of their CIP students about this characteristic of the course on the end-of-year questionnaires. The educators are also clearly curious about the culture of volunteerism with which their students come into the CIP program; hence, the question regarding previous volunteer work. Furthermore, in an addendum to this question, they also ask about which organizations respondents have been involved with and type of work they have done. The question about what the students learned or gained from completing CIP also complements the educators' desire to raise the awareness of the students about the reality around them. While educators like Deniz claim that "our priority is university students," the question about the benefit to the community complements the idea that "we are very much willing to do good stuff for all of this [sic] children, elderly, environment, rights, everything" (Deniz, interview, January 14, 2011). While the questionnaire is formal and required of all CIP participants, informal measures such as observation or anecdotal evidence also complements the gathering of a holistic picture of the program's impact as is seen in a 2008 study by Çetindamar and Hopkins.

Çetindamar and Hopkins (2008) looked at additional measures of effectiveness when exploring the impact of CIP as well as looking at CIP alumni. First, the authors included students who, after completing the mandatory CIP requirement, continued their academic work in CIP-related areas. Second, they researched graduates who made an effort to bring social responsibility into their corporate careers. Furthermore, the authors looked at successful exportation of the program to other universities. Finally, the students' feedback on the program was gathered through the use of surveys administered to all the students involved in CIP such as in the 2010–2011 evaluation described above. The surveys asked such questions as what the students thought about the requirement of CIP and the value of the coursework. The authors offered mostly anecdotal evidence of the positive impact on the lives of the graduates of CIP and Sabancı, pointing to graduates who "implement a comprehensive recycling program...[and another] who is completing a Ph.D. in Development Economics" (p. 407). In reporting on the current students' opinions on the value of CIP as well as its required nature, the authors reported that "85% consistently agree that the projects should be mandatory...[a student said] 'If I did not have to continue with my project, I would not have...had the satisfaction and warmth that I had from working with these children whose lives are more difficult than I could have imagined'" (p. 408). In contrast, another study by Hopkins (2007) points out that "Turkish university personnel and students are not convinced that civic engagement-like courses are academically or socially worthwhile" (Brabant, 2010, p. 120).

The inherent challenges in evaluating the course are substantial, including the admission that "it is not easy to measure the success of such a program, and it certainly would not be easy or credible to do so from within our own structure" (Hopkins & Terzioglu, 2011, p. 83). The sheer size of the program also complicates any evaluation that goes deeper than the superficial level of questionnaires to additionally include interviews and observations. The size of the program is due to the fact that all first-year university students at Sabancı are expected to go through the course and 683 students were enrolled in CIP in the 2010–2011 academic year. The CIP staff is small, consisting of only six full-time employees, and one part-time consultant. Any evaluation that were to be conducted by this staff, whose other duties include the facilitation, advisement, and coordination of the projects with the students and with civil society organizations, would be an enormous task.

Thus, CIP relies heavily on experiential and transformative learning, emphasizing the importance of process over knowledge. As one educator stated,

> Knowledge and Skills? Probably our biggest weakness. Not a lot of theory. We tried to do some with training, knowledge background. I personally felt that and still feel that there is so much out there in theory and facts that it's pretty accessible but not so much in practice. But I say let's get on with it. If they are interested they will pursue it. (Ella, September 6, 2010)

Because of this emphasis on process, any evaluation must be mostly observational. The CIP staff work closely with supervisors and students, and gain this deep insight from their daily work and from reports that supervisors file at the end of the year.

While two different evaluations stress different findings (Çetindamar & Hopkins, 2008; Hopkins, 2007), the interviews I conducted with the students during the 2010–2011 academic year revealed both convergence with and divergence from the narrative of the educators. Many of the students, including Sedef and Canan, adhered to the school of thought as delineated by one educator, Bahar, above: that CIP was designed to help the more unfortunate, the impoverished, the children, the environment, and the helpless. This rests within the idea of volunteerism as helping the helpless with compassion because one wants to.

> I think it's to give something back. Because almost everyone of us, we are very privileged kids. (Sedef, November 24, 2010)

> I think we have good opportunities but there are some people who are not lucky like us so we want to share this luck with them. Our aim is this. We want to make them happy. (Canan, November 24, 2010)

In contrast, students like Elif saw the purpose of CIP as "contributing social responsibility to university students" (Elif, December 1, 2010). As another student Ecesu said, "the aim is to make those students aware, so I think it is going pretty good" (Ecesu, December 17, 2010).

Thus, there are two goals that are emerging from the discourse of students involved with CIP. The first is the awareness of Turkey's realities within a privileged, elite student body. The second is a positive impact on the society with whom those university students are working. A missing component of the evaluation is this impact on the second population involved in CIP, however indirectly; the schoolchildren, the refugees, the children with disabilities, and the other sectors with which the CIP projects are involved. One CIP educator noted that there is little follow-up with the external communities except that "some of our [Sabancı] students keep in touch with some of the kids...writing postcards" (Işıl, December 10, 2010). In 2010, I observed a summer project in a rural community in the eastern part of Turkey. During my observation, I discovered that one CIP student kept in touch with two of the schoolkids with whom she had been working. This limited follow-up is left to the initiative of the CIP students.

This lack of focus on the broader community can be a significant weakness when evaluating the impact of CIP as the program does not exist in isolation. With the dual purposes of the course, raising awareness and creating a culture of volunteerism, a broader evaluation is necessary; one that measures not only if, but also how and to what extent CIP students continue their relationship with the specific schoolchildren with whom they were working, for instance, and with volunteerism in general. Furthermore, examining how the broader community experiences CIP could also illuminate weaknesses in the CIP format. The mandatory nature of the course can also create a negative impact that must be included in the evaluation and remains a challenge for the evaluation of CIP. This impact could manifest firstly on the university students themselves, and secondly, on the communities and civil society organizations with whom they work.

This unexplored impact may also be worthy of examination when considering a comprehensive evaluation of CIP. One trainer who was involved in training CIP students who were to work with children shared her surprise about the Sabancı students when she said, "So many of them were antagonistic, it was clear they didn't want to be there" (Aygul, interview, July 21, 2011). Her concern was with the schoolchildren that the university students were working with as she feared this antagonism might harm the schoolchildren. This kind of information is vital for a robust evaluation of the strengths and weaknesses of the program and for remaining clear-eyed about the challenges that remain in educating for awareness, creating sustained volunteerism, and promoting a culture of peace.

CONCLUSION

Creative curricular approaches to inculcating respect for a culture of peace draw on social justice, peace education, human rights, and global civics. They remain an emerging, ever-shifting development in pedagogy globally and with this protean nature comes significant challenges to successful and meaningful evaluation. This chapter aims to present an overview of the life of an academic community by providing a picture of the goals of the Civic Involvement Projects as well as the program's attempt to evaluate its impact. While the educators' words were primarily stressed in this work, it is my hope that the students' voices have also been represented in order to give an added depth to the program.

Nevertheless, the primary purpose of this chapter is to highlight the challenges and difficulties that face peace education evaluation in this higher education context. Courses such as the Civic Involvement Projects are ambitious in their scope and goals, and evaluation that is equal to its ambition becomes a necessarily significant undertaking. In the case of CIP, this evaluation is confined primarily to brief questionnaires administered to the students enrolled in the course. Others involved in the CIP process, such as the external trainers or the community members with whom the university students work, are not included in this evaluation, thus overlooking potentially critical insight into CIP and its impact beyond Sabancı—an insight particularly critical due to its unique structure.

The Civic Involvement Projects occupy a unique place in Turkish education; however, its influence on the education system in the post-2005 reform context continues to increase. Stronger evaluation techniques for both depth and breadth are necessary for this course as it is exported to other institutions and at lower education levels in this period of education reform. Further research on how CIP adapts to and learns from its increasing pedagogical popularity and its long-term impact on both CIP students and the community is also recommended for a more robust evaluation of the program. Last but not least, as such education reforms give students in primary and secondary school more opportunity to engage in community service, how the changing educational background of students entering Sabancı University changes or reinforces the need for programs such as CIP can illuminate the face of peace education in Turkey.

REFERENCES

Altınay, A. G. (2004). *The myth of the military nation: militarism, gender, and education in Turkey*. New York: Palgrave Macmillan.

Bar-Tal, D. (2002). The elusive nature of peace education. In G. Salomon & B. Nevo (Eds.), *Peace education: The concept, principles and practice in the world* (pp. 27–36). Mahwah, NJ: Lawrence Erlbaum.

Brabant, M. (2010). Service-Learning: An exportable pedagogy? In T. Stewart & N. Webster (Eds.), *Problematizing service-learning: Critical reflections for development and action* (pp. 107–128). Charlotte, NC: Information Age Publishing.

Çayır, K., & Bağlı, M. T. (2011). 'No-one respects them anyway': Secondary students' perceptions of human rights education in Turkey. *Intercultural Education, 22*(1), 1–14.

Çetindamar, D. & Hopkins, T. (2008, November). Enhancing students' responsibility towards society through civic involvement projects. *Innovations in Education and Teaching International, 45*(4), 401–410.

Harris, I. M., & Morrison, M. L. (2003). *Peace education*. Jefferson, North Carolina and London: McFarland and Company, Inc.

Hopkins, T. (2007). *Measuring effectiveness of civic participation at the university level in Turkey: A case study of the Civic Involvement Project at Sabanci University.* St. Louis: Center for Social Development, Global Service Institute, Washington University.

Hopkins, T., & Terzioğlu, T. (2011). Civic involvement in a Turkish university. In H. Altınay (Ed.), *Global civics: Responsibilities and rights in an interdependent world* (pp. 79–86). Washington, D.C.: Brookings Institute.

Kolouh-Westin, L. (2004). *Learning democracy together in school? Student and teacher attitudes in Bosnia-Herzogovina.* Stockholm: Institute of International Education, Stockholm University.

Mandry, A. (2012). *Thinking locally about global human rights: A case study of a Turkish university.* (Unpublished doctoral dissertation), Teachers College, Columbia University, New York.

Milli Eğitim Bakanlığı [Ministry of National Education] (2005, February). *Tebliğler Dergisi: Sosyal Etkinlikler Yönetmeliği* [Regulation on Social Activities], sa. 2569. Retrieved January 5, 2011 from http://digm.meb.gov.tr/belge/yonetmelik_SosyalEtkinlikler.doc

Nevo, B., & Brem, I. (2002). Peace education programs and the evaluation of their effectiveness. In G. Salomon & B. Nevo (Eds.), *Peace education: The concept, principles, and practices around the world* (pp. 271–282). Mahwah, NJ: Lawrence Erlbaum.

Ramirez, F. O., Suárez, D. F., & Meyer, J. W. (2006). The worldwide rise of human rights education, 1950–2005. In A. Benavot & C. Braslavsky (Eds.), *The changing contents of primary and secondary education: Comparative studies of the school curriculum* (pp. 35–52). Hong Kong: CERC.

Sabancı University. (2005). *Sabancı University civic involvement projects. In Sabancı University.* Retrieved January 29, 2009, from http://www.cip.sabanciuniv.edu/eng/?Tdp/Tdp.html

Sabancı University. (2009). *Sabancı University, About us.* In Sabancı University. Retrieved May 1, 2009, from http://www.sabanciuniv.edu/eng/?genel_bilgi/ genel_bilgi.html

CHAPTER 8

PEACE EDUCATION IN HIGHER EDUCATION

Using Authentic Assessment Practices to Build Peace

Rajashree Srinivasan

INTRODUCTION

Peace education (knowing peace and doing peace) is not an act of remembering facts about non-violence and peace, but includes the inculcation of a rigorous, creative, and critical understanding about peace and the practice of it. The process of building critical understanding places enormous responsibility on the part of peace educators to facilitate the process of knowledge construction and address the valuable and distinctive resources that each learner brings to the table. Furthermore, the nature and content of peace education, shaped by contexts, make the task of teaching peace a complex activity. Therefore, developing cognitive flexibility, empathetic understanding, and moral thinking to address the vastness of human experience requires progressive pedagogies and sophisticated assessment practices. Such learning can neither be measured nor tested. The use of authentic assessment practices as one of the tools to prepare reflective peacebuilders is ex-

Peace Education Evaluation: Learning from Experience and Exploring Prospects,
pages 117–129.
Copyright © 2015 by Information Age Publishing
All rights of reproduction in any form reserved.

amined in this chapter. By authentic assessment, I refer to learning experiences/ opportunities provided to learners to help them establish the connections between the real world of contextualized practice and the realm of generalizations and theoretical frameworks. Several teacher education programs use a wide repertoire of authentic assessment practices to prepare reflective teachers. As a teacher educator, engaged in the task of preparing reflective teachers, I used collaborative inquiry and reflective journal writing as authentic assessment tools. I highlight in this chapter my experience of using these in an elementary teacher education program in the Indian context. Drawing lessons from the use of such authentic assessment practice in teacher education, the chapter highlights the possibilities of its potential use in building peace among adult learners through its efficacious alignment with contextualized content and reflective inquiry as a teaching learning approach.

CONTEXT

The interface between curriculum, assessment, and teaching-learning is now widely recognized in classroom life across the world. The importance of learner progress and agency, and the value of active learner participation assume paramount importance in assessing the multiple dimensions of human efforts in education that include experiences, dispositions, skills, knowledge, and praxis. Traditional testing has also come under heavy criticism because of its inauthentic nature and its inability to assess range of learning experiences. Its excessive engagement with measuring and 'labeling' students has led educators to explore alternatives to conventional assessment. It is in this complex context that authentic assessment practices provide a pathway for exploring alternatives to facilitate student learning.

The first formal use of the term 'authentic' in the context of learning and assessment appears to have been by Archbald and Newmann (1988, cited in Cummings and Maxwell, 1989). Their reference was to authentic achievement. They identify achievement as having three characteristics—knowledge production, disciplined inquiry, and value beyond assessment. Cumming and Maxwell (1989) in their analysis of the progress of the construct of authentic assessment observe tentatively that it was Wiggins (1989) who made the first reference to authentic assessment. Wiggins (1989) particularly stressed that authentic and realistic assessment needs to reflect the intellectual work of practicing professionals, and is characterized by active engagement, exploration, and inquiry on the part of the student, as the main criteria for authentic assessment. Researchers such as Newmann and Archbald (1992), Ingvarson and Marrett (1997), Karge (1998), Morris (2001), Prestidge and Glaser (2000) and Darling-Hammond (2000) describe a variety of authentic assessment tools that are intended to increase students' engagement and make learning more relevant. These include role play and drama, concept maps, student portfolios, reflective journals, and group work.

Authentic assessment is first and foremost formative in nature and is intended *for* learning as opposed to a mere assessment *of* learning. It is based on the premise that education is not simply a matter of memorization but must be informed by critical thought and connected to the authentic or real world. It allows the students and teachers to take critical stances about their work and helps students understand how their work is shaped by social, historical, and political processes. It is an important avenue for students to take ownership of their learning. Authentic assessment provides a complete portrait of student's acquisition of content knowledge and the students' emotions, cognition, and competencies. Their usefulness in curriculum development and teaching-learning has led many disciplines, including peace education, to explore the possibility of adopting these empowering tools.

Teaching peace is a complex activity. It does not entail the mere transmission of knowledge. It involves a spectrum of nuanced thinking and action. Peace education is directed toward capacitating active citizen-learners with the necessary skills and knowledge to understand, confront, resist, transform, and ultimately eliminate violence in all its multiple forms and manifestations (Jenkins, 2007). Such transformations are not easily facilitated, nor can they be mandated or dictated. Horton and Freire (1990) remind us that such social change cannot be forced upon people. It is highly dependent on the students' commitment to change as an individual and as a responsible citizen. This implies a willingness on the part of students to change their ways of thinking and acting, thereby nurturing moral sensibilities required for their transformation. Assessing the 'change' brought out by peace education programs is challenging but nevertheless crucial for strengthening the impact and refining the curriculum. The transformative agenda in teaching for democracy and human rights, nonviolence, social and economic justice, gender equality, environmental sustainability, disarmament, traditional peace practices, international law, and human security calls for a tough scrutiny of the curricular content, teaching learning practices, and the assessments engaged in by peace educators.

Cabezudo and Haavelsrud (2007) describe the integral interrelationship between form, content, and context in peace education. They argue that for peace education to be relevant and valuable to a given population, the content and form of that education must take into consideration the social, cultural, political, and educational context of the learner. In deciding the form, content, and context, question are raised regarding the relationship between theory and practice in peace education. A practice-oriented field of study always suffers the "divide tension" and attempts to address this divide in several ways. Theory (knowing about peace) gives the learners the concepts and tools to look at practice (doing peace) in a more informed way. And it is from the experiences of the practitioner that we can clearly grasp where ideas collide or cohere (Gopinath, 2008). Building a synergy between peace education theory and the journeys of people towards realization of these ideas is an imperative for peace education. Therefore, establishing linkages between *knowing about peace* and *doing peace* is possible through the path of reflective inquiry.

The field of peace education can draw lessons from several teacher education programs across the world that highlights the importance of reflective inquiry and the role of authentic assessments in such inquiry-oriented programs. The following is an analysis of my experience as a teacher educator in one of the Elementary Teacher education programs of India, whose vision was to create reflective teachers. I will reflect on my experience of using collaborative inquiry and journal writing as authentic assessment practice in teacher education.

AUTHENTIC ASSESSMENT IN TEACHER EDUCATION: AN INDIAN EXPERIENCE

Darling-Hammond (2000) observes that teacher education programs use authentic assessments of teaching as one set of tools to help novice teachers create, in a principled fashion, bridges from generalizations about practice to apparently idiosyncratic, contextualized instances of learning. She characterizes authentic assessments as those that sample the actual knowledge, skills, and dispositions of teachers in teaching and learning contexts; require the integration of multiple types of knowledge and skill; rely on multiple sources of evidence collected over time and in diverse contexts; and are evaluated using codified professional standards.

I taught in a four-year pre-service elementary teacher education program in India offered at Lady Shri Ram College, a premier women's college in India. The program is based on the premise that a deep critical understanding of the curriculum, knowledge, and pedagogy is a pre-condition in the making of a teacher who will have the potential to contribute to the transformation of school education. The students were oriented to work with the public education system in India, which is largely attended by students from the socially and economically disadvantaged sections. The vision of the program was to prepare student teachers to be reflective practitioners.

One of the important learning opportunities of the pre-service teacher experience is the internship. The aim of the internship program was to help students gain actual experience teaching children, explore innovative pedagogic practices, and understand the functioning of the school as a system located in a socio-political context. I was involved as an internship supervisor for nearly seven years. The intensive structured process of teaching in elementary grades (eleven weeks in primary and six in the upper primary classrooms) provided them with the physical and psychological space for evolving innovations in teaching. I was assigned six students whom I guided, supervised, and mentored. I made observations and analyses of the student interns' class twice a week. Following four days of teaching, the students met me once a week as a group. Drawing from their experience in the authentic task—i.e., the school classroom setting—I engaged in collaborative inquiry as pedagogy and as an assessment tool. The practice of both supporting and challenging young interns is integral to promoting professional orientations and relationships. The experience of my interns helped me learn more about the fluid and evolving nature of pedagogy. I also assessed students through reflective journals which they wrote daily after their school teaching practice

Collaborative inquiry is a collective process of learning, which consists of episodes of reflection and practice. Through a dialogic process, students understand about contexts and experiences of people. I used collaborative inquiry for three reasons. First, to facilitate students to examine their experiences, assumption, beliefs, and attitudes towards various aspects of children and teaching and learning. Second, to challenge the teacher-learner's point of view and help them to reconsider/question existing knowledge in the light of their experiences. Third, to encourage the practice of reflection through the linking theory and practice. I also believed strongly that collaborative inquiry could strengthen the sense of identity, collegiality, and community amongst student-teachers. During these collaborative inquiry sessions, students shared about their teaching experience, problems in classroom management, challenges of dealing with the school as a system, problems in teaching diverse children, etc. The classes began with quizzing, probing and questioning about differences between their interpretation of episodes and mine, and there were times when I moved away from my previously central role as students took charge. They shared what motivated, irritated, excited, or confused them. The reflection that took place led to agreements, disagreements, and tensions. By questioning the process of teaching and learning, there was a refining, qualifying, or deconstructing and reconstructing experience, which helped them generate new knowledge and diverse conceptions. The students realized that they need to suspend their beliefs and stereotypes and consider the perspectives of others and understand processes as located in the historical, socio-cultural, and political context. Most importantly, the students began to see the power of how the experience or comment of one person served as a catalyst in generating new ideas and understandings. One of the student interns remarked:

> We were encouraged to challenge the status-quo of the society and the education systems. Each of us had different views about the way an issue can be looked. But I think through such spaces to debate and dialogue and write about our thinking, I understood that multiple perspectives can co-exist.

As these interns were teaching in schools that had mostly students from disadvantaged areas, the student teachers were encouraged to reflect upon their own positions in society vis-à-vis gender, caste, class, linguistic variation, disability, equity, and justice.

Another student shared about moving away from personal survival to addressing needs of students:

> When internship began, I was focusing on how to be a 'good teacher' and how can I do things rightly. It is these debriefing sessions along with my professor and peers,

did I learn to look at the contexts of my children more keenly and my teaching more critically. Through these sessions, I began to see the importance of being inclusive in my classroom.

Most importantly the collaborative inquiry strengthened the personal side of the teachers. Knowles, Coles, and Presswood (1994) say that, "pre-service programs should reveal inquiry into "self, contexts and relationships" as an essential and lifelong aspect of professional development; among other things, such inquiry fosters personal and professional development (p. viii). One of the students shared:

> Due to exploring, analyzing and reflecting in small groups and close student-teacher interactions, I could see a new personality developing within me—of someone in charge of myself and my role as a teacher. I have begun to gain more confidence in dealing with children and their behaviour.

The sixteen week internship period aimed specifically at maximizing links between theory and practice, with a view of promoting an inquiry approach to teaching. As all faculty are involved in internship supervision, they see firsthand what is happening in the schools and are able to discuss these examples during the collaborative sessions. Specific learning instances in practice situations are theorized. General principles are illustrated with practical examples. There is a constant attempt to connect theoretical understandings with practice, exercising great caution in making them understand that practice is not merely application of a theory.

Confusion and conflicts constantly emerged and as a teacher educator I had to be "prepared for uncertainty" as students argue and contest notions. At several points in time, I realized that their views also challenged my own assumptions and it refined my pedagogy. As we advanced together, contesting the prescribed knowledge terrains, we also began generating personal theories. Using collaborative inquiry as pedagogy and an authentic assessment practice helped me understand how students learnt, what was bothering them, and how they actually dealt with classroom problems. I was able to engage the student interns in a meta-cognitive process and thereby sharpen the reflective skills/attributes of the students. It helped me to track their progress and growth as individuals, as student teachers, and as prospective professionals. Reflection had come to be an integral part of learning for both my student teachers and for myself.

Supplementing communal inquiry was writing reflective journals. Interns were required to maintain reflective journals in which they recorded their daily experiences, feelings, and analyses of their teaching, connecting their teaching experience to theories and concepts learnt in their College classrooms. Writing is a context for Schon's (1987) "reflection-of-action". Expectations from journal writing and the criteria for assessment were clearly conveyed to the students. The journals were interactive in the sense that I regularly responded to concerns raised by the interns by writing back in these journals. It is through these bidirectional conversations that I gained entry into the pre-service teachers' thinking and understanding. It helped me assess their current understanding and beliefs, values, and assumptions that influence their teaching.

Reflective journal writing enveloped within a context of collaborative inquiry provided me great insights into their real world of teaching and learning. Both require a safe and secure learning environment where students feel confident to express their views and opinions. Writing journals after their teaching helped students re-live that experience and generate lessons from that experience. One of the students shared:

> I did not value Vygotsky's theory till I began to see the importance of scaffolding in my interaction with the children. It is only through my writing, when I step back and look at my day in the light of what I learnt do I realize the importance of theories.

It suggests, there is great value in writing as it provides a context for stepping outside of one's role to view the situation and, hence, the journal becomes an "insider's view from outside". Most students allude to the use of journal writing as an important tool to help link their understanding of theory with practice.

However, using reflective journals as an authentic assessment tool is fraught with several challenges. Students do not become reflective just because we extol the value of reflection to them and ask them to do reflective writing assignments (Spalding & Wilson, 2002). Most students coming out of a system that is predominantly transmission-oriented found the idea of reflection disturbing to engage in. Dewey (1933) points out that one can think reflectively only when one is willing to endure suspense and to undergo the trouble of searching, and to many persons both suspense of judgment and intellectual search are disagreeable; they want to end them as soon as possible. To be genuinely thoughtful, we must be willing to sustain and protract the state of doubt which is the stimulus to thorough inquiry. Therefore, facilitating reflection is a deliberate activity. It requires a competent mentor who is able to move students along the reflection continuum.

I consistently wrote feedback to the students, raised questions, commended them on their practices, guided them on classroom management, and strengthened their thinking on the realities of everyday teaching. As one of the students wrote about her experience:

> Writing journals is something that I never enjoyed initially. But when I began seeing my supervisor's comments and questions, I knew I was being guided with prompts to scaffold my reflective practice. I have begun to see that there are several alternatives to the way we approach teaching.

Detailed written feedback is important for enhancing their levels of reflectivity. Feedback consisted of positive comments appreciating the students efforts (e.g., "your efforts at sustaining children's interest in the activity are deeply appreciated"), raising questions to provoke their thinking further, helping them see theory and practice linkages, making them connect their thinking to the larger social, political, and educational processes. Further, the teacher educators' expressions of personal connection to the content of students' journal entries ("I can understand how you feel about this issue—I am struggling to understand it as well") also encourage students.

Assessment of reflective journals in teacher education has been commented upon by several scholars (Crème, 2005; Moon, 1999; Varner & Peck, 2003). Detailed assessment criteria plays a central part, as they provide the structure and foundation for what is expected of the students through the writing. Clarity of expectations assists students to move beyond descriptive accounts of their experiences. Therefore, development of rubrics for assessment is important for the faculty and the students to observe the development of reflective practice. Rubrics are structures that make explicit the basis on which judgments of quality are made. The purpose of rubrics is to guide student learning by creating a common language for discussing what distinguishes one level from another. The rubrics developed to assess the students' authentic experiences were classified as Descriptive, Analytical, and Reflective (see Table 8.1). The criteria for assessment included analysis and reflections on classroom practices and experiences, which included reflections on process of transaction, children's involvement and learning, time management, responding to individual differences, learners' socio-economic background and their responses, and relationship between children's learning and the pedagogy used. The second criterion focused on students' understanding of the linkages between classroom practice and theory. The third criterion was growth in the intern's reflection. Although not included in the rubrics, the fourth criterion was regularity of submitting journals.

Descriptive journals just gave details of the student's day in the classroom and the activities carried out. The analytical journals would examine certain themes, look at some episodes in the classroom, and analyze them but would never indicate any reflection on what could be done further. The third journal type was the critical reflective journal, which was a rarity. These journals outlined the challenges in the classroom teaching learning processes, looked at the transaction of content and pedagogy, reflected on the large processes of the institution, incorporated learning from previous classroom interactions, explored alternatives, and connected theory and practice. There were instances when the reflective journals slip from level of 'reflection' to 'analytical' as well. The greatest challenge, however, were the descriptive journals; enormous amounts of time need to be spent on these students to help them identify instances and issues of the classroom. Resistance to push their thinking beyond the "comfort zone" may be a factor because thinking and acting in new ways can be threatening. There are risks in undertaking reflection. Moreover, if students did not see the benefits of reflection, they would make no progress in the quality of the reflection. While working on students who show progress in reflection was an easier task, there is certainly a great need to research what approaches teacher educators can adopt to enhance the levels of those who struggle with reflection.

TABLE 8.1.   Rubrics for Assessment of Reflective Journals

		Levels		
		Descriptive	**Analytical**	**Reflective**
Criteria	Classroom Practices and Experiences	Describes the here and now of the classroom Discusses one's own teaching; is not critical of one's teaching Unable to see linkages between one's teaching and student's learning	Engages in criticism of one's teaching, perceives relationship between one's teaching and learner's responses, recognizes that changes to one's practice is needed. Recognize the learners and learning as embedded in context	Engages in critical reflection on one's teaching and offers alternatives for future practice, is analytical about the relationship between one's teaching and children's learning; analyses the range of factors that impinge on the classroom practice; critically analyzes the role of social milieu in learning
	Linkages between theory and practice	Does not see linkages between theory and practice	Recognizes the relationship between some concepts and practice; is unable to be critical about the linkages	Articulates conceptual understanding to practice, applies theoretical understandings to practice, enriches theoretical understanding with experiences from practice
	Growth in critical reflection	Does not question commonly held beliefs, is unable to reflect on the growth of the self, does not reflect on past learning	Questions beliefs and assumptions but does not offer alternatives, partially reflects about one's self, refers minimally to past learning	Challenges the assumptions and offers alternatives, keenly reflects on one self, constantly relates past experiences and learning to present.

Thus authentic assessment practices such as journal writing through a dialogue between the teacher and learner have immense value in enhancing their professional knowledge, challenging the norms and ways of thinking about the society, developing sensitivity towards diverse children, and creating agency among the student teachers. The self-assessment involved in authentic assessments such as the reflective journals helps students take upon themselves the onus for their learning and development. Developing self-awareness helps shape one's identity as a teacher. Such processes that integrate the heart and the head humanize the education processes. Thus, authentic assessment practices have an invaluable potential to direct the students towards becoming critical thinkers.

AUTHENTIC ASSESSMENT AND BUILDING PEACE

The students who enter peace education programs in higher education institutions are adult learners. It is assumed that an effective peace education program will seek to infuse the sensibilities of theory and practice of peace education amongst its learner. Fostering an understanding about linkages between knowing about peace and doing peace is indeed always challenging. One of the many important ways of establishing this understanding is through collaborative reflective inquiry and journal writing.

Students bring with them a baggage of historical and social experiences that may include assumptions, beliefs, stereotypes and biases about various facets of life—of conflicts, violence, identity, religion, caste, culture, oppression, and inclusion, among others. Students' knowledge and understanding about the structures and systems in which they live need to be continuously challenged. While their existing knowledge is being challenged, the students realize that they need to suspend their beliefs and stereotypes. They learn to consider the perspectives of others and understand processes as located in the historical, socio-cultural, and political contexts. This process could lead to strengthening the content of peace education. Moreover, peacebuilding practice is fraught with difficulties, contradictions, and dilemmas. Therefore, inquiries into these contexts make students understand how challenging, dynamic, and sensitive issues of conflict are. Such reflections help them begin to seek alternatives. Such inquiries can be done during the theoretical study, of course, or after their fieldwork. Such inquiry has the transformative potential to develop the necessary cognitive capacities, emotional dispositions, and ethical stances required to foster peaceful coexistence. A dialogic process and a safe and secure environment free of judgment and ridicule is crucial to elicit reflective learning.

When reflective inquiry is used as a pedagogic practice in peace education, it becomes pertinent to use assessment practices that are sensitive to these subtleties and complexities of human thinking and understanding, and to the role such processes play in transformation. The nature of peace education renders summative assessment practices obsolete. Authentic assessment of learning, its quality, significance and relevance is most truly and usefully performed by the learner, not the teacher or those who have authorized her (Reardon & Snauwert, 2011). It is towards facilitating reflective peace learning that journal writing as an authentic assessment practice can be used in peace education. Connecting conceptual understanding to situations in practice and revisiting theory with experiences from practice allows for the development of cognitive flexibilities, empathetic understanding, and moral thinking, which form the bedrock of reflective practice in peace education. Developing reflective capacities through authentic learning opportunities allows for education to play a "peace sustaining role".

Reflective journal writing in peace education can be viewed from three dimensions. One is from a point of creating learner agency. The overarching purpose is to create a sense of personal ownership about one's learning. The learner's reflection about one's self and others in the society and community becomes the central point of inquiry. From a motivational perspective, students adopt intrinsic moral and social standards as they begin to gain ownership over their learning. Gaining these moral standards is the basis for the practice of peace. Writing journals, from a cognitive perspective, requires peacebuilders to juxtapose the content, the context, and their experiences as a learner into a coherent understanding and learning about peace. From a meta-cognitive perspective, students develop insights about their abilities, the tasks they perform, and the strategies that are useful in their journey towards peacebuilding. Therefore the importance of reflective inquiry and authentic assessment is an imperative for peacebuilding.

Evaluation of peace education may gain greatly from the modes of inquiry that has been outlined by Reardon (2011). She articulates three types of inquiry: critical/analytic, moral/ethical, and contemplative/ruminative. They are comprehensive and non-hierarchical. It may be worthwhile for peace educators/researchers to research and explore the possibility of developing assessment rubrics based on these different forms of inquiry, which may help understand and assess students of peace education better.

CONCLUSIONS

The notion of reflective inquiry requires only reaffirmation in the discipline of peace education as the pioneers of the discipline were progressive educators like John Dewey, Maria Montessori, Paul Freire, and Elise Boulding who extolled, among other things, the virtue of reflection and experience. The emphasis of peace education is not just about transmission of knowledge but on connecting knowledge and practice. Adult learners engaged in building peace need to understand the definite linkage between knowing peace and doing peace. This chapter presents a case for systematic reflection and use of reflective journals as an important component of peace education. In order to prepare peacebuilders for this complex and diffuse nature of peace education, peace educators need to plan reflective exercise as part of their instruction.

Also, the prospects of promoting reflective practice and authentic assessments without adequate attention being paid to the conceptual underpinnings will lead to a murky understanding of reflective practice in peace education. It is a challenge indeed to foster an understanding of the symbiotic relationship between practice and theory. As peace education professionals we need to present a compelling case for authentic assessments to foster reflective practice. Peace educators must also be trained to use these assessment practices. While authentic assessment is distinct in terms of perspective, task design, and context and criteria for assessment, it is extremely time consuming and human resource intensive. Stringent institutional policies on assessment can also be deterrents to using such assessment practices. The interdependency between the content, pedagogy, and assessment is important for enhancing the validity of authentic assessment practice. Ambiguities and contradictions will exist as we venture into this new terrain. More research will need to be carried out to take forward these forms of less-known but highly useful forms of assessment for learning. A conviction that such forms of assessment are important for building peace will allow for carving newer landscapes in the discipline.

REFERENCES

Archbald, D.A., & Newmann, F.M. (1988). *Assessing authentic academic achievement in secondary schools*. Reston, VA , National Association of Secondary School Principals.

Cabezudo, A., & Haavelsrud, M.(2007). Rethinking peace education. In C. Webel & J. Galtung (Eds.), *Handbook of peace and conflict studies* (pp. 279–298). New York: Routledge.

Crème, P. (2005). Should student learning journals be assessed? *Assessment & Evaluation in Higher Education, 30*(3), 287–296.

Cumming, J. J., & Maxwell, G. S. (1999). Contextualizing authentic assessment. *Assessment in Education, 6*, 177–194.

Darling-Hammond, L. (2000). Authentic assessment of teaching in context. *Teaching and Teacher Education, 16*, 523–545.

Dewey, J. (1933). *How we think*. New York: Heath.

Gopinath, M. (2008). Towards a praxis of possibility: Experiences from the field. In S. Kakran, N. Sinha, & M. Sewak (Eds.), *Education for peace and multiculturalism: A Report* (pp. 48–68). New Delhi: WISCOMP.

Horton, M., & Freire, P. (1990). *We make the road by walking: Conversations on education and Social Change*. In B. Bell, J. Gaventa, & J. Peters (Eds.). Philadelphia: Temple University Press.

Ingvarson, L., & Marrett, M. (1997). Building professional community and supporting teachers as learners: The potential of case methods. In L. Logan, & J. Sachs (Eds.), *Meeting the challenge of primary schooling for the 1990s*. London: Routledge.

Jenkins, T. (2007). Rethinking the unimaginable: The need for teacher education in peace Education. *Harvard Education Review, 77*(3), 366–369. Retrieved August 8th 2010 from www.jstor.org.

Karge, B. (1998). Knowing what to teach: Using authentic assessment to improve classroom instruction. *Reading & Writing Quarterly, 14*, 319–331.

Knowles, J. G., Cole, A., & Presswood, C. (1994). *Through preservice teachers' eyes: Exploring field experiences through narrative and inquiry*. New York: Merrill.

Moon, J. A. (1999). *Reflection in learning and professional development: Theory and practice*. London: Kogan Page.

Morris, R. V. (2001). Drama and authentic assessment in a social studies classroom. *Social Studies, 92*, 41–44.

Newmann, F. M., & Archbald, D. (1992). The nature of authentic academic achievement. In H. Berlak, F. M. Newmann, E. Adams, D. A. Archbald, T. Burgess, J. Raven, & T. A. Romberg (Eds.), *Toward a new science of educational testing and assessment*, (pp. 71–84). Albany, NY: SUNY Press.

Prestidge, L. K., & Williams Glaser, C. H. (2000). Authentic assessment: Employing appropriate tools for evaluating students' work in 21st-century classrooms. *Intervention in School & Clinic, 35*, 178–182.

Reardon, B. A. (2011). Concerns, cautions and possibilities for peace education for political efficacy. In B. Wright & P. Trifonas (Eds.), *Critical peace education: Difficult dialogue*. Springer.

Reardon, B. A., & Snauwaert ,D. T. (2011). Reflective pedagogy, cosmopolitanism, and critical peace education for political efficacy: A discussion of Betty A. Reardon's assessment of the field.*Factis Pax: Journal of Peace Education and Social Justice*, *5*(1),1–14.

Schon, D. (1987). *Educating the reflective practitioner*. San Francisco: Jossey-Bass.

Spaulding, E., & Wilson, A. (2002). Demystifying reflection: a study of pedagogical strategies that encourage reflective journal writing. *Teachers College Record*, *104*(7), 1303–1421.

Varner, D., & Peck, S. (2003). Learning from learning journals: The benefits and challenges of using learning journal assignments. *Journal of Management Education*, *27*(1), 52–77.

Wiggins, G. P. (1989). *A true test: Towards more authentic and equitable assessment*. Phi, Delta, Kappan, 70, 703–713.

NARRATIVE METHOD FOR EVALUATION OF STUDENTS' TRANSFORMATIVE LEARNING IN A PEACE AND CONFLICT RESOLUTION PROGRAM

Zulfiya Tursunova

INTRODUCTION

This chapter presents an analysis of the evaluation of a graduate peace and conflict studies program using personal narratives of program students. The narrative method used in this evaluation helps to determine the problems and challenges for the lived application of the program content that the students were learning—for example, cross cultural communication, negotiation, mediation, and other peace methods in transformative learning. The students' reflections about conflicts and their resolution, the meaning of rituals, and social events generate a bottom-up understanding of perspectives important to educators and administrators involved in decision-making and design of the curriculum. The data derived from a narrative

Peace Education Evaluation: Learning from Experience and Exploring Prospects,
pages 131–144.
Copyright © 2015 by Information Age Publishing
All rights of reproduction in any form reserved.

evaluation tool is critical for programs as they develop the curricula and social learning environment conducive to students' needs.

This chapter describes the encounters of 80 post-graduate level students from a wide spectrum of cultural and demographic backgrounds representing about 25 countries. These students were enrolled in a graduate-level Peace and Conflict Resolution program at a European university. The participants of this study include students of different ages, professions, marital status, and social and economic upbringing. The university curriculum is based on the examination of three forms of violence as popularized by peace researcher, Johan Galtung (1996): direct violence, or the visible hurting and killing of people; structural violence, or the manifestations of suffering caused by unjust structures of society that lower potential life enhancement for a particular group; and cultural violence, or the justification of direct and structural violence through nationalism, racism, sexism, and other forms of discrimination and prejudice in education, the media, literature, science, and the arts, among other areas. The students studied together for two semesters and then spent their third semester away writing their theses. The students lived in one dormitory building where classes were held and cooking and other socio-cultural activities took place. An overarching purpose of the program is for students to acquire knowledge, practice, and skills that will assist them in their efforts to foster peace, social justice, and equality in the countries from which they came, as well as on-site at the university.

In this chapter, I explore transformative learning processes and actions of the participants of the study who evaluated their application of peace and conflict theories learned in the classroom in daily practice and future plans. I also discuss the advantages and challenges of using narrative inquiry in relation to the evaluation of higher education peace and conflict studies programs.

THEORETICAL BACKGROUND

This research was inspired by the transformative learning approach of Jack Mezirow (2000) as well as narrative or life story approaches of the study of groups (Archibald, 2008; Maoz et al., 2002; Senehi, 2000, 2002; Tursunova, 2008). Transformative learning relates to the processes by which people transform their own and others' tacit frames of reference of values, attitudes, and assumptions, and reflect constructively on them to generate beliefs and opinions underlying in their actions (Mezirow, 2000). Transformation relates to a "movement through time of reformulating reified structures of meaning by reconstructing dominant narratives" (Mezirow, 2000, p. 19). In this study, transformation relates to how people learn to negotiate and act on their own purposes, values, feelings, and meanings, rather than those that they integrate uncritically from others, with the purpose of achieving greater control over their lives as socially responsible agents (Mezirow, 2000). The main implication of this research to the field of peace and conflict resolution education is that transformative learning is crucial in terms of students and soon-to-be peacebuilding practitioners acquiring new skills, values, and tools for self-awareness by transforming pre-existing frames of mind (Kegan, 2000).

Learning involves increasing knowledge, skills, and extending cognitive capacities, all vital in enhancing one's frame of reference. Such learning is transformative in terms of bringing new content into existing ways of knowing. In addition, learning is aimed at changes of not only *what* is known but also in *how* knowing take places. These types of learning are invaluable; the first type refers to a pre-existing frame of mind and the second relates to the reconstruction of that very frame. It is vital for program developers to understand transformative learning as the process of how student knowing takes place and how a new frame of reference is negotiated and generated to foster social change.

Learning is influenced by personal or folk stories, a widespread form of communication in this unique post-graduate communal learning and living setting. Storytelling enables communities to be created and recreated. It helps people to define social identity, produce shared knowledge, negotiate power relations, generate emotions, and educate others. Besides these *constructive* aspects, storytelling can be *destructive* as it encodes and transfers understandings of conflict by intensifying, perpetuating, or further embedding conflict in culture (Senehi, 1996, 2002). Stories can also be neutral, told and retold without addressing conflicts or problems (McDrury & Alterio, 2002). Furthermore, stories can be rejected by the listeners for a variety of reasons (Gubrium & Holstein, 1997; Rosenwald & Ochberg, 1992; Tursunova, 2012).

The narrative, or storytelling, helps people to understand and negotiate intangible dimensions of conflicts. However, storytelling does not address structural injustices and asymmetries of power in socio-economic and political contexts. In this research, I was as interested in what participants were learning in the classroom as what they were learning and putting into practice in social situations outside of the classroom. The university is a unique educational setting where students take classes and live together in a multicultural environment. Hence, I examine transformative processes in participants and group dynamics, which shed light on identities, cultures of conflict, and power relations in a social learning environment.

Mixed methods were used to evaluate the processes and outcomes of participants' transformations, but this chapter focuses on the use of the narrative method. Data provided the possibility of examining participants' reflections of transformative learning moments in applying peace and conflict studies into daily practice.

NARRATIVE METHOD

Since the study conducted explored the complex dimensions of transformative learning and self-evaluation of participants, mixed methods for collecting data were used. These methods included: (1) narrative and storytelling inquiry to allow sixteen students, who volunteered to participate in the study, to interpret their experiences, reflect about peace and conflict resolution practices, and make meaning of them; (3) case studies of conflict stories related to food rituals and other social activities; and (4) informal conversations and participant observation while the author was a student at the university. I provide pseudonyms for the names of participants to preserve their anonymity. The participants were asked to consent to the research and were told that their confidentiality would be preserved, that they had the choice to withdraw, and that their written information would be returned upon request.

The narrative approach enabled me to listen to participants' voices and understand their meaning when they interpreted inner transformations from their life experiences. The participants' key indicators—such as their understandings of peacefulness, conflict, inclusion, exclusion, privilege, and power—guided the categorization and coding used to interpret and make sense of the data collected. The data analysis helped me to find the relations among events and ideas, and to determine commonalities, patterns, and differences among participants' responses. The data collected from surveys, interviews, observations, artifacts, and literature was then divided into themes.

Written accounts of 16 participants allowed me to amass data on the importance of stories told, rituals performed, and the conflict resolution methods that students applied within community settings outside of, but informed by, classroom learning. To understand the experiences of students, the questions focused on why participants engaged in particular rituals (social, religious, healing, secular) and storytelling activities; what were their goals and hopes for their use of these activities? The students were asked to reflect on the significance of the stories told during classes, leisure time, and rituals, such as prayer, communal worship, playing soccer, hiking, going to the spa, meals, and the celebration of religious holidays, as well as students' birthdays. The participants responded to questions related to their favorite stories, and to who initiated rituals and storytelling: students, administration, board members, professors, visiting lecturers, or other individuals. Finally, the participants wrote about the tools of conflict resolution methods they applied inside and outside the classroom and throughout their social lives, along with their impact on relationships among students, professors, and administrators. The students were also encouraged to reflect on the kinds of destructive elements of their experience.

This study was based on my personal participant observation lasting a year and a half aimed at familiarizing the author/researcher with activities and issues discussed, as well as to discover important but taken-for-granted aspects of the school and classroom. Participant observation yielded a detailed explanation of how people addressed conflicts and communicated their needs. Participation in the university's academic and socio-cultural life enabled me to become deeply immersed in order to understand the student participants. I interacted with students to gain a better understanding of events and context, including people, place, acts, activities, events, objects, goals, time, and feelings expressed by participants.

RESEARCH FINDINGS AND DISCUSSION

Understanding Conflict Analysis, Conflict Resolution, and Peacebuilding practices through Narrative Methodology

Using a narrative method helped me to identify the ways students comprehend knowledge and enact their transformative learning in everyday life. In their stories, the participants listed such methods as mediation, negotiation, non-violent communication (Rosenberg, 2005), alternative dispute resolution design, non-violent action, and the ABC (attitudes, behaviour, contradiction) model (Galtung, 2004), which they used to transform conflicts. Katerina indicated that:

> The issues were solved by individual confrontation, long house discussions, gossip, or lots of passive aggression. Many meetings such as house meetings could have been meaningful if, as one student suggested, there was stronger facilitation, guiding everyone to be aware of the plan and the life-serving purpose of the meetings. In spite of the wide use of the non-violent communication model, sometimes it was successful and sometimes it was not.

The students' stories showed that the evaluation of peacefulness of the social context indicates the success but also challenges in applying conflict resolution theories to social behaviour and interactions at interpersonal level. The participants' evaluations show that learning about peace did not always transform into education for peace when introspection of theory and practice was required. Data collected through this narrative methodology enabled me to understand what a peace education program, based on learning, meaning and capabilities of each person to influence transformative learning, might look like.

Evaluation of conflict resolution methods revealed the processes and qualities of inter—and intra-personal peacebuilding. Some of the student participants considered going to church and praying by themselves as being of high importance for them. Healing rituals as meditations and candle-light were practiced by students. Social activities such as biking, going to the spa, sightseeing, and hiking were often considered important parts of relationship-building.

The evaluation of the social life revealed that narrative in this case is about meaning-making about life and becoming aware of the impact of the experience on the individual student. Jessica indicates that "people cling too tightly to something that worked magically once and do not understand when it does not work again in reality, making both sides resentful and angered. Gratitude ceremonies never allowed us to be honest about rejecting gratitude." There is an apparent gap between the external ritual actions and the meaning these actions convey to the individual. In the statement above, Jessica is disappointed that a ceremony at the end of a meeting in which everyone thanks the others present and comments on how important the ideas expressed were to them did not leave room for criticism of the ideas presented or the way in which they were expressed. Rituals highlight the need to go more deeply into the creation of attitudes, which are rarely linked to transformative learning and knowledge production.

Ceremonies can only be understood when people are open, transparent, and conscious about issues. Rituals and symbolism can transform people's thinking and action when human virtues such as honesty and transparency permeate rituals and storytelling. Building relations and connecting to the reality of life are important in making rituals and storytelling constructive. Rituals and stories have a potential to re-order space, moving from disharmony to peace. These strategies may question existing frames of reference, which may deconstruct old knowledge and produce new knowledge significant for conflict resolution practitioners. In evaluating transformative learning in a peace and conflict studies program, examining relationships expressed in rituals and stories can highlight a culture in which there are conflicts and deep power relations that participants may not initially take into account.

Student participants also indicated that storytelling and rituals helped to transform conflicts sometimes before they became evident. These strategies facilitated the connection and understanding among students. Sabrina pointed out that "the key was to talk about the rituals." She said that rituals, when not talked about were sometimes misinterpreted. As she indicated:

> In such a diverse environment where cultural rituals are so important for communication, the rituals we participated in were all important in coming to an understanding of one another. Back at home in the U.S., I find some rituals unimportant, or less important, because they lose meaning and become things we do without thought or understanding of why we do them. For example, asking people on the street, 'how are you?' has become a ritual that has lost its original meaning. We ask out of habit rather than because we really want to know how someone is doing. Another example is of handshakes—we shake people's hands because it is expected of us, not because it means anything. Here we were forced to look at the meaning of these rituals because they are not practiced by everyone and are therefore curious to some. We explained the meaning behind rituals to our friends and that was what gave them meaning in that setting. Thus, understanding the use of rituals in a multicultural context is an important tool for broader understanding and cross-cultural communication.

Cultural resources such as knowledge of rituals, use of body language, space, and meaning were crucial in transformative learning. Conflict resolution methods were also symbolic; sometimes when students had a disagreement they would end it with hug. Transformative learning took place with changes of values, attitudes, and better understandings of fellow students.

The evaluation of the educational curriculum by students revealed that the course on cross-cultural communication was helpful in understanding differences between high-context and low-context cultures.[1] However, the curriculum focused strongly on the examination of conflicts and predominantly Western methods of conflict resolution with the exception of Ho'oponopono[2] and Ubuntu[3] (Tutu, 1999). Courses about rituals, storytelling, and indigenous conflict resolution methods were not part of the curriculum and could have built on the multicultural knowledge of students coming from 25 countries of the world.

Interpreting and Reconstructing Gendered Conflicts and Stories

Storytelling empowers participants to unpack multilayered conflicts and bring about systematic changes, which in turn affect relationships among women and men and their experiences of those relationships. Listening to women's voices enables all participants to explore the process of articulating deep culture and structure of gender-based violence perpetuated in attitudes and behavior of men. When conflicts about sexual harassment and assault of women arose, female students met together informally and developed a sexual harassment policy and enforced its implementation through policy design. Non-violent collective action and mediation helped to stop sexual violence. This social action, which addressed gender-based violence, speaks to the transformative character of learning and the social change agenda of gender equality and social justice.

In retelling stories, participants selected and represented specific episodes related to sexual assault and their human agency and standpoint on the issues. One of the students wrote that he tried to mediate a conflict between a perpetrator and a victim, which was difficult. These life experiences showed how individuals can "talk back" and reconstruct their learning in the act of telling stories—creating meaning and a shared vision of the space free from gender-based violence.

---

[1] Edward T. Hall (1977) explains differences between high and low context cultures. He indicates several conceptions that are different in high and low context cultures: 1) time (polychromic with loose schedules and last minutes changes in plans vs. tight schedules); 2) space and tempo (synchrony where everyone moves with others and in harmony with nature vs. low synchrony; 3) reasoning (comprehensive logic where knowledge is gained through intuition and spiral logic vs. linear logic with knowledge gained through analytical reasoning); 4) verbal messages where restricted codes are encoded in nonverbal and contextual meaning vs. direct verbal communication modes; 5) social roles (tight vs. loose social structure where behavior is not predictable); 6) interpersonal relations (group interests are important vs. individual interests are paramount; and 7) social organization (customary laws and oral agreement vs. formal written procedures, rules, and regulations).

[2] Ho'oponopono is an ancient Hawaiian practice of reconciliation and forgiveness (Galtung, 1996).

[3] The Ubuntu philosophy defines the quality of human relations people should nurture in order to live in harmony. Desmond Tutu (1999) specifies that "a person with Ubuntu is open and available to others, affirming of others, does not feel threatened that others are able and good, for he or she has a proper self-assurance that comes from knowing that he or she belongs in a greater whole and is diminished when others are humiliated or diminished, when others are tortured or oppressed (p. 31). Ubuntu represents the central values of African ontologies and fosters a sense of belonging, friendship, compassion, forgiveness, generosity, interdependency, sharing, and cooperation (Kamwangamalu, 1999).

Sharing gendered and cultural issues in the intercultural communication course provided a space to unpack differences in proxemics, haptics, and interpersonal spatial distance between men and women in a multi-cultural context. In a setting where students live in one building, socialize, and spend time together, social interactions caused tensions. Some Muslim girls felt that they were touched, hugged, or were expected to become girlfriends with no consent or wanted to be "tasted" by men because they were more racially or culturally different. Conversations among female students showed how tensions and miscommunications were rampant. Listening to some examples, such as greetings between genders dependent on age, relationship, religion, and country of origin and residence, provided an opportunity for students to talk about the differences in observing distance, touching, and movements across cultures and religions.

Exploring Conflict Stories: Social Space, Identity, and Group Boundary Construction

Narrative methodology is vital in grasping students' evaluations of the social activities taking place outside of the classroom. Students' conflict stories related to food rituals and other social activities demonstrate learning experiences that enabled students to reinforce cultural identity boundaries and, at other times, walk through building relations and developing transformative skills and knowledge. For example, each semester students divided themselves into five to seven cooking groups, such as vegetarian or based on different ethnic backgrounds (i.e. African, South Asian, Latin American). The group affiliations were primarily based on the cultural identity of participants with the exception of few students.

The students said that cooking food in a small kitchen was meaningful because they had to cooperate and learn from each cultural cooking style. Cooking and tasting traditional cuisine was another learning experience in the diverse cross-cultural setting. Anna wrote:

> Food really presents diversity of cultures and connects to everyone's life. It created so many problems for students to solve together—foods disappearing, nobody washes the dishes, dirty floor. Many students had to learn something new—many learned to cook for the first time. Students shared their cultures through food—learning to cook a different dish, tasting it, and seeing so many different spices.

Yet, division into a vegetarian group, consisting mostly of European and North American students, and non-vegetarian groups, consisting of students from Africa, Asia, and a few Europeans, drew visible boundaries among communities across racial lines. The eating space was divided into two groups—the first consisting mostly of Caucasian students and the second group consisting of students of other races. These racial borders were preserved during the semesters and reinforced divisions of students coming from the global North and South.

Stories also revealed how participants overcame these racial borders inscribed in space during cultural events when all students shared the eating space and ate the food served by students who organized the event. To provide exposure to other cultures, the students organized European, Asian, and African cultural nights and also celebrated Halloween, Ramadan, Hanukkah, and other holidays. As Brittany described, "The cultural nights were perhaps the most significant for me because I felt I was getting a glimpse into various cultures from around the world. Those experiences have stayed with me." Carrying out cultural nights required preliminary preparation of the menu, responsibilities taken by each student, and one day of cooking for an evening feast accompanied by cultural performances and, later on, dancing.

Narratives also disclosed the apparent gap among separate specific cultural constructions such as Asian, African, and European, and the change processes needed to celebrate multiculturalism. After the celebration of several cultural nights, the idea of carrying out an interfaith dialogue emerged, but was not implemented. The cultural nights, which celebrated the richness of each culture, provided the impetus to organize a multicultural night to appreciate the diversity and richness of many cultures. Cultural nights brought a sense of "unity in diversity" in which cultures were celebrated instead of being rejected, ignored, and devalued.

Conflict Stories, Food Rituals, and Gender Roles

Conflict stories showed that traditional gender roles and expectations need to be renegotiated in participants' interactions. Conflicts sometimes enabled female students to urge men to change gender expectations and perform traditional women's roles such as cooking and cleaning. One male student who was not helping at all said that he was a manager during the Asian cultural night. A female student told him: "We do not need managers; we need people who will do the job." She asked him to prepare the tables, arrange the chairs, and help out.

In retelling stories, female students showed how they bridged the gap between conflict analysis and transformation, and how they moved from a status of subordination to the exercise of agency and having power. They used food preparation as a catalyst for transforming gender roles by changing the behavior of male students who did not know how to cook. In one case, Ryan was standing and watching while Fatima was cooking. Fatima had been cooking for Ryan for two weeks. After two weeks, Ryan told her that he had servants to cook food in his house. She told him, "I am not a servant and, from now on, cook your food yourself!" This epiphany shows the break-up of a cycle of conflict embedded in meaning making, knowledge production, and transformative learning for both students.

Storytelling

Because lives are understood and influenced by narratives, narrative approaches help individuals inquire about their experiences at the same time. In reflecting about personal stories in the peacebuilding process, the respondents pointed to the personal story of a professor who was abducted and abused by rebels. Students were also moved by the stories and experiences of a professor who uses nonviolent methods of transforming conflicts and drawing the attention of the public to injustice in society. The story of a professor working in peace education was also an inspiration for those working in the field of peace education. These stories had an empowering impact. As one respondent indicated, "These types of stories empower me by their example—if others can make it through tough times and still work for justice, so can I."

Alternative space, such as the Dialogue group set up by two students, became a place of encounter for a group of about ten people in which participants could be open and honest about intimate topics that were not dealt with in class, or were only done so superficially. It was characterized by storytelling, alternating with conceptual abstraction and reflections. Matthew, one of the organizers of the group, wrote:

> Our hope was to build community, give support at the ego level and strengthen our dialogical skills!!! Over time it sort of became a ritual for some of us. The impact of this Dialogue group in terms of conflict resolution practices is that many of participants in the Dialogue group sessions acknowledged to have widened their views and understanding of self and other individuals and cultures. Thus at a deep ego level it certainly improved the capacity to transform conflict.

Students explored diverse issues such as tense family relations or patterns of relationship break-ups. Many did not have clear pathways of conflict transformation, but through narration and reflective thinking when questioned, they developed ways to improve, avoid, and/or end destructive relations and behaviors.

Participants also felt that some faculty members overdid the stories by constantly repeating them. Stories were told so often that they lost the impact that they could have had on students. One student said that one of the professors often spoke in anecdotes at every opportunity, making it difficult to communicate with him in reality, whereas other professors used a story sparingly (and effectively) to illustrate a point. The students rejected some stories and outlined destructive aspects of storytelling. I observed that students did not directly express discontent with a huge number of stories and continued in some way to reinforce professors' power.

Narrative Method in Peace and Conflict Studies Evaluation

Based on this research into using a narrative method as an evaluative instrument, I consider that the methodology is important in the evaluation of higher education-level peace and conflict studies programs. First, narrative methodology focuses on students' knowledge production and meaning-making of inequalities and inequities across lines of social identity, race, ethnicity, marital status, class, power relations, and country of origin. Learning about peace and how peacebuilding can take place is a transformative learning goal of reframing points of reference. Narrating, examining, and bridging theories with practices that take place in the learning environment and during social activities provide insight into the processes of knowledge production and transformative learning processes and actions.

Second, narrative methodology is participatory. It enables participants to be part of the evaluation of the educational program in peace and conflict studies. Narrative methodology is a bottom-up approach of evaluating the quality and essence of experiences of transformative learning that is vital for future peace-builders.

Third, narrative inquiry enables participants to create *self-awareness* and *critical thinking,* and to influence power structures at personal, interpersonal, and institutional levels. Narrative creates a space to voice gendered issues, reflect critically, and develop self-awareness. The narrative method shows how transformative learning can occur and help to reorganize social space for equality and justice.

Fourth, narrative inquiry is about *power sharing* and *co-management* of transformative learning process and outcomes. The evaluation of learning by students decenters control of learning and places transformative learning control in the hands of students. Power sharing and co-management places students' needs at the centre of peace and conflict educational programs.

Sixth, narrative inquiry in evaluation is visionary as it fosters change. Storytelling has a potential to generate a transformative agenda and determine priorities in social change. It can require a response to feedback and make necessary changes in program planning and management. It can help to manage the transition and foster team-building and commitment of stakeholders.

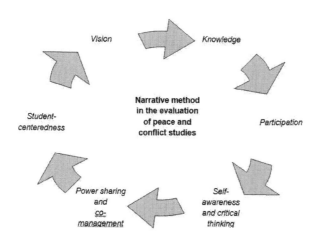

FIGURE 9.1.   Narrative Method in the Evaluation of Peace and Conflict Studies

Narrative method in program evaluation can fail if the management in organizations is authoritarian, does not respond to students' needs, and is not flexible to change.

CONCLUSION

Narrative methodology is an effective evaluation tool to address areas of concern in fostering transformative learning outcomes in peace and conflict studies. It can also be destructive if members of organizations do not share power, information, and resources to address students' needs. The narrative methodology is a bottom-up approach to evaluation which can assist in curriculum development and strategic planning of organizations. It can foster new knowledge production at all levels of the organization, which can constructively influence students' learning outcomes.

The evaluation of content of the curriculum and social activities revealed cohesive change of the students' peacebuilding skills, knowledge, and practice. Social lives were enriched by social, cultural/social, secular, and religious rituals that enabled students to widen their worldview and better understand others' meaning of rituals. Shared rituals speak to the universality of rituals in terms of creating meaning, empowering, and transforming relationships. These rituals enable students and faculty to create community and strengthen and renew its ties with faculty members. Yet, the practice of rituals and storytelling require transparent meaning as well as genuine expression and sincere building of relationship that are vital for conflict transformation. Exclusion and marginalization in the participation of some of the small social activities across ethnicities, races, and countries of origin have also been visible and require critical examination and discussion by students themselves.

Transformative learning requires an application of the newly acquired skills and knowledge in peace and conflict resolution into practice. In spite of the successful examples of the application of conflict resolution skills through the program, the students in this program faced the challenge of applying newly acquired skills. To decrease the gap between the content of the curriculum and practice, additional time should be allocated to the discussion of the difficulties students face in resolving conflicts. The feedback will help to improve the content of the curriculum and, more importantly, the knowledge and skills of the practitioners.

Stories can be seen as joint actions between the storyteller and the audience to create a peacework which is vital in transformative learning in peace and conflict resolution studies. Stories were not "just stories," but real experiences of students and faculty that were constructive in terms of sharing emotions and experiences, empowering students to serve humanity and work for peace. However, student participants felt that sometimes stories were repetitive and thus, became meaningless. Stories can be destructive if power in storytelling is not shared equally between the storyteller and the listeners. Transformative learning requires communication and mutual feedback to make learning enriching and effective in everyday practice.

Transformative learning in an educational setting can also be informed by rituals and narrative theory and practice that allow students to recount their experiences. Ritual and stories can provide opportunities to develop intellectual, physical, spiritual, and healing powers to evaluate thoughts and actions, solve conflicts, and provide avenues for conflict resolution. However, these methods may also not be a panacea to all human problems, especially if stories and ritual do not address structural inequalities and inequities of the participants engaged in transformative learning.

ACKNOWLEDGEMENTS

The author would like to thank the students for their support of this project. I also wish to thank Rene Wadlow, formerly Professor and Director of Research, Graduate Institute of Development Studies, University of Geneva, for his comments.

REFERENCES

Archibald, J. (2008). *Indigenous storywork: Education the heart, mind, body, and spirit.* Vancouver, Canada: UBC Press.

Galtung, J. (1996). *Peace by peaceful means: Peace and conflict, development and civilization.* London, UK: Sage.

Galtung, J. (2004). *Transcend and transform: An introduction to conflict work.* London, UK: Pluto Press.

Gubrium, J. F., & Holstein, J. A. (1997). *The new language of qualitative method.* New York, NY: Oxford University Press.

Hall, E. T. (1977). *Beyond culture.* New York, N.Y.: Anchor Books.

Kamwangamalu, N. M. (1999). Ubuntu in South Africa: A sociolinguistic perspective to a pan-African concept. *Critical Arts: South-North Cultural and Media Studies, 13*(2), 24–41.

Kegan, R. (2000). What 'form transforms?: A constructive-developmental approach to transformative learning In J. Merizow (Ed.), *Learning as transformation:' Critical perspectives on a theory in progress* (pp. 35–69). San Francisco, CA: Jossey-Bass.

Maoz, I., Steinberg, S., Ban-On, D., & Fakhereldeen, M. (2002). The dialogue between the 'Self' and the 'Other': A process analysis of Palestinian—Jewish encounters in Israel *Human Relations, 55*(8), 931–962.

McDrury, J., & Alterio, M. (2002). *Learning through storytelling in higher education: Using reflection and experience to improve learning.* London, UK: Kogan Page.

Mezirow, J. (2000). Learning to think like an adult: Core concepts of transformation theory. In J. Mezirow (Ed.), *Learning as transformation: Critical perspectives on a theory in progress* (pp. 3–34). San Francisco, CA: Jossey-Bass.

Rosenberg, M. B. (2005). *Speak peace in a world of conflict: What you say next will change your world.* Encinitas, CA: Puddledancer.

Rosenwald, G. C., & Ochberg, R. L. (Eds.). (1992). *Storied lives: The cultural politics of self-understanding.* New Haven, CT: Yale University Press.

Senehi, J. (1996). Storytelling and conflict: A mater of life and death. *Mind and Human Interaction, 7*(3), 150–164.

Senehi, J. (2000). Constructive storytelling in intercommunal conflicts: Building community, building peace. In S. Byrne & C. L. Irvin (Eds.), *Reconcilable differences: Turning points in ethnopolitical conflict* (pp. 96–114). West Hartford, CT: Kumarian Press.

Senehi, J. (2002). Constructive storytelling: A peace process. *Peace and Conflict Studies, 9*(2), 41–62.

Tursunova, Z. (2008). The role of rituals in healing trauma and reconciliation in post-accord peacebuilding. *Journal of Human Security, 4*(3), 54–71.

Tursunova, Z. (2012). *Livelihood, empowerment and conflict resolution in the lives of indigenous women in Uzbekistan.* (Doctoral dissertation). The University of Manitoba, Winnipeg, Canada.

Tutu, D. (1999). *No future without forgiveness.* London, UK: Rider.

CHAPTER 10

EDUCATION FOR PEACE IN BOSNIA AND HERZEGOVINA

How Do We Know It Is Working?

H. B. Danesh

INTRODUCTION

There is limited literature on the nature of effectiveness of programs included under the banner of peace education (see e.g. Nevo & Brem, 2002). Peace education is not a unitary concept and includes a wide range of approaches dealing with such divergent and partially related issues as human rights and freedom, nonviolent communication, conflict resolution, causes of violence, types of peace, international and cultural studies, environmental protection, and cross-cultural studies, among others. This diversity of perspectives on peace education has its genesis in the fact that both issues of conflict and violence and the concept of peace itself have, thus far, eluded a universally agreed-upon understanding and definition. In order to provide a point of reference for the presentation of the conceptual foundation of the Education for Peace program, its methodology, and the outcome of its implementation in schools thus far, first some of the prevailing views on issues of conflict, violence, and peace are briefly reviewed.

Peace Education Evaluation: Learning from Experience and Exploring Prospects,
pages 145–161.
Copyright © 2015 by Information Age Publishing
All rights of reproduction in any form reserved.

CONFLICT, VIOLENCE, AND PEACE EDUCATION

Throughout human history and in almost all societies, two parallel and oppo-site conditions—the presence of violence and yearning for peace—have existed. While the quest for peace is ever-present, the much more broadly accepted view is that conflict and violence are inherent aspects of human nature and life; that through culture and education some of the most destructive aspects of the human proclivity to conflict and violence can be reduced; and that when violence is con-trolled, partial and temporary peace can be achieved.

Views on conflict, though varied, are fundamentally based on the notion that conflict is not only inevitable, but even necessary and desirable. Galtung and Ja-cobsen (2000) comment that "conflict, incompatible goals, are as human as life itself; the only conflict-free humans are dead humans" and that "war and violence are like slavery, colonialism, and patriarchy; however, they come and they go" (p. vii). Muldoon (1996) states that "conflict is the spice that seasons our most intimate relationships" (p. 9). Other notions are that conflict is useful for identity development, social change, and creativity. These views are generally based on the idea that there are basic human needs that require satisfaction, and conflict arises when these needs are either unmet or have negatively affected others in the same pursuit. The belief in the primacy of the role of conflict in human life is often encapsulated in the notion of the *survival of the fittest* that informs both the biological theory of evolution put forward by Charles Darwin and social Darwin-ism. Likewise, views on violence although varied, also point to its inevitability in human life. Among these are the views that aggression is a weapon of choice in a competitive world (Stone & Kelner, 2000, p. 569), that there is a genetic predis-position to violence in humans (Kinder, 2011), and that education plays a major role in human violence (de Waal, 2002, p. 25).

The Challenge of Peace Education

In 1964, Galtung (1964) proposed the concepts of negative peace—the ab-sence of violence and war—and positive peace—characterized by "the integration of human society" (p. 2). Later, Galtung (Galtung & Høivik, 1971; Galtung 1990) added the concepts of structural, direct, and cultural violence to his formulation of peace. With regard to the all-important issue of the relationship among peace, conflict, and violence, Galtung (1969) asserts that the "statement peace is absence of violence shall be retained as valid" (p. 167). Likewise, Claske Dijkema and Saint Martin d'Hères (2007) consider peace as well-managed social conflict.

This symbiosis of conflict, violence, and peace makes both peace creation and peace education activities unduly dependent on how we deal with conflict and vi-olence. A representative example of this relationship is the ten (10) goals of peace education identified by Ian Harris and Mary Lee Morrison (2003) in their book, *Peace Education*. It is remarkable that all ten goals of peace education identified by the authors, directly or indirectly, are related to the issues of conflict and violence. Gavriel Salomon and Edward Cairns (2010) likewise observe that various definitions and conceptions put forward by leading scholars of peace and peace education "share in common the idea that peace education is to negate violence and conflict and to promote a culture of peace to counter a culture of war" (p. 5). Consequently, the purpose of peace education has become unduly dependent on the study of conflict and violence and strategies on how to effectively deal with them. As such, peace as an independent and valid subject of study takes a secondary seat to those of conflict and violence.

It is in this context that the conceptual theories of the Education for Peace (EFP) program assume their relevance and importance.

Conflict, Violence, and Peace: A Re-Appraisal

In the Education for Peace (EFP) program, the concepts of conflict, violence, and peace are viewed within the framework of the Integrated Theory of Peace (ITP), which defines peace as a psychosocial and political, as well as moral and spiritual, condition within the framework of a unity-based worldview. Education is regarded as the most effective tool for developing a unity-based worldview and for creating both a culture of peace and a culture of healing (Danesh, 2006). ITP identifies *unity* as the primary force of existence and affirms that *unity, not conflict,* is the main dynamic power in human relationships and the main prerequisite for creating peace. Within this framework, unity is defined as a:

> conscious and purposeful condition of convergence of two or more unique entities in a state of harmony, integration, and cooperation to create a new evolving entity(s), usually, of a same or a higher level of integration and complexity. The animating force of unity is love, which is expressed variably in different conditions of existence (Danesh & Danesh, 2002, p. 68).

The concept of unity and its significance to peace education is more readily understood in the context of the role of *worldview* with regard to issues of conflict, violence, and peace. Worldview here refers to the framework through which we understand reality, human nature, the purpose of life, and laws of human relationships. Our thoughts, feelings and actions are shaped by our individual and collective worldviews, which reflect the nature and the process of development of our consciousness and our unique identities. Worldviews are formed on the basis of our personal life stories and collective histories in the context of prevailing influences of religion, science, ideologies, and environmental conditions (Danesh & Clarke-Habibi, 2007).

Within this dynamic context of individuality and universality, in the EFP curriculum three metacategories of worldview are identified—Survival-Based (authoritarian), Identity-Based (adversarial) and Unity-Based (integrative) (Danesh, 2002, 2006, 2007). The most common and all-pervasive worldview in human history is the *survival-based worldview,* which directly relates to the insecurities of life at both individual and collective levels in the context power-seeking, domination, and authoritarian and dictatorial practices at home, in the institutions of the society (including schools), and in the modes of governance.

As we gradually mature, both individually and as communities of people, a new mindset, correspondent with the age of adolescence, begins to shape our thoughts, feelings, and actions. The central theme of this mindset—*the identity-based worldview*—is the process of formation of individual and group identity and frequent episodes of volatile conflicts, power-struggle, and competition (Simmel, 1956) in the context of the notion of the *survival of the fittest*, individualism, and the quest to win.

Although these two worldviews are most prevalent and strongly defended in the contemporary world, nevertheless, they are proving incapable of meeting the needs of humanity. It is within this context that a new worldview—the *unity-based worldview*—is gradually emerging in all areas of human life. Within the framework of the unity-based worldview the legitimate concerns of both survival-based and identity-based worldviews, such as individual and group security, identity validation, and mutual respect and opportunity are met. In addition, such fundamental objectives as equality, justice, and freedom from prejudice and oppression can best be accomplished within the operation of the unity-based worldview.

In summary, the EFP Curriculum, formulated within the framework of ITP, states that:

- *Unity* is the fundamental law of existence and all human relationships;
- *Conflict is the absence of unity*;
- *Unity* is the fundamental prerequisite of *peace*;
- *Peace* is an independent state of being;
- *Violence is the absence of peace*;[1] and,
- *Human proclivities* to peace and violence are shaped by our respective *worldviews*. (Danesh, 2008b)

BRIEF HISTORY OF EFP

The Education for Peace (EFP) Program started its implementation in Bosnia and Herzegovina (BiH) in 2000 in six schools—one primary and one secondary school each in three cities: Banja Luka, Sarajevo, and Travnik—involving some 6,000 students, 400 teachers and staff, and several thousand parents. Since then, based on its evident effectiveness, at the invitation of the BiH education authorities and with the support of the International Community, the EFP program has been systematically introduced to more schools. In 2012, as a specific component of the education reform in BiH, three distinctive activities are underway: incorporation of the EFP program into the curricula of all of BiH's 1,000+ schools (K-12) with over half a million students; ongoing in-service training of all teachers (about

---

[1] This formulation is the mirror image of Galtung's view that asserts that peace *is the absence of violence.*

70,000) by all ten Pedagogical Institutes, and the training of future teachers (pre-service) in the EFP concepts and methodologies by all eight public universities.

MAIN EFP OBJECTIVES AND METHODOLOGY

Based on the concepts outlined above, in the course of the past decade, a comprehensive peace-based education curriculum with four interrelated components—Education for Peace (EFP), Conflict-Free Conflict Resolution (CFCR), Leadership for Peace (LFP), and Youth Peacebuilders Network (YPN)—have been developed and implemented. The main objectives of the EFP program are to create a:

- *Culture of Peace* in and among the participating school communities;
- *Culture of Healing* (from the negative impacts of sustained conflict and violence) in and among the participating school communities; and
- *Culture of Excellence* (academic and behavioral) in the participating schools.

At the start of the pilot project in 2000, EFP's sole objective was to create a *culture of peace* in and among the participating schools with a focus on fostering interethnic understanding, providing training in peace-based conflict resolution, and creating violence-free environments. The second objective—creating a culture of healing—was added when, after 18 months (three semesters) of the implementation of the EFP program in the six pilot phase schools, it became evident that considerable personal and inter-group healing among these highly traumatized post-war populations had taken place (Danesh, 2008a). The third objective—creating a culture of excellence—was added based on unsolicited reports by students, teachers, parents, and school administrators about the positive impact of the EFP program in their schools. They reported that, both to their surprise and delight, they had noticed appreciable increase in the academic performance of the students, generally, and "under-achievers" particularly. They also reported a remarkable decrease in the episodes of bullying and fighting among students and an increase in their participation, cooperation, and enthusiasm. These positive developments became evident after at least one full semester of implementation of the EFP program in the classrooms and the schools as a whole.

Based on lessons learned thus far, four prerequisite conditions for an effective peace-based education program are identified:

- Condition I: Truly effective peace-based education takes place in the context of a unity-based worldview.
- Condition II: Peace-based education best takes place within the context of a culture of peace.
- Condition III: Peace-based education best takes place within the context of a culture of healing.

- Condition IV: Peace-based education is most effective when it constitutes the framework for all educational activities and involves the whole school population and all areas of study, throughout the year (Danesh, 2006).

ELEMENTS OF THE EFP CURRICULUM

The main elements of the EFP curriculum, both with respect to its conceptual formulation and application methodologies, are subsumed under four main categories: *integrative and inclusive, universal and specific, peace-based framework,* and *peaceful/healing environment.* The *integrative/inclusive* component refers to the program's focus on engaging all members of the schools community in study of all subjects within the framework of the universal principles of peace. The *universal/specific* aspect aims to inform all members of the school community of the *universal* principles of peace as formulated in the EFP Curriculum—that humanity is one, that the oneness of humanity is expressed in diversity, and that the greatest task before humanity is to strengthen its oneness and safeguard its

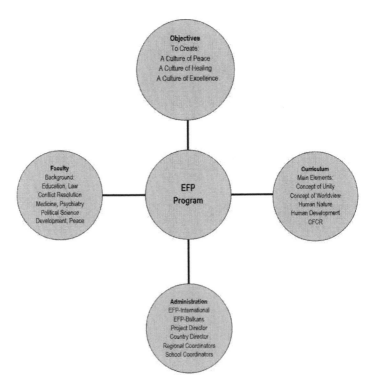

FIGURE 10.1. Organization Components of the EFP-BiH Program

diversity. The *specific* aspect refers to the fact that EFP curriculum is specifically designed for each new community with the full participation of their educators and scholars.

Peace-based framework refers to the requirement to study all subjects—history geography, biology, literature, physics, etc.—from the perspective of peace rather than conflict as is the practice now. For example, when students begin to study geography, the teacher helps them to fully comprehend the fact that the Earth is fundamentally one and environmentally an indivisible entity and that division of the world with distinctive boundaries is arbitrary.

Peaceful/healing environment component refers to the fact that the entire school community becomes engaged in learning how to create a culture of peace and a culture of healing in their school and classrooms and how to share these insights and skills with others in their homes and communities (Danesh, 2007; 2008a; 2008b). These elements of the EFP curriculum are put into practice in the framework of organization of the EFP program as depicted in Figure 10.1.

OUTCOME

Thus far, the EFP program has gone through three stages of expansion, with a fourth stage now being anticipated.

As Table 10.1 demonstrates, the EFP program is currently being fully integrated into all primary and secondary schools and many preschools with the active participation of all BiH universities and Pedagogical Institutes and with the approval of all Ministries of Education. This massive expansion of the EFP-BiH program was accomplished through specific tasks including:

- training of all teachers and staff in all schools in EFP concepts and methodologies;
- introductory lectures to all students;
- lesson-planning workshops with all teachers;
- introduction of EFP concepts and methodologies to all classrooms by all teachers;
- personal study of the book *Peace Moves* (Danesh, 2004) by students in grades 6 and higher;
- participation of all students in the *Peace Events* in every school;
- introduction of Conflict-Free Conflict Resolution (CFCR) and decision-making practices to the school teachers, staff, and students;
- school-wide community consultation opportunities; and
- meeting the needs of traumatized children and adults through creation of a *Culture of Peace* and a *Culture of Healing* in every school (Danesh, 2009).

TABLE 10.1. Chronology of Introduction of the EFP Program into BiH Educational Institutions

PHASE	Mode of Instruction	Number of Schools	Number of Students	Number of Teachers and Staff	Outcome
Phase I Pilot Phase 2000–2002	Intensive Model	12 Schools 7 Primary 5 Secondary	10,000 proportionally from Bosniak, Croat, Serb populations	800 All teachers, administrators, support staff	Request by the BiH/ Government & International Community to expand
Phase II Expansion Phase 2003–2006	EFP Multimedia Model	100 Secondary Schools in 65 cities & towns across BiH	80,000 proportionally from Bosniak, Croat, Serb populations	5,000 teachers, administrators, support staff	Full partnership with all 13 BiH Ministries of Education & 10 Pedagogical Institutes (in-service training)
Phase III Integration Phase 2007–2012 →	Peace-Based Curriculum Model	All 1000+ BiH primary and secondary schools+ some preschools	Over 500,000	Over 70,000	Full partnership with all 8 BiH public universities (pre-service training)
Phase IV EFP-World Phase 2012→	EFP eLearning Model	Open to all schools globally	Open to all students globally	Open to all teachers/ parents/ educators globally	Global promotion of peace-based education **Free of Charge**

EVALUATION AND RESEARCH

The evaluation part of the EFP program has consisted of three components: on-going systematic internal evaluation by teachers, school administrators, students, and EFP faculty; periodic external evaluations performed by experts appointed by the major funding agencies; and research projects.

From the onset, specific criteria were established to provide the necessary information and feedback regarding the four dimensions of a successful peace education program: the cognitive, the affective, the volitional, and the behavioral (Harris & Morrison, 2003). This information was obtained through a variety of means: specifically designed questionnaires; periodic individual interviews; group evaluation discussions involving teachers, students, and administrators; discussion groups with the parents; and through the evaluation of the presentations by all students during their school's respective *Peace Events*. These events are occasions in which the cognitive, the affective, the volitional, and the behavioral aspects of the EFP program can be readily reviewed and evaluated (Danesh, 2009).

As described, all teachers and staff of the participating schools receive basic training in the principles and methodologies of EFP prior to the start of the academic year. Then, every teacher, in every classroom, endeavors to conduct his/her class, regardless of the subject of study, within the framework of universal principles of peace. Simultaneously, students in higher grades (6–12) are encouraged to study *Peace Books,* an interactive, easily accessible book based on a dialogue among nine young students from around the globe who attempt to see if peace was possible, and if so, how. Based on instructions by the teachers and study of *Peace Moves*, every classroom, involving all students, under the direction of teachers, is assisted to make a presentation on the essential concepts of peace as they apply to the subject of their study.

Students are encouraged to make their presentations through visual, literary, and performing arts. These presentations are evaluated with regard to the message they convey, the understanding of principles of peace they may reflect, and the effectiveness with which they are presented. This latter element is affected both by the depth of insight and commitment inherent in the presentation and by its artistic merit.

Peace Events proved to be valuable instruments for evaluation of the effectiveness of the EFP program. They allowed assessment of all aspects of the EFP program. By employing the medium of the arts, students have the opportunity to convey their newly acquired intellectual and emotional insights to a large audience of fellow students, teachers, shool staff, parents and relatives, and community leaders, as well as the media. In doing so, students in each classroom assume the role of teachers and have the opportunity to see the impact of their new learning on both themselves and others. This exercise demands deep learning and commitment on the part of students and provides them with a totally engaging process of learning, where all faculties of the participants are called into action—they are intellectually stretched, emotionally vitalized, socially engaged, artistically invigorated, and spiritually enriched. *Peace Events* also render each classroom transparent. On various evaluation occasions, the impact of *Peace Events* were volunteered in statements such as the following by a teacher of an "ethnically segragated" (since the war of 1992–1995) primary school:

> The pupils increasingly participate in free activities with a lot of creativity and their own ideas, all aiming at their better preparation for the Peace Events. A cooperative spirit is developed in them, which contributes to the pupils mutually exchanging their ideas and complementing on them. In this way, the pupils train themselves for independent and creative work. For the purpose of more animation of the whole society, I believe that better cooperation with the media should be established through the TV broadcasts of Peace Events and the organisation of radio and TV programmes in which parents, pupils and teachers could participate.

The above statement addresses two major challenges with regard to the education system in BiH—school segregation and pedagogical rigidity. School ethnic segregation is a post-war phenomenon in BiH referring to the use of the same school building separately for different ethnic populations. The *Peace Events* bring these school communities together. The comment about the impact of *Peace Events* in increasing creativity, cooperation, and motivation in the student body is an oblique reference to the established rigid pedagogical practices that are still very common in BiH schools and are being modified through implementation of EFP in their schools.

In addition to their educational values, *Peace Events* also proved of value in evaluation of the effectiveness of the program. At the start of the pilot project there was a lesser degree of universal positive response, particularly in the more nationalistic and antagonistic communities. This fact became evident primarily when the *Peace Events* were held and clearly demonstrated the differences among various classes through their presentations. Some presentations showed good understanding of the principles of peace on the part of the students, whereas others were clearly on the opposite pole, and many in between were struggling. Those on the opposite pole continued to focus on the ethnic differences, resentments, and grievances and discouraged focus on points of harmony and unity that had characterized the pre-war dynamics of interpersonal and community relationships in BiH. Thus, *Peace Events* became occasions of objective self-evaluation by many students, their teachers, school administrators, and parents. A marked positive change was observed in each school after each new *Peace Event*.

EVALUATION RESULTS

Pilot Phase (2000–2002)

The internal evaluation component included questionnaires and brief interviews with randomly selected students, staff, and parents in each school four times a year during the two years of the pilot project. The purpose of these questionnaires and interviews was to collect feedback about the participants' general impressions, their understanding of the goals of the project, the effects of EFP on the teaching process in the school, the effects of the *Peace Events* on the wider community, and what participants had learned during the project. The first set of interviews was quite revealing. While in each school there were about 30% of teachers and support staff who were quite positive about the program, there were about 30% who were equally negative, and the remaining 40% had assumed a wait-and-see attitude, neither fully committed to nor actively rejecting the program.

However, there were particular characteristics and attitudes discernible in each ethnic population. The staff of the two schools in the Sarajevo region with mixed but primarily Bosniak populations, who perceived themselves as the main victims of the war, showed either acceptance and support for the program or approached EFP as something that was needed by the *other* two ethnic groups. As the "victims," they did not see any need to receive peace education themselves. The attitude of this group dramatically changed when they attended the first countrywide *Peace Event* in Banja Luka and saw the manner in which all students had embraced the program and the transformations that had taken place in the staff of the schools in the other two cities.

The two schools in Banja Luka were also similarly divided among the three groups—about a third positive, a third negative, and a third partially committed to the program. Those who supported the program were passionate about it and supported it in the face of considerable pressure and even threat. Those who were against the program were equally passionate in their antagonism. Many of them have been, either directly or indirectly, involved in the atrocities of the war in which the Serb army played a very active role. However, a sizeable number of participants, similar to those from Sarajevo, were bewildered and questioning their leaders, communities, and themselves. For the Banja Luka participants likewise, the turning point was the *Peace Event*, which helped them to rediscover some of their sense of dignity and humanity lost in the course of the war in which they were the dominant aggressors.

In Travnik schools, a considerable departure from the attitudes and responses of the schools in the other two cities was noticed. The school populations in Sarajevo and Banja Luka were primarily mono-ethnic; in Travnik one school was almost exclusively Bosniak and the other all Croat. In both Sarajevo and, particularly, Banja Luka, the staff of the two schools receiving their EFP training together were primarily from the same ethnic backgrounds and, therefore, their concerns and objectives were rather similar. However, in Travnik the two groups receiving EFP training together were either almost exclusively Bosniak or Croat. This mixed ethnic configuration changed the character of the training sessions. At first, the participants were tense and polite, later searching but cautious, then joyously surprised, as they began to rediscover their past harmonious relationships. This process resulted in the development of significant levels of intergroup harmony and healing between these schools and their respective communities at a faster rate than in the schools in Banja Luka and Sarajevo. The following are some sample responses to the EFP program from across BiH:

> As a result of participating in the EFP project, my way of teaching has changed, my relationships with students has changed, and my relationship with my family has changed...all for the better.

> —*Teacher, Secondary School, Banja Luka (2001)*

> In this project we learned many new things: new approaches to resolving conflicts, how to create our own lives, and how to make our own decisions. But the most important thing that we learned is to be at peace with ourselves and teach other people to be peaceful. Our society doesn't have many projects like this.

> —*Student, High School, Travnik (2002)*

This project has changed our vision and worldview. I feel that the vision of every teacher and student in this school has been in some way changed through this project.

—Literature Teacher, High School, Sarajevo (2002)

The children all over the world are in need of peace and security. On the occasion of the Summit devoted to the children, we recommend this program [EFP] to all the nations for consideration, as a model of society oriented towards peace, cooperation, and development.

—From a letter addressed by the BiH Government to the Special Session (8–10 May 2002) of the United Nations General Assembly on Children

This is a unique project. It will teach how to create a violence-free environment, in homes and schools and in the country as a whole.

—The Senior Deputy High Representative, Ambassador Dr. Matei Hoffmann, 28 June 2000

This invaluable project was conceived in such a way that the soul-searching process of reflection which the participants undergo as the project unfolds—be they pupils, teachers, parents, administrators, ordinary school workers—results, largely speaking, as we have ascertained ourselves, in a heightened holistic awareness of the war period and its tragic consequences, and indeed triggers the desire amongst them to become authentic peace-makers, and precisely provides them with the necessary tools to achieve this goal...

—Claude Kieffer Senior Education Advisor, Office of the High Representative, BiH (2002)

Expansion Phase (2003–2007)

When the project obtained a major grant from the Swiss Agency for Development and Cooperation (SDC) to design and implement a multimedia version of the EFP Program in 100 new schools, a similar evaluation program was employed. EFP-MULTIMEDIA is a pilot guided e-learning program, using a "blended learning" model of computer-based and person-to-person training strategies.

A comprehensive external evaluation was performed by a two-person team of experts commissioned by SDC midway through their four-year grant (2002–2006). Below are excerpts from this evaluation:

It must be looked at as an achievement that all of the 13 Ministers of Education had agreed to participate in this EFP programme as well as the Directors of the 8 [later10] pedagogical institutes and one hundred directors of secondary schools. The Ministers, Deputy Ministers, Directors of Pedagogical Institutes and Directors of secondary schools, met by the evaluation team, talked positively about the programme.... The teachers interviewed mentioned first of all the opportunity to be trained by the EFP program through a new educational framework which offers new didactical possibilities: more interaction between students and teachers, an open forum for discussion between students and teachers, and the relief for students of not having a heavy memory load with drill exercises...To be a "peacemaker" was declared as an important learning target by many teachers.

Almost all students interviewed referred to the impact of EFP in positive terms. Some students mentioned that EFP had been used as a common topic to discuss with their parents...The most important part of the project seems to be that it has brought people together across nationalities and languages; it has provided a place to meet. Several persons said that in the education sector there was no other project like this...

The project seems to have had—and still continues to have—a healing effect on a war-torn nation. One of the teachers said: "The biggest impact was on the psychological level. People got an opportunity to express their emotions. We need this type of therapy. It had to do with the atmosphere created..."

There seems to be little doubt that the project has had great impact on many of the participants, both on teachers, support staff, administrators and students involved. The most important impact seems to have been on the personal level, the meeting of people across nationalities and languages. The evaluation team heard several touching stories from teachers about their own experiences and the experiences of parents and children gained especially during the pilot phase of the project. (SDC, 2006)

RESEARCH FINDINGS

Thus far, three research projects have been conducted on the EFP-BiH program. Below are summaries of these research activities.

EFP-Longitudinal Research Project

The longitudinal plan of study of the effectiveness of the program which was initiated at the start of the pilot project included a detailed specially-designed questionnaire, aimed at having an in-depth look at the issue of psychosocial transformation from conflict-based to peace-based worldviews, which is at the core of the EFP approach. The questionnaire was initially given to 80 teachers and 80 students, randomly chosen from all participating schools. In addition to the questionnaire, these teachers and students were interviewed individually (60–90 minutes depending on translation requirements) and participated in "focus group" discussions.

When we collected the completed questionnaires, we noticed that a good number of questions were either left without any response or were answered in a very scanty manner. When, in the course of individual interviews we shared this observation, the answer given by a very large and diverse number of teachers and school directors was: *We Bosnians are private people and do not share our personal and private thoughts, feelings, or beliefs.* They stated that in the Bosnian society, people have considerable fear and hesitation to express themselves openly and frankly, and when they feel obliged to answer, they would respond according to what they think is expected of them, rather than what they really think and feel.

The hesitation to reveal oneself openly and freely; the fear of being discovered, particularly with respect to one's thoughts and feelings; and the tendency to conform to the wishes of those in positions of authority and power are among the main characteristics of authoritarian and unsafe societies (Adorno et al. 1950, Goertzel, 1987, Petty, Wegener & Fabrigar 1997, among others). The people of BiH have lived under authoritarian rulers, some benign and others malicious, for centuries. Therefore, the responses of the teachers and some students gave to the questionnaire were not surprising. The discussions in the focus groups were either general and unrevealing or a reiteration of jargon about human rights, tolerance, freedom, democracy, and peace that they assumed the researchers wanted to hear. In fact, in two of the focus groups, the participants openly stated *"if you want to hear the 'real things' you have to take us out of Bosnia. Then it will be safe to talk!"* These sentiments were voiced by the majority of the participants in spite of frequent and emphatic reassurances on the part of the research team that the data was not only anonymous, but also strictly confidential.

In the light of these findings, we decided to apply another approach—the Most Significant Change (MSC) research method—to our research plans. The MSC evaluation technique has several features that makes it particularly appropriate for the evaluation of EFP project. Among these features is the fact that MSC is a structured and continuous process that categorizes, collates, and examines the information in order to assess change based on the actual impact of the project. It is a participatory monitoring and evaluation technique, which engages the participants to objectively evaluate each others' subjective experiences in the program.

'Most Significant Change' Research Project

This research was conducted by Sophia Close (2011). Below is a summary of her findings:

> The evaluation responses represent a broad cross-section of BiH; Bosniaks, Croats and Serbians, men and women, children and adults. The written stories are tremendous; often breathtakingly honest...

> Results indicated that the evaluation participants have begun to understand key principles of unity in diversity and conflict resolution, and to apply this to their everyday lives...

> Results indicate that EFP has positively altered participants' family, peer and student-teacher relationships, and has built the foundations of an inter-ethnic harmony in each of the school communities involved...

Overall, the initial evaluation process, occurring after EFP has been implemented in the four schools for nine months, indicates that EFP is on track to provide the framework, through new curriculum methodology, for participants to re-think and review their existing worldviews. EFP creates spaces that actively praise an individual's endeavor to participate in, and reflect on, inter-ethnic harmony and peace...

The role of education in peacebuilding was highlighted by many participants: "Peace is not granted, peace needs to be learned about. I have realized that special attention should be paid to such a kind of education. From the earliest stages of life, children should learn about fundamental principles of peace: unity, equality, and beauty of diversity. This project does not impose those ideas. It guides children, through games and creativity, to experience and realize these principles by *themselves*"...

Furthermore, this evaluation confirms the value of a participatory, community-based initiative focused on peace education and peace building: and its potential to produce positive change, especially in conflict-ridden communities... (pp. 278–279)

Columbia University Research Project

The purpose of this research was to see how the EFP program affected psychological reconstruction in post-conflict BiH and whether it was effective in developing positive intergroup attitudes and behaviors that foster a sense of social inclusion and social stability. The research sought to demonstrate the impact of the EFP Program in BiH and whether or not it verified the validity of Universal-Diverse Orientation and Intergroup Contact theories. The findings of the research are based on a cross-sectional study examining positive intergroup outcomes among 444 Bosnian youth representing the Bosniak, Croatian, and Serbian ethnic groups. The roles of Intergroup Contact and of Universal-Diverse Orientation were examined as "two potentially important factors for predicting a number of heretofore unexamined positive intergroup outcomes in the post-conflict setting of Bosnia and Herzegovina. The positive outcomes studied included interethnic hope, positive intergroup attitudes, intergroup friendship, and intergroup peace-building intentions" (Lowe, 2011, p. 183–184).

SUMMARY

Based on the extensive evaluation and research performed on the Education for Peace Program in Bosnia and Herzegovina in the course of 12 years, there is ample evidence that EFP is a very effective peace-based education program with evident transformative properties. This success has its genesis in the distinctive conceptual formulations and all-inclusive and comprehensive implementation strategies of the program. The emphasis on transformation from conflict-based to unity-based worldviews, study of all subjects within the framework of the universal principles of peace, unity building as the main approach to conflict prevention and resolution, and the requirement for inclusion of all members of the school community—all students, teachers, staff, and parents (to the extent possible)—in creating a peace-based school community are among the main features of this unique peace-based education program. The program is being incorporated in the curricula of all BiH schools (K-12) and the teacher-training programs of all eight public universities. EFP, now in its fourth phase of development, plans to offer its curriculum as a comprehensive, state of art, interactive, multi-media and multi-lingual study program, globally and free of charge.

REFERENCES

Adorno, T. W., Frenkel-Brunswick, E., Levinson, D. J., & Sanford, R. N. (1950). *The authoritarian personality.* New York: Harper and Row.

Close, S. (2011). Education for peace: An evaluation of four schools in Bosnia and Herzegovina. In H.B. Danesh (Ed.). *Education for peace reader* (pp. 269–281). Victoria, Canada: EFP Press. Retreived from: http://www.efpinternational.org/images/stories/publications/efp_reader.pdf

Danesh, H. B. & Danesh, R. (2002). Has conflict resolution grown up? Toward a new model of decision making and conflict resolution. *International Journal of Peace Studies, 7*(1), 59–76.

Danesh, H. B. (2002) Breaking the cycle of violence: Education for peace. In H. B. Danesh (Ed.), *African civil society organization and development: Re-evaluation for the 21st century.* New York: United Nations.

Danesh, H. B. (2004). *Peace moves: An exploration for young people.* Sarajevo, Bosnia & Herzegovina and Victoria, Canada: EFP Press.

Danesh, H. B. (2006). Towards an integrative theory of peace education. *Journal of Peace Education, 3*(1), 55–78.

Danesh, H. B. (2007). Education for peace: the pedagogy of civilization. In Z. Bekerman & C. McGlynn (Eds.), *Addressing ethnic conflict through peace education: International perspectives.* New York: Palgrave Macmillan.

Danesh, H. B., & Clarke-Habibi, S. (2007). *Education for peace curriculum manual: A conceptual and practical guide.* Vancouver, Canada: EFP Press.

Danesh, H. B. (2008a). Creating a culture of healing in multiethnic communities: An integrative approach to prevention and amelioration of violence-induced conditions. *Journal of Community Psychology, 36*(6), 814–832.

Danesh, H. B. (2008b) The education for peace integrative curriculum: Concepts, contents, and efficacy, *Journal of Peace Education, 5*(2), 157–173.

Danesh, H. B. (2009) Unity-based peace education: Education for peace program in Bosnia and Herzegovina—A chronological case study. In G. Salomon & E. Cairns (Eds.), *Handbook of peace education.* New York: Taylor & Francis Group.

de Waal, F. (2002). Primitive behavior and human aggression. In W. Ury (Ed.) *Must we fight? From the battlefield to the schoolyard—a new perspective on violent conflict and its prevention.* San Francisco: Jossey-Bass.

Dijkema, C., & d'Hères, S. M. (2007). *Conflict: A knot to be untangled.* IRENEES Dossier File 10/13. Retrieved September 11, 2001 from http://www.irenees.net/en/fiches/notions/fiche-notions-185.html.

Galtung, J. (1964). An editorial. *Journal of Peace Research, 1*(1), 1–4.

Galtung, J. (1969). Violence, peace, and peace research. *Journal of Peace Research, 6*(3), 167–191.

Galtung, J. (1990). Cultural violence. *Journal of Peace, 27*(3), 291–305.

Galtung, J., & Høivik, T. (1971) Structural and direct violence: A note on operationalization, *JPR, VIII*(1), 73–76.

Galtung, J., & Jacobsen, C. G. (2000). *Searching for peace: The road to TRANSCEND.* London, UK: Pluto Press.

Goertzel, T. (1987). Authoritarianism of personality and political attitudes. *J. Social Psy. 127,* 718.

Harris, I. M., & Morrison, M. L. (2003). *Peace education.* Jefferson, NC: McFarland and Company, Inc.

Kinder, C. (2011). *The roots of violence in society.* Curriculum unit, Yale-New Haven Teachers Institute. Retreived September 15, 2011 from http://www.yale.edu/ynhti/curriculum/units/2002/6/02.06.02.x.html#c.

Lowe, J. K. (2011). Fostering positive psychological outcomes in post-conflict settings: universak-diverse orientation and intergroup contact in Bosnia and Herzegovina. In H. B. Danesh (Ed.), *Education for peace reader.* Victoria, Canada: EFP Press.

Muldoon, B. (1996). *The heart of conflict.* New York: Perigree.

Nevo, B. & Brem, I. (2002). Peace education programs and evaluation of their effectiveness. In G. Salomon & B. Nevo (Eds.), *Peace education: The concept, principles, and practices around the world.* Mahwah, NJ: Lawrence Erlbaum Associates.

Petty, R. E., Wegener, D. T., & Fabrigar, L. R. (1997). Attitudes and attitude change. *Annual Review of Psychology. 48,* 609–647.

Salomon, G., & Cairns, E. (2010). *Handbook on peace education.* New York, NY: Taylor & Francis Group.

Simmel, G. (1956). *Conflict and the web of group affiliation.* K. H. Wolff (Trans.). Glenco, IL: FreePress.

Stone, R. & Kelner, K. (2000). Violence: No silver bullet. *Science, 289*(5479), 569.

CHAPTER 11

EVALUATING SEEDS OF PEACE

Assessing Long-Term Impact in Volatile Context

Ned Lazarus

INTRODUCTION

For peace educators working in contexts of intractable conflict, impact is the inevitable question. Sometimes it is asked genuinely, with recognition of good intentions. More often, it is a rhetorical trump card—a dismissal delivered with the authority of a verdict. In the Middle East, the impact question often evokes a skepticism accumulated over decades of impotent diplomatic interventions. In such situations, peacebuilders are constantly challenged to justify their practice: "So people participated in your program—so what? Did that resolve the conflict?" This is, therefore, precisely the question that practitioners must answer convincingly in order to build legitimacy among key audiences: funders, scholars, activists, mainstream educators, and most importantly, the communities in which they work.

The good news is that evaluation and scholarship are beginning to establish avenues of effective response to this inevitable question. Every evaluation process offers the opportunity to articulate a grounded vision of a specific intervention, requiring practitioners to identify attainable goals, concrete outcomes, meaningful

Peace Education Evaluation: Learning from Experience and Exploring Prospects,
pages 163–177.
Copyright © 2015 by Information Age Publishing
All rights of reproduction in any form reserved.

indicators, and tangible results—intended and unexpected—of their work. These are challenging but rewarding tasks, which clarify the distinction between a project's value-orientation (e.g., peace; conflict transformation) and its actual scope and content (e.g., training teachers; inspiring critical thinking among students). This process empowers practitioners to speak authoritatively on the basis of empirical evidence—and to bring the question of impact down to earth. "Resolving the conflict is beyond the scope of our project," one can simply say; "Here are our actual goals—and despite the failures of political leaders on the macro-level, here is what our work has accomplished on the ground." The significance of this process extends beyond individual initiatives. As evaluation becomes integrated into peacebuilding practice, impact can be considered in light of a track record of empirical studies and practical experience.

This chapter presents key findings from a recent evaluative study of a prominent peace education initiative, the Seeds of Peace program (SOP) (Lazarus, 2011).[1] The study is of unprecedented scope and size and proposes a new indicator of long-term impact. Rather than conceptualize impact primarily in terms of short-term attitudinal changes among peace education participants, this study traces *peacebuilding activity* among hundreds of Israeli and Palestinian SOP graduates from adolescence through adulthood—over periods of eight to fifteen years.[2] The longitudinal framework is designed to measure the endurance of program impacts and to highlight the influence of profound changes in personal, organizational, and political contexts. It is presented here not solely as an assessment of this particular program, but as part of the empirical record of peace education and a potential framework for evaluating interventions, models, and the wider field.

EVALUATING MIDDLE EAST "PEACE CAMPS": THE CASE OF SEEDS OF PEACE

Since 1993, several thousand Israeli and Palestinian youth have participated in the Seeds of Peace international camp program in Maine, USA, and in regional follow-up activities in the Middle East. SOP is one of at least 20 North American summer programs of this kind established in recent decades, 15 of which involve Israeli and Palestinian participants (Lazarus, 2011, p. 29). Each has its own *gestalt*; some emphasize arts, others media, while others adopt a traditional American camp curriculum. All of the programs, however, espouse a common theory of change: Offering Israeli and Palestinian youth a program of dialogue and shared experience, in an idyllic American setting, will humanize their perceptions of the "enemy" and inspire them to return to the Middle East as committed peacemak-

---

[1] The study is the author's doctoral dissertation, Lazarus, N. (2011). *Evaluating peace education in the Oslo-Intifada generation: A long-term impact study of Seeds of Peace 1993–2010.* (Doctoral dissertation). This article presents a brief summary of certain findings; for greater depth on the issues discussed here, please refer to the complete dissertation.

[2] Adulthood is defined, for the purposes of this study, as 21 years of age and above.

ers. The study presented here is the first large-scale, long-term assessment of a program based on this theory of change.

SOP is a prominent case as it is the largest and longest running of the North American peace camps; its alumni population, aggregate fundraising, and media coverage exceed those of all the other programs combined (Boorstein, 2006; Posner, 2006). SOP's first group of youth participants attended the historic signing of the Oslo Accords, the first Israeli-Palestinian diplomatic agreement, on the White House lawn in 1993. At the ceremony, President Clinton declared that "no one is more important than the Arab and Israeli children gathered here."[3] Since that auspicious public relations debut, leading U.S. media sources have featured stories on SOP, alongside myriad local, global, and online sources.

The framing of media coverage of SOP, however, has varied with the vicissitudes of the conflict. The image of young Israelis and Palestinians gathered alongside Yitzhak Rabin, Yasser Arafat, Shimon Peres, and Bill Clinton in 1993 became an icon of hope in the heyday of the Oslo peace process. Yet, after the collapse of negotiations led to the most lethal escalation of Israeli-Palestinian violence in generations, the euphoric images from the White House lawn came to evoke a fateful naïveté. History thus shaped two storylines that define popular conceptions of the impact of SOP—which, in turn, color perceptions of peace education as a whole.

A heroic narrative adopts the program's own promotional rhetoric, portraying participants as "ambassadors of peace" and "leaders of tomorrow," and the camp as "empowering the next generation" and transforming enemies into friends (Seeds of Peace). SOP's late founder John Wallach claimed that, "When [participants] return home, they are on their way to becoming leaders of a new generation... as committed to fighting for peace as their predecessors were in waging war" (Wallach, 2000, p. 13). A veteran journalist with close ties to American, Arab, and Israeli political elites, Wallach often spoke of a future in which SOP graduates would become Israeli and Palestinian leaders and bring an end to bloodshed between their nations.[4] This narrative shaped media coverage of SOP during the Oslo years (1993–2000) and endures in some contemporary reports (Engstrom, 2009).

Since the eruption of the second Palestinian *intifada* in late 2000, however, a dismissive narrative has emerged in parallel, conflating the outcomes of peace education programs with the failures of the official Israeli-Palestinian negotiations—in essence, throwing the "Track Two" baby out with the "Track One" bath-

---

[3] Full text of President Clinton's speech available at Israel Ministry of Foreign Affairs. "Declaration of Principles on Interim Self-Government Arrangements." Accessed June 2, 2011. http://www.mfa.gov.il/MFA/Foreign%20Relations/Israels%20Foreign%20Relations%20since%201947/1992-1994/108%20Dfeclaration%20of%20Principles%20on%20Interim%20Self-Gove.

[4] Author's personal observation.

water.[5] An October 2008 *San Francisco Chronicle* article, entitled "Peace Camps Show Few Results," adopts the language of impact evaluation to advance this dismissive narrative. The *Chronicle* asserts that "impact, if any, fades… activities expire with the end of the first meeting… programs have failed to produce a single prominent peace activist" (Kalman, 2008).

These are not critiques of program content, but explicit factual claims. Yet empirical study reveals these claims to be as explicitly false. Indeed, despite contradictory conclusions, the heroic and dismissive narratives share common elements. Each frames the question of impact in terms of post-intervention peacebuilding activity—or a lack thereof—by "peace camp" graduates; yet neither is based on a systematic study of actual results.[6] The present study was designed to replace facile narratives about peace education with grounded assessments, based on an empirical record of actual program outcomes.

OVERVIEW OF THE STUDY: BACKGROUND, DESIGN, FINDINGS

From 1996–2004, I served as Middle East program director for Seeds of Peace, based in Jerusalem. My experiences in the field led me to recognize both heroic and dismissive narratives as caricatures of complex outcomes. In those years, my colleagues and I worked to facilitate hundreds of SOP graduates crossing borders and checkpoints to continue dialogue and understand each others' realities. Teen-aged alumni drove the transformation of Seeds of Peace from an American summer camp to a year-round, cross-conflict youth movement in the Middle East. The organization's role was supportive—enabling graduates to implement their ideas. SOP provided funding, logistics, transportation, and staff to perform three functions in particular: securing permits from the Israeli military for Palestinians to move through the Occupied Palestinian Territories (OPT) and Israel, reassuring parents that their children would be safe on "the other side," and then facilitating actual encounters.

With this follow-up support, SOP graduates initiated homestay exchanges between Israelis, Palestinians, Egyptians, and Jordanians; joint presentations in each others' schools; and dialogue groups, overnight seminars focused on arts, media, and issues at the core of the conflict. During the height of the *intifada*, when cross-checkpoint visits were impossible, graduates initiated uni-national meetings and service projects in their own communities. Alumni also devised other means to continue cross-conflict communication: exchanging videotaped messages between Israelis and Palestinians in the OPT and initiating dialogues

---

[5] *Track One* refers to diplomacy conducted at the official, governmental level; Track Two refers to non-governmental forums of international engagement, also referred to as *citizen diplomacy* or *unofficial diplomacy*, among other terms. See Diamond. and McDonald (1996).

[6] Indeed, prominent media sources—such as the *60 Minutes* and *Nightline* news programs, among others—have alternated between heroic and dismissive narratives on SOP, always in line with shifts in the macro-political context. See Lazarus, 2011, p. 6–7.

between Palestinian and Jewish citizens of Israel (Al-Jundi & Marlowe, 2011). As adults, alumni spurred SOP to sponsor Conflict Resolution training courses and used the training to work for SOP and dozens of other peace initiatives (Maddy-Weitzman, 2004).

The enthusiasm of SOP camp graduates led the program to open a "Center for Coexistence" in Jerusalem, inaugurated with a 1999 ceremony attended by more than 500 Egyptian, Israeli, Jordanian, and Palestinian alumni. Yet, only a year later, this hopeful community was confronted with tragedy. Early in the *intifada*, Aseel 'Asleh, a 17 year-old Palestinian citizen of Israel and highly active SOP graduate, was killed by Israeli police—one of 13 Arab demonstrators killed in protests and riots that swept Israel in October 2000.[7] In the aftermath, I watched as Aseel's death and escalating violence drove many graduates to drop out of the program. Other alumni, however, remained dedicated peacebuilders into adulthood, while many alternated between periods of activity and alienation.

These experiences inspired me to move from practice to research; I left the organization in order to independently conduct the present study.[8] The research questions focus on the scope and fluctuations of alumni activity over time. First, have Israeli and Palestinian SOP graduates engaged in Middle East peacebuilding over the long term? Second, how have changes in personal, organizational and political contexts affected graduates' participation? The design combines qualitative and quantitative approaches, aiming for a methodology sensitive to the asymmetric and dynamic social contexts of its subjects.

To establish an empirical baseline, I first sought to track the peacebuilding activity of all 824 Israeli and Palestinian graduates of SOP's first ten summer programs (1993–2002), over periods of 8–15 years.[9]

---

[7] Seventeen year-old Aseel 'Asleh was shot and killed by Israeli police on October 2, 2000, at the site of a protest that developed into a confrontation between a crowd of Arab youth and police, near his home in the Galilee village of Arabeh. Aseel was one of 12 Arab citizens of Israel and one Palestinian killed by police fire during such confrontations at the onset of the second intifada (one Israeli Jew was killed in a separate incident by stone-throwing during the same period). An Israeli governmental Commission of Inquiry headed by Supreme Court Justice Theodor Or found no justification whatsoever for the killing of Aseel, or for the police use of live ammunition in his case and numerous others. Police and eyewitness testimonies to the commission confirmed that Aseel stood alone, far from the crowd, was not personally involved in confrontation with the police at the scene, yet was chased and shot at close range. For information on Aseel's death and October 2000, see Lazarus (2011, pp. 329–339, 367–374, 387–392). See also Judicial Authority of the State of Israel (2003); Abu-Baker, K. and Rabinowitz, D. (2005); Lazarus, N. (2005, November 17); Lazarus, N. (2001, November 17); Lazarus (2011, Chapters 7 and 8).

[8] I engaged full-time in the research and writing processes from 2004–2011; since leaving in 2004, I have had no official affiliation with the SOP organization. For detail, please refer to Lazarus, 2011, chapters 1 and 2.

[9] For the purposes of the study, I defined peacebuilding activity in a broad sense, as voluntary participation of SOP graduates in any form of non-violent, cross-conflict (i.e. Arab/Jewish or Israeli/Palestinian) engagement aimed at transforming perceptions and sociopolitical relations between Israeli Jews and Palestinian Arabs and contributing to resolution of the conflict. This definition encompasses a wide spectrum of activities aimed at conflict transformation, including advocacy, dialogue, human rights

Using the program's database and consulting with former colleagues and alumni, I classified each graduate's level of peacebuilding activity at different stages of life, according to a three-point scale: Active, In-Touch, or Out-of-Touch. *Active* graduates engaged frequently in cross-conflict peacebuilding activities, with SOP and other initiatives; *In-touch* graduates engaged occasionally in such activities; *Out-of-touch* graduates were not involved.

Once classified, I compared participants' activity rates according to gender, nationality, and year of SOP camp participation, from adolescence to adulthood. Longitudinal tracking granted the study context-sensitivity, allowing comparison across shifting personal, organizational, and political situations. I then complemented quantitative measures with qualitative research, asking more than 200 *adult* SOP alumni to articulate the program's impacts on their lives in their own terms.[10]

My quantitative findings affirmed the complexity of outcomes and the influence of changing contexts. Through longitudinal tracking, I was able to identify patterns of alumni engagement over time. In terms of personal trajectories, majorities of Israeli and Palestinian SOP alumni were active during the first year after camp and remained active or in-touch through the remainder of high school—evidence of high initial motivation sparked by the camp program, and partially sustained through follow-up in the Middle East. Ages 18–21, however, were defined by the compulsory military enlistment of Israeli Jewish graduates during *intifada* conditions, and correlated with sharp declines in activity across the board. For some graduates, these years constituted a "breaking point." Others described this period as, in one graduate's words, "three years of disconnection"—yet they returned to peacebuilding as adults. Indeed, at least 144 adult graduates (17.5% of alumni ages 21–30) actively engaged in diverse forms of peacebuilding with SOP and more than 40 other cross-conflict initiatives.

Table 11.1 details the trends of alumni peacebuilding participation over time.

Together, these findings indicated that the SOP camp experience was initially inspiring for a majority of participants; that the conflict context gradually eroded impact for many alumni, over several years; but that follow-up restored or sustained motivation among a core group, who displayed long-term commitments to peacebuilding. These findings echo conclusions of previous studies: a) that extended cross-conflict encounters can have transformative initial impact on participants (Hammack, 2006a; Risen, 2011); b) that intractable conflict context exerts a power-

---

and humanitarian work, peace education, and non-violent protest. This is in concert with growing international recognition that diverse activities contribute to the goals of transforming conflict, reducing violence, and building more just and peaceful societies. As explained in a 2006 World Bank report, "Peacebuilding is now understood more broadly. It often covers all activities related to preventing outbreaks of violence, transforming armed conflicts, finding peaceful ways to manage conflict, and creating the socio-economic and political pre-conditions for sustainable development and peace." See Or Commission (2003), Smith (2002). Civil society and peacebuilding: potential, limitations, and critical factors. Report no. 36445-GLB, p. 12. For practical examples of Israeli and Palestinian peacebuilding from across the full spectrum of approaches, see Just Vision. (n.d.)

[10] For detail of methodology, please refer to Lazarus, 2011, chapters 1 and 2.

TABLE 11.1. Alumni Peacebuilding Activity, by National Identity and Personal Context

PCI[1] (n=87)	First-Year	HS	Post-HS (64)[2]	Adult[3]
Active	36%	27%	15%	16.2%
In-touch	32%	20%	21%	n/a
Out-of-Touch	32%	53%	64%	n/a
Israeli (425)	**First-Year**	**HS**	**Post-HS (367)**	**Adult**
Active	50%	34%	11%	16.7%
In-touch	25%	24%	27%	n/a
Out-of-Touch	25%	42%	62%	n/a
Palestinian (312)	**First-Year**	**HS**	**Post-HS (282)**	**Adult**
Active	46%	25%	20%	18.9%
In-touch	24%	24%	29%	n/a
Out-of-Touch	30%	51%	51%	n/a
All Alumni (824)	**First-Year**	**HS**	**Post-HS (713)**	**Adult**
Active	44%	29%	15%	17.5%
In-touch	27%	23%	27%	n/a
Out-of-Touch	29%	49%	58%	n/a

[1] Palestinian citizens of Israel.
[2] The number in the Post-HS column represents total graduates ages 18-21 at the time of coding (2003–04).
[3] For adult graduates (ages 21-30), data were available only for "active" graduates, not "in-touch."

ful "erosion effect" against peacebuilding motivation (Salomon, 2004; Hammack, 2006b); but c) that follow-up activity can mitigate this erosion or restore motivation for some participants (Maddy-Weitzman, 2004; Salomon, 2010).[11] The importance of follow-up was further emphasized by my comparisons of long-term activity between different camp classes. As the next section illustrates, youth who joined SOP in later years, when the program offered follow-up support in the Middle East, displayed greater rates of long-term peacebuilding activity.

PROGRAM AND CONFLICT CONTEXTS

In the period under review, Israeli and Palestinian alumni grew from adolescents to adults, from students to professionals, from children to parents, and for many Israeli Jews, from youth, to soldiers, to veterans. SOP grew from a start-up summer camp to an internationally recognized NGO with year-round programming

---

[11] As Salomon (2010) explains, "Those changes that can be brought about by a relatively short-term intervention can be as easily changed back by the prevailing socio-political forces… [yet] attitudinal and perceptual changes that become eroded by external socio-political forces can be restored" by follow-up activity (pp. 9–10).

in the U.S., the Middle East, and other conflict regions. The Israeli-Palestinian conflict transformed from a context of historic negotiations, to horrific escalation, to "unilateral separation" and stalemate, with no apparent prospect of resolution.[12] These changes implied qualitative differences in the "SOP experience" of each group of participants, in terms of camp program, political environment, and the scope and quality of follow-up activities available in the Middle East.

I studied the influence of program and conflict contexts through comparisons of peacebuilding activity by different camp classes, tracking graduates according to their original year of camp participation. These comparisons led to a striking finding: Factors related to the program content—rather than conflict conditions—correlated most significantly with long-term outcomes, in both peace process and *intifada* contexts. This finding was illustrated by comparison of alumni activity between three eras during SOP's first decade, each characterized by different program and conflict conditions:

- 1993–96: *Early years, experimental program*—During this era, historic Palestinian-Israeli interim agreements generated both hope for peace and violent opposition. SOP ran two-week camp programs, with little organized follow-up for participants in the Middle East.
- 1997–99: *Best of Times*—During this era, the peace process atmosphere remained stable if stagnant; negotiations stalled, yet levels of conflict violence were (relatively) low.[13] The SOP program thrived: SOP camp drew hundreds of participants to 3–4 week sessions, and graduates engaged in year-round follow-up programs in the Middle East.
- 2000–02: *Worst of Times*—During this era, the eruption of the *intifada* led to hundreds of Israeli and thousands of Palestinian casualties, creating a hostile atmosphere for peacebuilding. After severe initial shocks, SOP gradually re-established previous levels of camp and follow-up programming, making adjustments necessitated by the situation.

Table 11.2 links the different conflict and program conditions prevailing in each era with the levels of long-term participation displayed by SOP graduates of the same period.

These findings illustrate that program factors, particularly the provision of follow-up support, had decisive impact *even in the most difficult conflict conditions*. The 1993–96 groups, who had no organized follow-up, displayed low levels of subsequent activity, despite experiencing a more hopeful political context. The 1997–99 and 2000–02 groups each displayed similar—and higher—long-term activity rates, despite drastically different conflict contexts. The 2000–02 graduates attended camp in a vastly more violent, polarized environment than the 1997–99

---

[12] See chapters 8 and 9 in Dowty, D. (2007) and Khalidi, R. (2007).

[13] The emphasis is on "relative"; these brief descriptions do not, of course, fully reflect the complexity of the situation. For further detail, see Lazarus, 2011, p. 139–168.

TABLE 11.2. Alumni Peacebuilding Participation in Different Conflict and Program Contexts[1]

Era Conflict Context Program Context	First year Participation	High School Participation	Ages 18–21 Participation
1993–96: Early Years Peace Process; No Regional Follow-up	54%	30%	29%
1997–99: Best of Times Peace Process; Regional Follow-up	85%	65%	54%
2000–02: Worst of Times Intifada; Regional Follow-up	82%	66%	55%

[1]Participation rates here include graduates ranked "active" and "in touch."

group. Yet graduates of both eras engaged in peacebuilding at much higher rates than 1993–96 graduates. Organized support for regional follow-up was the common denominator between these 1997–99 and 2000–02 eras.

The factor that correlated most significantly with long-term activity, moreover, was a form of follow-up participation entirely at the program's discretion: the selection of some alumni, by SOP staff, to return to camp a second time as a "Peer Support" (PS). During the decade in question, 240 alumni earned this status (29%

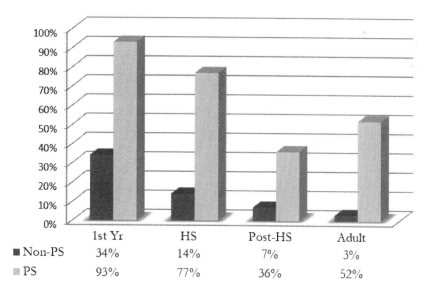

	1st Yr	HS	Post-HS	Adult
■ Non-PS	34%	14%	7%	3%
▨ PS	93%	77%	36%	52%

FIGURE 11.1. Percentage of Active Graduates by Life-Stage, PS/Non-PS

of all graduates). As Figure 11.1 illustrates, PS selectees were much more active than other alumni. The PS selection process established two sets of graduates on divergent paths of long-term peacebuilding engagement.

A third comparison affirms both the influence of conflict context and the restorative potential of follow-up. To study the effects of rapid shifts in context, I compared participation rates during a period of escalating conflict (2002–May 2003) with a period of de-escalation marked by a tenuous cease-fire (June 2003–2004). In terms of programming, during the escalation, SOP featured no programs for adult graduates; during the de-escalation, by contrast, SOP established training courses for adult alumni. As Table 11.3 illustrates, the latter period is characterized by increased activity for all groups. This shift reflects the improvement of conflict context. Yet the return to activity of many alumni, after a period of inactivity, also indicates an enduring salience of latent motivation. This finding is strengthened by the enrollment of adult graduates, often after substantial periods of inactivity, in peacebuilding training courses. Thus, conflict escalation diminished, but did not erase, the motivation of many graduates. Alumni engagement was influenced by conflict conditions, but also very much *by the program's responses to those conditions.*

From the data presented here, it remains possible to draw a range of conclusions regarding the program's impact. Whether these figures constitute success remains in the eye of the beholder. Yet facile generalizations become impossible, complicated by a documented record of diverse outcomes evolving dynamically in context over time. The data provide a foundation for empirically grounded evaluation.

QUALITATIVE FINDINGS: THE PEACEBUILDER'S PARADOX

Extensive qualitative research remained an essential complement to these quantitative findings; having established a baseline of *what* happened, I investigated

TABLE 11.3.   Changes in Alumni Participation by Group During Improved Context

Group	% Active	% In-touch	% Out-of-touch	Peacebuilding Activity Increase 2003–04
PCI 02-03	12%	29%	59%	
PCI 03-04	34%	29%	37%	+22%
ISR 02-03	17%	26%	57%	
ISR 03-04	26%	26%	48%	+9%
PAL 02-03	20%	29%	51%	
PAL 03-04	27%	27%	46%	+5%
Overall 02-03	16%	28%	56%	
Overall 03-04	29%	27%	44%	+12%

why alumni engaged or disengaged from peacebuilding at different moments in the conflict and in their own lives.[14] Drawing upon my contacts among SOP's first ten camp classes, I engaged in correspondence and conversations with a total of 305 alumni, and conducted formal interviews with 70 Israeli and Palestinian graduates who had been "active" for some time after their initial summer. Inspired by the "Most Significant Change" evaluation method, I asked interviewees strictly open-ended questions in order to allow graduates to describe the program's impacts in detail, nuance, and crucially, in their own terms (Davies & Dart, 2005).

Alumni testimonies added complexity to the picture. The vast majority of graduates described their personal experiences in the program in superlative terms, as the source of valuable experiences, friendships, networks, perspectives, and skills. In the words of numerous graduates, SOP was "the best thing that ever happened to me," "a gift," "the root of all my interests, political and academic," "one of the most central elements that shaped me, as a social and political activist, in every sense." Such sentiments even characterized most graduates no longer involved with SOP. One Palestinian graduate, now involved only in explicitly politicized activism, opened her interview by stating, "I'm gonna start by saying that I do not regret joining Seeds of Peace and when I have kids in the future I will send them, 'cause I want them to get that experience... SOP have changed my life and if it's not for [SOP]... I don't think I would have accomplished what I have accomplished in my life."

Yet the same graduates told of enduring harsh criticism from family, peers, and educators. Indeed, the more SOP encouraged alumni to engage in peacebuilding, the more it placed them at odds with the dominant consensus of their societies and the intractable realities of the conflict—a "peacebuilder's paradox" (Abu-Nimer & Lazarus, 2008). This dynamic found different expressions in the asymmetrical realities of Israeli Jews and Palestinians. Each group articulated a distinct "national dilemma"; Israeli Jews experienced crises of conscience regarding compulsory military service, while Palestinians debated whether dialogue with Israelis constituted "normalization" of the Israeli military occupation (Salem, 2005). All, however, experienced a constant struggle for social legitimacy due to SOP affiliation. At the organizational level, moreover, many of the graduates most dedicated to peacebuilding lambasted SOP's U.S. leadership for alleged detachment from Middle Eastern realities, and for episodes of organizational conflict that alienated veteran alumni and staff.[15] From graduates' points of view, SOP's impacts were multiple, both positive and negative; there was no simple bottom line.

Nonetheless, for the overwhelming majority, there was no question that the program had profound and lasting impact at the personal level. When asked whether it was ethical to confront youth with such difficult dilemmas, an Israeli

---

[14] For detail of qualitative findings, please refer to Lazarus, 2011, chapters 4–9.

[15] It is important to note that critiques were directed towards the leadership of the period up to 2009; since then, a new leadership cadre has hired graduates as program directors and addressed some key points of critique. See Lazarus 2011, p. 428–432.

alumna explained that, "My educational ideology is to teach children to ask questions and to doubt. It's to educate a generation of people that doesn't take for granted the dictates of their society... The fact that it's difficult, and that it makes [one] a more conflicted young person... my own children, I'll definitely educate this way." The same alumna has indeed devoted her adult career to fulfilling this "educational ideology," by working as a dialogue facilitator and peace educator with SOP and numerous other peacebuilding initiatives. Her work illustrates the potential of generating impact beyond the immediate micro/participant-level; long-term active graduates often engage in multiple campaigns and programs over time, contributing to local peacebuilding networks in diverse ways.

In the peacebuilding evaluation literature, "impact" is sometimes strictly defined as generating change in the macro-conflict, or contributing to "peace writ-large" (Anderson & Olsen, 2003). Neither this nor any peace education project can claim impact at that level; of course, neither can the leaders of the world's most powerful states or international institutions whose explicit mandate is conflict prevention and resolution. I contend with d'Estree et al. (2001) and others that grassroots educational initiatives should aspire—and be judged by—linkage of micro-outcomes to *meso*-level impacts: contributions to local civil society movements, networks, and organizations (Nan, 2008; Spurk, 2008). I conclude by considering implications of these findings for peace education practice and evaluation.

CONCLUSIONS

The findings detailed above speak to a pair of core questions in the peace education literature, each a variation on the issue of impact. The first is the practitioner's question, aptly embodied by the title of Salomon's article: "Does peace education make a difference in the context of an intractable conflict?" (Salomon, 2004). The second is the evaluator's question—whether this kind of "making a difference" can be measured. In both cases, this study indicates that the answer can be a qualified yes—given a focus on *long-term peacebuilding activity rather than short-term attitudinal change*, on the part of educators and evaluators. In each case, sustained follow-up support must be considered a sine qua non of effective practice.

In a 2005 study of peace education, Liyanage and Malhotra lament the "paucity of research on long-term impact" in difficult contexts, observing that rigorous long-term studies "tend not to be situated in the arena of violent or extreme ethnopolitical conflict; rather, they tend to be in relatively peaceful climates" (Malhotra & Liyanage, 2005, p. 910). Previous studies in protracted conflict contexts have tracked participants over spans of a few months to two years post-intervention. The present study documents a potential for longer-term impact, extending over periods of at least three years for a majority of subjects studied, and over ten years for a committed minority—through volatile conflict conditions.

Liyanage and Malhotra further note that "'follow-up' interventions that might boost the impact of initial, intensive interventions..." have been all but "ignored

TABLE 11.4. Peacebuilding Initiatives in which Adult SOP Graduates Participated/ Worked

Dialogue/Negotiation	Advocacy/Protest	Education/Media/Mixed
• Al-Quds University/Peace Now Dialogue	• Alternative Information Center	• Multiple Conflict Resolution MA/PhD programs
• Creativity for Peace	• American Task Force on Palestine	• Campus for All
• Crossing Borders	• Bat Shalom	• Faculty for Israeli-Palestinian Peace
• Givat Haviva	• B'tselem	
• Hands of Peace	• The Campus is Not Silent	• Geneva Initiative
• Heartbeat Jerusalem	• Coalition of Women for Peace	• IPCRI
• Independent dialogues at multiple Israeli, U.S. universities	• HaMoked	• Just Vision
	• Holy Land Trust	• Jerusalem Stories
• Israeli-Palestinian Negotiating Partners	• International Solidarity Movement	• Olive Tree Program
		• One Voice
• New Story Leadership	• Middle East Nonviolence and Democracy	• Palestine Note
• Peace Camp Canada	• New Profile	• Search for Common Ground
• Peace it Together	• Palestinian Campaign for the Right of Entry/Re-Entry	• Sixty Years, Sixty Voices
• Peres Center for Peace		• Zochrot: Remembering the Nakba in Hebrew
• Sulha Peace Project	• Peace Now	
• Alternative Information Center	• Student coalition at Tel-Aviv University	

in the contact literature" (Malhotra & Liyanage, 2005, p. 920). This study illustrates the value of a longer-term approach to both intervention design and evaluation. Echoing Hammack (2006a,b) and Salomon (2010), I conclude that in contexts of long-term conflict, short-term interventions alone are likely to inspire short-term effects. Peace educators and evaluators must approach the initial encounter and its immediate cognitive effects as an essential spark for change—but devote attention and resources to keeping the fire burning.

This long-term commitment may seem unrealistic for peacebuilding initiatives living by the whims of donors and the calendar of the project cycle, perpetually stretched in terms of personnel and financial capacity. In this regard, one finding from this study can illustrate the value of an integrated vision of the field. As Table 11.4 details, Israeli and Palestinian SOP graduates have served as activists, directors, facilitators, participants, and staff for at least 40 other Israeli-Palestinian peacebuilding initiatives of diverse content and political orientations, in addition to building the follow-up programs sponsored by Seeds of Peace. Among active adult graduates, some have continued with dialogue and peace education; others moved to politicized approaches such as advocacy and nonviolent direct action. Nearly all active alumni, however, cited experiences from SOP as their original sources of inspiration—in the words of one Palestinian graduate, "it was the beginning of peace activism." This path from adolescent encounter experiences to adult civil society activism embodies the potential contribution of micro-level peace education to meso-level impact. While each specific initiative is limited in content and capacity, all can connect motivated participants to larger movements, networks, and organizations engaged in cross-conflict peacebuilding.

REFERENCES

Abu-Baker, K., & Rabinowitz, D. (2005). *Coffins on our shoulders: The experience of the Palestinian citizens of Israel.* Berkeley: University of California Press.

Abu-Nimer, M., & Lazarus, N. (2008). The peacebuilder's paradox and the dynamics of dialogue: A psychosocial portrait of Israeli-Palestinian encounters. In J. Kuriansky (Ed.), *Beyond bullets and bombs: Grassroots peacebuilding between Israelis and Palestinians* (pp. 19–32). Westport, CT: Prager.

Al-Jundi, S., & Marlowe, J. (2011). *The hour of sunlight: One Palestinian's journey from prisoner to peacemaker.* New York: Nation Books.

Anderson, M., & Olson, L. (2003). *Confronting war: Critical lessons for peace practitioners reflecting on peace practice projects.* Cambridge, MA: Collaborative Development Action.

Boorstein, M. (2006). *A measure of peace: The role and impact of people-to-people in the Israel-Palestine conflict* (Master's thesis). New York University, New York.

Davies, R., & Dart, J. (2005). *The 'most significant change' (MSC) technique: A guide to its use.* Retrieved May 27, 2011 from Monitoring and Evaluation News: http://www.mande.co.uk/docs/MSCGuide.pdf

d'Estree, T. P., Fast, L., Weiss, J., & Jakobsen, M. (2001). Changing the debate about 'success' in conflict resolution efforts. *Negotiation Journal, 17*(2), 102–113.

Diamond, L., & McDonald, J. W. (1996). *Multi-track diplomacy: A systems approach to peace.* Sterling, VA: Kumarian Press.

Dowty, D. (2007). *Israel/Palestine.* New York: Polity Press.

Engstrom, C. (2009). Promoting peace, yet sustaining conflict? A fantasy-theme analysis of Seeds of Peace publications. *Journal of Peace Education, 6*(1), 19–35.

Hammack, P. (2006a). Identity, conflict and coexistence: Life stories of Israeli and Palestinian adolescents. *Journal of Adolescence, 21* (3), 323–369.

Hammack, P. (2006b). *The narrative stalemate: Conflict, identity, and the cultural psychology of Israeli and Palestinian adolescence* (Doctoral dissertation). University of Chicago, Psychology, Chicago.

Judicial Authority of the State of Israel (2003). *Report of the Governmental Commission of Inquiry into Clashes Between the Security Forces and Israeli Citizens in October 2000.* Retrieved March 3, 2010 from http://elyon1.court.gov.il/heb/veadot/or/inside_index.htm (Hebrew). In English, see Official Summation of the Or Commission Report. (2003, September 1). *Haaretz.* Retrieved March 3, 2010 from http://www.haaretz.com/hasen/pages/ShArt.jhtml?itemNo=335594.

Just Vision. (n.d.). *Visionaries.* Retrieved June 2, 2011 from http://www.justvision.org/visionaries.

Kalman, M. (2008, October 19). Peace camps show few results. *San Francisco Chronicle.*

Kuriansky, J. (Ed.). (2007). *Beyond bullets and bombs: Grassroots Peacebuilding between Israelis and Palestinians.* Westport, CT: Greenwood.

Khalidi, R. (2007). *The iron cage: The story of the Palestinian struggle for statehood.* Boston: Beacon.

Lazarus, N. (2005, November 17). For *Justice, Please Hold*. *Haaretz*. Retrieved March 3 from http://www.haaretzdaily.com/hasen/pages/ShArt.jhtml?itemNo=646967

Lazarus, N. (2001, November 17). Jerusalem Diary Part 5. *Slate*. Retrieved March 20, 2011 from http://slate.msn.com/id/2058163/entry/2058168/.

Lazarus, N. (2011). *Evaluating peace education in the Oslo-Intifada generation: A long-term impact study of Seeds of Peace 1993–2010*. Ph.D. Dissertation, American University, International Relations, Washington, D.C.

Maddy-Weitzman, E. (2004). *Waging peace in the holy land: A qualitative study of Seeds of Peace 1993–2004*. Ph.D. Dissertation, Boston University, Psychology, Boston.

Malhotra, D., & Liyanage, S. (2005). Long-term effects of peace workshops in protracted conflicts. *Journal of Conflict Resolution , 49*(6), 908–924.

Nan, S. A. (2008). Conflict resolution in a network society. *International Negotiation, 13* (1), 111–131.

Or Commission. (2003). *Report of the governmental commission of inquiry for investigation of clashes between security forces and Israeli citizens in October 2000*. Jerusalem: State of Israel Judicial Authority.

Posner, A. (2006). *Teaching peace while living war: Obstacles to effective peace education by non-governmental organizations—the case of Israel/Palestine 2000–2004* (Doctoral dissertation). Tufts University, Fletcher School of Diplomacy, Boston.

Risen, J. (2011). *Attitudinal study of Seeds of Peace participants* (Unpublished manuscript). University of Chicago.

Salem, W. (2005). The anti-normalization discourse in the context of Israeli-Palestinian peacebuilding. *Palestine-Israel Journal of Politics, Economics and Culture, 12*(1), 100–109.

Salomon, G. (2010). *A summary of our findings: Recent research findings by the Center for Research on Peace Education*. Working Paper, University of Haifa, Center for Research on Peace Education, Haifa.

Salomon, G. (2004). Does peace education make a difference in a context of intractable conflict? *Peace and Conflict: Journal of Peace Psychology, 10* (3), 257–274.

Seeds of Peace. (n. d.). Retrieved December 22, 2011 from http://www.seedsofpeace.org

Smith, D. (2002). *Towards a strategic framework for peacebuilding: Getting their act together*. Overview Report of the Joint Utstein Study of Peacebuilding. Oslo: Royal Norwegian Ministry of Foreign Affairs.

Spurk, C. (2008). Forget impact. *New Routes, 13*(3), 11–14.

Wallach, J. (2000). *The enemy has a face: The Seeds of Peace story*. Washington, D.C.: United States Institute of Peace.

CHAPTER 12

THE OLIVE TREE INITIATIVE

Lessons Learned about Peace Education through Experiential Learning

Daniel Wehrenfennig, Daniel Brunstetter, and Johanna Solomon

INTRODUCTION

Peace education is widely perceived as a means to help contribute to the resolution of conflicts. The United States Institute of Peace, for example, states that its mission is "to teach, train, inform policymakers, practitioners, students and the public about the challenges of conflict prevention, management and resolution and how to respond to those challenges" (United States Institute of Peace, n.d.). Education can lead to understanding and trusting the "other" by promoting perspective taking and intercultural communication skills founded in empathy, open-mindedness, and respect (Abu-Nimer, 1999; Kelman, 2005; Millora, 2011; Williams & Assay, 2003). Ultimately, the desired outcome of peace education programs is a move away from individual and community relations defined by polarization, de-legitimization, and dehumanization towards tolerance and reconciliation.

This chapter focuses on peace education grounded in experiential education, dialogue, and contact theories (Bekerman, 2007; Helman, 2002; Hewstone, 1996). Despite a rich theoretical and experimental heritage, relatively few empirical studies in peace education exist. Currently, the growing field suffers from a

Peace Education Evaluation: Learning from Experience and Exploring Prospects,
pages 179–191.
Copyright © 2015 by Information Age Publishing
All rights of reproduction in any form reserved.   **179**

dearth of academic discussion regarding the challenges facing those who seek to create or evaluate these programs (Bekerman, 2007; Millora, 2011; Schimmel, 2009; Schulz, 2008; Walter and Paul, 2004). Without this dialogue, critics are skeptical of the positive effects of such "uncritically acclaimed" programs, claiming the "optimism on which these theories are predicated is far from proving itself justified" (Bekerman, 2007, p. 24; Salomon 2003; Stephan & Stephan 1996). How do we evaluate peace education programs? What challenges face those who design these programs and the researchers who test their effectiveness?

To provide insight into these questions, we examine one experiential educational program—the Olive Tree Initiative (OTI) at the University of California, Irvine. OTI is a diverse student, faculty and community initiative promoting dialogue and understanding about the Israeli-Palestinian conflict through experiential learning. Its educational philosophy centers on the belief that dialogue and prolonged contact between conflicting groups, whether in the region or among participating students, can change local conditions (in this case, on UCI's campus) through empowerment, empathy, and perspective taking.

OTI has received many local, state, and national awards that point to the perceived merits of the OTI program in promoting co-existence and understanding. These include the Interfaith Peace Ministry of Orange County Paul S. Delp Peace Award, the University of California President's Award for Outstanding Leadership, the U.S. Center for Citizen Diplomacy (in cooperation with the U.S. Department of State) "Top Ten" Higher Education Program Award, and a California State Assembly Resolution for outstanding contributions to the community.

In this chapter, we explore the internal evaluation procedures used to test the effectiveness of OTI. These include qualitative analyses of interviews, quantitative analyses of surveys and course evaluations, feedback from student group and board retreats, as well as initiation of longitudinal evaluations of alumni. Specifically, this chapter works through some of the challenges that the directors and researchers faced as they sought to evaluate the OTI program in these ways.

We proceed by briefly presenting the fundamental educational philosophy of OTI, followed by a discussion of the internal methods used to evaluate the program. We then highlight several potential challenges facing evaluators of experiential peace education programs, including: operationalizing the notion of success, methodological limitations of qualitative and quantitative evaluations such as small N and selection bias, difficulties in tracking long-term benefits to participants, and dilemmas linked to community response and funding. Our hope is that in examining the strengths and weaknesses of the evaluation protocol established by OTI, advances can be made in developing and evaluating similar programs.

PEACE EDUCATION:
A CASE STUDY OF THE OLIVE TREE INITIATIVE

The Olive Tree Initiative was born out of conflict, or more accurately, the reaction to the Israeli-Palestinian conflict on the campus of the University of California, Irvine and in the surrounding Jewish and Arab/Muslim diaspora communities of Orange County. Protected by first amendment rights of freedom of speech and assembly, student and community activism has produced a campus climate characterized by passion, but also mired in tense polarization between pro-Israel and pro-Palestinian groups. Even though diaspora groups are not physically ensconced in the day to day reality of the conflict, members of diaspora communities have important ties to the region through family, history, finances, and social and religious identification. Some scholars suggest that diaspora communities are strong, identity-based groups and may hold more radical and entrenched positions than those who live in the region, who may instead focus on daily issues of resources and safety (Al Omari, 2010).

Within this polarized context a diverse group of UCI students, in partnership with several faculty and community members, founded the Olive Tree Initiative in 2007. Participants were from Christian, Druze, Jewish, Muslim, and non-religious backgrounds with varying—and often polarized—perspectives on the Israeli-Palestinian conflict. In reaction to tensions on campus, these students created a safe forum where they could discuss and plan an educational trip to the Middle East to learn from people living the conflict. Some students wanted to prove to the "other" side that they were right and others just wanted to learn more. In September 2008, after a year and a half of challenging preparations, fifteen students and three advisors (two professors and one graduate student) traveled to Israel and the West Bank for two weeks to learn first-hand about the conflict. The group was about one third self-identified pro-Israeli, one third self-identified pro-Palestinian and one third individuals without strong preferences. They met with politicians, academics, students, religious leaders, journalists, activists, and everyday people. Every effort was made to balance the itinerary, which was decided upon by the students and faculty advisors, so that participants felt that all relevant narratives were heard and that all the important, accessible places were seen.

Since 2008, there have been four student trips and two community trips. Upon their return, students share the knowledge they gained on campus and in the surrounding communities. Examples include a yearly welcome back event, monthly dialogue sessions and debates, mock negotiations, a film festival, high school outreach, hosting speakers from the region, and presentations at local synagogues, churches, and mosques. The students also write a reflective article for publication in a campus-sponsored journal.

The Olive Tree Initiative program, in cooperation with the School of Social Sciences at the University of California, Irvine has also developed academic components to better support the experiential component. Participating students not only meet weekly to discuss current events and plan activities, but also take courses within the newly established Certificate Program in Conflict Analysis and Resolution. For this program, students take a core course and an elective in three modules: Theory and Methods of Conflict Analysis and Resolution; Culture, History and Politics of Conflict Zones; and Application of Theory and Methods.

EVALUATING OTI: CHALLENGES AND METHODS

From the very beginning, OTI has been committed to evaluating its educational activities. During this process, we identified several evaluative challenges that we have faced.

Operationalizing Success

The first challenge lies in defining "successful". Without an operationalized definition and, therefore, a specified goal associated with a peace education program, it is impossible to judge whether expectations are met. In the peace education literature, disagreement exists regarding the goals of peace education programs. Some scholars postulate that success should be measured by whether significant change occurs in local conditions. These scholars criticize those programs that do not lead to broad positive interactions between antagonistic groups (Abu-Nimer, 1999; Bekerman, 2007; Halabi & Sonnenshein, 2000). While theoretical work has suggested success could be defined on an individual basis if contact with the "other" led participants to change attitudes from intolerant to tolerant (Allport, 1954; Pettigrew, 1998), recent scholarship warns that when individuals return to their communities after a dialogue program they face profound challenges in the application of lessons learned (Abu-Nimer, 2004). Other scholars discuss "success" in terms of prompting widespread inter-communal engagement (Schimmel, 2009) or activism that strives for socio-political change (Bar-Tal, 2004; Hager et al., 2011; Salomon, 2004).

Based on our own experience, there are problems with each of these understandings of "success". Judging a program on whether it brings "peace to the Middle East", or even to the participants' communities, ignores too many exogenous factors and sets the bar far beyond short-term practicality. Alternatively, expecting every participant to renounce prejudices oversimplifies factors that inhibit such change (such as in-group pressures), and downplays the time it takes for student participants to integrate into leadership positions for community dynamics to change. Finally, defining success in terms of activism assumes there are easily identifiable right and wrong views and agreed upon notions of justice. Such a perspective can be counterproductive in cases of entrenched conflict. In the case of the Israeli-Palestinian conflict, there are conflicting and deeply entrenched narratives, as well as competing views of justice and victimization (Juneau & Sucharov, 2010; Maoz & Bar-On, 2002). We found that insisting on change or justice may actually serve to reify identity and strengthen stereotypes (Helman, 2002). That said, OTI's general goals of providing dialogue tools and experience with the "other" are not enough to label a program successful. We believe the essential question is not whether dialogue programs will bring peace, but rather: what can they provide to improve inter-group relations?

OTI provides students with an option other than local polarization—a space for cultural interaction and learning. From its inception, OTI's goal has been threefold: to develop dialogue skills; to encourage the acquisition of knowledge about multiple narratives of the conflict leading to a better understanding of the self, the other, and the nuances of the conflict; and to provide mentoring that leads to the development of future community leaders. These three learning outcomes are embedded in the OTI program and have been institutionalized in UC Irvine's academic program in Conflict Analysis and Resolution.

First, in the class *Introduction to Conflict Analysis and Resolution*, students learn skills in dialogue techniques and familiarize themselves with theories of conflict resolution. They become equipped with necessary tools—how to ask questions, how to be an attentive listener, how to communicate respectively one's own views, how to engage with those that hold differing viewpoints, and how to put all of this learning in a larger theoretical context. Success is measured by participants' ability to use these skills in both in-group discussions and in discussions with out-group community members.

Second, in *Narratives of the Middle East,* students acquire knowledge about the different narratives of the conflict and are exposed to the complexity of the situation. This helps them to distinguish propaganda that reproduces stereotypes from perspectives that provide for common ground. Success in knowledge acquisition is not a measurement of "fact" intake. Rather, we place emphasis on exposing participants to the multiplicity of narratives and complexities of the conflict. We theorize that this increase in cognitive perspective taking, coupled with acquisition of more detailed knowledge, will encourage students to move away from thinking in monolithic stereotypes and holding a zero-sum view of the conflict towards possessing an attitude where multiple narratives and truths could simultaneously be deemed valid, and thus an environment in which deep discussions of local nuances could be undertaken.

Finally, students take classes in *Scholarship and Leadership Development,* which helps to build leadership skills. Building off of their developed skill sets in dialogue, and their exposure to alternative narratives, students are required to undertake projects that promote dialogue and understanding in the local community. Through mentorship from faculty advisors, they are empowered to build bridges of positive engagement and understanding between conflicting groups.

One of the biggest factors leading to animosity between conflicting groups is a lack of positive contact, which allows for a continuing lack of trust and facilitates the dehumanization of the "other". A successful dialogue program can help to diminish this separation by humanizing the "other" by building positive contact channels and trust between individuals and communities. OTI participants return to their communities with dialogue skills, deep knowledge of the conflict, and a more empathetic view of the "other side".

Measuring Dialogue Skills, Knowledge Acquisition of Multiple Perspectives, and Efficacy of Mentoring Efforts

In measuring the success of OTI, we found it useful to think in two phases: short-term and long-term. As noted in the literature, many dialogue programs show positive effects while participants are part of the program, but these effects may decline over the long-term as participants return to their communities (Schimmel, 2009). This suggests that it is important to evaluate not only whether the program achieves its educational goals, but also the propensity of participants to retain the program's teachings. Indeed, in a recent case study of a peace education project between Israeli, Palestinian, and Swedish students, Michal Schulz remarked that the biggest challenge facing program directors is "to design a methodological study that can follow a process of reconciliation through the stages before, during, and after an educational program" (2008, p. 47). Our evaluation process aims to meet this goal by measuring different levels of success at multiple time points before, during the program, and beyond.

OTI focuses on educating the student participants to provide them with the skill sets, knowledge, and experience to become future leaders. It is important to focus our current analysis on measurable short-term elements that impact the students, with an eye toward future work on long-term individual, campus, and community level changes.

Short-Term Measurement

The Olive Tree Initiative employs a number of evaluation techniques to analyze whether students understand the content and theory as intended. First, course evaluations lend insight into teaching and learning dynamics. In addition to standard course evaluations employed by the university, OTI faculty members have developed an additional evaluation that more specifically addresses the goals of the program. These classes are open to all UCI students and the anonymous evaluations are provided to all who take the class. They ask open-ended questions such as: What did you learn from this course that you will remember at a later date? What did you learn that you will use in your daily life? How effective was this class in providing a balanced perspective on the Middle East? Feedback gives an idea of what the students learned from the courses, which is compared to pedagogical expectations.

Second, OTI conducts two yearly reflective retreats: one with community board members (and student representatives) and one with students. During these retreats, focus groups concerned with specific elements of the program—such as education, fundraising, and social dynamics—carefully evaluate where the program is presently and new directions for the future. The retreats last between one and two days. The goal is to critically discuss the program, assess its strengths and weaknesses, and make appropriate improvements based on student and community input.

Finally, OTI participants voluntarily take part in a multi-year quantitative and qualitative study based on a psychological model predicting that change in perspective taking will increase empathy, decrease prejudice, and increase pro-social behaviors toward the out-group, resulting in more positive inter-group relations (Batson & Ahmad, 2009; Betancourt, September 1, 1990). The study, developed in 2010, is designed to measure these specific psychological changes (in empathy, perspective taking, ethnic and religious prejudice), which mirror OTI's core goals as discussed above. The study has three main components: a survey measure, an open-ended interview, and participant observation.

The mixed methods approach described here represents a pilot evaluation tool. Our discussion here aims at analyzing the procedures to provide a deeper understanding of the benefits and challenges of peace education programs. The design used to evaluate OTI is quasi-experimental, using control and treatment groups when possible. During the first year of the protocol, researchers capitalized on a natural experiment to form both control and participant groups. Because there were more interested participants than spots available, and because factors such as year at the university and participation in fundraising—as opposed to character or prior beliefs—entered into the decision of who was able to go on the trip, a natural control group exposed to OTI but not the intervention (trip) was formed. While this may not be applicable to all peace education programs, as it was not in subsequent years, other forms of control including matched pairs or true random assignment are sometimes available and provide results that control for historical factors.

The quantitative survey measures included a modified empathy scale and a test of implicit prejudice toward relevant groups including Israelis, Palestinians, Jews, and Muslims (see Aron, Aron, & Smollan, 1992 for openness scale; Greenwald, Poehlman, Uhlmann, & Banaji, 2009 for IAT). These tests afforded researchers insight into how participants view themselves in comparison to others with reduced self-report bias.

The qualitative element of this study consisted of open-ended interviews. Questions focus on participants' perceptions of the history of the conflict, the most pressing current issues in the Middle East, victimhood and aggression both in the local community and in the region itself, and plans for involvement in the community. Responses were associated with goals of the program—perceptions of narratives, perspective taking, empathy, prejudice, efficacy, behavior toward out-groups and community involvement. Interviews provided insight into how participants perceived change within themselves and the impact of the program on these changes, as well as methodological insight into the statistical results.

The researchers contextualized the views expressed by participants through participant observation (see Schulz, 2008 for similar use of this method). The close relationship between the researchers and the participants throughout the process—before, during and after the trip—allowed the researchers to closely observe the participants' behavior, which facilitated their interpretation of the scope of individual and group level change across time.

Methodological Challenges

Program evaluation posed three notable methodological challenges. First, one important limitation of OTI and other such interventions is the risk of self-selection bias. As scholars of similar programs note, participants in peace education programs tend to be open to dialogue and actively seek out such opportunities; those who do not believe in dialogue thus tend to be excluded (Bar Tal, 2004; Schimmel, 2009, p. 53). This may lead to selection on the dependent variable, which is problematic to analyses, making it difficult to reliably quantify the changes purported to have occurred.

We address this challenge by attempting to recruit students with divergent views to participate in the group. The process of active recruitment targets students whose views would add to the group dynamic, some of whom are skeptical of OTI's value to community concerns. While students must show willingness to sit at the table, this fact alone does not ensure positive outcomes; one need only look at the history of failed peace negotiations between Israelis and Palestinians to see that willingness to sit down to talk is not a sufficient condition for positive change. We acknowledge that we are not able to include people with extreme positions who are unwilling to hold discussions with the "other". However, many participants, despite agreeing to join the group, initially hold mistrustful views of the "other" and are skeptical of the legitimacy of other narratives. This means that developing a more empathic view of the "other" or developing a greater appreciation of competing narratives marks a significant change.

This challenge is compounded by the small number of participants, which ranges from 15–32 per year. While a necessary limiting factor in order to facilitate group dialogue, and because of funding constraints in this and similar interventions, small participant numbers constrain the effectiveness of statistical analyses. With fewer than forty participants per iteration, the researcher is unlikely to find statistically significant changes even if the majority of participants do show a shift in attitudes or behaviors. Ideally this problem can be overcome by evaluating multiple cohorts in a multi-level statistical model. In the meantime, we supplement the quantitative analyses with in-depth qualitative studies to tease out the causal effects at play. Following Millora (2011), qualitative studies can provide overlapping evidence to support claims about acquisition of knowledge as well as the experiences and processes that facilitate appreciation of the "other". Absence of such overlapping evidence in the interviews would bring into question the validity of the claims drawn from the statistical analyses.

A related challenge to small numbers lies in recruitment of students to participate in the study. For ethical reasons, participation in OTI cannot be contingent on participation in any study. Moreover, forced study participation might cause already divided and distrustful students representing more extreme viewpoints to avoid the group altogether. However, recruitment of as many students as possible into the study remains necessary for quantitative measures to be valid given the small N and carefully balanced participant group. While an impartial or third party researcher is often ideal for the reduction of bias, we found that a participant observer stance facilitates trust between the researcher and the participant that facilitates both participation in the student and honest reporting of sentiments. For example, students expressed being more confident that what they reported would not be taken out of context if the research was disseminated publicly and that confidentiality would be maintained because of the trusting relationship with the researchers.

Qualitative studies also pose challenges. As receiving institutional support and funding depends on showing positive results, concerns of biased interpretation of results may be raised when it is in the researchers' interest for the program to succeed. To avoid seeing change where it did not occur, we have made every attempt to be honest and critical in our assessment. We must conduct any study with a stance of wanting to find both strengths and weaknesses in order to grow and improve. Moreover, any publications will undergo peer review in academic journals, and our evaluation processes helps ensure a system of checks and balances such that measurement of success, and hence funding, does not hinge on one test, but rather on a series of markers over time.

One last note in the study of these programs must be made: as academics, results gained from these studies are not only for internal use, but also geared toward creating a shared knowledge base through publication and public dissemination of our findings. In a small and active community where participants and program leaders are known entities, several difficulties can arise: a bias toward only publishing positive results, negative feedback (and possibly withdrawn funding) if anything perceived to be negative toward a specific community is written, and fear from participants that quotes or data might be misused by the university administration or surrounding community organizations to punish student clubs or judge participants. This is a challenge specific to many educational programs—one we approach with caution. We seek to ensure that every document produced is as unbiased as possible and only shown in its final form. For example, we do not post preliminary working papers on websites or blogs. Moreover, we provide participants the opportunity to see what has been written before the public has access to the published paper to ensure they are aware of results. Finally, we use pseudonyms and follow all IRB guidelines to ensure confidentiality.

Long-Term Success

If short-term success is measured in teaching students dialogue skills, a better understanding of the other, and leadership development, how do we measure long-term outcomes? Students participate in the program for a year or two by taking classes and traveling to the region. Upon their return, students often experience in-group and community pressure simply for having engaged the "other".

They then graduate and enter the world. Do the skills students learn help them in the future? Does empathy for the "other "remain after they leave the nurturing environment of the peace education program?

Scholars have observed that once program participants leave the dialogue group and return to their communities, the effects of the program diminish or are forgotten within a few months, prompting participants to fall back into the attitudinal and behavioral norms of their community. Social pressures, in the form of mocking, questioning and marginalization, and entrenched social norms have been identified as causes of this shift (Abu-Nimer, 2004, p. 54; Schimmel, 2009). Many OTI students face internal pressures from their in-group peers and are viewed with distrust due to their participation in OTI. One challenge is therefore having students retain increased perspective taking and openness to the "other" after they leave the program or university.

We believe that they best way to preserve the benefits of this educational program is to keep students actively involved in the program even after they return or graduate. To this end, we have developed several strategies. First, we try to keep returning students involved by placing them in leadership roles in the initiative. For example, students are nominated by their peers to be OTI board members, serving as meeting, fundraising, social, or outreach chairs. In addition, returning students are also required to take the leadership and scholarship development class where they plan and carry out an outreach project related to the values of OTI. Returning students also organize events such as talks at local community and religious centers, speaker series, educational dialogues and teach-ins, mock debates, and a yearly inter-campus summit. Program alumni are also actively involved in recruitment and training of the next OTI cohort. Second, OTI has an online dialogue group that alumni can participate in from wherever they are in the world. The forum is limited to OTI participants, encouraging a continuation of open dialogue based on the shared trust and values developed through participation in OTI. Third, as alumni move on to graduate school and professional careers, we maintain an alumni network whereby past and present OTI members are made aware of professional opportunities. We also invite alumni to return to give presentations about their professional experiences and to serve as mentors to new students. Lastly, we encourage alumni to "sponsor-an-OTI-student" by making a nominal yearly contribution to help a new student travel to the region. By encouraging them to give back, the lessons of OTI, we hope, will remain.

As a relatively young program, we have not fully been able to test the program and these retention methods to garner their long-term effects. We have conducted a brief alumni survey and are in the process of developing a more detailed long-term evaluation survey. To further build longitudinal measures, we plan to conduct surveys and interviews at later intervals to gain insight into retention over time.

One strong retention indicator is found in the professional choices students who participate in OTI make after participation. Approximately one third of all OTI students have changed their majors/educational outlook to concentrate more on the Middle East and/or conflict resolution in general. Furthermore, looking at the choices of post-graduate activities of participants, we find that a majority of our forty alumni who have graduated (many participants are still students) to date stay involved in this field by either continuing with graduate studies in conflict resolution or international affairs (12), focusing on the themes related to the Middle East in other programs including law and journalism (5), starting a professional career in the Middle East or a position dealing with the Middle East (7), while others are in the application process for such programs and professional opportunities (7). In-depth follow up interviews with these alumni about how OTI shaped their professional careers and interactions in the future would provide greater insight into the long-term benefits of the program.

CONCLUSION: A WORD OF CAUTION AND LESSONS FOR THE FUTURE

The purpose of this chapter has been to present the Olive Tree Initiative as a peace education initiative and explore the challenges that emerged from attempts to evaluate it. We identified several challenges, including operationalizing success, tracking long-term success, and methodological limitations of evaluation procedures. Our findings suggest that, in the particular case of OTI, success is measured primarily on an individual level—development of dialogue skills, acquisition of nuanced knowledge or perspective taking that breaks down stereotypes, and leadership development. Finally, we provide suggestions for measuring and preserving the benefits of the initiative in the long-term.

As we look to the future, a word of caution is in order. Critics of peace education programs see in the failure of peace to emerge in the conflict region the inefficacy of peace education programs as a whole. However, it is dangerous to generalize in such a way because to do so denies the particularities and contexts of each specific program. Absent a nuanced meta-analysis of all such programs to evaluate their general effectiveness, a general condemnation is not (yet?) warranted; unless initiatives define "peace in the Middle East" as their goal, they should not be judged on this criterion. That said, education initiatives need to be very clear about their goals, and these goals need to both be theoretically grounded and mark a change from the status quo. OTI is one such initiative and we hope that this study provides some insight into the challenge of evaluating similar programs. While we do not make claims of generalizability to all such programs, we hope this chapter has provided some insight into what OTI's program leaders face so others may use this as they think about the future.

To this end, we provide key lessons for the future from our experiences with OTI. First, the evaluation process serves first and foremost as a means to improve the program by receiving feedback from participants and adjusting the program to ensure it meets stated expectations. Second, no evaluation procedures are perfect. However, employing a variety of quantitative and qualitative approaches provides for a more robust evaluation process. Third, should the results point to limitations and challenges, such evidence should not be used to undermine the value of such programs, but rather, should be seen as providing constructive criticism that can help strengthen the program and improve learning outcomes. Finally, should the results point to positive outcomes, peace program leaders should not rest on their laurels, but should continue to build off of initial successes to expand the scope and learning power of the educational experience.

REFERENCES

Abu-Nimer, M. (1999) *Dialogue, conflict resolution, and change: Arab-Jewish encounters in Israel.* Albany, NY: State University of NY Press.

Abu-Nimer, M. (2004) Education for coexistence and Arab-Jewish encounters in Israel: Potential and Challenges. *Journal of Social Issues.* 60(2), 405–22.

Al Omari, G. (2011, May 26). *The Arab Spring and its implications on the peace process.* Lecture conducted at University of California, Irvine, International Studies Public Forum.

Allport, G. W. (1954). *The nature of prejudice.* Cambridge, MA: Addison-Wesley Pub. Co.

Aron, A., Aron E. N., & Smollan, D. (1992). Inclusion of other in the self scale and the structure of interpersonal closeness. *Journal of Personality and Social Psychology.* 63(4), 596–612.

Bat-Tal, D. (2004) Nature, rationale, and effectiveness of education for coexistence. *Journal of Social Issues, 60*(2), 253–71.

Betancourt, H. (September 01, 1990). An attribution-empathy model of helping behavior: Behavioral intentions and judgments of help-giving. *Personality and Social Psychology Bulletin, 16*(3), 573–591.

Batson, C. D., Ahmad, Y. N. (2009). Using empathy to improve intergroup attitudes and relations. *Social Issues and Policy Review, 3*(1), 2009. 141–177.

Bekerman, Z. (2007) Rethinking intergroup encounters: rescuing praxis from theory, activity from education, and peace/co-existence from identity and culture. *Journal of Peace Education. 4*(1), 21–37.

Greenwald, A. G., Poehlman, T. A., Uhlmann, E., & Banaji, M. R. (2009). Understanding and using the Implicit Association Test: III. Meta-analysis of predictive validity. *Journal of Personality and Social Psychology, 97*, 17–41.

Hager, T., Saba, T., & Shay, N. (2011) Jewish Arab activism through dialogical encounters: changing an Israeli campus. *Journal of Peace Education, 8*(2), 193–211.

Halabi, R., & Sonnenshein, N. (2000). Consciousness, identity, and challenge to reality, educational approaches at the Neveh Shalom School for Peace. In A. Halabi (Eds.) *Identities in dialogue* (pp. 16–27). Tel Aviv: Hakibbutz Hameuchad Publishing House.

Helman, S. (2002). Monologic results of dialogue: Jewish-Palestinian encounter groups as sites of essentialization. *Identities, Global Studies in Culture and Power, 9*, 327–354.

Hewstone, M. (1996). Contact and categorization: Social psychological interventions to change intergroup relations. In C. N. Macrae, C. Stagor, & M. Hewstone (Eds.), *Foundations of stereotypes and stereotyping* (pp. 323–368). New York: Guilford.

Juneau, T., & Sucharov, M. (2010). Narratives in pencil: Using graphic novels to teach Israeli-Palestinian relations. *International Studies Perspectives, 11*, 172–83.

Kelman, H. C. (2005). Building trust among enemies: The central challenge for international conflict resolution. *International Journal of Intercultural Relations, 29*, 639–50.

Millora, M. L. (2011). This is how life can be different: How U.S. student experiences in international education programs facilitate civic and global engagement. *Journal of Student Affairs Research and Practice, 48*(2), 299–245.

Maoz, I., & Bar-On, D. (2002). From working through the Holocaust to current ethnic conflicts: Evaluating the TRT group workshop in Hamburg, *Group* 26(1),115–25.

Pettigrew, T. F. (1998). Intergroup contact theory. *Annual Review of Psychology, 49*, 65–85.

Schimmel, N. (2009). Towards a sustainable and holistic model of peace education: A critique of conventional modes of peace education through dialogue in Israel. *Journal of Peace Education, 6*, 51–68.

Schulz, M. (2008). Reconciliation through education—Experiences from the Israeli-Palestinian conflict. *Journal of Peace Education, 5*(1), 33–48.

Salomon, G. (2003). *The effects of participation in coexistence programs supported by the Abraham Foundation on Jewish and Arab youngsters.* Haifa, Israel: University of Haifa.

Salomon, G. (2004). A narrative based view of coexistence education. *Journal of Social Issues. 60*(2), 273–87.

Stephan, W. G., & Stephan C. W. (1996). *Intergroup relations.* Boulder, CO. Westview.

United States Institute of Peace. (n.d.). About USIP. Retrieved from: http://www.usip.org/about-us

Walter, S. G., & Paul, V. W. (2004). *Education programs for improving intergroup relations: Theory, research, and practice.* New York, Teachers College, Columbia University.

Williams, M. N., & Assay, S. M. (2003). The world as a classroom: The impact of international study experiences on college students. *College Teaching, 51*(4), 141–147.

CHAPTER 13

HOW DO WE KNOW WE ARE BUILDING PEACE?

A Reflection On What is Good Youth Peace Monitoring and Evaluation

Meghann Villanueva, Lillian Solheim,
Imke van der Velde, and Eefje van Esch[1]

INTRODUCTION

The experience of many youth workers involved in peace education is often that evaluation is perceived as something which is donor-imposed, difficult, and time consuming. Yet, it is considered that "evaluation is something that is natural for human beings. We do it all the time. We collect information, we process it, we give it a meaning and a value and we act or react according to it" (Kloosterman, Giebel & Senyuva, 2007, p. 7). Why, then, is evaluation perceived negatively by youth workers? Could there simply be different ways of evaluation taking place? There is a need for a deeper and better understanding of how youth workers evaluate their peace education activities.

[1]United Network of Young Peacebuilders (UNOY Peacebuilders)

Peace Education Evaluation: Learning from Experience and Exploring Prospects,
pages 193–205.
Copyright © 2015 by Information Age Publishing
All rights of reproduction in any form reserved.

This chapter examines and reflects on the evaluation practice of non-formal peace education initiatives, especially with regard to youth initiatives. A specific characteristic of non-formal education is the use of experiential learning, in which learning does not occur through didactic means but through the processing of one's own experience from activities initiated, and relating it to reality. Within youth organizations, this is achieved through several methods, such as peer-to-peer learning, simulations, and games. Through peer education, youth organizations are particularly instrumental in achieving successes in peace education. We can see, however, that due to the nature of these organizations and the dynamics of the youth peacebuilding field in which they operate, follow-up and evaluation is a challenging task. How do youth organizations take on monitoring and evaluation of their peace education projects? What are the challenges and the opportunities?

This article argues that although monitoring and evaluation is often seen as imposed by the donor, investing in the right monitoring and evaluation tools should result in opportunities for learning and further development. This article does not aim to create a new framework or a strategy for monitoring and evaluation of youth organizations, but highlights the challenges and ideas for further exploration for youth organizations. After providing a short introduction to why monitoring and evaluation is important for youth organizations, we consider some key challenges and realities for monitoring and evaluation of youth peace education initiatives. This section provides an overview of the challenges youth organizations face, the solutions they come up with to address these, and their ways of monitoring and evaluating. This will lead to some final conclusions and ideas for further consideration for actors in the field.

The article is based on the experience of United Network of Young Peacebuilders (UNOY), a youth peace network with over 60 member organizations worldwide, the personal experiences of the authors, and a survey done among youth workers, activists, and relevant youth organizations. In total, 34 persons responded to the questionnaire. The respondent organizations are from 22 countries, on five continents.[2]

YOUTH, PEACE, AND M&E

Youth peacebuilding organizations are important actors in educating for a Culture of Peace (Adams et al., 2010). To consider the role of young people in peacebuilding initiatives and conflict transformation means speaking of young people not only as victims or perpetrators and instigators of violence, but also (and rather) as active agents of change. Peace education is particularly important for young

---

[2] All survey respondents are members of UNOY Peacebuilders and are youth-led and youth-focused CSOs/NGOs working in the field of peacebuilding and conflict transformation on a local, national, regional, and/or international scope. These organizations are based in the following countries: Armenia, Azerbaijan, Belarus, Benin, Cameroon, DR Congo, Egypt, Eritrea, Germany, Greece, Italy, India, Kenya, Mexico, Nepal. Nigeria, Northern Ireland, Pakistan, Spain, Switzerland, Uganda, the United Kingdom, and the United States of America.

people as they have the potential to transform their societies over subsequent generations. Organizations run by youth are often better able to assess the needs and priorities of young people and to formulate and get their messages across in accessible and appealing ways. Peer pressure is a major factor in adolescent behavior and decision-making and it can also play out positively in the context of peer-to-peer learning. Youth are able to creatively think of innovative ways to bring the message of peace education to their peers—this is what makes them instrumental in promoting social transformation. By joining peace networks and initiatives, their capacities and effectiveness of actions can be increased and its multiplier effect reinforced. However, as youth organizations are often characterized by high energy and the dynamism of moving from one project to another and taking on many projects, the time to evaluate successes and build on them are sometimes overlooked.

Evaluating the impact of peacebuilding interventions in general is difficult since peacebuilding is a complex process having no common understanding and often being centered on developing quite intangible outcomes, requiring long-term monitoring rather than short-term (PricewaterhouseCoopers, 2007). For youth organizations, this poses a first particular difficulty. At times, due to lack of long-term financial and human (and sometimes institutional) resources, youth peace education projects tend to be sporadic, and too short-term to be extensively monitored and evaluated. It is this nature of youth peace projects that makes monitoring and evaluating a challenging process. Nevertheless, monitoring and evaluation of non-formal youth peace education is important. And, as we will show, monitoring and evaluation does play a key role in the projects run by youth organizations in this field in order to assess successes, challenges, and strengths, and to identify new opportunities and improvements for future endeavors.

M&E REALITIES IN YOUTH PEACE ORGANIZATIONS

In general, reasons and explanations for monitoring and evaluation do not seem to differ much between youth organizations and mainstream/regular organizations. Monitoring and evaluation as a requirement by donors is, also in the youth field, a major impetus to engage in M&E. The benefits are considered the same: to learn from the activities done and to improve future implementation and organizational capacity. Monitoring and evaluation is done to "learn from practice, to theorize practice and to improve practice."[3] According to the survey results, the reasons for monitoring and evaluation are overlapping. Notably, some youth organizations appear to make no distinction between monitoring and evaluation, for example when stating that monitoring is done to consider impact.

Most respondents, though, use monitoring to ensure that quality standards are in place and to track progress of projects with the aim of adjusting them where needed. However, it is also emphasized that monitoring is less common than eval-

---

[3] Survey respondent from Mexico.

uation—although every project is evaluated, especially short-term projects (trainings, courses, events) are not monitored. If they are, this is mostly done through daily surveys/questionnaires or reflection groups to follow through the flow of the training. We often see that youth organizations use creative group exercises and visual methods to monitor the progress and group dynamic in training courses.[4] Long-term projects are monitored because of the need for interim reports (to funders), to develop publications and to improve partnership commitments.

Evaluation in turn is done to identify gaps and learning opportunities, to reflect upon results and changes, and to review whether the implemented outcomes of the project are in line with the outlined vision, mission, and objective of the project and organization. Interestingly, many organizations point out that they evaluate and report not only for internal learning or to adhere to donor requirements, but also to disseminate their results to other stakeholders and (youth) organizations. As one respondent shares: "innovative knowledge production and learning are the primary reasons of evaluation of peacebuilding. These stocks of knowledge may help develop sound policies and best management of the limited resources. It can also be a recipe (best practice) for other countries in conflict."[5] Other rationales for evaluation focus on assessing effectiveness and efficiency of strategy and funding, and on long-term aspects of impact and sustainability.

MAIN CHALLENGES IN MONITORING AND EVALUATION

Impact and Sustainability

Just like many other NGOs, youth organizations are puzzled by the question of how to measure whether we are creating peace. The nature of peacebuilding interventions are that such projects cannot easily be quantified, and it is difficult to isolate impact in the short-term from the complex political, economic and social contexts in which they are located (Brun et al., 2009; Brusset, 2006; Fast & Neufeldt, 2005). Did we contribute to a positive change in human values, attitudes, and modes of behavior? How do we know that our efforts prevented violent conflict? Can we ever claim credit for a more social and just society?

A majority of respondents underlined and recognized the importance of impact evaluation: "and finally, the most important thing is the fact that we assess also the general impact of the project which is a sophisticated process of the assessment of the projects focused mainly on the long-term aspects and sustainability of our projects."[6] An interesting statement—have youth peacebuilding organizations found the key to measuring impact in peace? On the contrary; by the nature of youth projects, often these "demand short-term results and outcomes, rather than paying attention to reflexive evaluation" (Del Felice & Solheim, 2011, p. 1103). Indeed, as one youth worker stresses, "we get busy again with new projects

---

[4] See for examples: Kloosterman, Giebel, & Senyuva, 2007, p. 68-117.
[5] Survey respondent from Nepal.
[6] Survey respondent from Egypt.

and forget about looking into the impact of the other projects."[7] There is a rush for youth organizations driving attention away from reflexive evaluation. One respondent mentioned that "although the desired vision is peace, it is not necessarily the desired output. Peace is a very long-term goal and the indicators for deciding when peace has been achieved are very difficult to identify."[8] In general, impact evaluations are the exception rather than the norm.[9]

Human and Financial Resources

While most youth organizations are clearly aware of the importance given to impact, in practice it proves hard for youth organizations to undertake impact assessments due to constraints in finances, human resources, and skills. Finding the right indicators for the process of measuring changing behaviors and attitudes requires concrete knowledge and skills, and investing in M&E is both costly and time-consuming (Del Felice & Solheim, 2011). In addition, the existing structures and tools are often considered very technical and not easily transferrable from large programs to small youth initiatives (Brun et al., 2009).

In general, youth organizations lack the fundamental M&E experience in its human and financial resources, as underlined by a majority of the survey respondents. After all, one major attribute of youth organizations is having a workforce with limited years of work experience and qualifications. Often running on volunteers and interns and with only few paid positions, youth organizations do not have the luxury of offering paid positions to M&E experts. Instead, monitoring and evaluation comes as part of everyone's job, without a specific budget allocated to collecting the necessary data. And at times it is "unclear whose responsibility it is."[10] A particular challenge for youth organizations also lies in the high turnover of volunteers, interns, and staff. Coupling the lack of relevant knowledge and skills to the loss of institutional memory, it becomes difficult to imbed and maintain a sound monitoring and evaluation structure.

While many youth organizations are aware of these lags, it is simply the reality that they have to deal with. Sometimes youth organizations rely on project funding only, and need to make sure that by the time one activity finishes, they are already busy implementing another one to secure the sustainability of their organization. This does not leave much time for reflection and evaluation and for opportunities to learn from previous projects. In terms of sustainability of the projects we can, therefore, see a gap between policy and practice.

---

[7] Survey respondent from Spain.
[8] Survey respondent from Eritrea.
[9] As is reflected in both the survey data and the authors' experiences
[10] Survey respondent from United Kingdom.

Donor Versus Recipient Expectations

Additionally, monitoring and evaluation is also seen as something that is imposed by the donor, and hence done only under the terms as required by the donor (Brun et al., 2009). One respondent said that "one-sided donor requirements miss the specific context and need,"[11] whereas another respondent claims that "donors are only interested to check their own indicators."[12] Often, the requirements and indicators are drawn without consulting the target group and stakeholders and how best to monitor and evaluate, and does not take into account the situation and reality of youth and youth work. This contributes to donors and recipients having different expectations and perspectives; while donors try to ensure that their funds were efficiently administered and that the programs were making the intended impact, recipients of the funds often regard monitoring and evaluation as an opportunity to reflect on how to improve their work, but also sometimes as a distraction from their work. They may not see the necessity for evaluation, but will nevertheless conduct it. As a result of this lack of priority or ownership, the organization does not really learn anything from the experience. One respondent claimed that unless the "donor listens to the local implementer, the community is not empowered to run their affairs after completion of the project."[13]

The dialogue between funding institutions and youth organizations could be improved. It is felt that there are few funding institutions focusing or even only understanding youth organizations, and their specific contexts. Almost all respondents indicated that there is little appropriate support from donors when it comes to M&E. As some youth organizations believe donors impose short deadlines and strict requirements, this goes against youth organizations often being somewhat ad-hoc and unstructured—with a specific need for flexible conditions.

Strategy and Structure

The lack of resources and donor-imposed requirements is only part of the picture. A main obstacle for youth organizations is that the great majority of them are activity-oriented structures. Often, especially from the point of view of organizations, projects are well-supported during preparation and implementation, but the monitoring and evaluation phase is not given as much importance. This may be due to a lack of monitoring and evaluation structures in the organizations, as well as a lack of clear direction and strategy with regards to how and what to monitor and evaluate. Most respondents replied that M&E is done on ad-hoc or project basis, and only one indicated having an overarching "M&E Reporting and Learning Framework" in place.[14] Moreover, it shows that not all youth organizations are aware of the relation between monitoring and evaluation and strategic planning

---

[11] Survey respondent from Nepal.
[12] Survey respondent from Pakistan.
[13] Survey respondent from Pakistan.
[14] Survey respondent from Kenya.

for the entire organization. At least eight respondents mentioned they were not sure how M&E helped their organization in its strategic development, or found the question to be not applicable.

Youth peace organizations are a specific type of organization. Differing in size and structure, most have started as grassroots (activist) organizations or private initiatives, growing over time in scope and objectives. With an initial focus on hands-on social action and transformation and no direct intention to create an enterprise with a core business, for many organizations the structural development through strategy and policy formulation comes at a later stage. Twenty years down the line, UNOY Peacebuilders is still in the development phase when it comes to specific policies, such as the M&E policy that was adopted not too long ago. As action has often played a bigger role than reflection—even in the historical sense of the structural development of youth organizations—perhaps this explains why the action mentality still flourishes on the level of project cycle management. According to one respondent, "there is a challenge in planning for results and impact from the beginning of the project stage. Youth organizations should first clearly plan their activities by outlining the result-based impact or output they would like to achieve."[15]

A lack of strategic vision and/or funding sets organizations up to implement one project after another in most cases without seeing and observing the linkage between them. In the worst cases, they do not see the link between their projects. Working in that way causes trouble for the evaluation process as it becomes difficult to see what has been changed during the previous activity and how these changes might affect further projects or activities. This deprives organizations of self-evaluation, which is the most valuable tool for peace-oriented organizations to measure the effects of their projects and to try to learn lessons from their own experience and build on the results achieved.

Another reason is brought about by the lack of sufficient time and commitment to implement M&E measures within the duration of the project itself. The lack of commitment is often extended to the target group and participants, and some organizations report that it is difficult to make evaluation interesting and exciting for participants, getting youth to fill out surveys and questionnaires in a reflective manner.

CONSCIOUS AND UNCONSCIOUS: YOUTH M&E PROCESSES

As seen above, a number of external and internal challenges make monitoring and evaluation a challenging and often ignored task and process. Current monitoring and evaluation tools and techniques are often not well suited for evaluation of non-formal peace education by and for young people. However, despite the various challenges and the lack of structured monitoring and evaluation, it is also in our experience that young people do reflect on the effect of their work. This happens in both a planned and an ad-hoc manner. Consciously or unconsciously, youth organizations learn from their projects. In other words, there is learning and

---

[15] Survey respondent from Eritrea.

evaluation taking place, individually and as a group, even if this is not part of a conscious or structured process.

Unstructured learning processes are vital for youth organizations. Many youth organizations are learning by doing. The main issue is that these processes are less visible, less well documented, and less likely to be considered as proper monitoring and evaluation. Yet monitoring and evaluation is quite natural in youth projects, and those characteristics identified as challenging contexts for youth organizations also hold major benefits and are simultaneously its strengths. Yes, youth organizations are often unstructured. But this also means that they are flexible, tending to adjust easily to changing contexts. The process by which this is done, however, is perhaps not clearly recognized by youth organizations themselves as monitoring. As youth organizations often face many challenges, they are almost inherently sharp and constantly adapting. The youthful target groups, their audience, are often not afraid of giving constructive criticism. High staff turnover means a lot of fresh ideas and innovation. There is no time to develop tunnel vision.

For example, being confronted with often tight budgets and little room to maneuver inherently requires close financial monitoring. Youth projects are often implemented with no frills, and in terms of efficiency, many adult-led organizations could learn from youth organizations' capabilities to creatively search for effective alternatives. In the eyes of youth organizations themselves, however, this efficient implementation and close monitoring of a budget derives from a given situation, and not an externally formulated desire or rationale to be more efficient. Likewise, as many youth organizations collaborate in projects, there is a mutual dependency and shared responsibility. Many contact moments are necessary in this situation where reflecting on the process is common.

Finally, using non-formal education methodologies means giving ownership to participants and actively listening and adjusting projects to their needs. Based on informal talks and daily moments for reflection, many youth organizations will recognize how they adjusted projects last-minute or during the project to better connect with participants' needs. Because this comes so innately for youth organizations, they are not likely to qualify it as proper monitoring and evaluation, believing there must be much more to it.

TOOLS IN DEVELOPMENT

Most respondents indicate that they use common methods for monitoring and evaluation focusing on qualitative aspects. Oral reports through staff meetings, face-to-face meetings, and field visits are most preferred. This, again, is a less visible method than the mid-term or end reports, which are less mentioned. Two respondents[16] mentioned the use of logical frameworks. Interestingly, some respondents are very much involved in new media and artistic tools, such as monitoring through online tools (e.g., Google forms), or arts, games, and exercises for evaluation and video/

---

[16] Survey respondents from Nepal and Nigeria.

photography as the main reporting method. In addition, the more regular forms of reporting are often accompanied by a bottom-up participatory approach; some respondents mentioned having informal talks with the community, organizing focus group discussions, and mapping qualitative experiences of participants as key in their monitoring and evaluation. Lastly, while one respondent uses good practices as case studies in their reports to donors, another respondent is actively using "most significant change stories to monitor and evaluate the changes that have occurred."[17] This means that they use less standardized methods in which indicators have been set a-priori, and are much more focused on the process of the projects that they undertake. This makes sense, as non-formal education is much often more focused on behavior and values than on fixed results.

Also, we have seen that youth organizations sometimes develop their own tools for monitoring and evaluation. For instance, UNOY Peacebuilders developed a short and concise evaluation toolkit[18] in order to "develop youth-specific criteria for evaluation, as the available evaluation toolbox seemed to be inadequate" (Del Felice & Solheim, 2011, p. 1101), while another respondent mentioned their development of an "Advocacy Progression Index and Results Framework", tracking their own results. Interestingly enough, this is the same respondent from Kenya that has an official M&E strategy in place. Other respondents use simpler existing methods like a problem tree analysis, SMART-objectives, and/or a context analysis as methods for planning and reviewing these for their monitoring and evaluation processes. One respondent uses the GANNT chart[19] to keep track of progress. However, while these examples show youth responding to the evaluation challenge with their own tools and answers rather than being driven only by external demands, this seems rather exceptional. Additionally, as long as youth organizations value M&E as something externally-driven and too complex for their levels of knowledge and skills, this will remain exceptional.

GOOD PRACTICES

In order not to simply count the number of projects or look for the long-term impact of the work, it has also proved useful to look at the personal and team elements as well as the social context of a project, and to assess whether the personal motivation, the organization, and the context are aligned with the principles and mission of the organization (Del Felice & Chludova, 2005). As youth organizations try to achieve peace through behavioral change and awareness, we should acknowledge that youth peace organizations are not only creating peace externally through their educational projects. Educational activities give reciprocal shape to values, attitudes, and behavior, of all youth involved. In that aspect, youth organi-

---

[17] Survey respondents from Nigeria.

[18] See Del Felice & Chludova (2005).

[19] Survey respondent from Italy. GANNT is a project management tool which illustrates the different phases and the work breakdown structure of a project.

zations are often schools in democracy, providing relevant skills and awareness to the volunteers and interns while creating social capital. This accounts for a major benefit and good practice of youth organizations: not only are youth organizations educational implementers, but they are also their own target audience, changing attitudes and beliefs and building the skills of youth workers themselves.

The above insight is not consciously present within youth organizations. Looking at good practices as identified by the respondents, it is surprising that fifteen organizations felt they had no good practices to share, either due to a mere absence of examples or to modesty. Others share how monitoring in general led to identification of problems and adjustments of projects. However, from all data gathered, some other good practices or recipes for good practices can be distilled, even if not being identified by the owners as such.

Relating to the above analysis aiming to look at team elements and social contexts, it seems that some youth organizations are aware of the potential of using M&E for human resource matters, as respondents mentioned occasions in which M&E led to the identification of training needs of staff and volunteers. It seems, however, that there are no M&E-structures in place to monitor and evaluate the acquired knowledge of the organization's human capital in the sense of youth organizations being schools of democracy for staff itself.

Two respondents describe how it must be ensured that all those who are impacted by projects and who could provide an impact to make projects a success should have a chance to voice their opinions and evaluations in M&E.[20] And as analyzed before, indeed many youth organizations do employ participatory approaches to their M&E. In addition, two other respondents describe how a comprehensive (and mixed-methods) approach will contribute to good practices in M&E—using a combination of storytelling, tally sheets, checklists, client cards, evaluation forms, discussion sessions, follow-up interviews, and so on.[21]

Another respondent mentioned how receiving training on M&E actually provided momentum for reflecting upon their own M&E system, making the youth organization see the importance of participatory methods, as he states: "Yes, initially before my training…I thought that the tools of just collecting data was enough. But not until my training on using problem tree analysis and focus group discussions, so since recently all these tools are always used whenever I am monitoring a project.[22] He then continues to explain how this has been "a tremendous experience…and the more I use the tools, the more exciting it is to me to do more."

IDEAS FOR DEVELOPMENT

The last example brings us to one of the ideas for development. It is essential that youth organizations have access to appropriate training, specifically suited to the needs and concerns of youth organizations. However, budget constraints

---

[20] Survey respondents from Belarus and Northern Ireland.
[21] Survey respondents from Nigeria and DR Congo.
[22] Survey respondent from Nigeria.

often limit the possibilities for real-life training. In this case, it is valuable to look at other alternatives and forms, e.g. an online/distance learning platform, or through the development of a comprehensive but concise M&E toolkit tailored to youth organizations. Using existing networks such as UNOY Peacebuilders as a platform for the exchange of knowledge and good practices will help youth organizations learn from each other and develop their own M&E structures and strategies accordingly. Moreover, in networks and especially through projects in partnerships, we create opportunities to learn from each other, to transfer skills, and exchange experiences in this area.

Additionally, it is important for youth organizations to consciously consider how a monitoring and evaluation strategy serves their organization. Some respondents outlined how the board is involved in overall M&E of the organization, while another respondent mentioned how they have an M&E Committee concerned with overseeing all sporadic efforts.[23] It is such bodies that could not only develop a strategy, but also begin translating policy into practice—and it is the practice where most youth organizations have their difficulties. When aiming to develop a policy and framework for monitoring and evaluation, it is important to keep it as simple as possible. If you have limited resources, chose to evaluate a few crucial things rather than trying to evaluate everything. Consider what you want to achieve from your efforts and chose the tools accordingly. Youth organizations often have a high turnover and hence a need for structures in place to evaluate, document the outcomes, and create organizations conducive to learning. However, it is important that these structures and systems set in place do not become too overwhelming.

It is similarly important that M&E loses its stigma of being a bureaucratic and boring burden. Youth organizations should start a dialogue with their funding organizations to discuss what each of them wants from the project and how to assess this. We recommend letting youth organizations adjust the M&E strategy to better fit the nature of their projects and to develop these in dialogue with the donor, while simultaneously acknowledging the necessity for youth organizations to understand the importance of sound monitoring and evaluation. Both donors and youth organizations can formulate M&E requirements in ways that are more interesting to youth and more suited to the needs of the youth organization. As one respondent suggested: "for example, they can propose activities that would be interesting for youth to do and through which they would be performing monitoring and evaluation under a different name without even knowing it."[24] Close to this is the need for youth organizations to realize that they are already undertaking M&E activities that should be defined as such, and that M&E is an integral part of the whole project cycle. Still, it should be remembered that the focus lies on the change process and that M&E is only a means to an end.

As mentioned earlier, youth organizations fill not only a role in implementing peace education projects. Youth organizations themselves are, in a way, important

[23] Survey respondent from the United Kingdom.
[24] Survey respondent from Armenia.

schools of peace where young people learn democratic principles, participation, and civic engagement. Youth are the champions of participatory education, which also means veering away from the traditional indoctrination style of education and instead, encouraging youth to contribute to the development of knowledge, skills, and attitudes necessary for democratic citizenship (Harris & Morrison, 2003). This is an aspect often overlooked, and youth organizations should look at the role they have in this, and how they can use this knowledge and position to their benefit.

CONCLUSIONS

Youth peace work is a way of evolving and learning. Youth organizations—although their M&E strategy or efforts may sometimes be scattered—have a valuable place in peace education efforts. Evaluation can help to form "good practices" for other organizations, although every project and every situation will be different. As for any other organization, it is important to review and see what is really achieved compared with expected outcomes. It can help to learn lessons and develop good strategies. It can help to enhance organizations' performance and can help to prioritize wisely. Evaluation and monitoring can raise the responsibility of project staff members and participants to increase quality, thereby enhancing organizations' performance. It helps to become holistic, more flexible, and reliable.

As for the role of UNOY Peacebuilders, we will continue to strengthen the network and to work on M&E. Many of the survey respondents mentioned a lack of specialists and experienced people who can support them in their monitoring and evaluation. The network could solve this issue and provide links between the member organizations so they can, for instance, express their need to the network for a specialist and ask for support from within the network. It is also important to continue sharing experiences and good practices.

Finally, there is no blueprint for evaluation and monitoring in youth peace work organizations and we should not try to aim for one. Youth peacebuilding initiatives in themselves are also not always straightforward and do not have a blueprint that can be transferred from one reality to another. Hence, one of the key recommendations is to formulate a flexible monitoring and evaluation strategy that supports and enables the organization to reach its goal and objectives through their project cycle management, instead of an overly technical and static piece that does not do justice to the type of work and scope of youth organizations.

ACKNOWLEDGMENTS

Thanks to Sybylla Anderson for working on the concept note of this chapter, and to Edgar Khachatryan and Ana Afonso for valuable resources. Thanks to Matilda Flemming for valuable input. Finally, we highly appreciate the respondents/ UNOY members who participated in our survey.

REFERENCES

Adams, D., Estrada, M., Barbeito, C., Delfin, N., Jani, S., Jinadasa, H., Ospina, J., Rizzi Carlson, O., Roitenburd, M., Solheim, L., & Villanueva, M. (2010). *Report on the decade for a culture of peace: Final civil society report on the united nations international decade for a culture of peace and non-violence for the children of the world (2001–2010).* Retrieved from http://escolapau.uab.cat/img/programas/cultura/mundiali.pdf

Brun, S., Cseke, B., Forges, O., Shahnazaryan, L., Solheim, L., & Tanase, A. (2009). *Partners for peace. A toolkit for setting up European Youth Peace Projects in partnership.* The Hague: UNOY Peacebuilders.

Brusset, E. (2006). *Literature overview of evaluation tools for conflict prevention,* Londonderry: INCORE.

Del Felice, C., & Chludova, L. (2005). *What is good youth peace work? A Guide to evaluation.* The Hague: UNOY Peacebuilders.

Del Felice, C., & Solheim, L. (2011). Youth organizations as learning organizations: exploring special contributions and challenges. *Development in Practice, 21*(8), 1094–1108.

Fast, L., & Neufeldt, R. (2005). Envisioning success: Building blocks for strategic and peace-building impact evaluation. *Journal of Peace-Building and Development, 2*(2), 24–41.

Harris, I. M., & Morrison, M. L. (2003). *Peace education* (2nd ed.). Jefferson, NC, & London, UK: McFarland & Company, Inc., Publishers.

Kloosterman, P., Giebel, K., & Senyuva, O. (2007). *Educational evaluation in youth field* (T-Kit 10). Strasbourg: Council of Europe. Retrieved from http://youth-partnership-eu.coe.int/youth-partnership/publications/T-kits/10/Tkit_10_EN

PricewaterhouseCoopers. (2007). *A monitoring and evaluation framework for peacebuilding* (Special EU Programmes Body). UK: PricewaterhouseCoopers LLP. Retrieved from http://www.seupb.eu/Libraries/PEACE_Programme_Evaluations/PWC.sflb.ashx

EVALUATING PEACE EDUCATION PROGRAMS: QUANTIFYING ATTITUDINAL AND BEHAVIORAL CHANGE

Lessons Learned from the Youth Theater for Peace Programs

Susan Armitage

It is better to see once than to hear a hundred times.

—*Focus group discussant, Kyrgyzstan*

INTRODUCTION

The United Nations defines peace education as education "directed to the full development of the human personality and to the strengthening of respect for human rights and fundamental freedoms." It promotes "understanding, tolerance and friendship among all nations, racial or religious groups" (Article 26, Universal Declaration of Human Rights) (UN, 2000). This understanding of peace

Peace Education Evaluation: Learning from Experience and Exploring Prospects,
pages 207–221.
Copyright © 2015 by Information Age Publishing
All rights of reproduction in any form reserved.

education implies an end goal of fostering lasting change in individual attitudes and behaviors around conflict and diversity. Yet accurately measuring the degree of this change remains a daunting task for many practitioners who need reliable data to improve their own programs and justify their work to donors. Peace educators can cite numerous examples of impact, but making the leap from anecdotes to quantifiable data is a major challenge for the field.

While it is easy to count the number of people trained or educational manuals distributed by a program, the "full development of the human personality" occurs over an individual's entire lifespan, and any peace education intervention is time-limited. This challenge is particularly relevant for peace education programs that target youth. Young people are growing and changing, developing a system of personal values that continues to evolve over time in response to experience. Thus, the full impact of a peace education intervention may not be visible until years later when students have had a chance to test transformed ideas and approaches in the context of lived realities. However, donor funding mechanisms rarely support longitudinal evaluation after activity completion. Even when a study can be done, it is difficult not only to locate program participants, but also to assign attribution to a specific peace education intervention.

Capturing accurate baseline data on participants' attitudes is another central challenge to evaluating peace education programs. Despite the reality of conflict, peace and tolerance are widely held values in cultures around the world. Thus, self-reporting bias can cloud data; one can assume that few individuals would be inclined to report their own prejudiced thinking, even if they do recognize it as such. Participants' desire to give the "right" answers on a survey can inflate baseline results, especially among youth beneficiaries and in cultures with a deeply held sense of respect for authority. An overly positive baseline can result in false negative change reported after the intervention, when participants have in fact developed perspective and a sense of trust that allows them to comment more honestly.

This chapter will discuss learning from IREX's Youth Theater for Peace programs in Central Asia, that, through a highly participatory peace education methodology, promote conflict prevention among young people, educators, and other youth-serving adults. Youth in conflict prevention programs are often framed in the context of their vulnerability as potential instigators or victims of violence. Yet through effective peace education, youth may undergo a transformative experience that empowers them to serve as leaders and ambassadors for peace within their families, schools, and communities. This chapter relates IREX's practical experience in quantifying the effects of this potentially transformative experience.

CENTRAL ASIAN CONTEXT

The Youth Theater for Peace (YTP) programs in Tajikistan and Kyrgyzstan work to promote sustainable conflict prevention at the community level using a participatory theater methodology called Drama for Conflict Transformation. IREX designed the YTP model in response to USAID's request for people-to-people approaches that create opportunities for contact and exchange between adversarial groups and has implemented the programs since 2010 in collaboration with local NGO partners. Kyrgyzstan and Tajikistan became independent from the Soviet Union in 1991 and have suffered from conflict since transitioning into sovereignty. Both countries have large youth populations that are increasingly removed from economic and educational opportunity, have few positive extracurricular outlets, and are at risk of becoming involved in violence.

Kyrgyzstan: Following the April 2010 revolution in which former President Kurmanbek Bakiyev was ousted amidst protests and violence, southern Kyrgyzstan erupted into brutal ethnic conflict that took hundreds of lives. Kyrgyz citizens are deeply bruised and ever more reluctant to engage with those of different ethnic backgrounds (Trautman, 2011). In addition to the outflow of young men seeking work abroad, internal migration of ethnic Kyrgyz escaping the poverty and instability of the south continues to disrupt the demographics of already-settled communities in the northern provinces. Disputes that begin over resources, land use, employer relations, and crime frequently escalate along ethnic lines and are rebranded and perpetuated as such.

Peace education has the potential to play a key role in mitigating the effects of the conflict on youth and building an enduring culture of peace. Nearly 70% of youth report fear, dissatisfaction, or apathy about the future as the prevailing attitudes in society (UNDP, 2010, p. 20). The high prevalence of labor migration means many youth are being raised by extended family members while their parents work abroad. In this vacuum of identity, security, and opportunity, young people—especially boys—are easy targets for violent criminal and extremist groups. Yet youth remain highly concerned about security in their country, ranking "peace" as their second most valued concept, a unique result among Kyrgyzstan's more stable neighbors (UNDP, 2010, p. 20).

Tajikistan: Long the poorest of the former Soviet republics, Tajikistan has been labeled a country at risk of becoming a failed state, with potentially violent consequences that could destabilize the entire region (International Crisis Group, 2009). Root causes of conflict in Tajikistan include economic, resource, and border issues, which are complicated by ethnic and religious differences. While the country has made some economic strides over the past several years, 53% of the population still lives below the poverty line and 17% below the extreme poverty line (World Bank, 2009). The brutal civil war from 1992 to 1997 ravaged the country's already inadequate infrastructure, with particular aftereffects for rural populations. Such challenging economic conditions can inflame even modest undercurrents of ethnic tension, as individuals and communities seek to blame those viewed as "other" for their plight. Dependent on outdated and deteriorating irrigation systems, farmers on either side of the border between Tajikistan and Kyrgyzstan point fingers at each other over water shortages (EurasiaNet, 2009). Tajikistan's southern Khatlon region also faces a complex set of challenges, including residual animosities from the war; long, largely unpatrolled borders with Afghanistan; ethnic tensions; and risk of conflict between entrenched regional groups.

As in Kyrgyzstan, labor migration affects a large number of families in Tajikistan, weakening the connections between youth and their parents. In many rural areas, enrollment declines in the final years of secondary school; many girls drop out to get married after the 9th or 10th grades, while boys join a continuous flow of Tajik labor migrants to Russia. In contrast to the relative openness IREX has experienced in Kyrgyzstan, the government of Tajikistan is reluctant to acknowledge the presence of or potential for conflict in the country. To operate effectively in Tajikistan, IREX framed its program in the wider context of youth development and community issues and did not promote YTP locally as a conflict prevention program.

DRAMA FOR CONFLICT TRANSFORMATION AS A PEACE EDUCATION METHODOLOGY

Theater is a form of knowledge; it should and can also be a means of transforming society. Theater can help us build our future, instead of just waiting for it.

—*Augusto Boal, Games for Actors and Non-Actors (p. 16)*

Drama for Conflict Transformation (DCT) is a unique people-to-people approach to peace education. DCT establishes a safe space to allow members of conflicting groups to break down barriers through personal contact and build strong personal relationships; provides people with tools to identify and address issues of mutual concern, establishing common ground for cooperation and coexistence; and provides a vehicle for individuals to serve as peace promoters, advocating for a culture of peace.

DCT is a flexible set of tools that unlock the creative power of individuals and communities to adopt new perspectives around conflict and develop novel solutions. IREX's approach draws on the work of Dr. Augusto Boal, a Nobel Peace Prize-nominated Brazilian director, activist, and educator who pioneered the Theater of the Oppressed methodology, and adds elements of Playback Theater, developed by Jonathan Fox and Jo Salas, as well as Michael Rohd's Hope is Vital methodology. IREX has applied the Youth Theater for Peace model in the diverse settings of Tajikistan, Kyrgyzstan, Indonesia, and Kenya to create a framework for exploring local conflict dynamics. Since the content depends entirely on the life experience of participants, DCT can address many types of conflict, from ethnic and religious to resource-based.[1]

---

[1] Under the current YTP project, play topics include: ethnic/regional conflict; school fights/bullying; racketeering; family problems/domestic violence; crime; gender issues, and suicide.

> **Example Forum Theater Play:** A teenage girl wins a scholarship to continue her education. Her father supports her, but her stepmother and stepbrother vehemently oppose further study. The stepmother arranges the girl's marriage to a wealthy man without consulting the bride-to-be or her father. Given the tough economic circumstances, the father decides not to stop the betrothal. After the wedding, the girl is forced to abandon her educational goals and accept an unhappy existence ridden by physical abuse from her new mother-in-law.
>
> BOX 14.1.

A key theme of the DCT approach is what Boal described as the "rehearsal for reality" (Boal, 2002, p. 48). DCT provides an arena where participants can act out and practice peace-promoting behaviors, which they internalize and apply to their daily lives. The crux of the methodology is Forum Theater, in which a group of actors create a play based on a real-life conflict issue. The play is structured to end on an unresolved note of conflict, and should possess in its cast at least one potential ally for the protagonist, as well as multiple "turning points" where an individual character's actions could change the outcome of the scenario. The play is performed once in its original form; next, a trained facilitator, the Joker, prompts the audience to consider the events that they have just seen on stage. The play is then repeated from the beginning, but the audience members are invited to demonstrate their ideas for preventing or resolving the conflict by making an "intervention" in the performance. This process is facilitated by the Joker, who invites the audience to yell "Stop!" to signal the moment in which they want to intervene. Once "Stop!" has been called, the actors freeze and the Joker guides the audience member onstage to replace a chosen character, then restarts the action. Following each intervention, the Joker facilitates a discussion to analyze the impact of the demonstrated action—positive or negative—and whether or not it is represents a realistic option. IREX's Youth Theater for Peace model promotes sustainable conflict prevention by achieving the following objectives:

1. Youth-serving professionals develop skills and attitudes to engage youth in DCT.
   - Training of Trainers: IREX trains educators and others doing youth work to facilitate the DCT methodology by first experiencing it as "players."
2. A cadre of youth from adversarial groups is mobilized and empowered to share DCT with the larger community.
   - Youth Camps: The adult mentors trained at the TOT implement the methodology with youth at intensive DCT summer camps, with support from a DCT expert.
   - Theater Tours: Participants form theater groups and Drama Clubs following the summer camps and take their performances on the road, sparking dialogue about local conflict issues.

> Before we came to the Youth Theater for Peace camp, if someone said there is a problem in society we thought it was not our job, but now our worldview has changed. Everything is in our hands.
>
> —*Youth participant, Kyrgyzstan*

BOX 14.2.

3. Trained program participants institutionalize DCT methodologies in their schools, NGOs, workplaces, and other institutions.
   - Sustainability Workshop and Grants: IREX provides seed funding, capacity-building training, and ongoing coaching to promote the sustainability of participants' DCT projects.

The Youth Theater for Peace model operates using the following theory of change: *If the participants change their attitudes and behaviors through DCT training and if they engage others in constructive dialogue about conflict issues, then audience members will change their attitudes and behaviors and promote peace more broadly.* To test this theory of change and evaluate the effects of the programs in Central Asia, IREX has created a monitoring and evaluation (M&E) system. The indicators and data collection tools are designed to measure impact beyond basic output tracking, such as the number of audience members and performances staged.

IREX's key indicators for the YTP program include increases in empathy for members of 'other' groups, in the ability to speak openly and in a balanced way about conflict issues,[2] and in an individual's sense of personal agency to positively affect conflict situations. The latter is particularly relevant in Central Asia, where the legacy of Soviet rule has contributed to pervasive feelings of individual powerlessness. As an adult participant noted in a focus group in Tajikistan, "Our performances opened people's eyes in the communities we visited. People realized that waiting for somebody to solve their problems doesn't make sense anymore. They should think about and find solutions to their problems on their own."

EVALUATION METHODOLOGY

IREX's Performance Monitoring and Evaluation Plan (PMEP) for Youth Theater for Peace established indicators for each program objective, targets for each indicator, and a protocol and timeline for data collection. The IREX Senior Program Officer, M&E Program Officer, and Deputy Director in Washington, DC, developed the evaluation tools in collaboration with the independent M&E con-

---

[2] Speaking about conflict in an *open* and *balanced* way is defined with the following rubric: s/he can: explain his/her opinion on the local causes of conflict in a logical and calm manner; speak in a fair and calm way about members of other ethnic, religious, or regional groups; does not use stereotypes or inflammatory language; speaks knowledgably about both sides of the issue; is comfortable with critiques of his/her opinions.

TABLE 14.1

Tool	Target Group	Completed By	Collection Schedule
Baseline survey	Adult participants (mentors)	Participants	Beginning of TOT
Post-TOT survey	Adult participants (mentors)	Participants	End of TOT
Assessment of TOT participants' knowledge, skills, and attitudes	Adult participants (mentors)	DCT experts	End of TOT
Baseline survey	Youth camp participants	Participants	Beginning of youth camp
Post-camp survey	Youth camp participants	Participants	End of youth camp
Assessment of youth camp participants' knowledge, skills, and attitudes	Youth camp participants	Adult participants (mentors)	End of youth camp
Forum Theater performance monitoring report forms	Output monitoring	IREX/partner NGO staff (or adult participants, if staff were unable to attend a performance)	Ongoing throughout Theater Tours and Sustainability Grants
Orally-administered final survey	Youth/adult program participants and a comparison group of demographically similar non-participants	Independent evaluator and partner NGO staff (with training and oversight by independent evaluator)	Final evaluation (September-October 2011)
Focus group discussions	Community members who attended Forum Theater performances	Independent evaluator and partner NGO staff (with training and oversight by independent evaluator)	Final evaluation (September-October 2011)
Semi-structured interviews	Key informants (community leaders and local officials, sustainability project leaders, adult program participants)	Independent evaluator and partner NGO staff (with training and oversight by independent evaluator) Final evaluation (September-October 2011)	
Participatory self-assessment exercise	IREX's NGO partners	Independent evaluator	Final evaluation (September-October 2011)

sulting firm Social Impact. The Senior Program Officer oversaw the data collection conducted by IREX field staff and partners in Tajikistan and Kyrgyzstan and coordinated data analysis and reporting to USAID. The final program evaluation was designed and conducted by Vadim Nigmatov, an independent evaluation consultant based in Tajikistan.

An overview of the major data collection tools used is provided in Table 14.1. The pre—and post-event surveys and the tools used in the final evaluation provide the most substantive assessments of attitudinal and behavioral change.

Pre- and Post-Event Surveys: IREX's pre—and post-event surveys asked participants to rate their level of agreement with several statements using a Likert scale,[3] such as "I have more confidence in my ability to positively affect conflict situations" and "I am able to speak more openly and in a balanced way about the conflicts in my community." Participants were also asked to respond to other statements on a yes/no basis, such as "Now, I can have better conversations with people of other ethnicities, religions, or nationalities." The survey findings suggest the DCT camps had a positive effect on participants:

- 94% of youth reported *increased personal agency* in conflict situations following the DCT training.
- 90% of youth also reported they *could speak more openly and in a more balanced way* about conflict issues following the camp, and 91% of these youth were assessed by their local adult mentors as able to do so.
- 85% of youth reported *increased empathy for 'other' groups.* (To measure empathy, participants were asked if they had gained more understanding of the situation, feelings, motives, and ideas of people of other ethnicities, religions, or national origins.)
- 88% of youth reported *more positive interactions with those from other ethnic or religious backgrounds.*

It is important to note that these increases were reported by participants who were asked to reflect on change in their own attitudes following the event. However, a comparison of the baseline and post-event data for questions such as "With my help, adults and community leaders can find effective and peaceful solutions to problems in my district," actually indicated a slight decrease in personal agency for participants from Tajikistan. Meanwhile, participant interviews reflected the opposite: "Being involved in YTP made me believe that I can work with people of different nationalities and I can undertake bigger responsibility," an adult mentor commented. "When I joined the program, my relationship changed with people around me," a youth participant shared. "I gained lots of confidence and people around me became confident in my ability to widen my knowledge and share it with my peers. I started to be a goal oriented person and I see that I am capable to achieve my goals that I set up for myself."

This unexpected decrease likely reflects an inflated baseline; participants' responses implied they felt a great deal of personal agency, since they sensed this was the 'right' answer. Program staff also noted that many youth participants had difficulty completing the pre—and post—event surveys and that the purpose of the data collection was not clear. While the data collection team did state that the

---

[3] Options included *strongly agree; agree; undecided; disagree; strongly disagree.*

surveys were anonymous, participants could answer however they wanted, and the information would be used to improve the program, these explanations do not always resonate in an environment like Tajikistan, where the government tightly controls narratives of conflict.

To increase the accuracy of baseline data in future programs, IREX will consider piloting surveys with a smaller, demographically similar group to refine wording before collection begins, as well as reducing the length of program surveys and tailoring the survey language more specifically to youth.

Final Evaluation

The findings of the pre—and post-event surveys, as well as anecdotal observations and statements gathered throughout program implementation, indicated changes in participants' attitudes and behaviors. To further assess the program's performance and progress towards its goal and objectives, IREX hired an independent evaluator to investigate the following research questions:

- To what extent has YTP accomplished its stated goals and objectives? What factors have contributed to or prevented success?
- What effects has YTP had on target youth, institutions, and communities?
- What effects has the YTP program had on the capacity of IREX's partner organizations to conduct effective conflict prevention programs and engage youth in conflict transformation?

The evaluation utilized a variety of tools to assess, verify, and triangulate information from participants, audience members throughout the community, local partners, project staff, and other stakeholders.

Participant and Comparison Group Survey

To determine if changes in attitudes and behaviors could be attributed to the program, the evaluator used a quasi-experimental design to compare program participants with a demographically similar group of non-participants (hereafter referred to as the "comparison group"). The primary tool was an orally-administered survey given to participants and the comparison group. "The survey was designed to assess and compare attitudes and behaviors of program participants and the comparison group towards conflict issues and towards those of other ethnicities, religions, and nationalities, to assess abilities and confidence in having a positive impact on solving community and interpersonal conflicts in a peaceful manner, and to evaluate abilities and confidence in speaking in front of groups of people and community leaders," the evaluator noted in his report (Nigmatov, 2011, p. 7). "In addition, the survey intended to evaluate if the DCT methodology had any effects on program participants in regard to positive changes in their communications and interactions with those of other ethnicities, religions, and nationalities. The questionnaires included a number of open and closed-ended questions.

Sampling Methodology

Tajikistan:
59 program participants
59 comparison group
Kyrgyzstan:
60 program participants
60 comparison group
Total respondents: 238

BOX 14.3.

For most of the questions, respondents were asked to rate the level to which they agreed with a number of statements. The questions were formulated in a way which best allowed data to feed into YTP program progress indicators" (Nigmatov, 2011, p. 7).

Key Findings

Participants reported higher levels of confidence, personal agency, and empathy, and more positive interactions with people of other ethnic, religious, or national origins, in contrast to their comparison group counterparts:

- 100% of program participants in Tajikistan and Kyrgyzstan reported being very confident or confident in their ability to help resolve interpersonal disagreements or conflicts in a peaceful way, compared to approximately 37% in Tajikistan and 55% in Kyrgyzstan of comparison groups.
- Nearly 98% of program participants in both countries responded being confident in positively affecting any conflict situation in their community, compared to about 15% of comparison group respondents in Tajikistan and 31% in Kyrgyzstan.
- 100% of participants in Tajikistan and about 98% in Kyrgyzstan reported being able to communicate well with people of other ethnicities, religious groups, or nationalities, compared to 44% of the comparison group in Tajikistan and about 81% of the comparison group in Kyrgyzstan.
- 100% of program participants in Tajikistan and 98% in Kyrgyzstan reported having better conversation, friendship, and trust with people of other ethnicities, religions, and nationalities. Almost all of the respondents claimed that the changes in their empathy towards and interactions with those of other groups were incited by their participation in YTP program.
- Approximately 90% of program participants in Tajikistan and Kyrgyzstan reported confidence in speaking in front of large audiences (25+ people), compared to about 10% of the comparison group in Tajikistan and 17% in Kyrgyzstan.
- About 83% of program participants in Kyrgyzstan and 81% in Tajikistan reported feeling confident while speaking in front of governmental officials or community leaders, as opposed to 15.5% of the comparison group in Kyrgyzstan and 8.5% in Tajikistan.

The evaluator noted that while participants in Kyrgyzstan and Tajikistan displayed nearly identical results, the comparison group in Kyrgyzstan displayed generally higher levels of confidence, personal agency, and empathy than the comparison group in Tajikistan. This may be reflective of different political and socio-economic conditions and levels of openness in the two societies.

Limitations

The evaluator acknowledged the possibility of selection bias, noting that since participants had taken initiative to become involved in YTP, it was likely they would have started the program with 'better' attitudes and behaviors around conflict and tolerance issues. To address this limitation, he noted that the survey asked program participants to state whether or not their program participation was the primary reason for the reported attitudinal or behavioral change. In addition, the multi-lingual environment of some communities presented a challenge; where respondents spoke Uzbek or Kyrgyz, surveys were conducted with the help of translator, which could influence results. Finally, staff of IREX's partner NGOs served as survey enumerators in some cases, which may have inherently encouraged the participants to talk about the programs' effects more favorably. However, the decision was made to involve partner staff in order to build their evaluation capacity, and because they had already gained the trust of participants and community members; this provided the evaluation team with greater access to subjects for data collection and may have also yielded more open responses.

Audience Member Focus Groups and Semi-Structured Interviews with Key Informants

The evaluation also included focus group discussions with adult and youth community members who had attended Forum Theater performances staged by YTP participants, but were not involved directly in the program's DCT training events. The focus groups were conducted by the evaluator and staff of IREX's partner organizations, who were trained to use a structured focus group guide with key questions. The evaluator accompanied and provided oversight to partner staff implementing the focus groups in order to verify the quality of their data collec-

---

Focus Group Sampling Methodology

Tajikistan:
12 focus groups
81 discussants
Kyrgyzstan:
12 focus groups
79 discussants
Total focus groups: 24
Total discussants: 160

BOX 14.4.

Interview Sampling Methodology

Tajikistan:
9 community leaders
7 sustainability project leaders
Kyrgyzstan:
6+ community leaders
sustainability project leaders
Total key informants interviewed: 29

BOX 14.5.

tion. The goal of including partners in implementing the evaluation was to build their capacity to evaluate their own peace education programs in the future.

In order to further evaluate YTP program impact on community members and schools where Drama Clubs were established, the evaluation team also conducted key informant interviews with relevant community leaders (local authorities and school principals in the target schools where Drama Clubs were formed). Semi-structured interviews with randomly selected leaders of sustainability grant projects were also conducted with the goal of evaluating YTP's effects on 'secondary beneficiaries,' the new program participants trained by direct YTP participants who attended the TOT and camps.

Key Findings

Based on an analysis of findings from the focus groups, the evaluator concluded that YTP had certain effects not only on direct program participants but on wider community members as well, through events organized by program participants (Forum Theater plays):

- 100% of the focus groups reported that the DCT methodology had a visible positive effect on community relations as they relate to conflict issues and local problems.
  - "Forum Theater is like a mirror," a community member in Tokmok, Kyrgzystan, commented. "We can see ourselves and how we make emotional mistakes which result in conflicts. Forum Theater performances allow us to look at our problems and our behavior from an outsider's viewpoint" (Nigmatov, p. 50).
  - In Tajikistan, where girls often marry at 15 and 16, Mr. Nigmatov reported that a number of respondents mentioned that parents had started to change their attitudes, allowing their daughters to continue their education. One focus group discussant shared an example of a girl who was about to be married without her consent. When a Forum Theater performance at her school sparked dialogue about early marriage and its consequences, the girl took a video of the play on her mobile phone. She used the video to launch a discussion with her parents at home, and successfully persuaded them to delay her marriage and let her continue her education (Nigmatov, 2011, pp. 24–31).
- The majority of focus group participants stated that Forum Theater plays performed by the YTP participants had an impact on their attitudes towards conflict issues, and particularly towards individuals of other ethnicities, religions, and nationalities.
  - "I feel that I have changed myself thanks to Forum Theater," commented an ethnic Kyrgyz girl from a border community in southern Kyrgyzstan. "Before, I perceived Tajiks who live near to our communities very negatively. But now I understand them more and

behave more patiently and tolerantly towards them" (Nigmatov, 2011, p. 50).

- About 60% of adult community members and about 67% of youth audience members in Kyrgyzstan and Tajikistan who saw one or more YTP Forum Theater plays were assessed by the focus group facilitators as able to speak about conflict issues in their community in an open and balanced way. (Focus group facilitators determined the number of participants able to speak in an open and balanced way, based on a rubric provided in the focus group guide.)

Based on analysis of the key informant interviews, focus groups, and semi-structured interviews with leaders of sustainability projects, Mr. Nigmatov also concluded that YTP's sustainability grant projects have had visible positive effects on secondary beneficiaries and the target institutions (primarily schools), although the projects were still being implemented at the time of the evaluation. His report notes that numerous examples were cited of behavioral and attitudinal changes among the secondary beneficiaries trained by the direct program participants. These included improved academic performance among new participants, no fights between students at the target schools, comments that youth have become more 'open,' and reports of improved communication, and even friendship, between young people of different ethnic groups.

Limitations

While IREX had collected some baseline data on community members' ability to speak openly and in a balanced way about conflict, this information was insufficient to make a comparison with the focus group results. The evaluator also acknowledged that due to the subjective nature of focus groups, the findings could be influenced by the evaluator's own views. To overcome this limitation, he involved a representative of the local partner organization in each focus group discussion and they discussed the findings together in a de-brief meeting. As noted earlier, language was a challenge in some communities. As Mr. Nigmatov does not speak Uzbek or Kyrgyz, focus groups in these languages were conducted through a translator, which could influence both the facilitation and the results.

CONCLUSIONS AND RECOMMENDATIONS

Overall, the evaluation of IREX's Youth Theater for Peace program found that "the YTP approach and the DCT methodology are effective tools in promoting lasting attitudinal and behavioral changes in youth and adults in relation to conflict issues on community level, relations within community, and particularly in relation to people of other ethnicities, religions and nationalities" (Nigmatov, 2011, p. 10). The DCT methodology was also recognized as likely to have a positive effect on self-confidence and leadership skills in both youth and adults. Additionally, communities expressed a high level of interest in continuing DCT activities, which bodes well for future sustainability.

IREX's experience evaluating the effects of Youth Theater for Peace has yielded several lessons learned that can be of value for the wider peace education community.

Change in attitudes and behaviors can be measured, even on a budget. While IREX had allocated funding to hire an external evaluator, the pre—and post-event surveys designed primarily in-house also quantified attitudinal and behavioral change. By carefully selecting indicators and creating effective data collection tools, including series of questions designed to elicit attitudes indirectly, peace educators can evaluate the deeper effects of their work beyond the basic output level.

Tools and techniques for effective baseline data collection are still an outstanding need. IREX's evaluation could have been further strengthened if the audience focus group data was compared against a solid baseline that measured community members' attitudes around conflict. Additionally, the baseline data on participants for some indicators in Tajikistan does not appear to be an accurate reflection of participants' true attitudes and behaviors when triangulated with observations and focus group and interview data.

Peace educators should focus on building evaluation capacity in colleagues and partners. The training for local partners that IREX incorporated into the final evaluation plan allowed partner staff to participate more fully, practicing evaluation skills that they can apply to other peace education programs in the future. A major lesson IREX learned during this process was to start building capacity earlier in the program, as during the training the evaluator noted that partners were not well aware of the overall program Performance Monitoring and Evaluation Plan PMEP) and its indicators. While the partners had been collecting data throughout the program, they did not understand why they had been required to collect all the data and how it fit within an overall M&E framework. While IREX involved partner organizations in developing some of the data collection tools, more substantial involvement earlier in the program would likely have increased buy-in and contributed to M&E capacity building efforts.

REFERENCES

Boal, A. (2002). *Games for Actors and Non-Actors* (2nd ed). (Adrian Jackson, Trans.) London and New York: Routledge.

EurasiaNet. (2009). *Kyrgyzstan: Ambiguous Kyrgyz-Tajik border increases risk of conflict*. Retrieved from http://www.eurasianet.org/departments/insightb/articles/eav020209b.shtml

International Crisis Group. (2009). *Asia Report No. 162, Tajikistan: On the Road to Failure.*

Nigmatov, V. (2011). *Final evaluation report for youth theater for peace programs. IREX.* Accessible at http://www.irex.org/news/youth-transformed-final-evaluation-youth-theater-peace-released

Trautman, T. (2011, June 13). Kyrgyzstan's ethnic wounds still close to the surface. *World Politics Review.* Retrieved January 20, 2011 from http://www.worldpoliticsreview.com/articles/9140/kyrgyzstans-ethnic-wounds-still-close-to-the-surface

United Nations (UN). (2000). *Peace education: Origins.* Retrieved from http://www.un.org/cyberschoolbus/peace/frame2.htm

United Nations Development Program (UNDP). (2010). *Kyrgyzstan: Successful youth, successful country.*

World Bank. (2009). *Tajikistan country brief 2009.* Retrieved from http://go.worldbank.org/JI1AOY9RZ0

CHAPTER 15

THE ROLE OF DONORS IN POST-CONFLICT RECONCILIATION PROCESSES

Balancing Material and Behavioral Dimensions

Ruerd Ruben

INTRODUCTION

Studies regarding the donor support provided to post-conflict reconciliation processes consider a wide array of activities and efforts that might contribute to prevention, mitigation, management or transformation of the underlying dynamics of conflict. Since conflict resolution and peacebuilding have become part of the mandate of international development organizations, questions regarding their effectiveness and sustainability are considered increasingly relevant. On the other end, private organizations and diaspora communities also tend to play a major role in conflict resolution processes but these efforts are rarely evaluated in similar terms.

The literature on both types of interventions and supportive activities has been largely disconnected. International aid tends to be associated to the public arena (i.e. state building, security systems) whereas remittances from diaspora networks

Peace Education Evaluation: Learning from Experience and Exploring Prospects,
pages 223–237.
Copyright © 2015 by Information Age Publishing
All rights of reproduction in any form reserved.

are usually linked to expenditures at private and local community level. In a similar vein, public aid efforts are strongly oriented towards physical reconstruction activities (e.g., road rehabilitation, energy and water provision, repatriation and demining), while private resources are mostly devoted to community dialogue processes and local capacity building that focus on behavioral change (sometimes also called: peacebuilding from below).

Notwithstanding the emerging 'division of labor' between different types of donor support, in practice public and private activities strongly interact in post-conflict reconciliation processes. Effective complementarities between both types of support are also required in order to guarantee a balanced attention to the different underlying dimensions of the conflict. Material deficiencies and deficits in livelihoods due to exclusion and conflict can be addressed through the mobilization of support systems and service provision. However, structural inequalities, power imbalances and polarized attitudes cannot be mitigated only from the supply side, but also need to be addressed in direct interaction with the agents involved. This requires the emergence of new and legitimate forms of governance that are able to deal with the behavioural dimensions of the conflict.

Complex societal problems are usually better addressed if balanced attention is given to the different material and behavioral drivers that shape the nature of human interaction. Following the seminal work by Binswanger and Rosenzweig (1986), we distinguish between (i) the access and ownership to resources (land, employment, housing, water and energy) and institutions (markets, state, community networks) as part of the material framework for individual decision-making, and (ii) the socio-cultural engagement between people and the trust relationships amongst societal groups that provide incentives that guide behaviour within the transactional network. While traditional (neo)Marxist and institutional theories would predict a rather linear relationship from the material to the behavioral realm with a predominant focus on contextual factors, contemporary approaches to development acknowledge the multifaceted and nested interaction between material and behavioral forces and thus strongly encourage an interdisciplinary analysis of processes of peacebuilding, reconciliation and negotiation (Ramsbotham, Woodhouse, & Miall, 2008).

We rely on a comparison of two distinctive evaluation studies in Southern Sudan and Rwanda where the international donor community has been actively involved in the process of post-conflict reconciliation. Recognizing the many structural differences between both countries in their historical settings, there are also striking similarities in the performance of the donor community and their perception on the nature of local conflicts. This leads to an essentially different mix, composition and sequence of donor efforts, and particular views regarding the importance of socio-economic development and governance and justice-oriented reconciliation activities. Most bilateral and multilateral donors exhibit a relatively strong orientation towards investments for the reconstruction of physical infrastructure and rehabilitation of service provision. Activities by (inter)national and local non-governmental organizations are mainly devoted to livelihood reconstruction and therefore acknowledge the importance of decentralized execution and local governance. Diaspora networks and related remittances bypass many formally established institutions but exhibit an important influence on the reconstruction of social capital and the establishment of new social norms. In theory, these different 'channels' could reinforce each other, but it is equally possible that trade-offs occur in specific settings.

The remainder of this article is structured as follows: section 2 provides a short overview of the literature on the dynamics of post-conflict reconciliation and summarizes the available evidence regarding the different contributions of donors to this process. In section 3 we discuss the role of donor support in post-conflict reconciliation processes, focusing attention on the cases of southern Sudan and Rwanda that illustrate marked differences in the attention given to the underlying drivers of political and socio-economic nature. Section 4 presents a general analysis of the roles of donors in post-conflict reconstruction and reconciliation, distinguishing between the potential impact of public, civic and private donors in reshaping the different material and behavioural dimensions that influence the multifaceted nature of the conflicts. In section 5 we discuss in more detail the contributions of peace education. Finally, section 6 concludes with some implication for program design and policy evaluation.

THE NATURE OF CONFLICT AND THE DYNAMICS OF POST-CONFLICT PROCESSES

Many current approaches to conflict resolution and post-conflict reconciliation and reconstruction are usually based on the contradiction between socio-cultural values and the political economy structure. The nature and dynamics of the interactions between structural, attitudinal and behavioural dimensions of conflicts has been outlined originally by Galtung (1975) and is further elaborated by Azar (1990). The central idea is that conflict de-escalation and resolution requires balanced concerns for both the direct needs and the underlying interests and power relations that shape the objective and subjective realm of the conflict.

Support to post-conflict reconciliation processes tends to be based, however, on different views and perceptions regarding the precise nature of the interactions between these different underlying conflict dimensions. Collier and Hoeffler (2004) devote major attention to the greed and grievance motives for conflicts and consider the struggle on natural resources and (ethnic or political) inequalities as key drivers for civic war. Scarcity and deprivation accompanied by (youth) underemployment may provide a particular breeding ground for resource-based conflicts.

On the other end, authors like Duffield (2008) emphasize the importance of situating conflicts in their socio-cultural context, pointing to the role of opposing or conflicting identities as a root causes for structural violence. The different views are schematically outlined in Table 15.1.

These different interpretations of conflict dimensions are essentially based on opposing views regarding the interactions between the material and behavioural dimensions of societal change. Binswanger and Rosenzweig (1986) developed an early framework for analyzing these interactions in rural areas of sub-Sahara Africa, where risk and information constraints are considered driving forces for shaping the social exchange and the material production relationships. In a context of ill-functioning markets and open unemployment, insurance against risk can only be provided through interlinked transactions and social institutions. These social exchange mechanisms (like reciprocity in sharecropping and inter-linked contracts) are thus considered as a fundamental requirement for enabling resource-poor households to participate in societal progress. In the absence of market-based insurance mechanisms (like credit and lease arrangements), most resource exchange takes place between social strata based on partnership trust.

The importance of trust for maintaining social cohesion is further elaborated by Ostrom and Walker (2003), paying due attention to the risks of erosion of social capital in more heterogeneous societies. The degradation of generalized trust in society will be further enhanced by the segmentation of (in)formal exchange networks that takes place in settings of declining trust between social groups. These mechanisms are likely to gain more force in societies with a high degree of resource inequalities and low level of education. At a more personal level, this translates into a loosing sense of legitimacy regarding the state and a declining sense of belonging to the society at large. In the absence of (in)formal social bonds, latent conflicts based on wealth, racial or ethnic divisions can easily escalate into violent conflicts.

The patterns of interaction between material exchange mechanisms and behavioral trust can be considered as a useful framework for further analyzing processes of post-conflict reconciliation. Whereas the mix and sequence of activities and interventions aiming to support the reconciliation process will certainly vary between different settings, it is considered of primary importance to maintain a clear view of the different logics underlying the conflict as perceived by the main actors. The role of third party agents—both external donors and private parties—in mediation and reconstruction activities may differ according to the type of conflict

TABLE 15.1. Dimensions of Conflicts

Material dimensions	Behavioral dimensions
Unequal land distribution	Ethnic or religious divisions
Limited access to resources	Low (personal & institutional) trust
Scarcity of infrastructure	High risk & scarce reciprocity
High un/underemployment	Weak governance structures
Low educational participation	Conflicting identities
Scarce health care provision	Limited legitimacy

and the degree of separation of social identities and the feelings of trauma. The transition from containing conflict (peacekeeping) and ending a violent conflict (peacemaking) to post-war reconstruction and reconciliation requires a careful engagement with all parties involved (see Ramsbotham et al., 2008 for a detailed discussion). International development agencies tend to become involved initially through humanitarian aid but in subsequent stages also play a role in the transformative process.

Donors may provide leverage to the reconciliation and reconstruction activities, but this also involves serious risks of becoming a party in the process (Keen, 2008). Public donors tend to be highly preoccupied with quickly instituting democracy through general elections, whereas the local setting might asks for other dynamics to ensure stability and create legitimacy. Private voluntary agencies (NGOs) and individual (diaspora) networks usually maintain stronger local linkages and may therefore play an important complementary role in strengthening behavioural relations in post-conflict settings.

EVALUATING POST-CONFLICT RECONCILIATION IN RWANDA AND SOUTHERN SUDAN

In order to better understand the logic and dynamics of post-conflict reconciliation processes we draw on the comparison of different types of evaluations of support activities to post-conflict reconciliation and peacebuilding in two different settings: Southern Sudan (2005–10) and Rwanda (1995–2010). Special attention is given to the analysis of the nature and understanding of the underlying conflict, the role of different—internal and external—actors in the reconciliation process, and the importance attached to material and behavioural factors in mitigating and addressing the post-conflict situation.

Southern Sudan

For Southern Sudan, the comprehensive situational analysis made by Johnson (2003) informed many studies on the underlying factors of the conflict. Much attention was given to historical factors that lead to socio-economic (resource-based) and political (power-based) conflicts. Subsequent analyses of the Sudan conflict point attention to several other factors, like the clash of cultural identities, the manipulation of tribal interests, the prevalence of old and new patronage systems and intra-elite competition (de Waal, 2007). This multiplicity of conflict causes makes the local situation extremely difficult to understand to outsiders.

The multi-donor evaluation conducted by Bennett et al. (2010)—using the Conflict Prevention and Peacebuilding (CPPB) categories inspired by the joint Utstein study of peacebuilding (Smith, 2004)—provided a mapping of four key factors underlying the conflict (social, economic, political and security) and indentifies which factors are susceptible to donor interventions. This innovative approach to conflict analysis clearly illustrates that major political problems are related to value systems and ideological positions vis-à-vis the state where donors can exercise little direct influence. Donor support to the reform of justice and security institutions, the promotion of good governance and for strengthening the culture of justice, truth and reconciliation received in practice far less attention compared to support activities in the material development sphere.

In fact, 79% of all donor funding (actual expenditures of approximately US $3 billion) was devoted to socioeconomic development (i.e. roads, education and health care, water and sanitation, agricultural production). Efforts to enhance state building, support to the reintegration of returnees, strengthening local governance regimes are qualified as largely insufficient and incoherent. The static nature of many bi/multilateral funding mechanisms hinders an adequate and pro-active response to local sources of conflict. The expected 'peace dividend' through the provision of basic services can therefore not directly be translated into higher societal trust.

Rwanda

Rwanda provides a typical example of a country in which civil society actors and ordinary members of society are actively included in reconstruction processes (see e.g., Fred-Mensah, 2004; Paffenholz & Spurk, 2006). The country has known violent conflict for many years, which has resulted in serious erosion of social ties. Since 1994, Rwanda has been in the process of reconstruction to attain sustainable economic growth and peace. However, for Rwanda to recover, the challenge is to balance economic development with social development in a manner that simultaneously enables a nation to find its way out of poverty, while encouraging new social relations across class, ethnic, and gender divides (Colletta & Cullen, 2000).

To restore national unity, large-scale, state-led reconciliation programmes have been launched. Popular courts (called *Gacaca)* are used extensively to enhance local reconciliation. Rwanda's citizens are encouraged to engage in reconciliation committees and solidarity camps, and the government has labelled itself as "the government of national unity and reconciliation". However, the effects of these policies are still unclear, and feelings of interpersonal distrust still prevail. Even though Rwanda has made a remarkable economic recovery, still almost 60% of the population lives below the poverty line and inequality is increasing (Ansoms, 2005).

In response to the 1994 genocide and earlier conflicts, massive migration flows emerged, involving over 2 million Rwandans. Most of these migrants fled to neighbouring countries such as Congo, Tanzania and Burundi, and approximately 200,000 migrants fled to Europe. Although some of them returned, many Rwandans still continue to live in exile. These Rwandans who remain scattered over the world but strongly influence post-conflict processes. Rwandan migrants direct large flows of remittances to Rwanda: in 2007, the country received about US$21 million in individual remittances from abroad (World Bank, 2008). Households with family members abroad that receive remittances are able to generate substantially higher standards of living and experience more food security (Koster, 2008). Official Development Assistance to Rwanda totalled approximately USD 603 million in 2006, being equivalent to some 27% of GDP and financing over half of the public budget.

A recent evaluation on the role of remittances in the Rwandese process of reconstruction and reconciliation—relying on attitudinal field surveys and experimental methods (Caarls et al., 2012)—revealed that the regular inflow of resources from family and relatives can effectively support material reconstruction, but also tend to de-motivate receiving households to take part in the socio-cultural reconciliation process. This study was largely motivated from an academic interest—the EU-funded INFOCON program—with the explicit purpose to increase understanding on the role of transnational communities in peacebuilding. In fact, some crowding-out effects are registered for remittances-receiving households that appear to be less willing to become engaged in community activities, thus undermining the intrinsic motivation of individuals to cooperate with other members of the local community.

Evaluation Principles & Practices

The substantial foreign aid for post-conflict assistance programs has been subject of several evaluations. Different approaches have been used to assess the impacts on both economic recovery and conflict recidivism. The multi-donor evaluation of conflict prevention and peacebuilding in Southern Sudan relied mainly on the structural analysis of drivers and constraints of the conflict and consequently assessed multiple—mostly complementary—pathways for intervention. In a different way, the appraisal of individual motivations for reconciliation and engagement in reconstruction activities in Rwanda is based on the bottom-up identification of suitable incentives for (and constraints of) collective action and a careful assessment of the role of (inter)national networks that may support or limit collective action. Donors thus try to tailor interventions to the post-conflict environment by selecting activities and agents capable in addressing simultaneously the before-outlined material and behavioural dimensions. Evaluations on the impact of multilateral donors—including the World Bank—on post-conflict assistance yield rather ambiguous results. Flores and Nooruddin (2009) conclude in their systematic evaluation of 170 grants comprising 20–25% of lending operations under the World Bank post-conflict assistance facility that the Bank's 'Framework for involvement in post-conflict reconstruction' (issued in 1997) pays overwhelming attention to economic recovery but gives little explicit recognition to the underlying political obstacles. Moreover, the Bank also risks aggravating post-conflict tensions if it pressures governments to implement policies that exacerbate short-run distributional conflicts. In fact, for a long time post-conflict situations were essentially treated similar to recovery from natural disasters.

Monitoring and evaluation in post-conflict settings face a number of structural constraints that ask for a more tailored framework. Fragility and conflict-prone situations require a deep understanding on how development interventions can affect economic, social, and political cleavages. Moreover, specific indicators for measuring fragility are needed to track levels of (and changes in) the legitimacy and effectiveness of nation-states. Critical contextual elements that shape the dynamics of M&E in different types of post-conflict situations include the level of political interests, the role or presence of the military, the ongoing security situation, and the nature of the peace agreement. There is almost always tension (and sometimes confusion) in post-conflict programs between pressures for immediate impact and reconstruction and the need for longer-term capacity building and structural reform (USAID, 2006). From the perspective of M&E, these tradeoffs are often represented as different levels of objectives and indicators (outputs, intermediate results, and strategic objectives) or as pertaining to different phases in the post-conflict process (stabilization, reconstruction, and development). There are also related tensions between sector-specific outcomes and outcomes relating to the reduction of fragility and increase of stability. In this regard, the most common tradeoffs are between results relating to the perceived effectiveness of the host government and those relating to its legitimacy.

In practical terms, time frames for programs that should demonstrate 'quick wins' and more structural interventions that support trust and social coherence are mostly difficult to reconcile. Rapid adjustments may become necessary under changing security conditions. Basic data for baseline studies are often unavailable and novel techniques and approaches should be used to assess impact. In fact, incremental progress is usually a more feasible goal, and flexible arrangements are critical to be able to respond to changing conditions on the ground. The institutional complexity—with large number of foreign donors and weak national agencies—also asks for innovative evaluation approaches, relying on media analysis, geo-referenced surveys, story-telling and behavioural gaming.

DONOR SUPPORT TO RECONCILIATION

The international donor community has been actively engaged in the reconstruction and reconciliation processes both in Rwanda and in Southern Sudan. However, the role of donor support widely differs depending on the funding modalities and the partnership relationships established. We therefore compare the roles of bi/multilateral donor mostly supporting public agencies with the engagement of private donors from the NGO and diaspora communities that maintain stronger engagement with civic and network activities in post-conflict societies.

Southern Sudan

The multi-donor evaluation of the support to conflict prevention and peace-building activities in Southern Sudan (Bennett et al., 2010) is highly critical of donor coordination and registers the lack of alignment of interventions amongst bilateral donors. Several pooled funding were established to increase aid effectiveness, efficiency and flexibility. Pooled funding reduced transaction costs and also provided predictability, enabling development partners to engage in long-term planning. Concerns about corruption and limited public management experience of the Southern Sudan public authorities led donors to choose multilateral channels of support.

The assessment shows market differences in disbursements of bilateral, multi-donor trust funds (administered by the World Bank) and pooled funding arrangements depending on fund management regimes. Funds managed by private contractors that can be held accountable for their performance show most favorable performance. MDTF-funded projects for road infrastructure and rural water and sanitation delivered according to expectations. UN-managed pooled funds are, however, very slow, overly bureaucratic and charge high overhead costs (up to approximately 16%). Moreover, direct involvement of public agencies remained limited and local counterpart contributions proved difficult to meet. In comparison, the DFID-initiated Basic Services Fund (BSF) aimed at strengthening the delivery of basic services (primary education, primary health care and basic water, sanitation and hygiene education) via NGOs to most underserved populations reports quite impressive results.

At a more systematic level, it remains questionable whether the focus on service delivery is helpful to alleviate the multiple drivers of conflict. Few efforts were made to strengthen the cultural and institutional resilience necessary for managing conflicts without violence (Bennett, op cit., p. 74). In fact, donors placed great emphasis on principles of coordination, but this impaired their attention for state building. The discourse around 'post-conflict recovery' obscured the fact that there is little to recover and that many conflict arenas still prevail (p. 76). Much of the aid is driven largely by donors themselves and based on mistaken assumptions that gave greater priority to socioeconomic issues while disregarding the importance of local dispute resolution, transitional justice and community dialogue.

Rwanda

Donor support to the reconciliation and reconstruction process in Rwanda devoted much attention to the process of state building. It was recognized that the exclusionary character of the state was at the roots of its fragility. The current government argues a politics of consensus and inclusion. The Unity and Reconciliation Commission played a key role in rebuilding community cohesion, social trust and harmony, which was severely shattered during the genocide.

International donors have given the government substantial room to maneuver and have been careful not to overly interfere with domestic political processes (Putzel and Golooba-Mutebi, 2009). Initially, the government held several round-tables in 1995/96 but relations with donors remained strained. NGOs delivering humanitarian aid were hesitant to collaborate with the government, and finally almost 250 NGOs were expelled. Some bilateral donors decided to pay off the arrears with the World Bank to enable new lending operations. The consultative process launched by the government for the elaboration of the first Poverty Reduction Strategy Paper (Government of Rwanda, 2002) convinced donors that there was a comprehensive strategy. Some donors started to grant budget support, but most aid was focused on social sector programmes and little support was extended to the productive sector. Since limited poverty alleviation took place and inequality increased considerably, the government elaborated the second PRSP, the Economic Development and Poverty Reduction Strategy (EDPRS), focusing on increasing investment in four areas to promote economic growth: agriculture, human resources, infrastructure, and the financial sector. Donor-state dialogue became intensified, with bi-monthly meetings of the Development Partners Consultative Group and joint budget support review twice a year. State officials show a clear recognition and appreciation for the crucial role foreign assistance has played in the reconstruction of the country, but also expresses a profound desire to graduate from "aid dependence" and a widespread concern about all 'off-budget' aid.

Long-term commitments by donors have been crucial to the government's ability to establish long-term planning in its state-building project. In addition to state building, due attention was given to state-society relations. Donors and International NGOs were carefully kept outside this process. Strict controls on corruption, maintaining rule of law and the state's capacity to guarantee security and peace are critical for establishing legitimacy. Less attention is given to mechanisms of civic participation and voice. On the other end, consistent efforts are made to contribute to the "healing" from trauma, enabling local communities to address reconciliation and express forgiveness (Staub et al., 2003; Staub et al., 2005). These efforts are usually supported by NGOs and are sometimes also related also to diaspora groups. However, since the diaspora communities are still frequently involved in long-distance nationalism, they tend to be less prepared for reconciliation. Their willingness to return and to obtain citizenship is still badly constrained by the authoritarian state building process.

Donor Roles

Comparing the post-conflict reconciliation and reconstruction experiences in Southern Sudan and Rwanda provides us with some important lessons. First, the fundamental importance of state building to enhance legitimacy and confirm the leading role of established public institutions in the reconstruction process. Second, the importance of establishing an adequate balance between physical reconstruction activities (infrastructure and services provision) vis-à-vis socio-cultural conflict management programs to enhance social cohesion, identity and trust. Third, the crucial role played by (highly coordinated) donor efforts in creating a commitment for long-term resource support to sometimes dialectically developing national reconciliation processes.

TABLE 15.2. Donor Support Programs

	Material dimensions	Behavioral dimensions
Multilateral donors & multi-donor trust funds	• Infrastructure (roads, electricity) • Land rehabilitation/registration • Demining & civil disarmament • Public finance & taxation	• Insurance regimes • Land distribution • Law enforcement (police, customs, etc.)
Bilateral donors	• Water & sanitation • Education & Health Care	• Decentralization • Human rights promotion
Non-Governmental Organizations (NGO's)	• Community services • Repatriation	• Community dialogue & trust • Cooperative development • Civil protection & customary law • Local governance (CBO's)
Diaspora networks	• Housing reconstruction • Small-scale self-employment	• Community facilities • Citizenship

Donor coordination in post-conflict settings may be reinforced when different agencies are able to recognize their comparative advantages. Table 15.2. provides a tentative framework for a balanced appraisal of specific donor roles, both in the area of material support and in the sphere of behavioral relationships. Whereas full specialization is certainly not warranted, some complementarities can be reached based on the recognition of particular opportunities in local settings. In many post-conflict situations it remains an utmost challenge to establish an adequate balance between state-building activities (providing security, rule of law, access to justice, taxation, economic development and essential service delivery) and civil society engagement (enhancing identity, social trust and feelings of justice). Donors can contribute to this balance through a well established mix of material support services and behavioral incentives.

PEACE EDUCATION

Peace education and capacity building are critically important in post-conflict situations. In addition to physical reconstruction of educational facilities, due attention should be given to special training modules, including psychosocial support for students and teachers), peace education and human rights, reduction of household and gender-based violence, landmines awareness, and other health and safety issues. Progress in these areas is usually measured with process and quality indicators. Many post-conflict programs emphasize the governance as well as the methodological benefits of participatory and community-based M&E methods.

Schools provide a general sense of wellbeing and a safe haven. In post-conflict situations with large movements of displaced persons, people prefer to settle in locations where there are functioning schools. In addition to aggregate measures of access and enrollment, it is essential that M&E of education in post-conflict settings disaggregate and closely track data on the equity of access and enrollment across any ethnic, geographic, or regional cleavages characterizing the conflict. Measures of educational quality and educational relevance are also critical, whether the goal is seen in purely educational terms or in terms of stabilization and reconciliation. In most post-conflict settings, simply tracking test scores, completion rates and other standard measures of educational results is often premature.

From the behavioural point of view, peace education at community level is considered of critical importance. The process of acquiring the values, the knowledge and developing the attitudes, skills, and abilities to be able to deal with conflicts through negotiation, mediation and communication requires more process-oriented efforts that are difficult to evaluate with standard approaches. Assessing progress in trust building and power balancing efforts usually starts with improved insights and transparency regarding existing structural and motivational constraints. Many of these interventions are conducted at a rather local, community level and based on participatory approaches to evaluation.

The robust evaluation of the role of peace education programs on conflict prevention and reconciliation meets several constraints. Due attention should be given to the tracing of changes in attitudes, values and behaviour that are influenced by multiple—partly external—factors. Full-fledged impact studies are difficult to pursue due to the absence of baselines and complications to find a suitable counterfactual. Moreover, most available studies are school-based and tend to disregard broader societal interactions and the multi-facetted causes of violence (Harris, 2003). Instead, the effectiveness of peace education on violence prevention and conflict resolution abilities and trust building can be also be analyzed with in-depth attitudinal studies that rely on experimental approaches. This also enables to compare the usefulness of different instruction methods and to assess the importance of the frequency of meetings and the group size on attitudinal performance. Such formative evaluation will substantially contribute to insights in opportunities to improve program design.

Finally, it remains extremely difficult to appreciate the impact of peace education at higher system levels. Most evaluations are limited to attitudinal change and seldom assess further impact on actual behaviour outside the school environment. Moreover, the role of peace education in societal processes of trust building and justice reinforcement, based on tolerance, identity and respectful behaviour is still only partially understood. The underlying theories of change are often rather mechanical in nature and fail to understand the intrinsic linkages between behavioural change and societal development (Ashton, 2007). This mimics to a certain extent the earlier mentioned difficulties in the design of peace-oriented development programs.

LESSONS AND OUTLOOK

Reconstruction and reconciliation are two important constituents of peace building processes, where the (re)building of social capital and trust represent central elements. Strategies for reconciliation and reconstruction in post-conflict areas are largely based on establishing credible institutions and restoring social ties and networks, which are both considered critically important constituents for preventing future outbreaks of violence (Colletta & Cullen, 2000; Knack & Keefer, 1997).

Programs to support post-conflict reconstruction usually address the creation and restoration of physical infrastructure and facilities, minimal social services, and structural reform and transformation in the political, economic, social, and security sectors. This implies that post-conflict reconstruction encompasses not only an economic rebuilding of the country, but also a reconstruction of public institutions and social networks. Paying simultaneously attention to both the material and the behavioural aspects of post-conflict societies is key for successful peacebuilding. This also requires particular M&E approaches that address changes in attitudes and behaviour at individual and societal level.

While the necessity of so-called 'local participation' in post-conflict reconstruction processes is increasingly recognized (Paffenholz & Spurk, 2006), the design and evaluation of such efforts asks for a thorough analysis of the intangible aspects of reconstruction programmes, rather than solely focusing on activities aimed to foster economic recovery. As already acknowledged by Galtung (2001, p. 54): "To limit reconstruction to rehabilitation and rebuilding is to commit the fallacy of (badly) misplaced concreteness … It means being mesmerized by visible at the expense of invisible effects." The rebuilding of trust and social capital represents a vital and essential element in the reconciliation process.

Peace education is a vital—albeit sometimes neglected—aspect in conflict prevention and reconciliation programs. Large-scale programs tend to emphasize investment for the recovery of educational facilities and improved access to schools as major achievements. Far less attention is usually given to the content of educational programs and training in peace enforcing attitudes. This asks for substantial investments in teacher training and curriculum development tailored to local conditions. Moreover, due attention should be given to popular education in non-formal settings in order to enable wider participation in awareness-raising programs. The adequate understanding of the interface between material and behavioural incentives remains a key factor for successful peacebuilding programs.

We learn from the documental evidence derived from evaluation studies on post-conflict reconciliation in Southern Sudan and Rwanda that different donors can play distinctive and possibly complementary roles in this process. While bilateral donors and multi-donor trust funds provide wide opportunities for large-scale public investments that enable the state to improve its service provision, additional efforts are required for strengthening the legitimacy of the state agencies themselves. Therefore, support for civil society development, identity building and the strengthening of local community networks is equally required to support peacebuilding from below. The precise mix and sequence of donor support for these mutually related priorities remains to be negotiated in each particular setting.

REFERENCES

Ansoms, A. (2005). Resurrection after civil war and genocide: growth, poverty and inequality in post-conflict Rwanda, *The European Journal of Development Research, 17*(3), 495–508.

Ashton, C. V. (2007). Using theory of change to enhance peace education evaluation. *Conflict Resolution Quarterly, 25*(1), 39–53.

Azar, E. (1990). *The management of protracted social conflict: Theory and cases.* Aldershot: Dartmouth.

Bennett, J., Pantuliano, S., Fenton, W., Vaux, A., Barnett, C., & Brusset, E. (2010). *Aiding the peace: A multi-donor evaluation of support to conflict prevention and peacebuilding activities in Southern Sudan 2005–2010.* London: ITAD Ltd.

Binswanger, H. P., & Rosenzweig, M. R. (1986). Behavioural and material determinants of production relations in agriculture. *Journal of Development Studies, 22*(3), 503–539.

Caarls, K., Fransen, S., & Ruben, R. (2012). Can Migratory Contacts and Remittances Contribute to Reconciliation and Reconstruction in Rwanda? *International Migration.* doi:10.1111/j.1468-2435.2012.00747.x

Colletta, N.J. and Cullen, M. J. (2000). *Violent Conflict and the Transformation of Social Capital. Lessons from Cambodia, Rwanda, Guatemala, and Somalia.* Washington D.C: The World Bank.

Collier, P., & Hoeffler, A. (2004). Greed and grievance in civil war. *Oxford Economic Papers,* 56 (4): 563–595.

de Waal, A. (2007). *Sudan: What kind of state? What kind of crisis?* Crisis States Research Centre. London: London School of Economics.

Duffield, M. (2008). *Development, security and unending wars: The merging of development and security.* Cambridge: Cambridge University Press.

Flores, T. E., & Nooruddin, I. (2009). Financing the peace: Evaluating World Bank postconflict assistance programs. *Review of International Organization, 4*(1), 1–27.

Fred-Mensah, B. K. (2004). Social capital building as capacity for postconflict development: The UNDP in Mozambique and Rwanda. *Global Governance, 10,* 437–457.

Galtung, J. (1975). Three approaches to peace: peacekeeping, peacemaking and peacebuilding. In J. Galtung (Ed.). *Peace, war and defense: essays in peace research (*282–304). Copenhagen, Denmark: Christian Eijlers.

Galtung, J. (2001). After violence, reconstruction, reconciliation, and resolution. In M. Abu-Nimer (Ed.), *Reconciliation, justice, and coexistence: Theory and practice.* Lanham, MD: Lexington Books.

Government of Rwanda. (2002, June). *Poverty reduction strategy paper.* National Poverty Reduction Programme. Washington, DC: International Monetary Fund.

Harris, I. (2003, April). *Peace education evaluation.* Paper presented at annual meeting of the American Educational Research Association, Chicago.

Johnson, D. H. (2003). *The root causes of the Sudan's civil wars.* Oxford/Bloomingston/ Kampala: International African Institute.

Keen, D. (2008). *Complex emergencies.* Cambridge: Polity Press.

Knack, S., & Keefer, P. (1997). Does social capital have an economic payoff? A cross-country investigation. *The Quarterly Journal of Economics, 114*(4), 1251–1288.

Koster, M. (2008). *Fragmented Lives: Reconstructing rural livelihoods in post-genocide Rwanda* (Doctoral dissertation). Wageningen University.

Ostrom, E., & Walker, J. (2003). *Trust and reciprocity: Interdisciplinary lessons for experimental research.* New York, NY: Russell Sage Foundation.

Paffenholz, T., & Spurk, C. (2006). *Civil society, civic engagement, and peace building.* Working Paper, No. 36, Conflict Prevention and Reconstruction Unit in the Social Development Department, Washington, DC.: The World Bank.

Putzel, J., & Golooba-Mutebi, F. (2009). *Statebuilding in fragile situations—How can donors 'do no harm' and maximise their positive impact? Country case study—Rwanda. Joint study by the London School of Economics, Institute of Policy Analysis and Research, Rwanda (IPAR) and PricewaterhouseCoopers LLP.* Paris: OECD.

Ramsbotham, O., Woodhouse, T., & Miall, H. (2008). *Contemporary conflict resolution.* Cambridge, MA: Polity Press.

Smith, D. (2004). *Towards a strategic framework for peacebuilding—Getting their act together. Overview of the Joint Utstein Study of Peacebuilding,* Commissioned by the Royal Norwegian Ministry of Foreign Affairs. Oslo: PRIO-International Peace Research Institute.

Staub, E., Pearlman, L. A., Gubin, A., & Hagengimana, A. (2005). Healing, reconciliation, forgiving and the prevention of violence after genocide or mass killing: An intervention and its experimental evaluation in Rwanda. *Journal of social and clinical psychology, 24*(3), 297–334.

Staub, E., Pearlman, L. A., & Miller, V. (2003). Healing the roots of genocide in Rwanda. *Peace Review: A Journal of Social Justice, 15*(3), 287–294.

USAID (2006). *Monitoring and evaluation in post-conflict settings.* USAID Report PN-ADG-193. Washington, D.C.: Management Systems International.

World Bank (2008). *Migration and remittances factbook 2008.* Washington D.C.: World Bank.

CHAPTER 16

ASSESSING PEACE EDUCATION AT THE NATIONAL LEVEL

Challenges and Possibilities

Cécile Barbeito Thonon and Johanna Ospina

INTRODUCTION AND PREVIOUS CONSIDERATIONS

Around the world, peace education initiatives address interpersonal and structural issues.[1] When it comes to evaluation, however, a majority of programs focus their efforts on assessing change at the interpersonal level. Typical questions asked include: how were the sessions implemented? What did participants learn? It is less common to assess the effects that peace education programs have on the structural level. Thus, questions left to the wayside include: to what extent is peace education included in formal or non-formal curricula? To what extent do its effects decrease militarism or armament spending in a country? Do peace education initiatives succeed in preventing war or decreasing negative perceptions between peoples? In order to fill this gap, this chapter focuses on evaluation of peace edu-

---

[1] The structural level refers to how structures such as organizations, states, and world systems enshrine laws, rules, policies, or practices.

Peace Education Evaluation: Learning from Experience and Exploring Prospects,
pages 239–253.
Copyright © 2015 by Information Age Publishing
All rights of reproduction in any form reserved.

cation initiatives at a structural level, by tackling some methodological challenges of creating and using national indicators of peace education.

Three methodological dilemmas will be addressed:

- In relation to the theoretical framework, how can we define peace education in a way that is feasible for research, but at the same time reflects the variety of conceptualizations of peace education?
- Concerning the programs, how can we analyze them without designating overly simplistic comparisons that only lead to broad generalizations? How can we set standards among countries and territories while being context sensitive?
- Regarding the outcome indicators, how can we take into account multiple factors and, at the same time, isolate the key factors that foster peace education?

In order to address these dilemmas, the chapter will first relate them to the three basic principles of the theory of complexity defined by Edgar Morin (1995). Together, these three principles offer a comprehensive and flexible lens that enriches our reflection and raises new questions. Second, the chapter analyzes ten yearbooks with country-level indicators and indexes in order to examine their approaches to solving these dilemmas. This analysis and discussion of such practices allows for a final section of conclusions and recommendations.

REFLECTIONS THROUGH THE COMPLEXITY LENS: PRINCIPLES AND CHALLENGES

Complexity as a theory and paradigm aims at overcoming the *simplism* of the positivist paradigm that tends to universalize, hegemonize, and unify reality, and of the interpretativist and socio-critical paradigms that have a narrow scope as they seek to analyze very concrete phenomena. Although the first contributions of complexity theory come from physics, it has influenced other fields of knowledge and has been defined by different disciplines (Ashby, 1962; John Neumann, 1966; Weaver, 1948). Complexity has been defined by Edgar Morin as a weave of events, actions, interactions, feedback, and determinants that together constitute the world. Complex thought is an alternative perspective that applies a multidimensional view to what it analyzes. Morin's (1995) complex thought is based on three main principles that are related and interdependent: the *dialectic principle*, the *hologramatic principle*, and the *recursiveness principle* (pp. 105–109). They help to approach complex processes such as learning, teaching, and assessment. These three principles are analyzed to reflect on three above-mentioned challenges faced when creating and using country-level peace education indicators for evaluation purposes.

The Challenge of a Conceptual Framework: The Dialectical Principle

A consensual definition of peace education is the first challenge for the design, implementation, and evaluation of peace education programs. While peace education can be conceived in diverse ways, it also needs a practical working definition. Different historical and cultural contexts have expanded its contents and perspectives. Classical research requires, therefore, a definition of the conceptual framework on which the indicators will be based.

However, one of Morin's three principles of complexity, namely the *dialectical principle,* suggests that each phenomenon implies a dialectic relation among the parties. This infers that there is not one unique theory, that is absolutely valid, but a diversity of positions and interpretations that, despite seeming contradictory, can contribute from their particularity to the construction of knowledge. The foundations of knowledge, then, do not depend on reaching consensual definitions that allow for the analysis of a coherent reality, but on analyzing synergies among differing if not opposing views that make up a whole.

This first principle questions the assumption that it is preferable to have one single conception of peace education that is applied worldwide. It suggests, instead, that varying measures and points of view of peace education, including contradictory ones, could be considered for the country-level indicators. What is the conceptual approach of peace education used in different contexts? What are the conditions of peace in each of them? Should national indicators of peace education use one single definition of peace education or culturally-differentiated ones?

To answer these questions, it is relevant to consider that "peace education" is composed of two terms: *peace* and *education*. What each of these terms means has been a major point of debate among authors and disciplines throughout history. In the case of education, different conceptions can be associated with the three classical epistemological paradigms of social sciences (Bredo, 1982; Pop-

Classical research   **Paradigm of complexity**

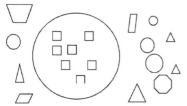 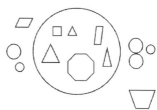

The conceptual framework defines a coherent whole.   **Contradictions are allowed in the studied subject**

FIGURE 16.1.

kewitz, 1988). The *positivist paradigm* considers education a process aimed at developing people's physical, intellectual, and moral abilities, enabling them to make achievements in a specific environment (Durkheim, 2003, p. 70). The *interpretativist paradigm* views education as an interdependent process among students and teachers who interact in educational and social contexts (Young, 1971; Popkewitz, 1988). The *socio-critical paradigm* understands education as a process in which actors participate in equal conditions; it is a critical, reflective and emancipatory approach, overtly political and committed with the transformation of societies (Carr, 1990, pp. 144–145).

Peace has been defined in negative and positive conceptions, and also in its inner or social dimensions—in the eastern and western cultures respectively (Galtung, 1985). Some focus on peace of the elites such as princes, empires, and countries, or those at the grassroots community level. Others relate it the achievement of liberal conditions, such as the market economy and democratic elections, whereas others consider it a personal and social emancipatory process.[2] The term peace encompasses all of these views and contradictions.

These discussions are reflected, consequently, in the conceptualization of peace education, as presented in the following classification:

Peace education's **negative approach** understands peace as the absence of war and focuses, therefore, on the prevention of war (Jares, 1999). In this approach, peace education should avoid problems and seek good behavior and harmony in personal and social relations (Haavelsrud, 1996; Reardon, 1988).

Peace Education's **positive approach** assumes conflict as an opportunity to transform societies nonviolently. Thus, peace education is understood as a continuing and permanent process of human empowerment through competencies useful for building peaceful societies at all levels (Harris, 2003; Jares, 1999; Reardon, 1988).

Through its **structural approach,** peace education seeks a society without the structural violence that exists among different relationships of societies (Borelli & Haavelsrud, 1993). Therefore, peace education does not only prevent war, but also prevents violence forged by institutions, including educational organizations, through their policies and socialization processes (Borelli & Haavelsrud, 1993; Jares, 1999).

At the **interpersonal level**, peace education aims at overcoming everyday violence where people and social groups interact with each other. This perspective considers as a core issue understanding structural and psychosocial causes of conflict, and transforming them (Iglesias, 2007).

Structural and interpersonal levels are interdependent, as interpersonal relationships are determined by social, cultural, economic, and political aspects of societies (Haavelsrud & Cabezudo, 2007).

---

[2] It is not an objective of this article to reflect on the epistemology of peace. However, for reflections on those different conceptions of peace, see Galtung, 1975 or Richmond, 2006.

While some advocate for the inclusion of peace education in formal education, others consider that it must stay completely outside of this system, because educational institutions are instruments of power to serve the elites and reproduce structural violence (Burns, 1981; Galtung, 1985; Haavelsrud, 1976; Jares, 1999). Therefore, they propose a "de-scholarized" peace education, developed in alternative contexts through non-formal education.

In an attempt to reconcile these perspectives, peace education will be defined including different approaches, as an educational process that contributes to building sustainable peace by training for the needed competencies to contribute to preventing and transforming all forms of violence.

These diverse approaches demonstrate the complex nature of the concept of peace education, shapes and nourishes its content and contributes to its purpose. This way, peace education can be considered: as negative (disarmament education) and positive (nonviolence and peacebuilding), interpersonal (conflict transformation) and structural (human rights and development education). These approaches can be considered in the formal, non-formal, and informal educational arenas.

The Challenge of Contextualizing: The Hologramatic Principle

One of the maxims of complexity is to take into account that every context has its own specificity. This would mean that country-level indicators—which can lead to generalizations and comparisons—might not be the most accurate methodological option. If this is true, another principle of the paradigm of complexity, the hologramatic principle, can justify the added value of having country indicators. *The hologramatic principle* states that the part is included in the whole and that the whole is reflected in the part. This means that to understand a part we must take into account the whole, in a way that "transcends reductionism that sees only the parts, and holism that can't see more than the whole" (Morin, 1995, p. 107).

This principle justifies the need to consider both macro and micro levels. The process of a peace education project will necessarily be determined by the context in which it is developed. Despite this obvious idea, few peace education initiatives take into account, while defining monitoring or evaluating, the context in which they are developed.

Some peace education authors have highlighted the importance of analyzing contexts. As some insist, the educational objective needs to be related to the particular conditions prevailing in a society; these conditions determine the specific needs and goals of a particular peace education program (Bar-Tal, 2002). The analysis of contextual conditions allows understanding the existing possibilities to transcend violence and to develop desirable visions of the future and possibilities for action (Haavelsrud & Cabezudo, 2007).

An analysis of the context to define a peace education project needs to be reflected, therefore, in the monitoring and evaluation process. Accordingly, Solomon and Kupermintz (2002) advocate for a peace education evaluation model that

Classical research

Paradigm of complexity

or

and

Classical research focuses either on micro (interpretativist and socio-critical paradigms) or on macro (positivism) levels.

Complex research complements the micro with the macro points of view.

FIGURE 16.2.

takes into consideration the socio-political context where the project takes place, as a way to evaluate whether the program is adapted to the context.

As the hologramatic principle suggests, evaluation needs to assess how the context (the whole) determines a peace education project (the part), but also how a peace education project (the part), has an impact in its context (the whole). The attempt to evaluate peace education at micro and macro levels leads us to consider the following ethical and methodological aspects: How can we measure whether peace education projects respond successfully to the needs of each context? In analyzing such different contexts, how can indicators be set that describe a global image and, at the same time, take into account the specificity of each country? Is it ethical to compare countries? Does it make sense methodologically? If not, how do we measure countries' improvements in peace education without unjustly comparing them?

For example, using the same standard in schools to measure the learning process of students coming from different cultural or socio-economic backgrounds can seem inappropriate. Similarly, at a global level, it can be just as unfair to apply the same standard to countries that are in starkly divergent situations. It might make sense, then, to avoid homogenizing the analysis into one single standard, and referring each country's performance to the context of violence it is facing.

In this direction, Salomon and Cairns (2010) suggest to analyze the challenges that peace education programs face in various contexts by differentiating the socio-political conditions in which these programs take place: a) context of belligerent ethno-political conflicts (e.g., Kosovo); b) a context of nonviolent intergroup tension involving issues (e.g., immigration in France) and; c) contexts of relative tranquility (e.g., the Nordic countries).

The Challenge of Identifying the Factors of Change: The Recursiveness Principle

To identify good practices and to promote more effective programming in peace education projects, some evaluation theories use methods to identify the positive factors that cause a situation to change (e.g., Most Significant Change, Appreciative Inquiry, Learning from Success). Identifying these factors helps in establishing relationships of cause and effect. But establishing cause-consequence synergies in a broader scale poses methodological problems, as it is difficult to isolate external factors and to guarantee that if a social factor has been transformed, it is exclusively due to the analyzed peace education program, and not to an external variable.

It is also problematic to suggest that social change has been the consequence of a program, and not its cause. If a country legislates peace education, should we consider this law a cause or a consequence of the existence of peace education initiatives? Did a peace education program lead to a law on peace education? Or did the peace education law provide the ground for more peace education programs?

The *recursiveness principle* means that the same phenomenon can be both the cause and the consequence of a process. Comparing it to an eddy that is simultaneously being moved and generating movement, Morin explains that "a recursive process is the one in which products and effects are, at the same time, causes and producers of what is producing them" (1995, p. 106). The recursiveness principle invites a focus on the synergies of factors, without an attempt to identify if every factor is a cause or a consequence of a reality. Recursiveness, moreover, is not a circular process, but rather a spiral one, as all the factors involved generate new situations different from the starting point.

Peace and peace education can be considered recursive, as they are conceived as perfectible realities, not defined as fixed states, but as an everlasting process of improvement of human conditions (Muñoz, 2001). Methodological questions, in this regard, would not be: What are the causes of significant change? or What are the consequences (outputs and impacts) of a peace education program? but rather: What phenomena create virtuous spirals of peace education? How can we identify and measure them?

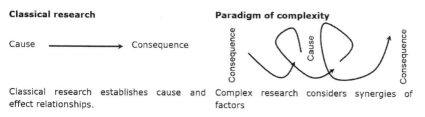

Classical research

Cause ———————→ Consequence

Classical research establishes cause and effect relationships.

Paradigm of complexity

Complex research considers synergies of factors

FIGURE 16.3.

Dialectical principle	• Do they use a definition applied universally or culturally differentiated ones? • Do they question this fact or propose any alternative?

BOX 16.1.

The key factors that lead to effective and transformative peace education can be identified and measured through interviews (interpretivist-qualitative technique), and through data correlations (positivist-quantitative technique). In both cases, it is necessary to discuss which values will be given to each phenomenon. Following these three principles and previous reflections, an analysis of already existing indicators will identify which types of indicators can contribute to the evaluation of peace education programs at the national level.

AN APPROACH TO THE ANALYSIS OF INDICATORS ON PEACE EDUCATION

Despite the large number and diversity of peace education programs that take place around the world, there are only isolated efforts to monitor and evaluate such programs. (Adams, 2010; Harris, 2003; Salomon & Cairns, 2010; Salomon & Nevo, 2002). With the purpose of identifying indicators to evaluate peace education programs at the national level, and according to the above-mentioned complex principles, some relevant indexes have been analyzed. Criteria in choosing them was that they cover educational and peace arenas in their different conceptions (positive/negative, social/inner peace education, formal/non formal), their multi-disciplinarity, and the diversity of methodologies and data collection strategies used (quantitative/qualitative, official state sources/civil society reports).

The analyzed indicators and indexes are: Social Watch's Basic Capacities Index (2011), DeRivera's Culture of Peace Indicators (2004), Freedom House's Freedom of the World, The Institute for Economic & Peace's Global Peace Index, UNDP's Human Development Index (2011), The UNICEF' Multiple Indicator Cluster Survey (UNICEF, 2011), UNESCO's Education for All Development Index (2011), the European Multi-Stakeholder Steering Group on Development Education's (2010) DE Watch, and the Fund for Peace's Failed States Index. Each of these instruments has been analyzed in a way to respond to the aforementioned questions.

What Do Existing Indicators Say about the Conceptual Framework?

Eight of the analyzed national indicators specify concretely the subject they are observing, while only one has opted for a variety of definitions.

Indexes coming from the international agencies—UNESCO, UNDP and UNICEF—are built on concepts set out in the framework of international instruments protecting human rights, such as the Universal Declaration of Human Rights and other international programs that contribute to the states' respect and guarantee of rights. This parameter concept assumes the universality of human rights according to Vienna's World Conference on Human Rights (United Nations, 1993) which states that human rights are "universal, indivisible and independent." However, the question remains whether human rights can be defined from a particular cultural and ethical conception setting common standards, or whether it is possible, instead, to support different notions of human dignity.

Aware of this debate, the Freedom of the World Index recognizes that it "does not maintain a culture-bound view of freedom," but applies a similar standard "to all countries and territories, irrespective of geographical location, ethnic or religious composition, or level of economic development" (Freedom House, 2011). Applying the same definition globally implies the risk of being ethnocentric or "single-viewed."

This reflection is relevant in the case of the Freedom of the World Index, which is based on the perceptions of individuals, and thus might be considered more variable than other more objective indicators. As Freedom House states, "the survey operates from the assumption that freedom for all peoples is best achieved in liberal democratic societies" (Freedom House, 2011). Although it is important to clarify on which values an indicator is based (and making them explicit is already a way to show awareness that an assumption might not be shared by everyone), there is still a risk of generalizing views that could not be globally valid.

Similarly, the Global Peace Index (GPI) explains its difficulty to attain the concept it aspires to measure: while recognizing the positive conception of peace, the GPI focuses on "the measurement of peace as the 'absence of violence' that seeks to determine what cultural attributes and institutions are associated with states of peace" (IE&P, 2011, p. 5). Its decision to adhere to one single aspect of peace is justified because it is "the simplest way of approaching" the term. To overcome the contradiction of conceiving positive peace but measuring negative peace, the GPI develops further work to relate it to other indicators of positive peace such as political participation, civil liberties, freedom of the press, and women in parliaments.

On the other hand, the European Development Education Monitoring Report (2010) DE Watch reflects on the definition and application of the concept of development education (DE). In order to analyze this concept in European countries, the report establishes a typology of DE through two main approaches: a) an unrecognized approach to DE: DE as public relations for development aid; and b) recognized approaches to DE. The latter includes three dimensions: 1) DE as awareness raising 2) DE as global education: which focuses on local-global interdependence and involves participation by the target audience; and 3) DE as enhancement of life skills. This enables the report to include a diversity of approaches to development education.

TABLE 16.1.

	One definition	Different Definitions	One Definition with Different Views
Pros	• Delimits the study framework • Adds coherence in the analyzed subject	• Reflects diversity of views • Builds knowledge through dialectics	• Allows diversity of views • Demonstrates complexity of concepts and their different approaches
Contras	• Does not recognize other views, exclusive • Universalizing and hegemonic knowledge	• Its broad scope might complicate research • It is more difficult to make comparisons between different peace education initiatives	• Can lead to too broad a scope of analysis • Difficult to apply to a specific phenomenon

Using one definition that includes different views seems to be an interesting option in order to respect the dialectical principle in peace education.

What Do Existing Indicators Say about being Context Sensitive?

Some of the analyzed reports synthesize their indicators into indexes that allow rankings of countries (HDI, GPI) from best to worst performers. Other indexes rank the countries using qualitative categories (HDI, Freedom House Index), while others do not compare countries (Social Watch). If ranking countries allows us to compare their situation with a similar standard, it can also be questioned whether it makes sense to compare such different situations.

The Education for All Development Index—EDI (UNESCO)—ranks countries and territories according to their level of EDI, classifying them into three categories: high, medium, and low EDI. This shows progress and setbacks with regard to education. However, due to problems collecting data in countries and territories in conflict or with inaccurate data sources, not all are included. For this reason, the Index cannot provide a global and regional overview of the full realization of the right to education.

An interesting approach comes from UNDP's Human Development Index (HDI), which analyzes two main dimensions: global and regional reports. Global yearly reports analyze and compare countries and territories, setting the following ranking: Very High Human Development, High Human Development, Medium Human Development, and Low Human Development. In Regional Human Devel-

Hologramatic principle	• How to have a global overview while being context sensitive? • How do we measure countries' improvements in peace education without making comparisons among countries?

BOX 16.2.

TABLE 16.2.

	Rankings	Groupings	No Classification
Pros	• Synthesizes the analysis very concretely • Puts more pressure on states to take effective measures	• Less competitive than rankings • Gives an idea of trends among the countries	• Avoids comparing countries that are too different • Allows a consideration of different views of a phenomenon
Contras	• Competitive logic • It compares with the same standards realities that have unequal contexts	• Less concrete than rankings	• Does not give global information about a phenomenon • Less useful for research purposes

opment yearly reports, classification based on geographic criteria by sub-regions analyze aspects of Human Development. The HDI can be adapted to the national level as well as the subnational level to compare differences among various groups of the population of each country or territory.

Some of the analyzed national indicators, on the contrary, do not rank countries and, therefore, avoid comparing different realities. Social Watch yearbook, for example, analyzes each country's trend in comparison to the same country in the previous year, but does not compare countries. This strategy allows for knowing the situation of each country, analyzing trends and, at the same time, prevents easily fabricated comparisons that would not take into account the specificity of each context. The evaluation of peace education at a national level can lead to the comparison of countries in order to grade the relative conditions of each of them and brings with it the risk of establishing unfair rankings. It is necessary to reflect, then, on how to set appropriate classification criteria in order to compare countries and territories.

Most of the analyzed indicators and indexes rank countries according to the classification of their own index (GPI, HDI, etc.). Only one (UNDP regional reports) groups countries according to another criteria than the ranking itself (geographical criteria). Similarly, there could be groupings according to a country's performance on peace education, or groupings according to other criteria, such as the level of violence within the context of where peace education programs are implemented (Salomon, 2010). This second option, where peace education programs would be analyzed with a lens that takes into account the context in which it is developed) would respect the hologramatic principle.

What Do Existing Indicators Say about Identifying the Factors Of Change?

Most reports choose their indicators according to a theoretical statement, selecting the ones that intuitively seem to be the key factors of change of the defined subject. Some reports (Social Watch, the Failed States Index) choose their

| Recursiveness principle | • What phenomena create virtuous spirals of peace education?
• How can we identify and measure them? |

BOX 16.3.

indicators according to their own theoretical definition. Others follow the criteria of international agreements. UNESCO's Education for All Development Index follows the criteria of the Dakar Framework for Action, where states agreed on six education goals to be met by 2015. UNICEF's Multiple Indicator Cluster Survey (MICS) has considered various agreements, such as twenty of the Millennium Development Goals (MDGs). None of the analyzed reports justify the selection of indicators by a different method than a theoretical statement (such as statistical calculations or other means).

Once the indicators are chosen, some reports use indicators as such, not pondered in an index. Freedom of the World, for example, gathers seven indicators, and DeRivera (2004) identifies thirteen Culture of Peace Indicators. UNICEF's MICS is composed of a range of indicators in six areas related to child welfare; this allows for the production of statistics and estimates of internationally comparable data. Some other reports resume indicators in a synthesized value (index) in which each indicator has a weight of one. EDI is composed of four indicators (weighted 1/4) that provide an overall assessment of a country's education system in relation to goals agreed upon. The Basic Capacities Index, and the Human Development Index synthetize three indicators (weighted 1/3) each.

Some others give weigh each indicator depending on how much they contribute to the analyzed phenomenon (GPI). The Global Peace Index applies a weight of 60% to measure internal peace and 40% for external peace. Inside each of these dimensions, every indicator has a range from one to five. In any of those cases, the weight given to every item seems determined by the experts' intuition "following robust debate" (IE&P, 2011, p. 7). While qualitative information can be as valid as more positivist methods, using intuition to decide on the weight of each indica-

TABLE 16.3.

	Independent indicators	Index without giving weight to indicators	Index with weight given to indicators
Pros	• Includes a wide range of different dimensions	• Prioritizes a few determinant indicators • More synthesized approach than indicators	• Allows for having a diversity of indicators • More synthetized approach than indicators
Contras	• General overview of a phenomenon. • Less focused than an index	• Mainly useful for very specific phenomena	• More subjective measurement than if weight is decided intuitively

tor, can lead to the reproduction of classical rankings where the most developed countries score better.

Having an index with weighted indicators seems to be a more adequate method of reflecting the complexity of multiple factors that together add up to peace. However, what is more important is to take into consideration that criteria for choosing and weighting indicators should not be exclusively subjective, as this might interfere in the identification of the key drivers of peace education.

Linking indicators to a theoretical definition offers one option for establishing some criteria for the selection of indicators. As always, there might certainly be other criteria and/or methods that could be applied to ensure the identification of other factors of change.

CONCLUSIONS AND REFLECTIONS

Considering the main principles of the paradigm of complexity defined by Edgar Morin, and analyzing how various national indicators and indexes respond or not to those principles, it has been possible to identify some criteria for a future development of peace education indicators at a national level. These criteria are:

- To include different perspectives on the concept, according to the *dialectical principle*. The inclusion of opposing views contributes to organization and complexity; thus an option could be to use one definition that comprehends different understandings to the concepts of peace education, and to make sure that all of those conceptions are reflected in the indicators. The set of indicators should include information about peace education at the formal, non-formal, and informal levels, data related to positive, negative, interpersonal and structural peace education.
- To analyze data taking into consideration context differences, according to *the hologramatic principle*. It seems important to avoid homogenizing different realities of the countries and territories, and to instead take into

TABLE 16.4.

Regarding the Peace Education Concept	Positive	Negative
Interpersonal	Personal social freedoms (Freedom House)	Vengeance-seeking group grievance (Fund for Peace)
Structural	• Access to the right to education (UNESCO) • Life expectancy at birth (HDI: source UNDP) • Relations with neighboring countries (GPI) • Index of Democratization (DeRivera: source PRIO)	• Military spending (GPI: source SIPRI) • Number of external and internal conflicts (GPI)

account their particularities. For this, it might be useful to set typologies of context scenarios sensitive to the fact that those countries and territories experience different situations of violence and peace. In this respect, the GPI itself could be used as an indicator of the country situation that could be used to define categories of countries.

- To identify the drivers of peace education through a variety of means, according to the *recursiveness principle*. To identify which practices and factors better contribute to peace education, it can be useful to analyze different factors—whether included in the definition of peace education or not—and evaluate to what extent they are or are not key factors.

Such indicators could be uneven economic development with ethnic, religious, or regional disparities (Fund for Peace, 2010), the percentage of seats in parliaments held by women (DeRivera, 2004: source UNDP), the legitimacy of the state, corruption, and lack of representativeness of the state (Fund for Peace), among others.

REFERENCES

Adams, D. (Ed.) (2010). *World report on the culture of peace.* Barcelona: Fundación Cultura de Paz.

Ashby, R. (1962). Principles of the self-organizing system. In H. Foerster & G. Zoopf (Eds.), *Principles of self-organization: Transactions of the University of Illinois Symposium.* London: Pergamon Press.

Bar-Tal, D. (2002). The elusive nature of peace education. In Salomon, G. & Nevo, B. (Eds.), *Peace education: The concept, principles and practice in the world.* (pp. 27–36). Mahwah, NJ: Lawrence Erlbaum

Borelli, M., & Haavelrsud, M. (1993). *Peace education within the archipielago of peace research 1945–1964.* Norway: Arena.

Bredo, E. (1982). *Knowledge and values in social and educational research.* Philadelphia: University Press.

Burns, R. (1981): Educación para el desarrollo y educación para la paz. *Perspectivas, 9*(2), 135–151.

Carr, W. (1990). *Hacia una ciencia crítica de la educación.* Barcelona, Spain: Laertes.

DeRivera, J. (2004). Assessing the basis for a culture of peace in contemporary societies. *Journal of Peace Research, 41*(5), 531–548.

Durkheim, E. (2003). *Educación y Sociología.* Barcelona, Spain: Península.

European Multi-Stakeholder Steering Group on Development Education (2010). *European development, education monitoring report—DE watch.* Brussels, Belgium: Deep.

Freedom House (2011). *Freedom in the world.* Retreived May 15, 2012 from http://www.freedomhouse.org.

Fund for Peace (2010). *The failed states index 2011.* Arlington, VA: Fund for Peace.

Galtung, J. (1975). *Essays in peace research, I. Peace: Research, education, action.* Oslo: Prio.

Galtung, J. (1985). *Sobre la paz.* Barcelona, Spain: Fontamara.

Haavelsrud, M. (1976). The hidden connection. In J, Xesús (Ed.), *Educación para la Paz. Su teoría y su práctica.* Madrid, Spain: Popular.

Haavelsrud, M. (1996). *Education in developments,* Tromso, Norway: Arena Publishers.

Haavelsrud, M., & Cabezudo, A. (2007). Rethinking peace education. In J. Galtung & C. Webel (Eds.), *Handbook of peace and conflict studies.* Trowbridge: The Cromwell Press.

Harris, I. (2003). *Peace education evaluation.* Paper presented American Educational Research Association (AERA), Chicago, IL.

IE&P (2011). *Global peace index. Methodology, results & findings.* Sydney, Australia: Institute for Economics & Peace.

Iglesias, Á. (2007). *Educar pacificando. Una pedagogía de los conflictos.* Santiago de Compostela, Spain: Seminario Galego de Educación para la Paz.

Jares, X. (1999). *Educación para la Paz. Su teoría y su práctica.* Madrid, Spain: Popular.

Morin, E. (1995). *Introducción al pensamiento complejo.* Barcelona, Spain: Gedisa.

Muñoz, F. (2001). *La paz imperfecta.* Granada, Spain: Instituto de la Paz y los Conflictos.

Neumann, J. (1966). *Theory of self-reproducing automata.* Urbana, IL: University of Illinois Press.

Popkewitz, T. (1988). *Paradigma e ideología en investigación educativa.* Madrid, Spain: Mondatori.

Reardon, B. (1988). *Comprehensive peace education. Educating for global responsibility.* New York, NY: Teachers College Press.

Richmond, O. (2006). The problem of peace: understanding the 'liberal peace.' *Conflict, Security & Development, 6*(3), 291–314.

Salomon, G., & Cairns, E. (Eds.). (2010). *Handbook on peace education.* New York, NY: Taylor and Francis.

Salomon, G., & Kupermintz, H. (2002). *The evaluation of Peace education programs: Main considerations and criteria.* Haifa, Israel: Center for Research on Peace Education.

Salomon, G., & Nevo, B. (2002). *Peace education, the concept, principles and practices around the world.* Mahwah, NJ: Lawrence Erlbaum Associates.

Social Watch—Plataforma 2015 y Más (2011). *Las políticas globales importan. Informe Social Watch 2010.* Madrid, Spain: Iepala.

UNDP (2011). *Human development report 2011, sustainability and equity: A better future for all.* New York, NY: UNDP.

UNESCO (2011). *EFA global monitoring report, the hidden crisis: armed conflict and education.* Paris, France: UNESCO.

UNICEF (2011). *The state of the world's children 2011: Adolescence an age of opportunity.* New York, NY: UNICEF.

United Nations. (1993). *Vienna Declaration and Programme of Action.* Adopted by the World Conference on Human Rights in Vienna on 25 June 1993. Office of the High Commissioner for Human Rights. Retrieved from http://www.ohchr.org/EN/ProfessionalInterest/Pages/Vienna.aspx

Weaver, W. (1948). Science and complexity. *American Scientist, 36,* 536–644.

Young, M. (1971). *New directions in sociological theory.* London, UK: Collier-Macmillan.

PART 3

IDEAS FOR EXPERIMENTATION AND "NEXT MOVES"

CHAPTER 17

RE-CONCEPTUALIZING IMPACT

Assessing Peace Education through a Social Movement Lens

Karen Ross

INTRODUCTION

Peace education has been used for many years as a way of improving relationships between individuals and groups. While it is practiced in a variety of different contexts, peace education has an especially important role to play in areas of intractable conflict—conflicts which, broadly defined, are resistant to de-escalation or resolution, and often characterized by periods of acute violence and negative inter-group relationships (Coleman, 2000). In areas of intractable conflict, peace education is one of many tools that are utilized in attempts to improve relationships between conflict groups and contribute to the transformation of societal or national conflict. Although the objectives of individual programs vary, ultimately peace education in intractable conflict areas aims to contribute to "peace writ large" (Chigas & Woodrow, 2009), or what Church and Shouldice (2002) define as "peace in the big picture or overall situation in the country" (p. 38).

This far-reaching aim, as well as the urgency of transforming entrenched conflicts that have continued for years or decades, suggests that it is critical for schol-

Peace Education Evaluation: Learning from Experience and Exploring Prospects, pages 257–271.
Copyright © 2015 by Information Age Publishing
All rights of reproduction in any form reserved.

ars and practitioners alike to understand whether peace education programs are achieving what they set out to do. Up until now, however, the success of peace education—its impact—has largely been measured in relatively narrow terms, providing a sense of how it can potentially change individuals over the short term but not how it contributes to broader peacebuilding processes. Thus, it is important to define alternative frameworks, both conceptual and methodological, for understanding the impact of peace education. To start, we should think about impact as encompassing a broader range of concepts and constructs, from a variety of disciplinary and epistemological perspectives, than has been utilized up until now in peace education evaluation. Improving understanding of peace education's consequences also requires expanding the lens through which we conceptualize the very implementation of peace education. By broadening these lenses, we widen the landscape for researching the impact of, and for addressing other empirical questions about, peace education.

This chapter presents initial thoughts about alternative approaches that can be used to expand an understanding of what success might look like in the field of peace education, and consequently, the impact of peace education implemented in conflict settings. I suggest, first, that the conception of the term *impact* should be broadened beyond its current use as an indicator of internal, individual-level change to include institutionalization of peace education, or its embeddedness in the conflict-ridden societies where it is implemented, as well as the way that peace education changes individual participants in the long-term. I then offer using concepts from social movement research as one potential framework for exploring impact, and examine the conceptual fit of several of the concepts utilized in social movement scholarship with research on the impact of peace education.

PEACE EDUCATION IN INTRACTABLE CONFLICT

The current state of peace education might best be described as chaotic. At the moment, the field consists of numerous initiatives, lacking a clear connection except for the use of the word "peace" to describe them all. Within the academic realm, as several authors have pointed out (Basiga, 2004; Harris, 2004; Reardon, 2000; Salomon & Kupermintz, 2002), the concept of peace education is used to cover disparate topics relating to, among other things, human rights education, the learning of conflict resolution techniques, environmental education, multicultural education, and education about war. In areas of intractable conflict, however, the goals of peace education are described in much more concrete terms. Specifically, scholars suggest that peace education programs in conflict regions are perceived to be:

> …an attempt to change the individual's perception of the other's collective narrative, as seen from the latter's point of view, and consequently of one's own social self, as well as to relate practically, less hatefully, and more trustingly toward that collective other. (Salomon, 2002, p. 9)

In other words, peace education in conflict zones aims to ameliorate relations between collective groups so as to contribute to a larger transformation of society away from conflict norms.

To achieve this, Bar-Tal (2000) suggests that each group in a given conflict must change beliefs about its own goals and abolish "the societal dreams and visions, expressed in specific goals, that caused the intergroup conflict" (p. 357). Bar-Tal suggests that education—including formal schooling—can be utilized in order to help change societal beliefs; yet, this requires institutional support for endeavors that run contrary to prevailing societal norms. In societies characterized by intractable conflict, such support rarely exists—in fact, peace education in any form may be considered a subversive activity in such contexts (Salomon, 2011). Thus, most peace education programs in intractable conflict settings are implemented outside of formal school systems.

RESEARCHING PEACE EDUCATION

Whether implemented in or out of schools, educational endeavors aiming to promote peace, tolerance, and coexistence between youth in conflict settings have been the focus of much academic scholarship. Research on peace education includes scholarship focusing on issues such as the process of its implementation (Maoz, 2004; Maoz, Bar-On, Bekerman & Jaber-Massara, 2004) and on the relationship between peace education and identity (Bekerman & Maoz, 2005; Hammack 2006, 2009). However, the so-called million-dollar question with respect to peace education is: "does it really make a difference?" (Salomon, 2006, p. 37).

In attempting to answer this question, much of the scholarship on peace education examines its effectiveness within the framework of Gordon Allport's contact hypothesis (1954), which suggests that when certain conditions are met, intergroup contact can be effective in reducing negative outgroup stereotypes (Pettigrew, 1998). Thus, most impact evaluations on peace education focus on individual effects, such as change in attitudes (e.g., Kupermintz & Salomon, 2005; Malhotra & Liyanage, 2005; Maoz, 2004), and suggest that programs are successful if students demonstrate positive attitudinal or behavior shifts. While this scholarship is important, a number of gaps limit the utility of existing impact research on peace education. For example, evaluations demonstrating a positive effect of participation in peace education on participants focus almost entirely on change as measured immediately following completion of programs (Salomon, 2011), with little attention paid to whether or how long individual-level change is maintained over time. Moreover, existing literature (e.g., Maoz, 2003; Yablon, 2007) often ignores the mechanisms that lead from intervention to outcome and the external social structures that can facilitate or constrain program consequences. Finally, in assessing peace education's effects, most research (e.g., Biton & Salomon, 2006; Malhotra & Liyanage, 2005) does not address the broader political context in which programs are implemented. Thus, current scholarship tells us little about whether, beyond immediate individual-level changes, peace education makes a difference in transforming societies away from an ethos of conflict and towards peace—and, if it does, how this process occurs.

Given the lofty objectives of peace education in conflict contexts, it seems that most evaluative research fails to measure whether these goals have been achieved. Why the discrepancy? In other words, what is the reason for the gap between desired outcomes (such as contributing to "peace writ large") and the way in which evaluation research measures the impact of peace education programs in conflict settings? This question can be answered in part by looking at the techniques often used to assess impact; research relying on self-reported questionnaire responses by program participants, or on interviews conducted immediately following participation in a time-bound program, tells us little beyond how these programs shape individual program participants in the short-term. At a broader level, however, the problem may be with the way in which evaluation, and evaluative research, is defined and perceived by the peace education community. In academic circles, evaluators of peace education are largely tied to traditional assessment methods that follow educational research more broadly in defining the "gold standard" (Delandshere, 2004) as research using randomized control groups and/or quasi-experimental design.

This approach has certain strengths—namely, the potential for generalizing to a larger population and, therefore, clear application to policy in the educational realm. However, the methods and conceptual frameworks currently in use by peace education researchers are ineffective as a means of fully understanding how well the broad objectives of peace education programs in conflict areas are being met. Moreover, these approaches define impact in peace education programs narrowly within the framework of positivist research. The indicators of peace education outcomes used in most research suggest a conception of impact narrower even than the definition provided by evaluation scholar Carol Weiss (1998), who defines impact as encompassing both long-term outcomes of a program, and the effects of programs on the larger community (p. 8). Such a narrow conceptualization of impact significantly limits the possibilities for understanding the role peace education can play in transforming the landscape of intractable conflicts. Thus, it is imperative that scholars of peace education broaden both the conceptual and the methodological lenses through which they evaluate peace education programs and organizations.

NEW APPROACHES TO PEACE EDUCATION AND PEACE EDUCATION EVALUATION

A first step in broadening these frameworks is to re-examine the mechanisms of peace education in intractable conflict. While Salomon's (2002) definition provides a nuanced understanding of the immediate goals of peace education in intractable conflict contexts, it is necessary to think about how peace education programs are linked to broader, societal-level peacebuilding processes and how peace education differs from education aimed at other types of learning and outcomes, such as formal school subjects like mathematics or geography. Moreover, as scholars in the field point out (Bar-Tal & Rosen, 2009; Salomon, 2011), much of the peace education work implemented in areas of ongoing conflict occurs outside of schools and school settings. In fact, in these settings, where official policies and/or societal norms contradict the goals of peace education, programs generally are implemented through grassroots or civil society organizations; these groups often function in tandem with other organizations to challenge established policy and work to shift society away from conflict and towards peace (see e.g., Hall-Cathala, 1990). In other words, organizations implementing peace education in areas of intractable conflict are often, though not always, linked to other organizations in peace movements.[1,2] Given this proximity, therefore, a more encompassing definition of peace education organizations might include them within the sphere of *social movement organizations* (SMOs). Such a definition captures the breadth of this field in a way that transcends the limitations of conceptualizing peace education solely in educational terms.

Viewing peace education organizations as part of broader social movements fits well with recent scholarship on collective action, such as literature on the multi-institutional politics model of social movements (Armstrong & Bernstein, 2008). In their work in this area, Armstrong and Bernstein challenge one of the dominant theoretical approaches to social movement research: political process theory (also known as political opportunity theory). This theory emphasizes the importance of favorable political contexts in enabling the success of social movement endeavors (McAdam, 1982). Armstrong and Bernstein suggest that in order to more comprehensively encompass phenomena falling outside the scope of traditional social movement categories, scholars should conceptualize domination or hegemony as organized not only around the state, as suggested by political process theory, but also around other formal institutions and cultural norms. Such an approach enables social movement theory to include organizations such as peace education organizations that challenge dominant discourses in conflict societies, rather than necessarily directly targeting educational or other state institutions. The multi-institutional approach to social movement scholarship also aligns with elements of what Polletta (2006) calls "awkward movements," specifically, groups that traditionally have been difficult to place within the framework of existing social movement research.

---

[1] This is true not only of peace education organizations in areas of intractable conflict. For example, Howlett and Harris (2010) point to the evolution of peace education in the United States and its close link during the late 19th century and early 20th century to organizations involved in international understanding, peacebuilding, and anti-militarism.

[2] Although Hall-Cathala classifies programs dedicated to Arab-Jewish contacts as a part of the Israeli peace movement, others have argued that this link is an ad hoc and ambiguous one, reflected primarily through the dual role played by individuals who work for peace education programs and are activists within other peace movement organizations (Abu-Nimer, 1999).

In addition to expanding the scope of social movement actors, conceptualizing peace education organizations as agents of social movement action significantly broadens the landscape for evaluating peace education programs. Specifically, conceptualizing peace education in this way suggests that empirical questions about success, or impact, might be addressed by examining varying facets of social movement outcomes. In the following pages, therefore, I utilize frameworks from the social movement literature to make the case for expanding the definition of impact in peace education, and discuss methodological approaches for understanding the link between mechanisms at play in peace education interventions and the impact of those interventions. I focus on the following social movement frameworks, which have particular relevance for understanding impact in peace education: *social movement success,* as defined in terms of political legitimacy; *the creation and maintenance of social networks,* as key factors in recruitment to and sustained participation in social movements; and other *factors leading to social movement recruitment.* The relevance of these particular frameworks stems from their conceptual fit, both with social movement research generally and with what scholars of peacebuilding and conflict resolution define as the potential outcomes of peacebuilding interventions.

Political Legitimacy

As discussed above, peace education programs in intractable conflict contexts are often initiated outside of formal educational institutions. In many cases, these programs directly contradict explicit and implicit messages conveyed in the curricula, which generally serve to reinforce group identity and the societal ethos of conflict (Bar-Tal, 2000), and thus minimize the potential for improving intergroup relations (Ben-Porath, 2006; Bush & Saltarelli, 2000). Therefore, programs implemented by peace education organizations lie outside of the realm of interventions that educational or other state institutions typically support. However, scholarship suggests that in order to successfully disseminate their ideology—and to simply survive—it is necessary that these organizations receive some level of institutional support (Anderson, 2001; Gawerc, 2010). As Brint, Contreras, and Matthews (2001) state, political or institutional legitimacy is essentially a prerequisite of success for educational endeavors: in other words, these endeavors are rarely successful unless, eventually, they receive state or institutional support. Moreover, institutionalization of peace-related messages means that there is greater potential for their widespread dissemination and, therefore, for these messages to have a significant influence on what and how students are taught about conflict and peace. Anderson (2001) suggests, "institutionalization as an indicator points to changes at the level of the larger society" (section 4).

Salomon (2011) points out that while peace education seeks to change the dispositions and values of individuals, those individual-level attributes are rooted in much broader social norms, indicating that for peace education "to have any lasting effect, it must affect the societal ethos" (p. 48). In order to understand the impact of peace education, therefore, it is important to focus not only on the way such programs impact individuals—or, in other words, the political effects of such programs—but also on the political legitimacy accorded to organizations implementing peace education programs and the extent to which they have been institutionalized. Such legitimacy is an indicator that organizations implementing peace education programs have gained adherents or supporters from within the system who might then utilize existing power structures to potentially enable broader change.

Methodologically, examining impact defined as political legitimacy requires a far different tactic from individually focused approaches utilized most often in evaluative research on peace education. Specifically, data collection and analysis methods such as the examination of organizational documents, interviews with key figures in educational policy, and analysis of public perceptions towards the organization(s) in question, can provide a richer understanding of whether and how peace education programs and organizations have become politically legitimized and/or part of mainstream educational institutions. Existing literature on the adoption of curricular and other educational reforms (e.g., Binder, 2000) uses these and similar data sources and methods in order to understand *how*, and *to what extent*, challengers to mainstream education have been accepted in the public eye as well as by decision-makers within the educational system.

Beyond the literature on educational reforms, research on the impact of peace education programs and organizations implementing them can draw on methods used in empirical research asking about the institutionalization of non-dominant collectivities—i.e., how social movements, broadly defined, succeed, and what that success means. Two examples from the social movement literature point to the potential of such an approach, as well as to the importance of comparison in how it is utilized. First, Armstrong and Crage's (2006) examination of why the Stonewall riots became a central part of gay collective memory addresses the question of what distinguished Stonewall from other similar events and, in doing so, delineates the analytical strength of comparing cases similar in their processes in order to isolate what differentiates them. The use of deliberate comparison strengthens the authors' overall conclusions about causal factors that enabled Stonewall to become an event of such importance in the gay collective memory. Second, Ganz's (2000) analysis of the unionization of California agriculture compares organizations with similar objectives and working during the same time period, drawing upon these similarities to highlight differences in what he calls strategic leadership. Ganz suggests that these differences are the causal reasons for one group's success in unionization relative to the other. Beyond the use of comparison, these examples both illustrate that success in social movement action is defined at least in part by the political and/or public recognition that is accorded to these movements. Examination of impact in peace education, therefore, might be well served by examining organizations through this lens, as well as by using similar methodological techniques.

Social Networks

In addition to focusing on the political legitimacy accorded to peace education, knowledge about the impact of peace education programs would be enhanced by more clearly understanding the degree to which social ties or networks are formed and maintained, both between individual participants in peace education programs and between the organizations themselves. The existence of social ties has been shown to be important in social phenomena, such as the creation of social capital (Putnam, 1995); within the literature on social movements, moreover, research suggests that these networks play an important role in both the recruitment of social movement participants (McAdam & Paulsen, 1993) and in their continued participation in movement activities (Passy 2002; Passy & Giugni, 2001; Stryker, 2000).

In the literature on conflict and conflict resolution, social networks have also taken on an increasingly important role in recent years, with a particular emphasis on networks at the organizational level. As Ricigliano (2003) points out, peacebuilding processes are inherently a combination of structural, social, and political elements, each of which, iteratively and in combination, help societies in conflict move towards stable peace. Specifically, Ricigliano states that networks of peacebuilding organizations are important because they:

> Promote information exchange between political, social, and structural actors working on a specific conflict, between official and unofficial actors, and between international actors and local partners. This information exchange will promote improved and integrated situation assessments and program design. (p. 452)

Thus, Ricigliano points to the importance of networks among organizations working at social, structural, and political levels, and argues that it is necessary for changes to occur at all three levels simultaneously in order for peacebuilding processes to fully take hold.

As Nan (2008) points out, networks can be either exclusive or inclusive. Exclusive networks, in conflict areas, often reinforce existing conflict dynamics rather than helping transcend them (p. 127). On the other hand, research has demonstrated that inclusive peacebuilding networks are particularly important for promoting positive societal shifts. For example, Gamson and Modigliani (1963) suggest that the level of tension between two entities is captured conceptually by the ratio of disintegrative to integrative ties; increasing the ratio of integrative ties when few are present, they argue, can have a significant influence on reducing tension and ensuring stability. Similarly, case study research on the Global Partnership for the Prevention of Armed Conflict (GPPAC), a worldwide network of civil society representatives focused on ending armed conflict, points to a number of factors important for assessing the success of networks and their ability to positively impact peace building processes (Verkoren, 2006), including network inclusiveness. As a whole, this scholarship thus suggests that among the most important issues in assessing the potential impact of peace education networks is establishing "how far a network helps foster coordinated, reciprocal action" (Church et al., 2003, p. 2).

Methodologically, both qualitative approaches and structured, quantitative analysis can be undertaken to help understand the potential role of peace education networks in contributing to broader peacebuilding processes. For example, interviews with key network members can be used to assess the formation of social capital within collaborative groups (e.g., Mandarano, 2009). Social network analysis techniques can also be utilized to map attributes such as network density, centrality of actors, and network structure. This analysis can be undertaken at the organizational level to understand the connections among peace education organizations and between such organizations and other central actors in the peacebuilding field. This helps to assess the existence and extent of cross-cutting ties among peace education organizations, and thus the potential impact these organizations might have on peacebuilding at the societal level.

At the individual level, social network analysis can provide information about the extent to which network ties exist among participants of peace education programs. Given the importance of network ties for social movement recruitment and participation, the density of these ties is a strong indicator of the potential impact participation in peace education programs can have on providing the kind of support necessary for individuals to continue working for peace beyond the scope of the educational programs in which they participate. Here, too, both quantitative and qualitative methods can be used to assess the strength of network ties as well as their continuity over time. For example, Passy and Giugni's (2000) study of participation in the Swiss solidarity movement utilized life history interviews in order to "unveil structures of meaning" (p. 126) about the way networks facilitated or hindered sustained commitment of individuals to the movement. Similar methods can be used with participants in peace education programs in order to enable greater understanding of the way relationships formed through program participation influence commitment to peacebuilding. Alternatively, McAdam and Paulsen's (1993) analysis of the networks of Freedom Summer participants points to the potential of numerical analysis techniques for assessing the potential impacts of networks, utilizing network analysis of survey data in order to provide a more basic understanding of the number of relationships between program participants and their relative strength.

Links to Continued Peace Activism

Finally, an important, yet under-researched, indicator of peace education impact is continued engagement in collective social action for peace. According to Salomon (2002), in addition to creating short-term changes in attitudes and behaviors, peace education should result in a disposition among participants to engage in nonviolent activities. Others in the peacebuilding field echo this sentiment. For example, Galtung (1983) has written that peace education has to be more than teaching that war is not good: it also must "be concerned with what to do about it" (p. 283). Likewise, Anderson and Olson (2003) suggest that one of the main indicators of the effectiveness of peacebuilding initiatives is that participants in these programs develop their own initiatives for peace.

The necessity of connecting individual participation in peace education to the broader socio-political context and change over time exemplifies the inherent flaws in measuring only short-term and/or attitudinal change among participants. Yet, given the complexity and fluidity of life courses and choices, experimental or longitudinal studies of participants in peace education programs are both logistically and methodologically difficult to pursue as an approach to understanding the ways participation in such programs conditions participants in the long-term.

The social movement literature, again, hints at both substantive and methodological possibilities for addressing these complexities. Research in this field implicitly suggests that isolated transformational experiences, such as participation in educational programs, can create the impetus for ongoing and active participation in social movements. For example, in his discussion of participation in high-risk activism, McAdam (1986) presents a model for recruitment that leads back to two fundamental factors: families, and what he terms, "other socialization influences" (see chart, p. 69). What constitutes these "other socialization influences" remains vague and largely unexamined in social movement literature; however, this concept could potentially include participation in educational programs, particularly in light of other sociological research demonstrating that social activism can be affected by singular experiences such as encounters with new movements or exposure to activism (Corning & Myers, 2002; Downton & Wehr, 1998). In addition to providing evidence of what McAdam's "other socialization influences" might look like, these studies indicate that specific experiences can lead to the social-psychological state of "cognitive liberation" necessary for activism (Nepstad, 1997): in other words, the shift in consciousness from accepting the system to perceiving it as unjust, and from feeling powerless to believing in one's own efficacy or ability to instigate change. They thus illustrate the potential role peace education programs might play in recruiting students to peace movements and continued peace activism.

In order to assess the extent to which peace education programs fulfill this potential role, evaluation methods can be used that can link participation in these programs to continued involvement in peace movement activities. Longitudinal research is one approach that can provide insight into peace education programs and subsequent choices and worldviews of their participants over time. Yet, the logistics of longitudinal research make it methodologically problematic. In particular, the funding necessary for sustaining a longitudinal study over a period of years and decades is out of reach for most organizations and funders interested in assessing the impact of peace education programs. Thus, another approach for examining the link between program participation and participation in broader social movement activities is the use of retrospective interviewing or life history research. Although some recent scholarship in the field of evaluation has dismissed qualitative methods as insufficiently rigorous (Harris, 2008), the retrospective/ life history approach has been used by well-established social movement scholars and sociologists of education to demonstrate how participation in specific events is significant at later life stages. For example, in McAdam's (1988) seminal study, retrospective interviews of Freedom Summer participants were used to understand how participation in these events influenced their later commitments to social activism. Likewise, in a study on the long-term impact of school desegregation, Holme, Wells, and Revilla (2005) conducted in-depth interviews with graduates of desegregated schools in order to assess the influence of students' experiences. According to the authors, "graduates only came to understand what they learned from their high school experience *after* they left high school" (p. 14). Finally, recent research on North American peace education programs for Israelis and Palestinians (Lazarus, 2011; Lazarus, chapter 11, this volume) serves to exemplify the potential of in-depth, retrospective data for assessing the influence of participation in peace education programs upon participants' willingness to engage in continued activism. The in-depth, open-ended interviews necessary for collecting information about how program participants attribute meaning and influence to their involvement with peace education hold tremendous potential for enabling researchers to understand the connection between participation in peace education programs and long-term impacts of that participation.

CONCLUSIONS

In the preceding pages, I have highlighted some of the limitations of current evaluation research on peace education and suggested that in order to fully understand the impact of peace education in conflict areas, we need to expand the conceptual and methodological lenses utilized for research in this field. Scholars have made it clear that evaluative scholarship must move beyond narrow input-output models and that it should measure change beyond the immediate, short-term, individual level (Salomon, 2011).

A major limitation to achieving this is the fact that the impact of peace education, like that of conflict resolution interventions as a whole, is contingent on a complex interplay of factors ranging from internal affective states to the broad, macro-level context in which programs are implemented. Yet, even while acknowledging the Sisyphean endeavor it entails, inroads must be made into addressing the "methodological anarchy" of evaluative research in the peacebuilding field (Hoffman, 2004, p. 12). Despite their limitations, I suggest utilizing concepts from research on social movements as one approach to better understand the potential of peace education programs to transform societies and help move them from intractable conflict towards peace. These concepts are helpful in particular for providing a lens for viewing impact that acknowledges the institutional as well as individual nature of peace education programs in conflict contexts, and for addressing both the mechanisms linking intervention to outcome and the relationship between micro—and macro-level processes inherent in this type of endeavor. Thus, while at the moment it may be "impossible for peace educators to claim that the world is more peaceful as a result of their endeavors" (Harris, 2008, p. 260), engaging with this more expansive palate of research methodologies might help us better comprehend peace education's role in the creation of a more peaceful and just society.

REFERENCES

Abu-Nimer, M. (1999). *Dialogue, conflict resolution, and change: Arab-Jewish encounters in Israel.* Albany, NY: State University of New York Press.

Allport, G. (1954). *The nature of prejudice.* New York: Doubleday Anchor Books.

Anderson, M. (2001). *Measuring peace: Indicators of impact for peace practice.* Boston, MA: The Collaborative for Development Action, Inc.

Anderson, M. B., & Olson, L. (2003). *Confronting war: Critical lessons for peace practitioners.* Cambridge: The Collaborative for Development Action, Inc.

Armstrong, E. A., & Bernstein, M. (2008). Culture, power, and institutions: A multi-institutional politics approach to social movements. *Sociological Theory, 26*(1), 74–99.

Armstrong, E. A., & Crage, S. M. (2006). Movements and memory: The making of the stonewall myth. *American Sociological Review, 71*(5), 724–751.

Bar-Tal, D. (2000). From intractable conflict through conflict resolution to reconciliation: Psychological analysis. *Political Psychology, 21*(2), 351–365.

Bar-Tal, D., & Rosen, Y. (2009). Peace education in societies involved in intractable conflicts: Direct and indirect models. *Review of Educational Research, 79*(2), 557–575.

Basiga, B. (2004). Globalization and peace education. *Canadian Social Studies, 38*(3), 18.

Bekerman, Z., & Maoz, I. (2005). Troubles with identity: Obstacles to coexistence education in conflict-ridden societies. *Identity: An International Journal of Theory and Research, 5*(4), 341–357.

Ben-Porath, S. R. (2006). *Citizenship under fire: Democratic education in times of conflict.* Princeton, NJ: Princeton University Press.

Binder, A. (2000). Why do some curricular challenges work while others do not? The case of three Afrocentric challenges. *Sociology of Education, 73*(2), 69–91.

Biton, Y., & Salomon, G. (2006). Peace in the eyes of Israeli and Palestinian youths as function of collective narratives and participation in a peace education program. *Journal of Peace Research, 43*(2), 167–180.

Brint, S., Contreras, M. F., & Matthews, M. T. (2001). Socialization messages in primary schools: An organizational analysis. *Sociology of Education, 74*(3), 157–180.

Bush, K. D., & Saltarelli, D. (2000). *The two faces of education in ethnic conflict: Towards a peacebuilding education for children.* Florence, Italy: UNICEF Innocenti Research Centre.

Chigas, D., & Woodrow, P. (2009). Envisioning and pursuing peace writ large: a response. In B. Schmelzle & M. Fischer (Eds.), *Peacebuilding at a crossroads? Dilemmas and paths for another generation* (pp. 47–58). Berlin, Germany: Berghof Conflict Research.

Church, C., & Shouldice, J. (2002). *The evaluation of conflict resolution interventions: Framing the state of play.* Londonderry, UK: Initiative on Conflict Resolution and Ethnicity (INCORE).

Church, M., Bitel, M., Armstrong, K., Fernando, P., Gould, H., Joss, S., et al. (2003). *Participation, relationships and dynamic change: New thinking on evaluating the work of international networks* (Working Paper #121). London, UK: Developing Planning Unit, University College London.

Coleman, P. T. (2000). Intractable conflict. In M. Deutsch & P. T. Coleman (Eds.), *The handbook of conflict resolution: Theory and practice* (pp. 428–50). San Francisco, CA: Jossey-Bass.

Corning, A. F., & Myers, D. J. (2002). Individual orientation toward engagement in social action. *Political Psychology, 23*(4), 703–739.

Delandshere, G. (2004). The moral, social and political responsibility of educational researchers: Resisting the current quest for certainty. *International Journal of Educational Research, 41*, 237–256.

Downton, J., & Wehr, P. (1998). Persistent pacifism: How activist commitment is developed and sustained. *Journal of Peace Research, 35*(5), 531–550.

Galtung, J. (1983). Peace education: Learning to hate war, love peace, and to do something about it. *International Review of Education, 29*(3), 281–287.

Gamson, W. A., & Modigliani, A. (1963). Tensions and concessions: The empirical confirmation of belief systems about soviet behavior. *Social Problems, 11*(1), 34–48.

Ganz, M. (2000). Resources and resourcefulness: Strategic capacity in the unionization of California agriculture, 1959–1966. *American Journal of Sociology, 105*(4), 1003–1062.

Gawerc, M. (2010). *Israeli Palestinian peace-building partnerships: Stories of adaptation, asymmetry, and survival* (Doctoral dissertation). Boston College.

Hall-Cathala, D. (1990). *The peace movement in Israel, 1967–87.* New York, NY: St. Martin's Press.

Hammack, P. L. (2006). Identity, conflict, and coexistence: Life stories of Israeli and Palestinian adolescents. *Journal of Adolescent Research, 21*(4), 323–369.

Hammack, P. L. (2009). Exploring the reproduction of conflict through narrative: Israeli youth motivated to participate in a coexistence program. *Peace and Conflict: Journal of Peace Psychology, 15*(1), 49–74.

Harris, I. (2004). Peace education theory. *Journal of Peace Education, 1*(1), 5–20.

Harris, I. M. (2008). The promise and pitfalls of peace education evaluation. In J. Lin, E. J. Brantmeier, & C. Bruhn (Eds.), *Transforming education for peace* (pp. 245–263). Charlotte, NC: Information Age Publishing.

Hoffman, M. (2004). *Peace and conflict impact assessment methodology.* Berghof Research Center for Constructive Conflict Management.

Holme, J. J., Wells, A. S., & Revilla, A. T. (2005). Learning through experience: What graduates gained by attending desegregated high schools. *Equity & Excellence in Education, 38*(1), 14–24.

Howlett, C. F., & Harris, I. M. (Eds.), (2010). *Books, not bombs: teaching peace since the dawn of the republic.* Charlotte, NC: Information Age Publishing.

Kupermintz, H., & Salomon, G. (2005). Lessons to be learned from research on peace education. *Theory Into Practice, 44*(4), 293–302.

Lazarus, N. (2011). *Evaluating peace education in the Oslo-Intifada generation: a long-term impact study of Seeds of Peace 1993–2000* (Doctoral dissertation). American University, Washington DC. (ProQuest Publication Number 3465403). Retrieved October 3, 2011 from ProQuest database.

Malhotra, D., & Liyanage, S. (2005). Long-Term effects of peace workshops in protracted conflicts. *Journal of Conflict Resolution, 49*(6), 908–924.

Mandarano, L. A. (2009). Social network analysis of social capital in collaborative planning. *Society & Natural Resources, 22*(3), 245–260.

Maoz, I. (2003). Peace-building with the hawks: Attitude change of Jewish-Israeli hawks and doves following dialogue encounters with Palestinians. *International Journal of Intercultural Relations, 27*(6), 701–714

Maoz, I. (2004). Coexistence is in the eye of the beholder: Evaluating intergroup encounter interventions between Jews and Arabs in Israel. *Journal of Social Issues, 60*(2), 437–452.

Maoz, I., Bar-On, D., Bekerman, Z., & Jaber-Massarwa, S. (2004). Learning about 'good enough' through 'bad enough': A story of a planned dialogue between Israeli Jews and Palestinians. *Human Relations, 57*(9), 1075–1101.

McAdam, D. 1982. *Political process and the development of Black insurgency, 1930–1970.* Chicago, IL: University of Chicago Press.

McAdam, D. (1986). Recruitment to high-risk activism: The case of freedom summer. *American Journal of Sociology, 92*(1), 64–90.

McAdam, D. (1988). *Freedom summer.* New York, NY: Oxford University Press.

McAdam, D. & Paulsen, R. (1993). Specifying the relationship between social ties and activism. *American Journal of Sociology, 99*(3), 640–667.

Nan, S. A. (2008). Social capital in exclusive and inclusive networks: Satisfying human needs through conflict and conflict resolution. In M. Cox (Ed.), *Social capital and peace-building* (pp. 172–185). New York, NY: Routledge.

Nepstad, S. E. (1997). The process of cognitive liberation: Cultural synapses, links, and frame contradictions in the U.S.-Central American peace movement. *Sociological Inquiry, 67*(4), 470–487.

Passy, F. (2002). Social networks matter. But how? In M. Diani & D. McAdam (Eds.), *Social movements and networks: Relational approaches to collective action* (pp. 21–48). Oxford, UK: Oxford University Press.

Passy, F., & Giugni, M. (2000). Life-Spheres, networks, and sustained participation in social movements: A phenomenological approach to political commitment. *Sociological Forum, 15*(1), 117–144.

Passy, F., & Giugni, M. (2001). Social networks and individual perceptions: Explaining differential participation in social movements. *Sociological Forum, 16*(1), 123–153.

Pettigrew, T. F. (1998). Intergroup contact theory. *Annual Review of Psychology, 49*, 65–85.

Polletta, F. (2006). Mobilization forum: Awkward movements. *Mobilization: An International Journal, 11*(4), 475–478.

Putnam, R. D. (1995). Bowling alone: America's declining social capital. *Journal of Democracy, 6*(1), 65–78.

Reardon, B. A. (2000). Peace education: A review and projection. In B. Moon, S. Brown, & M. Ben Peretz (Eds.), *International companion to education* (pp. 397–425). New York, NY: Routledge.

Ricigliano, R. (2003). Networks of effective action: Implementing an integrated approach to peacebuilding. *Security Dialogue, 34*(4), 445–462.

Salomon, G. (2002). The nature of peace education: Not all programs are created equal. In G. Salomon & B. Nevo (Eds.), *Peace education: The concept, principles, and practices around the world* (pp. 3–14). Mahwah, NJ: Lawrence Erlbaum Associates.

Salomon, G. (2006). Does peace education really make a difference? *Peace and Conflict: Journal of Peace Psychology, 12*(1), 37–48.

Salomon, G. (2011). Four major challenges facing peace education in regions of intractable conflict. *Peace and Conflict: Journal of Peace Psychology, 17*(1), 46–59.

Salomon, G., & Kupermintz, H. (2002). *The evaluation of peace education programs: Main considerations and criteria.* Haifa, Israel: Center for Research on Peace Education, University of Haifa.

Stryker, S. (2000). Identity competition: Key to differential social movement participation? In S. Stryker, T. J. Owens, & R. W. White (Eds.), *Self, identity, and social movements* (pp. 21–40). Minneapolis, MN: University of Minnesota Press.

Verkoren, W. (2006). *Networking for peace: Opportunities for the global partnership for the prevention of armed conflict.* The Hague, The Netherlands: European Centre for Conflict Prevention/International Secretariat of the Global Partnership for the Prevention of Armed Conflict.

Weiss, C. H. (1998). *Evaluation.* Upper Saddle River, NJ: Prentice Hall.

Yablon, Y.B. (2007). Cognitive rather than emotional modification in peace education programs? Advantages and limitations. *Journal of Moral Education 36*(1), 51–65.

CHAPTER 18

PEDAGOGY OF ADDRESSIVITY

Peace Education as Evaluation

Naghmeh Yazdanpanah

INTRODUCTION

There is an intrinsic similarity among the constituent components of the triad "peace education evaluation." In spite of the prevailing analytical scrutiny and formal procedures which set the connotation of the terms today, education and evaluation are inherently interwoven in the fabric of life. John Dewey's (1997) assertion that "any social arrangement that remains vitally social, or vitally shared, is educative" perhaps most eloquently conveys the inseparability of education from life (p. 9). Evaluation, as well, has primordially been part of human life, allowing for the survival of the human species and underlying the numerous decisions people make on a daily basis (Stake, 2004). Peace, the final component of the triad, again reiterates this link to life by highlighting the element of serving life and improving its quality.

The purpose of this chapter is to discuss the present state of peace education evaluation in view of the innate affiliation it has to life and vouch for re-examination of the notion so that it can fully capture this linkage to life. The chapter begins with a critical overview of current trends in peace education evaluation in

Peace Education Evaluation: Learning from Experience and Exploring Prospects,
pages 273–286.
Copyright © 2015 by Information Age Publishing
All rights of reproduction in any form reserved.

relation to ways that the broader literature on evaluation research has evolved. Drawing on the tradition of transformational peace education, it highlights the inherently evaluative nature of peace education and suggests that peace education itself is a constant evaluation of the quality of life. Finally, the chapter sets to reveal the pedagogical and epistemological premises within peace literature which endorse this evaluatory nature of peace education by putting the thoughts of Michael Bakhtin, Paulo Freire, and M. K. Gandhi in dialogue with one another, using their points of convergence to propose an evaluatory peace education: a pedagogy of addressivity.

EVALUATION RESEARCH AND PEACE EDUCATION

There is growing agreement about the importance and necessity of evaluation in peace education (Ashton, 2004; Bar-Tal, 2002), although actual practice and theoretical richness has yet to mirror this level of recognition and recommendation. The available literature is partly concerned with the small proportion of educational programs that makes use of evaluation (Jenkins, 2008; Nevo & Berm, 2002) and the limited availability and exchange of information about extant evaluations, which inhibit professional dialogue on the subject (Ashton, 2004; Church, 2008). Far from being an integrated part in the design process of peace education programs, evaluation is still mainly viewed as a post-hoc activity (Ashton, 2007; Rothman, 1997). When discussing theoretical implications, the literature's most immediate focus is on the difficulties in evaluating peace education and the challenges of assessing programs' outcomes and finding appropriate criteria for evaluation (Ashton, 2004; Fountain, 1999; Harris, 2008). Relatively few studies move beyond achievement of program outcomes and impacts to examine other fundamental issues involved in peace education evaluation (Austin, Fischer, & Wils, 2003; Kupermintz & Salomon, 2005). To better understand the state of peace education evaluation, it is useful to view it in the context of the broader field of evaluation studies.

Since the emergence of evaluation as a systematic field of research,[1] there has been tremendous debate, revision, and transformation in the field's founding assumptions and premises. Earlier approaches attributed the value of a program to the extent that stated objectives had been achieved (Nevo, 1983; Stufflebeam & Shinkfield, 2007) and were mostly governed by a technical, positivist perspective in which only information that could be measured quantitatively was deemed valid (Mabry, 2010; Potter, 2006). As a result of increased awareness of the social implications of evaluating, this approach's claim to value-free objectivity was contested and key questions were raised: valuable to whom? in what contexts?

---

[1] The emergence of evaluation studies as a discipline is often attributed to the 1960s when the launch of various educational and social programs in the United States brought the need for their evaluation to the foreground. Nonetheless, the history of the field can be traced back to some 150 years prior to this period (Stufflebeam & Madaus, 2000).

according to which sets of values? and how are those values constructed? In response to these questions, a diverse range of theories and persuasions were put forward, making the field more dynamic and bringing about more interpretive and critical modes of inquiry.

In the discourse on peace education evaluation, there is little sign of direct reference to or serious engagement with this valuable body of work and the fundamental questions it poses. When issues such as the importance of process, participation and ownership, and power relations arise, they are often mentioned in such cursory a manner that their implications are hardly articulated. Most peace educators are attentive to and aware of the social and political complexities about which they need to be sensitive. However, when it comes to evaluation, an epistemological shift seems to occur by which these issues are, for the most part, taken for granted. This exposes peace education evaluation to the risk of remaining confined to a technical approach and losing its aliveness so that it becomes a mere external pressure and a "burdensome imposition" (Rothman, 1997, p. 452).

Peace Education as Evaluation

The challenge of transcending the narrow positivist and objectives-based notion of evaluation and invigorating peace education evaluation may be partly addressed through more rigorous consideration of the broader literature and discussion on the theory and practice of evaluation. Nevertheless, there is also a need to delve deeper into the mutual implications that exist between the ways that peace education is conceptualized and the manners through which it is evaluated, as well as to examine how the reciprocal bearing that they have on one another opens the possibility for both notions to be re-defined.

Peace education can be approached from different perspectives. Betty Reardon (1988) identifies three historical phases of *reform, reconstruction,* and *transformation,* each of which has different assumptions about knowledge and learning. In the reform and reconstructive approaches, peace knowledge is assumed to be a substantive package of information and norms, the successful transmission of which would result in the desired behavioral or institutional changes. These approaches, consequently, think of learning as accumulation of data and lean towards instruction as their main mode of pedagogic practice. The transformative approach is guided by the principle of mutual responsibility for creation of knowledge and opts for the *edu-learning* pedagogic mode in which learning is a lifelong process of "doing, acting, and becoming... within a consciousness of ever-expanding spheres of complexity and constant change" (Reardon, 1988, p. 48).

In view of these epistemological and pedagogic distinctions, objectives-based evaluation is in alignment with the non-transformative approaches. What binds these approaches together is their shared positivist predisposition towards technical proficiency which attempts to tame life by defining peace education and its evaluation in terms of given, a-historical truths and preordained goals and standards. With its emphasis on means and processes instead of ends and goals, however, the conversational mode of inquiry in transformative peace education embraces the multi-faceted nature of truth and aims to capture the flow of life in all the changes and transformation through which it proceeds.

The close connection of peace, education, and evaluation to life, with which the opening lines of this chapter began and to which the transformative approach refers, provides the possibility to view these components in a new light. Peace can be construed as an unceasing process of critique and envisioning geared towards serving life through transformation of what diminishes its quality. In this sense, not only is any peace process inherently educational, but also peace education is by nature evaluative. To make this statement even bolder, it is possible to play with the Gandhian maxim and claim that, in fact, *there is no way to evaluate peace education; peace education is evaluation.* This is to say that far from a mechanical process or a lifeless object of measurement, peace education itself is a constant evaluation of individual and communal well-being.

The concept of peace education as evaluation emerges when the idea of peace education as transmission is replaced by peace education as an open-ended process of discovery. An evaluatory peace education, as an ongoing meditation on life in terms of what enriches or tarnishes it, is much less concerned with articulation and achievement of any specific way of life than it is intent on perceiving the qualities of life as experienced from different perspectives and angles. Within such a framework, the educational process and its evaluation become coterminous activities (Schwandt, 2001); not only does the pedagogy realign itself to life in continuous cycles of evaluation, but the evaluation practice also can itself be described as pedagogic.

FOUNDATIONAL TENETS:
BETWEEN BAKHTIN, FREIRE, AND GANDHI

When peace education is regarded as a constant evaluation of life and how it can be enriched, the boundaries between education and evaluation fall apart. This is reflected in how Reardon considers *evaluation* to be one of the three significant transformative learning processes next to *speculation* and *integration* (Reardon, 1988). The theories of evaluation which emphasize interpretation, deliberation, and value pluralism have much to contribute to an educative-evaluative peace practice (Guba & Lincoln, 1989; House & Howe, 1999). Nevertheless, what are the conceptual premises within peace literature from which the possibility of such a practice can be inferred?

This section intends to respond to this question by putting the thoughts of Mikhail Bakhtin, Paulo Freire, and M. K. Gandhi in dialogue with each other. Notwithstanding their evident differences, there are common threads and thematic similarities between their systems of meaning which are consistent with what has been iterated thus far about transformative education and its linkage to life and which can provide a conceptual foundation in support of peace education as evaluation. These points of convergence have been organized under three tenets of *diversified truth, unity in multeity,* and the *dialogic self.* Working in relation to one another, these tenets encompass the epistemological shifts of consciousness that make an evaluatory peace pedagogy possible. Before moving to the discussion of how these tenets work to create such pedagogy, this section focuses on these tenets and how they are reflected in the thoughts of each of the thinkers.[2]

Diversified Truth

For Gandhi, truth is the ultimate reality and "the sole justification for existence" (2001, p. 38). This is manifested in his reference to the notion of *Sat-Chit-Anada* (Truth-knowledge-bliss), which is usually ascribed to the Brahman (the supreme and universal spirit) and indicates that human salvation rests upon the full-hearted devotion to truth. It is in this light that the fearless practice of truth is regarded a religious as well as an ontological duty and becomes the shaping force behind Gandhi's entire social and political vision.

Nevertheless, as resounding as his conviction in the all-encompassing nature of truth might be, so is Gandhi's emphasis on the human limitations in understanding it. He contends that perfect eternal Truth can never be fully comprehended. Because the human mind functions though numerous media, different people conceive of truth differently, so that the only available manifestation of truth is "what the voice within tells you" (Prabhu & Rao, 1946). According to Gandhi, while the search for truth can be pursued amid these relative understandings of it, "no one has the right to coerce others to act according to his own view of truth" (1933, p. 157).

Bakhtin (1984) believes that truth is by nature dialogic, asserting that truth does not belong to any single individual but is rather "born *between people* collectively searching for truth, in the process of their dialogic interactions" (p. 110). Bakhtin views the world as an event which is always experienced from a unique temporal/special site, giving each person a specific *field of vision,* or consciousness, that can never merge into consciousnesses present in other sites. Therefore, rather than existing "in-themselves," thoughts, and truth itself, always belong to a particular consciousness and field of vision, and thus has a particular valid voice (p. 31).

For Bakhtin, this dialogic notion of truth and plurality of independent voices is manifested in the polyphonic novel[3] mainly because it recognizes that its own language is not the center of the ideological world. The author allows her charac-

---

[2] Far from an attempt to exhaust the theoretical dimensions of these systems of thought, the ideas and concepts referred to in this section are merely used so as to provide a general understanding of the thinker's theories as well as to clarify how the tenets fit within the constellation of their thoughts. The chapter, thus, does not claim to present or expect from the reader a thorough comprehension of these theories and their pertinent terminology.

[3] As a literary critic, Bakhtin carefully studied the genre of novel, and more specifically the polyphonic novel, which he thought can offer new insight into the "human consciousness and the dialogic sphere of its existence" (1984, p. 270). In effect, Bakhtin's thoughts on language and the novel can

ters' consciousness and voice to develop without subordinating one to another or finalizing their fates in her own authorial vision. The polyphonic novel, thus, embodies a plenitude of languages of everyday life "all of which are equally capable of being 'languages of truth,' but, since such is the case, all of which are equally relative, reified, and limited" (Bakhtin, 1981, p. 367).

Freire's thoughts about truth are found in his writings about humans' ability to actively perceive reality. He points out that people "find themselves rooted in temporal-spatial conditions which mark them and which they also mark" (1972, p. 100). Humans are always "in a situation," and their consciousness of their situation is shaped dialectically in their relation with the world in each historical epoch. Freire believes that understanding this historicity, which he calls the solidarity between the world and humans, help humans perceive reality as a dynamic process of transformation and creation.

For Freire, learning is a process of creation and invention and knowledge emerges only through "continuing, hopeful inquiry human beings pursued in this world, with the world and with each other" (2000, p. 72). He polemically asserts that on this journey of inquiry "I cannot think *for others*, or *without others*, nor can others think *for me*" (1972, p. 100). This forms the basis of the problem posing approach to education in which the learners' historical condition and their awareness of it are presented as questions to be investigated with active participation of the learners as *co-investigators*.

Unity in Multeity

Yet another similarity among these thinkers is their search for a sense of organic unity in the midst of the provisionality and polyphony of truth. For Bakhtin, human life and language are governed by two opposing forces. While the *centrifugal* forces, whose power rests on the dialogic nature of meaning, stratify life into "a multitude of concrete worlds and verbal-ideological belief systems" (1981, p. 288) by orienting each utterance[4] towards the myriad of possible meanings it can have (Holquist, 1990, p. 69), the *centripetal* forces try to unify life with "processes of socio-political and cultural centralization" (Bakhtin, 1981, p. 271). They attempt to counteract the dialogizing effects of centrifugal forces by creating a unitary language.

Thus although Bakhtin regards existence as the "unified event of being," his views about the irreducible polyphony of life make his concept of unity quite distinct from what the term may usually convey. He mentions that in monologic worldviews the unity of existence is taken as the unity of consciousnesses so

---

be taken as a metaphor from which his higher philosophy about the human self and the world can be deduced.

[4] The utterance can be considered as the basic unit of studying language within Bakhtin's dialogic philosophy of language, as opposed to the sentence. Rather than containing only what is said, the utterance should better be understood as an actively performed speech act.

that a *single* consciousness becomes the benchmark of what is true, delegating whatever is different into categories of *irrelevance* or *error* (1981, p. 80). Then, in a passage that demands to be quoted, he constructs a different relation between unity and truth:

> It is quite possible to imagine and postulate a unified truth that requires a plurality of consciousnesses, one that cannot in principle be fitted into the bounds of a single consciousness, one that is... by its very nature full of event potential and is born at a point of contact among various consciousnesses. (1984, p. 81)

Unity in diversity within Gandhian thought is the result of the relation between ultimate truth and the relative understandings of it. Being (Sat) is at the etymological root of truth (Satya), and therefore, "nothing is or exists in reality except truth" (Gandhi, 2001, p. 38). This notion of eternal truth, all else being momentary, is what appeases the mind of the seeker in the face of the infinite multeity of human truths for even though the relative personal perspectives on truth might appear incompatible, they are in reality "like the countless and apparently different leaves of the same tree" (2001, p. 34).

Gandhi's acknowledgment of unity in diversity can also be partly contributed to his interpretation of *Advaita Vedanta* i.e. non-dual Hinduism (Collinson et al., 2000; Richards, 1986). Most relevant here is the general Vedic notion of "thou art that" which contends that even though humans might posses separate bodies, the unified soul of humanity, or the divine inner self (Atman), is identical to the substratum of the universe (Brahman). In spite of various differences in his philosophy from classical Advaita (Gier, 1993; Richards, 1986), Gandhi asserts that he believes in "the essential unity of man [humanity] and for that matter of all that lives" (as quoted in Richards, 1986, p. 2).

For Freire, unity is closely linked to the idea of being with the world and other humans. It is, thus, deeply rooted in the Brazilian educator's humanist creed. Freire (1972) asserts that to be in solidarity with people is to enter into their situation, to enter into *communion* with them, and go beyond perceiving them as abstract entities (p. 34). For him, the prime site of unity in diversity is true dialogue, where people come together as equal subjects committed to expressing themselves through naming the world all the while they receive others with trust, love, and humility.

The seemingly contradictory character of dialogue is that its ability to unite is contingent on its capacity to recognize diversity and difference. In an interview, Freire elaborates on the possibility of speaking from one's location and at the same time staying open to negotiation, stating that one's particular location is, at once, a point of reference for better understanding of one's own footing as well as a point of departure towards understanding other locations. Therefore, while our historical location conditions us, it also enables us to "make linkages with other historical events so as to gain greater comprehension of reality" (Leistyna, 2004, p. 21).

The Dialogic Self

Another shared topic of deliberation among the thinkers is the *self* as the subject of knowledge. As a humanist, Freire's most pressing question concerns the conditions for becoming more fully human through transforming the oppressive relations that turn the oppressed into "beings for others." For him, humans are beings of praxis through which they simultaneously create history and are shaped as historical-social beings. In this sense, the condition of being a human, being a self, is that of a historically conditioned being capable of going beyond its conditioning through active intervention (1998, p. 115).

Humans are always in the process of becoming—"unfinished beings in and with a likewise unfinished reality" (Freire, 1972, p. 72). This unfinishedness renders human existence in the world a state of "being with" others. The self, Freire mentions, is a relational presence which "in recognizing another presence as 'not-I,' recognizes itself as a presence" (1998, p. 26). The high esteem Freire has for dialogue, regarding it as the primary process through which humans become *authentic subjects*, is mainly because of the opportunity it provides the self and the other to encounter, for "it is the otherness of the 'not-I' or the 'you' that makes me assume the radicality of the *I*" (1998, p. 46).

In spite of his belief in the oneness of humanity, Gandhi also allocates great primacy over individuality as the locus from which the ultimate reality of oneness can be served. "Individuality is and is not," he says to describe this double-sidedness, "even as each drop in the ocean is an individual and is not" (Gandhi, 1930, p. 38). For Gandhi, the self is inter-connected to others within an extended network of connections (Roy, as cited in Gier, 1993, p. 42), as a result of which it becomes responsible towards others, and in return, they become indispensable companions for the self in the search for truth.

In the search for truth in the light of this "relational self," one needs a considerable measure of self-discipline and has to reach out to others through practice of nonviolence and active love. The two pivotal aspects of Gandhi's practical philosophy of nonviolence, ahimsa and self-suffering, can only be understood in view of this relational notion of self as it is because of this interconnectedness that one can conceive of pain inflicted on others as one's own pain. If one's suffering can effectively break the karmic imbalance created by an act authored by another person, it is only because, in view of the ultimate reality, there is no difference between me and that other.

In Bakhtin's dialogic philosophy, the positionality of the self, in terms of categories of time and space, means that the self is not a unitary entity but rather a triad consisting of a center, a non-center, and the relation between them (Holquist, 1990, p. 29). Thus, a second set of categories is created: that of the self and the other. These categories relate to one another so that while the time/space categories the self uses to model its own limits are always open and unfinished, the temporal and special categories it resorts to perceive the other are closed and finalized (Holquist, 1990, p. 22).

This openness of the self categories has two fundamental consequences. Firstly, the self becomes an on-going event, a flux of sheer becoming whose existence depends on a constant act of authoring (Holquist, 1990, p. 30). The world keeps addressing the self in the unique place it occupies and it has no other choice but to provide response. Gradually, these responses take a pattern, a text-like quality, which is called life. Secondly, this openness makes the self unable to understand itself, as any understanding requires a level of fixation in time and space; it is only from a position outside something that it can be perceived. Consequently, in order to gain any self-knowledge, the self is required to view itself through the categories of the other. Just as the word, according to Bakhtin, is always in need of a future answer-word to form its concept[5] (1981, p. 279), the existence of the self is also dialogically dependent on the other and her or his response.

In spite of the evident differences among these three systems of meaning in their origin, orientation, and discourse, the three tenets above summarize their overlapping points, which, in a sense, distinguish them from other discourses and systems. Their shared critique of the self-sufficient subject as well as their emphasis on positionality of knowledge indicates a departure from the Cartesian essentialist legacy. Nonetheless, the thinkers retain the belief in the possibility for some form of union, even if this sense of unity can only bear meaning in reference to the innate heterogeneity of the world.

PEDAGOGY OF ADDRESSIVITY

The question of values is at the heart of evaluation. Relying on positivistic assumptions about neutral objectivity, objectives-based evaluation largely avoids this question, unconsciously reducing its value palate to those embedded in the stated goals. No sooner is the value-laden nature of evaluation accepted than the question of whose values should be represented resurfaces. In response, some resort to uniform standards (Joint Committee, 1994) and explicit criteria, whereas others vouch for more interpretive approaches that attend to the values of all involved parties. Nevertheless, both of these approaches have shortcomings: while the former might "bring injustice and constrain creativity" (Stake, 1981, p. 149), the latter's optimistic assumption about the possibility of consensus building can at times have counter-intended effects (Mabry, 2010).

The crux of this question about values is how the quest for reaching a shared understanding of the segment of life being focused on (the evaluand) can be bal-

---

[5] Here is another manifestation of the parallel between Bakhtin's broader philosophical scheme and his philosophy of language. According to Bakhtin, due to the internal dialogism which presides over the structure of the word and its semantic aspects, the meaning of any word is not self-contained, but rather shaped in a dialogic relation with the word's object as well as the answer every word, Bakhtin believes, is directed towards. This is then mirrored in how the self forms itself in dialogic relation to the other.

anced with the need to make room for the various voices and value positions that pertain to it. The three tenets outlined in the previous section can be used to develop a pedagogical foundation for the evaluatory approach to peace education, which enables it to tackle this dilemma. Put within the framework of Bakhtin's theory of addressivity, this pedagogical scheme reveals how the *self*, as the subject of evaluatory inquiry, is positioned between the ever diverse forces of *truth*, and the inclination of social life towards *unity*.

Let's start our examination of this pedagogic frame with an explanation of addressivity. The term, as Bakhtin (1986) understands it, is the condition of being and communicating in a dialogic world where every utterance belongs to a specific person and her site of perception as well is directed towards an addressee and his responsive utterance (p. 95). For Bakhtin, "there is neither a first nor a last word" but a chain of meaning in which each utterance is a rejoinder of an infinite dialogue (p. 168). Every utterance is, in this sense, a response and awaits a response. The notion, of course, is not limited to language; just as there is a dialogic trace of other words in every word, the self also bears the traces of Others (Murray, 2000). Within the realm of addressivity, life becomes a dialogue between the events that address the self and the responses they invoke. "To be is to communicate dialogically. When the dialogue ends, everything ends" (Bakhtin, 1984, p. 252).

Also pertinent here is the notion of evaluation in Bakhtinian thought.[6] The utterance is never neutral; it always reflects an extra-verbal reality and expresses an evaluative attitude towards it (1986, p. 90). This evaluative orientation of the utterance determines its meaning to the extent that "a change in meaning is, essentially, always a *reevaluation*" (Voloshinov, 1986, p. 105). These evaluations are determined by the specific conditions and goals of their contextual area of human activity and speech genre (Bakhtin, 1986, p. 60) and are imbued with the evaluative purview of the social group to which they belong (Voloshinov, 1986, p. 106). The value-laden utterance, nonetheless, always goes beyond mere expression of what is already given to create something, "something new and unrepeatable" (Bakhtin, 1986, p. 120).

Here lies the fundamental character of the utterance as the point where centrifugal and centripetal forces are brought to bear (Bakhtin, 1981, p. 272). Being at the threshold of what is said and that which is yet unsaid, the utterance opens a site of event potentiality for the speaking subject, giving her a relative sense of freedom to author her relationship with existence. The dynamics of the pedagogy of addressivity as a concurrently educative-evaluative process rests on this dialogic character of the human life, which similar to the utterance, is "always a border incident" (Holquist, 1990, p. 28). It allows the evaluator to craft a new

---

[6] There are some doubts about the authorship of some texts produced within what is known as "the Bakhtin Circle" as it is disputed whether Bakhtin has published these books under his friend and colleague's names (Medvedev, Voloshinov, Kanaev) in order to avoid censorship or whether they were in fact written by those colleagues.

response by establishing a dialogic relation between the existing traditions, modes of meaning and codes of practice which he inherits from the field and the unique requirements of life as manifested in the case at hand, here and now.

In this fashion, the pedagogy of addressivity develops a set of qualities that empower it to perform the two often-cited functions of evaluation, namely, learning and accountability. The first quality is that of the dialogic nature of this pedagogy and the notion of learning as dialogue. Rich metaphors help us see a subject of inquiry in new and clearer ways (Kliebard, 1982). The metaphor of dialogue reintroduces the role of teacher and students and, correspondingly, evaluator and stakeholder, as equal interlocutors who cooperate on a joint project in which not only the topic at hand but also the participants themselves are transformed.[7]

As a result of this quality, the pedagogy of addressivity is bestowed with a democratic character which requires the involvement and participation of stakeholders. In addition to the fact that obtaining a sound evaluative account of a process requires responsiveness to the needs and value positions of all involved parties, the process of collaborative evaluation itself can be considered an educative and political community practice. In this sense, the pedagogy of addressivity can assist the creation of what can be called learning communities, which are not merely a community of individuals who are gathered to learn a specific subject, but communities that adopt a dialogic concept of learning as the prime mode and goal of their social interactions and affairs.

Yet another important quality of this form of pedagogy is its ability to go beyond repressive rationalist tendencies, which many have warned against as a possible pitfall of peace education (Ellsworth, 1989) and evaluation (Nevo & Brem, 2003). The theory of addressivity itself stems from Bakhtin's critique of rationalism and "its cult of unified, exclusive reason" (1984, p. 82), which he deemed responsible for consolidation of monologic patterns in different spheres of life. The pedagogy of addressivity realizes that the opposite of reason is not non-reason, but always another body of equally valid alien reason. Informed by addressivity, to understand the world involves becoming perceptive of the manifold rational and non-rational processes such as narration and metaphoric exchanges.

Added to these qualities, the pedagogy of addressivity allows the authority of life as the prime criterion for any evaluation to reemerge. In this sense, before any standard or predetermined criteria, the evaluative point of reference would be how the first-hand living experience of those involved has been affected and improved. An illustrative example of this shift in focus is seen in Restorative Circles, a dialogue-based restorative practice in which parties to a conflict gather to reflect on their shared experience of conflict and form action-plans to improve their situation. One of the most emphasized points within the frame of the evaluatory session devised in this system is that the session should not be turned into a

---

[7] Ove Karlsson (2001) and Tineke Abma (2001) offer two outstanding case studies that demonstrate how dialogue can be used in evaluation to provide the opportunity for collective reflection and learning.

trial of whether the action-plans were carried out or not but rather remain focused on the well-being of the participants and the conditions they face[8] (Barter, 2008).

Finally, the pedagogy of addressivity also provides the possibility to replace the concept of accountability with the more dynamic notion of *answerability*. Bakhtin (1993) calls the sense of responsibility and commitment which stems from the state of addressivity answerability. An answerable act, according to him, arises from the acknowledgment of one's unique participation in existence from one's unique place in it (pp. 42–43). Only I am addressed by the world in the place that I alone occupy in the world and, therefore, no one else can provide a response from that site. As a result, whereas conventional accountability is determined retrospectively and with reference to some external criteria or standard, viewed from the perspective of addressivity, all the requirements that hold an act accountable are already present in the act at the time when it is performed. Within the structure of answerability, an act is prior to any other criteria answerable to life itself.

CONCLUSION

The central idea of this chapter is the organic evaluative and educative quality of life; the chapter examined the possibility of a peace pedagogy that can break the boundaries between education and evaluation and embrace their natural linkage to life. It attempted to present a brief general outline of the founding premises and resulting implications of such an evaluatory peace pedagogy using Bakhtin's dialogic philosophy of addressivity, in the hopes that it will initiate a dialogue in which the subject can be explored more thoroughly in the future.

REFERENCES

Abma, T. A. (2001). Reflexive dialogue: A story about the development of injury prevention in two performing-art schools. *Evaluation, 7*(2), 238–252.

Ashton, C. (2007). Using theory of change to enhance peace education evaluation. *Conflict Resolution Quarterly, 25*(1), 39–53.

Ashton, C. (2004, March). *The case of peace education evaluation as a strategy for supporting sustainability.* Paper presented at the ISA 2004 Annual Meeting. Montreal, Canada. Retrieved August 20, 2011 from: http://www.allacademic.com/meta/p74211_index.html

Austin, A., Fischer, M., & Wils, O. (Eds.). (2003). *Peace and conflict impact assessment: Critical views on theory and practice.* Berghof handbook dialogue series. Retrieved September 14, 2011 from: http://www.berghof-handbook.net/documents/publications/dialogue1_pcia_complete.pdf

Bakhtin, M. M. (1981). *The dialogic imagination: Four essays.*(C. Emerson & M. Holquist, Trans.) Austin, TX: University of Texas Press.

Bakhtin, M. M. (1984). *Problems of Dostoevsky's poetics.* (C. Emerson, Ed. & Trans.). Minneapolis, MN: University of Minnesota Press.

---

[8] For more information about Restorative Circles visit: http://www.restorativecircles.org.

Bakhtin, M. M. (1986). *Speech genres and other late essays*. (C. Emerson & M. Holquist, Eds., V.W. Mcgee. Trans.). Austin: University of Texas Press.

Bakhtin, M. M. (1993). *Toward a philosophy of the act* (V. Liapunov & M. Holquist, Eds., V. Liapunov, Trans.). Austin, TX: University of Texas Press.

Bar-Tal, D. (2002). The elusive nature of peace education. In G. Salomon & B. Nevo (Eds.), *Peace education: The concepts, principles, and practices around the world.* (27–36). Mahwah, NJ: Lawrence Erlbaum.

Barter, D. (2008, March 18). *Introduction to restorative circles tele-course.* Lecture conducted by Bay Area Nonviolent Communication (BayNVC).

Church, C. A. (2008). Peacebuilding evaluation: From infancy to teenager. *New Routes: A Journal of Peace Research and Action, 13*(3), 3–6.

Collinson, D., Plant, K., & Wilkinson, R. (2000). *Fifty Eastern thinkers.* New York, NY: Routledge.

Dewey, J. (1997). *Democracy and education: An introduction to the philosophy of education.* Retrieved on March 29, 2009, from: http://www.gutenberg.org/etext/852

Ellsworth, E. (1989). Why doesn't this feel empowering? Working through the repressive myths of critical pedagogy. *Harvard Educational Review, 59*(3), 297–324.

Fountain, S. (1999). *Peace education in UNICEF.* New York, NY: UNICEF.

Freire, P. (1972). *Pedagogy of the oppressed.* New York, NY: Herder and Herder.

Freire, P. (1998). *Pedagogy of freedom: Ethics, democracy, and civic courage.* Lanham, MD: Rowman & Littelfield.

Freire, P. (2000). *Pedagogy of the oppressed* (P. D. Macedo & M. B. Ramos, Trans.). New York, NY: Continuum International Publishing Group.

Gandhi, M. K. (September 8, 1930). Letter to P.G. Mathew. *Collected works of Mahatma Gandhi,, 50*(53), 38.

Gandhi, M. K. (November 11, 1933). Speech at Deoli. In *Collected works of Mahatma Gandhi, 62*(173), 156–157.

Gandhi, M. K. (2001). *Non-violence resistance* (Satyagraha). New York, NY: Dover Publications.

Gier, N. F. (1993). Gandhi, ahimsa, and the self. *Gandhi Marg, 15*(1) 24–36. Retrieved on May 1, 2010, from: http://www.class.uidaho.edu/ngier/490/gahs.pdf

Guba, E. G., & Lincoln, Y. S. (1989). *Fourth generation evaluation.* Beverly Hills, CA: Sage.

Harris, I. (2008). The promises and pitfalls of peace education evaluation. In J. Lin, E. Brantmeier & C. Bruhn (Eds.), *Transforming education for peace.* (pp. 245–264). Charlotte, NC: Information Age Press.

Holquist, M. (1990). *Dialogism: Bakhtin and his world.* London, UK: Routledge.

House, E. R., & Howe, K. R. (1999). *Values in evaluation and social research.* Thousand Oaks, CA: SAGE.

Jenkins, T. (2008, October 15). *Evaluating peace education (EPE): An initiative of the International Institute on Peace Education, a special project of Global Education Associates.* Retrieved on October 28, 2011, from: http://www.iprafoundation.org/grant_tony_jenkins.shtml

Joint Committee on Standards for Educational Evaluation. (1994). *The program evaluation standards: How to assess evaluations of educational programs* (2nd ed.). Thousand Oaks, CA: Corwin Press.

Karlsson, O. (2001). Critical dialogue: Its value and meaning. *Evaluation, 7*(2), 211–227.

Kliebard, H. M. (1982). Curriculum theory as metaphor. *Theory into Practice, 21*(1),11–17.

Kupermintz, H., & Salomon, G. (2005). Lessons to be learned from research on peace education in the context of intractable conflict. *Theory into Practice, 44*(4), 293–302.

Leistyna, P. (2004). Presence of mind in the process of learning and knowing: A dialogue with Paulo Freire. *Teacher Education Quarterly, 31*(1), 17–29. Retrieved on May 19, 2009, from: http://www.teqjournal.org/backvols/2004/31_1/leistyna.pmd.pdf

Mabry, L. (2010). Critical social theory evaluation: Slaying the dragon. In M. Freeman (Ed.), *Critical social theory and evaluation practice. New directions for evaluation, 127*, 83–98. Published online on Wiley Online Library, DOI: 10.1002/ev.341.

Murray, J. W. (2000). Bakhtinian answerability and Levinasian responsibility: Forging a fuller dialogical communicative ethics. *Southern Communication Journal,* 65(2–3), 133–150.

Nevo, D. (1983). The conceptualization of educational evaluation: An analytical review of the literature. *Review of Educational Research, 53*(1), 117–128.

Nevo, B., & Brem, I. (2002). Peace education and the evaluation of their effectiveness. In G. Salomon & B. Nevo (Eds.), *Peace education: The concepts, principles, and practices around the world.* (pp. 271–282). Mahwah, NJ: Lawrence Erlbaum.

Potter, C. (2006). Program evaluation. In M. Terre Blanche, K. Durrheim & D. Painter (Eds.), *Research in practice: Applied methods for the social sciences* (2nd ed., pp. 410–428). Cape Town, South Africa: University of Cape Town Press.

Prabhu, R. K., & Rao, U. R. (Eds.). (1946). *The mind of Mahatma Gandhi.* Retrieved on May 25, 2010, from: http://www.mkgandhi.org/momgandhi/momindex.htm

Reardon, B. A. (1988). *Comprehensive peace education: Educating for global responsibility.* New York, NY: Teachers College Press.

Richards, G. (1986). Gandhi's notion of truth and the Advaita tradition. *Religious Studies, 22*(1),1–14.

Rothman, J. (1997). Action evaluation and conflict resolution training: Theory, methods and case study. *International Negotiation, 2*(3): 451–470.

Stake, R. E. (1981). Setting standards for educational evaluators. *American Journal of Evaluation, 2*(2), 148–152.

Stake, R. E. (2004). *Standard-based and responsive evaluation.* Thousand Oaks, CA: Sage.

Stufflebeam, D. L., & Madaus, G. F. (2000). Program evaluation: A historical overview. In D. L. Stufflebeam, G. F. Madaus, & T. Kellaghan (Eds.) *Evaluation models: Viewpoints on educational and human services evaluation.* (2nd ed., pp. 3–18). Boston, MA: Kluwer Academic Publishers.

Stufflebeam, D. L. & Shinkfield, A. J. (2007). *Evaluation theory, models, and applications.* San Francisco, CA: Jossey Bass.

Schwandt, T. A. (2001). Understanding dialogue as practice. *Evaluation, 7*(2), 228–237.

Voloshinov, V. N. (1986). *Marxism and the philosophy of language.* (L. Matejka & I.R. Titunik, Trans.). Cambridge, MA: Harvard University Press.

CHAPTER 19

IMAGINE THERE IS NO PEACE EDUCATION

An Exploration in Counterfactual Analyses

Thomas de Hoop and Annette N. Brown

> Imagine there's no countries. It isn't hard to do. Nothing to kill or die for.
> And no religion, too. Imagine all the people. Living life in peace.
> —*John Lennon (1971)*

INTRODUCTION

The last few years have witnessed a heated debate between those who promote rigorous impact evaluation methods and those who call for a more pluralist evaluation approach in the evaluation of development programs (e.g., Banerjee & Duflo, 2011; Deaton, 2010; Woolcock, 2009). However, in peace education evaluation the debate between quantitatively and qualitatively oriented researchers has been less prevalent, possibly because of the less dominant position of economists, who tend to favor quantitative methods, in the peace education evaluation field. Nevertheless, a number of quantitative researchers have paid attention to the evaluation of peace education programs in the last decade (e.g., Biton & Salomon,

Peace Education Evaluation: Learning from Experience and Exploring Prospects,
pages 287–297.
Copyright © 2015 by Information Age Publishing
All rights of reproduction in any form reserved.

2006; Blattman, Hartman & Blair, 2011; Malhotra & Liyanage, 2005), thus laying the ground for a similar discussion on methodological approaches in peace education evaluation.

This chapter aims to introduce the advantages and disadvantages of rigorous impact evaluation to peace education practitioners who are not (yet) familiar with the quantitatively-oriented counterfactual analysis employed in rigorous impact evaluations. Counterfactual analysis focuses on what would have happened with the beneficiaries of a peace education program in the absence of the program. It is never possible to observe the counterfactual. That is, if a person is a participant, you cannot observe that same person as a non-participant at the same point in time. Rigorous impact evaluation methods seek to mimic the counterfactual as closely as possible with help of statistically sound analyses in order to estimate what happens in the counterfactual situation. That is, rigorous impact evaluation methods "imagine" that the participant did not participate, or more generally, "imagine" the counterfactual.

While we can "imagine there's no countries", there is no way to estimate statistically the outcomes of that imagined state. With rigorous impact evaluation methods, though, we can statistically estimate the counterfactual outcomes for the beneficiaries of many programs, allowing us to compare these "non-participant" outcomes to the observed outcomes of the participants. Rigorous impact evaluations have been conducted on education programs for many years now (e.g., Duflo, Hanna & Ryan, 2012; Filmer & Schady, 2008; Glewwe et al., 2004; Kremer, Miguel, & Thornton, 2009). These studies typically use a comparison group of individuals or households as the foundation for the counterfactual. It is important to note that counterfactual analysis requires more than just a comparison group of non-participants. It includes efforts to make the comparison group resemble the participant group as closely as possible. We believe there are many opportunities for applying rigorous methods for assessing the counterfactual to peace education evaluation, which could help the field to increase significantly the knowledge and understanding concerning the impact of peace education programs.

We begin by presenting an example of a peace education evaluation that attempts to analyze the counterfactual without rigorous methods (Fauth & Daniels, 2001). Although the evaluation offers important lessons, we conclude that the evaluation methods do not permit conclusions regarding the causal effects of the peace education program. To explain the benefit of rigorous methods for counterfactual analysis, we present examples from the few rigorous impact evaluations of peace education programs that are currently available. Following this discussion, we argue that although impact evaluations of peace education programs have an important role to play in peace education, researchers need to be careful with the measurement of both attitudes and behaviors. For this reason, we finalize the chapter with several recommendations to improve the practice of measurement in rigorous impact evaluations. These recommendations should prove helpful to evaluators who engage in impact evaluations of peace education programs but who struggle with the measurement of outcome variables.

AN EVALUATION OF A PEACE EDUCATION PROGRAM IN SIERRA LEONE

Peace education evaluations have not all ignored counterfactual questions. Instead, some evaluators have tried to assess the causal impact of peace education programs by directly asking participants in such programs for a self-assessment of what their situation would be in the absence of the program. One example comes from an evaluation of the Youth Reintegration Training and Education for Peace (YRTEP) program implemented by Management Systems International for the United States Agency for International Development in Sierra Leone. The YRTEP program provided non-formal education activities, livelihood skills development, and basic literacy and numeracy skills to targeted ex-combatants and other war-affected youth (Fauth & Daniels, 2001). The program focuses on delivering messages about peace and reconciliation. Taking into account these messages and the focus on education, we are confident to categorize this program as a peace education program.

The evaluation assesses the program impact on the behavior and the attitudes of the participants. Ex-combatants and war-affected youth were interviewed by two consultants and were asked a series of questions regarding how their behavior has changed as a result of the peace education program (Fauth & Daniels, 2001). To analyze the counterfactual for the ex-combatants and war-affected youth, the consultants simply asked the participants whether their attitudes and behavior would be different in the absence of the program.

This direct approach of asking the participants to imagine their own counterfactual instead of constructing one based on a comparison group is susceptible to cognitive biases, which are described in more detail by White and Phillips (2012) in their overview of methods for evaluating programs where it may not be possible to construct a comparison group. Two possible biases here fall under the category of respondent bias. One is courtesy bias, where the respondent gives the answer that he or she feels that the interviewer wants to hear. A similar bias, which could also be at play here, is social acceptability bias, where the respondent gives the answer he or she believes is considered the socially correct answer.

Considering these possible biases, it is not surprising that respondents almost unanimously (99%) responded that they were able to manage conflicts as a result of the training. Additionally, of those who responded that they were able to manage conflict, 81% said that their conflict management skills had improved, while 17% considered their conflict management skills somewhat better and 3% a little better (Fauth & Daniels, 2001). Moreover, 99% said that they were better able to manage stress and 98% said that they were better able to solve problems as a result of the peace education program, while 99% of the participants stated that they were more self-aware and self-confident as a result of the program. Finally,

77% of the respondents stated that they would not have planted crops or started a business in the absence of the program. Fauth and Daniels (2001) argue that "not coincidentally, these correspond with the emphasis placed on agriculture and income generation options in the program" (p. 10).

However, even in the absence of respondent biases, there could easily be errors of attribution in the participants' responses regarding the impact of the program. That is, they may indeed have experienced some of the changes reported but may be incorrectly attributing the cause of those changes to the program. For example, several recent studies indicate that the common response to a traumatic event is resilience (e.g., Bonanno et al., 2012; Neria et al., 2010). Resilience is characterized by decreases in stress in the years after a traumatic event. The respondents for the evaluation of the YRTEP program could have been mistaking their own increased resilience for an impact of the program, resulting in an overestimate of the impact of the program.

We believe that some combination of respondent bias and errors of attribution very likely resulted in a large overestimate of the impact of the program and conclusions that are too good to be true. Without identifying a comparison group and using it to construct a counterfactual, the consultants were not able to estimate what would have happened to the participants in the absence of the program. This is not to say that the program did not have any positive impact. There simply are no data to measure attributable impacts of the program.

Nevertheless, the responses also reveal that the beneficiaries of the peace education program were quite satisfied, indicating that the program was well implemented. Otherwise, the respondents would most likely object to statements suggesting that their attitudes and behavior changed positively as a result of the program. The evaluation thus provides valuable lessons concerning implementation of the program even though it is unable to rigorously assess the causal impact of the program. The next section discusses the use of comparison groups in rigorous impact evaluations. We also present examples of rigorous impact evaluations of peace education programs.

RIGOROUS IMPACT EVALUATIONS

Rigorous impact evaluations are studies that measure the net impact of a program by identifying a counterfactual to estimate the outcomes of program beneficiaries in the absence of the program and compare those to the observed outcomes of the beneficiaries. By placing emphasis on the counterfactual in our definition of impact evaluation, we use a definition of impact evaluation that is generally shared by economists (White, 2009). Observed and reported changes in outcomes over time can usually be explained by multiple causes. Therefore, a counterfactual based on a comparison group is required to measure the net impacts that can be directly attributed to programs such as peace education programs.

Rigorous impact evaluations may use either experimental methods (i.e. randomized controlled trials) or quasi-experimental methods (Ravallion, 2001;

White, 2009) to establish the counterfactual. In randomized controlled trials, the program, such as a peace education program, is allocated randomly across a group of actors, after which the estimate of the average impact can be obtained by comparing the mean outcome of those in the group who received the program with those in the group who did not. Randomized controlled trials are a solution for the problem of selection-bias, resulting from the beneficiaries being selected into the program based on characteristics that may also influence the measured outcomes. If the method of selecting beneficiaries into the program results in the beneficiaries being systematically different from the non-beneficiaries, it is difficult to differentiate the effects of those differences from the effects of the program. Randomized controlled trials solve this problem by making selection into the program random and thus eliminating systematic differences between the beneficiaries and the non-beneficiaries of the program. Randomized controlled trials should not be confused with random sampling of the beneficiaries and non-beneficiaries. The latter approach does not solve problems related to selection-bias, whereas randomized controlled trials do.

Quasi-experimental methods aim is to compare the outcomes of the beneficiaries of a program with the outcomes of a comparable, but not randomly chosen, comparison group. Different statistical techniques can be used to obtain the impact estimate of a program using a quasi-experimental research design.[1]

EXAMPLES OF IMPACT EVALUATIONS
OF PEACE EDUCATION PROGRAMS

Although scarce, examples of rigorous impact evaluations of peace education programs exist. In order to demonstrate the possibilities for rigorous impact evaluations of peace education programs, this section presents two examples of these impact evaluations. Each analyzes the impact of a typical peace education program by comparing the beneficiaries of the program with an arguably comparable group of non-beneficiaries: the counterfactual. Both evaluations discuss programs that focus on delivering messages about peace and reconciliation, leading us to argue that both programs can be considered peace education programs. In both evaluations, the comparison group is selected by analyzing the observable characteristics of the participants in the peace education program and by comparing them with the observable characteristics of non-beneficiaries. Both studies can be considered quasi-experimental evaluations of peace education programs.

In the first example, the impact of a school-based peace education program among Jewish Israeli and Palestinian adolescents was assessed by comparing

---

[1] Propensity score matching and regression discontinuity design methods are two examples of quasi-experimental methods. A full explanation of these methods is outside the scope of this chapter. Caliendo and Kopeinig (2008) provide practical guidance to the use of propensity score matching for evaluating interventions, while Imbens and Lemieux (2008) review most of the practical and theoretical issues in implementing regression discontinuity design methods.

the attitudes of the participants in a peace education program with a comparison group that was selected from a group of Israeli-Jewish tenth-grade male and female youngsters (ages 15–16) and a group of same-age Palestinian male youngsters (Biton & Salomon, 2006). A pre-test before the program ensured that the beneficiaries of the program were similar in terms of age and gender as the non-beneficiaries in the comparison group, thus making the comparison group a more reliable counterfactual. The evaluation compared the associations to the concept of peace between the comparison group and the participants in a peace education program focusing on the relations between Palestinian and Jewish Israeli youth.

Without the counterfactual, an evaluation might have given the (wrong) impression that the peace education program had no effect on the attitudes of the Palestinian youth because their hatred of Jews (as assessed by several attitudinal statements) had not changed between the pre-test and the post-test. However, a comparison with the counterfactual suggests that the peace education program did have a positive effect on the attitudes of the Palestinian youth. Mistrust and hatred of Jews among the Palestinian adolescents that were not part of the program doubled between the pre-test and the post-test, most likely as a result of the Intifada that took place between the pre-test and post-test (Biton & Salomon, 2006). Arguably, the peace education program resulted in a prevention of increased mistrust and hatred of Jews among the Palestinian participants (Biton & Salomon, 2006). This example thus shows that the lack of a counterfactual can result in an underestimate of the impact of peace education programs just as it can result in an overestimate of the impacts as argued for the evaluation of Fauth and Daniels (2001) above.

The previous result demonstrates the impact of peace education programs on the attitudes of participants. Rigorous impact evaluations of peace education programs can also demonstrate the impact of these programs on behavior. In our second example, a rigorous impact evaluation of a peace education program in Sri Lanka focuses on the effects of a peace workshop on the donating behavior of participants (Malhotra & Liyanage, 2005). It demonstrates the value of creative measurement by comparing donations to help poor people of another ethnicity (both Tamil and Sinhalese) between participants and non-participants in peace education workshops (Malhotra & Liyanage, 2005). The results show that participants in a peace workshop donate more money to the other ethnicity than non-participants who applied for the workshop but did not participate (Malhotra & Liyanage, 2005). This example shows the importance of a counterfactual as well as the importance of the creative measurement of outcome indicators, on which we focus in the next section.

MEASUREMENT PROBLEMS

As shown in the previous examples, rigorous impact evaluations of peace education programs require creativity in the use of measurement tools for deriving the impact of peace education programs on relatively soft indicators. One objection to using rigorous methods to evaluate peace education and other peace-building interventions is that the desired impacts of these interventions are qualitative (e.g. decreased mistrust) and not quantitative (e.g., increased incomes), and thus cannot be analyzed using quantitative methods. This distinction confuses the issues, however. In order to apply the methodologies of rigorous impact evaluation, it is true that one must be able to observe and measure one or more outcomes, but the measurement need not be represented as a number on a scale. There are statistical techniques that allow for both binary outcomes and categorical outcomes. In addition, with the increasing use of rigorous methods for evaluating peace-related interventions, researchers have developed innovative ways for meaningfully measuring the desired qualitative outcomes. In this section, we present examples of peace education outcome measures according to three categories: self-reported attitudes and perceptions, self-reported behaviors, and observed behaviors. We also provide recommendations for measuring and evaluating peace education outcomes.[2]

Measuring attitudes is a key element in most, if not all, evaluations of peace education. Inherent in the education aspect of these peacebuilding interventions is a theory of change that involves changing people's knowledge, attitudes, and perceptions. The altered knowledge, attitudes, and perception are then expected to influence behaviors. Even when the behavioral outcomes can be observed and measured, one cannot unpack the causal chain without information on attitudes and perceptions. For example, Paluck (2009) found that a peace messaging radio program in Rwanda transformed perceptions of social norms and behaviors *without* changing personal beliefs, thus calling into question presumptions that observed behavioral changes are the result of transformed attitudes, at least for similar interventions.

The measurement of attitudes and perceptions necessarily relies on self-reported data collection. Self-reported data suffer from numerous potential biases, as described by White and Phillips (2012). In addition to courtesy bias, social acceptability bias, and errors of attribution as discussed above, there may be self-serving bias (respondents take credit for good things and blame others for bad things) and self-importance bias (respondents overestimate their role in events). In addition, surveyor biases may affect the collection of self-reported attitudinal data.

Nevertheless, these data can be useful if collected and analyzed carefully. In the Malhotra and Liyanage (2005) impact evaluation of the long-term effects of peace workshops, the authors measured attitudes using an empathy scale adapted from psychology research. The scale is based on responses along a "completely agree" to "completely disagree" scale for five statements regarding concern for the "other" group. The comparison of participants to non-participants shows that participants had greater empathy. Blattman, Hartman, and Blair (2011) employ a similar method for measuring attitudes in their impact evaluation of the Community Empowerment Programme, which provided peace trainings to community

---

[2] The discussion in this section draws on Samii, Brown, and Kulma (2011).

members in Liberia. Their survey asked a set of questions under several themes (e.g. women's rights, ethnic bias) with respondents indicating *agree* or *disagree*. The responses are combined into indexes for each theme. Using these measures, the impact evaluation provides only weak evidence of the effects of peace trainings in Liberia on relevant attitudes. In both studies, the questions are designed to be relatively concrete in an attempt to reduce biases—for example, a question is "which tribe do you think is most likely to keep their [sic] place dirty?" as opposed to "how do you feel about tribe X?"

Slightly less problematic are self-reported measures of behaviors. The intent of these measures is to capture information that is objective—did you do something, rather than what do you believe. However, even in the cases of development programs where the outcomes are more straightforward, self-reported measures can be misrepresent reality. For example, a question such as "did you work for wages last week?" could still suffer social acceptability bias or not be understood in the same way by respondents as by the researchers. For the behaviors that evaluators want to measure for peace education interventions, it is easy to understand how social acceptability bias might distort responses. In their study of a school-based curriculum for reducing violence in the United States, Farrell and Meyer (1997) construct scales for violent behavior, problem behavior, and drug use using the responses to survey questions about the frequency of certain behaviors. The violent behavior scale incorporates the self-reported frequencies of "been in a fight in which someone was hit" and "brought a weapon to school" among others. It is easy to imagine that, in spite of the surveyors' promises of confidentiality, the respondents may not answer honestly. Self-reported behavior data can provide valuable outcome measurements, though. In the same Farrell and Meyer (1997) evaluation, the authors report several methods employed to increase the validity of the data and show that the impact of the program on the violent behavior of girls was different from the impact on the violent behavior of boys.

In order to address the limitations of self-reported data, researchers are increasingly measuring outcomes using observed behavior data, usually as a complement to the measures from the self-reported data. These measures fall on a continuum from observed "real" behaviors (e.g., closed-circuit cameras that record violent altercations in public) to observed "artificial" behaviors, typically measured through the use of constructed games. Most data fall somewhere in the middle of the continuum. For example, Malhotra and Liyanage (2005) paid respondents a show-up fee and then informed respondents of a fictional fundraiser to benefit poor children from the "other" group. Respondents could donate to the fundraiser from their show-up fee and were asked to record the amount of their donation. The authors use these monetary values as observed behavior measures of respondents' empathy toward the "other."

With some creativity and innovation, credible measurement of peace education outcomes is possible. What follows are some cautions and recommendations. First, due to the qualitative nature of peace education outcomes, triangulation among measures is important. In an ideal situation, a researcher would have self-reported attitude data, self-reported behavior data, and observed behavior data to measure a key concept. Measuring outcomes in a variety of ways also increases the possibility of analyzing the causal chain, in particular to examine whether changes in attitudes are necessary (or sufficient) for changes in behaviors.

At the same time, researchers should be careful to avoid the "indicator soup" problem and "multiple comparisons" problem when they measure a large number of outcomes. The indicator soup problem is the difficulty of organizing and interpreting the results with large numbers of measures. The multiple comparisons problem is that in any large group of tests, statistical probability suggests that a few will come back with statistical significance even when there is no change in reality. Particularly if researchers follow our first recommendation, peace education impact evaluations may often include a large number of outcome measures. Samii, Brown, and Kulma (2012) find that 11 of the 24 peacebuilding impact evaluations, identified through an extensive search, report more than 25 different outcome measurements.

King, Samii, and Snilstveit (2010) suggest some strategies for dealing with these problems. To address indicator soup, researchers can clearly map out the theory of change for the intervention and then link the measured outcome to points along the map in order to distinguish clearly the different hypothesis tests conducted. An approach to dealing with multiple comparisons is to establish at the beginning of the study how indicators will be aggregated in order to test core hypotheses. These hypotheses and the methods for aggregating the indicators should be clearly laid out in advance of data collection and analysis. Casey, Glennerster, and Miguel (2011) provide an excellent example of this strategy in their impact evaluation of a community-driven development intervention in Sierra Leone.

Our third recommendation is to build on established approaches, particularly those that are theoretically based, when developing or aggregating measures. For example, Malhotra and Liyanage's (2005) empathy scale is adapted from the Interpersonal Reactivity Index from the field of psychology. Biton and Salomon (2006), in their impact evaluation of peace education for Palestinian and Israeli youths, draw heavily on a questionnaire developed by other researchers and used to study youth understandings of peace across a large number of countries. Basing measures on existing approaches increases their credibility and also facilitates the synthesis of findings across different impact evaluations. Indexes are quite easy to make up. However, they are rarely meaningful to interpret.

RIGOROUS EVALUATION OF PEACE EDUCATION: DIFFICULT BUT POSSIBLE

This chapter demonstrates the potential use of counterfactual analysis in peace education evaluation by introducing rigorous impact evaluation. We show several examples demonstrating that oftentimes a proper comparison group is a necessary condition for counterfactual analyses in peace education evaluation. Currently, however, only few peace education evaluations use a comparison group to construct a counterfactual for the assessment of the effectiveness of the program. Without a counterfactual, peace education evaluations can certainly provide useful lessons on processes. To attribute the impacts of a peace education evaluation, however, the use of a proper counterfactual is a necessary condition.

Outcome measures of peace education programs are often not easily measurable. For this reason, evaluators of peace education programs should focus strongly on measurement issues when applying counterfactual analyses. The examples in this chapter demonstrate that measurement issues are a difficult but possible-to-overcome hurdle for most impact evaluations in the field of peace education. Future peace education evaluations could thus certainly benefit from rigorous impact evaluation methods, but only when evaluators pay sufficient attention to measurement issues in their research design.

REFERENCES

Banerjee, A. V., & Duflo, E. (2011). *Poor economics: A radical rethinking of the way to fight global poverty.* Cambridge, MA: MIT Press.

Biton, Y., & Salomon, G. (2006). Peace in the eyes of Israeli and Palestinian youths: Effects of collective narratives and peace education program. *Journal of Peace Research, 43*(2), 167–80.

Blattman, C., Hartmann, A., & Blair, R. (2011). *Can we teach peace and conflict resolution? Results from a randomized evaluation of the community empowerment program (CEP) in Liberia: A program to build peace, human rights, and civic participation.* New Haven, CT: Innovations for Poverty Action.

Bonanno, G. A., Galea, S., Bucciarelli, A., & Vlahov, D. (2012). Psychological resilience after disaster: New York City in the aftermath of the September 11th terrorist attack. *Psychological Science, 17*(3), 181–86.

Caliendo, M., & Kopeinig, S. (2008). Some practical guidance for the implementation of propensity score matching. *Journal of Economic Surveys, 22*(1), 31–72.

Casey, K., Glennerster, R. & Miguel, E. (2011). *Reshaping institutions: Evidence on external aid and local collective action.* NBER Working Paper no. 17012. Cambridge, MA: National Bureau of Economic Research.

Deaton, A. (2010). Instruments, randomization and learning about development. *Journal of Economic Literature, 48*(2), 424–55.

Duflo, E., Hanna, R., & Ryan, S. P. (2012). Incentives work: Getting teachers to come to school. *American Economic Review, 102*(4), 1241–78.

Farrell, A. D., & Meyer, A. L. (1997). The effectiveness of a school-based curriculum for reducing violence among urban sixth-grade students. *American Journal of Public Health, 87*(6), 979–84.

Fauth, G., & Daniels, B. (2001). *Impact evaluation: Youth Reintegration Training and Education for Peace (YTREP) Program.* Washington DC: USAID.

Filmer, D., & Schady, N. (2008). Getting girls into school: Evidence from a scholarship program in Cambodia. *Economic Development and Cultural Change, 56*(3), 581–617.

Glewwe, P., Kremer, M., Moulin, S., & Zitzewitz, E. (2004). Retrospective vs. prospective analyses of school inputs: The case of flip charts in Kenya. *Journal of Development Economics, 74*(1), 251–268.

Imbens, G. W., & Lemieux, T. (2008). Regression discontinuity designs: A guide to practice. *Journal of Econometrics 142*(2), 615–35.

King, E., Samii, C., & Snilstveit, B. (2010). Interventions to promote social cohesion in Sub-Saharan Africa. *Journal of Development Effectiveness, 2*(3), 336–70.

Kremer, M., Miguel, E., & Thornton, R. (2009). Incentives to learn. *Review of Economics and Statistics, 91*(3), 437–56.

Lennon, J. 1971. Imagine. On *Imagine*. UK: Apple.

Malhotra, D., & Liyanage, S. (2005). Long-term effects of peace workshops in protracted conflicts. *Journal of Conflict Resolution, 49*(6), 908–924.

Neria, Y., Besser, A., Kiper, D. & Westphal, M. (2010). A longitudinal study of posttraumatic stress disorder, depression, and generalized anxiety disorder in Israeli civilians exposed to war trauma. *Journal of Traumatic Stress, 23*(3), 322–30.

Paluck, E. L. (2009). Reducing intergroup prejudice and conflict using the media: A field experiment in Rwanda. *Journal of Personality and Social Psychology, 96*(3), 574–87.

Ravallion, M. (2001). The mystery of the vanishing benefits: An introduction to impact evaluation. *World Bank Economic Review 15*(1), 115–40.

Samii, C., Brown, A., & Kulma, M. (2011). *Evaluating stabilization interventions.* International Initiative for Impact Evaluation (3ie) white paper.

White, H. (2009). *Some reflections on current debates in impact evaluation. 3ie working paper no. 1.* New Delhi: International Initiative for Impact Evaluation.

White, H., & Phillips, D. (2012). *Addressing attribution of cause and effect in small n impact evaluations: Towards an integrated framework. 3ie working paper no. 15.* New Delhi, India: International Initiative for Impact Evaluation.

Woolcock, M. (2009). Toward a plurality of methods in project evaluation: A contextualised approach to understanding impact trajectories and efficacy. *Journal of Development Effectiveness, 1*(1), 1–14.

CHAPTER 20

EVALUATION OF PEACE EDUCATION TRAINING PROGRAMS

Promoting Consistency between Teaching and Content

Maria Lucia Uribe Torres

INTRODUCTION

Educators play a significant role in the success of peace education programs[1]. In this field, more than in any other, the success lies on the capacity of educators to internalize the principles of peace education, become role models and use ap-

---

[1] A study conducted by a team of students at the School of International and Public Affairs - Columbia University on the impact of an inter-Agency "Peace Education Program - PEP", concluded that the failure of success of the program lies on the teachers and on the quality training provided to them. It recommends ongoing teachers training and supervision to ensure its success. Additionally, it stresses that unless facilitators and teachers themselves demonstrate the skills, values and attitudes of PEP, they cannot help students to acquire those skills. The PEP was jointly developed and implemented by UNHCR and the Inter-Agency Network for Education in Emergencies – INEE- as a rights-based approach for both formal and non-formal learning, designed to promote skills that build positive and constructive behaviors for peace and conflict prevention and minimization. The program was implemented in more than 13 countries.

Peace Education Evaluation: Learning from Experience and Exploring Prospects,
pages 299–316.
Copyright © 2015 by Information Age Publishing
All rights of reproduction in any form reserved.

299

propriate methodologies (Baxter & Ikobwa, 2005). However, educators training evaluations are still applied in informal ways, often not prioritized, lack systematization and validation. As in most peace education programs, evaluation is often considered an add-on that takes a back seat to program implementation, generally not included in the program design process. Additionally there is little consistency in the evaluation standards or methods used (Ashton, 2007).

Educators training programs in formal and non-formal educational settings aim at equipping participants with the necessary competencies to implement and facilitate peace education. The evaluation of these training programs need to take into consideration not only the skills and knowledge acquired but also the internalization of concepts and principles, their application after the training and how educators demonstrate attitudes and behaviors conducive to creating a culture of peace.

The implementation of training program evaluations should provide participants with the tools to look at themselves, their attitudes and behaviors and how those impact the people they work with. Those tools can help them self-assess their own learning, changes, new perceptions and experiences, serving as a mechanism for individual transformation. A continuous and systematic evaluation process of educators training programs is needed to relate their own changes with the learning of their students,[2] to the development of proper learning environments and with the use of appropriate methodologies.

The evaluation model suggested in this paper presents a holistic view of evaluation of educators training programs in peace education. It takes into consideration elements of other models applied in the education and training fields and additionally places the educator at the heart of the evaluation process. It is developed considering the essential role self-reflection plays in critically assessing how educators' attitudes, behaviors and contradictions affect the implementation of peace education programs. It uses Johan Galtung's conflict triangle as a tool to encourage individual transformations in educators but also to leverage the success of peace education programs.

EVALUATION OF TRAINING PROGRAMS

The initial models for the evaluation of peace-building projects came from the strong tradition of monitoring and evaluation in the development assistance field (PricewaterhouseCoopers LLP, 2007, p. 8)[3], primarily due to the experience gained in this area providing evidence of success to different stakeholders and donors. In the area of peace education and human rights training programs, much on evaluation have been developed based on models used by the private sector,

---

[2] Students are hereafter referred as beneficiaries of peace education programs conducted by educators, and used interchangeably.

[3] This report was commissioned to independent consultants from PricewaterhouseCoopers by the Special EU Programmes Body and the PEACE II Monitoring and Evaluation Working Group.

research institutions and also influenced by the development field. Even though these models provide a good framework for evaluation, it is important to ask: Are these models sufficient to measure the impact of education programs that aim to contribute to peace building? Can they be used to evaluate the changes in attitudes and behaviors participants go through peace education training programs? And do those models share the same objectives as peace education training programs?

Studies in the development area conclude that evaluation has four main purposes (Weiss, 1995): 1) Guidance for action: the direct instrumental use of findings; 2) Reinforcement of prior beliefs: enhancing confidence of those who press for change; 3) Mobilization of support for desired change; and 4) Enlightenment: increase in understanding.

These purposes are defined from the perspective of the organization and from an administrative, financial and donor-satisfaction point of view. They may rather refer to different types of uses that can be given to the evaluation of a program but not necessarily to the main objectives to execute one.

In academic training courses, according to Bramley and Newby (1984), evaluation is conducted with the purpose to gain feedback on the linkages between learning outcomes and objectives and to consider the cost-effectiveness of the program. Evaluation also serves as a research mechanism to determine the relationships between learning, training and transfer to the job, and to assess the impact of the interventions on a specific context. These purposes though more conducive to understand the impact on the beneficiaries of a program still lack emphasis on the ongoing learning process educators go through.

The purpose of a peace education training program evaluation for educators should be formulated from the perspective of the participants, i.e. educators, in order to direct the focus of the evaluation to the process and not only to the results. It should encompass the following purposes:

- To understand the process of change at different levels: personal, group and community.
- To identify the effectiveness of the program in the provision of knowledge and development of skills.
- To assess the internalization of attitudes and behaviors that are consistent with the principles of peace education in relation to participants' contexts and realities.
- To measure the effectiveness of the training program to enhance the learning of the final beneficiaries.

Focusing on the educators will allow a better design of the evaluation from the beginning of the program. It can promote more innovative ways for monitoring and evaluation and better assessment of the long-term impact of the program.

EVALUATION OF PEACE EDUCATION TRAINING PROGRAMS

In many educators training programs on peace education, the focus of the evaluation is placed on their satisfaction of the training, their plans to use what was learned, and the implementation of programs after the training. It measures quantitatively how many lessons or workshops were implemented and the number of participants and graduates. It also evaluates the cost of the venue, the number of trainers available, and the outcome of the training measured by the number of educators who claim behavior change. Qualitatively, it measures educators' satisfaction, appropriateness of activities and methodologies used, and types of programs initiated by the educators after the training. It takes into account the suitability of the venue, the manner of the trainer, the group dynamics and the type of behavior change claimed by educators in the community (UNESCO, UNHCR and INEE, 2005, p. 22).

Often these evaluations do not concretely measure how much and how educators have internalized concepts and apprehended principles, and the possible influence they have in the student's learning. There are, however, studies that examine the influence and contribution of ongoing educators training to students' learning. Case studies from Bangladesh, Botswana, Guatemala, Namibia and Pakistan have provided evidence that ongoing professional development, especially in the early years after initial preparation of educators and then continuing throughout their career, contribute significantly to student learning and retention (Craig, Kraft, & du Plessis, 1998). The more educators learn about peace education, reflect about its principles and internalize them in their daily lives, the better they can design, plan and deliver their programs.

Internalization requires that educators go through a process of learning and unlearning that is only possible through self-reflection. An evaluation questionnaire can openly ask educators if they think they have changed any behavior or attitudes towards others or if they are respectful with their students; but do these questions allow them to reflect about their own bias or unconscious violent behaviors or attitudes? Is an evaluation questionnaire enough to foster unlearning and internalization in educators?

Many training programs do include self-reflection activities in their evaluation processes. EURED is an example that relies on a model of self-reflection developed by Ben Chetkov-Yanoov. The model assesses learning objectives for educators, including: 1) Getting to know oneself: self-understanding with respect to one's own attitudes to violence and peace; 2) Getting to know the subject: knowledge about the factors of war and peace and peace education; and 3) Learning to communicate the subject: objectives and methods of peace education (EURED, 2002, p. 29).

There is, however, lack of correlation between educators' attitudes and behaviors and the delivery of peace education programs. How much emphasis the educator gives to listening to students, how dialogue is created, the type of questions the educator asks -open-ended, guiding, instructive or closed-, the space given to students to think by themselves, and how trust is developed in the group. These factors should encompass the attitudes and behaviors of educators regarding acceptance of difference, respect for diversity, empathy and non-violence.

Especially in contexts affected by a strong cultural and structural violence, where violent behaviors are normalized in the lives of individuals and commonly accepted and supported by society and its institutions, there is a tangible need to foster self-reflection skills and spaces for educators. It is also important that evaluation processes examine the correlation between educators' attitudes and behaviors with the learning of students in a peace education program.

Evaluation should not only be a tool to be used at the end of a training program but a continuous mechanism for educators to evaluate themselves *vis-à-vis* their first assessment on attitudes, values, knowledge and behaviors. Additionally this ongoing process of evaluation should allow them to continuously reflect on how they apply the principles of peace education, their own apprehension of the content in relation to their individual realities, and the challenges applying it. Consequently educators will be more prepared to promote social transformations in their society and be role models for their students.

EVALUATION MODELS

In most education programs, evaluation is done using two types of approaches: formative and summative (Equitas, 2007).

Formative evaluation seeks to strengthen or improve a program or intervention by examining, amongst other things, its delivery, the quality of its implementation and the organizational context, personnel, structures and procedures. It is mainly a change oriented evaluation approach, especially attuned to assessing in an ongoing way, any discrepancies between the expected direction and outputs of the program and what is happening in reality, in order to implement it better (Stern, 2003, p. 1).

Summative evaluation refers to evaluation activities that are conducted after a training session or program has been completed in order to assess its overall effectiveness (OHCHR & Equitas, 2011, p. 81). In relation to training of educators, summative evaluations consider if the learners acquired the knowledge and skills that they were supposed to as stated in the objectives of the program. It examines how possible changes in attitudes and behaviors can influence their work and impact their students.

Several models have been developed to evaluate training programs; the most commonly applied are the ones proposed by Kirkpatrick (1975), Hamblin (1974) and Warr, Bird and Rackham (1970). The latter represents a wider picture of evaluation as a total system that not only measures results but also processes, including the training needs analysis of the program and participants, the final assessment and the report on the achievement of the program (Rae, 2002).

The Kirkpatrick Model is the one that perhaps has received the most attention in the training field. It suggests four levels of evaluation (Kirkpatrick Partners, 2011):

1.   Reaction—Were the participants satisfied with the training? What are the participants' feelings regarding the content, structure and methods? The information at this stage is collected at the end of the training program.
2.   Learning—What did the participants learn from the training? Did the participants learn what was intended to be taught in terms of knowledge, skills and attitudes?
3.   Behavior—Did the participants change their job behavior and performance based on what was learned? Are they more competent to perform their job?
4.   Results—Did the behavioral change have a positive effect in the work context or organization? To what degree targeted outcomes occur as a result of the training program.

In peace education programs, this model can serve as the basis for a process-oriented evaluation that correlates behavioral and attitudinal changes with outcomes.

Critics of the Kirkpatrick model have suggested two additional levels to evaluate. The first one suggests the inclusion of activities before the learner attends the program, including the development of a baseline to measure the work level of the participants before attending the program and as a way to validate its success (Rae, 2002, p. 4). In peace education training programs, it is important to understand where the learners are coming from, in order to know whether they have moved to another level, if they are aware of changes in their attitudes, knowledge and skills and how they can improve their work behavior.

The second level suggested by his critics is to include the financial assessment of the level 4—results—as they affect the return on the investment. This is especially important from the business point of view, however, in the case of peace education training programs this needs to be seen in terms of social return on the investment, i.e. capacity building for schools, creation of social capital, contribution to social change through individuals that are not only good professionals but respectful parents, committed peace workers and good citizens.

Other approaches to evaluation tend to be an extension or variation of the original Kirkpatrick model. For example, Newby (1992) additionally describes a context evaluation approach, which focuses on the different environmental and contextual features in which the program takes place. Torres (1999) uses evaluative inquiry, as a participatory learning experience through dialogue, reflection, asking questions and clarifying values, beliefs, assumptions and knowledge collectively.

In peace education training programs, evaluative inquiry has a particular added value. It provides the opportunity to engage in dialogue across gender, generational and cultural backgrounds to assess the learning through a collaborative methodology. Therefore, the methodology itself is a reflection of some of the principles of peace education. This moves the evaluation from a vertical approach where a group of individuals assess the learning of others, to a horizontal evaluation where everyone involved participates and critically assesses what needs to be improved, how they benefited from it and through inquiry generates self-introspection and collective reflection.

The assessment of reactions during the program is crucial for the evaluation of peace education training programs for educators. Through an ongoing reaction evaluation is possible to recreate an environment that enables a process of un-learning violent attitudes and behaviors. This can be done by prompting educators to reflect about factors that trigger off thoughts, memories and reflections about their own experiences and realities. Many programs use learning logs for participants to reflect about their own experiences during the program. Even though, learning logs are, in many cases, not labeled as a kind of reaction evaluation but as self-assessment tools, they could be used to create dialogues with participants, through voluntary participation, about their own reflections and reactions to particular activities during the program.

These models show consistently that there should be an impact of the program on the individual learning, on the development of new behaviors and attitudes and on the organization and society.

The following section describes a proposed model of evaluation of peace education training programs, which takes into consideration some of the ideas highlighted above, builds on in the gaps to meet the particular needs of peace education and proposes a way to consider evaluation in a holistic way.

A MODEL FOR EVALUATION OF PEACE EDUCATION TRAINING PROGRAMS FOR EDUCATORS

The proposed model includes formative and summative evaluations, and impact assessment mechanisms. It proposes as main component the use of a self-reflection tool to assess the learning process each educator goes through. This tool acts as a mechanism to correlate educator's attitudes, knowledge and skills to content delivery, methodologies used and impact of the program on the beneficiaries. The self-reflection tool is integrated with other components of the evaluation process and acts as the backbone of the evaluation model.

While summative and formative evaluations mostly document cognitive changes, they do not necessarily assess changes in dispositions, attitudes and behaviors that may occur as a result of peace education trainings. Considering the importance in peace education of role modeling and the development of critical thinking, it is a *sine qua non* for educators to be able to develop meta-cognitive skills that allow them self-assess their own learning process and changes.

The proposed evaluation model is composed of the following components:

a. *Self-reflection* developed throughout the program.

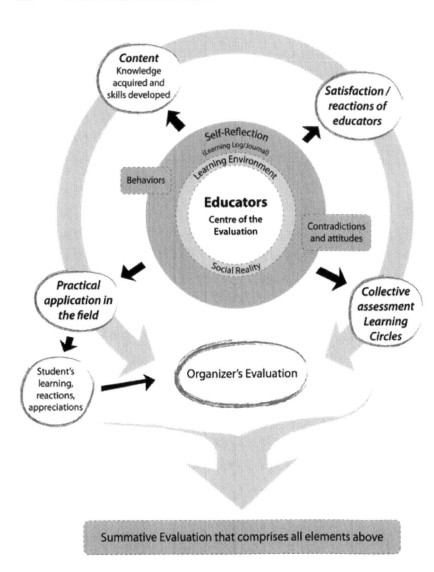

FIGURE 20.1. Components of the suggested evaluation model

b. Assessment of the *content* in terms of knowledge acquired and skills developed.

c. *Practical application* of what was learned. How the acquired skills are applied in the development, content and delivery of peace education programs, and the coherence of educators' attitudes and behaviors with peace education principles

d. *Ongoing collective reflection* through learning circles.

e.   *Educators' satisfaction* in terms of reactions and sense of intellectual, personal and emotional growth at different stages.

f.   *Impact in secondary beneficiary group*—group of students who will be affected by the educator.

g.   *Organizer's evaluation.* Assessment of the effectiveness of the training program, training team, delivery, logistics, and usefulness of mechanisms put in place to support educators' development and learning.

There are two additional cross-sectional components: *learning environment and social context and reality*. These components are analyzed in order to understand their influence on the overall evaluation.

EXPLANATION OF THE MODEL

Educators become aware of their own possible violent behaviors and attitudes through daily *self-reflection* spaces that allow them to identify, examine and at best deal with their inner contradictions. Self-reflection acts as a catalyst for individual transformation and for generating a comprehensive evaluation system.

From the beginning and throughout the training program educators evaluate their own changes, new understandings and challenges, and reflect on the unlearning process they go through and how to improve. The ongoing self-reflection process nourishes the other evaluation components creating a feed back/forward system that enriches educators' competencies. A good evaluation is prospective and forward-looking, anticipating where evaluation feedback will be needed rather than just reacting to situations as they arise (OHCHR & Equitas, 2011, p. 21). The evaluation becomes a tool for transformation and not just a measure of current/ acquired competences, weaknesses and strengths.

The following pages review each of the components of the proposed model and provide an in-depth explanation of the self-reflection process.

Content—Knowledge Acquired and Skills Developed

Educators assess the *knowledge acquired and the skills developed during the training* through self-inquiry questions. For instance if participants are learning about non-violent alternatives, the evaluation of content will focus on how they use those in daily life, how they develop their creativity and what may be hindering their capacity to find concrete and practical non-violent alternatives. The evaluation in this area is not in terms of listing a number of non-violent alternatives, for example, but identifying creative non-violent ways of responding to specific situations in the classroom, with parents, colleagues, family and in society.

Some programs ask open questions to educators to assess their knowledge and skills. For example the Learning to Live Together program developed by GTZ (Sinclair, Obura, & Tibbitts, 2008, pp. 110–115) includes questions like: What has the course added to your knowledge, or has it given you new ideas and concepts? What special skills have you learned during the course? How has the course changed your own or other trainees' values and attitudes? Do the educators think they will play (or have already played) a more active role as citizens, peace builders, mentors for youth, etc., as a result of this training? Is there any change in how you and your fellow trainees feel about people who are from a different social group to you? Or in how you behave towards them? After the first year of the course or after specific lessons, did you find any change in your behavior towards others, and if so, what do you think caused it?

These questions are appropriate to assess changes, though could be accompanied by action-oriented questions that trigger further reflection like: How would you use the new skills you acquired? How do you think your behavior changes will benefit your performance as educator and your students? What challenges do you find in applying peace education principles and how could you overcome them?

The process of self-reflection works as a way to contrast what was learned, what was discovered and acquired in the training program, with educators' previous experiences, current practices and improvements needed.

Practical Application

Peace education training programs are most of the times combined with *practical experience* where educators develop and facilitate their own programs and apply what they learn. An evaluation of the *application* is needed to measure how educators' skills, knowledge and attitudes are put into practice, how they are able to incorporate them into content and methodologies, and are integrated in their role as peace educators.

As with the other components in this model, the evaluation of the application is also combined with self-reflection, allowing educators to reflect on the challenges they experience. For instance: listening fully to children, trusting their capacities, giving students more responsibilities, treating girls and boys equally, applying disciplinary measures that do not imply corporal punishment, etc. What is hindering educators' capacity to apply the principles of peace education in their interactions with students? Educators become aware of their own unknown or hidden violent attitudes by practicing and reflecting back on the experience and their own behaviors.

This part of the evaluation needs to be supported by peer review through dialogue spaces. Participants provide mutual feedback on their performance, share their own assessment and receive mutual advice on how their performance could have been improved.

Beneficiaries' Evaluation

During the practical implementation of programs by educators, it is important to conduct *evaluations to the students or beneficiaries*. It is important that evaluation covers a post-program phase in order to evaluate the learning of beneficiaries.

Most peace education programs apply a baseline to participants, which is checked at the end of the program through questions mostly related to knowledge and skills. In this model it is important to consider how students' learning is influenced by the knowledge, skills and attitudes of their educators. Most of the times this correlation is not made, and the learning of students is only associated with the content and methodologies used in the programs. An explanation of the correlation of factors is provided in the section on Factoring relations.

A practical way of conducting these evaluations is by asking questions such as: was the learning environment conducive to dialogue and sharing? Were you encouraged to participate and take further responsibilities? Did the program allow spaces for challenging your views and ideas? Did you feel that your opinions were respected and taken into account by the educator? Did you feel included in the discussions? Did the explanations help you broaden your understandings?

It is additionally necessary to create spaces for educators and students to enter in horizontal dialogue to exchange views about the program and provide mutual feedback. Students have a role to play in the self-reflection process of their educators by sharing their expectations, needs, frustrations, satisfaction and easiness or discomfort with the learning process. This dialogue can positively support educators' professional and personal development. Although this is a necessary component for a holistic evaluation process, it is not an easy task. It requires the creation of a proper space for dialogue, trust, respect, openness and the willingness and capacity of the educator to listen empathically without judgment and reprisals against students. Educators need to be encouraged to create *sharing circles* with their students where they can freely express their views about the program; and to hold continuous one-on-one dialogue, within the parameters of a respectful and at the same time professional educator-student relationship.

Educators' Satisfaction

During certain moments of the training program, it is important to evaluate the *satisfaction of the educator*. How they feel in relation to the activities carried out, what was hard, what challenged them, what was rewarding and motivating. Did they enjoy the activities? Did the activities allow them to relate to their reality and context? Was the methodology conducive to reflection and learning? Some of these questions are part of formative evaluations and others are part of reaction's evaluations, as suggested in Kirkpatrick's model.

It is sometimes difficult to weight reactions into the evaluation process, however, their assessment works as a thermometer to measure motivation, educators' ownership of the program and engagement with the content.

Collective Assessment—Learning Circles

The evaluation process is complemented with continuous *learning circles*[4] with other educators to share fears, discoveries, experiences, ideas and challenges. Learning circles are open and yet safe spaces to share participants' experiences and help awakening unconscious attitudes and unexplored contradictions that can affect their role as peace educators. *Collective reflection* through dialogue helps collectively evaluating how the concepts and principles of peace education are applied individually, with students and in society.

Learning circles can be organized around a specific topic, for instance, gender relations, creativity, violence in society, frustration, etc. A facilitator is appointed to open and close the circle and facilitate the sharing. Educators engage in dialogue about experiences, discoveries during the training and ideas to overcome challenges, and how to consistently apply the principles of peace education in their lives and as educators. Each learning circle ends with a few ideas for improvement or actions that can be used by each educator. Learning circles are not spaces for advising the other on how he/she should act; they are spaces to collectively assess common challenges, come to realizations about possible bias, violent behaviors and attitudes and obtain ideas to move forward.

After the training program participants can continue meeting periodically to assess their changes overtime, their new perceptions on a specific topic and how they take action.

Learning Environment and Social Reality

An analysis of the learning environment and social context is developed in parallel to the evaluation process. *The learning environment factor* takes into consideration the place where educational activities are conducted and available facilities. Aspects like distance for the educators to the place where the training is conducted, availability of boards, paper, and pens, accessibility of learning sites, adequate training hours and security and safety of training places, may influence the attendance, level of attention, interest in the programs, among others, that can indirectly influence the learning of educators.

The social context and reality refers to a conflict-sensitive analysis that takes into consideration the direct, structural and cultural violence that shape the society. What kind of conflicts does society face? What kind of violence children, young people and adults are confronted with? How are the relations between groups of people? How media influences the views of people? Is the country

---

[4] Learning circles, generically described, are small diverse, democratic groups of people (generally 6–12) who meet regularly over a specified period of time to focus their different perspectives into a common understanding of an issue or problem. The discussion takes place in an atmosphere of mutual trust and understanding. The goal is to achieve deeper understanding by the participants and their efforts are often directed towards the construction of a final product or recommendation for a course of action. Riel (2006).

politically stable? What kind of past experiences influence the collective memory of its people? By understanding the dynamics of society, it is possible to develop reflection questions to be asked during the learning circles and deconstruct learning together.

An analysis of the learning environment and social reality provides elements to improve the program during the training. It acts as a warning system to make sure the program is contextualized and responds to the needs of the group.

Organizers' Evaluation

Once all the above areas have been evaluated, it is recommended that organizers assess the fulfillment of the objectives, logistics, teamwork, challenges and improvements needed. The *organizer's evaluation* is complemented with 1) Evaluation forms and the results of other activities used to assess the overall learning from a session and the training program;[5] 2) The information obtained and discussions from the collective assessment or learning circles;[6] 3) Answers given in the evaluation of knowledge acquired and skills developed and 4) Observations made from the practical application. All findings are then contrasted with the learning environment and social context and reality.

The organizer's evaluation helps developing a summative evaluation that takes into consideration all factors expressed in the model and helps making decisions based on a comprehensive and holistic picture of the training program. It can provide concrete ideas to follow up educators' performance and initiate a longitudinal evaluation process.

SELF-REFLECTION PROCESS (IN DEPTH-EXPLANATION)

The proposed evaluation model requires that educators go through a self-reflection process before, during and after the training, to assess what is strengthening, hindering or challenging their performance as peace educators. This process is particularly important to reflect on how preconceived ideas, individual and collective experiences, and cultural understandings shape their own way of thinking and behaving. It helps examining what might affect their ways of teaching, of relating to students, approaching a topic or even understanding their own and students' social context. Self-reflection can generate unlearning and critical thinking which are fundamental elements of peace education.

The self-reflection process proposed is based on the conflict triangle developed by Prof. Johan Galtung (1990, p. 294) that aims to understand how conflicts take place and can be transformed. The triangle (Figure 20.2) is composed of

---

[5] OHCHR & Equitas (2011) provides an end-of-training summary evaluation samples to assess the effectiveness of a training session or program, p. 181- 228.
[6] This input does not take into consideration individual reflections but common challenges and ideas developed during the learning circles. It helps examining the main-common constraints of educators and their ability to transform them.

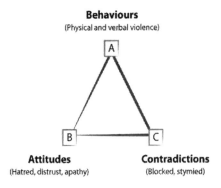

FIGURE 20.2.   Conflict Triangle—adapted from Galtung (1990)

attitudes, behaviors and contradictions. The behaviors are found in the manifest level, which can be observed and are conscious, while the attitudes and contradictions are in the latent level, which are usually unconscious and inferred. Attitudes and contradictions need inner dialogues to create consciousness about them, be understood, reflected upon and transformed.

By using the conflict triangle, educators are prompted and constantly reminded to look at their inner contradictions and how those can affect their performance as educators. They can reflect about unconscious violent behaviors reflected in physical and verbal aggression to students, and about unaware attitudes reflected in apathy and distrust. It is important for peace educators to reflect on how previous experiences, upbringing, their context and unconscious attitudes, manifest in undesired behaviors and could provoke or be the source of contradictions, that if not dealt adequately can negatively impact their programs.

Table 20.1 provides examples to consider in each area of the triangle that can be included in the self-reflection process. These examples are based on situations that may contribute to inner conflicts and consequently have a negative impact on the peace education program and on the learning of students. The purpose is to help educators reaching a level of *conscientization* of forgotten or repressed experiences[7] and to help them become conscious subjects of their role as peace educators.

EXAMPLES FOR EACH AREA OF THE CONFLICT TRIANGLE

The self-reflection process is not the same as an evaluation baseline, which should also be used to know the level of each educator in terms of knowledge and skills related to peace education and its principles. This is a more holistic process to be

---

[7] References to processes of *conscientization* are made by Galtung (1996), p. 74, in relation to Paulo Freire's pedagogy of the oppressed.

TABLE 20.1

Behaviors	Attitudes	Contradictions (expressed in situations that might cause conflicts)
Preferences for a particular gender, ethnic or cultural groups	Resentment against a specific group of people	Past violent experiences
Lack of attention to children's ideas and proposals	Lack of trust	Economic difficulties
Aggressive communication with students	Lack of empathy	Emotional instability
Use of corporal punishment	Pessimism	Emotional loss
Difficulties engaging in dialogue with students	Indifference	Unbearable responsibilities
Make fun of children's ideas and actions	Lack of creative thinking	Dysfunctional family
Use of patronizing language	Lack of self-esteem and confidence	Lack of life fulfillment
Put children's ideas down	Patronizing and paternalism	Frustration

used throughout the program, individually and collectively. It does not have an end and fixed answers. It is a process of self-discovery, of developing critical thinking and understanding their role as peace educators. The main way of carrying out this self-reflection process is through journals or learning logs and then sharing voluntarily during the learning circles. Questions can be integrated into other components of the evaluation and even in the content of the training sessions.

FACTORING RELATIONS

It is important for organizers, donors and educators to look at ways in which the development of and changes in attitudes, skills and knowledge may have a concrete impact on the beneficiaries. The impact could be measured through three lenses: proper delivery of content and methodologies, creation of an effective learning environment and the actual learning of students.

Factoring the results should be conducted after the training program takes place, if possible, in the framework of a longitudinal performance evaluation process. Peace educators are evaluated in terms of the competencies (knowledge, attitudes and skills) needed to perform their jobs and capacity to impact successfully the learning of their students. Evaluations should take into consideration particular competencies designed for the program and their acquisition needs to be analyzed through the process of self-reflection, as explained in the suggested model.

Table 20.2, although not exhaustive, shows some examples of how changes/ acquisition of knowledge, attitudes and skills in educators may have an impact on

TABLE 20.2

	Content	Methodologies	Learning environment
Knowledge	By understanding micro and macro level conflicts, peace educators manage to connect the individual learning of students to their realities and social context.	By understanding how participatory methodologies help achieving a particular objective, peace educators become more creative in delivering a program and can easily engage students in the learning process.	By understanding the psychological development of a child and the importance of participatory learning, peace educators can create more respectful environments for learning and encourage the development of critical thinking.
Attitudes	By being empathic to children's needs, ideas, dreams and expectations, peace educators can customize the content better which in turn will support the engagement and participation of students.	By being respectful to all ethnic groups, gender and religions, peace educators can select methodologies that support inclusive education and use them to build bridges of trust and reconciliation.	By being coherent in personal life with the principles of peace education, educators can inspire students to become peacemakers and more easily learn what peace and peace-building mean.
Skills	By being resourceful and creative, peace educators can easily adapt the materials to the context and realities children face, taking into consideration the dynamics of conflict situations and different actors.	By communicating respectfully and empathically, and by using non-violent alternatives to solve conflicts in the classroom, students will emulate the same pattern of communication, which in turn makes them more prompted to engage in dialogue.	By listening to students and creating trust in the group through a horizontal relationship, students can recreate a peaceful environment, become active participants in the learning process and get confidence to participate and propose new ideas.

the success of peace education programs. It also helps visualizing the importance of evaluating these three elements consistently.

CONCLUSIONS

Peace education training programs for educators are a fundamental building block in the success of peace education activities. The role that educators play in recreating a conducing environment for reflecting about peace, non-violent alternatives, conflicts, violence and relationships is extremely important in the effectiveness of the programs. Therefore, peace education training program evaluations should be centered on the attitudes and behaviors of the educators as role models and on how those are translated into the delivery of their programs, and consequently may impact their students.

Although fundamental, there are several challenges related to the application of evaluation of training programs in peace education. One main challenge is related to financial resources. In the non-formal education sector, most of the times donors are more interested to evaluate the short or long term impact on the population that will benefit from the programs that educators will implement, rather than on the process educators goes through to develop themselves. Therefore, a budget line is not allocated to run long term and in-depth evaluations of educators. Three ways to overcome these challenges are: 1) Make educators' evaluation a clear part of the program design, including it in the content of the program. 2) Qualify the importance of role modeling as a building block in the success of larger peace education programs. This can be done by developing case studies, interviews with educators and students and recording some of the learning circles. 3) Build online mechanisms to follow up educators' performance and changes that can be more cost-effective than physical meetings.

In many cases, including formal education, organizers of training programs overlook the importance of evaluating attitudinal changes assuming that educators are *per se* already skilled to teach and facilitate any content, as long as they obtain the knowledge about it. However, in the case of peace education programs, educators not only need to know pedagogical tools and have knowledge of peace education, but they also need to be role models, critical thinkers and embed in their own behaviors, worldviews and attitudes, the principles of peace education.

Although it is important to consider the difficulties attributing direct relation between the role of educators, their performance in the classroom and the impact on the learning of students, it is necessary to understand to what extent role modeling and the creation of peaceful and respectful learning environments affect the impact of the program on students. Evaluations, therefore, should not downplay the role that educators play in transforming individuals even if the immediate effects cannot be seen.

It is precisely because of the nature of peace education that a paradigm shift in its program evaluation is needed, starting by bringing educators to the front of the evaluation, articulating the design of the program with an ongoing evaluation centered on self-reflection, and creating mechanisms to follow up and support the continuous changes educators go through. Evaluation should not only be a technical tool but a transformational instrument at individual and organizational levels.

REFERENCES

Ashton, C. (2007). Using theory of change to enhance peace education evaluation. *Conflict Resolution Quarterly, 25*, 39–53.

Baxter, P., & Ikobwa, V. (2005). Peace education: why and how? *Forced Migration Review 22*, 28–29.

Bramley, P., & Newby, A. (1984). The Evaluation of training part I—Clarifying the concept. *Journal of European Industrial Training , 8*(6), 10–16.

Craig, H., Kraft, R., & du Plessis, J. (1998). *Teacher development: Making an impact.* USAID Advancing Basic Education and Literacy Project and World Bank, Human Development Network, Effective Schools and Teachers. Washington, D.C.: ABEL Clearinghouse for Basic Education.

Equitas. (2007). HRE for social change: Evaluation approaches and methodologies. *International Human Rights Education (HRE) Evaluation Symposium* . Montreal, Quebec: Equitas, Office of the United National High Commissioner for Human Rights .

EURED. (2002). *The EURED teacher training programme. Design for a European peace education course.* Vienna, Austria: EURED.

Galtung, J. (1990). Cultural violence. *Journal of Peace Research , 27*(3), 291–305.

Hamblin, A. C. (1974). *Evaluation and control of training.* Maidenhead, UK: McGraw-Hill.

Kirkpatrick, D. L. (1975). Techniques for evaluating training programs. In D. L. Kirkpatrick (Ed.), *Evaluating training programs.* Alexandria, VA: ASTD

Kirkpatrick Partners. (2011). *The Kirkpatrick philosophy.* Retrieved November 16, 2011 from Kirkpatrick Partners. The One and Only Kirkpatrick: http://www.kirkpatrickpartners.com/OurPhilosophy/tabid/66/Default.aspx

Newby, A. (1992). *Training evaluation handbook.* Toronto, Canada: Pfeiffer & Company.

OHCHR & Equitas. (2011). *Evaluating human rights training activities. A handbook for human rights educators.* Montreal, Canada: International Centre for Human Rights Education and the Office of the United Nations High Commissioner for Human Rights.

PricewaterhouseCoopers LLP. (2007). *A monitoring and evaluation framework for peacebuilding.* London.

Rae, L. (2002). *Assessing the value of your training: The Evaluation process from training needs to the report to the board.* England: Gower Publishing Limited.

Riel, M. (2006). *Learning circles teachers' guide.* International Education and Resource Network. Retrieved February 10, 2012 from http://www.iearn.org/circles/lcguide/p.intro/a.intro.html#Concept

Sinclair, M., Obura, A., & Tibbitts, F. (2008). *Learning to live together—Design, monitoring and evaluation of education for life skills, citizenship, peace and human rights.* (G. a. Development, Ed.) Eschborn, Germany: Deutsche Gesellschaft für Technische Zusammenarbeit (GTZ) GmbH.

Stern, E. (2003, December). *Evaluating socio economic development, Sourcebook 2: Methodkation.* Retrieved 11 16, 2011 from ec.europa.eu/regional_policy/.../sb2_formative_evaluation.doc

Torres, R. (1999). *Building capacity for organizational learning through evaluative inquiry.* California: Developmental Studies Center.

UNESCO, UNHCR, and INEE. (2005). *Inter-Agency peace education program. Skills for constructive living.* Paris, France: UNESCO.

Warr, P., Bird, M., & Rackham, N. (1970). *Evaluation of management training.* London, UK: Gower Press

Weiss, C. (1995). Nothing as practical as a good theory: exploring theory-based evaluation for comprehensive community initiatives for children and families. In J. Connell, A. Kubisch, L. Schorr, & C. Weiss (Eds.), *New Approach in Evaluating Community Onitiatives.* Washington DC: Aspen Institute.

CONCLUSION

This volume's authors offer a variety of opinions and valuable insights. Our learnings and questions have been too many to count since the inception of the idea for this volume; three stand out in particular. First, in considering internal capacities, existing tools and the interest for peace education evaluation, is the push for evaluation externally demand-driven? Or are there stories of evaluation that are genuinely developed and grown from the inside? Second, how is the imperative for accountability and quest to learn balanced in the drive for peace education evaluations? And third, how does peace education evaluation practice reflect the principles of peace education?

Regarding the first issue, we have departed from the assessment that evaluation in the field of peace education was mainly demand-driven, either by donor or by educational authorities. Having gathered numerous examples of peace education evaluation experiences, we now observe that educators and organizations are internally leading evaluation exercises and reflections. This is an important step towards the recognition and strengthening of evaluation as an integral part of any educational endeavour. Though we believe external demands and frameworks continue to prevail, this book shows that there are rich experiences from which to learn, such as teachers and activists developing their own tools of assessment adapted to the realities and constraints that they face.

Peace Education Evaluation: Learning from Experience and Exploring Prospects,
pages 317–320.
Copyright © 2015 by Information Age Publishing
All rights of reproduction in any form reserved.

Second, several authors touch on the delicate balance between evaluation for accountability and evaluation for learning. Authors show both the difficulty and the possibility to achieve this balance in light of the needs of each educational experience and context. Evaluation exists not as a burden, but as an intrinsic part of the educational program and a valuable path through which educators and participants could acquire and sharpen necessary critical-thinking skills. Educational criteria should be at the center of any evaluation. Efficacy criteria should be linked to the needs and expectations of all involved, but most importantly to the participants and the communities in which the activities take place.

Third, this volume's authors offer a variety of reflections related to evaluation itself serving as a model of peace education. Authors converge on the idea that any evaluation exercise related to peace education should remain loyal to the principles and values which inspire the field, namely respect for diversity and cultural responsiveness, critical awareness about power relations, and participation of all involved in the decision-making process. The volume also provides several examples which keep participants at the center of an empowering educative evaluation experience. Keeping the principles of peace education central to evaluation efforts requires deep reflection on epistemological and methodological issues. Respect for those involved and their diversity of opinions and identities may imply changes in methodological choices. Chapters in this book show the use of a wide variety of methodologies and strategies on the spectrum of positivist-interpretive approaches. They provide detailed explanations of methodological options given the context, opportunities and constraints of each educational program.

Overall, we hope that this volume offers compelling insights and action-oriented momentum for multiple stakeholders whose presence and practice in peace education is varied. We hope that this book serves as a resource for many, from the student to the funder, from the policy maker to the practitioner. From our perspective as educators, this volume offers teachers and practitioners tools and experiences from different parts of the world. Given their deep contextual knowledge, we recognize that fellow educators are the most pertinent actors in the evaluation community for assessing how effectively and efficiently tools work in any given situation. As educators and researchers, we are deeply touched by teachers and how they live the lives they lead in disparate and sometimes desperate situations. We have found that narratives of productive, internally-driven evaluations by fellow educators inspire and encourage our own experimentation and hope that this volume likewise serves as a resource for our peers around the world.

Through this volume, grant foundation administrators, funding managers and policy makers who support peace education efforts might become more acquainted with non-traditional assessment methods and acquire a more nuanced understanding about the invaluableness of the peace education programs they support. We hope that this audience might be encouraged by these chapters to thoughtfully assess the demands or constraints regarding evaluation placed on peace education grantees and make strides for more inclusive and adaptive reporting mechanisms for non-conventional educational programs. We could not have lasted as long as we have without financial and other resources bestowed in both faith and contract by funders to conduct research, implement programs and pursue educational opportunities in the fields of peace education, conflict resolution and international development about which we are most passionate. We are hopeful that this volume acts in part as remuneration for such support.

We are not immune to the fact that there is much to be read and not enough time for seeming indulgence; our own bookshelves, housing unopened books, stand as evidence to such a reality. Yet, we remain intentionally optimistic that educational researchers and evaluators will find particularly elucidating the detailed descriptions of methodological tool boxes presented by these diverse voices. Such reading can assist to garner ideas for future experimentation in how to most effectively and thoughtfully assess peace education and similar programs. We are moreover encouraged that this volume models the reality of the peace education field in which actors—such as ourselves—wear and bear multiple identities: educator, evaluator, researcher, sometimes even funder! This model can serve as an alternative to the consistent "theory and practice" divide that persists in both education and international development.

Lastly, we hope that this volume reaches students of peace and conflict studies, international educational development, comparative and international education, conflict resolution and research methods among other fields, given that we were all once those eager and confused students and now continue to work with student populations. Through this volume, we hope that students become acquainted with various experiences from around the globe through new voices and are introduced to evaluation as an integral part of educational practice. This resource serves as well to situate peace education evaluation as one of the lenses through which students can observe and know the reality in which they are engaged as practitioners and researchers. As you might imagine given our education-based careers, the three of us have a soft spot for students and we especially look forward to hearing how this work moved, challenged, incensed or inspired them beyond critique to critical action.

In conclusion, from our perspective, some lines of action and future reflection emerge from the chapters of this book. We acknowledge a need to further learn and discuss evaluation experiences and the challenges involved. Dedicated seminars and new publications will help the peace education community to create the necessary spaces for learning and exchange. We see the need for all stakeholders to engage in dialogue about the various understandings and expectations of peace education. We also sense the desire to further experiment with new methodologies and ideas. Evaluation exercises need to be implemented in new and engaging participatory ways so as to make them integral parts of the educational practice. Evaluation can and should be peace education. Such a model encourages accountability to all stakeholders, participation and a genuine deep reflection on our reasons and assumptions of how personal transformation and social change occur.

We hope this volume contributes to this process of reflection, experimentation and action.

In some small way, the original impetus for this volume was selfish, as educators Celina and Andria in 2006 struggled to maintain vision and momentum in their peace work without the existence of resources that provided encouragement and basic, helpful information. Our own challenges and celebrations in the field of peace education have been possible only by the many who have taught and continue to teach us, whether it be a youth participant sitting on the grass in a small peace education program in rural Liberia or a professor at the front of a grand lecture hall in the Netherlands or New York City. It is both our desire and expectation that this volume serves as a resource for current peace education programs and motivation for deeper investigations and case studies of peace education evaluation. More importantly, this volume—and the heartbeats, time, passion, and unrestrained optimism that is encapsulated in these pages by all of these authors—stands as a testimony of hope both for and in a world that is every day less violent and more peaceful than the last.

ABOUT THE AUTHORS

Chapter 1

Hakim Mohandas Amani Williams received his doctorate of education in International Educational Development/Peace Education at Columbia University. He has many years experience in after-school programming, has served on several research teams (at CPRE and NCRECE), and taught a graduate online course on peace education at Drexel University for two years. At present, he is an Assistant Professor of Africana Studies (Caribbean focus), Education and Globalization Studies at Gettysburg College. Research interests include human rights/ peace education, school/structural violence, and educational inequity..

Chapter 2

University Professor Werner Wintersteiner, Ph.D., is the founding director of the "Centre for Peace Research and Peace Education" at Klagenfurt University, Austria. He is director of the Master's program in Global Citizenship Education, a teacher trainer for German, a peace educator, and member of the Austrian Competence Centre for Education (German) at Klagenfurt University. His main re-

Peace Education Evaluation: Learning from Experience and Exploring Prospects, pages 321–329.

Copyright © 2015 by Information Age Publishing
All rights of reproduction in any form reserved.

search fields include: peace education and global citizenship education, culture and peace, and (transcultural) literature education. He is a member of the editorial board of the "Journal of Peace Education" as well as a member of the Council of the Peace Education Commission (PEC) of IPRA (International Peace Research Association).

Chapter 3

Helga Stokes holds a doctorate in instructional systems and comparative and international education from the Pennsylvania State University. She taught in the K-12 system, in traditional and innovative schools. Her main interest is in school improvement from an international and comparative perspective, in particular in the innovative design of learning environments Her international experience includes having lived in various South American countries, West Africa and Puerto Rico. Currently, at the School of Education of Duquesne University, she collaborates in the evaluation of educational programs and teaches evaluation and research methods.

Rodney K. Hopson is Professor, Division of Educational Psychology, Research Methods, and Education Policy, College of Education and Human Development, George Mason University. He received his Ph.D. from the Curry School of Education, University of Virginia, and has done post-doctoral/sabbatical studies in the Faculty of Education, University of Namibia, the Johns Hopkins Bloomberg School of Public Health and Centre of African Studies, Cambridge University. Hopson's research and funded projects raise questions that 1) analyze and address the differential impact of education and schooling on marginalized and underrepresented groups in diverse global nation states and 2) seek solutions to social and educational conditions in the form of alternative and democratic paradigms, epistemologies, and methods for the way the oppressed and marginalized succeed and thrive despite circumstances and opportunities that suggest otherwise.

Chapter 4

Cheryl Woelk is a language instructor and peace educator working in multicultural contexts. She taught most recently at Eastern Mennonite University's Intensive English Program in Harrisonburg, Virginia, USA, where she developed curriculum for various courses, including the Intensive English for Peacebuilding for the Summer Peacebuilding Institute. After obtaining a B.A. in English at Canadian Mennonite University, Cheryl worked for several years with English and peace education curriculum at the Korea Anabaptist Center in Seoul, South Korea. She also has experience in teaching and curriculum development in Canada, China, and East Timor, and most recently with the Northeast Asia Regional Peacebuilding Institute in South Korea and Japan. She has a certificate in TEFL, an MA in

Education concentrating on Curriculum and Instructional Strategies, and a graduate certificate in peacebuilding from Eastern Mennonite University's Center for Justice and Peacebuilding. She currently lives in Saskatoon, Canada with her spouse Hong Soek (Scott) Kim.

Chapter 5

Erin Dunlevy is the Restorative Justice Coordinator at the Urban Assembly School of Design and Construction at Park West Campus in New York City. She has been an educator with the Department of Education for twelve years and holds a master's degree in international education from New York University. Erin has partnered with The Center for the Theatre of the Oppressed, The Restorative Way, the International Institute for Restorative Practices, and Educators for Social Responsibility to implement strategies for violence-prevention in New York City public schools.

Christina Procter was an English teacher, grade team leader, and Restorative Practices facilitator for four years at the High School for Arts, Imagination, and Inquiry. With previous teaching experience in the UK and Argentina, she holds an MA in Adolescent Education of English from Hunter College and a BA in Literature and Creative Writing from the University of Warwick. She has partnered with the International Institute for Restorative Practices and Educators for Social Responsibility and has studied Group Therapy at Fordham University. Christina now lives in Santa Fe, New Mexico, where her social justice work has shifted into efforts to mitigate climate disruption, especially in areas disproportionately affected. She is the Editor of EcoSource magazine as well as the Administration and Communications Manager of nonprofit New Energy Economy.

Chapter 6

Roberta A. Heydenberk, Ed.D has extensive experience in the areas of conflict resolution, bullying prevention program design and multicultural education. Roberta has conducted bullying, bias, and conflict resolution research in wide ranging settings and age groups. Roberta's research has appeared in peer reviewed journals, magazine articles, and in a textbook. Roberta has shared her research at more than 30 national and international conferences, and she is a recipient of awards for her initiatives in bullying and conflict resolution. Roberta worked for Educational Testing Service as a test-essay analyst, she is research director for a nonprofit organization, she founded a nonprofit organization to benefit Sudan's schools, and she has served on several education boards. Roberta teaches conflict resolution, guides independent research studies, and is chair of a student club as an adjunct professor in the College of Education at Lehigh University.

Warren R. Heydenberk, Ed.D has extensive experience in conflict resolution and bullying prevention programs. Warren has conducted conflict resolution and bullying research which has been disseminated in academic journals, magazine articles and in a textbook. Warren has taught in elementary, secondary, alternative education, and higher education. Warren has served on several education nonprofit boards. Warren is faculty emeritus at Lehigh University where he teaches conflict resolution and language arts within the College of Education.

Chapter 7

Antonia Mandry has a Doctorate in International Educational Development with a concentration in Peace Education from Teachers College, Columbia University (2012). Her research interests include education in the Middle East, human rights and citizenship. She also served as Senior Editor for Current Issues in Comparative Education and former Managing Editor of the Society of International Education Journal. She received her Master's of Education in Curriculum, Instruction and Educational Psychology in 2001 from Loyola University of Chicago. She previously taught at Middle East Technical University from 2004 to 2007, where she developed an expertise in ELT teaching. She has also worked with international organizations such as UNESCO, UNHCR and UNICEF, having worked with UNICEF in Chad, South Sudan and Turkey.

Chapter 8

Rajashree Srinivasan is an Associate Professor at the Azim Premji University, Bangalore, India. She is currently the Coordinator of the Master's in Teacher Education Program of the University. She has a decade of experience in teacher education. She worked at the Department of Elementary Education at Lady Shri Ram College, Delhi University as a teacher educator. She has worked on a collaborative project that aimed to develop a plan for India's University Grants Commission to increase inclusivity in higher education country-wide. She collaborated on a project on liberal arts education with the Institute of Higher Education Policy, Washington. She has significant expertise in pedagogic practices in teacher education and her other research interests are peace education and diversity issues in higher education.

Chapter 9

Zulfiya Tursunova is an Assistant Professor in the Department of Social and Economic Development at Algoma University in Canada. She has expertise in development, women's empowerment, health, and peace studies. Her professional experience is focused on community development, indigenous issues, and feminist research. Zulfiya received her Ph.D. in Peace and Conflict Studies from the University of Manitoba. Her recent work examines women's and their household members' livelihood constraints and the choices they make and diversification in response to land tenure and socio-economic changes in rural development in post-Soviet Uzbekistan. Zulfiya's research emphasizes how the conflict resolution practices of women are woven into their everyday life, and function autonomously from the hierarchical elite-driven Women's Committees and state court systems established in Soviet times.

Chapter 10

Dr. H. B. Danesh is the founder and president of the International Education for Peace Institute (Canada). He is a retired professor of conflict resolution, peace education, and psychiatry. Dr. Danesh is the author and creator of the internationally acclaimed Education for Peace Program—first piloted in Bosnia and Herzegovina—and the main author of its multi-volume curriculum. He teaches peace education, peace studies, peace-based conflict resolution, peace-based leadership and governance, and peace-based family at several institutions of higher education in Europe, North America, and India.

Chapter 11

Ned Lazarus is Visiting Professor of International Relations at The George Washington University's Elliott School of International Affairs. A conflict resolution scholar, practitioner and evaluator specializing in Israeli-Palestinian peacebuilding, Ned has conducted recent evaluations of more than 50 Israeli-Palestinian civil society peace initiatives on behalf of USAID, the United States Institute of Peace, and the European Union. Ned has taught Conflict Resolution at George Mason University, Georgetown University and the University of Massachusetts-Boston. Ned earned his doctorate in international relations from American University's School of International Service in 2011; his dissertation assesses the long-term impacts of peace education for more than 800 Israeli and Palestinian youth before, during and after the second intifada. Before entering the academic field, Ned served as Middle East Program Director for Seeds of Peace, based in Jerusalem, from 1996–2004.

Chapter 12

Daniel Wehrenfennig, Ph.D. is the Executive Director of the Olive Tree Initiative, an award-winning international experiential learning program that brings students and community members on annual educational fact-finding trips to conflict zones around the world (Middle East, Caucasus). He also directs the Certificate Program in Conflict Analysis and Resolution at the University of California, Irvine (UCI). He has produced a documentary film for civic education in Malawi/Africa. His recent work has been published by *Peace Review, Communication Theory*, the University of California Press, Lexington Books and Studies in Ethnicity and Nationalism.

Daniel Brunstetter is Associate Professor of political science at UC Irvine. His research interests include questions of identity and just war theory. He has published in journals such as *Political Studies, International Relations, Ethics and International Affairs, and Review of Politics*. He is also co-director of the Olive Tree Initiative, and co-founder of the undergraduate certificate program in Conflict Analysis and Resolution.

Johanna Solomon is a Ph.D. candidate in political science at UC Irvine. She participated in the third Olive Tree Initiative trip to Israel/Palestine and Jordan in the fall of 2010. She holds master's degrees in both political science and counseling psychology.

Chapter 13

The United Network of Young Peacebuilders (UNOY Peacebuilders) is an international network connecting 60 youth peace organizations across 35 countries. Our goal is to create a world where young people have the opportunity and skills to contribute to peace. We work to strengthen youth-driven peacebuilding initiatives based on the needs of our members, facilitate a safe space for dialogue and conflict transformation, develop the organizational capacities of our members and to bring the voices of young people to policy makers on a regional and global level.

Chapter 14

Until July 2012, Susan Armitage was responsible for providing management oversight, as well as technical input and support, to the USAID-funded Youth Theater for Peace programs in Kyrgyzstan and Tajikistan. There, she oversaw the work of program staff based in Bishkek and Dushanbe and liaised with local partners to meet deliverables. Susan has contributed to the development of the Performance Monitoring and Evaluation Plan (PMEP) for the program, designed quantitative and qualitative M&E tools, and analyzed data for reporting. She has extensive experience working on the ground in Central Asia and has served as a trainer at Youth Theater for Peace events. Prior to her employment at IREX, Susan served as a youth and community development volunteer in Russia and Ukraine. She holds a bachelor's degree in English from Oberlin College and a master's degree in journalism from the CUNY Graduate School of Journalism. Susan is currently Deputy Managing Editor-International at BuzzFeed.

Chapter 15

Ruerd Ruben holds a PhD in development economics from Free University Amsterdam. He lived and worked for 14 years in several Central American countries (Nicaragua, Honduras, Costa Rica, El Salvador) being engaged in programs of land reform, cooperative development and smallholder agriculture. Hereafter he was appointed at Wageningen University to coordinate a multidisciplinary research and training program on food security and sustainable land use in sub-Saharan countries (Mali, Burkina Faso, Kenya, Ethiopia). He started an innovative program on the prospects for smallholder incorporation in tropical food value chains. In 2006 he obtained the chair in development studies at Radboud University Nijmegen to conduct further research on voluntary organizations and the impact of fair trade value chains. Since 2010 he has served as director of the independent Policy and Operations Evaluation Department (IOB) at the Netherlands Ministry of Foreign Affairs.

Chapter 16

Cécile Barbeito Thonon works at the Escola de Cultura de Pau (School for a Culture of Peace) as a trainer and researcher on Peace Education. She has published two books, and applied research reports on peace research. She has also participated as a teacher in MA degrees as well as grassroots trainings. Her experience in peace education evaluation is related to the peace education courses she participates in at university level, where she has applied innovative techniques of evaluation such as observation through Theatre of the Oppressed techniques, and portfolios as a tool of self evaluation. She has also participated in a comparative field research of evaluation of peace education projects in contexts of armed conflict in Palestine, Ivory Coast, and Colombia. She holds an MA in Research on Educational Methodologies, Training, And Educational Evaluation (Universitat de Barcelona) and is currently working towards her Ph.D.

Johanna Ospina is Ph.D. candidate at Carlos III University in Madrid, Spain. Her thesis project is "The Concept of Peace Education in Armed Conflict Situations, the Case of the Occupied Palestinian Territories." She holds a Master's degree in Human Rights and has participated as lecturer for a specialization in Citizen Education and Human Rights at Carlos III University. Her experience in peace education comes from her work for several organizations where she has participate as researcher, project assistant and trainer on topics such as the right to education, citizenship education, education and human rights and peace and conflict studies. She also has participated as author in different publications about topics such as peace process in Colombia, peace education, culture of peace, the right to education in Gaza.

Chapter 17

Karen Ross is Assistant Professor of Conflict Resolution at the University of Massachusetts-Boston. Karen received her Ph.D. in Inquiry Methodology and Comparative & International Education at Indiana University, and is a long-time practitioner of peacebuilding and dialogue in conflict regions. Her research interests lie at the intersection of education, peace-building, and social activism, with a geographic focus on Israel-Palestine. Karen is particularly interested in methodological questions relating to the assessment of peace-building interventions.

Chapter 18

Naghmeh Yazdanpanah is a peace worker and educator based in Iran. She received her BA in anthropology from University of Tehran, and her MA in peace and conflict studies from the European Peace University in Austria. Her work has been guided by a desire to converge the theoretical insights of philosophy and social sciences with the more practical orientation of peace activism and community education. She has worked with different age and social groups in diverse settings from Iran and Afghanistan to Denmark and Austria. Restorative justice, Theater of the Oppressed, and Nonviolent Communication are among her main areas of professional interest.

Chapter 19

Thomas de Hoop serves as a Research and Evaluation Specialist for American Institutes for Research in Washington, DC. Dr. de Hoop has several years of experience coordinating impact evaluations in South Asia, sub-Saharan Africa and Latin America. He has applied a wide variety of statistical and econometric techniques and is an expert in using theories of change for rigorous impact evaluation. Additionally, he has advised a wide range of academics on the appropriate use of statistical techniques and mixed-methods research when he was an evaluation specialist at 3ie. His current research focuses on impact and process evaluations of education programs in India and the Philippines. In previous work he has analyzed the relationship between social norms and the impact of development programs in Ghana, India and Peru. As an evaluation specialist for 3ie, Dr. de Hoop was responsible for coordinating the review and quality assurance of 10 impact evaluation grants with a total value of $5 million awarded under the Social Protection Thematic Window funded by DFID. He also managed the quality assurance of 20 impact evaluation grants awarded under the Open and Policy Window. Further, he is a member of the Peer-Review Group for the Impact Evaluation of the Millennium Villages Project in Northern Ghana.

Dr. Annette Brown serves as Deputy Director of the International Initiative for Impact Evaluation (3ie) in charge of Advancement and Impact Evaluation Services, and she is Head of the 3ie Washington office. She also heads 3ie's HIV/AIDS evidence programs. She established and continues to lead 3ie's programs for impact evaluation replication and registration, and she is currently launching 3ie's new joint Evidence for Peace initiative with IPA and the World Bank. She is also responsible for planning and managing 3ie's advancement strategy, which encompasses fundraising and membership recruitment and engagement. Until May 2012, she also served as Chief Evaluation Officer, for which she directed 3ie's evaluation office and oversaw grants management and quality assurance for all primary study research funded by 3ie. Earlier in her career, Brown was Assistant Professor of economics at Western Michigan University and held research positions at the World Bank and the Stockholm Institute for Transition Economics. She holds a Ph.D. in economics from the University of Michigan. Her current research projects are on the topics of peace-building, governance, HIV/AIDS prevention, and internal replication. Brown serves on the Boards of Directors for Equal Access, an international non-profit implementing communications for social change projects in Asia and Africa, and for Experiments in Governance and Politics, an organization of scholars and practitioners engaged in field experiments on topics of governance, politics, and institutions.

Chapter 20

Maria Lucia Uribe Torres is the Director of Arigatou International in Geneva, an international NGO that works to secure the rights of children and foster children's well-being. She serves as the Secretary General of the Interfaith Council on Ethics Education for Children. Before her appointment, she served as Coordinator and Deputy Coordinator for Education and Fragility for the Inter-Agency Network for Education in Emergencies (INEE), where she provided technical support and expertise on issues relating to education, conflict and peacebuilding within INEE. Maria Lucia has over 12 years of international experience working in global, intercultural, interfaith, human rights, child rights and peace education. Maria Lucia holds a Master in Peace and Conflict Transformation from the University of Basel in Switzerland, a specialization in Economic, Social and Cultural Rights and a Bachelor's degree in International Relations and Finance.

62457186R00195

Made in the USA
Lexington, KY
07 April 2017

C0-AWC-676

GRECO-ROMAN CULTURE AND THE GALILEE OF JESUS

Greco-Roman Culture and the Galilee of Jesus, the first book-length investigation of this topic, challenges the conventional scholarly view that first-century Galilee was thoroughly Hellenized. Examining architecture, inscriptions, coins, and art from Alexander the Great's conquest until the early fourth century CE, Chancey argues that the extent of Greco-Roman culture in the time of Jesus has often been greatly exaggerated. Antipas's reign in the early first century was indeed a time of transition, but the more dramatic shifts in Galilee's cultural climate happened in the second century, after the arrival of a large Roman garrison. Much of Galilee's Hellenization should thus be understood within the context of its Romanization. Any attempt to understand the Galilean setting of Jesus must recognize the significance of the region's historical development as well as how Galilee fits into the larger context of the Roman East.

MARK CHANCEY is Assistant Professor in the Deparment of Religious Studies at Southern Methodist University, Dallas. He is author of *The Myth of a Gentile Galilee* (2002, SNTS Monograph No. 118).

SOCIETY FOR NEW TESTAMENT STUDIES

MONOGRAPH SERIES

General Editor: John M. Court

GRECO-ROMAN CULTURE AND THE GALILEE OF JESUS

MARK A. CHANCEY

Southern Methodist University, Dallas, Texas

CAMBRIDGE
UNIVERSITY PRESS

CAMBRIDGE UNIVERSITY PRESS
Cambridge, New York, Melbourne, Madrid, Cape Town, Singapore, São Paulo

Cambridge University Press
The Edinburgh Building, Cambridge CB2 2RU, UK

Published in the United States of America by Cambridge University Press, New York

www.cambridge.org
Information on this title: www.cambridge.org/9780521846479

© Mark A. Chancey 2005

This book is in copyright. Subject to statutory exception
and to the provisions of relevant collective licensing agreements,
no reproduction of any part may take place without
the written permission of Cambridge University Press.

First published 2005

Printed in the United Kingdom at the University Press, Cambridge

A catalogue record for this book is available from the British Library

ISBN-13 978-0-521-84647-9 hardback
ISBN-10 0-521-84647-1 hardback

Cambridge University Press has no responsibility for the persistence or accuracy of URLs for
external or third-party internet websites referred to in this book, and does not guarantee that
any content on such websites is, or will remain, accurate or appropriate.

DS
110
.G2
C52
2005

For Tracy Anne

Contents

Preface

The need for a new synthesis and analysis of the evidence for Greco-Roman culture in Galilee during the time of Jesus became apparent to me while working on my study on Galilee's population, *The Myth of a Gentile Galilee*. In particular, I was struck at the importance of context, both geographical and chronological, for understanding the region as a whole as well as the significance of individual artifacts and buildings. When reading about particular archaeological finds, I wanted to know if they were typical or atypical within Galilee, the larger area of Palestine, and elsewhere in the Roman East, as well as within their own time periods. I also wanted to contextualize investigations of Galilee within the larger scholarly conversation about Romanization. In this work, I have tried to collect and present the archaeological data from Galilee in a concise, accessible form, while also directing the reader to parallel finds from other regions and to standard reference works on specific categories of material culture. Fuller bibliographies for individual sites can often be found in my previous book, *Myth*. I have written primarily for scholars who are interested in understanding the setting of Jesus, but I also hope this book will prove useful to scholars specializing in Early Judaism, Syro-Palestinian archaeology, and the Roman Near East.

When discussing specific sites, I have sometimes used the Greek name and sometimes the Hebrew, depending on which is better known. My transliteration of Hebrew names usually follows the general-purpose style outlined in Patrick H. Alexander et al., eds., *The SBL Handbook of Style for Ancient Near Eastern, Biblical, and Early Christian Studies* (Peabody, Mass.: Hendrickson, 1999), 28–29. Thus, *khet* is typically represented by *h* or *kh* and *alef* and *ayin* by a ';

underdots are omitted. I have provided map coordinates for sites not included on the map, when possible. As for my use of Josephus, translations are typically from the Loeb edition.

I am greatly indebted to the people who read portions of the manuscript and offered suggestions for improvement: Tracy Anne Allred, Jeremy Bakker, Joshua Ezra Burns, Jaime Clark-Soles, Richard W. Cogley, Johan Elverskog, Steven Fine, Sean Freyne, Adam Marshak, Dale B. Martin, Byron R. McCane, Eric M. Meyers, and Adam Porter. I also owe special thanks to Mordechai Aviam, who helped me gather data on Galilee's inscriptions; Eric M. Meyers, Steven Fine, and David Hendin, for providing me with access to forthcoming works; and C. Thomas McCollough, James F. Strange, and Morten Hørning Jensen, all of whom provided me with copies of or information from conference papers. I continue to profit from the wise counsel of Eric M. Meyers and E. P. Sanders, my mentors at Duke University, and Richard W. Cogley, my department chair at Southern Methodist University. Eric M. Meyers first introduced me to the joys of archaeological fieldwork. The Dorot Foundation and the Endowment for Biblical Research helped fund my participation in the Sepphoris Regional Project in the 1990s, and the SMU University Research Council provided grants for research in the libraries of Duke University and for travel to Italy to study Roman architecture. A Research Fellowship from SMU allowed me to take a sabbatical semester in the fall of 2003 to devote to writing. This book would not have been possible without the invaluable assistance of Billie Stovall of the Fondren Library Interlibrary Loan Office. Katharina Brett, my editor, has been an extremely helpful source of guidance and advice, and I am grateful to John Court for the opportunity to contribute again to the SNTS series. I am extremely thankful for the careful attention my work received from copy-editor Tony Rainer. The members of my family continue to provide me with welcome support. My students are a perpetual source of inspiration.

I began work on this project a few weeks before my wedding, and it has been an all-too constant companion with me and my wife, Tracy Anne Allred, in the early years of our marriage. Tracy Anne has been an unfailing source of encouragement, good humor, and healthy perspective throughout the stages of this book's preparation. I dedicate this work to her.

Abbreviations

ABD	David Noel Freedman et al., eds., *Anchor Bible Dictionary*, 6 vols. (New York: Doubleday, 1992)
ADAJ	*Annual of the Department of Antiquities of Jordan*
AJA	*American Journal of Archaeology*
AJC	Ya'akov Meshorer, *Ancient Jewish Coinage*, 2 vols. (Dix Hills, N. Y.: Amphora Books, 1982)
ANRW	*Aufstieg und Niedergang der römischen Welt* (Berlin and New York: Walter de Gruyter, 1970–present)
BA	*Biblical Archaeologist*
BAR	*Biblical Archaeology Review*
BASOR	*Bulletin of the American Schools of Oriental Research*
Beth She'arim	*Beth She'arim* Benjamin Mazar, vol. 1, *The Catacombs 1–4* (New Brunswick: Rutgers University Press, 1973) Moshe Schwabe and Baruch Lifshitz, vol. 2, *The Greek Inscriptions* (New Brunswick: Rutgers University Press, 1974) Nahman Avigad, vol. 3, *The Excavations 1953–1958* (New Brunswick: Rutgers University Press, 1976)
BTB	*Biblical Theology Bulletin*
CBQ	*Catholic Biblical Quarterly*

CHJ	*The Cambridge History of Judaism* W. D. Davies and Louis Finkelstein, eds., vol. 1 (Cambridge: Cambridge University Press, 1984) W. D. Davies and Louis Finkelstein, eds., vol. 2 (Cambridge: Cambridge University Press, 1989) William Horbury, W. D. Davies, and John Sturdy, eds., vol. 3 (Cambridge: Cambridge University Press, 1999). Steven T. Katz, ed., vol. 4 (Cambridge: Cambridge University Press, in press)
City-Coins	Ya'akov Meshorer, *City-Coins of Eretz-Israel and the Decapolis in the Roman Period* (Jerusalem: Israel Museum, 1985)
CRBS	*Currents in Research: Biblical Studies*
ESI	*Excavations and Surveys in Israel*
GLI	Clayton Miles Lehmann and Kenneth G. Holum, eds., *The Greek and Latin Inscriptions of Caesarea Maritima* (Boston, Mass.: The American Schools of Oriental Research, 2000).
Gush Halav	Eric M. Meyers, Carol L. Meyers, with James F. Strange, *Excavations at the Ancient Synagogue of Gush Halav* (Winona Lake, Ind.: Eisenbrauns, 1990)
HA	*Hadashot Arkheologiyot*
HSCP	*Harvard Studies in Classical Philology*
HTR	*Harvard Theological Review*
HUCA	*Hebrew Union College Annual*
IEJ	*Israel Exploration Quarterly*
INJ	*Israel Numismatic Journal*
JBL	*Journal of Biblical Literature*
JJS	*Journal of Jewish Studies*
JPOS	*Journal of the Palestine Oriental Society*
JSJ	*Journal for the Study of Judaism in the Persian, Hellenistic, and Roman Periods*
JSS	*Journal of Semitic Studies*

Khirbet Shema'	Eric M. Meyers, A. Thomas Kraabel, and James F. Strange, *Ancient Synagogue Excavations at Khirbet Shema', Upper Galilee, Israel, 1970–1972* (Durham: Duke University Press, 1976)
LA	*Liber Annuus*
Meiron	Eric M. Meyers, James F. Strange, and Carol L. Meyers, *Excavations at Ancient Meiron, Upper Galilee, Israel 1971–1972, 1974–1975, 1977* (Cambridge, Mass.: The American Schools of Oriental Research, 1981)
Millar, *RNE*	Fergus Millar, *The Roman Near East: 31 BC–337 CE* (Cambridge, Mass. and London: Harvard University Press, 1993)
MPI	Ruth Ovadiah, and Asher Ovadiah, *Hellenistic, Roman, and Early Byzantine Mosaic Pavements in Israel* (Rome: Lerva di Bretschneider, 1987)
Nagy, *Sepphoris*	Rebecca Martin Nagy, Carol L. Meyers, Eric M. Meyers, and Zeev Weiss, eds., *Sepphoris in Galilee: Crosscurrents of Culture* (Winona Lake, Ind.: Eisenbrauns, 1996)
NEA	*Near Eastern Archaeology*
NEAEHL	Ephraim Stern et al., eds., *The New Encyclopedia of Archaeological Excavations in the Holy Land*, 4 vols. (Jerusalem: The Israel Exploration Society and Carta, New York: Simon and Schuster, 1993)
NTS	*New Testament Studies*
OEANE	Eric M. Meyers, ed., *The Oxford Encyclopedia of Archaeology in the Near East*, 5 vols. (New York & Oxford: Oxford University Press, 1997)
PEQ	*Palestine Exploration Quarterly*
QDAP	*Quarterly of the Department of the Antiquities in Palestine*
RB	*Revue biblique*

RPC	*Roman Provincial Coinage* Andrew Burnett, Michel Amandry, and Pere Paul Ripollès, eds., vol. 1 (London: British Museum Press, Paris: Bibliothèque Nationale, 1992) Andrew Burnett, Michel Amandry, Ian Carradice, eds., vol. 2 (London: British Museum Press, Paris: Bibliothèque Nationale, 1999)
SEG	*Supplementum Epigraphicum Graecum*
TA	*Tel Aviv*
TJT	*Toronto Journal of Theology*
Treasury	Ya'akov Meshorer, *A Treasury of Jewish Coins* (Jerusalem: Yad Ben Zvi Press; Nyack, N.Y.: Amphora Books, 2001)
WA	*World Archaeology*
ZPE	*Zeitschrift für Papyrologie und Epigraphik*

Josephus:

Ant.	*Jewish Antiquities*
War	*Jewish War*

Rabbinic works:
The abbreviations for rabbinic references are taken from Patrick H. Alexander et al., eds., *The SBL Handbook of Style for Ancient Near Eastern, Biblical, and Early Christian Studies* (Peabody, Mass.: Hendrickson, 1999).

Galilee and northern Palestine

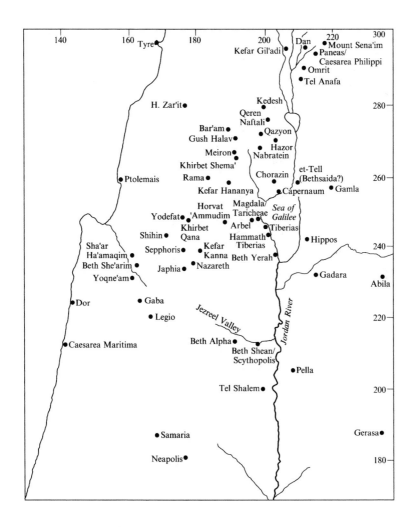

Introduction

By the time of Jesus, all Judaism was Hellenistic Judaism. Martin Hengel's dictum, articulated in his massive book *Judaism and Hellenism* and elaborated upon in follow-up projects, has been enormously influential.[1] His review of evidence from the Persian through the early rabbinic periods demonstrated that Hellenistic influence was felt in many spheres of Jewish life in Palestine: linguistic, literary, educational, architectural, religious, philosophical, artistic, political, economic, and military. Collectively a tour de force, his works exposed the problematic nature of sharp differentiations between Judaism in the Mediterranean Diaspora and Judaism in Palestine. Hengel argued that any use of the phrase "Hellenistic Judaism" that excludes Palestinian Judaism is inappropriate, and any effort to portray Palestinian Judaism as more "orthodox" than Diaspora Judaism on the basis of its supposedly lesser Hellenization is doomed to failure. Hengel has had his critics,[2] but his main point

---

[1] *Judaism and Hellenism*, trans. John Bowden, 2 vols. (Philadelphia: Fortress, 1974), especially vol. 1, 104; *Jews, Greeks and Barbarians: Aspects of the Hellenization of Judaism in the Pre-Christian Period*, trans. John Bowden (Philadelphia: Fortress, 1980); *The 'Hellenization' of Judaea in the First Century after Christ*, trans. John Bowden (London: SCM Press, Philadelphia: Trinity Press International, 1989); "Judaism and Hellenism Revisited," in John J. Collins and Gregory E. Sterling, eds., *Hellenism in the Land of Israel* (Notre Dame, Ind.: University of Notre Dame Press, 2001), 6–37.

[2] Samuel Sandmel, "Palestinian and Hellenistic Judaism and Christianity: The Question of the Comfortable Theory," *HUCA* 50 (1979): 137–148; Samuel Sandmel, review of Martin Hengel, *Judentum und Hellenismus: Wissenschaftliche Untersuchungen zum Neuen Testament* (Tübingen: J. C. B. Mohr [Paul Siebeck], 1973), *Journal of Ecumenical Studies* 11:4 (1974): 701–702; Louis H. Feldman, "How Much Hellenism in Jewish Palestine?" *HUCA* (1986): 83–111; Louis H. Feldman, "Hengel's *Judaism and Hellenism* in Retrospect," *JBL* 96 (1977):

is rightly accepted as conventional wisdom in most sectors of New Testament scholarship: Palestinian Judaism must be understood as a part of, not apart from, Hellenistic Judaism. Judaism in Galilee was no exception. It, too, felt the impact of Greek culture, and no one can any longer imagine Jesus living, as it were, on an isolated and untouched island of Semitic culture in a sea of Hellenism.[3] Like the rest of Palestine, it came under the influence of yet another empire's culture when it fell into the orbit of Rome, a point that Hengel and others also correctly made. Many scholars regarded archaeological finds in the 1980s and 1990s as further confirmation of Hengel's arguments. Images of the region had varied in earlier scholarship, with some portraying it as thoroughly Hellenized and others as backwater and uncultured.[4] The weight of majority view has now shifted towards the view that Galilee fully exhibited key aspects of Greco-Roman culture. Hengel had argued that Greek was widely used in Palestine; excavations in Galilee found numerous Greek inscriptions. Hengel had drawn attention to the presence of Greco-Roman architectural forms; archaeologists uncovered new examples of such buildings in Galilee. Hengel had noted the importance of Greco-Roman artistic influence; projects in Galilee discovered mosaics, frescoes, figurines, and other artifacts reflecting that influence.

Excavations at Sepphoris, located less than four miles from Nazareth, took pride of place in discussions of the region, at least within New Testament scholarship. A theater had been uncovered there in 1931, and more recently, bathhouses, a basilical building,

---

371–382; cf. also Tessa Rajak, "Judaism and Hellenism Revisited," in *The Jewish Dialogue with Greece and Rome: Studies in Cultural and Social Interaction* (Leiden: Brill, 2001), 1–11 and Lester L. Grabbe, *Judaism from Cyrus to Hadrian*, 2 vols. (Minneapolis: Fortress, 1992), vol. 1, 148–153.

[3] The metaphor's phrasing is from Hengel, *Judaism and Hellenism*, vol. 1, 311; cf. Wayne A. Meeks, "Judaism, Hellenism, and the Birth of Christianity," in Troels Engberg-Pedersen, ed., *Paul Beyond the Judaism/Hellenism Divide* (Louisville, Ken.: Westminster John Knox Press, 2001), 17–27, esp. 24–25.

[4] The most famous depiction of Galilee as rural and bucolic is found in Geza Vermes's *Jesus the Jew* (Philadelphia: Fortress Press, 1975). For a review of scholarship on Galilee, see Mark A. Chancey, *The Myth of a Gentile Galilee* (Cambridge: Cambridge University Press, 2002), 16–22; Halvor Moxnes, "The Construction of Galilee as a Place for the Historical Jesus – Part I," *BTB* 31 (2001): 26–37 and "The Construction of Galilee as a Place for the Historical Jesus – Part II," *BTB* 31 (2001): 64–77.

and an aqueduct have been excavated. At least some of the city's streets were shown to be organized in a grid pattern, a characteristic feature of both Greek and Roman cities. The city's spectacular mosaics contained Dionysiac imagery, including a depiction of a procession in honor of Dionysos as well as a symposium with Heracles. Another mosaic showed flora and fauna of the Nile, and yet another portrayed Orpheus. These mosaics bore Greek inscriptions, as did the city's coins, a market weight, and other objects.[5]

Though Sepphoris received the lion's share of attention, numerous other sites were also excavated and older digs attracted renewed interest.[6] The necropolis at Beth She'arim had been investigated in 1936–1940 and 1953–1958, but the full report had not been translated from Hebrew into English until the 1970s. With nearly three hundred inscriptions, the catacomb complex was increasingly cited as an exemplar of the region's Hellenistic milieu. So was Tiberias, though the presence of the modern city by the same name made it difficult to excavate. On the basis of several categories of evidence – architecture, coins, various forms of art, inscriptions, Greek and Latin loanwords and names in Jewish sources, the presence of imports from elsewhere in the Mediterranean – Lower Galilee, especially, was increasingly seen as no less Hellenized and urbanized than anywhere else in the Roman world.[7]

[5] Eric M. Meyers, Ehud Netzer, and Carol L. Meyers, "Sepphoris: Ornament of all Galilee," *BA* 49 (1989): 4–19; James F. Strange, "Sepphoris," *ABD*, vol. 5, 1090–1093; Eric M. Meyers, "Roman Sepphoris in Light of New Archaeological Evidence and Recent Research," in Lee I. Levine, ed., *The Galilee in Late Antiquity* (New York and Jerusalem: The Jewish Theological Seminary of America, 1992), 321–338. For more recent reviews, see Mark Chancey and Eric M. Meyers, "How Jewish was Sepphoris in Jesus' Time?" *BAR* 26:4 (2000): 18–33, 61; Mark A. Chancey, "The Cultural Milieu of Ancient Sepphoris," *NTS* 47:2 (2001): 127–145; Chancey, *Myth*, 69–83.

[6] J. Andrew Overman provides a thorough overview in "Recent Advances in the Archaeology of the Galilee in the Roman Period," *CRBS* 1 (1993): 35–57.

[7] The following works, many by scholars who later revised their positions, have often been cited to support the view of a thoroughly Hellenized Galilee: Eric M. Meyers, "The Cultural Setting of Galilee: The Case of Regionalism and Early Judaism," in *ANRW* 2.19.1, 686–702; Eric M. Meyers and James F. Strange, *Archaeology, the Rabbis, and Early Christianity* (Nashville: Abingdon, 1981), 31–47; J. Andrew Overman, "Who Were the First Urban Christians? Urbanization in Galilee in the First Century," in J. David Lull, ed., *SBLSP 1988* (Atlanta: Scholars Press, 1988), 160–168; Douglas R. Edwards, "First-Century

In light of these findings, few New Testament scholars would seriously dispute that Galilean culture indeed reflected Greek and Roman influences. Yet, if consensus exists on that basic point, confusion abounds about how extensive those influences were at different times and about the specific ways in which they were manifested. As impressive and influential as Hengel's work has been, some of his specific claims were oversimplified. Furthermore, much subsequent scholarship has gone well beyond Hengel in its characterizations of Greco-Roman culture in the world of Jesus. A review of statements often made about Jesus, his earliest followers, and their Galilean setting highlights issues that merit further examination.[8]

Scholars have frequently suggested, on the basis of numismatic and other inscriptions, that Greek was frequently spoken in the region, though it did not displace Aramaic as the dominant tongue.[9] The use of Greek was not limited to the cities of Sepphoris and Tiberias; it might be heard in other Galilean communities as well, such as Capernaum, Magdala/Taricheae,[10] and Chorazin.[11] Overall, it was proposed, the language was as common in Galilee as it was in Egypt and Asia Minor.[12] The fact that at least two of Jesus' disciples,

Urban/Rural Relations in Lower Galilee: Exploring the Archaeological and Literary Evidence," in Lull, *SBLSP 1988*, 169–182; Douglas R. Edwards, "The Socio-Economic and Cultural Ethos of the Lower Galilee in the First Century: Implications of the Nascent Jesus Movement," in Levine, *Galilee*, 39–52; Howard Clark Kee, "Early Christianity in the Galilee: Reassessing the Evidence from the Gospels," in Levine, *Galilee*, 3–22; James F. Strange, "Some Implications of Archaeology for New Testament Studies," in James H. Charlesworth and Walter P. Weaver, eds., *What has Archaeology to do with Faith?* (Philadelphia: Trinity Press International, 1992), 23–59.

[8] Many of the claims below have antecedents in earlier scholarship, but they have drawn new life from Hengel's influence and recent excavations. They are illustrative of certain types of arguments made about Galilee and are not intended to represent the full spectrum of scholarship.

[9] Robert W. Funk, *Honest to Jesus: Jesus for a New Millennium* (San Francisco: HarperSanFranciso, 1996), 33–34, 78–79; Howard Clark Kee, *Jesus in History: An Approach to the Study in the Gospels*, 3rd ed., (Orlando, Fla.: Harcourt Brace & Company, 1996), 248; Kee, "Early Christianity"; Marcus J. Borg, *Meeting Jesus Again for the First Time: The Historical Jesus & the Heart of Contemporary Faith* (San Francisco: HarperSanFrancisco, 1994), 26–27.

[10] On the two names, see Chancey, *Myth*, 98–100.

[11] John E. Stambaugh and David L. Balch, *The New Testament in its Social Environment* (Philadelphia: Westminster Press, 1986), 92–93.

[12] Heinz O. Guenther, "Greek: The Home of Primitive Christianity," *TJT* 5 (1989): 247–279, esp. 250–251.

Andrew and Philip, had Greek names showed that the language had gained usage even among the lower socio-economic classes.[13] It was thus quite likely that Jesus himself spoke at least a little Greek, raising the possibility that the gospels preserved some of his sayings verbatim. It was also now more easily imaginable that one or more of the gospels, perhaps Matthew or Mark, had been written in the region.[14] An even earlier document, Q, believed by many to have been composed in Greek, might also have originated there.[15]

The proximity of Sepphoris to Nazareth made it likely that Jesus was exposed to the full range of Greco-Roman culture. He would have needed Greek to communicate with the city's diverse population, one that included a large number of gentiles. Antipas's construction projects could have created employment opportunities for a *tekton* like him, and the city, like others in the area, included many buildings characteristic of Greco-Roman urbanization – temples, bathhouses, a theater, and other monumental architecture. Jesus might have sat in the theater, watching classical plays. He might also have heard popular philosophers preaching on the city's corners.[16]

---

[13] Hengel, *'Hellenization'*, 16.

[14] Anthony J. Saldarini, "The Gospel of Matthew and Jewish-Christian Conflict in the Galilee," in Levine, *Galilee*, 23–38; Aaron M. Gale, "Tradition in Transition, or Antioch versus Sepphoris: Rethinking the Matthean Community's Location," in *SBLSP 2003* (Atlanta: Scholars Press, 2003), 141–156.

[15] James M. Robinson, "History of Q Research," in James M. Robinson, Paul Hoffmann, and John S. Kloppenborg, *The Critical Edition of Q* (Minneapolis: Fortress Press; Leuven: Peeters Publishers, 2000), xix–lxxi; John S. Kloppenborg, "The Sayings Gospel Q: Recent Opinion on the People Behind the Document," *CRBS* 1 (1993): 9–34; John S. Kloppenborg Verbin, *Excavating Q: The History and Setting of the Sayings Gospel* (Minneapolis: Fortress Press, 2000), 214–261; Jonathan L. Reed, "The Social Map of Q," in John S. Kloppenborg, ed., *Conflict and Invention: Literary, Rhetorical, and Social Studies on the Sayings Gospel Q* (Valley Forge: Trinity Press International, 1995), 17–36; Jonathan L. Reed, *Archaeology and the Galilean Jesus: A Re-Examination of the Evidence* (Harrisburg, Penn.: Trinity Press International, 2000), 170–196; Christopher M. Tuckett, *Q and the History of Early Christianity* (Edinburgh: T & T Clark, 1996), 102–103; William E. Arnal, *Jesus and the Village Scribes* (Minneapolis: Fortress Press, 2001), 52–59; Leif E. Vaage, *Galilean Upstarts: Jesus' First Followers According to Q* (Valley Forge: Trinity Press International, 1994).

[16] Compare, for example, the various points made by Kee, "Early Christianity"; Funk, *Honest*, 33, 79; Overman, "Who were the First Urban Christians?" and by Richard A. Batey in three works: "'Is Not This the Carpenter?'" *NTS* 30 (1984): 249–258; "Jesus and the Theatre," *NTS* 30 (1984): 563–574; and *Jesus and the Forgotten City: New Light on Sepphoris and the Urban World of Jesus* (Grand Rapids, Mich.: Baker Book House, 1991).

Sepphoris was not alone in its mixed population. Tiberias, too, was home to a considerable number of gentiles, and the region as a whole could be characterized as "semipagan."[17] Jesus need not leave Galilee to encounter non-Jews; he would have had frequent interaction with them throughout his life. Some of these pagans were indigenous Galileans, while others were Phoenicians, Arabs, or descendents of Greek settlers.[18] The region's roads were major trade routes that bustled with merchant convoys and other travelers.

Galilee, like the rest of Palestine, was occupied by the Roman army, perhaps even settled by Roman colonists, according to some scholars.[19] Two gospels preserve a memory of Jesus' encounter with a Roman centurion (Matt. 8:5–13 and Luke 7:1–10). Roads built and paved by the Roman army and marked by Roman milestones crossed the region.[20] Sepphoris itself was a Roman administrative and military center.[21] After finishing their lengthy terms of service, some Roman soldiers chose to stay in Antipas's Galilee, retiring there.[22] The region's Romanization was thus no less thoroughgoing than its Hellenization.

In light of Galilee's cosmopolitan and diverse cultural atmosphere, a wholesale re-imagining of Christian origins was in order. Both Jesus and his earliest followers – according to influential reconstructions of the earliest stratum of Q, a rootless, itinerant group of Galileans[23] – could be best understood as Cynic-like philosophers.[24] The

---

[17] Funk, *Honest*, 33, 79; cf. Strange, "Some Implications."

[18] The influence of this view, which pre-dates recent archaeological work, is reflected in many Bible dictionary articles (Chancey, *Myth*, 1 n. 2).

[19] James F. Strange, "First-Century Galilee from Archaeology and from the Texts," in Eugene H. Lovering, Jr., ed., *SBLSP 1994* (Atlanta: Scholars Press, 1994), 81–90; Marianne Sawicki, *Crossing Galilee: Architectures of Contact in the Occupied Land of Jesus* (Harrisburg, Penn.: Trinity Press International, 2000), 82–85, 88, 92–96, 178–179. On the characterization of Galilee as a colony or of the Roman "occupation" as "colonial," see Sawicki, *Crossing Galilee*, 7, 27, 82, 88–89, 133, and Borg, *Meeting Jesus*, 52.

[20] Sawicki, *Crossing Galilee*, 112; cf. Funk, *Honest*, 12, 99–100.

[21] Kee, "Early Christianity"; Batey, *Jesus*, 14, 81, 140.

[22] Sawicki, *Crossing Galilee*, 141.

[23] Burton L. Mack, "Q and a Cynic-Like Jesus," in William E. Arnal and Michel Desjardins, eds., *Whose Historical Jesus?* (Waterloo, Ont.: Wilfrid Laurier University Press, 1997), 25–36 and *The Lost Gospel: The Book of Q and Gospel Origins* (San Francisco: HarperSanFrancisco, 1993); Vaage, *Galilean Upstarts*; Arnal, *Jesus*.

[24] John Dominic Crossan, *The Historical Jesus: The Life of a Mediterranean Jewish Peasant* (San Francisco: HarperSanFrancisco, 1991), 74–88, 338–341; *Jesus: A Revolutionary Biography*

argument has sometimes been framed as one of influence: Jesus had heard the teachings of Cynic philosophers at Sepphoris or while he traveled through the region. Though explicit evidence of Cynics in Galilee was lacking, to imagine a Cynic-free Galilee would be to imagine a Hellenism-free Galilee – and thus, by implication, an impossibility. If all Hellenism was Hellenistic Judaism, and Galilee's architecture, art, and inscriptions confirmed the region's full participation in the larger culture of the Greco-Roman world, then envisioning Jesus as a Jewish Cynic was not a problem. One scholar even suggested that protestations that Cynics were unlikely to be found in Galilee were, in fact, covert apologetic attempts to defend early Christianity's uniqueness.[25] At other times, the proponents of the Cynic thesis have utilized an argument of analogy: regardless of whether or not Jesus and the Q community actually encountered any Cynics, they were much like them and a comparison with them was especially illuminating. This argument, too, has frequently been accompanied by appeals to the high level of Hellenization purportedly attested in the archaeological record.

Such positions have not been universal, of course, and their conflation above for brevity's sake should not be interpreted as suggesting that a scholar who holds one also holds the others. Some of these statements, as will be seen in the course of this study, are quite reasonable, but most are built on shaky foundations. They sometimes seem to reflect one or more of several assumptions: that Greek and Roman cultures were homogenous across the Mediterranean region; that more evidence of those cultures has been found in

(San Francisco: HarperSanFrancisco, 1994), 114–122; "Itinerants and Householders in the Earliest Jesus Movement," in Arnal and Desjardins, *Whose Historical Jesus?* 7–24. In *The Birth of Christianity* (San Francisco: HarperSanFrancisco, 1998), 333–335, Crossan backs away from some of his earlier arguments, and the comparison with Cynics is missing entirely from his recent work with Jonathan L. Reed, which exhibits a more nuanced portrayal of Galilee (*Excavating Jesus: Beneath the Stones, Behind the Texts* [San Francisco: HarperSanFrancisco, 2001]). F. Gerald Downing has collected parallels between Jesus' teachings and those of the Cynics in numerous works, including *Cynics and Christian Origins* (Edinburgh: T & T Clark, 1992); *Christ and the Cynics* (Sheffield: JSOT, 1988); *Jesus and the Threat of Freedom* (London: SCM, 1987). Note also Burton L. Mack, *A Myth of Innocence: Mark and Christian Origins* (Philadelphia: Fortress Press, 1988), 53–77; and Robert W. Funk, Roy W. Hoover, and the Jesus Seminar, *The Five Gospels: The Search for the Authentic Words of Jesus* (New York: Macmillan, 1993), 33.

[25] Vaage, *Galilean Upstarts*, 13, 145 n. 58.

early first-century CE Galilee than is actually the case; that finds in Jerusalem, the coastal cities, and the Decapolis were representative of Galilee; or that evidence from the second or later centuries accurately reflects the situation in the early first century. The last assumption is especially common. At times, depictions of the Galilee of Jesus have relied so heavily on late data that is it almost as if Jesus were being contextualized within the third century, rather than the first.[26]

If we are to understand the particularity of the Galilean context of Jesus and his followers, we must acknowledge the significance of chronological development, regional variations, and class distinctions in the ways Hellenistic, Roman, and local cultures interacted. With these factors in mind, this study investigates the emergence of certain aspects of Greco-Roman in Galilee and the significance of that cultural interaction for the Historical Jesus and early Judaism. The chief challenges to such a project are deciding what phenomena to include within the terms "Hellenistic" and "Roman" and determining how to envision the interaction of those cultures with local ones.

Writing specifically of "Hellenism," Hengel pointed out that the word is so broad and all encompassing that it is not always useful: "it says too much, and precisely because of that it says too little."[27] As several scholars have noted, "Hellenistic" can be used to indicate a wide variety of things:

- the speaking of Greek (from minimal ability to full fluency)
- familiarity with Greek philosophy and literature
- distinctively Greek architectural forms (i.e., stadiums, theaters, gymnasia)
- use of imported Greek tableware and cookware, or, at least, local imitations
- civic organization like a polis, with a Greek constitution, *boule*, and officials.

---

[26] Mark A. Chancey, "Galilee and Greco-Roman Culture in the Time of Jesus: The Neglected Significance of Chronology," *SBLSP 2003* (Atlanta: Scholars Press, 2003), 173–188.

[27] Hengel, *'Hellenization'*, 54.

The word "Roman" lends itself just as easily to ambiguity. Studies that use terms like these must be explicit in identifying which specific aspects of culture they are investigating, careful not to imply that other phenomena should be excluded from the meanings of the terms, and mindful of the danger of lapsing into essentialism. A brief survey of related studies shows how other scholars have handled such issues.

G. W. Bowersock has argued that many studies of Hellenistic culture start with a problematic model: an understanding of "Hellenization" as "the deliberate or inevitable imposition of Greek ways over local ones." In his view, the concept of "Hellenization" is "a useless barometer for assessing Greek culture" because it implies the replacement of one culture by another, a process that rarely actually occurred. Local cultures did not disappear under the weight of Greek culture but instead found new ways to express themselves by adopting aspects of that culture. If "Hellenization" is a misleading word, the concept of "Hellenism" is nevertheless quite helpful. "Hellenism . . . represented language, thought, mythology, and images that constituted an extraordinarily flexible medium of both cultural and religious expression." Thus, "it provided a new and more eloquent way of giving voice" to various peoples.[28]

Lee I. Levine provides another possibility, describing "Hellenism" as the "cultural milieu (largely Greek) of the Hellenistic, Roman, and – to a somewhat more limited extent – Byzantine periods," and "Hellenization" as "the process of adoption and adaptation of this culture on a local level."[29] Other cultures also spread beyond their points of origin in the "Hellenistic world," that is, the territories conquered by Alexander and his successors, and distinctions should be made "as to the degree of receptivity in each area [aspect of culture], as well as from region to region and from class to class."[30] At particular places, particular groups might adapt specific aspects of Greek culture to their own needs, while other groups might reject

[28] G. W. Bowersock, *Hellenism in Late Antiquity* (Ann Arbor: University of Michigan Press, 1990), quotations from xi and 7; cf. Eric M. Meyers, "The Challenge of Hellenism for Early Judaism and Christianity," *BA* 55 (1992): 84–91.

[29] Lee I. Levine, *Judaism and Hellenism in Antiquity: Conflict or Confluence?* (Peabody, Mass.: Hendrickson Publishers, 1998), 16–17.

[30] Levine, *Judaism*, 22.

those aspects. Furthermore, Levine emphasizes the importance of chronology, noting that evidence of Hellenism increases with the passing of each century.

The most thorough recent examination of the interaction of Hellenism and Judaism is that of John M. G. Barclay.[31] Focusing on the Diaspora, Barclay defines Hellenism as a fusion of cultures after Alexander, characterizing it as "common urban culture in the eastern Mediterranean, founded on the Greek language . . . typically expressed in certain political and educational institutions and largely maintained by the social élite."[32] Noting several different spheres of culture (political, social, linguistic, educational, ideological, religious, and material culture), he argues that Jews might engage Hellenism in one area of life while ignoring it in others, and that there were differences in the degree of engagement. To deal with these phenomena, he utilizes the sociological concepts of assimilation, acculturation, and accommodation. He defines assimilation as the extent of social integration and interaction between Jews and non-Jews and acculturation as the level of familiarity with various aspects of Greek culture. Accommodation is conceptualized as the use to which acculturation is put, whether to embrace Greek culture fully, or to resist it by reinterpreting and expressing Jewish distinctiveness in new ways.[33] Barclay applies this model to describe the interplay between Judaism and Hellenism in various regions, with considerable attention to class differences. He might be critiqued on some points; he does not always differentiate clearly between Hellenistic and Roman cultural elements, and his discussion does not always pay sufficient attention to chronological developments.[34] His overall project, however, is a significant contribution, precisely because his guiding model is inherently flexible enough to handle diverse responses.

James F. Strange has addressed the issue of how Romanization affected material culture in Jewish Palestine. He suggests that we

[31] John M. G. Barclay, *Jews in the Mediterranean Diaspora: From Alexander to Trajan (323 BCE–117 CE)* (Berkeley: University of California Press, 1996).

[32] Barclay, *Jews*, 88.

[33] Barclay, *Jews*, 82–124, especially 90–98.

[34] Leonard V. Rutgers, "Recent Trends in the Study of Ancient Diaspora Judaism," in *The Hidden Heritage of Diaspora Judaism*, 2nd edn. (Leuven: Peeters, 1998), 15–44.

envision certain features of material culture – the Jerusalem temple, synagogues, particular styles of tombs, and symbols like the menorah – as a Hellenistic Jewish foundation, upon which the Romans imposed an "urban overlay," one that was itself also influenced by Hellenism. That overlay included "baths, hippodromes, theaters, amphitheaters or circuses, odeons, *nymphaea*, figured wall paintings, statues, triumphal monuments, temples," and other features. The overlay and foundation interacted to produce a new cultural atmosphere that was distinct from either one alone.[35]

Two recent important studies on the Romanization of the Near East, one by Fergus Millar, the other by Warwick Ball, approach their topic from fundamentally different perspectives.[36] For Millar, Roman culture largely obliterated local cultures, replacing them with Roman buildings, Roman coins, Roman art, and Roman inscriptions. Palestinian Judaism was a rare exception to this process, in that Jews managed to maintain a culturally distinctive ethnos, despite being subsumed into the Roman Empire. But Ball offers a strong critique of Millar's work. For him, Roman culture was little more than a veneer laid over local indigenous cultures, cultures that continued to survive and to express themselves in the new media of Roman culture. Ball argues, for example, that scholars have over-emphasized the uniformity of so-called "Roman" monumental architecture in the Near East, while neglecting aspects of that architecture that were distinctive to each sub-region or that in some cases originated in the Near East, not in Rome.

These discussions of the interaction between Hellenism, Roman culture, and Judaism have conceptual points of contact with ongoing conversations about the nature of Romanization in other parts of the Empire.[37] The major starting point of those studies is

---

[35] Strange, "Some Implications," esp. 31–34.
[36] Fergus Millar, *The Roman Near East: 31 BC–337 CE* (Cambridge, Mass. and London: Harvard University Press, 1993); Warwick Ball, *Rome in the East: The Transformation of an Empire* (London and New York: Routledge, 2001).
[37] For reviews of the scholarship, see Jane Webster, "Roman Imperialism and the 'Post Imperial Age'," in Jane Webster and Nicholas J. Cooper, eds., *Roman Imperialism: Post-Colonial Perspectives* (Leicester: University of Leicester, 1996), 1–17; Jane Webster, "Creolizing the Roman Provinces," *AJA* 105 (2001): 209–225; Richard Hingley, "The 'Legacy' of Rome:

the work of F. Haverfield, who analyzed the influence of the Romans on the Celts in Great Britain.[38] Haverfield concluded that the Romans deliberately spread their culture – language, pottery, architecture, art, civic organization – and that locals enthusiastically adopted it. This new culture did not wholly subsume the old; instead, Celtic and Roman cultures mixed, though the latter was dominant. Haverfield took seriously the differences between regions, and he recognized that the Greek East never fully adopted Roman ways. But in the west, the spread of Roman culture was nothing less than the spread of civilization. The Romans, he suggested, should thus be credited for bringing progress to the natives.[39]

Scholarly dissatisfaction with this Romano-centric perspective was inevitable. The backlash was especially notable in post-World War II scholarship focusing on geographical areas that had been colonial possessions of the modern European empires, such as North Africa. Many of these scholars argued that though the Roman impact on indigenous populations might be highly visible in the material culture, it was only a veneer superimposed on local culture, a model similar to those of Ball and Strange. In many cases, indigenous ways continued with only minimal change under the Romans; in others, subject peoples actively rejected Roman domination. Thus, for example, Marcel Bénabou's review of the historical development of Roman rule in North Africa and its impact on religion, language, personal names, and

---

The Rise, Decline, and Fall of the Theory of Romanization," in Webster and Cooper, *Roman Imperialism*, 35–48; Roel Brandt and Jan Slofstra, eds., *Roman and Native in the Low Countries: Spheres of Interaction* (Oxford: BAR, 1983), especially J. Slofstra's study, "An Anthropological Approach to the Study of Romanization," 71–104; Greg Woolf, *Becoming Roman: The Origins of Provincial Civilization in Gaul* (Cambridge: Cambridge University Press, 1998), 1–23; D. J. Mattingly, ed., *Dialogues in Roman Imperialism: Power, Discourse, and Discrepant Experience in the Roman Empire* (Portsmouth, R. I.: Journal of Roman Archaeology, 1997).

[38] F. Haverfield, *The Romanization of Great Britain* (4th ed., Oxford: Clarendon Press, 1923; 1st edn. in 1906).

[39] That this perspective was strikingly similar to how the British perceived their own administration of empire has not gone unnoticed among social historians of scholarship. Much of the early discussion about Romanization was deeply influenced by the modern contexts of European colonialism.

city organization emphasized the ways Africans resisted Roman culture.[40] Martin Millett has advanced a different model. Focusing on Britain, he argues for a high level of acculturation to Roman ways. In his view, the Romans encouraged acculturation and locals willingly accepted it. Provincial elites Romanized to maintain their positions of status and power, and many of the lower classes copied them. Millett terms this process "progressive emulation." His study devotes considerable attention to the Roman military presence, their organization of territory into administrative districts (*civitates*), their reliance on local tribal leaders, the emergence of Roman civic planning and architecture, and economic changes.[41]

Jane Webster, who has also worked primarily with Celtic materials, strongly criticizes Millett's model as merely an updating of Haverfield's. She points out that many provincial elites and even more of the masses refused to embrace Roman culture. For her, the notion of "progressive emulation" does not do justice to differences within and between regions and within and between social classes. Furthermore, she emphasizes, failure to adopt Roman ways should not necessarily be viewed as merely a reflection of a slow rate of acculturation; it might also be interpreted as a form of local resistance against the Romans. "Romanization," in her opinion, is a wholly inadequate term, precisely because it glosses over such variations. She proposes "Creolization," understood as resistant adaptation, as a substitute that more appropriately conveys the mixing and fusion of local and Roman elements.[42] Webster's sentiments have

---

[40] Marcel Bénabou, *La résistance africaine à la romanisation* (Paris: François Maspero, 1976); cf. David J. Mattingly, "From One Colonialism to Another: Imperialism and the Maghreb," in Webster and Cooper, *Roman Imperialism*, 49–69.

[41] Martin Millett, *The Romanization of Britain: An Essay in Archaeological Interpretation* (Cambridge: Cambridge University Press, 1990) and "Romanization: Historical Issues and Archaeological Interpretation," in Thomas Blagg and Martin Millett, eds., *The Early Roman Empire in the West* (Oxford: Oxbow Books, 1990), 35–41. Ramsay MacMullen's survey emphasizes the roles of legions and colonists in Romanizing the provinces, but he also notes the enthusiasm of the local elites, an argument with obvious points of contact with Millet's thesis (MacMullen, *Romanization in the Time of Augustus* [New Haven and London: Yale University Press, 2000]).

[42] Webster, "Roman Imperialism"; "Creolizing"; "Necessary Comparisons: A Post-Colonial Approach to Religious Syncretism in the Roman Provinces," *WA* 28:3 (1997): 324–338; "Art

been echoed in other studies that apply the insights of postcolonial methods[43] and that emphasize the particularity of specific regions.[44] The interactions of Greek, Roman, and local cultures in the ancient world were too complex for any one of these models to be considered universally valid. There were simply too many variations. Roman culture, for example, was sometimes merely a veneer upon local culture; at other times the two cultures mingled to produce something quite different from what either one had been alone. The masses sometimes emulated both the indigenous elites and the Romans themselves; on other occasions they rejected what they saw as the pretensions of the upper classes. Roman ways were sometimes embraced and sometimes resisted by a broad spectrum of society. As will be seen, the nature of our information about Galilee makes it difficult to insert the available data smoothly and consistently into any of these models. Instead of choosing one of them and then trying to force our evidence into its parameters – an effort doomed to look artificial – it might prove more profitable to be intentional in drawing from all of them, keeping their different insights and questions in mind as we survey Galilee's ancient cultural landscape. Their most important implications, summarized, are the following:

• Any consideration of either Hellenization or Romanization must specify which aspects of culture are being examined (i.e., architecture, language, numismatics, education, philosophy, economics, technology, etc.).

---

as Resistance and Negotiation," in Sarah Scott and Jane Webster, eds., *Roman Imperialism and Provincial Art* (Cambridge: Cambridge University Press, 2003), 24–52.

[43] Hingley, "'Legacy'"; Peter van Dommelen, "Colonial Constructs: Colonialism and Archaeology in the Mediterranean," *WA* 28:3 (1997): 305–323; Brad Bartel, "Colonialism and Cultural Responses: Problems Related to Roman Provincial Analysis," *WA* 12 (1980): 11–26; Mattingly, *Dialogues*; Scott and Webster, *Roman Imperialism*; Webster and Cooper, *Roman Imperialism*.

[44] Brandt and Slofstra, *Roman and Native*; Karen Meadows, Chris Lemke and Jo Heron, eds., *TRAC 96: Proceedings of the Sixth Annual Theoretical Roman Archaeology Conference* (Oxford: Oxbow Books, 1997); Susan E. Alcock, ed., *The Early Roman Empire in the East* (Oxford: Oxbow Books, 1997); D. Mattingly, "Being Roman: expressing identity in a provincial setting," *JRA* 17 (2004): 5–25; Mattingly, "From One Colonialism"; Blagg and Millett, *Early Roman Empire*.

- Hellenization or Romanization in one aspect of culture should not be automatically interpreted as evidence for Hellenization or Romanization in another aspect of culture.

- Neither Hellenization nor Romanization should be understood to indicate total replacement of local, indigenous cultures.

- Neither Hellenistic nor Roman culture was wholly uniform across the affected geographical areas; there were considerable differences between regions.[45]

- Within a specific region, different social classes and other groups might have widely varying attitudes toward and degrees of acceptance of Hellenization and Romanization.

- Attention to chronological development is necessary for an understanding of how these processes played out in a given locale.

- We should specify, when possible, which parties sponsored the adoption of particular aspects of Hellenistic and Roman culture – e.g., outside rulers and administrators, occupying military forces, client kings, provincial and civic elites, the masses, or, at least, subgroups within the masses. These parties themselves should not necessarily be assumed to be homogenous.

- Social elites might sometimes choose to emulate Greek or Roman ways, and commoners might sometimes choose to emulate elites, but we should not assume that such emulation was the universal norm.

- Failure to adopt certain aspects of Hellenistic or Roman culture might sometimes be regarded as resistance to those dominant cultures, as might efforts to develop and express distinctive local and ethnic identities.

- Locals might sometimes appropriate the cultural symbols and vocabularies of larger Hellenistic and/or Roman culture to express their own identities; they might even employ those symbols and vocabulary to express resistance to those cultures.

Remembering these insights will help us to skirt a surprisingly common pitfall, the "all or nothing" mindset that the possibilities are

---

[45] Eric M. Meyers has long championed this approach by drawing attention to the differences and similarities between Lower Galilee and Upper Galilee ("Cultural Setting"; "Galilean Regionalism as a Factor in Historical Reconstruction," *BASOR* 221 [1976]: 93–101; "Galilean Regionalism: A Reappraisal," in W. S. Green, ed., *Approaches to Ancient Judaism* [Missoula, Mont.: Scholars Press for Brown University, 1978], vol. 5, 115–131).

limited to full Hellenization and/or Romanization, on the one hand, or full isolation, on the other. Casting a comparative eye at other regions, mostly those near Galilee but occasionally more distant ones, will sharpen our perception of the ways in which Galilee was similar and dissimilar to other parts of the Mediterranean world. Differentiating archaeological evidence by time period will help us to avoid anachronistic conclusions about the early first century CE.

I will argue here for a more tempered view of the influence of Hellenistic and Roman culture in Galilee in the early first century CE than is often found. In doing so, I build on a foundation already laid by scholars like E. P. Sanders,[46] Eric M. Meyers,[47] Sean Freyne,[48] and Martin Goodman.[49] My argument should not be interpreted in any way as a claim that Galilee was *sui generis*. To the contrary, it is an argument that takes seriously both the evidence we have from Galilee itself as well as what we know of Hellenization and Romanization elsewhere. Though I focus primarily on published archaeological data, I also make considerable use of the gospels, the writings of Josephus, and rabbinic sources. The project's chronological scope ranges from the late Persian period (late fifth and early fourth centuries BCE) to the early fourth century CE, with particular emphasis on how the material culture of Galilee in the second and third centuries CE differed from that of the first.[50]

Studies like those described above remind us of the importance of establishing basic working definitions at the outset of our

---

[46] E. P. Sanders, *The Historical Figure of Jesus* (London: Allen Lane, Penguin Press, 1993), 33–48; "Jesus in Historical Context," *Theology Today* 50 (1993): 429–448; "Jesus' Galilee," in Ismo Dunderberg, Kari Syreeni, and Christopher Tuckett, eds., *Fair Play: Diversity and Conflicts in Early Christianity: Essays in Honour of Heikki Räisänen* (Leiden: Brill, 2002), 3–41.

[47] Eric M. Meyers, "Jesus and his Galilean Context," in Douglas R. Edwards and C. Thomas McCollough, eds., *Archaeology and the Galilee: Texts and Contexts in the Graeco-Roman and Byzantine Periods* (Atlanta: Scholars Press, 1997), 57–66.

[48] Sean Freyne, *Galilee from Alexander the Great to Hadrian: 323 BCE to 135 CE* (Wilmington, Del.: Michael Glazier; Notre Dame, Ind.: University of Notre Dame Press, 1980; reprint, Edinburgh: T & T Clark, 1998); *Galilee, Jesus, and the Gospels* (Philadelphia: Fortress Press, 1988); and *Galilee and Gospel* (Boston and Leiden: Brill Academic Publishers, 2002).

[49] Martin Goodman in "Galilean Judaism and Judaean Judaism," in *CHJ*, vol. 3, 596–617 and *State and Society in Roman Galilee, AD 132–212* (Totowa, N. J.: Rowman and Allanheld, 1983).

[50] I do not attempt here to provide a full overview of the fourth century CE or of the transition from the Roman to the Byzantine periods.

investigation. I will sometimes use the words "Hellenistic" and "Roman," along with "Persian" and "Byzantine," to indicate chronological parameters.[51] In this regard, I follow the standard practice of Syro-Palestinian archaeology:

Persian Period	539–332 BCE
Early Hellenistic Period	332–198 BCE
Late Hellenistic Period	198–63 BCE
Early Roman Period	63 BCE–135 CE
Middle Roman Period	135–250 CE
Late Roman Period	250–360 CE
Byzantine Period	360–640 CE

Note that this schema is something of a hybrid based on both political events[52] and on changes in material culture (particularly pottery) that occurred for a variety of reasons.[53] The terminology can be somewhat confusing, since a reference to the "Hellenistic period" need not imply the literal presence of Greeks and a reference to the "Roman period" does not necessarily indicate the presence of Romans.

Defining the chronological sense of the terms, however, is the easiest of our tasks; creating workable definitions for the larger cultural phenomena proves more difficult. Words like "Hellenism," "Hellenization," and "Romanization" all have their ideological baggage,[54] but each serves as a "convenient shorthand"[55] nonetheless. In

[51] See Walter E. Rast, *Through the Ages in Palestinian Archaeology* (Philadelphia: Trinity Press International, 1992).
[52] For example, the conquest of Alexander c. 332 BCE, the arrival of Pompey c. 63 BCE, the Bar Kochbah War c. 135 CE, the Arab conquest c. 640 BCE.
[53] That is, destruction from war or earthquakes.
[54] On the social history of scholarship on Hellenism and Judaism, see the essays in Engberg-Pedersen, *Paul*, especially Meeks, "Judaism, Hellenism"; Dale B. Martin, "Paul and the Judaism/Hellenism Dichotomy: Toward a Social History of the Question," 29–61; Philip S. Alexander, "Hellenism and Hellenization as Problematic Historiographical Categories," 63–80; Collins and Sterling, *Hellenism*; Seth Schwartz, *Imperialism and Jewish Society, 200 BCE to 640 CE* (Princeton and Oxford: Princeton University Press, 2001), 12, 22; Lester L. Grabbe, "Hellenistic Judaism," in Jacob Neusner, ed., *Judaism in Late Antiquity*, part 2 (Leiden: E. J. Brill, 1995), 53–83; and Levine, *Judaism*, 6–33.
[55] The phrase is from Woolf, *Becoming Roman*, 7.

the most obvious sense, "Hellenism" refers to the presence of Greek culture. There is no comparable single word to denote the presence of Roman culture ("Romanism" would be the equivalent, but it finds no users). "Hellenization," in my usage, denotes the processes, in all their variety, of interaction between Greek and local cultures, and "Romanization," likewise, the processes, in all their variety, of interaction between Roman and local cultures. As already noted, neither implies the erasure of local culture. The term "Greco-Roman" is useful to indicate the blending of these two cultures. Already the imperfections of such terminology are apparent. "Hellenistic" can apply to cultural phenomena still occurring centuries after what archaeologists call the "Hellenistic period." Furthermore, in the eastern half of the Mediterranean region, the Romans encouraged Hellenistic culture, already present to varying degrees, as a unifying force. Thus, "Romanization" there often included "Hellenization" in ways that "Romanization" in Western Europe did not. Another drawback to all of these terms, admittedly, is that they emphasize the cultures of the dominant political powers rather than those of indigenous peoples.

The addition of "paganism" to the terminological mix complicates matters further, since "pagan" has often been used as a substitute for "Greek" or "Roman." In my usage, "pagan" denotes only the worship of a god or gods other than the one worshipped by Jews and Christians. Those deities might be from the Greek or Roman pantheon, but they might also be local or imported from beyond the Greco-Roman world.[56]

Nor can we pretend that the meaning of the term "Judaism" is uncontested. My usage reflects the influence of E. P. Sanders's argument that most forms of Judaism in the ancient world can be conceptualized together as "common Judaism," indicating a shared emphasis on covenantal monotheism, continuity with the history of Israel, Sabbath observance and other distinctive (though not always unique) customs like circumcision and dietary restrictions.[57] While this notion of Judaism emphasizes common practices and

---

[56] Compare Chancey, *Myth*, 7–8.
[57] E. P. Sanders, *Judaism: Practice and Belief: 63 BCE–66 CE* (London: SCM Press; Philadelphia: Trinity Press International, 1992) and *Historical Figure*, 33–48.

beliefs, it should not be interpreted as suggesting there was no diversity within it.

One dimension of Galilee's cultural milieu is becoming increasingly clear: despite occasional claims to the contrary, Galilee's population in the first century was predominantly Jewish, with gentiles only a small minority. Scholars like Eric M. Meyers, E. P. Sanders, and Sean Freyne have long advocated this position,[58] and recent studies by Peter Richardson and Mordechai Aviam, Jonathan L. Reed, and myself confirm it.[59] Archaeological data suggests that a population shift occurred in Galilee after the Hasmonean conquest (late second or early first century BCE), with many older settlements abandoned and new settlements established. The gospels and Josephus describe the region's inhabitants as mostly Jewish, and the amount of archaeological evidence for Jews – stone vessels, ritual baths, and ossuaries – far outweighs the surprisingly little evidence for pagan cultic practices. These generalizations hold true for both smaller communities as well as larger ones like Sepphoris and Tiberias. Any consideration of the interaction of Greco-Roman and local Galilean cultures in the early first century must acknowledge the region's Jewish character and not exaggerate the number or influence of pagans.

Josephus defines Galilee as the region between Mount Carmel and the territory of Ptolemais on the west, Samaria and the territory of Scythopolis to the south, Gaulanitis and the territory of Hippos and Gadara to the east, and the territory of Tyre, which extended as far inland as Kedesh, to the north.[60] These borders also roughly correspond to the limits of Herod Antipas's territory. This study

---

[58] Meyers, "Jesus"; Sanders, "Jesus," "Jesus' Galilee," *Historical Figure*, and *Judaism*; Freyne, *Galilee from Alexander* and *Galilee, Jesus, and the Gospels*.

[59] Mordechai Aviam and Peter Richardson, "Josephus' Galilee in Archaeological Perspective," in Steve Mason, ed., *Flavius Josephus: Translation and Commentary* (Leiden: Brill, 2001), vol. 9, 177–209; Reed, *Archaeology*, 23–61; Chancey, *Myth*. See also Rafael Frankel, Nimrod Getzov, Mordechai Aviam, and Avi Degani, *Settlement Dynamics and Regional Diversity in Ancient Upper Galilee: Archaeological Survey of Upper Galilee* (Jerusalem: Israel Antiquities Authority, 2001) and my "Archaeology, Ethnicity, and First-Century CE Galilee: The Limits of Evidence," forthcoming in Margaret Daly-Denton, Brian McGing, Anne Fitzpatrick McKinley, and Zuleika Rodgers, eds., [title not yet known].

[60] *War* 3.35–44; see also Chancey, *Myth*, 9–10 n. 26 and Mordechai Aviam, "Borders between Jews and Gentiles in the Galilee," in *Jews, Pagans and Christians in the Galilee* (Rochester: University of Rochester Press; Woodbridge, Suffolk: Boydell & Brewer, 2004), 9–21.

relies primarily on Josephus's description for an obvious reason: he provides an informed first-century perspective, and my goal is to illuminate first-century Galilee. Any decision about how to define Galilee's borders has ramifications for how data is organized – what is regarded as within Galilee, and what is portrayed as outside it.[61] Though my choice to rely on Josephus's description affects the presentation of my data, it does not affect the substance of my argument. Regardless of exactly where one draws the lines of Galilee's boundaries, the overall pattern of evidence is the same, with differences (of varying degrees of significance) between the material culture of most of Galilee and that of cities and areas on its perimeter.

I have argued elsewhere that Galilee's role as a crossing ground for long-distance travelers and traders has been greatly overstated. The region was certainly integrated into the economic network of the larger Roman world, as finds of imported goods make clear, and its roads did connect it with both surrounding regions and more important trade routes. There appears to be little reason to suggest, however, that its highways were especially full of merchants and other travelers from afar. Most people traversing Palestine would have bypassed Galilee, though some would have passed nearby. An investigation of its cultural milieu must not exaggerate the influence of outsiders, though it should acknowledge that some Galileans, particularly in the border regions, would have had contacts with the peoples of neighboring territories.[62]

With those points in mind, this study investigates the expression of Greek and Roman cultures in Galilee in public and monumental architecture, inscriptions, coins, and various forms of art. These specific categories of evidence receive the bulk of my attention not because they are the only or the inevitable ways in which Greco-Roman influence might be expressed (that is definitely not the case) but because they are the types of findings most often cited in discussions of Galilee in New Testament scholarship. By

---

[61] Thus, for the purposes of this project, I treat the coastal plain, most of the Jezreel Valley, and Paneas as beyond Galilee's borders (contrary to some modern usages of the term "Galilee").

[62] Chancey, *Myth*, 155–165.

focusing on them, I am trying to address some of the questions most frequently posed about Galilee and to correct some of the more frequently repeated misperceptions. Along the way, I consider other aspects of Galilee's cultural climate, such as the construction of Roman roads and cities' adoptions of names that honored the emperor.

Though this project charts the varied rates of appearance in Galilee and elsewhere of certain artifacts associated with Greco-Roman culture, there are numerous other pertinent issues equally worthy of scholarly exploration. Rabbinic texts provide ample material for examining relations with Roman administrators and the extent of the rabbis' familiarity (if not always that of the commoners) with Hellenistic and Roman legal thought, philosophy, and educational practices.[63] The archaeological record allows opportunities for pursuit of a myriad of other topics, such as changes in technology; shifts in settlement patterns; typologies of domestic architecture;[64] use and distribution of imported wares; imitation of imported goods by local manufacturers; continuity, change, and the development of particularly Galilean forms in various categories of material culture;[65] and the use of luxury goods such as jewelry and gems. The need remains for a full treatment of the economic impact of Romanization on Galilee.[66] Many developments within

---

[63] Goodman, *State and Society*; Peter Schäfer, ed., *The Talmud Yerushalmi and Graeco-Roman Culture*, 3 vols. (Tübingen: Mohr Siebeck, 1998–2002); Daniel Sperber, *The City in Roman Palestine* (New York: Oxford University Press, 1998); Lee I. Levine, *The Rabbinic Class of Roman Palestine in Late Antiquity* (Jerusalem: Yad Izhak Ben-Zvi; New York: Jewish Theological Seminary of America, 1989); Saul Lieberman, *Hellenism in Jewish Palestine: Studies in the Literary Transmission, Beliefs and Manners of Palestine in the I Century B. C. E.–IV Century C. E.* (New York: Jewish Theological Seminary of America, 1950).

[64] Peter Richardson's study ("Towards a Typology of Levantine/Palestinian Houses," *JSNT* 27 [2004]: 47-68) is an important contribution in this regard.

[65] Two articles provide examples of how productive examining such categories can be: Andrea M. Berlin, "Romanization and anti-Romanization in pre-Revolt Galilee," in Andrea M. Berlin and J. Andrew Overman, eds., *The First Jewish Revolt: Archaeology, History, and Ideology* (London and New York: Routledge, 2002), 57–73 and Jonathan L. Reed, "Stone Vessels and Gospel Texts: Purity and Socio-Economics in John 2," in Jürgen Zangenberg and Stefan Alkier, eds., *Zeichen aus Text und Stein: Studien auf den Weg zu einer Archäologie des Neuen Testaments* (Tübingen and Basel: A. Francke Verlag, 2003), 381–401, esp. 393.

[66] Such a study would require a thorough review of recent scholarship on ancient urban–rural relations (rather than an over-reliance on one or two models), a search for patterns in the region's numismatic evidence, a site-by-site sifting for examples of trade, a

Judaism can be interpreted (to varying degrees) as reactions to growing Hellenistic and Roman influence: the increasing emphasis on ritual purity, as demonstrated by the rising use of stone vessels and ritual baths; sectarianism; revitalization and revivalist movements; and, of course, the events leading up to the two Jewish revolts. There is thus no shortage of questions about Greco-Roman culture in Galilee or about Galilean Judaism in general, but there is a practical limit to what any one project can do.[67] I make no attempt to address these issues in detail, though I touch upon some of them.

As with all studies that focus on archaeological materials, the conclusions drawn here are provisional, always subject to revision in light of future finds and publications. Nonetheless, we have sufficient data to talk with some confidence about the ways in which Galileans adopted, adapted, and rejected certain aspects of Greek and Roman culture, and thus about how the Galilee of Jesus fits into the larger context of the Greco-Roman world. My discussion proceeds along the following lines: Chapter One is devoted to the encounter with Greek culture in the late Persian and the Hellenistic periods in Palestine as a whole and Galilee in particular. In Chapter Two, I describe the history of the Roman military presence in Galilee, highlighting the lack of long-term garrisons there until the second century CE. Chapter Three examines the period from the Romans' arrival in the mid-first century BCE to the Jewish revolt in 70 CE, devoting special attention to the role of the Herodian client kings in spreading Greco-Roman culture. The transformation of Galilean cities in the second and third centuries is discussed in Chapter Four. Chapter Five investigates what we can determine about the languages spoken in Galilee, especially the extent of the use of Greek. Chapter Six considers the information

---

serious grappling with the problems posed by extracting information about social conditions from parables, and an investigation of the economic obligations of client kings to Rome.

[67] D. Kennedy raises similar questions about the larger Roman Near East ("Greek, Roman, and Native Cultures in the Roman Near East," in J. H. Humphrey, ed., *The Roman and Byzantine Near East* [Portsmouth, R. I.: Journal of Roman Archaeology, 1999], vol. 2, 76–106).

provided by Galilee's numismatic record about the region's Hellenization and Romanization. Chapter Seven provides an overview of several categories of art found in Galilee, including mosaics, frescoes, statues, and figurines, a body of evidence which demonstrates that Galileans were noticeably more comfortable with Greco-Roman media and motifs in the second and later centuries CE than in the first. My conclusion summarizes the implications of the study's findings.

CHAPTER I

Galilee's early encounter with Hellenism

By the time of Jesus, it is often observed, Galilee's encounter with
Hellenism was centuries old. Greek culture had made its way to
Palestine even in the Persian period, and it had been spread further
by Alexander the Great and his successors, the Ptolemies and
Seleucids. In some respects, the Maccabees and Hasmoneans embraced it.[1] The fact that all of the foregoing statements are true does
not change another fact: our actual *evidence* for Hellenistic culture in
Galilee in the last few centuries before the Common Era is strikingly
limited. The poor preservation of Hellenistic-era strata is partly
to blame for that circumstance, but not solely. The evidence that
has survived suggests that while Hellenistic culture was present in
Galilee, it was not as widespread as might be thought. Overall, in
fact, its inroads were quite modest. In this chapter, I will provide a
chronological overview of Galilee's early encounter with Hellenism,
as well as that of the rest of Palestine.[2]

BEFORE ALEXANDER

Palestine's contacts with Greek culture did indeed predate the
arrival of Alexander. Some cities had imported Greek goods as early

---

[1] For convenience, I reserve the term "Maccabees" for Judas and his brothers and "Hasmoneans" for the dynasty that began with Simon's son, John Hyrcanus I.
[2] Rami Arav's masterful overview of Hellenistic Palestine includes sites on Galilee's fringes
(Beth Yerah, Scythopolis, Tel Anafa, and Tel Dan) but notes very little evidence from the
region itself (*Hellenistic Palestine: Settlement Patterns and City Planning, 337–31 BCE*
[Oxford: BAR, 1989], 97–105); cf. Andrea M. Berlin, "Between Large Forces: Palestine
in the Hellenistic Period," *BA* 60:1 (1997): 2–57, esp. 12 on the third century; Mordechai
Aviam, "Galilee: The Hellenistic to Byzantine Periods," *NEAEHL*, vol. 2, 453–458,

24

as the eleventh century BCE, and by the sixth century, Aegean pottery and Athenian black- and red-glazed wares had made their way there. Persian rule of Palestine did not prevent the growth of Greek cultural influence.[3] The importing of Greek pottery continued and coins minted by distant Greek cities circulated.[4] Persian and local civic coins often imitated Greek designs, depicting, for example, the owl, long associated with Athens, and the griffin.[5] The port city of Dor became one of the first cities in Palestine to lay streets at right angles, and further north, Tel Abu-Hawam and Shiqmona did likewise.[6] This type of city plan, called a Hippodamian grid even though it predates the famous architect Hippodamus (fifth century BCE), is a telltale sign of Hellenistic influence.[7]

Overall, Persian Galilee has provided less evidence for Hellenistic culture than some other parts of Palestine. Galilee had been sparsely populated since the Assyrians deported the Israelite tribes in the late eighth century.[8] In the Persian period, however, new settlements began appearing. Phoenician pottery in the western region suggests

esp. 453–454; Frankel et al., *Settlement Dynamics*, 108–110; Eric M. Meyers, James F. Strange, and Dennis E. Groh, "The Meiron Excavation Project: Archeological Survey in Galilee and Golan, 1976," *BASOR* 230 (1978): 1–24.

[3] Ephraim Stern, *Archaeology of the Land of the Bible, vol. 2: The Assyrian, Babylonian, and Persian Periods, 732–332 BCE* (New York: Doubleday, 2001); Ephraim Stern, "Between Persia and Greece: Trade, Administration and Warfare in the Persian and Hellenistic Periods (539–63 BCE)," in Thomas E. Levy, ed., *The Archaeology of Society in the Holy Land* (New York: Facts on File, 1995), 432–445; Ephraim Stern, *Material Culture of the Land of the Bible in the Persian Period, 538–332 BC* (Warminster: Aris & Phillips; Jerusalem: Israel Exploration Society, 1982); Eric M. Meyers, "Second Temple Studies in the Light of Recent Archaeology: Part I: The Persian and Hellenistic Periods," *CRBS* 2 (1994): 25–42; Hengel, *Hellenism and Judaism*, vol. 1, 32–35; Hengel, *Jews*, 4.

[4] Stern, *Material Culture*, 141, 232, 283–286.

[5] Stern, *Archaeology*, 556–570; *Treasury*, 1–19; Uriel Rappaport, "Numismatics," in *CHJ*, vol. 1, 25–59.

[6] Ephraim Stern, "Stratigraphical Summary of Architectural Remains," in Stern, *Excavations at Dor, Final Report*, 2 vols. (Jerusalem: Hebrew University and Israel Exploration Society, 1995), vol. 1, 29–48; Stern, *Material Culture*, 230.

[7] Ball (*Rome*, 248–256) strongly emphasizes the pre-Greek origins of urban grids.

[8] Frankel et al., *Settlement Dynamics*, 104–107; Zvi Gal, *Lower Galilee during the Iron Age* (Winona Lake, Ind.: Eisenbrauns, 1992); Chancey, *Myth*, 31–34. Only a few Galileans would have been descendants of the Israelites, *contra* Richard A. Horsley in *Galilee: History, Politics, People* (Valley Forge, Penn.: Trinity Press International, 1995) and *Archaeology, History and Society in Galilee: The Social Context of Jesus and the Rabbis* (Valley Forge, Penn.: Trinity Press International, 1996).

that settlers there were arriving from the coast.[9] In the northeast, around Mt. Meron, quite different pottery, called "Galilean Coarse Ware," suggests that people of an unidentifiable ethnicity dwelt there.[10] Most Galilean communities were quite small.[11] Large buildings appear to have been rare; a pagan temple at Mizpeh Yamim, a columned administrative building at Kedesh, and a citadel at Hazor were the exceptions in this regard, not the norm.[12] Imported Greek goods were rarer than in the coastal cities.[13] Coins, mostly of Tyre and Sidon, circulated in Galilee, though in smaller quantities than adjacent areas.[14]

GALILEE UNDER THE GREEKS

Alexander the Great and his Macedonian army swept down the coast of Palestine in 332 BCE while en route to Egypt. They passed through Palestine again the following year as they moved north and then east into Mesopotamia. On his first trip through the region, Alexander besieged Tyre and Gaza and, according to legend, he visited Jerusalem.[15] On his second journey through the region, his

---

[9] Stern, *Archaeology*, 373–379; note also Phoenician-style masonry at Yoqne'am (Amnon Ben-Tor, Yuval Portugali, and Miriam Anissar, "The Third and Fourth Seasons of Excavations at Tel Yoqne'am, 1979 and 1981," *IEJ* 33 [1983]: 30–53).

[10] Frankel et al., *Settlement Dynamics*, 106–108, 110.

[11] On sites in and near Galilee with Persian-era remains, see Frankel et al., *Settlement Dynamics*, 107; Stern, *Material Culture*, 1–14; Stern, *Archaeology*, 373–379; Zvi Gal, "Galilee: Chalcolithic to Persian Periods," in *NEAEHL*, vol. 2, 450–453; and the following in Nagy et al., *Sepphoris*: Michael Dayagi-Mendels, "Rhyton," 163 and "Persian-Period Incense Burners," 164–165; Matthew W. Stolper, "Vase Fragment," 166–167; and Rafael Frankel, "The Mizpeh Yamim Hoard," 168–170.

[12] Rafael Frankel and Raphael Ventura, "The Mispe Yamim Bronzes," *BASOR* 311 (1998): 39–55 (Mizpeh Yamim is at map coordinates 193/260); Sharon C. Herbert and Andrea M. Berlin, "A New Administrative Center for Persian and Hellenistic Galilee: Preliminary Report of the University of Michigan/University of Minnesota Excavations at Kedesh," *BASOR* 329 (2003): 13–59, esp. 46–48; Stern, *Material Culture*, 1–4; Yigael Yadin, "Hazor: Excavation Results: First Four Seasons (1955–1958)," *NEAEHL*, vol. 2, 595–603. A structure at Ayelet ha-Shahar (map coordinates 195/246) has sometimes been dated to the Persian period, but see Amnon Ben-Tor's reservations in "Hazor: Fifth Season of Excavations (1968–1969)," *NEAEHL*, vol. 2, 604–605.

[13] Greek imports have, however, been discovered at Hazor and Ayelet ha-Shahar (Stern, *Archaeology*, 216).

[14] Stern, *Archaeology*, 561 and *Material Culture*, 217–228; see discussion in Chapter Six.

[15] *Antiquities* 11.336 provides one version of the legend; on the visit's historicity, see Grabbe, *Judaism*, vol. 1, 181–183.

army suppressed a revolt in Samaria.[16] Aside from these battles, though, his immediate impact on the region is difficult to gauge.

Traditions and inscriptions from the Roman and Byzantine periods associate him and his officers with the foundation of numerous cities,[17] such as Samaria,[18] Gerasa,[19] Dium, Pella,[20] and Capitolias.[21] Whether the history of any of these cities actually goes back to Alexander is almost impossible to determine; however, some of Samaria's fortifications date to c. 300 BCE, showing, at the least, that the site was occupied shortly after his conquest.[22] It was fashionable for cities to assert such links to famous figures of history and myth,[23] and their claims of connections with Alexander should probably be interpreted primarily as affirmations of their "Greekness."[24]

---

[16] Grabbe, *Judaism*, vol. 1, 205–208.

[17] Hengel, *Jews*, 9; A. H. M. Jones, *The Cities of the Eastern Roman Provinces* (2nd ed., Oxford: Oxford University Press, 1971), 238–239; cf. also Emil Schürer, *The History of the Jewish People in the Age of Jesus Christ*, rev. and ed. Geza Vermes, Fergus Millar, and Matthew Black, 3 vols. (Edinburgh: T & T Clark, 1973–1987), vol. 2, 146–149.

[18] Curtius Rufus, a Roman biographer (first or second century CE), reports that Alexander settled Macedonians at the city of Samaria (4.8), but Eusebius (c. 260–c. 340 CE) names Alexander's general Perdiccas, rather than Alexander himself, as the founder of a Greek city there (*Chronicle* 123). Josephus claims that Alexander granted the Samaritans permission to erect a temple on nearby Mt. Gerizim (*Ant.* 11.321–324).

[19] According to a scribal gloss on the commentary on Nicomachus by Jamblichus, Alexander founded Gerasa by stationing a group of elders (*gerontes*) there. Most scholars have rejected this report as merely a strained etymology for the city's name (Carl H. Kraeling, "The History of Gerasa," in Carl H. Kraeling, ed., *Gerasa: City of the Decapolis* [New Haven: American Schools of Oriental Research, 1938], 27–72, esp. 28). Because a third-century CE statue-base inscription there mentions Perdiccas, some scholars have suggested that he was regarded as the city's founder (C. B. Welles, "The Inscriptions," in Kraeling, *Gerasa*, 355–496, specifically, 423 no. 137; Kraeling, "History," 28–29; Jones, *Cities*, 238–239). Note also the third-century CE coin that calls Alexander "founder" (*City-Coins*, 94 no. 256).

[20] The sixth-century text of Stephanus of Byzantium identifies Dium as a foundation of Alexander, and a gloss on that text makes the same claim about Pella (Schürer, *History*, vol. 2, 145–148).

[21] *City-Coins*, 86 no. 232; Augustus Spijkerman, *The Coins of the Decapolis and Provincia Arabia* (Jerusalem: Franciscan Printing Press, 1978), 102 no. 15.

[22] Berlin, "Between," 10; J. W. Crowfoot, Kathleen M. Kenyon, and E. Sukenik, *The Buildings at Samaria* (London: Palestine Exploration Fund, 1942), 24–27.

[23] Hengel, *Judaism and Hellenism*, vol. 1, 57. In his discussion of cities in Asia Minor, Getzel M. Cohen treats such claims from the Roman and later periods skeptically (*The Hellenistic Settlements in Europe, the Islands, and Asia Minor* [Berkeley: University of California Press, 1995], 420–423).

[24] Compare Zaphra Newby's observation that in the second and third centuries CE, cities throughout the east associated themselves with Greek culture by claiming historical links

Alexander's death in 323 BCE brought with it the splintering of his empire among his dominant officers.[25] Palestine went first to the Seleucids, but for only two decades, too brief a time to leave an identifiable imprint in the archaeological record. The Ptolemies seized it c. 301 BCE, and while most of it would remain in their hands throughout the following century, some territory occasionally changed hands with the Seleucids.[26] After their victory at the Battle of Paneas (c. 200 BCE), the Seleucids regained control over all of Palestine.[27] Numerous cities took Greek names in this era. Under the Ptolemies, the port city Acco became Ptolemais, and Beth Shean, at the eastern end of the Jezreel valley, became Scythopolis. In the Transjordan, Pella was renamed Berenice and Rabbat-Ammon, Philadelphia. Philoteria, probably named for the sister of Ptolemy II, may have been an entirely new foundation.[28] The foundation and refoundation of cities continued under the Seleucids.[29] In the Huleh, north of Galilee, Seleucia was built.[30] Roman-period coins and inscriptions show that Abila took the name Seleucia[31] and that

---

to Athens, Sparta, and other important Greek cities ("Art and Identity in Asia Minor," in Scott and Webster, eds., *Roman Imperialism*, 192–213, esp. 193–194). Julian M. C. Bowsher suggests that such claims indicate only that a city had a Greek-style constitution ("Civic Organisation within the Decapolis," *ARAM* 4:1 & 2 [1992]: 265–281, esp. 267–268).

[25] For historical overviews, see Hengel, *Judaism and Hellenism*, vol. 1, 6–12; Hengel, *Jews*, 1–48; Freyne, *Galilee from Alexander*, 27–35; Berlin, "Between."

[26] During the Fourth Syrian War (219–217 BCE), for example, Antiochus III briefly held Tyre, Ptolemais, Philoteria, Scythopolis, Atabyrion (Mt. Tabor), Gadara, Abila, Pella, and other places (Polybius, *Histories*, 5.65.2, 5.70.3–12, 5.71.1–3; Freyne, *Galilee from Alexander*, 30–31; Hengel, *Jews*, 7).

[27] On the third-century BCE conflicts between the Ptolemies and the Seleucids, see H. Heinen, "The Syrian-Egyptian Wars and the New Kingdoms of Asia Minor," in F. W. Walbank, A. E. Astin, M. W. Frederiksen, R. M. Ogilvie, eds., *The Cambridge Ancient History* (Cambridge: Cambridge University Press, 1984), vol. 7, pt. 1, 412–445.

[28] On the renaming of these cities, see Victor Tcherikover, *Hellenistic Civilization and the Jews* (Philadelphia and Jerusalem: Jewish Publication Society of America, 1959; reprint, Peabody, Mass.: Hendrickson, 1999), 102; Jones, *Cities*, 242; Freyne, *Galilee from Alexander*, 104–114. Little is known of Philoteria, though ruins at Beth Yerah might be its remnants (Ruth Hestrin, "Beth Yerah," *NEAEHL*, vol. 1, 255–259).

[29] Jones, *Cities*, 252–253.

[30] Josephus, *Ant.* 13.393, *War* 1.105, 4.2; cf. *Life* 37. For discussion of possible locations of Seleucia, see Aviam and Richardson, "Josephus' Galilee," 193 and Freyne, *Galilee from Alexander*, 113–114. Tcherikover argued that a city named Antioch was also built in the Huleh (*Hellenistic Civilization*, 101–102; cf. *Ant.* 13.394, 17.23; *War* 1.105).

[31] Spijkerman, *Coins*, 48–57.

Hippos[32] and Gerasa[33] adopted the name of the Seleucids' capital city, Antioch.[34] The sixth-century historian Stephen of Byzantium notes that Gadara was known as both Antioch and Seleucia.[35] Ptolemais kept its name, which honored the Seleucids' rivals, but its coins from the mid-second century and later proclaimed its citizens "Antiocheans who are in Ptolemais."[36] It could have been under the Seleucids that Scythopolis became Nysa, a name that honored not only the nurse of the god Dionysos, but perhaps also a member of the Seleucid household.[37] Many Galileans would have been familiar with these new names, especially those of nearby cities like Ptolemais, Hippos, and Scythopolis. But how much can we deduce about life in those cities on the basis of Greek names? Taking a new name does not indicate that colonists arrived, that commoners began speaking Greek, or that construction of Hellenistic architecture soon followed. Nor does it tell us to what extent or how quickly a city adopted a Greek form of civic government. We find ourselves largely in the dark on such matters.

It is difficult to discuss Ptolemaic and Seleucid governance of Galilee in anything but the most general of terms.[38] Papyri from Egypt suggest that the Ptolemies typically divided their territory into nomes, and their nomes into toparchies. Villages were, in turn, administratively assigned to the toparchies. Sometimes the Ptolemies sent their own officials to govern; sometimes, they relied upon indigenous leadership, particularly at the local level.[39] The Zenon papyri, a collection of letters, contracts, and other business documents from a Ptolemaic official's journey through Palestine and southern Syria in 259 BCE, suggest that they established a

[32] Spijkerman, *Coins*, 170–179.

[33] Welles, "Inscriptions," nos. 30, 56–57, 251.

[34] Cohen discusses the popularity of the names Antioch and Seleucia in the Seleucid Empire (*Hellenistic Settlements*, 428–431).

[35] Jones, *Cities*, 252.

[36] *City-Coins*, 12.

[37] Freyne, *Galilee from Alexander*, 34. A city in western Asia Minor was also named Nysa; see Cohen, *Hellenistic Settlements*, 256–257 on the name's origin.

[38] Hengel, *Judaism and Hellenism*, vol. 1, 18–28; Freyne, *Galilee from Alexander*, 27–35; Roger S. Bagnall, "Palestine, Administration of (Ptolemaic)," *ABD*, vol. 5, 90–92; Thomas Fischer, "Palestine, Administration of (Seleucid)," trans. Frederick H. Cryer, *ABD*, vol. 5, 92–96; Herbert and Berlin, "New Administrative Center," 48–54.

[39] Hengel, *Judaism and Hellenism*, vol. 1, 18–32; Arav, *Hellenistic Palestine*, 124–127.

similar system in Palestine.[40] Seleucid provinces appear to have been divided into hyparchies, to which towns and villages were assigned. Like the Ptolemies, the Seleucids relied on a combination of their own and local personnel to administer their holdings. Several Hellenistic-era fortresses in western Lower Galilee attest to some military presence in the region,[41] but nothing in the literary or the archaeological record suggests that large numbers of Ptolemaic and Seleucid administrators, soldiers, or colonists arrived there.[42] With no major cities at the time, Galilee probably received fewer officials than other regions.

We are fortunate to have a few inscriptions from northern Palestine that shed a little light on officials in the Seleucid period. One is a Greek inscription found near Ptolemais recording a dedication offered by a Seleucid governor to Zeus Soter c. 130 BCE.[43] Another Greek inscription is found on a limestone stele near Scythopolis. Dating to c. 202–195 BCE, it records several orders and memoranda from Antiochus III, his son Antiochus IV, and the region's *strategos* and chief priest, Ptolemaios.[44] Two other inscriptions from Scythopolis provide rare early proof of Greek-style officials. One lists the priests of an Olympian deity, probably Zeus (the inscription is fragmentary), showing that Greek deities – or, at least, Hellenized forms of local deities – were worshiped.[45] The second, a lead weight

[40] Xavier Durand, *Des Grecs en Palestine au IIIe Siècle avant Jésus–Christ: Le Dossier Syrien des Archives de Zénon de Caunos (261–252)* (Paris: J. Gabalda, 1997); William Linn Westermann, Clinton Walker Keyes, and Herbert Liebesny, *Zenon Papyri: Business Papers of the Third Century BC Dealing with Palestine and Egypt* (New York: Columbia University Press, 1940); P. W. Pestman et al., *A Guide to the Zenon Archive*, 2 vols. (Leiden: E. J. Brill, 1981); Tcherikover, *Hellenistic Civilization*, 60–73. Several of these papyri mention Beth Anath, a site possibly in Upper Galilee (Hengel, *Judaism and Hellenism*, vol. 1, 22; Durand, *Des Grecs*, 67–68; Berlin, "Between," 14; Pestman et al., *Guide*, vol. 2, 481 on Βαιτάνατα).
[41] Mordechai Aviam, "Hellenistic Fortifications in the 'Hinterland' of 'Akko-Ptolemais'," in *Jews*, 22–30.
[42] Chancey, *Myth*, 35–36.
[43] Y. H. Landau, "A Greek Inscription from Acre," *IEJ* 11 (1961): 118–126; cf. J. Schwartz, "Note complémentaire (à propos d'une inscription grecque de St. Jean d'Acre)," *IEJ* 12 (1962): 135–136.
[44] Y. H. Landau, "A Greek Inscription Found Near Hefzibah," *IEJ* 16 (1966): 54–70; *SEG* 29.1613, 39.1636, 40.1509, 41.1574.
[45] *SEG* 8.33; Alan Rowe, *The Topography and History of Beth-Shan* (Philadelphia: University of Pennsylvania Press, 1930), 45.

from 117/116 BCE, demonstrates that the market overseer was known by the Greek title, *agoranomos*.[46] Inscriptions from Galilee itself are lacking, however, with the possible exception of an ostracon from Sepphoris. Excavators interpreted the first five of its seven letters אפמלסלש as the transliteration of the Greek *epimeletes*, a common title with a wide range of meanings.[47]

Greek influence in Palestine under these two kingdoms is reflected in numerous aspects of the material culture. Hellenistic-style fortifications, with buttresses and towers, were built at several cities, including Beth Yerah (probably under the Ptolemies),[48] and Sepphoris (probably under the Seleucids).[49] Peristyle buildings (i.e., buildings with column-lined courtyards) have been found at Gezer, Maresha, Samaria, Beth Zur, and, nearer to Galilee, Tel Anafa.[50] A few more cities, such as Maresha[51] and perhaps the one at Beth Yerah, adopted some degree of orthogonal planning.[52] The famous three orders of Greek columns, Ionic, Doric, Corinthian, began to

---

[46] *SEG* 27.1451. That the title was also already in use elsewhere in Palestine is shown by a market weight from Maresha dated 107–106 BCE (*SEG* 27.1439) and weights at Scythopolis (no author, *Inscriptions Reveal: Documents from the Time of the Bible, the Mishna and the Talmud* [Jerusalem: Israel Museum, 1972], 110 no. 224 and Alla Kushnir–Stein, "New Hellenistic Lead Weights from Palestine and Phoenicia," *IEJ* 52 [2002]: 225–230).

[47] Eric M. Meyers, "Sepphoris on the Eve of the Great Revolt (67–68 CE): Archaeology and Josephus," in Eric M. Meyers, ed., *Galilee through the Centuries: Confluence of Cultures* (Winona Lake, Ind.: Eisenbrauns, 1999), 109–122, esp. 112–113; Joseph Naveh, "Jar Fragment with Inscription in Hebrew," in Nagy, *Sepphoris*, 170; Joseph Naveh, "Epigraphic Miscellanea," *IEJ* 52 (2002): 240–253, esp. 242–243. In Josephus, *epimeletes* often refers to the administrator of a large piece of territory; Herod the Great is described as the *epimeletes* of the Jews (*Ant.* 14.127) and of all Syria (*Ant.* 14.280) (E. Meyers, "Sepphoris on the Eve," 113). In later inscriptions, it refers to civic and religious positions (John D. Grainger, "'Village Government' in Roman Syria and Arabia," *Levant* 27 [1995]: 179–195, esp. 183ff). See more Roman-period examples in Chapter Five.

[48] Hestrin, "Beth Yerah"; for other cities, see Marie-Christine Halpern-Zylberstein, "The Archeology of Hellenistic Palestine," in *CHJ*, vol. 2, 1–34, esp. 3–13; Arav, *Hellenistic Palestine*, 156.

[49] Meyers, "Sepphoris on the Eve," 110–111.

[50] Halpern-Zylberstein, "Archeology," 3–17; Arav, *Hellenistic Palestine*, 167; Robert W. Funk, "Beth-Zur," *NEAEHL*, vol. 1, 259–261; Sharon C. Herbert, "Occupational History and Stratigraphy," in Herbert, ed., *Tel Anafa, I: Final Report on Ten Years of Excavation at a Hellenistic and Roman Settlement in Northern Israel*, 2 vols. (Ann Arbor: Mich.: Kelsey Museum, 1994), vol. 1, 26–182, esp. 31ff.

[51] Amos Kloner, "Mareshah," *OEANE*, vol. 3, 412–413; Berlin, "Between," 6–8.

[52] Arav, *Hellenistic Palestine*, 98.

make their appearance.[53] Greek imports increased, and local potters imitated Greek styles, making fishplates and glazed pots.[54] Stamped amphora handles discovered throughout Palestine reflect a taste for imported wines.[55] The Hellenistic custom of burials in *loculi* (niches cut inside tombs so that the bodies lay perpendicular to the walls) was introduced.[56] People would have been exposed more and more to the Greek language through its presence on coins and occasionally other government inscriptions (although, as we will later see, whether they could actually read these inscriptions is debatable).[57] Bathing facilities were built at a few sites, such as Kedesh,[58] Tel Anafa,[59] and Beth Zur (south of Jerusalem).[60]

As important as these developments are, it is essential to keep them in perspective.[61] While a few cities began constructing orthogonal streets, most of our evidence for that type of civic planning in Palestine dates to the Roman, not the Hellenistic, era. Many of the buildings associated with Hellenistic cities elsewhere are absent from Palestine. Theaters, common in Greece since the classical period and in Asia Minor and the Aegean islands since Alexander, are nowhere to be found,[62] and the hippodrome is entirely missing.[63] We have no evidence for a gymnasium, the central cultural and educational institution of Greek culture, until c. 175 BCE, when one was famously

---

[53] Moshe L. Fischer, *Marble Studies: Roman Palestine and the Marble Trade* (Konstanz: Universitätsverlag Konstanz, 1998), 37.

[54] Halpern-Zylberstein, "Archeology."

[55] See Berlin, "Between," 5, 13 and the references in Chapter Five.

[56] Byron R. McCane, *Roll Back the Stone: Death and Burial in the World of Jesus* (Harrisburg: Trinity Press International, 2003), 34.

[57] Compare Chapter Five.

[58] A reference to a bathhouse in a letter of Zenon shows that one had been built by 259 BCE (Westermann, Keyes, and Liebesny, *Zenon Papyri*, 8 no. 61). Recent excavations have discovered a later bathing facility (probably mid-second century BCE) associated with an administrative center (Herbert and Berlin, "New Administrative Center," 35–38).

[59] A late second-century structure had bathing facilities with a primitive heating system that anticipated Roman technology (Herbert, "Occupational History," 62–72).

[60] The bath dates to the second century BCE (Robert W. Funk, "Beth-Zur," *NEAEHL*, vol. 1, 259–261).

[61] On this point, note in particular Arav's analysis in *Hellenistic Palestine*, 147–153.

[62] Margaret Bieber, *The History of the Greek and Roman Theater* (Princeton: Princeton University Press; London: Oxford University Press, 1961); Arthur Segal, "Theaters," *OEANE*, vol. 5, 199–203.

[63] The nearest known hippodrome was hundreds of miles to the north at Syrian Seleucia (Polybius, 5.49.1).

built in Jerusalem.[64] Greek-style baths were far more common in other regions.[65] Almost all of the evidence mentioned above comes from outside Galilee. Though coins and imported wares demonstrate that Ptolemaic and Seleucid Galilee was economically connected to the larger Levant, the region was not a hotbed of Hellenism. There was no massive influx of Greek settlers, apparently few Greek inscriptions, and little Hellenistic architecture. Hellenistic culture was the culture of cities, not villages, and Galilee as yet had no major cities.

THE HASMONEANS, HELLENISM, AND GALILEE

Judea, of course, had a major city: Jerusalem. Jews there gave Hellenism a mixed reception, one that ultimately culminated in the Maccabean Revolt. To reduce this revolt to a rebellion against Hellenism is to misrepresent and oversimplify its causes,[66] which included internal tensions within the Jewish community and reactions against the particular excesses of the Seleucid ruler Antiochus IV. To dismiss entirely the role of Hellenism in fomenting the revolt, however, would be to ignore our chief evidence for understanding it, the books of First and Second Maccabees.

Both works are polemical, written to depict in the worst possible light both the Seleucids and the Jews most receptive to Hellenism. Their strong and obvious biases leave them open to charges of exaggeration, distortion, and even outright fabrication. Yet they

---

[64] 2 Macc. 4:7–10. For evidence for gymnasia further north in Syria, see Fergus Millar, "The Problem of Hellenistic Syria," in Amélie Kuhrt and Susan Sherwin-White, eds., *Hellenism in the East* (Berkeley and Los Angeles: University of California Press, 1987), 110–133, esp. 117; Hengel, *Judaism and Hellenism*, vol. 1, 70.

[65] Inge Nielsen, *Thermae et Balnea: The Architecture and Cultural History of Roman Public Baths*, 2 vols. (Aarhus: Aarhus University Press, 1993), vol. 1, 6–9.

[66] Discussions of the causes of the revolt are numerous. Classic ones include Tcherikover, *Hellenistic Civilization* and Elias J. Bickerman, *God of the Maccabees: Studies on the Origin and Meaning of the Maccabean Revolt*, trans. Horst R. Moehring (Leiden: E. J. Brill, 1979). More recent treatments include Erich S. Gruen, *Heritage and Hellenism: The Reinvention of Jewish Tradition* (Berkeley: University of California Press, 1998), 1–40; Grabbe, *Judaism from Cyrus*, vol. 1, 246–259, 276–293; Jonathan A. Goldstein, "The Hasmonean Revolt and the Hasmonean Dynasty," in *CHJ*, vol. 2, 292–351; Daniel J. Harrington, *The Maccabean Revolt: Anatomy of a Biblical Revolution* (Wilmington, Del.: Michael Glazier, 1988); Schürer, *History*, vol. 1, 146–163.

seem reliable on a very basic point: some Jews in Jerusalem were more open to Hellenism than others. First Maccabees notes that Jewish "renegades" built a gymnasium in the city so that they could observe the "ordinances of Gentiles." Once the gymnasium was constructed, some of its visitors "removed the marks of circumcision," an apparent reference to an operation that made their lack of foreskins less noticeable when they exercised in the nude.[67] According to Second Maccabees, the high priest Jason attempted to "shift his compatriots to the Greek way of life."[68] The gymnasium was built adjacent to the temple and Jason organized an *ephebate*, a group of youths, probably the sons of the city's elites, to be educated at it.[69] He also attempted to enroll the city's inhabitants as "Antiochenes." The exact meaning of the word is unclear, but it suggests that he wanted the city to assume the name Antioch, as had other Seleucid cities. In an image that now seems almost comical, the author claims that priests neglected the sacrifices in the temple, so anxious were they to hurry over to the gymnasium's *palaestra* to watch wrestling. Whether this claim is accurate is beside the point; it effectively juxtaposes abandonment of the central rite of Judaism, temple sacrifice, with fascination with the activity symbolic of Hellenistic culture, gymnasium exercise. The book describes such abhorrent behavior as the height of "Hellenism" (4:13), providing us with the first known usage of the word.

Up to this point, though the city was not isolated from Hellenism, it was apparently not fully immersed in it, either. Despite having been under Greek rule for over 150 years, it had had no gymnasium and no *ephebate*. Archaeological finds suggest that it was not laid out on a Hippodamian grid or dotted with Hellenistic architecture and monuments. It has thus far yielded few Greek inscriptions from this period.[70]

---

[67] 1 Macc. 1:1–15. On skepticism regarding this claim, see Gruen, *Heritage*, 29–30 and Grabbe, *Judaism*, vol. 1, 278–279.

[68] 2 Macc. 4:10.

[69] 2 Macc. 4:7–17. According to 4:12, the gymnasium was "under the citadel," presumably the one overlooking the temple.

[70] Berlin notes only two inscriptions in Jerusalem from the time of Antiochus IV ("Between," 17).

The situation deteriorated rapidly under the next high priest, Menelaus. According to First Maccabees, Antiochus IV plundered both the temple and the city. He then, or so the book asserts, outlawed key practices of Judaism – animal sacrifice, circumcision, keeping the Sabbath, and possessing Torah scrolls. Furthermore, he ordered the construction of pagan shrines and the sacrifice of unclean animals.[71] Second Maccabees claims that Antiochus used the Jewish temple to worship the Olympian Zeus and forced Jews to participate in a festival of Dionysos.[72] The accuracy of these charges has been challenged, and the sequence of events is difficult to reconstruct.[73] What is undisputed is that the Maccabees harnessed popular outrage against the Seleucids and led their fellow Jews in revolt. The ultimate results of that rebellion are well-known: the capture and rededication of the temple c. 164 BCE; the beginning of a decades-long struggle against the Seleucids; the expansion of Jewish-controlled territory; and the establishment of a new dynasty of Jewish rulers, the Hasmoneans.

The Maccabees made only occasional forays into Galilee, which did not become a predominantly Jewish territory for decades.[74] Their earliest expedition there took place in the revolt's opening stages, when Simon led a mission to rescue Jews there from gentiles from Galilee and the coastal cities of Ptolemais, Tyre, and Sidon.[75] First Maccabees notes only that Simon battled the gentiles, driving them back as far as the "gate of Ptolemais" before gathering the region's Jews and bringing them down to the relative safety of Judea. The account, if accurate,[76] suggests that Jews were at the time a small minority in Galilee, in need of protection and capable of evacuation. A second campaign occurred there c. 144 BCE when Jonathan led his forces against the Seleucid king Demetrius II,

---

[71] 1 Macc. 1:41–61.

[72] 2 Macc. 6:2, 7. It is possible that these deities were Hellenized versions of Syrian gods (Grabbe, *Judaism*, vol. 1, 258–259).

[73] See Harrington, *Maccabean Revolt*, 92–97, and the other sources cited above.

[74] For an overview of Maccabean and Hasmonean activities in Galilee, see Mordechai Aviam, "The Hasmonaean Dynasty's Activities in the Galilee," in *Jews*, 41–50.

[75] 1 Macc. 5:9–23.

[76] 1 Macc. 5:21–22. On the historicity of this expedition, see Bezalel Bar-Kochva, *Judas Maccabeus: The Jewish Struggle against the Seleucids* (Cambridge: Cambridge University Press, 1989), 554 and Chancey, *Myth*, 39–40.

camping by the Sea of Galilee before meeting him at the plain of Hazor and driving his forces back to Kedesh.[77] The large building with a bath at Kedesh, probably a government archive of some sort, went out of use at approximately this time, suggesting that Seleucid troops abandoned Kedesh shortly after the battle.[78] Jonathan made another incursion to Galilee c. 143.[79] He first marched towards Beth Shean, where the forces of Trypho, a contender for the Seleucid throne, were encamped. He then fell for Trypho's trickery, accepting an invitation to be his guest at Ptolemais. Trypho seized him and attacked the troops he had left behind in Galilee. Within a few months, Jonathan was dead, executed in Gilead.[80]

The conquests of John Hyrcanus (135–104 BCE), Jonathan's nephew, extended Hasmonean territory northwards to Samaria[81] and, with the seizure of Scythopolis, to the borders of Galilee.[82] Most scholars assume that it was his successor, Aristobulus I (104–103 BCE), who annexed Galilee itself. Josephus writes that Aristobulus "made war on the Ituraeans and acquired a good part of their territory for Judaea and compelled the inhabitants, if they wished to remain in their country, to be circumcised and to live in accordance with the laws of Jews." He also cites a quotation of Timagenes in Strabo that states that Aristobulus "brought over to them a portion of the Ituraean nation, whom he joined to them by the bond of circumcision."[83] The whole passage is problematic, because it does not explicitly identify the geographical extent of Aristobulus's campaigns. If his conquests reached as far north as the primary Iturean territory, around Mt. Lebanon and Anti-Lebanon, then we

---

[77] 1 Macc. 11:63–74; cf. *Ant.* 13.158–162. On the possibility that 1 Macc. 9:1–2 alludes to an earlier battle in Galilee, see Chancey, *Myth*, 40.

[78] The interpretation of the building as an archive is supported by the presence of over 2000 stamped sealings, many with Greek mythological motifs (Herbert and Berlin, "New Administrative Center"; Donald T. Ariel and Joseph Naveh, "Selected Inscribed Sealings from Kedesh in the Upper Galilee," *BASOR* 329 [2003]: 61–80).

[79] 1 Macc. 12:39–53; cf. *Ant.* 13.187–193.

[80] 1 Macc. 13:23.

[81] *Ant.* 13.254–256, 275–281; *War* 1.64–66; Berlin, "Between," 31; Arav, *Hellenistic Palestine*, 91; Itzhak Magen, "Gerizim, Mount," in *NEAEHL*, vol. 2, 484–493.

[82] *Ant.* 13.280, *War* 1.66.

[83] *Ant.* 13.318–319; Chancey, *Myth*, 41–45; Sean Freyne, "Galileans, Itureans, and Phoenicians: A Study of Regional Contrasts in the Hellenistic Age," in Collins and Sterling, *Hellenism*, 184–215.

would expect to find destruction levels there, but thus far, none has been found. If the Itureans to whom Josephus refers were settlers who had drifted south into Galilee, as some scholars have suggested, then we would expect to find Iturean pottery there, but Iturean wares are largely absent in Galilee. The brevity of Aristobulus's reign and the fact that he minted no coins that we could use to date archaeological finds make it more difficult to understand what happened under him. It is possible, as Andrea M. Berlin has suggested, that Josephus and Timagenes are simply mistaken about Aristobulus's conquest of the Itureans. If so, then it was Aristobulus's brother Jannaeus who took Galilee.[84]

Like his predecessors, Jannaeus (103–76 BCE) enacted a policy of territorial conquest.[85] He struck first at Ptolemais, the port city closest to Lower Galilee.[86] His siege there was unsuccessful, but subsequent campaigns led to the seizure of a lengthy list of cities,[87] including Raphia, Anthedon, Straton's Tower, all on the coast;[88] Seleucia and Gamla in the Golan;[89] and Gerasa, Gadara, and Pella in the Decapolis region.[90]

Whether Jannaeus began the Judaization of Galilee or finished what his brother Aristobulus had started, Galilee was solidly Hasmonean territory by the end of his reign. His coins are scattered throughout the region, though many could have found their way there later. A new military presence is reflected in the construction or reuse of several fortifications.[91] Older sites were abandoned and

---

[84] Berlin, "Between," 38.

[85] Josephus claims that Alexander Jannaeus grew up in Galilee, sent there by his father Hyrcanus (*Ant.* 13.322).

[86] *Ant.* 13.324–355; *War* 1.86. See my discussion of the battles that ensued in Galilee (especially those involving Asochis/Shihin and Sepphoris) in *Myth,* 71, 83, 85.

[87] *Ant.* 13.395–397.

[88] *Ant.* 13.324–325.

[89] *Ant.* 13.393–394.

[90] *Ant.* 13.356–358, 394, 397; *War* 1.86–87, 104.

[91] Defenses at Yodefat were renovated, fortifications at Sha'ar Ha'amaqim, and Sepphoris were newly occupied, and those at Khirbet el-Tufaniyeh (map coordinates 174/261) were probably built (Israel Shatzman, *The Armies of the Hasmoneans and Herod: From Hellenistic to Roman Frameworks* (Tübingen: J. C. B. Mohr [Paul Siebeck], 1991), 83–87; David Adan-Bayewitz and Mordechai Aviam, "Iotapata, Josephus, and the Siege of 67: Preliminary Report on the 1992–1994 Seasons," *JRA* 10 [1997]: 131–165; Arthur Segal and Yehuda Naor, "Sha'ar Ha'amaqim," *NEAEHL*, vol. 4, 1339–1340; Chancey, *Myth,* 70–71; E. Meyers, "Sepphoris on the Eve").

new sites sprang up.[92] The findings of a survey of Upper Galilee undertaken from 1986–1990 are especially revealing.[93] In the northeast, Galilean Coarse Ware, used since the Persian period, began to disappear. In western Galilee, the boundary of the usage of Phoenician pottery began receding towards the coast.[94] Pagan cultic objects were shattered at Mizpeh Yamim and Beersheba (map coordinates 189/259).[95] These developments collectively suggest that population shifts occurred after the Hasmonean conquest, with pagans leaving the region as Jews moved in from the south. Archaeological data from the following decades and the information provided by Josephus and the canonical gospels suggest that after the Hasmonean conquest, Galilee was predominantly Jewish.[96]

Erich S. Gruen has recently emphasized how thoroughly the Maccabees and Hasmoneans embraced many aspects of Hellenistic culture. They "engaged regularly in diplomatic dealings with Greek kings, adopted Greek names, donned garb and paraded emblems redolent with Hellenic significance, erected monuments, displayed stelai and minted coinage inspired by Greek models, hired mercenaries, and even took on royal titulature."[97] Gruen is quite correct on these points, as his thorough discussion shows. First Maccabees and Josephus's *Antiquities* are full of references to diplomatic missions to and correspondence with foreign kings, contacts that often resulted in alliances.[98] John Hyrcanus gave Greek names to his sons

---

[92] New sites also appeared in Judea and in Samaria (Berlin, "Between," 28–29).

[93] Frankel et al., *Settlement Dynamics*, 108–110.

[94] Frankel et al., *Settlement Dynamics*, 108–114, 131–134.

[95] Frankel and Ventura, "Mispe Yamim Bronzes"; Frankel et al., *Settlement Dynamics*, 110. The destruction of cultic sites and expulsion and conversion of gentiles is consistent with earlier Maccabean and Hasmonean actions (1 Macc. 5:44, 68; 10:83; 13:47–48; *War* 1.66; *Ant.* 13.154–281, cf. 13.397).

[96] See the sources cited in my Introduction.

[97] Gruen, *Heritage*, 2; cf. 1–40. See also Tessa Rajak, "The Hasmoneans and the Uses of Hellenism," in Philip R. Davies and Richard T. White, eds., *A Tribute to Geza Vermes: Essays on Jewish and Christian Literature and History* (JSOT Supplement Series 100, Sheffield: JSOT Press, 1990), 261–280; Levine, *Hellenism and Judaism*, 37–46; Lee Levine, *Jerusalem: Portrait of the City in the Second Temple Period (538 BCE–70 CE)* (Philadelphia: Jewish Publication Society and Jewish Theological Seminary of America, 2002), 91–148; and Schwartz, *Imperialism*, 32–42.

[98] 1 Macc. 8:17–32, 12:1–23, 13:34–40; 2 Macc. 11:16–38. On the authenticity of the letters mentioned in 1 Maccabees, see Grabbe, *Judaism*, vol. 1, 260–261 and Tessa Rajak, "Hasmonean Kingship and the Invention of Tradition," in Per Bilde, Troels Engberg-Pedersen,

(Aristobulus, Antigonus, Alexander), starting a trend that continued until the end of the dynasty, though many Hasmoneans also had Hebrew names.[99] Simon wore royal purple and donned a crown, both gifts of the Seleucid King Alexander Balas.[100] The tomb he built at Mode'in for his brothers and parents reflects strong Hellenistic influence, with pyramids, columns, trophies of armor suits, and carvings of ships.[101] He also allowed the people of Jerusalem to erect a stele in Jerusalem with an honorific inscription.[102] Hyrcanus I and Alexander Jannaeus, in typical Hellenistic fashion, employed mercenaries, the latter recruiting Greeks from Asia Minor.[103] Hasmonean coins were free of human portraits, but their symbols were drawn from the standard repertoire of Hellenistic coinage. Those of Alexander Jannaeus and Mattathias Antigonus had Greek inscriptions, in addition to their Semitic ones.[104] The tactics of the Hasmonean armies reflected their familiarity with the military innovations of the Hellenistic period.[105] Hellenistic titles were common: Jonathan was named the "King's Kinsman" and "First Friend" by the Seleucids,[106] and John Hyrcanus received the title "Friend and Ally."[107] Aristobulus and Alexander Jannaeus both took the title "king,"[108] and Aristobulus proclaimed himself "Philhellene," or "Friend of the Greeks."[109] Following the practice of their Ptolemaic and Seleucid predecessors, the Hasmonean

Lise Hannestad, and Jan Zahle, eds., *Aspects of Hellenistic Kingship* (Aarhus, Denmark: Aarhus University Press, 1996), 99–115.

[99] Gruen, *Heritage*, 31–33; Schürer, *History*, 217; Goldstein, "Hasmonean Revolt," 330.

[100] 1 Macc. 10:20, 10:62.

[101] 1 Macc. 13:27–29. For discussion, see Steven Fine, *Art and Judaism in the Greco-Roman World: Toward a New Jewish Archaeology* (Cambridge: Cambridge University Press, 2005). Other tombs in and near Jerusalem from the late second century BCE to 70 CE also reflect Hellenistic influence, with their monumental scale, pyramid-shaped roof, and columns (Andrea M. Berlin, "Power and its Afterlife: Tombs in Hellenistic Palestine," *NEA* 65:2 [2002]: 138–148).

[102] 1 Macc. 13:25–30, 14:25–27.

[103] *Ant.* 13.249, *War* 1.65; *Ant.* 13.374–378, *War* 1.89–93; cf. Shatzman, *Armies*, 31–32.

[104] See discussion in Chapter Six.

[105] For example, the use of artillery and siege machinery (Shatzman, *Armies*, 24–25).

[106] 1 Macc. 10:89, 11:26–27.

[107] *Ant.* 13.247–249.

[108] *Ant.* 13.301, *War* 1.70; *Treasury*, 38–39.

[109] *Ant.* 13.318; cf. Rajak, "Hasmonean Kingship," 107. For other Mediterranean kings who took this title, see Aryeh Kasher, *Jews and Hellenistic Cities in Eretz-Israel* (Tübingen: J. C. B. Mohr [Paul Siebeck], 1990), 135n. 52.

rulers designated a considerable amount of land as "King's Land."[110] Hyrcanus and the kings who followed him devoted considerable resources to building palatial residences at Jericho, with multiple buildings, frescoed interiors, decorative gardens, columns, swimming pools, *mikvot*, aqueducts, and a bathhouse.[111]

That the Hasmoneans took on the trappings of the typical Hellenistic monarch is clear enough, but that their efforts led to a thoroughgoing Hellenization of Jewish society is not. Rami Arav has generalized that "even the most Hellenized sites in Palestine seem to have fallen behind the Hellenistic achievements" of other parts of the Mediterranean.[112] The gymnasium built by Jason in Jerusalem faded from history, never to be mentioned again in literary sources and never to be found.[113] With its demise, the *ephebate* presumably likewise crumbled. In Hasmonean territory, the number of imported goods dropped dramatically.[114] None of the Hasmoneans rebuilt Jerusalem on a Hippodamian grid or sponsored the construction of architectural symbols of Hellenism, such as a stadium or a theater. Hellenistic influence is much more visible in the Hasmoneans' private spaces, with their frescoes, colonnaded courtyards, Greek-style bathing facilities, than in the public eye. Though their subjects might have been aware of the extravagance of such palaces, they would hardly have been familiar with the details of their interiors. The primary place where the public would have glimpsed the Hasmoneans' affection for Hellenism was on their coins, and even there the Hasmonean statement was ambiguous.[115]

---

[110] Berlin, "Between," 33.

[111] Ehud Netzer, *Hasmonean and Herodian Palaces at Jericho: Final Reports of the 1973–1987 Excavations* (Jerusalem: Israel Exploration Society and Institute of Archaeology, 2001), vol. 1, 1–7; Ehud Netzer, "Jericho: Hellenistic to Early Arab Periods," *NEAEHL*, vol. 2, 681–691; Berlin, "Between," 34–35, 42; Arav, *Hellenistic Palestine*, 163–165.

[112] Arav, *Hellenistic Palestine*, 166.

[113] Duane W. Roller however, notes the possibility that the *xystos* (an exercise ground of some sort) adjacent to the temple at the time of the Revolt against Rome (*War* 2.344, 5.144) was related to the gymnasium (*The Building Program of Herod the Great* [Berkeley: University of California Press, 1998], 178).

[114] Berlin, "Between," 28–29, 42–43. Since by the time of Jannaeus the Hasmoneans held a number of ports (Joppa, Gaza, Straton's Tower), this change in trade patterns cannot be attributed to poor relations with the coastal cities.

[115] See discussion in Chapter Six.

Galilee displayed the same insularity as the rest of the Hasmonean territory. Tyrian and Sidonian coins attest to its continuing participation in a trade network including those cities, but there was little Phoenician semi-fine ware like that found in adjacent areas.[116] By the first century CE, the imported round, molded lamps and red-slipped Eastern Sigillata A pottery that had been used in earlier years had disappeared.[117] There was no dramatic increase in Hasmonean Galilee in the number of inscriptions (aside from coins) or Hellenistic-style urban planning. The overall impression is that while the Hasmonean conquest brought the Judaization of Galilee, it did not bring its rapid Hellenization.

A comparative look at the Phoenician settlement at Tel Anafa, northeast of Galilee in the Huleh, shows that such austerity was not inevitable.[118] Its inhabitants imported goods from all over the eastern Mediterranean and had a special fondness for Aegean wines. Their luxury goods included fine pottery, an unusually large number of molded glass bowls, even a small cache of gems. Figurines of Pan and perhaps Demeter show that they were familiar with the characters of Greek mythology.[119] The graffiti they carved onto their red-ware were in Greek,[120] and they cooked in Greek-style casserole dishes.[121] The most extravagant of their buildings, the one with the bathing facility, employed Phoenician- and Greek-style construction techniques.[122] Its courtyard was lined with Ionic and Corinthian columns, and its walls were painted and stuccoed. The settlement was abandoned c. 75 BCE, after the region came under Hasmonean influence.

---

[116] Andrea Berlin, "From Monarchy to Markets: The Phoenicians in Hellenistic Palestine," *BASOR* 306 (1997): 75–88.

[117] Berlin, "Romanization and Anti-Romanization."

[118] Berlin has drawn attention to the usefulness of this comparison ("Between"). On Tel Anafa, see Herbert, *Tel Anafa, I*; Sharon Herbert, ed., *Tel Anafa II, i: The Hellenistic and Roman Pottery* (Ann Arbor, Mich.: Kelsey Museum; Columbia, Mo.: Museum of Art and Archaeology of the University of Missouri, 1997); Kathleen Warner Slane, "The Fine Wares," in Herbert, *Tel Anafa II, i*, 247–418; Andrea Berlin, "The Plain Wares," in Herbert, *Tel Anafa, II, i*, ix–246; and sources cited in Chancey, *Myth*, 125–129.

[119] Sharon C. Herbert, "Tel Anafa, 1980," *Muse* 14 (1980): 24–30; Saul S. Weinberg, "Tel Anafa: The Hellenistic Town," *IEJ* 21 (1971): 86–109.

[120] Slane, "Fine Wares," 342–346.

[121] Berlin, "Plain Wares," 95.

[122] Sharon C. Herbert, "Introduction," in Herbert, *Tel Anafa, I, i*, 1–25, esp. 14–19.

Jannaeus's wife Alexandra Salome held the Hasmonean kingdom together for only a few years after his death. After she died in 67 BCE, it descended into civil war and chaos as her sons Hyrcanus II and Aristobulus II battled each other for the throne. Each probably looked back on the successes of the dynasty, the solidification of its power, and the expansion of its territory and assumed that similar glory awaited the victor of their struggle. Neither could have been fully aware of how drastically things were about to change.

CONCLUSION

We know far less of Hellenistic Galilee than we would like, and perhaps future excavations will fill in some of the gaps of our knowledge. On the eve of Rome's rise to power in the area, however, Hellenism's impact does not appear to have been very deep. Though some cities around Galilee publicly expressed their openness to Hellenistic culture by adopting Greek names, in most cases we can only speculate about the other ways they adopted and adapted Hellenism. It is tempting to attribute the lack of evidence from this period to the destruction of materials during the construction activity of later centuries, and we know that such destruction often occurred. That explanation alone, however, is probably insufficient. Writing of Syria in the Hellenistic period, Fergus Millar has argued that the absence of evidence is probably not solely due to accidents of survival and discovery, but rather to the slow pace of Hellenization there prior to the arrival of the Romans.[123] As will be seen, the same is true of Galilee.

---

[123] Millar, "Problem," 130. The ampleness of Mesopotamia's Hellenistic-period material culture provides a stark contrast (Malcolm Colledge, "Greek and non-Greek Interaction in the Art and Architecture of the Hellenistic East," in Kuhrt and Sherwin-White, *Hellenism*, 134–162).

CHAPTER 2

The Roman army in Palestine

The arrival in Palestine of the Roman general Pompey in 63 BCE
marks the beginning of a new chapter in the region's history.[1] The
following decades and centuries would bring drastic changes:
the end of the Hasmonean dynasty; proxy rule of Palestine by the
Romans through the Herodian client kings; the piecemeal annexation of the area and, with it, the implementation of direct Roman
rule through prefects and procurators; the establishment of a Roman
military presence; the destruction of the Jewish temple; and the slow
emergence of rabbinic Judaism. The Romans brought with them
the mixture of Roman culture and Hellenistic culture characteristic
of their eastern empire. To a large degree, then, Romanization
included Hellenization.

Understanding the chronological development of Rome's administrative and military presence in the region is crucial for understanding the spread of Greco-Roman culture there.[2] In this chapter, I
provide an overview of Rome's military activity in Palestine, paying
special attention to variations between regions and over time. I will
argue that because Galilee did not receive a long-term garrison until
c. 120 CE, contact with Roman soldiers in Galilee would have been

---

[1] On Rome's expansion east, see Ball, *Rome* and Millar, *RNE*.

[2] On the Roman army in Palestine, see Millar, *RNE*, 27–111; Benjamin Isaac, *The Limits of
Empire: The Roman Army in the East*, rev. ed. (Oxford: Clarendon Press, 1990), 427–435;
Lawrence Keppie, "Legions in the East from Augustus to Trajan," in Philip Freeman &
David Kennedy, eds., *The Defence of the Roman & Byzantine East* (Oxford: BAR, 1986),
vol. 2, 411–429; Menahem Mor, "The Roman Army in Eretz-Israel in the Years AD
70–132," in Freeman and Kennedy, *Defence*, vol. 2, 575–602; Zeev Safrai, "The Roman
Army in the Galilee," in Levine, *Galilee*, 103–114; Baruch Lifshitz, "Légions romaines en
Palestine," in Jacques Bibauw, ed., *Hommages à Marcel Renard* (Brussels: Latomus,
1969), 458–469.

uncommon in Jesus' lifetime, the story of his famous exchange with a centurion at Capernaum notwithstanding. As future chapters will demonstrate, a strong correlation exists between the arrival of Roman soldiers and the emergence of certain forms of Greco-Roman culture. Likewise, the relatively low profile of certain aspects of Greco-Roman culture in first-century Galilee is probably related, at least in part, to the absence of Roman soldiers.

THE BEGINNING OF ROMAN RULE

The Roman Senate had directed Pompey to rid the Republic of the threat of pirates, but he was not content with such a limited goal. He set out instead to expand Rome's territory, to create a relatively stable eastern frontier that would discourage the Parthians from venturing into Rome's sphere of interests, and, perhaps, to increase his own glory. Before his expedition was complete, he had conquered lands stretching from Pontus and Armenia in northern Asia Minor down the eastern Mediterranean coast all the way into Egypt.[3]

When Pompey marched into Palestine from Syria, he found the region in turmoil due to a dispute between the Hasmonean rivals Aristobulus and Hyrcanus. Each sent him gifts and embassies, hoping to turn him against the other,[4] but Hyrcanus was the more deferential of the two, and it was he who won Pompey's favor. Pompey named him high priest, imprisoned Aristobulus,[5] and besieged Aristobulus's followers in Jerusalem, an engagement that culminated, Josephus says, with the slaughter of priests in the temple.[6] Though Hyrcanus, as high priest, was nominal leader of the Jewish people, the days of the Hasmonean kingdom were over. Rome now ruled Palestine, which was placed under the care of the governor of the newly acquired Syria.

---

[3] On Pompey's eastern expeditions, see Robin Seagar, *Pompey the Great: A Political Biography* (2nd ed., Oxford: Blackwell, 2002), 53–62; A. N. Sherwin-White, *Roman Foreign Policy in the East, 168 BC to AD 1* (Norman: University of Oklahoma Press, 1983), 186–234.

[4] *Ant.* 14.34–47; *War* 1.131–132.

[5] *Ant.* 14.73; *War* 1.153.   [6] *Ant.* 14.58–73; *War* 1.138–151.

Little is known of the actions of the earliest Roman governors of Syria, but the fourth, Aulus Gabinius (57–55 BCE), made significant administrative changes in Palestine, dividing Jewish territory into five regional councils based at Jerusalem, Gadara, Amathus, Jericho, and Sepphoris.[7] The fact that Sepphoris was chosen suggests that it was already the most important city in Galilee; it does not, however, suggest that it hosted Roman troops and administrators. Josephus explicitly describes this arrangement as government by aristocrats – presumably local elites who ruled on Rome's behalf. The Romans themselves probably played little – if any – direct role in the councils, and there is no reason to suppose that a council required a strong Roman presence.[8] Within a few years, Gabinius reorganized the administration of Palestine again, placing power in the hands of Antipater, an Idumean who had supported Roman expansion and provided Gabinius with troops. The five councils were apparently disbanded; Josephus never mentions them again.[9]

On at least two occasions during this period, the Roman army conducted campaigns in or near Galilee. The first was under Gabinius, when the Romans defeated a pro-Hasmonean army at Mount Tabor.[10] Soon thereafter (53 BCE), the Parthians invaded in support of Aristobulus, and much of the combat occurred in Galilee. The Romans punished Jews who opposed them, enslaving some 30,000 people at Taricheae (Magdala), according to Josephus.[11]

Antipater maintained his position despite shifts in the political winds at Rome. Julius Caesar appointed him *epitropos* of Judea, and he, in turn, delegated authority to his two sons c. 47 BCE, appointing Phasael to govern Judea and Herod to govern Galilee.[12] Both Antipater and Phasael would be killed within a very few years,

---

[7] *Ant.* 14.91, *War* 1.170; Adam Porter, "Amathus: Gabinius' Capital in Peraea?" *JJS* 50 (1999): 223–229; Schürer, *History*, vol. 1, 244–245, 268 n. 5; E. Mary Smallwood, *The Jews under Roman Rule* (Leiden: E. J. Brill, 1976), 32–33.

[8] Compare Sanders, "Jesus' Galilee," 7.

[9] *War* 1.178; cf. Smallwood, *Jews*, 32–33. Sherwin-White provides a dissenting view, arguing that the councils lasted until the first revolt (*Roman Foreign Policy*, 275).

[10] *War* 1.177, *Ant.* 14.102.

[11] *Ant.* 14.120, *War* 1.180.

[12] *Ant.* 14.158; *War* 1.199–200, 203; Chancey, *Myth*, 49 n. 100.

Antipater by a political rival and Phasael by the Parthians. Herod's political career, however, was just beginning. While governing Galilee, he made a name for himself as an effective leader, collecting tribute from Galilean communities, defeating renegades who had raided border settlements, and routing Tyrian forces who had seized three Galilean fortresses in support of the Hasmonean Antigonus.[13] Herod later served as governor of Syria[14] and then as tetrarch of Judea, holding the latter position jointly with his brother Phasael.[15] In 40 BCE, however, a Parthian invasion brought the death of Phasael and the defeat of Herod's army. The Parthians appointed Antigonus king, and Herod fled, hoping to find sanctuary among the Nabateans. When they rejected him, he turned west to seek the aid of his patron in Rome, Antony.[16] His appeals were successful. The Senate, under Antony's influence, pronounced him king of Judea, not least because of his enmity toward Rome's rivals, the Parthians.[17] He sailed back to Palestine in 39 BCE, arriving at Ptolemais, bringing with him an army of Roman soldiers, and his forces grew as both gentiles and Jews (including many Galileans) joined them.[18] By 37 BCE, he had defeated the Hasmonean forces, seized Jerusalem, and claimed his throne. His territory encompassed most of the old Hasmonean kingdom, including Galilee and lands further northeast.[19]

When Herod died c. 4 BCE, Augustus divided his kingdom between his three sons. Galilee, along with Perea, went to Antipas.[20] Archelaus received Judea, Idumea, and Samaria; Philip was granted Batanea, Trachonitis, Auranitis, and other areas in the general vicinity of the present-day Golan Heights. The emperor allowed none of Herod's sons to take their father's title, *basileus*. Instead, Antipas and Philip each became tetrarch, literally, "ruler of a fourth," and Archelaus received the more prestigious title of

---

[13] *War* 1.204–205, 221, 238–239; *Ant.* 14.297–298.

[14] It is not clear what Herod's title was. *Ant.* 14.280 calls him *strategos* of Coile Syria; in *War* 1.225, he is *epimeletes* of "all Syria."

[15] *War* 1.244; *Ant.* 14.326.

[16] *War* 1.248–281, *Ant.* 14.330–380.

[17] *Ant.* 14.282–285; cf. Roller, *Building Program*, 11 n. 3.

[18] *Ant.* 14.394, *War* 1.290. Not all Galileans joined Herod; Josephus describes Herod's attacks on "bandits" at Arbel in *Ant.* 14.415–430 and *War* 1.305–313.

[19] Sanders ("Jesus' Galilee") provides a helpful overview of who held various cities in the transitions from Hasmonean to Herodian to Roman rule.

[20] *Ant.* 17.318–320, *War* 2.93–100.

ethnarch, "ruler of a people."²¹ From this point until the end of the first century CE, the political fortunes of the subregions of Palestine varied as territories shifted back and forth between client kings and Roman governors. Archelaus remained ethnarch in Judea for only ten years, after which the emperor removed him. In 6 CE, his territory became the province of Judea, administered by a Roman governor.²² It would remain provincial territory for the rest of the Roman period, with the brief exception of three years when it was granted to Agrippa I (41–44 CE).²³ After Philip's death in 33/34 CE, his territory passed briefly to the province of Syria before reverting back to the hands of client kings Agrippa I (37–44 CE), to the Romans again, then to Agrippa II (53–90s CE).²⁴

Galilee and Perea were ruled by Antipas for decades, until his brother-in-law Agrippa I convinced Gaius Caligula that Antipas was conspiring against him. Josephus implies that the charges were false, but c. 39 CE, Caligula banished Antipas to western Europe, giving his territory to Agrippa I.²⁵ After Agrippa's death in 44 CE,²⁶ Galilee was attached to the province of Judea, bringing it under direct Roman control for the first time in a century. In 61 CE, Claudius gave Agrippa II some of the lakeside cities of Galilee, including Tiberias and Taricheae, but they reverted back to the province of Judea at his death.

THE ROMAN MILITARY PRESENCE IN PRE-70 CE PALESTINE

From early in Herod the Great's reign until the first Jewish revolt, the Roman military presence in Palestine was small. Antony's troops had helped Herod seize the throne²⁷ and a legion remained in Jerusalem until 30 BCE,²⁸ but after that, Roman troops were not

---

²¹ *Ant.* 17.20–21. ²² *Ant.* 17.355, *War* 2.117.

²³ *Ant.* 19.274–275, *War* 2.215–216.

²⁴ Agrippa II died between 92/93 and 100 CE; see Schürer, *History*, vol. 1, 480–483; Millar, *RNE*, 91–92; Nikos Kokkinos, *The Herodian Dynasty: Origins, Role in Society and Eclipse* (Sheffield: Sheffield Academic Press, 1998), 396-399.

²⁵ In *Ant.* 18.245–252, Antipas is exiled to Lyon; in *War* 2.183, to Spain.

²⁶ *Ant.* 19.343–352; Acts 12:19–23; see discussion in Schürer, *History*, vol. 1, 452–453.

²⁷ *War* 1.288–294, 301–302, 317, 345–354; *Ant.* 14.394–395, 398, 434.

²⁸ *Ant.* 15.71–73.

regularly stationed in his territory. If his forces proved insufficient to deal with situations, he requested help from the governor in Syria, where four legions were typically stationed, mostly in the northern areas.[29] Thus, there were apparently no Roman soldiers in Trachonitis when Zenodorus allowed banditry c. 22 BCE,[30] none in Palestine when war broke out between Herod and the Nabateans in 12 BCE,[31] and none there when widespread chaos erupted at the death of Herod in 4 BCE.[32] In each of these cases, Roman legions marched down the coastal road from Syria, a pattern that would be repeated in first-century CE crises.[33]

At Herod's death, his army was probably split between his sons, and when Archelaus was deposed, his forces seem to have been converted to auxiliary units and passed to the Roman procurators. The backbone of the Roman forces in pre-70 CE Judea were based mostly at Caesarea, where the Roman prefect set up his head-quarters, and Jerusalem, where they were housed primarily in the Antonia fortress overlooking the Temple platform.[34] The troops assigned to the Antonia fortress must have been small in number, since the procurator Florus had to bring in forces from elsewhere as problems escalated in the city.[35] At the outbreak of the Jewish revolt, a few other garrisons were scattered across the region – Machaerus, Cypros, Ashkelon, Masada, and various places in Samaria.[36]

---

[29] Though four legions was the normal garrison, the number may have occasionally dropped to three or even two, particularly in the 50s when units rotated in and out of the province due to the war with the Parthians in Cappadocia. The Syrian garrison constituted about a sixth of Rome's total army (25 legions c. 14 CE, perhaps 28–29 by 70 CE). See H. M. D. Parker, *The Roman Legions* (Oxford: Clarendon Press, 1928), 92, 119, 128–129, 134–139, relying heavily on Tacitus, *Annals*; Lawrence Keppie, "The Army and the Navy," in Alan K. Bowman, Edward Champlin, and Andrew Lintott, eds., *The Cambridge Ancient History* (Cambridge: Cambridge University Press, 1996), vol. 10, 371–396, esp. 386–388; E. Dabrowa, "The Frontier in Syria in the First Century AD," in Philip Freeman and David Kennedy, eds., *The Defence of the Roman and Byzantine East* (Oxford: BAR, 1986), vol. 1, 93–108.

[30] *War* 1.398–400, *Ant.* 15.343–348.

[31] *Ant.* 16.271–299.

[32] *War* 2.16–19, 66–79; *Ant.* 17.250, 286.

[33] See especially Millar, *RNE*, 27–69.

[34] Some may have been stationed in the old Herodian palace (*War* 2.430, 440).

[35] *War* 2.430 for the Antonia fortress; *War* 2.296, 305, 318, 325–332, 430 on the use of troops stationed elsewhere.

[36] *War* 2.318, 408, 484–486; 3.9–28, 309; references collected in Schürer, *History*, vol. 1, 365.

Most of the rank and file "Roman" soldiers in Palestine were not from Rome or the Italian peninsula. Josephus suggests that they were locally raised, recruited from the pagan cities of Caesarea Maritima and Sebaste.[37] They were not in detachments from legions, whose members were all Roman citizens. Instead, they were in auxiliary units, whose members were usually not granted citizenship until after they were mustered out.[38] The combined provincial garrison was not especially large. At the death of Agrippa in 44 CE, it consisted of one *ala* and five *cohorts*, or approximately three thousand men.[39]

Though these were the main Roman units in Palestine, others may have occasionally passed through or been stationed there, as suggested by the book of Acts. Acts 10 refers to Peter's conversion of a centurion named Cornelius of the Italian Cohort at Caesarea Maritima c. 40 CE. We know of at least two units with similar names, the *Cohors I* and the *Cohors II Italica Civium Romanorum*. Both were auxiliary units attested to have been in Syria in the second half of the first century.[40] As their names imply, they were an unusual type of auxiliary unit, "citizen cohorts" whose members were already Roman citizens.[41] Their names imply that they originated on the Italian peninsula, but they would have acquired new recruits from the areas where they were stationed.[42]

---

[37] *Ant.* 19.356–366, 20.122, 20.176; *War* 2.236. Recruitment of auxiliaries from the provinces was typical throughout the empire.

[38] On the first-century Roman forces in Judea, see D. B. Saddington, *The Development of the Roman Auxiliary Forces from Caesar to Vespasian (49 BC–AD 79)* (Harare: University of Zimbabwe, 1982), 98–104. In contrast to legions, which were basically heavy infantry, auxiliary cohorts were light infantry, often specialty troops like archers and slingers. In addition, some auxiliary units were cavalry (*alae*), and others included both infantry and cavalry.

[39] *Ant.* 19.365; cf. *War* 3.66. Presumably, the garrison had shifted over to Agrippa I for his brief rule. After his death, it reverted back to the control of the Roman governor. Josephus refers to one *ala* and four cohorts during the reign of Cumanus (48–52 CE) (*Ant.* 20.122). See Saddington, *Development*, 50.

[40] Paul A. Holder, *Studies in the Auxilia of the Roman Army from Augustus to Trajan* (BAR International Series 70, Oxford: BAR, 1980), 66.

[41] D. B. Saddington, "The Development of the Roman Military and Administrative Personnel in the New Testament," *ANRW* 2.26.3, 2409–2435, esp. 2415–2416; Michael P. Speidel, "The Roman Army in Judaea under the Procurators: The Italian and the Augustan Cohort in the Acts of the Apostles," *Ancient Society* 13–14 (1982–1983): 233–240, esp. 233–237.

[42] Speidel ("Roman Army in Judaea") and Saddington ("Development") note that a gravestone discovered in Austria attests to the presence of an eastern recruit in such a unit.

Julius, Paul's centurion escort from Caesarea to Rome, was a member of the "Augustan Cohort" (*speira Sebaste*) (Acts 27:1).[43] It was almost certainly an auxiliary unit, as well. It is possible that its name was drawn from the city of Sebaste, an indication that the unit had been created there.[44] More likely, however, the name of the unit was the Greek equivalent of the Latin *cohors Augusta*. There were at least ten infantry cohorts with that name attested in the East, especially Syria, in the first century.[45] Regardless of the cohort's name or place of origin, it is not clear from Acts that the entire unit was stationed in Caesarea. The story claims only that Julius was present and available to escort the prisoner Paul.[46]

If the number of Roman soldiers in first-century Palestine was fairly small, the number of Roman colonists was even smaller – zero, in fact, in the lifetime of Jesus. Elsewhere in the Roman Empire (Spain, Gaul, North Africa, the Balkan coast, Greece, the southern part of Asia Minor), dozens of colonies and *municipia* had been founded by Julius Caesar and Augustus,[47] all serving as islands of Roman culture and agents of Romanization. The Levant, however, was not an area of focus of colonization efforts. The only colony in the Roman East at the time was at Berytus, planted by Augustus in 15 or 14 BCE.[48] No colonists would arrive in Palestine until two decades after Jesus' death.

JESUS AND THE CENTURION

In light of what we know about Roman troop deployments, there is little reason to believe that Roman soldiers were regularly stationed

---

[43] References to an infantry cohort and a cavalry unit in Acts 21–23 are presumably to the other aforementioned auxiliary forces.

[44] Saddington, *Development*, 50.

[45] Holder, *Studies*, 14–15, 23 n. 1–5; Saddington, *Development*, 172. Several *alae* also carried the name *Augusta*. An inscription in the Hauran suggests that one of the infantry cohorts was assigned to Agrippa II in the 80s CE; see discussion below.

[46] Speidel, "Roman Army in Judaea"; Saddington, "Development," 2417–2418; cf. M. H. Gracey, "The Armies of the Judaean Client Kings," in Freeman and Kennedy, *Defence*, vol. 1, 311–323, esp. 320 and the review of the history of one *cohors Augusta* in Michael P. Speidel, "The Roman Army in Arabia," in *ANRW* 2.8, 687–730, esp. 710–711.

[47] MacMullen, *Romanization*, 8–9, 32–33, 52–53, 94–95.

[48] Fergus Millar, "The Roman *Coloniae* of the Near East: A Study of Cultural Relations," in Heikki Solin and Mika Kajava, eds., *Roman Eastern Policy and Other Studies in Roman*

in first-century Galilee. The only case for a Roman presence hangs by the most slender of threads, the story of Jesus and the centurion at Capernaum (Matthew 8:5–13 and Luke 7:1–10).[49] In both versions of that story, presumably drawn from Q, Jesus enters the village and is approached by a gentile centurion whose servant is ill. Jesus offers to go to the centurion's house, but the officer protests that he is not worthy for Jesus to come under his roof. Instead, he expresses confidence that Jesus' word would be sufficient to heal his servant. When Jesus hears this, he marvels that he has not found such faith in Israel. He then heals the servant from a distance; the two apparently never meet. Each gospel adds its own redactional elements, but both share key emphases: the power and authority of Jesus, Israel's lack of a faithful response to Jesus, and Jesus' rewarding the faith of a gentile. The story is the only specific encounter between Jesus and a gentile in Galilee recorded in the New Testament.[50]

If the story has a historical basis, then soldiers stationed at Capernaum were led by a gentile officer. But does the pericope indicate that they were a Roman detachment? Probably not. Neither Matthew nor Luke identifies the centurion as a Roman; they portray him only as a gentile. The presence of a gentile soldier should come as no surprise, because we know that the Herodian kings employed them. Most famously, Herod the Great had foreign bodyguards (Gauls, Thracians, and Germans), as well as troops from Trachonitis and from a pagan city he founded, Sebaste.[51] After his death, Antipas may have acquired some of his gentile forces. In addition, Antipas's

---

History (Helsinki: Societas Scientiarum Fennica, 1990), 7–58; Millar, *RNE*, 36, 279; Isaac, *Limits*, 318–321. On the possible colonial status of Heliopolis near Berytus, see the studies by Millar.

[49] On Jesus and the centurion, see Chancey, *Myth* 101–102, 175–176 and Reed, *Archaeology*, 161–162. Scholars who have argued that the centurion is a Roman officer include Strange, "First-Century Galilee," 89–90; Kee, "Early Christianity," 18; Sawicki, *Crossing Galilee*, 183; Joel B. Green, *The Gospel of Luke* (Grand Rapids: William B. Eerdmans, 1997), 284–285; Thomas G. Long, *Matthew* (Louisville: Westminster John Knox Press, 1997), 89; Theodore W. Jennings, Jr. and Tat-Siong Benny Liew, "Mistaken Identities but Model Faith: Rereading the Centurion, the Chap, and the Christ in Matthew 8:5–13," *JBL* 123 (2004): 267–294.

[50] Jesus' other recorded encounters with gentiles occur outside Galilee (e.g., the Syro-Phoenician/Canaanite woman in the coastal region to the northwest [Mark 7:24–30/; Matt. 15:21–28], Pilate in Jerusalem).

[51] *War* 1.672, 2.58; *Ant.* 16.198–199, 266, 271; Gracey, "Armies," 312–313.

realm included not only Jewish Galilee but also Perea, which probably had a more mixed population[52] and could have provided him with pagan soldiers. It is also possible that Antipas occasionally recruited retired Roman officers, whether from the auxiliaries in Judea or the legions in Syria.

Furthermore, the term used in the gospels to identify the officer does not necessarily imply that he was the commander of a Roman detachment. English translations typically render the word "centurion," a Latin derivative with obvious Roman connotations. The Greek word in both versions of this pericope, however, is ἑκατόνταρχος. While it is sometimes used for Roman officers,[53] it also appears in reference to non-Romans. Most of Josephus's usages refer to Roman centurions, but others occur in his recounting of biblical stories, and in once case ἑκατοντάρχης is used for officers of the Jewish rebels.[54] In addition, the term appears frequently in the Septuagint, obviously in non-Roman contexts.[55]

Even if one were to argue that the term ἑκατόνταρχος reflected Roman-style military organization, that would still not show that the unit at Capernaum was Roman. Herod the Great had organized his troops along Roman lines, and it is highly likely that the Roman-educated Antipas did likewise.[56] The ἑκατόνταρχος at Capernaum could thus easily be one of Antipas's own officers.[57] This probability is strengthened all the more if the story in John 4:46–54, where Jesus

---

[52] Adam Lowry Porter stresses, however, that the Jewish population of Perea was sizable ("Transjordanian Jews in the Greco-Roman Period: A Literary-Historical Examination of Jewish Habitation East of the Jordan River from its Biblical Roots through the Bar-Kochba Revolt" [Ph. D. Dissertation, Duke University, 1999]).

[53] The Roman soldier at the foot of Jesus' cross is called a ἑκατόνταρχος in Matt. 27:54, a ἑκατοντάρχης in Luke 23:47, and a κεντυριων (a Latin loanword) in Mark 15:39.

[54] *Ant.* 6.40; 7.233, 368; 9.143, 148, 151, 156, and 188; for Jewish officers, *War* 2.578. See Karl Heinrich Rengstorf, ed., *A Complete Concordance to Flavius Josephus* (Leiden: E. J. Brill, 1975), vol. 2, 47–48.

[55] Ex. 18:21, 25; Num. 31:14, 48, 52, 54; Deut. 1:15; 1 Chron. 29:6, and elsewhere.

[56] Shatzman, *Armies*, 198–216; Keppie, "Army," 374; Gracey, "Armies," 314. In at least one case, Herod the Great employed a Roman officer (*War* 1.535). In *War* 2.52, 74, two of his officers have Latin names, though whether they are Romans or locals with Roman names is unclear.

[57] It is impossible to determine with certainty what type of officer the authors of Matthew and Luke had in mind when writing this story, or how their intended audiences understood the term ἑκατόνταρχος.

heals the son of a "royal official" (βασιλικός) from Capernaum, is based on a similar tradition.

There is no other evidence to which proponents of a Roman presence in Galilee in Jesus' lifetime might appeal, neither inscriptions nor passages in other ancient texts. Though some scholars have described Sepphoris as a Roman administrative and military center in this period,[58] Josephus provides no hint of such a role.[59] There were apparently no Roman troops at Sepphoris in 4 BCE when rebels raided the armory after Herod's death, and apparently none elsewhere in Galilee, since Varus had to bring down soldiers from Syria to quell the rebellions.[60] Nor, apparently, were Roman soldiers in Antipas's territory in the mid-30s CE when hostilities broke out between him and the Nabateans; the nearest forces, once again, were in Syria.[61]

Indeed, the stationing of Roman soldiers in the territory of a loyal client king like Antipas would have been somewhat unusual. Antipas and the emperor were on good terms.[62] The client king had been educated in Rome and probably had met Tiberius then. Josephus describes the two as friends.[63] When Agrippa I traveled to Rome to complain about Antipas, the emperor stood by Antipas.[64] Antipas was a key player in Roman diplomacy, participating in negotiations between the Parthians and the Romans.[65] When war broke out between Antipas and the Nabateans, Tiberius blamed Aretas, sending the general Vitellius to capture or kill him.[66] Antipas's status as a trusted figure in the emperor's court did not change until after Tiberius's death, when Agrippa convinced Caligula that Antipas was plotting against him.[67]

---

[58] See examples cited in my "Introduction."

[59] The piece of armor found at Sepphoris (part of a cuirass) tells us only that at some point a Roman had passed through the area, a fact none would dispute. On the armor, see James F. Strange, Dennis E. Groh, Thomas R. W. Longstaff and C. Thomas McCollough, "The University of South Florida Excavations at Sepphoris, Israel: Report of the Excavations: May 11 – July 14, 1998," at www.colby.edu/rel/archaeology/Sep98.html.

[60] *War* 2.56; *Ant.* 17.271, 288–289.

[61] *Ant.* 18.113–115.

[62] Morten Hørning Jensen discusses this material in "Josephus and Antipas: A Case Study on Josephus' Narratives on Herod Antipas," in Zuleika Rodgers, ed., *Making History: Josephus and Historical Method* (Leiden: E. J. Brill, 2005).

[63] *Ant.* 18.36–38.   [64] *War* 2.178.   [65] *Ant.* 18.101–105.

[66] *Ant.* 18.115.   [67] *Ant.* 18.247–252.

Client kingdoms were typically a source of manpower for the Romans, not additional territory for them to garrison.[68] Though Roman troops were occasionally assigned to such kingdoms if they faced internal or external threats, that situation was the exception, not the norm.[69] Thus it is not especially surprising to find an inscription from the mid-80s CE in the Hauran, part of the territory of Agrippa II, mentioning Lucius Obulnius, centurion of the cohort Augusta.[70] The area had not been entirely loyal to Agrippa in the Jewish Revolt, and the Romans may have sent troops to buttress him.[71]

For the troops at Capernaum to have been Roman, we would have to imagine a similar need for them – and there is none. We know of no serious threats to Antipas during Jesus' lifetime. His conflict with the Nabateans came in the mid-30s,[72] after Jesus' crucifixion, and those troubles apparently began and escalated without the Romans' awareness – a development difficult to explain if there were Romans at Capernaum. We might also ask why, assuming the Romans did place troops in Antipas's territory, they would choose Capernaum. The fishing village was located in the area where Galilee abutted Philip's territory, and the two client kings were not on bad terms. Perea, which bordered the Nabateans, would have been a more natural choice to receive troops if the Romans decided they were needed to safeguard Antipas from their other ally, Aretas. It has sometimes been suggested that Romans were needed at Capernaum to collect tolls on goods passing between Antipas's and Philip's territories, but such tolls would presumably have gone to the tetrarchs themselves, not to Rome.[73] Even if, however, one were to grant the unlikely prospect that Roman customs were

---

[68] Compare Jacobson, "Three Roman Client Kings," 26–27.

[69] David Braund, *Rome and the Friendly King: The Character of the Client Kingship* (London and Canberra: Croom Helm; New York: St. Martin's Press, 1984), 94; Edward N. Luttwak, *The Grand Strategy of the Roman Empire: From the First Century AD to the Third* (Baltimore and London: Johns Hopkins University Press, 1976), 20–40; Ball, *Rome*, 30.

[70] Speidel, "Roman Army in Judaea;" Gracey, "Armies," 320.

[71] Alternatively, the unit could have been from Agrippa's army, its name chosen to honor the emperor, but the possibility that it was Roman seems more likely since we know of Roman auxiliary units with similar names in the area.

[72] *Ant.* 18.109–115.

[73] Despite the frequency of scholarly references to Roman taxation of Galilee, we know little of it while Antipas reigned; direct Roman taxation apparently did not occur until after its

collected at this border, it would still strain credulity to suggest that Roman soldiers were required for the task. Why would the Romans need their own military personnel to collect taxes at the border of two client kings who were brothers, on generally amiable terms, and both unquestionably loyal to Rome? To do so would have been unnecessary and insulting.

In short, the gospels themselves do not present the centurion at Capernaum as the commander of Roman forces, and it is far more likely that he was a Herodian officer. In the absence of other evidence, this story is insufficient to demonstrate a Roman military presence in Galilee. Jesus' Galilee was not occupied by the Romans, and it is extremely unlikely that he encountered Romans soldiers there with any frequency.[74]

What, then, is one to make of one of the most famous of Jesus' sayings, his injunction that if one is commanded to go for one mile, he should go for two (Matt. 5:41)?[75] The passage has sometimes been interpreted as a reference to *angaria*, the Roman law that allowed soldiers to requisition transport.[76] The auxiliary forces in Judea may have used the right, and it is possible that Jesus and other Galileans heard of the practice from their southern neighbors or that they encountered it themselves when traveling to Judea. It is also possible that the saying simply did not originate with Jesus.

The lack of Roman troops in Galilee and the small number elsewhere in Palestine also has implications for how we interpret the story of the Gerasene/Gadarene demoniac (Mark 5:1–20/Matt. 8:28–34/Luke 8:26–39). In the pericope the demons cry out that they are so numerous that their name is "Legion." Jesus then exorcises them by sending them into a herd of swine, which casts itself into

---

incorporation into the province of Judea in 44 CE (Millar, *RNE*, 46–49; Schürer, *History*, vol. 1, 373–374).

[74] *Contra* Sawicki, *Crossing Galilee*, 141, there is no evidence that Roman soldiers retired to Galilee during the early first century.

[75] Jesus' advice to "go the extra mile" has sometimes been cited as a reference to Roman roads with Latin milestones (e.g., Robert W. Funk, *A Credible Jesus: Fragments of a Vision* [Santa Rosa: Polebridge Press, 2002], 99–100), but no such roads existed in Palestine in his lifetime.

[76] On *angaria*, see Isaac, *Limits*, 291–297.

the Sea of Galilee. John Dominic Crossan has shown how fruitful it is to interpret the name "Legion" as a symbolic reference to detested Roman forces. In this perspective, the story reflects the hostility of indigenous people toward their colonial occupiers, and Jesus' power over the demons symbolically represents the power of God's kingdom over that of Rome.[77] Any argument that this story originated in an occupied context, however, must reckon with the fact that the Roman presence in pre-70 CE Palestine was minimal.[78]

DIRECT ROMAN RULE AND THE OUTBREAK OF THE REVOLT

After the death of Agrippa I in 44 CE, the Romans assumed direct control of Galilee. They may have introduced administrative personnel into the region, but they probably relied mostly on local elites to manage their affairs. The single most famous inscription from Galilee may date to this time: a decree from Caesar prohibiting tomb robbery upon punishment of death.[79] The inscription is unusual in several respects. Unlike typical imperial edicts, it is in Greek, though it appears to have been translated from Latin. Though epigraphic and literary evidence demonstrates that laws against tomb spoliation were common, this is the only known inscription recording an imperial decree on the matter. Furthermore, its prescribed punishment, the death penalty, is harsher than

---

[77] Crossan, *Historical Jesus*, 313–318.

[78] David E. Aune suggests that the reference to pigs reflects awareness of the boar symbol on the emblem of the Legio X Fretensis, which was stationed in Syria before 70 CE and in Judea afterwards ("Jesus and the Romans in Galilee: Jews and Gentiles in the Decapolis," in Adela Yarbro Collins, ed., *Ancient and Modern Perspectives on the Bible and Culture: Essays in Honor of Hans Dieter Betz* [Atlanta: Scholars Press, 1998], 230–251).

[79] *SEG* 8.13, 13.596, 16.828, 20.452. The best recent review of the issues raised by this inscription is Adalberto Giovannini and Marguerite Hirot, "L'inscription de Nazareth: Nouvelle Interpétation," *ZPE* 124 (1999): 107–132; see also Craig Evans, *Jesus and the Ossuaries* (Waco: Baylor University Press, 2003), 35–37; Meyers and Strange, *Archaeology*, 83–84; J. N. Sevenster, *Do You Know Greek? How Much Greek Could the First Jewish Christians Have Known?* (Leiden: E. J. Brill, 1968), 117–121; Bruce Metzger, "The Nazareth Inscription Once Again," in E. E. Ellis and E. Grässer, eds., *Jesus und Paulus: Festschrift für Werner Georg Kümmel zum 70. Geburtstag* (Göttingen: Vandenhoeck & Ruprecht, 1975), 221–238; F. de Zulueta, "Violation of Sepulture in Palestine at the Beginning of the Christian Era," *JRS* 22 (1932): 184–197; and Frank E. Brown, "Violation of Sepulture in Palestine," *American Journal of Philology* 52 (1931): 1–29.

other such laws.[80] It is difficult to establish when it was erected; dates based on epigraphical grounds range from the mid-first century BCE to the second century CE. A new examination of its letters' morphology would be enormously helpful in this regard, particularly in light of the abundance of comparative material now available from Caesarea Maritima.

Most enigmatic of all are its origins. Franz Cumont found it in the Paris National Library, where it had long sat unnoticed, and published it in 1930.[81] It had been sent there from a private collection, and a brief notation in the inventory of that collection read only "Dalle de marbre envoyée de Nazareth en 1878." Because the inscription came from Nazareth, Cumont speculated that it must have been related to Jesus. He tentatively proposed that when the emperor heard reports of a Galilean troublemaker whose tomb was empty, he had issued this edict to squelch further robberies and rumors – a theory later popularized by F. F. Bruce.[82] Yet, as has often pointed out, the inscription's sparse accompanying documentation said only that it had been sent from Nazareth, not that it had been found there. Since Nazareth was heavily involved in the European antiquities trade, it would have been a natural place for the inscription's finder to take it. Theoretically, it could have come from anywhere; other proposed places of origin include Samaria[83] and Asia Minor.[84] It is more likely, however, that the inscription originated in or near Galilee than that it was discovered elsewhere and transported a long distance.

If the inscription is indeed from Galilee, we can probably rule out some of the earlier proposed dates and identify 44 CE, the beginning of direct Roman administration there, as a likely *terminus post quem*. The edict is best understood on its own simple terms: it is a law against grave robbery. With so many unanswered questions about it, any attempt to interpret it as a response to the story of

---

[80] Giovannini and Hirot, "L'inscription."

[81] Franz Cumont, "Un rescrit imperial sur la violation de sepulture," *Revue Historique 163* (1930): 241–266.

[82] F. F. Bruce, *New Testament History* (New York: Doubleday, 1969), 300–303. Erhard Grzybek and Marta Sordi revived this theory in "L'édit de Nazareth et la politique de Néron à l'égard des chrétiens," *ZPE* 120 (1998): 279–291.

[83] Zulueta, "Violation."   [84] Giovannini and Hirot, "L'inscription."

Jesus' empty tomb is far-fetched. Wherever and whenever it was posted, however, it advertised Rome's domination to all who saw it.

In the early or mid-50s, Palestine received its first Roman colony, a veteran settlement founded at the strategic site of Ptolemais. Aside from being an important port, Ptolemais connected the coastal route taken by soldiers marching south from Syria with the entrance to the Jezreel valley, a major east–west passage. The colony thus provided the Romans with a secure military base at an important junction as well as a reserve military force upon which to call, if necessary. Though there is some debate over which legions provided the settlers, they likely included the X Fretensis, VI Ferrata, and the XII Fulminata, all from the Syrian garrison.[85] The colonists took pride in their identity as Roman citizens. Two city coins depicted Nero ceremonially establishing the colony's boundaries by plowing with an ox; four legionary standards are visible in the scene's background.[86] Those coins, like others issued by Ptolemais for the next two centuries, had Latin inscriptions, in contrast to all of the city's preceding coinage, which had used Greek.[87] The colony also utilized Latin for other inscriptions. One shows that its territory was divided into *pagi*, the standard Roman administrative unit.[88] Another, a dedication to Nero, attests to the colony's usage of the Latin term *vici* for its villages Nea Come and Gedru. The number of colonists is difficult to estimate, but it could not have been very high – perhaps dozens, perhaps the low hundreds. Soon after the colony's foundation, the road connecting Ptolemais to Antioch was paved in the Roman fashion, as shown by a milestone dating to 56 CE.[89] This was not only the first Roman road in Palestine; it was also the earliest anywhere in the Near East.

---

[85] Shimon Applebaum, "The Roman Colony of Ptolemais-'Ake and its Territory," in *Judaea in Hellenistic and Roman Times: Historical and Archaeological Essays* (London: E. J. Brill, 1989), 70–96, esp. 85; *RPC*, vol. 1, 658; Millar, *RNE*, 65; Isaac, *Limits*, 322–323.

[86] *City-Coins*, 12; *RPC*, vol. 1, nos. 4749–4750. Such coins suggest that Nero established the colony, though Pliny places its foundation in Claudius's reign (*Natural History* 5.17.75).

[87] *City-Coins*, 13–15; Henri Seyrig, "Le monnayage de Ptolémais en Phénicie," *Revue Numismatique* (1962): 25–50.

[88] Michael Avi-Yonah, "Newly Discovered Latin and Greek Inscriptions," *QDAP* 12 (1946): 84–102, specifically 85–86, nos. 2–3; Applebaum, "Roman Colony," 70–75.

[89] R. G. Goodchild, "The Coast Road of Phoenicia and its Roman Milestones," *Berytus* 9 (1949): 91–127, esp. 112–113, 120 nos. 234A and 235; Isaac, *Limits*, 110.

Growing Jewish–Roman tensions erupted into widespread violence in 66 CE,[90] with initial hostilities occurring at Jerusalem and
Caesarea. The procurator Florus's few thousand auxiliary troops
proved inadequate to deal with the turmoil, forcing the Romans
once again to utilize their troops in Syria to deal with problems in
Judea. The war would bring a massive incursion by Roman soldiers
into Galilee and the rest of Palestine, and with it, a permanent
change in the ways in which Rome's eastern garrisons were
deployed.

To quell the rebellion, Cestius Gallus, legate of Syria, gathered his
forces at Antioch. His army included the XII Fulminata Legion, two
thousand soldiers from each of the other legions in Syria (the VI
Ferrata, X Fretensis, and perhaps the V Macedonica), ten auxiliary
units, and several thousand soldiers supplied by regional client kings
(Agrippa II, Antiochus of Commagene, Sohaemus of Emesa). As his
forces marched southwards along the coastal route to Ptolemais,
local gentiles joined them and swelled their numbers even further.[91]
The main target of Cestius Gallus was Jerusalem, but he did venture
into Galilee, pillaging the border town of Chabulon and other
nearby villages.[92] Later, soldiers from the XII legion entered Galilee
again, where Sepphoris gladly received them. After defeating rebel
forces at Asamon, a Galilean mountain, the soldiers rejoined the
main army at Caesarea.[93] Ultimately, Cestius Gallus suffered several
thousand casualties at Jerusalem and retreated to Syria.[94] After
describing Gallus's defeat, Josephus refers to an officer in charge
of forces in the Jezreel valley, but otherwise he provides no information about any Roman soldiers stationed in Galilee in the early
stages of the war.[95]

After the Gallus debacle, Nero appointed Vespasian, a veteran of
campaigns in Germany and Britain, to take charge of Roman efforts
against the Jews.[96] Vespasian, like his predecessor, gathered forces
at Antioch before marching to Ptolemais. His army included the V

---

[90] The activities of Roman troops in the revolt are summarized in Saddington, *Development*,
48, 101–103; Smallwood, *Jews*, 293–330. On the revolt in Galilee, see Horsley, *Galilee*,
76–88 and Chancey, *Myth*, 55–58.

[91] *War* 2.499–502; Saddington, *Development*, 101–102; Smallwood, *Jews*, 296.

[92] *War* 2.504–506.   [93] *War* 2.510–512; on Sepphoris's garrison, see *Life* 394.

[94] *War* 2.513–555.   [95] *Life* 115.   [96] *War* 3.1–5.

Macedonica and X Fretensis legions, twenty three additional cohorts, and several thousand troops from the client kings, including new troops sent by the Nabateans. When his son Titus arrived with the XV Apollonaris from Egypt, his forces numbered approximately 60,000 men.[97]

Vespasian was met at Ptolemais by a delegation from Sepphoris who requested that he assign a garrison to their city, as Cestius Gallus had. He responded by sending a thousand cavalry and six thousand infantry to the city.[98] Vespasian's main force attacked Gabara,[99] Japhia,[100] and Jotapata/Yodefat[101] before retiring for the winter. For that season, Vespasian initially quartered the V and X legions at Caesarea Maritima, though at least parts of these legions accompanied him later in the winter to Caesarea Philippi. The XV wintered at Scythopolis.[102] At winter's end, Vespasian reassembled his forces to march on the city of Tiberias, which he spared after the rebels abandoned it. He next seized Taricheae, executing some 1,200 Jews at the stadium and enslaving thousands more for Nero and Agrippa, according to Josephus.[103] The Roman army then defeated Jewish forces at Gamla,[104] Mt. Tabor,[105] and Gischala[106] before moving south to Jerusalem. At least some troops from the X Fretensis stayed behind to build a paved Roman road through the Jezreel, connecting Scythopolis to Ptolemais; a milestone dates it to 69/70 CE.[107]

At Jerusalem, the Romans were augmented further by the return of the XII Fulminata, the arrival of 2,000 men from the legions garrisoning Egypt, III Cyrenaica and XXII Deiotariana, more troops from client kings, and additional Syrian auxiliaries.[108] The Jewish rebels, divided amongst themselves, stood little chance against such an impressive assembly of forces, now led by Titus. Their inevitable defeat was accompanied by the even greater catastrophe of the destruction of the temple. Judaism would henceforth cease to be a sacrificial religion.

---

[97] *War* 3.29, 64–69.
[98] *War* 3.30–34, 59; cf. *Life* 411.
[99] *War* 3.132–134.
[100] *War* 3.289–306.
[101] *War* 3.141–288, 316–408.
[102] *War* 3.412–413, 443–444.
[103] *War* 3.445–505, 522–542.
[104] *War* 4.1–83.
[105] *War* 4.54–61.
[106] *War* 4.84–120.
[107] Benjamin Isaac and Israel Roll, *Roman Roads in Judaea I: The Legio–Scythopolis Road* (Oxford: BAR, 1982), 66 no. 1.
[108] *War* 5.40–47; Tacitus, *Histories* 5.1–2.

THE ARRIVAL OF THE ROMAN GARRISON

Previous outbreaks in Judea had led to only temporary increases in the Roman military presence. On this occasion, however, the Romans recognized that greater forces would be necessary to maintain stability and assigned the province to a governor of praetorian rank.[109] In contrast to the previous governors, who, as equestrians, typically controlled only auxiliary troops, the new governor received charge of a legion. The Legio X Fretensis, formerly part of the Syrian garrison, was selected to be Judea's legion,[110] an ironic choice, since its emblem was decorated with a boar, an unclean animal for Jews.[111] The legion and its auxiliary units made their main headquarters in devastated Jerusalem, and archaeological evidence of its activity has been found both there and at other Judean (that is, southern) sites.[112] The X Fretensis remained in Judea until the late third or early fourth century, when it moved to Aila, a port city on the Red Sea.[113] In addition, Vespasian settled eight hundred Roman veterans at Emmaus, only a few miles from Jerusalem[114] and elevated Caesarea to the status of a colony, as shown by inscriptions there recording its new name, Colonia Prima Flavia Augusta Caesarea.[115]

The other legions that had participated in the war were reassigned, two to Egypt and one to a station in northern Syria along the Euphrates.[116] The Syrian legion was soon supplemented by others, so that the bulk of Rome's eastern army continued to be grouped in that province.[117] The auxiliary troops raised in Caesarea and Sebaste that had been the primary Roman military presence in pre-war Judea were reassigned away from Palestine.[118]

---

[109] Smallwood, *Jews*, 331–334.   [110] *War* 7.1, 5, 17.
[111] *War* 7.17; Smallwood, *Jews*, 333.
[112] Isaac, *Limits*, 105–106, 427–430; Edward Dabrowa, "*Legio X Fretensis*," in Yann Le Bohec, ed., *Les Légions de Rome sous le Haut-Empire* (Lyon: Diffusion de Boccard, 2000), 317–325; Hillel Geva, "Jerusalem: The Roman Period," *NEAEHL*, vol. 2, 758–767.
[113] Smallwood, *Jews*, 534.
[114] *War* 7.217.
[115] Pliny the Elder, *Natural History*, 5.13.69; *GLI*, 6 and inscriptions nos. 3, 12, 24, 44, 122.
[116] *War* 7.5.
[117] L. J. F. Keppie, "The Legionary Garrison of Judaea under Hadrian," *Latomus* 32 (1973): 859–864; Keppie, "Legions"; Mor, "Roman Army"; Safrai, "Roman Army"; Isaac, *Limits*, 427–435.
[118] *Ant.* 19.366.

Roman forces in Judea were buttressed further in the second century by Hadrian, who established the Roman colony of Aelia Capitolina in Jerusalem. The colony was comprised primarily of veterans of the X Fretensis, though it is possible that some settlers came from other eastern legions.[119] Its formation, presumably interpreted by Jews as reducing the likelihood that their temple would be rebuilt, helped precipitate the Bar Kokhba revolt (132–135 CE).[120]

East of the Jordan, the extent of the Roman presence in the immediate aftermath of the first Jewish revolt is unclear. We have only hints. At Gerasa, one inscription from 75/76 CE honors M. Ulpius Trajan, the future emperor's father,[121] and another from 90/91 records the dedication of a theater by a Roman.[122] At Madytus in Asia Minor, an inscription refers to a Roman officer stationed in the "Decapolis of Syria" during Domitian's reign.[123]

By the early second century, Rome had absorbed the two remaining client kingdoms in the area, those of Agrippa II and of the Nabateans. After Agrippa's death, his territory was incorporated into the provinces of Syria and Judea. In 106, the Romans annexed the Nabatean territory, apparently without bloodshed. They reorganized it as the province of Arabia[124] and attached the old Decapolis cities of Gerasa and Philadelphia to it. The Nabatean royalist forces were converted into auxiliary troops,[125] and a Roman

---

[119] Benjamin Isaac, "Roman Colonies in Judaea: The Foundation of Aelia Capitolina," in *The Near East under Roman Rule* (Leiden: E. J. Brill, 1998), 87–108, esp. 100–103; Isaac, *Limits*, 323–325.

[120] At one time it was unclear whether the colony's foundation had preceded the revolt, as reported by Cassius Dio (69.12), or had followed it. The discovery of Aelia Capitolina's coins mixed with rebel coins in caves used by Jewish forces demonstrates that Cassius Dio was correct (Leo Mildenberg, *The Coinage of the Bar Kokhba War* [Aarau: Verlag Sauerländer, 1984], 100). See, however, Yoram Tsafrir's reservations in "Numismatics and the Foundation of Aelia Capitolina: A Critical Review," in Peter Schäfer, ed., *The Bar Kokhba War Reconsidered: New Perspectives on the Second Jewish Revolt against Rome* (Tübingen: Mohr Siebeck, 2003), 31–36.

[121] Pierre-Louis Gatier, "Governeurs et procurateurs à Gérasa," *Syria* 73 (1996): 47–56.

[122] *SEG* 27.1010.

[123] Benjamin Isaac, "The Decapolis in Syria: A Neglected Inscription," in *Near East*, 313–321.

[124] Cassius Dio 68.14.5; Millar, *RNE*, 92–95; G. W. Bowersock, *Roman Arabia* (Cambridge, Mass. and London: Harvard University Press, 1983), 81–82; and David Kennedy, *The Roman Army in Jordan* (London: Council for British Research in the Levant, 2000), 34–38.

[125] Millar, *RNE*, 92–93, 96–97; cf. G. W. Bowersock, "The Annexation and Initial Garrison of Arabia," *ZPE* 5 (1970): 37–47.

legion was sent to garrison the region. The VI Ferrata appears to have been briefly stationed there,[126] but it was soon replaced by the III Cyrenaica and its auxiliaries. Their principal base was at Bosra, though detachments were found elsewhere,[127] as abundant archaeological evidence shows.[128] In the late third and early fourth century, the III Cyrenaica was reinforced by a second legion, the IV Martia.[129]

Galilee, in contrast to Syria, the Transjordan, and geographical Judea, does not appear to have been occupied by Roman soldiers in the first decades after the temple's destruction. Perhaps the Romans felt that the combined might of the veteran colony at Ptolemais, the sympathetic city of Gaba (a military colony founded by Herod the Great),[130] and the nearby troops of Agrippa II (presumably converted to auxiliaries after his death) were sufficient to handle any minor troubles that erupted, and the X Fretensis could march north for major disturbances. By the early second century, however, circumstances had changed. In 115–117 CE, Jews revolted again, this time not in Palestine but in parts of the Diaspora.[131] The Romans decided to assign a second legion to the province of Judea, and this one was based in the Jezreel Valley and southern Galilee. The combined might of two legions and their auxiliaries were sufficient to handle most situations in Palestine, although the Bar Kokhba revolt required additional units.[132]

Exactly when the second legion arrived in Galilee is unknown, but it may have been as early as 117 CE. In that year, Hadrian named

---

[126] Inscriptions at Gerasa and Bosra attest to the presence of units of the VI Ferrata (Speidel, "Roman Army in Arabia," 698; Welles, "Inscriptions," 435 no. 171).

[127] Speidel, "Roman Army in Arabia;" Isaac, *Limits*, 118; Kennedy, *Roman Army*, 43–45.

[128] Bowersock, *Roman Arabia*, 105–109; Speidel, "Roman Army in Arabia"; Isaac, *Limits*, 122–128.

[129] Bowersock, *Roman Arabia*, 143–144; Speidel, "Roman Army in Arabia." The Legio I Parthica Philippiana may have been briefly been there in the mid-third century CE.

[130] *War* 3.36; *Ant.* 15.294; Chancey, *Myth*, 152–153.

[131] Smallwood, *Jews*, 389–427. Arguments that Galileans participated in this revolt are unpersuasive (*contra*, for example, Menahem Mor, "The Geographical Scope of the Bar Kokhba Revolt," in Schäfer, *Bar Kokhba War*, 107–131, esp. 127).

[132] Other forces involved in the Bar Kokhba war include a large number of auxiliary units, the Legio III Gallica, and detachments from at least five other legions. On the possible participation of the Legio XXII Deiotariana, see Smallwood, *Jews*, 428–466; L. J. F. Keppie, "The History and Disappearance of the Legion XXII Deiotariana," in *Legions and Veterans: Roman Army Papers 1971–2000* (Stuttgart: Franz Steiner Verlag, 2000), 225–232.

Quietus "consular legate" of Judea, a title that was normally reserved for governors who commanded more than one legion.[133] The earliest archaeological evidence is from only a few years later: a milestone recording the construction of the Sepphoris–Ptolemais road by the Legio II Traiana in 120 CE.[134] Another milestone, on the road connecting Sepphoris to Legio, dates to the same year. It, like most milestones in the area, does not identify the legion that erected it, but its wording is very close to that from the Ptolemais road, suggesting that it, too, was made by the II Traiana.[135]

The II Traiana had been redeployed to the Euphrates by 123 and was in Egypt c. 127.[136] It was replaced in Palestine by the Legio VI Ferrata and its auxiliaries, which were transferred from Arabia.[137] Exactly when the Legio VI Ferrata arrived is unclear, but it was probably responsible for roadwork in Galilee recorded on milestones dated to 129/130.[138] All that can be said with certainty is that it was in Palestine prior to the Bar Kokhba war in 132–135. Aside from occasional brief missions outside the province,[139] its units were based in Galilee and the Jezreel for a century or more. A coin of Damascus from the middle of the third century displays the legion's emblem, suggesting that at least part of it had been reassigned to Syria by that time.[140]

---

[133] Smallwood, *Jews*, 421–422; David L. Kennedy, "*Legio VI Ferrata:* The Annexation and Early Garrison of Arabia," *HSCP* 84 (1980): 283–309, esp. 307; Benjamin Isaac and Israel Roll, "Judaea in the Early Years of Hadrian's Reign," in Isaac, *Near East*, 182–197.

[134] Benjamin Isaac and Israel Roll, "Legio II Traiana in Judaea," in Isaac, *Near East*, 198–205. Note the challenge by J. R. Rea, "The Legio II Traiana in Judaea?" *ZPE* 38 (1980): 220–221 and Isaac and Roll's response in "Legio II Traiana in Judaea—A Reply," in Isaac, *Near East*, 208–210.

[135] On the 120 CE date, see Isaac and Roll, "Judaea," 184. Baruch Lifshitz had dated the milestone from the Sepphoris–Legio road to 130 CE ("Sur la date du transfert de la legio VI Ferrata en Palestine," *Latomus* 19 [1960]: 109–111).

[136] Isaac and Roll, "Judaea," 188. Smallwood notes the possibility that a detachment returned for the Bar Kokhba war (*Jews*, 447).

[137] Kennedy, "*Legio VI Ferrata.*"

[138] It is also possible that other units briefly passing through the region provided the labor; cf. Isaac and Roll, "Judea," 189–190.

[139] Smallwood, *Jews*, 481.

[140] Isaac, *Limits*, 139, 433 and Smallwood, *Jews*, 528–529. Hannah M. Cotton suggests, however, that the legion may have remained in northern Palestine beyond the mid-third century ("*Legio VI Ferrata,*" in Bohec, *Les Légions*, 351–357).

For the Bar Kokhba war, the two legions in Judea were joined
by a multitude of other Roman forces, including the III Gallica,
the III Cyrenaica, probably the XXII Deiotariana, and detachments from at least five other legions, and numerous auxiliary
units. This conflict seems to have been confined to Judea, and
there is no evidence of Galilean participation in it.¹⁴¹ After the
war, the Romans reduced their garrison in Judea back down to
two legions.

Rome's legions inscribed their presence on the land itself in the
form of new paved roads, constructed to facilitate troop move-
ments.¹⁴² The earlier roads in Palestine, the Ptolemais–Antioch
and Ptolemais–Scythopolis routes, were now integrated into a much
larger network. In addition to the roads of 120 CE connecting
Sepphoris with Ptolemais and Legio, roads were also built connecting Ptolemais with the Legio–Caesarea route at Gaba, as well as with
Tiberias and Bethsaida–Julias.¹⁴³ Further north, a road joined Paneas
with Tyre. Scythopolis was an important junction, with roads
shooting out in several directions. One connected it to Gerasa,¹⁴⁴
which itself became an important stop on the newly constructed
north–south Via Nova Traiana joining the Gulf of Aqaba to Bosra.¹⁴⁵
The road system in geographical Judea was even more intricate than
that in Galilee.¹⁴⁶

¹⁴¹ Smallwood, *Jews*, 428–466; on the Roman units involved, see 446–449 and Keppie,
    "History and Disappearance." Werner Eck and Gideon Foerster argue unpersuasively that
    a monumental inscription (which they associate with a long-gone arch) at Tel Shalem
    probably recorded a Roman military victory there ("Ein Triumphbogen im Tal von Beth
    Shean bei Tel Shalem," *JRA* 12 [1999]: 294–313). One does not have to postulate a battle to
    explain the presence of the inscription (Mor, "Geographical Scope" and Glen W. Bowersock,
    "The Tel Shalem Arch and P. Nahal Hever/Seiyal 8," in Schäfer, *Bar Kokhba War*, 171–180).
    Yuval Shahar's overview of cave hideouts in Galilee ("The Underground Hideouts in
    Galilee and their Historical Meaning," in Schäfer, *Bar Kokhba War*, 217–240) does not
    argue for their use in the Bar Kokhba revolt.
¹⁴² Isaac, *Limits*, 107–113; Isaac and Roll, *Roman Roads in Judaea I*; Mosche Fischer, Benjamin
    Isaac, and Israel Roll, *Roman Roads in Judaea II: The Jaffa–Jerusalem Roads* (Oxford: BAR,
    1996); Benjamin Isaac, "Milestones in Judaea: From Vespasian to Constantine," in Isaac,
    Near East, 48–68; Yoram Tsafrir, Leah Di Segni, and Judith Green, *Tabula Imperii
    Romani: Iudaea, Palaestina: Eretz Israel in the Hellenistic, Roman, and Byzantine Periods*
    (Jerusalem: Israel Academy of Sciences and Humanities, 1994); Chancey, *Myth*, 157–158.
¹⁴³ Fischer, Isaac, and Roll, *Roman Roads in Judaea II*, 4; Mordechai Aviam, "Two Roman
    Roads in the Galilee," in *Jews*, 133–138.
¹⁴⁴ Isaac and Roll, *Roman Roads in Judaea I*, 9.
¹⁴⁵ Ball, *Rome*, 67.   ¹⁴⁶ See sources already noted.

These roads transformed the landscape so that travelers could not help but recognize that even the pavement beneath their feet represented Roman military power and prowess. Each milestone bore a Latin inscription with the name and titles of the reigning emperor. Many had a second inscription in Greek indicating how far it was to the nearest city. Most people who used the roads, particularly nonsoldiers, would not have been able to read either the Latin or the Greek, but they would have understood the message of Roman imperial domination nonetheless. The milestones not only marked distances, they served to make sure that everyone knew just whose territory – Rome's – was being crossed. That the milestone inscriptions were made for such propagandistic purposes is strongly suggested by the fact that while they were frequently put up in densely populated areas, they were rarely erected in more sparsely settled areas.[147]

The VI Ferrata made its main headquarters at Legio,[148] built at the village of Kefar 'Otnay in the Jezreel Valley. Excavations of its ruins in the early twentieth century showed that the main part of the camp consisted of a small enclosure within a larger enclosure, with the whole complex large enough to house approximately a thousand men.[149] It had an amphitheater, probably built by soldiers for entertainment and training,[150] and an aqueduct system.[151] A discovery 2.5 kilometers away at Khirbet el Khazna reflects the soldiers' cultic practices: a white marble altar decorated with carvings of a legionary eagle, a Victory goddess standing on a globe, and two Latin inscriptions, one almost entirely gone but the other proclaiming a dedication to Serapis on behalf of the emperor by

[147] Isaac, *Limits*, 111–112; Millar, *RNE*, 108–109.

[148] Isaac, *Limits*, 432–433.

[149] G. Schumacher, *Tell El Mutesellim* (Leipzig, 1908), vol. 1, 188–190. Safrai provides the estimate of the camp's size ("Roman Army," 105).

[150] The poorly preserved structure is sometimes described as a theater, but the oval shape suggests it was an amphitheater (Schumacher, *Tell El Mutesellim*, vol. 1, 174, figure 259; Arthur Segal, *Theatres in Roman Palestine and Provincia Arabia* (Leiden: E. J. Brill, 1995), 52–53).

[151] Tsvika Tsuk, "An Aqueduct to Legio," in David Amit, Joseph Patrich, and Yizhar Hirschfeld, eds., *The Aqueducts of Israel* (Portsmouth, R. I.: Journal of Roman Archaeology, 2002), 409–411 and "The Aqueduct to Legio and the Location of the Camp of the VIth Roman Legion," *TA* 15–16 (1988–1989): 92–97.

a centurion.[152] Another Latin inscription, found closer to the main encampment, also comes from an altar.[153]

If Legio held only a thousand men, then several thousand others must have been assigned elsewhere in northern Palestine. Archaeological finds and rabbinic traditions shed some light on their deployment.[154] Soldiers of the VI Ferrata worked on the aqueduct at Caesarea Maritima under Hadrian,[155] and a fort at Beth Yerah was probably built by the unit.[156] A (second-century?) inscription records the presence of an auxiliary *ala* at Scythopolis.[157] Eleven kilometers southeast of Scythopolis, at Tel Shalem, a Roman fort stood for a few decades in the second century. Finds there include a Roman bath, two inscriptions (one Greek, the other the Latin inscription mentioned earlier), and forty-two fragments of a bronze statue of Emperor Hadrian.[158] A Latin inscription at Tiberias records the burial of a centurion from the VI Ferrata Legion;[159] a Greek one marks the interment of a centurion of the X Fretensis.[160] Another Greek inscription, this one on a sarcophagus found near Tiberias's city gate, identifies the interred as an army decurion, though it does not specify his unit.[161] Other Latin burial inscriptions of Roman soldiers have been found at Gabara,[162] Kefar Kanna and Acco.[163] Units also occasionally ventured further south; inscriptions

---

[152] Avi-Yonah, "Newly Discovered," 89–91 no. 6.

[153] Werner Eck and Yotam Tepper, "A Dedication to Silvanus near the Camp of the Legio VI Ferrata near Lajjun," *SCI* 20 (2001): 85–88; cf. Yotam Tepper, "Survey of the Legio Region," *HA* 115 (2003): 29-31.

[154] On the archaeological evidence, see Isaac, *Limits*, 427–435; Safrai, "Roman Army."

[155] *GLI*, 74 no. 29, 77 no. 54.

[156] B. Maisler, M. Stekelis, and M. Avi-Yonah, "The Excavations at Beth Yerah (Khirbet el-Kerak) 1944–1946," *IEJ* 2 (1952): 165–173, 218–229, esp. 222–223.

[157] Rosa Last and Alla Stein, "Ala Antiana in Scythopolis: A New Inscription from Beth-Shean," *ZPE* 81 (1990): 224–228.

[158] Isaac, *Limits*, 432; N. Tzori, "An Inscription of the Legio VI Ferrata from the Northern Jordan Valley," *IEJ* 21 (1971): 53–54; Eck and Foerster, "Ein Triumphbogen"; Bowersock, "Tel Shalem"; Gideon Foerster, "A Cuirassed Bronze Statue of Hadrian," *Atiqot* 17 (1985): 139–157.

[159] Avi-Yonah, "Newly Discovered," 91 no. 7.

[160] R. Cagnat and G. LaFaye, eds., *Inscriptiones Graecae ad Res Romanas Pertinenetes* (Paris: Academie des inscriptions et belles-lettres, 1906), vol. 3, no. 1204.

[161] Schwartz, *Imperialism*, 151.

[162] Avi-Yonah, "Newly Discovered," 88 no. 4.

[163] Mordechai Aviam, personal communication.

of the VI Ferrata have been found at Sebaste and as far away as Beth Govrin.[164] In contrast, the Romans do not appear to have ventured very far north into Upper Galilee; evidence of their presence there is minimal.[165]

Rabbinic sources refer often to encounters between Galilean Jews and Roman soldiers.[166] A few passages record the presence of a Roman camp overlooking Tiberias;[167] several others preserve memories of an incident in which soldiers from Sepphoris extinguished a fire at Shihin on the Sabbath.[168] A later tradition refers to a unit at Sepphoris in the fourth century.[169] It was said that no festival occurred at Sepphoris without the presence of a Roman patrol or at Tiberias without the presence of the governor or another official.[170]

The arrival of these soldiers greatly accelerated the Romanization of Galilee – an ironic fact, since very few of the soldiers themselves were from Rome or the Italian peninsula. By the early second century, legions throughout the empire were staffed mostly by non-Italians.[171] The VI Ferrata had been stationed in the eastern Mediterranean for decades, and its troops would have hailed from Asia Minor, Syria, and Arabia, though some may have been children

---

[164] Isaac, *Limits*, 431, 432.

[165] Roof tiles with the stamp of the Legio VI Ferrata were found at Horvat Hazon (map coordinates 187/257) and Kefar Hananya (D. Bahat, "A Roof Tile of the Legio VI Ferrata and Pottery Vessels from Horvat Hazon," *IEJ* 24 [1974]: 160–169; David Adan-Bayewitz, "Kefar Hananya 1986," *IEJ* 37 [1987]: 178–179). They do not necessarily reflect a Roman military presence at those sites, since the army could have sold tiles (cf. Ramsay MacMullen, *Soldier and Civilian in the Later Roman Empire* [Cambridge: Harvard University Press, 1963], 28–31).

[166] Aharon Oppenheimer, "Roman Rule and the Cities of the Galilee in Talmudic Literature," in Levine, *Galilee*, 115–139; Isaac, *Limits*, 115–118; Goodman, *State*, 141–146.

[167] *Y. Eruvin* 5, 22b; Safrai, "Roman Army," 105; Isaac, *Limits*, 435.

[168] *T. Shabbat* 13(14): 9; *m. Shabbat* 16:6; *b. Shabbat* 121a; *y. Shabbat* 16, 15d. Stuart S. Miller argues that the incident could have occurred any time between 70 CE and the mid-second century (*Studies in the History and Traditions of Sepphoris* [Leiden: E. J. Brill, 1984], 31–40). In light of what we know of Roman deployments, I would opt for the later end of that range, dating the fire no earlier than c. 120 CE (*contra* Safrai, "Roman Army," 105).

[169] *Y. Pesahim* 4, 31b; Miller, *Studies*, 40–45.

[170] *B. Shabbat* 145b; Oppenheimer, "Roman Rule," 122.

[171] The number of legionnaires recruited in Italy declined steadily after Augustus. By the time of Trajan, the proportion may have been as low as 21 percent, and after that it dropped further (Lawrence Keppie, *The Making of the Roman Army: From Republic to Empire* [Totowa, N. J.: Barnes & Noble Books, 1984], 180–181).

of earlier legionnaires recruited in Italy.[172] Regardless of his place of origin, though, every legionnaire was a Roman citizen, socialized in the ways and values of the Roman army and thus a bearer of Roman culture. Most soldiers in auxiliary cohorts and *alae* were not yet citizens, but they looked forward to citizenship as a reward at the end of their service. They, too, helped introduce Roman culture to Galilee on a new scale.

CONCLUSION

In the time of Jesus, there were no Roman army units, no colonists, and probably few, if any, Roman administrators in Galilee. Jesus did not frequently interact with Roman soldiers there, nor did Galilee suffer the political and economic consequences of actual occupation.[173] The overall Roman presence in Palestine was relatively small: an indeterminable number of administrators and a few thousand auxiliary soldiers, stationed primarily at Caesarea Maritima and Jerusalem.

The lack of a significant Roman presence in Galilee calls into question whether the term "colonial" is appropriate for understanding the political, social, and economic situation there before the early second century CE. We might likewise consider how helpful the language of "colony" and "colonial" is for describing pre-70 CE Judea, since most "Romans" in the region were recruited not from Rome, but from Palestine and, as auxiliaries, were not Roman citizens. At the very least, scholars who apply such terms to first-century Palestine should be explicit about what they mean (and do not mean) when using them.[174]

---

[172] J. F. Gilliam, "Romanization of the Greek East: The Role of the Army," in Gilliam, *Roman Army Papers* (Amsterdam: J. C. Gieben, 1986), 281–287.

[173] E. P. Sanders has effectively argued this point in "Jesus in Historical Context" and "Jesus' Galilee"; cf. Millar, *RNE*, 27–111; Schürer, *History*, vol. 1, 362–367; Lifshitz, "Légions romaines."

[174] For understandings of "colony," "colonial," and related terms, see Claire L. Lyons and John K. Papadopoulos, eds., *The Archaeology of Colonialism* (Los Angeles: Getty Research Institute, 2002). For a broader overview of the scholarly discourse on colonialism, postcolonialism, and imperialism, see Robert J. C. Young, *Postcolonialism: An Historical Introduction* (Oxford: Blackwell, 2001), 15–69.

By the early second century, circumstances were quite different. The entire area was now under direct Roman rule, the former client kingdoms split amongst the provinces of Syria, Arabia, and Judea, the latter renamed Syria Palaestina after the Bar Kokhba war. Roman legions were now found not only in Syria but also in Jerusalem and its environs, Galilee, and the Transjordan. Other changes were soon to follow.

CHAPTER 3

The introduction of Greco-Roman architecture

At the dawn of the Roman era, Hellenism had made only limited inroads into Galilean culture. Over the next few centuries, however, Hellenistic and Roman architecture became more common in Galilee and elsewhere in Palestine. In this chapter, I will focus on the construction activity in the early decades of Rome's rule, from 63 BCE to the first revolt in 66–70 CE, devoting special attention to the roles of the early Roman governors and the Herodian client kings, especially Herod the Great and Herod Antipas.

THE FIRST ROMANS

Whether Pompey and the early governor Gabinius initiated a wave of Roman construction in Palestine is unclear.[1] Pompey was well-known for sponsoring building projects elsewhere, such as a theater at Rome and the repair of the *bouleuterion* at Antioch. He had also founded and refounded numerous cities, especially in Asia Minor, though it is uncertain how much construction accompanied those foundations.[2] In Palestine, however, he refounded (*anaktizo*) only one city, Gadara, an action that likely did involve building, since Josephus specifically says that the city had been destroyed by Jewish forces.[3] Pompey also stripped other cities conquered by the Hasmoneans away from Jewish control. Josephus writes in *War* that Pompey "liberated from their rule all the towns . . . which they had not already razed to the ground, namely Hippos, Scythopolis,

---

[1] Isaac, *Limits*, 336–340.
[2] Roller, *Building Program*, 80–82; cf. William G. Fletcher, "The Pontic Cities of Pompey the Great," *Transactions and Proceedings of the American Philological Association* 79 (1939): 17–29.
[3] *War* 1.155.

Pella, Samaria, Jamnia, Marisa, Azotus, and Arethusa . . . Gaza, Joppa, Dora, and . . . Straton's Tower. All these towns he restored to their legitimate inhabitants and annexed to the province of Syria."[4] In *Antiquities*, Josephus adds Dium to this list.[5] The implication of these two passages is that, Gadara aside, any destruction at these cities had been minimal. Thus, the need for new building would also have been minimal.

The evidence for building activity by Gabinius is equally murky.[6] Josephus presents two lists of cities that received Gabinius's attention, lists that are similar, though not identical, to those of the cities that Pompey "liberated." In both, he writes that Gabinius went about the region "refounding" cities, again using the verb *anaktizo*. Though the verb can denote rebuilding, it is also subject to other interpretation. In the Roman period, as in the Hellenistic period, the refoundation of cities often as not involved only renaming and perhaps reorganization, not necessarily construction. Josephus says that a number of towns were resettled on Gabinius's orders.[7] Some of these cities, however, are the very ones that Josephus writes had already been restored to their inhabitants by Pompey, and one, Gamla, remained a Jewish village until its destruction in the first revolt. Noting these difficulties, Benjamin Isaac suggests that Josephus actually knew very little about the histories of these towns.[8]

Many cities honored Pompey and Gabinius for releasing them from Jewish rule, recording their gratitude on their coinage.[9] Gadara immediately adopted a new era, dating the city's foundation

---

[4] *War* 1.156.

[5] *Ant.* 14.75–76. Josephus's wording is made all the more curious by his earlier report that Pella had been razed by Jannaeus (*Ant.* 13.397). Archaeological evidence supports this report (Robert Houston Smith, *Pella of the Decapolis* [Wooster, Ohio: The College of Wooster, 1973], vol. I, 34–35; Robert H. Smith and Anthony W. McNicoll, "The 1982 and 1983 Seasons at Pella of the Decapolis," *BASOR Supplement* 24 [1985]: 21–50, esp. 29; cf. Ilan Shachar, "The Historical and Numismatic Significance of Alexander Jannaeus's Later Coinage as found in Archaeological Excavations," *PEQ* 136 [2004]: 5–33).

[6] *War* 1.165–166 and *Ant.* 14.88; on Gabinius, see Sherwin-White, *Roman Foreign Policy*, 271–279.

[7] That is, Scythopolis, Samaria, Anthedon, Apollonia, Jamnia, Raphia, Marisa, Adorus, Gamla, Azotus, and others.

[8] Isaac, *Limits*, 339.

[9] See my review of this material in "City Coins and Roman Power in Palestine: From Pompey to the Great Revolt," in Douglas R. Edwards, ed., *Religion and Society in Roman Palestine* (New York and London: Routledge Press, 2004), 103–112.

to Roman liberation; its coins from 64/63 BCE read "Year One of Rome."[10] Nysa-Scythopolis and Marisa soon adopted similar dating systems. In addition, the coins of Nysa-Scythopolis from the mid-first century BCE bear Gabinius's bust and show that the city renamed itself "Gabinia,"[11] and Marisa's coins from the same period bore the letters "GA," probably an abbreviation for a similar name.[12] Second- and third-century coinage of numerous other cities shows that at some point they, too, adopted the Pompeian era.[13] Cities that put such features on their coins were making strong statements that they (or, at least, their elites) identified themselves as Roman subjects and that their history began anew with their annexation by Rome.

Numismatic evidence and Josephus's remarks leave our questions about the extent of the construction activities of Pompey and Gabinius unanswered. Archaeological evidence provides little additional support for the idea that they began the architectural Romanization of the region. Though finds at Samaria, Azotus, and Scythopolis have been cited as possibly Gabinian,[14] very little can be traced with certainty to either him or Pompey – no buildings, no monuments, no Roman civic planning.[15]

HEROD THE GREAT: CLIENT OF THE ROMANS, PATRON OF GRECO-ROMAN CULTURE

A standard handbook on Roman architecture begins its discussion of the Eastern Mediterranean with Herod the Great.[16] This choice is certainly appropriate, since it was he, more so than Pompey or

---

[10] Spijkerman, *Coins*, 128–129, nos. 1–2.

[11] Rachel Barkay, "Coins of Roman Governors issued by Nysa-Scythopolis in the Late Republican Period," *INJ* 13 (1994–1999): 54–62.

[12] Shraga Qedar, "The Coins of Marisa: A New Mint," *INJ* 12 (1993): 27–33. In addition, Antioch's coins bore Gabinius's monogram (*RPC*, vol. 1, no. 4124), and second- and third-century coins of Canatha attest the name "Gabinia" (Barkay, "Coins" and "A New Coin Type of Dionysos from Canatha," *INJ* 11 [1990–1991]: 72–76).

[13] For example, Hippos, Philadelphia, Pella, Abila, Dium, Gerasa, Canatha, Gaba, Gaza, Dora, Apamea and Byblos (*RPC*, vol. 1, 672, 660–661, 676–677, 632, 647; Spijkerman, *Coins*, 316–317). Ptolemais adopted a similar system, dating its era to Julius Caesar's visit in 48/47 BCE (*RPC*, vol. 1, 658).

[14] Crowfoot, Kenyon, and Sukenik, *Buildings*, vol. 1, 31–32; Roller, *Building Program*, 81.

[15] Isaac, *Limits*, 339–340.

[16] J. B. Ward-Perkins, *Roman Imperial Architecture* (Middlesex: Penguin, 1981), 307–362.

Gabinius, who bore responsibility for bringing Roman culture to the region. His enthusiastic sponsorship of both Roman and Hellenistic architecture provided the example that his sons would follow.[17] A detailed description of his projects illustrates the extent of his impact and allows us to put into perspective the more meager activity that followed in Early Roman Galilee. It also provides an opportunity to discuss characteristic types of Hellenistic and Roman urban buildings.

Herod's visit to Rome in 40 BCE to seek Antony's support lasted only a week, but, as Duane W. Roller has commented, that week proved to be extraordinarily influential.[18] Roller's fascinating study shows the impact that this exposure to Roman culture had on Herod and, through him, on the whole Levant. When Herod arrived, Rome was a city at the initial stages of architectural renewal. Sulla, Pompey, and Julius Caesar had each sponsored the construction of new buildings, and the Rome of the monuments so well-known now was emerging. The previous decades had seen the rebuilding of the Capitoline Temple and the erection or renovation of numerous other basilicas, forums, and temples. Pompey's portico and theater (the latter, apparently the first permanent one in Rome) had been warmly received, and the foundations of another theater had already been laid. All of these new buildings, combined with the older assortment of temples and monuments, could not help but be impressive to a refugee who had been cast out from his own territory. Herod might have been powerless, but he knew where power lay, and discerning what the future held for his homeland could not have been difficult. Here at Rome, he perhaps saw a glimpse of the coming landscape of the Near East. By his next two visits, the first occurring between 19 and 16 BCE and the other in 12 BCE, Augustus's transformation of the city from one of bricks to

---

[17] On the Herodian dynasty, see Schürer, *History*, vol. 1, 287–483 and Nikos Kokkinos, *The Herodian Dynasty: Origins, Role in Society and Eclipse* (Sheffield: Sheffield Academic Press, 1998). On Herod's building projects, see Roller, *Building Program*; Peter Richardson, *Herod: King of the Jews and Friend of the Romans* (Columbia: University of South Carolina Press, 1996); Peter Richardson, *Building Jewish in the Roman East* (Waco: Baylor University Press, 2004), 225–240, 253–308.

[18] *War* 1.248–281, *Ant.* 14.330–380; Roller, *Building Program*, 16, 33–42.

one of marble would have been well underway – as were Herod's own building projects.[19]

After Herod returned to Palestine, he devoted much of the next three decades to sponsoring buildings that heightened the visibility of Hellenistic and Roman architecture and advertised his own wealth and generosity. He did not confine his attention to his own territory. Josephus's lengthy lists of Herod's donations show that they stretched from Judea up the Levantine coast, across Asia Minor, and into Greece.[20] Ascalon received baths, fountains, and peristyles; Tripoli, Damascus, and Ptolemais, gymnasia; Berytus and Tyre, stoas, temples, and agoras; Sidon and Damascus, theaters; Antioch, marble pavement and a lengthy colonnade; Rhodes, a rebuilt temple; Nikopolis, a number of public buildings. Inscriptions from Athens record both his gifts and his use of the titles *philoromaios*, "friend of the Romans," and *philocaesar*, "friend of Caesar."[21] He gave a sizable gift to the endowment of the Olympics, contributed to the taxation payments of towns in Asia Minor, and provided money to Cos for its *gymnasiarch*. Numerous other communities received land and corn. An inscription at Si'a, near Canatha, suggests that he donated to the temple of Baal Shamin.[22] Some of his gifts, such as the gymnasia, stoas, and agoras, had Hellenistic roots, while others, like the theaters and bathhouses, were Roman in style. While Herod may not deserve *all* of the credit for introducing such monumental architecture to the region, it seems obvious that he deserves *most* of it.[23]

Herod's accomplishments within his kingdom were no less impressive. Soon after Octavian emerged the victor of the Roman power struggles, Herod began work on a city honoring the new emperor. He built it at the site of the ancient city of Samaria and named it Sebaste, the Greek equivalent of Octavian's recently

[19] *Ant.* 16.6, 90–130; *War* 1.427, 452–455; Roller, *Building Program*, 66–75. Suetonius records Augustus's boast about turning Rome into a city of marble (*Augustus*, 28).

[20] *War* 1.422–425; *Ant.* 16.146–148; cf. Chancey, *Myth*, 50 n. 109; Richardson, *Herod*, 174–177; and Roller, *Building Program*, xii.

[21] For inscriptions in Palestine identifying Herod as *philocaesar*, see Richardson, *Herod*, 203–208 nos. 2, 6, 8).

[22] Richardson, *Herod*, 184, 206–207.

[23] Josephus does not identify who built a hippodrome he claims was in early first-century BCE Damascus (*Ant.* 13.389).

acquired title *Augustus*. Though several other cities eventually had similar names (Sebaste, Sebasteia, Sebastopolis), Herod's was the first. Many findings at Sebaste probably date back to the Herodian period: a temple (probably the one dedicated to Augustus and Roma that Josephus mentions), stadium, palace, streets aligned on a grid, and a colonnaded rectangular terrace that appears to have been a Roman-style forum, a highly unusual urban feature within Palestine. A basilica at the western end of the forum might also date to Herod, though some have dated it to the second century CE.[24]

Herod started work on another city honoring the emperor c. 22 BCE, calling it Caesarea.[25] Suetonius claims that each of Rome's client kings founded a city by that name, but Herod again appears to have been among the first.[26] He decided to make his new city a port, choosing the town of Straton's Tower as his site, even though the natural harbor there was hardly adequate for major shipping. Herod, however, was a man of no small ambition, and he set about to construct an artificial harbor on a scale that had never been done before. His engineers, probably aided by counterparts from Italy, devised two breakwater walls that together created a usable harbor.[27] They utilized the most advanced Roman technology, hydraulic concrete that would set underwater, imported in vast quantities from the Bay of Naples area.[28] The end-result of Herod's efforts was comparable in size to Athens's famous harbor, the Piraeus.[29] It was one of the earliest examples – perhaps *the* earliest – of a harbor

---

[24] *Ant.* 15.293, 296–298; *War* 1.403; Roller, *Building Program*, 209–212; James D. Purvis, "Samaria (City)," *ABD*, vol. 5, 915–921; Crowfoot, Kenyon, and Sukenik, *Buildings*, 41–50, 55–57, 62–67, 123–128; Clarence Stanley Fisher, "Architectural Remains," in George Andrew Reisner, Clarence Stanley Fisher, and David Gordon Lyon, *Harvard Excavations at Samaria: 1908–1910* (Cambridge: Harvard University Press, 1924), vol. 1, 91–223, esp. 211–219.

[25] Roller, *Building Program*, 89 n. 14.

[26] Suetonius, *Augustus*, 60; cf. David M. Jacobson, "Three Roman Client Kings: Herod of Judaea, Archelaus of Cappadocia and Juba of Mauretania," *PEQ* 133 (2001): 22–38, esp. 28–29.

[27] Avner Raban, "Caesarea: Maritime Caesarea," *NEAEHL*, vol. 1, 286–291; John Peter Oleson et al., *The Harbours of Caesarea Maritima*, 2 vols. (Oxford: BAR 1989, 1994); Avner Raban and Kenneth G. Holum, eds., *Caesarea Maritima: A Retrospective after Two Millenia* (Leiden: E. J. Brill, 1996).

[28] Roller, *Building Program*, 138; cf. *Ant.* 15.332.   [29] *Ant.* 15.332; cf. *War* 1.410.

built according to the methods described by the Roman architect Vitruvius.[30] Herod named his new port facilities Sebastos.[31]

Such an impressive harbor demanded an equally impressive city.[32] The buildings of Caesarea Maritima were, in Josephus's words, "constructed in a style worthy of the name which the city bore."[33] The city was organized on a grid, its streets intersecting at right angles and forming rectangular blocks to an extent very uncommon for its day. Its buildings included a theater, amphitheater, agoras, and, on a hill at the city's center, a temple to the emperor and Roma.[34] The temple's location ensured that it, along with the glistening white buildings that lined the shore, would be seen by visitors approaching by sea.[35] Herod placed a palace on a seaside cliff to maximize both its view and its visibility.[36] Fresh water was brought to the city by aqueduct, and seawater was utilized in an advanced underground sewage system. At the city's completion in 10 BCE, Herod instituted a series of quinquennial games that included the musical and athletic competitions and horse races typical of Greek festivals as well as animal shows and gladiatorial combat, forms of entertainment associated with the Romans.[37] These gladiatorial contests were the first ever held in the region. Ultimately, Caesarea was a state-of-the-art monument to the emperor, Rome, and Roman culture in general. It was also, of course, a monument to Herod himself.

---

[30] Raban, "Caesarea."

[31] *Ant.* 17.87; the name appears on coins of Agrippa I (*Treasury*, 232 no. 122) and on city coins issued c. 68 CE (*RPC*, vol. 1, nos. 4862–4864).

[32] Kenneth G. Holum, "Caesarea," *OEANE*, vol. 1, 399–404; Kenneth G. Holum, Avner Raban, et al., *NEAEHL*, "Caesarea," vol. 1, 270–291; Roller, *Building Program*, 133–144; Richardson, *City*, 104–129; Chancey, *Myth*, 144–148.

[33] *War* 1.415.

[34] Lisa C. Kahn, "King Herod's Temple of Roma and Augustus at Caesarea Maritima," in Raban and Holum, *Caesarea Maritima*, 130–145; Kenneth G. Holum and Avner Raban, "Caesarea: The Joint Expedition's Excavations, Excavations in the 1980s and 1990s, and Summary," *NEAEHL*, vol. 1, 282–285; Richardson, *City*, 112–114.

[35] *Ant.* 15.339; Richardson, *City*, 112–113.

[36] Richardson, *City*, 109, 115–117; Barbara Burrell, "Palace to Praetorium: The Romanization of Caesarea," in Raban and Holum, *Caesarea Maritima*, 228–250 and Kathryn Louise Gleason, "Rule and Spectacle: The Promontory Palace," in Raban and Holum, *Caesarea Maritima*, 208–227. Yosef Porat, however, argues that the palace dates to the early procurators, not Herod ("Caesarea – 1994–1999," *HA* 112 [2000]: 34–40).

[37] *War* 1.415, *Ant.* 16.136–149.

Herod honored his friends and patrons elsewhere in his kingdom, too. Buildings at Jerusalem and Jericho were named after the emperor and his supporter, Agrippa,[38] as was the city Anthedon, which became Agrippias.[39] Herod called a palace-fortress overlooking the Jerusalem temple Antonia, after his former patron.[40] He commemorated his own family members by naming the city of Antipatris for his father and Phasaelis for his brother.[41]

Jerusalem received considerable attention.[42] There, Herod constructed a lavish palace, an "amphitheater" nearby "out in the plain," and a theater.[43] The latter building, adorned with war trophies and inscriptions honoring Caesar, was used for wild animal fights and combat between criminals and animals, practices controversial to many Jerusalemites.[44] As he had at Caesarea, Herod instituted a set of quinquennial games. The city was also home to the best known of Herod's building projects, the Jewish temple. He expanded the entire precinct to twice its earlier size, making it the largest temple complex in the Mediterranean.[45] He surrounded the temple building itself with porticoes of marble columns;[46] the southernmost, with its four rows of 162 columns, outsized other basilical structures in the Roman world.[47] The renovations Herod began continued long his death, not reaching completion until 64 CE – just a few years before the building's destruction.

Other construction projects, especially fortresses and palaces, dotted Herod's kingdom.[48] He rebuilt several Hasmonean fortresses – Alexandreion, Hyrcania, Cypros, and Masada – and constructed

---

[38] *War* 1.402, 407.   [39] *War* 1.87, 118.   [40] *Ant.* 15.292.

[41] *War* 1. 417–418, *Ant.* 16.142–145.   [42] Levine, *Jerusalem*, 187–217.

[43] *Ant.* 15.268. On Josephus's possible misuse of the term "amphitheater," see discussion below.

[44] *Ant.* 15.267–279.

[45] Roller, *Building Program*, 176–178; Richardson, *City*, 138–146; *War* 1.401, 5.184–237; *Ant.* 15.380–425.

[46] *Ant.* 15.395, *War* 5.190–192; Roller, *Building Program*, 177.

[47] *Ant.* 15.411; Richardson, *City*, 141.

[48] For overviews, see Roller, *Building Program*, 125–238; Richardson, *Herod*, 197–202; Ehud Nezter, *The Palaces of the Hasmoneans and Herod the Great* (Jerusalem: Yad Ben-Zvi Press, Israel Exploration Society, 2001); Ehud Netzer, "Architecture in Palaestina Prior to and During the Days of Herod the Great," in Edmund Buchner et al., eds., *Akten des XIII internationalen Kongresses für klassische Archäologie: Berlin 1988* (Mainz: Verlag Philipp von

new ones at Machaerus and the immodestly named Herodium.[49] The round shape of the latter palace, which was intended to serve as his tomb, may have been inspired by reports of Augustus's mausoleum in Rome.[50] He also made the Hasmonean palace at Jericho his own, perhaps adding the amphitheater and a hippodrome there,[51] and he built a temple to the emperor at Paneas (later called Caesarea Philippi).[52]

The Roman-ness that so many of these buildings exhibited was strikingly new for the area. Theaters provide a prime example. None had appeared in Palestine in the Hellenistic era, despite their popularity elsewhere, but Herod built them at Caesarea, Jerusalem,[53] and Jericho.[54] He eschewed the features of the older Hellenistic-style theater, with its circular performance area at the bottom and seats wrapping around more than half of that circle. Instead, he constructed his theaters according to the Roman design, which was itself fairly recent. Each was shaped like a half-circle, with a decorative wall (*scaena frons*) stretched horizontally across the diameter. The performance area (*orchestra*) was thus itself approximately a half circle and smaller than the equivalent areas in Greek theaters. The upper seats (*summa cavea*) were supported by Roman barrel vaults, and halls (*vomitoria*) underneath the *summa cavea* led to the lower seats (*ima cavea*).[55] The construction

Zabern, 1990), 37–50; Mark Chancey and Adam Porter, "The Archaeology of Roman Palestine," *NEA* 64 (2001): 164–203, esp. 167–174.

[49] See Chancey and Porter, "Archaeology," 174 for other possible Herodian forts.

[50] *War* 1.419–421; *Ant.* 15.323–325, 17.196–199; Roller, *Building Program*, 72–73.

[51] Amphitheater: *War* 1.666; *Ant.* 17.161, 194; hippodrome: *War* 1.659, *Ant.* 17.175.

[52] *War* 1.404–406; *Ant.* 15.363–364. Scholars debate the temple's location: candidates include a building in front of the Pan grotto (Andrea M. Berlin, "Banias is Still the Best Candidate," *BAR* 29:5 [2003]: 22–24), another one hundred yards west (Ehud Netzer, "A Third Candidate: Another Building at Banias," *BAR* 29:5 [2003]: 25), and a tetrastyle structure excavated at Omrit (J. Andrew Overman, Jack Olive, and Michael Nelson, "Discovering Herod's Shrine to Augustus: Mystery Temple Found at Omrit," *BAR* 29:2 [2003]: 40–49, 67–68). John Francis Wilson reviews the possibilities in *Caesarea Philippi: Banias, The Lost City of Pan* (London and New York: I. B. Tauris, 2004), 14–16.

[53] *Ant.* 15.268.

[54] *Ant.* 17.161.

[55] On theater design, see Alexandra Retzleff, "Near Eastern Theatres in Late Antiquity," *Phoenix* 57 (2003): 115–138 and Bieber, *History*, 189.

of Herod's theaters was soon followed by that of several in the Nabatean kingdom.[56]

Amphitheaters and the combat sports for which they were designed were likewise Roman innovations. Some scholars have suggested that Josephus may have used the term "amphitheater" to refer to Hellenistic-style hippodromes, facilities built primarily for horse races, rather than to amphitheaters *per se*.[57] At Caesarea, they point to an elongated oblong structure found in the southern part of the city as a possible candidate for Herod's "amphitheater."[58] Similarly, some have argued that when Josephus mentioned an amphitheater at Jericho, he had in mind a long racecourse discovered there.[59] It is possible, however, that Josephus knew the difference between an amphitheater and a hippodrome and that the amphitheaters he mentions simply have not been discovered. If this is the case, and Herod's amphitheaters were, technically speaking, amphitheaters and not hippodromes, then Caesarea's may have been the first permanent one outside of Italy.[60]

---

[56] Segal, *Theatres*, 5–7.

[57] As used by archaeologists, the term "amphitheater" designates a circular or slightly oval entertainment building, as opposed to the semi-circular theater or the longer stadium or hippodrome. On amphitheaters as a Roman institution, see Ze'ev Weiss, "Adopting a Novelty: The Jews and the Roman Games in Palestine," in J. H. Humphrey, ed., *The Roman and Byzantine Near East* (Portsmouth, R. I.: Journal of Roman Archaeology, 1999), vol. 2, 23–50, esp. 39–40; Allison Futrell, *Blood in the Arena: The Spectacle of Roman Power* (Austin: University of Texas Press, 1997), 53–76; Thomas Wiedemann, *Emperors and Gladiators* (London and New York: Routledge, 1992), 41–46.

[58] On the possible ambiguity or misuse of the term "amphitheater" in antiquity, see Roller, *Building Program*, 140–141; Richardson, *Herod*, 186–187; Y. Porath, "Herod's 'amphitheatre' at Caesarea: a multipurpose entertainment building," in J. H. Humphrey, *The Roman and Byzantine Near East: Some Recent Archaeological Research* (Ann Arbor, Mich.: Journal of Roman Archaeology, 1995), 15–27, esp. 24–26 and Weiss, "Adopting," 34, 39. On the location of Caesarea's amphitheater, see Roller, *Building Program*, 140–141 and Porath, "Herod's 'amphitheatre.'"

[59] Rachel Hachlili, "Herodian Jericho," *OEANE*, vol. 3, 16–18; Netzer, *Palaces*, 64–67. Netzer has suggested that a building attached to the structure was used for receptions or as a gymnasium. Since there is no other evidence for gymnasia in Herod's territory, the latter option seems unlikely.

[60] A late source (the sixth-century CE writer Malalas in *Chronicle*, 216–217, 338, discussed by Roller, *Building Program*, 82) claims that Julius Caesar sponsored the construction of a theater, amphitheater, and baths at Antioch after his visit in 47 BCE. Isaac, however, strongly questions the reliability of Malalas, given how late he wrote (*Limits*, 335; cf. Roller, *Building Program*, 141).

Herod's palaces included Roman baths[61] – the first in Palestine and among the first anywhere in the eastern Mediterranean.[62] In contrast to earlier baths in the region, these used a hypocaust system to heat water for the *caldarium* (hot-room).[63] They sometimes included other rooms typical of the Roman bathhouse: the *apodyterium* (dressing room), *tepidarium* (warm room), and a *frigidarium* (cold room), the latter occasionally with a Jewish innovation, stairs that apparently allowed them to serve as ritual baths.

Herod also made extensive use of other Roman construction techniques. The warehouses at Caesarea, possibly built by him, utilized barrel vaults.[64] He often supplemented his typical style of masonry, courses of limestone ashlars dressed with bossing,[65] with techniques he would have encountered at Rome, *opus incertum* and *opus reticulatum*.[66] *Opus incertum* had been widely used in Italy for some time; *opus reticulatum*, only recently invented (late second century BCE), was used extensively by Augustus's builders.[67] Neither technique ever achieved much popularity in the eastern

---

[61] Baths have been found at Herodium, Jericho, Cypros, Machaerus, and Masada. In addition, excavators argue that a bathhouse found at Ramat Hanadiv, northeast of Caesarea, is Herodian (Yizhar Hirschfeld, "Architecture and Stratigraphy," 235–327 and Yizhar Hirschfeld, "General Discussion: Ramat Hanadiv in Context," 679–735, both in Yizhar Hirschfeld et al., eds., *Ramat Hanadiv Excavations* [Jerusalem: Israel Exploration Society, 2000]).

[62] Ronny Reich, "The Hot Bath-House (*balneum*), the Miqweh, and the Jewish Community in the Second Temple Period," *JJS* 39 (1988): 102–107; Ehud Netzer, "Herodian bathhouses," in J. De Laine and D. E. Mohnston, eds., *Roman Baths and Bathing* (Portsmouth, R. I.: Journal of Roman Archaeology, 1999), 45–55; Nielsen, *Thermae*, vol. 1, 93–99, 103–104.

[63] In the Roman hypocaust, heat from the furnace circulated between short pillars under the bath's floor (Fikret Yegül, *Baths and Bathing in Classical Antiquity* [New York: Architectural History Foundation; Cambridge and London: MIT Press, 1992], 356–362; Jean-Pierre Adam, *Roman Building: Materials and Techniques*, trans. Anthony Mathews [Bloomington and Indianapolis: Indiana University Press, 1994], 264–270).

[64] Holum and Raban, "Caesarea: The Joint Expedition's Excavations."

[65] With Herodian bossing, the outside face of each block was indented around its edges.

[66] Roller, *Building Program*, 99; Richardson, *Herod*, 183; for an example, see Nezter, *Palaces*, 48–63.

[67] With *opus incertum*, the facing of walls consisted of differently-shaped stones arranged in no discernible pattern. With *opus reticulatum*, the square faces of stones were arranged like diamonds, creating the visual impression of diagonal rows (Mario Torelli, "Innovations in Roman Construction Techniques between the First Century BC and the First Century AD," in Mario Torelli, *Studies in the Romanization of Italy*, ed. and trans. Helena Fracchia and Maurizio Gualtieri [Edmonton: University of Alberta Press, 1995], 212–245).

Mediterranean, and *opus reticulatum*, in particular, was uncommon outside of central Italy and Campania.[68] Their lack of diffusion makes Herod's employment of them all the more notable. The floors of some rooms in his mansions also reflected Roman tastes, with stone tiles of different colors (*opus sectile*).[69]

Herod was also fond of Roman-style decoration. The interior walls of his palaces were decorated with frescoes reminiscent of those found on the Italian peninsula. Stucco moldings covered walls, ceilings, and columns. Herod's mosaics, like contemporary ones in Italy, were made mostly of white tesserae, sometimes utilizing black or (less often) other colors to depict stripes, rosettes, or geometrical patterns. Unlike Italian art, however, Herod's decorations avoided representations of animals, people, and mythological figures.

Given Herod's penchant for construction, one might have expected him to lavish some of his gifts upon Galilee, where he had received his political start and support against Antigonus. This, however, does not seem to have been the case. Only once in Josephus do we find a reference to a Herodian building in Galilee, a royal palace (*basileion*) at Sepphoris raided by Judas the Galilean after Herod's death.[70] That structure has not yet been found, but given what we know of Herod's other palaces, it, too, probably incorporated Hellenistic and Roman construction techniques and stylistic features. Aside from this building and a military colony he established southwest of Galilee at Gaba,[71] however, Herod seems to have left the region almost wholly untouched. Its encounter with Roman architecture would not begin until the reign of his son, Antipas.

FROM ANTIPAS UNTIL THE WAR

When Antipas received Galilee, the region had only one major city, Sepphoris, which had suffered greatly after Judas the Galilean's

---

[68] Adam, *Roman Building*, 127–128; Torelli, "Innovations." Jacobson points out that *opus reticulatum* also appears in other client kingdoms ("Three Roman Client Kings," 28).

[69] *MPI*, 53 nos. 70, 69 nos. 94–95, 76–77 nos. 110–113, 109–110 nos. 181–183; on patterns see 150–151; Rachel Hachlili, *Ancient Jewish Art and Archaeology in the Land of Israel* (Leiden: E. J. Brill, 1988), 66–72.

[70] *Ant.* 17.271–272.   [71] *War* 3.36; *Ant.* 15.294.

assault.[72] Varus, Roman legate to Syria, had marched south to quell the Jewish uprisings, and Josephus claims that his troops had burned Sepphoris to the ground.[73] Antipas determined that he would resurrect the city as the "ornament of Galilee."[74] Though excavations have found no sign of widespread destruction, they have found considerable evidence of first-century construction.

Antipas had learned from watching his father how to flatter the emperor. He called his new Sepphoris Autocratoris,[75] a name with no known civic parallels. Some scholars have suggested that it indicated that the city had some degree of civic independence or "self-rule," but this seems unlikely. Cities with such independence (or pretensions of it) were called not "autocratoris" but "autonomous." *Autocrator*, however, was the Greek equivalent of the Latin *Imperator*, a title that Augustus received numerous times. Antipas thus appears to have named Sepphoris after an imperial title, just as his father had done with Caesarea and Sebaste. After Augustus died, Antipas built a wholly new city to honor Augustus's successor, Tiberias. At some point, he renamed the city of Betharamphtha in Perea as Julias, after Tiberius's mother and Augustus's wife.[76]

Antipas's work at Sepphoris and Tiberias apparently introduced Greco-Roman urban culture to Galilee for the first time, but to what extent? Sepphoris, in particular, has sometimes been represented in New Testament scholarship as the prototypical Roman city, but the actual evidence allows for only more modest interpretations. The first century was definitely a time of growth for the city, which spread from the acropolis eastwards onto a plateau. Its population, with perhaps 8,000–12,000 inhabitants, was large for the immediate region though not large by the standards of the

---

[72] *War* 2.56, *Ant.* 17.271–272.   [73] *War* 2.68, *Ant.* 17.289.

[74] *Ant.* 18.27; Chancey, *Myth*, 69–83; Chancey, "Cultural Milieu;" Chancey and Meyers, "How Jewish?"; Carol L. Meyers and Eric M. Meyers, "Sepphoris," *OEANE*, vol. 4, 527–536; Nagy, *Sepphoris*; E. Meyers, Netzer, and C. Meyers, *Sepphoris*; and Reed, *Archaeology*, 100–138.

[75] *Ant.* 18.27.

[76] *Ant.* 18.27; *War* 2.59, 168. Roller (*Building Program*, 183–184) suggests it was known as Livias until Augustus's death, when Livia Drusilla joined the Julian clan. It was definitely known as Livias in later centuries (Eusebius, *Onomasticon* 48.13–15); cf. footnote C at *Ant.* 18.27 in the Loeb edition.

empire as a whole.[77] Its streets were paved and at least two were built on a grid, though it did not yet have the main north–south cardo characteristic of Roman cities.[78] Numerous insulae have been excavated, and on the acropolis, a rectangular building with eight pools was found.[79] One of the city's aqueducts and the foundation of the basilical building on the eastern plateau date to the first century CE.[80]

Sepphoris's theater is particularly well-known among New Testament scholars. The archaeologists who discovered it on the northeastern side of the acropolis in 1931 thought that either Antipas or his father, Herod the Great, had built it.[81] In the 1980s, Richard A. Batey made the plausible suggestion that Antipas's exposure to theaters in Rome had prompted him to construct one of his own in his capital city. Batey raised the intriguing possibility that Jesus had attended Sepphoris's theater and watched performances of classical tragedies and comedies.[82] The image is evocative: Jesus, seated amongst the masses in the upper rows of the theater, looking down at the performers of a play of Sophocles or Euripides, soaking up the world of classical culture and mythology, the Beth Netofah valley as his backdrop. Perhaps it was there, Batey speculated, that Jesus had first learned the Greek word *hypocrite*, originally a theatrical term meaning "actor."[83] Perhaps his criticism of hypocrites who "disfigure/hide/disguise" (ἀφανίζουσιν) their faces (Matt. 6:16–18) alluded to the use of masks and paint by actors and mimes.

---

[77] Reed, *Archaeology*, 80; Crossan and Reed, *Excavating Jesus*, 81.

[78] C. Thomas McCollough and Douglas R. Edwards, "Transformations of Space: The Roman Road at Sepphoris," in Edwards and McCollough, *Archaeology*, 135–142.

[79] James F. Strange, "Six Campaigns at Sepphoris: The University of South Florida Excavations, 1983–1989," in Levine, *Galilee*, 339–356.

[80] James F. Strange, "The Eastern Basilical Building," in Nagy, *Sepphoris*, 117–121 and the numerous reports by James F. Strange, Dennis Groh Thomas R. W. Longstaff and C. Thomas McCollough at http://www.colby.edu/rel/archaeolo/Israel.htm; Tsvika Tsuk, "The Aqueducts to Sepphoris," in Amit, Patrich, and Hirschfeld, *Aqueducts*, 279–294.

[81] S. Yeivin, "Historical and Archaeological Notes," in Leroy Waterman, *Preliminary Report of the University of Michigan Excavations at Sepphoris, Palestine, in 1931* (Ann Arbor: University of Michigan Press, 1937), 17–34, esp. 29–30.

[82] Batey, "Jesus and the Theatre"; *Jesus and the Forgotten City*; "Sepphoris: An Urban Portrait of Jesus," *BAR* 18:3 (1992): 50–63.

[83] Matt. 6:2, 5, 16; 7:5; 15:7; 22:18; 23:13, 15, 23, 24, 27, 29, 51; Mark 7:6; Luke 6:42; 12:56; 13:15; Batey, "Jesus and the Theatre," 572 n. 1.

Not all archaeologists, however, have believed the theater existed in the early first century. Soon after the original excavation, W. F. Albright argued that a second- or third-century CE date was more in line with the majority of Palestine's theaters.[84] More recently, scholars have differed on the dating of pottery sherds found underneath the theater's stage and walls. James Strange and C. Thomas McCollough argue that the fragments are from the early first century.[85] Eric and Carol Meyers, Ehud Netzer, and Ze'ev Weiss date them to the late first century or later.[86] Publication of the fragments in question will enable other archaeologists to review the evidence and hopefully settle the debate.

Batey also portrayed the city as a Roman administrative headquarters and suggested that it, like Sebaste, Paneas, and Caesarea, would have had a temple to Roma and Augustus.[87] Yet, Josephus depicts the city as primarily Jewish, and he refers to no Romans there in the first century until the time of the revolt. No temple has been discovered, and there is little evidence of pagan cultic activity until the second century.

The presence in Galilee of a city like Sepphoris may explain why we find several references in the gospels to urban features: courts and prisons,[88] agoras,[89] wide streets (*plateias*) and narrow streets (*rumas*),[90] and gates, perhaps those in a city wall.[91] Sepphoris's acropolis was visible from the ridges that overlooked ancient Nazareth, and the two were in easy walking distance of each other. Batey has suggested that Antipas's construction projects could have provided employment for Jesus, whom Mark 6:3 identifies as a *tekton*, a word usually translated "carpenter" but with a range of meaning that

[84] W. F. Albright, review of Leroy Waterman, *Preliminary Report of the University of Michigan Excavations at Sepphoris, Palestine, in 1931*, in *Classical Weekly* 31 (1938): 148.

[85] Strange, "Six Campaigns," 342–343; C. Thomas McCollough, "The Roman Theater at Sepphoris: Monumental Statement of Polis at Play," unpublished paper presented at the ASOR/AAR/SBL Southeastern Regional Meeting, Knoxville, Tenn., March 1998.

[86] C. Meyers and E. M. Meyers, "Sepphoris," *OEANE*, vol. 4, 533; Ze'ev Weiss and Ehud Netzer, "Hellenistic and Roman Sepphoris: The Archaeological Evidence," in Nagy et al., *Sepphoris*, 29–37, esp. 32 and "Architectural Development of Sepphoris during the Roman and Byzantine Periods," in Edwards and McCollough, *Archaeology*, 117–130, esp. 122.

[87] Batey, *Jesus*, 56.

[88] Matt. 5:25/Luke 12:57–59.

[89] Matt. 11:16–17/Luke 7:32.

[90] Matt. 6:2, 5; 7:13; Luke 14:21.

[91] Matt. 7:13–14, Luke 13:23–24.

includes woodworker and stoneworker.[92] Whether Jesus ever worked there is, of course, impossible to determine (as Batey himself recognized). Despite Nazareth's proximity to the city, none of the gospels ever mentions it. Perhaps Jesus avoided it because he feared Antipas, particularly after the death of John the Baptist. Perhaps he was suspicious of Antipas's embrace of Roman culture, relatively limited though it was. Perhaps the city had poor relations with neighboring villages. Or, perhaps Jesus visited there regularly and we simply have no record of it. Whatever the case, it leaves us in the curious position of not knowing Jesus' stance towards the emergence of the first Greco-Roman city in Galilee.[93]

Sometime around 20 CE, Antipas founded a second city. With his inland territory, he did not have the option to build on the coast as his father had. He had, however, inherited a sizable lake, the Sea of Galilee, and it was on its western shore that he created Tiberias.[94] Like Autocratoris, less than twenty miles away, it was apparently the only city to bear its name; no other cities called Tiberias are known from the ancient world. The site chosen was located "in the best region of Galilee," as Josephus put it, overlooking the lake and not far from the hot springs at the village of Hammath. Unfortunately, it was atop an old graveyard, and many people refused to live there. Antipas had to forcibly settle the city, bringing in inhabitants from near and far. Josephus says that "no small contingent" of its population was Galilean, thus implying at the same time that a fair number of the new residents were not. Perhaps Antipas drew some of them from Perea, his other territory.

Tiberias was comparable in size to Sepphoris, with 6,000–12,000 inhabitants.[95] Less of it has been excavated than of Sepphoris,

---

[92] Batey, "'Is Not This the Carpenter,'" reviving a suggestion of Shirley Jackson Case, "Jesus and Sepphoris," *JBL* 45 (1926): 14–22.

[93] Willibald Bösen, *Galiläa als Lebensraum und Wirkungsfeld Jesu* (Basel and Vienna: Herder Freiburg, 1985), 69–75; Reed, *Archaeology*, 100–108.

[94] *Ant.* 18.36–38, *War* 2.168. The date of 20 CE is based on Antipas's coins that refer to the city and are dated to the 24th year of his reign, which began in 4 BCE (Yizhar Hirschfeld, "Tiberias," *OEANE*, vol. 5, 203–206 and James F. Strange, "Tiberias," *ABD*, vol. 6, 547). Michael Avi-Yonah argues for 18 CE, in "The Foundation of Tiberias," *IEJ* 1 (1950–1951): 160–169.

[95] Reed, *Archaeology*, 82. For overviews of Tiberias, see Hirschfeld, "Tiberias," *OEANE*, vol. 5, 203–206; Hirschfeld, "Tiberias," *NEAEHL*, vol. 4, 1464–1470; Gideon Foerster, "Tiberias,"

because it lies under the modern lakeside resort town of the same name. Josephus refers to a stadium at Tiberias, and archaeologists have recently discovered one,[96] but it is neither fully excavated nor published. He also mentions a palace with extravagant decorations that was built by the "tetrarch," which must mean Antipas.[97] The building was destroyed in the revolt because its artistic depictions of animals offended Jewish sensibilities, and it has never been found. Additional archaeological remains include a gate complex standing outside the ancient city, with a round tower bordering each side. The structure may have been a free-standing arch, serving more to signify Tiberias's status as a city than to defend it. It has usually been dated to Antipas's foundation of the city,[98] but this interpretation has been called into question. As Monika Bernett has pointed out, Josephus records that Vespasian tore down part of the southern wall to enable the entrance of his soldiers; the excavated gate, however, was quite broad – approximately 4.5 meters – more than wide enough for the passage of even heavy equipment. Furthermore, it does not even appear to have been connected to a city wall until the Late Byzantine period. Noting similarities to gates at Gerasa and Scythopolis, Bernett suggests that the excavated gate was built in the second century, not the first.[99]

Josephus was active in Tiberias during the revolt, and he mentions it frequently in *Life* and *War*. Furthermore, Tiberias was the home of Justus, who wrote a history of the revolt that was harshly critical of Josephus. Josephus devotes much of his autobiography to a refutation of Justus's charges, and the result is that we have a

---

NEAEHL, vol. 4, 1173–1176; Gideon Foerster, "Tiberias: Excavations in the South of the City," *NEAEHL*, vol. 4, 1470–1473; Strange, "Tiberias," 547–549; and Tessa Rajak, "Justus of Tiberias," *Classical Quarterly* 23 (1973): 345–368; Yizhar Hirschfeld, "Excavations at Tiberias Reveal Remains of Church and Possibly Theater," *BA* 54 (1991): 170–171.

[96] *Life* 331, *War* 2.618; no author, "Roman Stadium Found in Tiberias," *Jerusalem Post*, June 17, 2002.

[97] *Life* 65, 68. Josephus cannot have had Agrippa I or II in mind, since both were kings, not tetrarchs.

[98] For example, Yizhar Hirschfeld, *A Guide to Antiquity Sites in Tiberias* (Jerusalem: Israel Antiquities Authority, 1992), 25–26; Hirschfeld, "Tiberias," *OEANE*.

[99] Monika Bernett, "Der Kaiserkult als teil der Politischen Geschichte Iudeas unter den Herodianern und Roemern (30 v. – 66n. Chr.)" (Habilitationsschrift, Munich 2002), 202. I am greatly indebted to Monika Bernett and Rami Arav for their help in understanding this gate.

glimpse into the city's life that would have eluded us otherwise.[100] From Tiberias's earliest years, at least one office, the market over-seer, was known as the *agoranomos*, a traditional Greek title already used in other cities in Palestine and across the eastern Mediterra-nean.[101] Among the first at Tiberias to hold that office, appointed by Antipas himself, was Agrippa I, the future ruler of Palestine.[102] Two lead market weights, one from Antipas's reign (c. 31 CE) and the other from that of Agrippa II, further confirm the use of the title *agoranomos*.[103] Josephus also provides us with considerable detail about Tiberias's government. At the time of the revolt, it resembled that of an eastern Hellenistic (not western Roman) city, with ten *protoi*,[104] a *boule* of six hundred men,[105] and public assemblies to address serious issues. These assemblies met sometimes in the *pro-seuche*[106] and sometimes in the stadium, the latter large enough to hold thousands.[107]

The evidence we have for Tiberias exemplifies the methodological issues facing anyone trying to understand the Galilean context of Jesus. Almost all of our information comes from after Jesus' lifetime, though sometimes only by a few decades. Only the palace can be associated with certainty with Antipas. Though the other buildings could have been built by him, it is just as possible that they were constructed later.

Structures elsewhere in Galilee are equally difficult to date and identify. Underneath the fourth-century synagogue at Hammath Tiberias, famous for its mosaic of the twelve astrological signs,

---

[100] Rajak, "Justus."

[101] In addition to the Hellenistic-era examples mentioned in Chapter One, note a first-century CE weight from Tyre (Douglas R. Edwards and H. J. Katzenstein, "Tyre [Place]," *ABD*, vol. 6, 686–692); and two weights at Paneas, probably second-century CE and the other probably later (*SEG* 45.1941–1942). Richardson describes two from the period of Herod the Great (*Herod*, 204). For overviews of *agoranomoi* in Palestine, see Frederic Manns, *Some Weights of the Hellenistic, Roman and Byzantine Periods*, trans. Godfrey Kloetzli (Jerusalem: Franciscan Printing Press, 1984), 41–48 and Sperber, *City*, 32–47.

[102] *Ant.* 18.149.

[103] Shraga Qedar, "Two Lead Weights of Herod Antipas and Agrippa II and the Early History of Tiberias," *INJ* 9 (1986–1987): 29–35. The second weight mentioned above does not name a city, but probably comes from Tiberias, as does, perhaps, another weight discussed by Alla Kushnir-Stein, "Two Inscribed Lead Weights of Agrippa II," *ZPE* 141 (2002): 295–300; cf. *SEG* 42.1473, 43.1076.

[104] *Life* 69, 296; cf. *War* 2.639.   [105] *War* 2.639, 641; *Life* 64, 169, 279, 284.

[106] *Life* 277–280.   [107] *Life* 92, 331; *War* 2.618, 3.539–542.

archaeologists found the remnants of a rectangular columned build-ing from the first or second century. Noting the building's design, columns, and nearby water reservoirs and conduits, they suggested that the building was a gymnasium or palaestra. Because of the later synagogue, however, the structure was only partially excavated, and the full extent of its walls is not clear. The primary excavator acknowledged that it was difficult to determine the building's pur-pose, noting that it was also possible that it was an earlier syna-gogue.[108] A rectangular building at Magdala/Taricheae decorated with Doric columns was initially identified as a "mini-synagogue," but its purpose, too, remains unclear, and it has also been interpreted as a springhouse.[109] Regardless of how these buildings were used, their basic shape and use of columns reflect Greco-Roman influence.

At Beth She'arim, as at Sepphoris, remains from a first-century CE basilical building have been found underneath a later struc-ture.[110] Basilicas, rectangular buildings with interior rows of columns that formed long aisles, were a distinctly Roman architec-tural form. They were used for a wide range of purposes, from civil administration, legal proceedings, and merchant transactions. Un-fortunately, not enough evidence has survived from the earliest phase of either the Beth She'arim or Sepphoris building to determine their functions.[111]

We know from Josephus that the stadium at Tiberias was not the only example of sports architecture in Galilee; he also refers to a revolt-era hippodrome at Taricheae. This hippodrome, like

---

[108] Moshe Dothan, *Hammath Tiberias: Early Synagogues and the Hellenistic and Roman Remains* (Jerusalem: Israel Exploration Society, 1983), 15–19.

[109] Virgilio C. Corbo, "Scavi archeologici Magdala, 1971–1973," *LA* 24 (1974): 19–37; Morde-chai Aviam, "Magdala," *OEANE*, vol. 3, 399–400. E. Netzer interprets it as a springhouse in "The Synagogues from the Second Temple Period according to Archaeological Finds and in Light of the Literary Sources," in G. Claudio Bottini, Leah Di Segni and L. Daniel Chrupcala, eds., *One Land – Many Cultures: Archaeological Studies in Honour of Stanislao Loffreda* (Jerusalem: Franciscan Printing Press, 2003), 277–285; cf. Jürgen Zangenberg, "Magdala – Reich an Fisch und reich durch Fisch," in Gabriele Faßbeck, Sandra Fortner, Andrea Rottloff, and Jürgen Zangenberg, eds., *Leben am See Gennesaret* (Mainz am Rhein: Phillip von Zabern, 2003), 93–98, esp. 96, 98.

[110] *Beth She'arim*, vol. 1, 17.

[111] Sperber, *City*, 73–76. Note also the presence of a basilical structure at Gamla that may pre-date those of Galilee (Danny Syon and Zvi Yavor, "Gamla 1997–2000," *HA* 114 [2002]: 2–4).

Tiberias's stadium, was sometimes used for public assemblies.[112] Presumably, the same types of athletic competitions occurred in these buildings as took place in others in the Roman world: horse-races in the hippodromes and footraces and similar games in the stadium. There is no evidence at all of gladiator shows in these structures or anywhere else in first-century Galilee, just as there is no evidence for an amphitheater, the building where the bloody contests usually took place. It seems more than a stretch to argue, as one scholar has, that Jesus' disciple Simon grew up watching combat sports in the stadium at Tiberias, and, even less likely that this childhood interest lies behind his supposedly mercurial disposition and his nickname, Peter.[113]

No pagan shrine has yet been discovered from first-century Galilee,[114] but some have argued that Bethsaida, located within walking distance in the tetrarch Philip's territory, was home to a temple of the imperial cult.[115] The city is mentioned several times in the gospels, as the site where Jesus healed a blind man;[116] where he multiplied the loaves;[117] as the object of his rebuke;[118] and as the home of Philip, Andrew, and John.[119] If an imperial temple stood there, then Jesus' first followers would definitely have had some exposure to this key aspect of Roman culture.[120]

The exact location of Bethsaida is a matter of considerable dispute, but recent attention has centered on the site of et-Tell.[121] The excavation team there has proposed that a rectangular,

[112] *War* 2.599, *Life* 132–133.

[113] H. A. Harris, *Greek Athletics and the Jews* (Cardiff: University of Wales Press, 1976), 106.

[114] Note, however the Early Roman remains of a temple at Jebel Bilat in southern Lebanon (Aviam, "Borders," esp. 14).

[115] Though John (1:43–44; 12:21) and Ptolemy (*Geography* 5.71) regarded Bethsaida as part of Galilee, Josephus apparently did not (*War* 2.168, 2.252, *Ant.* 20.159; cf. *Ant.* 18.28, *Life* 399). The city passed to the province of Syria after Philip's death, and in 54 CE, it was given to Agrippa II (*War* 2.252, *Ant.* 20.159).

[116] Mark 8:22–26.

[117] Luke 9:10–17.

[118] Matt. 11:21–24/Luke 10:13–16.

[119] John 1:44, 12:21. In contrast, Mark 1:29 reports that James and John came from Capernaum.

[120] Whether Jesus was familiar with the building depends in part on the date of his death.

[121] Rami Arav, Richard A. Freund, and John F. Shroder, Jr., "Bethsaida Rediscovered," *BAR* 26:1 (2000): 44–56; Rami Arav, "Bethsaida," *OEANE*, vol. 1, 302–305; John F. Shroder, Jr.

columned, basalt building was an imperial shrine built by Philip.[122] Its different sections, they argue, correspond to the main parts of a typical Roman temple, with a porch, an approaching hall (*pronaos*), a main room (*naos*), and a room at the rear (*opisthodomous*).

Yet, in several respects, the building bears little resemblance to other temples in the Roman East. Those temples, particularly those that were the main ones in their cities, were often situated within a larger precinct, atop a large platform, or inside an enclosure wall, with a sizable ramp or flight of stairs leading up to their porch.[123] This structure, however, had none of those characteristics; in fact, it does not even appear to have had a paved floor.[124] Nor, actually, is its floor plan typical.[125] Furthermore, the fieldstones and slabs making up its walls[126] are quite different from the elegant courses of dressed ashlars in the imperial temples built by Philip's father, Herod.

Proponents of the identification of the building as a temple point for support to a small gray figurine found nearby that depicts a woman with curly, veiled hair – characteristics, they argue, that identify the woman as Augustus's wife, Julia.[127] The presence of

and Moshe Inbar, "Geological and Geographic Background to the Bethsaida Excavations," in Rami Arav and Richard A. Freund, eds., *Bethsaida: A City by the North Shore of the Sea of Galilee* (Kirksville, Mo.: Thomas Jefferson University Press, 1995), vol. 1, 65–98; James F. Strange, "Beth-saida," *ABD*, vol. 1, 692–693; and Chancey, *Myth*, 107 n. 243. My understanding of the issues regarding et-Tell was greatly enriched by conversations with R. Steven Notley.

[122] Rami Arav, "Bethsaida Excavations: Preliminary Report, 1994–1996," 3–113, esp. 19–24, in Rami Arav and Richard A. Freund, eds., *Bethsaida: A City by the North Shore of the Sea of Galilee* (Kirksville, Mo.: Truman State University Press, 1999), vol. 2; Rami Arav, "An Incense Shovel from Bethsaida," *BAR* 23:1 (1997): 32; Arav, Freund, and Shroder, "Bethsaida Rediscovered"; Fred Strickert, *Bethsaida: Home of the Apostles* (Collegeville, Minn: Liturgical Press, 1989), 103–105.

[123] Ball, *Rome*, 317–356.

[124] Arav carefully notes some of these objections in "Bethsaida Excavations," 23–24.

[125] Compare the floor plans in Ball, *Rome*, 317–356. Though the building appears to be different from most imperial temples, its basic rectangular shape is similar to ones at Messina and Ancyra (Heidi Hänlein-Schäfer, *Veneratio Augusti: Eine Studie zu den Tempeln des ersten römischen Kaisers* [Rome: Giorgio Bretschneider Editore, 1985], plates 30 and 40).

[126] Arav, "Bethsaida Excavations," 19; cf. Map no. 2 on the CD-ROM accompanying Arav, *Bethsaida*, vol. 2.

[127] Rami Arav, "Bethsaida Excavations: Preliminary Report, 1987–1993," in *Bethsaida*, vol. 1, 3–64, esp. 21; Strickert, *Bethsaida*, 106. Aside from the hairstyle, this figurine appears

a figurine of Julia would be significant, since Philip renamed Bethsaida Julias. Though Josephus says he named the city after Augustus's daughter Julia,[128] the excavators note that she had been disgraced in 2 BCE and suggest that Philip named it after the emperor's wife instead – thus the potential relevance of the figurine. The latter Julia died in 29 CE, and Philip honored her on his coins the following year. The city could have been renamed in her memory.[129] Yet whether the figurine is, in fact, Augustus's wife Julia is uncertain. Though she was often depicted with such hair and a veil, neither feature was unique to her.[130] The figurine could just as easily have been of someone else – or of no one in particular.

A bronze incense shovel, found nearby in a first-century CE refuse pit, has also been cited as strong evidence of emperor worship.[131] The responsibility for the association of such shovels with emperor worship lies partly with the great Yigael Yadin, who found similar shovels in Bar Kokhba period caves near the Dead Sea. Yadin claimed that other shovels had been found in "centers of pagan worship and in stations of the Roman Legions and Auxilia," but his own inventory of parallels does not support this

---

similar to a Hellenistic-period one at Yoqne'am (Renate Rosenthal–Heginbottom, "Stamped Jar Handles and Terracotta Fragments," in A. Ben-Tor, M. Avissar, Y. Portugali, et al., *Yoqen'am I: The Late Periods* [Jerusalem: Israel Exploration Society, 1996], 60–65, esp. 65).

[128] *Ant.* 18.28, *War* 2.168.

[129] John T. Greene, "The Honorific Naming of Bethsaida-Julias," in Arav and Freund, *Bethsaida*, vol. 2, 333–346; Mark D. Smith, "A Tale of Two Julias: Julia, Julias, and Josephus," in Arav and Freund, *Bethsaida*, vol. 2, 333–346; Strickert, *Bethsaida*, 91–107; Fred Strickert, "The Coins of Philip," in Arav and Freund, eds., *Bethsaida*, vol. 1, 165–189, esp. 181–184; *Treasury*, 229 no. 106.

[130] On Livia's hairstyles, see Elizabeth Bartman, *Portraits of Livia: Imaging the Imperial Woman in Augustan Rome* (Cambridge: Cambridge University Press, 1999), 5, 32–39; on the veil, see 41, 44. The depiction of the figurine in Arav, "Bethsaida Preliminary Report, 1987–1993," 21 suggests that the curly hair was divided into segments, a characteristic shared by only a minority of Livia depictions (e.g., Bartman's discussion of the "Diva Augusta" type in *Portraits*, 144–145.) The combination of the veil and the segmented, curly hair appears even rarer; for a possible parallel, see Rolf Winkes, *Livia: Octavia Julia* (Louvain-La-Neuve: Université Catholique de Louvain; Providence: Brown University, 1995), 132 no. 56.

[131] Strickert, *Bethsaida*, 105; Arav, "Bethsaida Excavations," vol. 2, 22; Arav, "Bethsaida Preliminary Report, 1994–1996," 22; Arav, "Incense Shovel"; Arav, Freund, Shroder, "Bethsaida Rediscovered," 56; and especially Richard A. Freund, "The Incense Shovel of Bethsaida and Synagogue Iconography in Late Antiquity," in *Bethsaida*, vol. 2, 413–460.

contention.[132] The reality is that of the several dozen known bronze shovels, few have been recovered in controlled archaeological contexts.[133] Their exact provenances and functions are largely unknown. Not a single one is recorded as having been unearthed at a temple of the emperor cult. Only one is known with certainty to have been discovered in a cultic context, a votive deposit underneath a Hellenistic-period temple at Beersheba in Judea.[134] The name "Serapis" on the handle of another also implies a cultic function.[135]

Incense was, of course, offered to the emperor and to other deities,[136] but this fact alone does not prove that incense shovels invariably should be associated with cultic acts. They may have had other functions: at least three are known to have been found in tombs – one of them Jewish – apparently placed there as funerary gifts.[137] Another bore the inscription "Good luck to the purchaser" – hardly evidence for temple use, though it does not preclude use in a household ritual.[138] It is entirely possible that such shovels were sometimes used merely for fumigation.[139] Furthermore, Jewish use of incense shovels is attested by rabbinic sources and suggested by Late Roman and Byzantine period synagogue mosaics.[140] A

---

[132] Yigael Yadin, *The Finds from the Bar Kokhba Period in the Cave of Letters* (Jerusalem: Israel Exploration Society, 1963), 58.

[133] Leonard Victor Rutgers, "Incense Shovels at Sepphoris," in Meyers, ed., *Galilee*, 177–198, esp. 197–198 and Yadin, *Finds*, 54–58. For the shovels most similar to that at et-Tell, see Yadin, *Finds*, 51 no. 5, 55 c and 57 d, f; Rebecca Martin Nagy, "Incense Shovel," in Nagy, *Sepphoris*, 179; and one described in David Gordon Mitten, "Two New Bronze Objects in the McDaniel Collection: An Etruscan Strainer and a Roman Incense Shovel," *HSCP* 69 (1965): 163–167.

[134] Yohanan Aharoni, "Excavations at Tel Beer-sheba," *TA* 2 (1975): 146–168, esp. 164 and pl. 36:1.

[135] K. Herbert, *Greek and Latin Inscriptions in the Brooklyn Museum* (Brooklyn: Brooklyn Museum, 1972), 14–16 no. 5, plate 5.

[136] S. R. F. Price, *Ritual and Power: The Roman Imperial Cult in Asia Minor* (Cambridge: Cambridge University Press, 1984), 208, 228.

[137] Rutgers, "Incense Shovels," 197–198; on the Jewish tomb, see A. Mazar, "A Burial Cave on French Hill," *Atiqot* 8 (1982): 41–45 (Hebrew; English summary on 5).

[138] J. H. Iliffe, "Greek and Latin Inscriptions in the Museum," *QDAP* 2 (1933): 120–126, esp. 123 no. 5, plate 46a.

[139] Nagy, "Incense Shovel."

[140] Though most of the rabbinic references are to temple practices, Freund has shown that Jews also burned incense in other contexts ("Incense Shovel"; cf. Rutgers, "Incense Shovels").

considerable number of incense shovels, albeit ceramic rather than bronze, have been discovered in Jewish domestic contexts at Sepphoris.[141] What all of this suggests is that the bronze incense shovel at et-Tell, like the figurine, provides less support for the identification of the building as a temple than might be thought, and even less support for a more specific identification as an imperial shrine. Because the shovel was found in a refuse pit, we can know little about its owner or purpose.

Likewise, the fact that a city was named in honor of the emperor or a member of his family does not guarantee that it had an imperial temple, as the apparent lack of such cults at first-century Sepphoris-Autocratoris and Tiberias shows. Any number of future finds could strengthen the arguments of the excavators of et-Tell, such as an altar, a statue, bones of sacrificed animals, dedicatory or other inscriptions, or indisputably cultic implements (recovered within the temple itself, rather than nearby). On the basis of the currently available evidence, however, it appears highly unlikely that this building was a temple dedicated to the emperor.

BEYOND GALILEE

Though Hellenistic and Roman cultures continued to impact architecture and urban organization elsewhere in Palestine, all too often first-century finds are too scarce to allow us to draw detailed conclusions. The overall impression is that between the death of Herod the Great and the first Jewish Revolt, local adaptation of Greco-Roman architectural conventions was sporadic and geographically spotty. The region's major Romanization in this regard was yet to come.

We do know that in Philip's territory, Paneas was renamed Caesarea Philippi and continued to grow.[142] At Gamla, a synagogue built in the first century BCE – one of the earliest synagogues in existence – continued to function until its destruction in the revolt.[143] Its rectangular shape, like the designs of later synagogues,

---

[141] Rutgers, "Incense Shovels."　　[142] *Ant.* 18.28.
[143] Steven Fine, "Gamla," *OEANE*, vol. 2, 382; Shemaryahu Gutman, "Gamala," *NEAEHL*, vol. 2, 459–463.

clearly reflected Greco-Roman influence.[144] Tel Anafa, in the Huleh, was re-occupied, and its new settlers showed a fondness for Italian-style pans and fine wares from Italy, Asia Minor, and Cyprus.[145]

Our knowledge of the coastal cities is limited, with the notable exception of Caesarea. Herod's prize city became the administrative capital of the new province of Judea and maintained its position as the most Roman city in Palestine. The king's seaside palace was converted to the governor's praetorium,[146] additional warehouses were built, and an amphitheater may have been constructed in the northeastern part of the city.[147] A Latin inscription demonstrates that Pontius Pilate (26–36 CE) built a shrine to emperor Tiberius.[148]

We are also largely in the dark regarding the extent of Hellenistic and Roman culture in the Decapolis cities. Josephus characterizes Gadara and Hippos (as well as Gaza) as Greek cities, but too few first-century remains have survived to allow us to determine exactly what that label meant.[149] Only Gerasa is known to have adopted orthogonal planning, which it did in the middle of the century. In this regard, it went beyond the Hippodamian grid of the stereotypical Hellenistic city by making one street its main thoroughfare – the *cardo maximus* of the Roman city. It also went beyond the typical Roman city of the time by lining that *cardo* with colonnades, anticipating a custom that would become even more common in the following century.[150] The city also built a new temple of Zeus Olympios, as demonstrated by an inscriptions recording gifts to it by a priest of Tiberius Caesar and the city's gymnasiarchs.[151]

---

[144] See discussion of this point in Chapter Four. [145] Berlin, "Plain Wares," 104–106.

[146] Burrell, "Palace." [147] Richardson, *City*, 108–110. [148] *GLI*, 67–70.

[149] *Ant.* 17.320, *War* 2.97; Gideon Foerster and Yoram Tsafrir note that an inscription on a second- or third-century altar at Scythopolis refers to it as a Greek city ("Nysa-Scythopolis – A New Inscription and the Titles of the City on its Coins," *INJ* 9 [1986–1987]: 53–58).

[150] Arthur Segal, *From Function to Monument* (Oxford: Oxbow Press, 1997), 5; Ball, *Rome*, 261–272. On the difference between Hellenistic and Roman city planning, see Ball, *Rome*, 248–256.

[151] Welles, "Inscriptions," nos. 2–4, *SEG* 35.1568–1569; cf. Welles, "Inscriptions," nos. 5–6.

As for Jerusalem, Josephus mentions that it had a hippodrome at the time of the Revolt, though he does not identify who built it.[152] He also makes several references to a *xystus*, an exercise trail of some sort, which he specifies as being physically connected to the temple; perhaps it stood at the location of the old Seleucid-era gymnasium.[153] The city used Greek titles for its officials. Josephus quotes a letter from Emperor Claudius to the "the officials, *boule*, and *demos* of Jerusalem"[154] and elsewhere refers to *dekaprotoi* and a *bouleuterion*, or meeting hall for the *boule*.[155] Some of the city's elites indulged themselves in the luxury of a hot bath; excavations have found four houses with private bathing facilities that included hypocaust systems and *mikvot*.[156]

CONCLUSION

Ironically, Pompey, Gabinius, and the early Roman governors apparently did less to introduce Hellenistic and Roman architecture to Palestine than did an Idumean Jew, Herod the Great. Herod's city Caesarea Maritima, in particular, combined features of both Greek and Roman cities in a fashion that was unprecedented at its time of construction. His enthusiastic sponsorship of Greco-Roman conventions also included Sebaste, Jerusalem, his many palaces, and cities throughout the eastern Mediterranean. Surprisingly, however, it does not appear to have extended into Galilee. When considering the first fifty years of the Roman era, it is important to keep in mind differences within Palestine between cities and between regions. Sepphoris was not Caesarea.

Antipas inherited the territory his father had neglected, and he poured his own efforts into it. Under his reign, Hellenistic and Roman influence became far more visible in Galilee's architecture than it had ever been before. When he rebuilt Sepphoris, at least

---

[152] *War* 2.44 and *Ant.* 17.255.
[153] *War* 2.344, 4.580–581, 5.144, 6.191, 6.324–325, 6.377; Roller, *Building Program*, 178; Harris, *Greek Athletics*, 39–40.
[154] *Ant.* 20.11.
[155] *Ant.* 20.11, 194; *War* 2.405, 5.532, 6.354; cf. Mark 15.43, Cassius Dio 66.6.2. Levine collects the references in *Jerusalem*, 266.
[156] Reich, "Hot Bath-House," 103–104.

some of its streets were laid on a grid, an indication of the urban planning that characterized both Greek and Roman cities. Presumably the planning was more extensive than the two streets intersecting at a right angle that archaeologists have discovered, but just how extensive is not yet clear. The basilica on the eastern plateau, though little of it remains from the first century, was a distinctively Roman building. Antipas probably reused his father's palace at Sepphoris, and he built another at his wholly new foundation, Tiberias. Probably both palaces reflected the mingling of Hellenistic and Roman characteristics that his father's had. Tiberias used Greek titles for positions within its civic government – *agoranomoi*, a *boule*, and *dekaprotoi*; Sepphoris probably did likewise. At some point, Tiberias acquired Hellenistic sports architecture, a stadium. These cities were a physical expression of Antipas's desire to express himself as a man of considerable stature who was fully in touch with the cultural currents of the Roman world. The names he bestowed upon them made his own loyalties and subservient status clear.

Greco-Roman architectural influence was not limited to the two main cities. A hippodrome stood at Magdala/Taricheae by the mid-60s, buildings there and in Hammath Tiberias used columns, and a basilical building was erected at Beth She'arim. Upper Galilee, with no major cities, did not yet reflect the new influx of Greco-Roman culture that was felt in Lower Galilee. In this regard, Eric M. Meyers' observations about the differences between the cultural climates of the two areas still stand.[157]

It is difficult to talk about how different sectors of Galilean society reacted to the newly arrived Greco-Roman architectural culture. Much of that culture was imposed from the top down, by Antipas. But when were the other buildings described above built, in his reign or afterwards? Who paid for them? If we had a larger corpus of inscriptions, perhaps we would be able to identify patrons from among the two Agrippas, or the cities' elites, or (after 44 CE) Roman administrators. But we have no such resource. Not a single first-century building inscription survives to tell us the name of a donor.

---

[157] See the sources cited in my Introduction.

As for the masses, how did they respond? Did they view these buildings as "progress" or merely as the visible expression of who had power and wealth and, by implication, who did not? Because the structures apparently had no precedents in the region, many people probably associated them with the new Roman domination, regardless of whether the styles of specific buildings were more properly characterized as Hellenistic or Roman, and whether they had been built by a Herodian client king or someone else. The images of animals in Antipas's palace at Tiberias were offensive enough to some that it was burned down in the angry, early days of the revolt – but apparently not offensive enough to have attracted a mob in the previous six decades. Exactly what types of competitions were held in Tiberias's stadium and Magdala's hippodrome, who competed in them, how often they took place, and who came as spectators – all these matters are wholly unknown. Presumably, any games were also viewed by some as a foreign innovation, but did that foreignness provoke hostility or curiosity? Many commoners apparently had no problem using the facilities for public meetings, if the need arose.

The Roman amphitheater made no appearance in Galilee in the first century, nor was it present elsewhere in Palestine aside from Caesarea and Jerusalem. Gladiatorial spectacles, a favorite entertainment of the Romans, would have been limited to those two cities; we have no evidence that any took place in Galilee. When Agrippa I decided to build an amphitheater, he built it not in his own territory but far to the north at the Roman colony of Berytus.[158]

Other buildings characteristic of Greco-Roman cities appear to have been uncommon, if present at all. The theater at Sepphoris was probably not constructed until after the Revolt, and Tiberias had not yet acquired one. No first-century temples have been found, unless future finds confirm arguments that one stood at nearby Bethsaida. Public bathhouses (as opposed to private baths, such as those in Jerusalem homes and Herodian palaces) made no inroads in Galilee or anywhere in Palestine.[159]

---

[158] *Ant.* 19.335–337.

[159] If the bathhouse at Ramat Hanadiv is post-Herodian, it is possible that it was a public facility, though more likely it was a private facility.

Thus when considering the "Greco-Roman" milieu of pre-70 CE Galilee, it is essential not to load the term with content imported from elsewhere. Both Sepphoris and Tiberias, for example, exhibited Greco-Roman urban architectural culture to a degree unprecedented for Galilee, but neither compared to Caesarea Maritima or Gerasa, much less to some of the other cities in the Roman world, like Pompeii, Herculaneum, Ostia, Ephesus, or Aphrodisias. Antipas's rebuilding of Sepphoris did not suddenly transform central Lower Galilee into a beacon of Roman culture. Though Antipas had introduced urban architecture to the region on an unprecedented scale, the interaction of Greco-Roman culture and local Galilean culture had only just begun.

CHAPTER 4

The transformation of the landscape in the second and third centuries CE

After the arrival of large, long-term Roman garrisons, Palestine's landscape was transformed as Greco-Roman urban and monumental architecture became common features in many cities. In this chapter, I will discuss some of the changes that characterized civic life in the second and third centuries. I begin with the adoption of new civic names and titles. Next, I provide an inventory of where Roman urban architecture appeared. Last, I consider the issue of who was responsible for the construction of these buildings. Throughout the chapter, I consider developments throughout Palestine in order to keep those in Galilee in perspective.

CIVIC TITLES AND NAMES

One effect of the heightened Roman presence in Palestine was the establishment of new colonies. Caesarea Maritima was elevated to colonial status by Vespasian shortly after the first revolt, taking the official name Colonia Prima Flavia Augusta Caesarea.[1] The Roman colony of Aelia Capitolina had been founded at Jerusalem by 132 CE.[2] Military veterans settled at both cities. Inscriptions show that Caesarea adopted Roman-style civic institutions, with *duumviri, decurions,* and *pontifices,*[3] and Aelia Capitolina probably did likewise. Both cities placed Latin inscriptions on their coins. In the late second century and throughout the first half of the third, numerous cities were awarded the status of colony[4] and a few

---

[1] See discussion in Chapter Two. [2] Cassius Dio 69.12.
[3] *GLI,* 6 and inscriptions nos. 3, 8, 10, 11, 15.
[4] Tyre (193 CE), Sebaste (197 CE), Petra (218 CE), Sidon (218 CE), Bosra (231 CE), Neapolis (244 CE), and Philippopolis (244 CE) (Arie Kindler, "The Status of Cities in The

received the still more vaunted title of "metropolis."[5] By then, however, the designation "colony" appears to have been purely honorific; the Romans had ceased to establish genuine colonies occupied by military veterans. According to a late rabbinic tradition, Judah ha-Nasi appealed to the emperor to have Tiberias granted the rank of colony, but the story may be legendary.[6] Archaeological evidence of colonial status is lacking.[7]

Other cities also adopted names that honored the Romans.[8] Joppa apparently added the name "Flavia," after the imperial dynasty,[9] and a new city, Flavia Neapolis, was founded at the bottom of Mt. Gerizim c. 81 CE by Vespasian.[10] Emmaus became Nicopolis c. 161 CE and then later Marcia Aurelia Antoninopolis Nicopolis.[11] Antipatris assumed a similar name.[12] In the third century, the names of numerous cities were changed to honor the Severan emperors, including Eleutheropolis and Diospolis (Lod).[13] At some point, Aelia Capitolina added a name honoring Commodus.[14] Second- and third-century CE coins from other cities show that they renamed themselves after individuals who had figured prominently in their histories. Gaba and Pella both took the name "Philippeia," probably after the proconsul of Syria c. 61/60 BCE, Marcius

---

Syro-Palestinian Area as Reflected by Their Coins," *INJ* 6–7 [1982–1983]: 79–87) and perhaps Scythopolis (early fourth century) (*SEG* 43.1073/ 20.1964).

[5] In Palestine, Caesarea Maritima (222 CE) received the title. Cities in adjacent areas that received the status include Tyre (93/94 CE), Petra (118 CE), Sidon (218 CE), and Bosra (244 CE) (Kindler, "Status").

[6] *B. Avodah Zarah* 10a; Millar, "Roman *Coloniae*," 10. Shimon Applebaum notes a *ketubah* from 347 CE that may refer to Tiberias as a colony ("Syria-Palaestina as a Province of the Severan Empire," in *Judaea*, 143–154, esp. 150–151 n. 51.).

[7] Meshorer argued that an early third-century coin of Tiberias had a faint and incomplete Latin inscription reading CO . . . TIBE, which he interpreted as a reference to colonial status (*City-Coins*, 35, 113 no. 86). Joshua Ezra Burns, however, recently inspected the coin in question and found no support for Meshorer's reading (personal communication).

[8] Millar, *RNE*, 354; Kindler, "Status," 84–85; A. H. M. Jones, "The Urbanization of Palestine," *JRS* 21 (1931) 78–85, esp. 82.

[9] *City-Coins*, 24.

[10] Isaac, "Roman Colonies," 95–96, *City-Coins*, 48–49.

[11] *City-Coins*, 56.

[12] Marcia Aurelia Antoniana Antipatris (*City-Coins*, 115 no. 150–152).

[13] Eleutheropolis became Lucia Septimia Severa Eleutheropolis (*City-Coins*, 64), and Diospolis (Lod) became Lucia Septimia Severa (*City-Coins*, 55).

[14] Ya'akov Meshorer, *The Coinage of Aelia Capitolina* (Jerusalem: Israel Museum, 1989), 62–63; cf. Smallwood, *Jews*, 492.

Philippus, and Canatha called itself "Gabinia." Gadara picked a more influential figure to commemorate, naming itself Pompeia.[15]

Galilee's cities participated in this trend. Beginning in 101 CE, the coins of Tiberias show that it proclaimed itself Claudiopolis.[16] It is possible that Tiberias had taken this name during Claudius's reign (41–54 CE), though if that were the case, one would have expected the name to have appeared on the city coins issued in 53 CE or on the coin Agrippa II minted with the city's name.[17] Perhaps the name change is associated with Tiberias's assignment to the Roman province of Judea after Agrippa's death. The city may have recognized its admission into the province by commemorating its earlier history under direct Roman governance (44–61 CE), naming itself after the first emperor who had ruled it directly.

During the revolt, Sepphoris had renamed itself Neronias (following the example of Caesarea Philippi, which had also adopted the name) and Eirenopolis ("City of Peace"),[18] but it appears to have quickly dropped both names after the war.[19] By the mid-second century, it was known as Diocaesarea, a name identifying "Caesar" as "Zeus." The new name does not seem to have been popular among Jews; the rabbis continued to refer to the city by its Hebrew name, Zippori.[20]

---

[15] Barkay "New Coin Types" and "Coins." The cities may have adopted these names earlier, but if so, it is unclear why they did not put the names on their coins until the second and third centuries.

[16] A. Kindler, *The Coins of Tiberias* (Tiberias: Hamei Tiberia, 1961), 55–57 nos. 3–6; *City-Coins*, 112–113 nos. 77–80. I interpret the inscriptions as Tiberias Claudiopolis, rather than as Tiberias Claudia (Meshorer's reconstruction) because one of the coins under Trajan reads ΤΙΒΕΡΙΕΩΝ ΚΛΑΥΔΙΟ (*City-Coins*, 112 no. 79). A coin from 186 CE has a fuller name, "Tiberias Claudiopolis which is in Syria Palaestina" (ΤΙΒ ΚΛΑ ΣΥΡ ΠΑΛ) (*City-Coins*, 113 no. 85).

[17] *Treasury*, 106–107, 177–178, 261. Cf. Gaba's renaming itself after Claudius in the first century (*City-Coins*, 113 no. 96).

[18] On Sepphoris, see discussion in Chapter Six. On Caesarea Philippi, see *Treasury*, 233 no. 132.

[19] Presumably Sepphoris discarded its wartime name "Neronia" shortly after Nero's death and the Roman Senate's proclamation of a *damnatio memoriae*.

[20] The name appears on second- and third-century coins; see discussion in Chapter Six. On literary references to the city, see Tsafrir, Di Segni, and Green, *Tabula Imperii Romani*, 227. Like many other city names adopted in the Roman and Byzantine periods, Diocaesarea would fade from use after the Arab conquest in the eighth century, replaced by a Semitic name, in this case, Saffuriyya.

Exactly when Sepphoris assumed the name Diocaesarea is difficult to determine. It is absent from city coins struck during Trajan's reign (98–117 CE) but appears on coins minted under Antoninus Pius (138–161 CE).[21] It is also found in a Greek inscription on the milestone from 120 CE on the Sepphoris–Legio road.[22] Whether the Greek inscription, which provides the distance to Sepphoris, is original or was added later is difficult to determine.[23]

The name Diocaesarea may have been chosen to honor Hadrian, who was identified with Zeus/Jupiter.[24] Many cities throughout the Empire, grateful for the emperor's visits or benefactions, renamed themselves after him.[25] If, however, Sepphoris chose "Diocaesarea" to flatter Hadrian, it was a unique selection; no other cities adopted that name.[26] Instead, cities that honored Hadrian typically called themselves Hadrianopolis, or added Hadriane to their old name (as Petra did, becoming Hadriane Petra).[27] Some scholars have suggested that Sepphoris adopted the name to honor Hadrian on his tour of Syria, Palestine, and Arabia in 130 CE,[28] but there is no evidence that he passed through Galilee.[29] Other explanations include A. H. M. Jones's proposal that the name reflected a decline in Jewish power at the city and perhaps a transfer of government

---

[21] Ya'akov Meshorer in "Sepphoris and Rome," in O. Mørkholm and N. M. Waggoner, eds., *Greek Numismatics and Archaeology: Essays in Honor of Margaret Thompson* (Belgium: Cultura Press, 1979), 159–171; "Coins of Sepphoris"; *City-Coins*, 36–37.

[22] Isaac and Roll, "Judaea."

[23] Though it is often assumed that Greek distance inscriptions on milestones are contemporary with the primary Latin inscriptions, no one (to my knowledge) has demonstrated this. The fact that the scripts of Greek inscriptions are often much cruder than those of the Latin inscriptions suggests they may be secondary; see Isaac and Roll, "Judaea," 184 n. 14.

[24] Mary T. Boatwright, *Hadrian and the Cities of the Roman Empire* (Princeton: Princeton University Press, 2000), 138–139.

[25] On Hadrian's benefactions, see Boatwright's excellent study, *Hadrian*.

[26] The name Diocaesarea predates Hadrian; a city in Cilicia and one in Cappadocia adopted it in the first century CE (T. S. McKay, "Diocaesarea," in Richard Stillwell et al., eds., *The Princeton Encyclopedia of Classical Sites* [Princeton: Princeton University Press, 1976], 275–276; cf. Jones, *Cities*, 74, 180, 210–213).

[27] Stephen Mitchell, "Imperial Building in the Eastern Roman Provinces," *HSCP* 91 (1987): 333–365, esp. 357–358; Boatwright, *Hadrian*, 104–105; Spijkerman, *Coins*, 218–222.

[28] For example, George Frances Hill, *Catalogue of the Greek Coins of Palestine (Galilee, Samaria and Judaea)* (London: British Museum, 1914), xi.

[29] Anthony R. Birley, *Hadrian: The Restless Emperor* (London and New York: Routledge 1997), 215–268.

from a Jewish *boule* to a gentile one[30] and Meshorer's suggestion that it reflected Hadrian's punishment of Sepphoris in the wake of the Bar Kokhba war – even though there is no evidence the city participated in that revolt.[31] Most likely, the name simply reflects the new political realities in Galilee after the arrival of Roman troops. The local *boule* probably adopted it as a gesture of loyalty to the occupying forces, possibly during Hadrian's reign but perhaps not until that of Antoninus Pius. One does not have to assume a transition from Jews to gentiles in the *boule*, one only has to assume savvy on the part of its members.

Because of a dearth of civic inscriptions, details about the governments of Sepphoris and Tiberias elude us.[32] Tiberias had been organized along Hellenistic (rather than Roman) lines, with its *agoranomos, protoi,* and *boule,* since at least the Revolt and probably for its entire history.[33] Presumably, Sepphoris had a similar administration (as my references above to its *boule* suggest), though a mid-second-century market weight referring to the *agoranomos* is our sole explicit archaeological evidence.[34] With Galilee's cities, we are in a quite different position than with Caesarea, with its inscriptions and Roman-style civic officials,[35] and Gerasa, where inscriptions mention the *epimeletes,*[36] *agoranomos,*[37] *grammateus, dekaprotos, archontes,* and other officials.[38]

---

[30] Jones, *Cities,* 279–280; Birley, *Hadrian,* 232.

[31] Meshorer, "Sepphoris and Rome," 159–171; "Coins of Sepphoris;" *City-Coins,* 36–37.

[32] On civic organization (especially the difference between Hellenistic and Roman), see Joyce Reynolds, "Cities," in David Braund, ed., *The Administration of the Roman Empire: 241 BC–AD 193* (Exeter: University of Exeter, 1988), 15–51; Hartmut Galsterer, "Local and Provincial Institutions and Government," in Alan K. Bowman, Peter Garnsey, and Dominic Rathbone, eds., *The Cambridge Ancient History* (Cambridge: Cambridge University Press, 2000), vol. 11, 344–360. On civic organization in the Levant, see Grainger, "Village Government" and Julian M. C. Bowsher, "Civic Organisation within the Decapolis," *ARAM* 4:1 & 2 (1992): 265–281.

[33] See discussion in Chapter Three.

[34] See Ya'akov Meshorer, "Market Weight," in Nagy, *Sepphoris,* 201; cf. his earlier "The Lead Weight: Preliminary Report," *BA* 49 (1986): 16–17.

[35] See discussion above.

[36] On *epimeletes* inscriptions at Gerasa, see Kraeling, "History," 60; *SEG* 39.1646, 1650; cf. those at Scythopolis, see *SEG* 37.1531/ 40.1509.

[37] Welles, "Inscriptions," 399–400 no. 53; *SEG* 46.2064.

[38] See discussion in Kraeling, "History," 44.

THE SPREAD OF GRECO-ROMAN URBAN ARCHITECTURE

From the late first century on, both of Galilee's cities saw extensive construction. Most of it was done with local materials, limestone and basalt, despite Palestine's greater integration into the marble trade network in the second and third centuries.[39] Other cities in Palestine, especially Caesarea Maritima and, to a lesser extent, Scythopolis, made greater use of the imported stone, and in them marble Corinthian columns and decorated cornices, friezes, and architraves became quite common.[40]

At Sepphoris, a new paved street was built along the northern edge of the acropolis running east toward the summit early in the late first or early second century, as was, perhaps, the theater.[41] A columned, monumental public building on the eastern side of the acropolis may also date to this period.[42] The city continued expanding onto the adjacent plateau, where a north–south *cardo* and an east–west *decumanus*, the hallmark streets of the Roman city, were constructed. The two streets, paved with limestone slabs, intersected at the basilical building, which itself underwent renovation in the second century. Both were lined with columns, a civic feature more characteristic of the Roman East than of the West, and shops.[43] Other streets and buildings, particularly on the plateau, were also built according to a grid pattern.[44] A second aqueduct system (parts of which are featured prominently at the modern site) was constructed, along with a sizeable reservoir tank and a pool (for swimming?).[45] Two Roman-style bathhouses (one late first- or

---

[39] Fischer, *Marble Studies*, 40–41, 263–265. Marble was not wholly absent from Galilee; some has been found at Sepphoris, though how much is not yet clear (Ze'ev Weiss, "Zippori 1999," *HA* 112 [2000]: 21–23; Ze'ev Weiss, "Zippori 2001," *HA* 114 [2002]: 23–24).

[40] In general, marble was used more often in Palestine than in the inland areas of Syria and Arabia but less often than in north Africa, western Europe, and the site of many of the quarries, Asia Minor (Fischer, *Marble Studies*, 47–131).

[41] Hoglund and Meyers, "Residential Quarter"; Weiss and Netzer, "Architectural Development"; and Weiss and Netzer, "Hellenistic and Roman Sepphoris."

[42] Ze'ev Weiss, "Zippori 2000," *HA* 113 (2001): 25–27.

[43] Ball, *Rome*, 261–272.

[44] McCollough and Edwards ("Transformations") describe the second-century paving of an earlier road on the plateau. A coin found under the pavement dates to 119/120 CE, suggesting this road was paved at the approximate time of the construction of the Sepphoris–Legio highway.

[45] Tsuk, "Aqueducts."

second-century, the other third- or fourth-century) benefited from the increased water supply. The latter was the larger of the two, with three *caldaria* and two *frigidaria*. Rabbinic sources refer to an upper and a lower agora.[46]

As of yet, no pagan temple has been found at Sepphoris. The foundation of a large public building (23 by 12 meters) could be from a temple, but it could also have supported a synagogue or some other structure.[47] Beginning with the reign of Antoninus Pius, Sepphoris's coins depicted temples,[48] but whether these symbols should be interpreted as representations of actual buildings is unclear. At other cities, excavations have often confirmed the presence of buildings depicted on coins – often, but not always. Sepphoris had a crucial characteristic that differentiated it from most other second- and third-century coin minting cities: a predominantly monotheistic population. Temple motifs were standard numismatic designs, and their presence at Sepphoris may merely reflect the desire of the *boule* to produce coins similar to those of other cities, or a propagandistic depiction of Roman culture.[49]

The domestic architecture of Sepphoris's elites also reflected growing Greco-Roman influence. Several peristyle houses, which are uncommon in Palestine, were built.[50] One, on the acropolis near the theater, dates to the early third century. A lavish, two-story residence, it is known for the Dionysos mosaic on its triclinium

---

[46] *B. Eruvin* 54b, *b. Yoma* 11a. On rabbinic references to Sepphoris, see Samuel Klein, *Beiträge zur Geographie und Geschichte Galiläas* (Leipzig: Verlag von Rudolf Haupt, 1906), 26–45.

[47] Weiss and Netzer, "Architectural Development" and "Hellenistic and Roman Sepphoris," 34.

[48] See discussion in Chapter Six.

[49] Compare Strange, "Some Implications," 38; Goodman, *State and Society*, 41, 46; Nicole Belayche, *Iudaea-Palaestina: The Pagan Cults in Roman Palestine (Second to Fourth Centuries)* (Tübingen: J. C. B. Mohr Siebeck, 2001), 38–44.

[50] Yizhar Hirschfeld, *The Palestinian Dwelling in the Roman–Byzantine Period* (Jerusalem: Franciscan Printing Press and Israel Exploration Society, 1995), 85–94; Eric M. Meyers, "Aspects of Everyday Life in Roman Palestine with Special Reference to Private Domiciles and Ritual Baths," in John R. Bartlett, ed., *Jews in the Hellenistic and Roman Cities* (London and New York: Routledge, 2002), 193–220; Eric M. Meyers, "Jewish Art and Architecture in Ancient Palestine (70–235 CE)," in *CHJ*, vol. 4 (forthcoming); Katharina Galor, "Domestic Architecture in Roman and Byzantine Galilee and Golan," *NEA* 66:1–2 (2003): 44–57, esp. 51; Jodi Magness, "Peristyle House," *OEANE*, vol. 4, 273.

floor.[51] On the eastern plateau, a peristyle house from the late third or early fourth century had mosaic panels depicting the god Orpheus and scenes from everyday life.[52] Another contained a decorative fountain.[53]

Tiberias underwent similar development.[54] As noted earlier, the southern gate complex often attributed to Antipas may actually date to the second century; it closely resembles arches erected elsewhere in the region during Hadrian's reign.[55] A *cardo* with a portico originated at a piazza inside the gate and ran north alongside the lake. Otherwise, topography limited the area where orthogonal planning could be applied, since there was only a thin strip of land between Mount Berenice and the shore. A large basilical building with columns and an eastern apse, built near the lake, may have been used for municipal functions. A second basilical building was built in the third century,[56] as was a rectangular public building with a *mikveh*. Other new structures include a semicircular *exedra* (date unknown), a theater (second–third century), a bathhouse with mosaics depicting animals and fish (fourth century), and an aqueduct (built between the third and fifth centuries).[57] The city's coins, like those of Sepphoris, depict temples. In this case, literary evidence corroborates the presence of a temple – or, at least, the partial construction of one. Epiphanius (c. 315–403 CE) refers to an uncompleted temple to Hadrian that the city's residents were trying to convert to a bathhouse.[58] As of yet, however, no remains of any temple have been found.

Roman-style construction was not limited to Sepphoris and Tiberias. At Beth She'arim, a two-story building, probably for civic

---

[51] R. Talgam and Z. Weiss, *The Mosaics of the House of Dionysos at Sepphoris: Excavated by E. M. Meyers, E. Netzer, and C. L. Meyer* (Jerusalem: Hebrew University, 2004), 17–33.

[52] Ze'ev Weiss, "Zippori (Sepphoris) – 1998," *HA* 110 (1999): 20–23.

[53] Weiss, "Zippori 2001."

[54] Unless otherwise noted, features described in this paragraph come from Hirschfeld, *Guide*, 15–33; Hirschfeld, "Tiberias"; and Hirschfeld and Foerster, "Tiberias."

[55] See discussion in Chapter Three.

[56] Eli Ashkenazi, "Researchers say Tiberias Basilica may have housed Sanhedrin," *Haaretz*, March 22, 2004 (www.haaretzdaily.com/hasen/spages/407113.html).

[57] Zalmon S. Winogradov, "The Aqueduct of Tiberias," in Amit, Patrich and Hirschfeld, *Aqueducts*, 295–304.

[58] Epiphanius, *Adv. Haereses* 30.12.1; discussed in Belayche, *Iudaea–Palaestina*, 93.

use, was erected in the late second century.[59] Capernaum saw the
appearance of sizable rectangular buildings and, in the second or
third century, a Roman bathhouse. Its four rooms were arranged
in a simple linear design, with a clearly identifiable *caldarium*,
frigidarium, and *tepidarium*; the fourth room could have served
as swimming pool or an *apodyterium*.[60] In the third or fourth
century, a bathhouse appeared at Rama, in the southernmost region
of Upper Galilee. Several times larger than the Capernaum bathhouse, this one contained a large courtyard, swimming pool, and
several side pools, in addition to the other standard rooms.[61]

At Kedesh, a Tyrian village on the northern fringe of geographical
Galilee, a massive pagan temple was built in the early second
century.[62] The 17.6 by 20 meter building stood approximately 12
meters high and was located within a large (55 by 80 meter) *temenos*.
Its decoration – some of it original, some added later – included
Corinthian and Ionic columns and elaborately decorated lintels.
Greek inscriptions show that it was in use by 117/118 CE and was
dedicated to the "Holy God of Heaven."[63] Mordechai Aviam notes
the remains of other temples across the northern limits of Galilee,
apparently beyond the area settled by Jews, at H. Zar'it, Jebel Bilat,
and Kh. ed Duweir, and two pagan inscriptions at Qeren Naftali
may also come from a temple.[64]

The most significant architectural development in Galilee in these
centuries is the proliferation of synagogue buildings.[65] The earliest
of these, at Nabratein, provides a helpful example of the varieties of

---

[59] *Beth She'arim*, vol. 1, 13–19.
[60] John C. H. Laughlin, "Capernaum: From Jesus' Time and After," *BAR* 19:5 (1993): 54–61.
[61] Vassilios Tzaferis, "A Roman Bath at Rama," *Atiqot* 14 (1980): 66–75.
[62] On Kedesh as a Tyrian village, see *War* 4.404.
[63] Asher Ovadiah, Moshe Fischer, Israel Roll, "Kedesh (In Upper Galilee): The Roman
Temple," *NEAEHL*, vol. 3, 857–859; Moshe Fischer, Asher Ovadiah, and Israel Roll, "The
Epigraphic Finds from the Roman Temple at Kedesh in the Upper Galilee," *TA* 13 (1986):
60–66; Moshe Fischer, Asher Ovadiah, and Israel Roll, "The Roman Temple at Kedesh,
Upper Galilee: A Preliminary Study," *TA* 11 (1984): 146–172; Mordechai Aviam, "Some
Notes on the Roman Temple at Kedesh," in *Jews*, 139–146; and other sources cited in
Chancey, *Myth*, 150–151.
[64] Aviam, "Borders," 14–16. Jebel Bilat and Kh. ed Duweir are both in southern Lebanon.
[65] For a review of scholarship on earlier synagogues at Masada, Herodium, and Gamla, see
Donald T. Binder, *Into the Temple Courts: The Place of the Synagogues in the Second Temple
Period* (Atlanta: Society of Biblical Literature, 1999), 4–22 and the sources cited in
Chancey, *Myth*, 66. Netzer mentions other early possibilities in "Synagogues."

synagogue design.[66] Originally built in the mid-second century, it was constructed in a "broadhouse" design, with the northern and southern walls longer than the other two (11.2 meters by 9.35 meters).[67] Two platforms on the southern wall suggest that the worshipers faced south, towards Jerusalem. One entrance was also located on the southern wall, another in the building's northeastern corner. It is not clear whether or not columns stood in the interior at this point.

In the second half of the third century, the synagogue was expanded and reoriented so that it ran lengthwise from north to south (11.2 meters by 13.85 meters). The southern wall (now one of the shorter ones) remained the focal point of worship and the main point of entry into the building. A portico of four columns stood outside that entrance, and two rows of three columns each ran lengthwise down the building's interior. With its columns and rectangular design, the renovated synagogue resembled Roman basilical buildings, and so synagogues of this style are typically called "basilical synagogues."[68] Destroyed by an earthquake in 306 CE, it was rebuilt again and continued to function until the mid-fourth century.

In the third century, additional synagogues appeared in both Upper and Lower Galilee. Most were basilical in design (Meiron,[69] Gush Halav,[70] Hammath Tiberias,[71] and Beth She'arim[72]), though one was a broadhouse (Khirbet Shema'[73]). Still more basilical synagogues

---

[66] Eric M. Meyers, James F. Strange, and Carol L. Meyers, "Preliminary Report on the 1980 Excavations at en-Nabratein, Israel," *BASOR* 244 (1981): 1–25 and "Second Preliminary Report on the 1981 Excavations at en-Nabratein, Israel," *BASOR* 246 (1982): 35–54.

[67] On synagogue typology, see Hachlili, *Ancient Jewish Art*, 99–102; Lee I. Levine, *The Ancient Synagogue: The First Thousand Years* (New Haven and London: Yale University Press, 2000), 296–302; Eric M. Meyers, "Ancient Synagogues: An Archaeological Introduction," in Steven Fine, ed. *Sacred Realm: The Emergence of the Synagogue in the Ancient World* (New York and Oxford: Yeshiva University Museum and Oxford University Press, 1996), 3–20, esp. 14–16; Meyers and Strange, *Archaeology*, 142–152.

[68] Basilical synagogues are also sometimes called "Galilean synagogues," though the design is not limited to Galilee.

[69] *Meiron.*

[70] *Gush Halav.*

[71] This synagogue was renovated in the fourth century (Dothan, *Hammath Tiberias*, 26, 67; cf. Dothan, "Hammath Tiberias," *NEAEHL*, vol. 2, 573–557).

[72] *Beth She'arim*, vol. 1, 18–19.   [73] *Khirbet Shema'.*

appeared in the fourth and fifth centuries[74] (Arbel,[75] Chorazin,[76] Capernaum,[77] Bar'am,[78] Horvat 'Ammudim,[79] Meroth,[80] and Japhia[81]). Like the renovated synagogue at Nabratein, most of these were arranged lengthwise from north to south. The entrance was located on one of the shorter walls (typically the southern one), often in the form of a façade with three portals. At some, columns decorated the façade. Inside, columns were arranged either in two parallel lines or in the shape of a "U." Stone benches for seating often lined two or three of the interior walls, and some synagogues had a second story.[82]

A monumental structure at Qazyon, famous for a Greek lintel inscription recording the honoring of the emperor Septimius Severus by a group of Jews,[83] has often been regarded as a synagogue. The building, however, had not only porticoes but also two pools – a feature that would have been unusual at synagogues. The building's design is similar to a temple, but the Jewish inscription is strong

---

[74] The identification of a fourth–fifth-century building at Beth Yerah as a synagogue (Hestrin, "Beth Yerah") has been disputed (Ronny Reich, "The Bet Yerah 'Synagogue' Reconsidered," *Atiqot* 22 [1993]: 137–144).

[75] Zvi Ilan and Avraham Isdarechet, "Arbel," *NEAEHL*, vol. 1, 87–89.

[76] Ze'ev Yeivin, *The Synagogue at Korazim: The 1962–1964, 1980–1987 Excavations* (Jerusalem: Israel Antiquities Authority, 2000), 29–31.

[77] Loffreda, "Coins" and the numerous studies cited in Chancey, *Myth*, 103–104.

[78] One synagogue might lie atop an earlier one (Mordechai Aviam, "The Ancient Synagogues at Bar'am," in *Jews*, 147–169).

[79] Lee I. Levine, "'Ammudim, Horvat," *NEAEHL*, vol. 1, 55–56; Lee I. Levine, "Excavations at the Synagogue of Horvat 'Ammudim," *IEJ* 32 (1982): 1–12; Doron Chen, "The Ancient Synagogue at Horvat 'Ammudim: Design and Chronology," *PEQ* 118 (1986): 135–137.

[81] Map coordinates 199/279; Avi Ilan, "Meroth," *NEAEHL*, vol. 3, 1028–1031.

[80] Dan Barag, "Japhia," *NEAEHL*, vol. 2, 659–660.

[82] Jodi Magness challenges the dating of several of these synagogues, placing the Khirbet Shema' one in the late fourth or early fifth century, the Gush Halav one in the second half of the fifth century or even the sixth century, and the Capernaum one in the sixth century ("Synagogue Typology and Earthquake Chronology at Khirbet Shema' in Israel," in *Journal of Field Archaeology* 24 [1997]: 211–220; "The Question of the Synagogue: The Problem of Typology," 1–48 and "A Response to Eric M. Meyers and James F. Strange," 79–91, both in Alan J. Avery-Peck and Jacob Neusner, eds., *Judaism in Late Antiquity: part 3, vol. 4: The Special Problem of the Synagogue* [Leiden: Brill, 2001]). The excavators of Khirbet Shema' and Gush Halav have offered a strong defense of their earlier dates (Eric M. Meyers, "The Dating of the Gush Halav Synagogue: A Response to Jodi Magness," 49–70 and James F. Strange, "Synagogue Typology and Khirbet Shema': A Response to Jodi Magness," 71–78, both in Avery-Peck and Neusner, *Judaism* 3.4).

[83] *CIJ*, vol. 2, no. 972.

evidence against that function. Perhaps it was some other form of public architecture.[84]

Other buildings besides basilicas have also been cited as the architectural inspiration for Galilee's synagogues: Nabatean, Syrian, and Roman temples, and Herodian triclinia.[85] Asher Ovadiah has suggested that a variety of building types, rather than any single one, most likely influenced synagogue designs.[86] Since all of the synagogues discovered in Galilee thus far were built in the late second century or later,[87] it seems difficult not to draw the general conclusion that they reflected the increased visibility of Greco-Roman architectural conventions. By the times of their construction, basilical buildings stood in Galilee's cities and other rectangular, columned buildings could be found both within the region and nearby.[88]

The proliferation of Greco-Roman architectural features in urban settings was characteristic of the Middle and Late Roman periods throughout Palestine, Arabia, and Syria. Several cities were at least partially re-aligned according to Roman orthogonal planning, with *cardos* and *decumani* (often accompanied by porticoes) and other streets built at right angles.[89] A few civic designs included

[84] Rachel Hachlili and Ann E. Killebrew, "Horbat Qazion," *HA* 109 (1999): 6–7; Aviam, "Borders," 17; Schwartz, *Imperialism*, 131.

[85] Hachlili, *Ancient Jewish Art*, 102–103; Magness, "Question"; G. Foerster, "Architectural Models of the Greco-Roman Period and the Origin of the 'Galilean Synagogue,'" 45–48 and E. Netzer, "The Herodian Triclinia—A Prototype for the 'Galilean-Type' Synagogue," 49–51, both in Lee. I. Levine, ed., *Ancient Synagogues Revealed* (Jerusalem: Israel Exploration Society; Detroit: Wayne State University Press, 1982).

[86] Asher Ovadiah, "Observations on the Origin of the Architectural Plan of Ancient Synagogues," in Asher Ovadiah, *Art and Archaeology in Israel and Neighbouring Countries* (London: Pindar Press, 2002), 77–86.

[87] On the possibility that architectural remains under the synagogue at Capernaum are those of a first-century CE synagogue, see Chancey, *Myth*, 103–104.

[88] Compare Richardson, *Building Jewish*, 140–143.

[89] That is, Aelia Capitolina, Abila, Ashkelon, Antipatris, Gadara, Hippos, Neapolis (Segal, *From Function*, 48–49; Joshua J. Schwartz, "Archeology and the City," in Sperber, *City*, 149–187, esp. 150–151; Ball, *Rome*, 264–266), Paneas (Wilson, *Caesarea Philippi*, 52), and Hippos (Arthur Segal, "Horbat Susita [A]," *HA* 114 [2002]: 5–8). Gerasa's column-lined cardo maximus is even earlier, dating to 76 CE (Segal, *From Function*, 5). Though Stanislao Loffreda has claimed that Capernaum exhibited orthogonal planning (*Recovering Capharnaum* [Jerusalem: Franciscan Printing Press, 1993], 24), Reed has demonstrated that this was not the case: the streets do not intersect at right angles, no *cardo* or *decumanus* has been identified, and blocks of buildings do not appear to be arranged along axes (*Archaeology*, 151–157).

market areas, either Hellenistic-style agoras or Roman *macella*.[90] Some acquired basilical buildings,[91] and numerous ones received new aqueducts.[92] If the city gate at Tiberias was, in fact, a second-century freestanding arch, its construction was part of a larger trend; similar-looking triumphal arches, a distinctively Roman form of propagandistic architecture, appeared at a few other cities.[93]

The construction of Galilee's two theaters was part of a larger regional trend.[94] Gerasa, Bosra, and Pella erected Roman-style theaters at the end of the first century or early in the second. By the third century, the number of theaters in Palestine had reached the thirties.[95] *Odea,* roofed theater-like structures often intended as music halls, appeared at Beth She'an and Antipatris.[96] In

---

[90] Agoras: Philadelphia (date unknown), Antipatris (perhaps early third century), Philippopolis (244 CE), Ashdod (pre-70 CE); *macella*: Gerasa (125 CE), Gadara (date uncertain), Bosra (second century CE?); an example at Petra may be even earlier, from the late first century BCE (Ball, *Rome*, 296; Segal, *From Function*, 55–67; J. Schwartz, "Archeology," 150).

[91] Ashkelon, Beth Shean, Tiberias, Dor, Paneas (J. Schwartz, "Archeology," 159); in addition, a late first-century palatial complex built by Agrippa II at Paneas included a two-story basilica (John F. Wilson and Vassilios Tzaferis, "Banias Dig Reveals King's Palace," *BAR* 24:1 [1998]: 54–61, 85; Wilson, *Caesarea Philippi*, 36–37).

[92] Amit, Patrich and Hirschfeld, *Aqueducts.*

[93] Gerasa, Bosra, Jerusalem, Suweda (Ball, *Rome*, 273–287; Segal, *From Function*, 129–140). Gerasa and Bosra each had two arches. Inscriptions show that one arch at Gerasa was dedicated to Hadrian, and one at Bosra was dedicated to the garrisoning legion. The Roman army outpost at Tel Shalem, near Scythopolis, may have built an arch (Bowersock, "Tel Shalem"; Eck and Foerster, "Ein Triumphbogen"). A gate with flanking towers, perhaps from the end of the first century, has recently been uncovered at Hippos-Susita (Arthur Segal, "Horvat Susita," *HA* 115 [2003]: 13–17).

[94] Segal, *Theatres*; Segal, "Theaters," *OEANE*; J. Schwartz, "Archeology," 166–169; Weiss, "Adopting," 31–33 and the map on 24; Ze'ev Weiss, "Buildings for Entertainment," in Sperber, *City*, 77–91, esp. 78–83. For theaters in the larger Roman world, see Hazel Dodge, "Amusing the Masses: Buildings for Entertainment and Leisure in The Roman World," in D. S. Potter and D. J. Mattingly, eds., *Life, Death and Entertainment in the Roman Empire* (Ann Arbor: University of Michigan Press, 1999), 205–255.

[95] Segal (*Theatres*, 4) notes Josephus's reference to the theater at Jerusalem and the archaeological remains of 30 in Palestine and the Transjordan from the first century BCE to the third century CE: Caesarea Maritima, Elusa, Sepphoris, Dor, Legio (perhaps an amphitheater), Scythopolis (2), Shumi (near Caesarea Maritima), Sebaste, Neapolis, Antipatris, Petra (2), Wadi Sabra, Sahr, Philippopolis, Kanawat, Hammat–Gader, Gadara (2), Abila, Adraa, Bosra, Pella, Gerasa (2), Birketein, and Philadelphia (2). The one at Tiberias should be added to this list. Weiss notes literary references to theaters at Gaza and Ashkelon ("Buildings," 78; "Adopting," 23; cf. J. Schwartz, "Archeology," 166–169; Retzleff, "Near Eastern Theatres.")

[96] Segal, *Theatres*, 60–61, 81–82; J. Schwartz, "Archeology," 169.

comparison to other theaters in the region, those at Sepphoris and Tiberias were mid-size, holding roughly 4,500 spectators each. They were larger than theaters like that at Hammat Gader, with room for 1,500–2,000, but significantly smaller than the Caesarea Maritima theater (renovated in the second century) and the primary theater at Scythopolis, both of which seated 6,000–8,000.[97]

Most of the entertainment in these theaters, as elsewhere in the Roman world, was probably by mimes, pantomimes, musicians, poets, and jugglers, though the tragedies and comedies associated with earlier eras might still be performed on occasion.[98] Rabbinic texts attest that rabbis and other Jews in Palestine were familiar with theaters; indeed, with so many of the buildings in the area, it would have been difficult not to have known something of the activities that occurred in them.[99] How high Jewish attendance was, however, is difficult to determine. One rabbinic passage, for example, records that Rabbi Meier prohibited Jews from going to theaters because of their association with idolatry;[100] another notes that adorning a theater was considered a sin.[101] The expression of such sentiments is sure proof that at least some Jews went to the theater – but who and how many, and how did habits vary among different cities?

The appearance of public bathhouses in Galilee likewise fits into a larger pattern.[102] In the second through fourth centuries, numerous

[97] Weiss, "Buildings," 79–82.

[98] Weiss collects literary and epigraphic references to mimes at Tyre, Berytus, Caesarea Maritima, Bosra and Gaza and to pantomimes at Caesarea and Hammat Gader ("Adopting," 31–33). See also Retzleff, "Near Eastern Theatres," 116; Mary T. Boatwright, "Theaters in the Roman Empire," *BA* 53 (1990): 184–192; Richard C. Beacham, *The Roman Theatre and its Audience* (Cambridge: Harvard University Press, 1992), 117–153; Bieber, *History*, 227–253. On the continuation of performances of comedies and tragedies, however, see C. P. Jones, "Greek Drama in the Roman Empire," in Ruth Scodel, ed., *Theater and Society in the Classical World* (Ann Arbor: University of Michigan Press, 1993), 39–52.

[99] Goodman, *State and Society*, 81–83; Martin Jacobs, "Theatres and Performances as Reflected in the Talmud Yerusahlmi," in Peter Schäfer and Catherine Heszer, eds., *The Talmud Yerushalmi and Graeco-Roman Culture* (Tübingen: Mohr Siebeck, 1998), vol. 1, 327–347.

[100] *T. Avodah Zarah* 2:5.

[101] *Y. Taanit* 1:4, 64b (cited in Weiss, "Adopting," 33).

[102] The second century, in particular, was the heyday of bathhouse construction throughout the Empire, especially in the east. See Garrett G. Fagan, *Bathing in Public in the Roman World*

baths were built throughout the southern Levant,[103] including cities surrounding Galilee such as Scythopolis,[104] Hammat Gader,[105] Kursi,[106] Ptolemais,[107] and Paneas.[108] Though a few private bathing facilities had been built in the pre-70 CE period, these bathhouses were apparently the first designed for broader use.[109] The bathhouse at Scythopolis and the eastern baths at Gerasa were among the largest in the eastern Roman Empire.[110] Bathhouses seem to have aroused little opposition among Jews. The potential for controversy was definitely there in the casual attitude towards nudity, the work required to heat water on the Sabbath, the typical adornment with statues.[111] Rabbinic traditions, however, reflect an awareness of the practices associated with bathhouses and an acceptance of them as a fact of life.[112]

(Ann Arbor: University of Michigan Press, 1999), 43; Inge Nielsen, "Early provincial baths and their relations to early Italic baths," in J. De Laine and D. E. Mohnston, eds., *Roman Baths and Bathing* (Portsmouth, R. I.: Journal of Roman Archaeology, 1999), 35–43. On the association of bathhouses with Roman culture, see Nielsen, *Thermae*, vol. 1, 1, 60 and Dodge, "Amusing the Masses," 219 and 243.

[103] For example, Dor, Gerasa, Gadara, Pella, Aelia Capitolina, Emmaus/Nicopolis, Kurnub/Mampsis (Nielsen, *Thermae*, vol. 2, 35–36, 41–42, 45–46; J. Schwartz "Archeology," 165–168); 'En Ya'el (Gershon Edelstein, "En Ya'el," *ESI* 5 [1986]: 30–33) and Kefar Sava (no author, "Kefar Sava-Nabi Yamin [Tomb of Benjamin]," *ESI* 1 [1982]: 63. Foerster reports remains of a bathhouse at Tel Shalem ("Cuirassed Bronze Statue"). Additional baths were built in the Byzantine period, such as those at Gerasa and (probably) Beth Yerah (B. Maisler, M. Stekelis, and M. Avi-Yonah, "The Excavations at Beth Yerah [Khirbet el-Kerak] [1944–1946]," *IEJ* 2 [1952]: 165–173, 218–229, esp. 218–223).

[104] Gaby Mazar and Rachel Bar-Hathan, "The Beth She'an Excavation Project, 1992–1994," *ESI* 17 (1998): 7–38, esp. 12.

[105] Yizhar Hirschfeld, *The Roman Baths of Hammat Gader* (Jerusalem: Israel Exploration Society, 1997).

[106] Judith Sudilovsky, "Bathhouse Uncovered at Kursi," *BAR* 29:1 (2003): 18.

[107] Moshe Dothan and Zeev Goldmann, "Acco: Excavations in the Modern City," *NEAEHL*, vol. 1, 23–27.

[108] Wilson mentions one built in the second or third century (*Caesarea Philippi*, 41). Vassilios Tzaferis and Shoshana Israeli describe another built sometime from the third to the sixth century ("Banias 1996," *HA* 109 [1999]: 1–2).

[109] The facility at Ramat Hanadiv is a possible exception; see discussion in Chapter Three.

[110] Elise A. Friedland, "The Roman Marble Sculptures from the North Hall of the East Baths at Gerasa," *AJA* 107 (2003): 413–448; on Scythopolis, see 419 n. 29.

[111] Reich, "Hot Bath-House"; Yaron Z. Eliav, "The Roman Bath as a Jewish Institution: Another Look at the Encounter between Judaism and the Greco-Roman Culture," *JSJ* 31 (2000): 416–454.

[112] Eliav, "Roman Bath"; Martin Jacobs, "Römische Thermenkultur im Spiegel des Talmud Yerushalmi," in Schäfer and Heszer, *Talmud Yerushalmi*, vol. 1, 219–311; Reich, "Hot Bath-House"; Goodman, *State and Society*, 83–84; and Sperber, *City*, 58–72.

Just as notable as the presence of certain forms of Greco-Roman urban architecture in Galilee is the absence of others.[113] Apparently, neither Sepphoris nor Tiberias constructed *nymphaea*, monumental fountains elaborately decorated with columns, carvings, and often statues, though nearby cities like Hippos, Scythopolis, and Gadara did.[114] No *tetrapyla* stood at the intersections of Galilean city streets, unless a large square pillar at Tiberias was once part of one.[115] As already observed, temples, a standard feature in the empire's cities, were rare in Galilee.[116] No amphitheaters, the characteristic building for Roman combat sports, were built within Galilee, though they were constructed at nearby Beth Shean, Caesarea Maritima, and perhaps Legio.[117] Nor did Galilee see the construction of any circuses or Hellenistic hippodromes to supplement the old stadium at Tiberias and hippodrome at Taricheae, though such facilities appeared at Caesarea Maritima, Tyre, Gadara, and Scythopolis (the one at the latter site rebuilt as an amphitheater in the fourth century).[118]

With so few sports facilities, watching athletic events was probably not a major part of Galilean life, though Taricheae and Tiberias

---

[113] The best synthesis of this material is Segal, *From Function*, to which I refer the reader for bibliographies of these sites. J. Schwartz's "Archeology" is also a helpful overview.

[114] Compare nymphaea at Gerasa, Canatha, Bosra, Philadelphia, Suweda, and Petra. Coins of Ptolemais and Pella depict *nymphaea*, though none has yet been discovered at either site (Segal, *From Function*, 151–168). An early interpretation of a monumental building at Hippos-Susita as a nymphaeum (Arthur Segal, "Horvat Susita," *HA* 113 [2001]: 14–18) has been rejected (Segal, "Horbat Susita [A]").

[115] Compare *tetrapyla* at Philippopolis, Bosra, Gerasa (2), Antipatris (Segal, *From Function*, 140–149); on the Tiberias pillar, see Hirschfeld, "Tiberias," *OEANE*, vol. 5, 204.

[116] On temple architecture in the Roman East, see Ball, *Rome*, 317–356.

[117] Compare also amphitheaters at Beth Guvrin/Eleutheropolis, Neapolis, and Bosra (Weiss, "Buildings," 78 and "Adopting," 24, 39–40; J. Schwartz, "Archeology," 169–170; Ball, *Rome*, 305). On the Legio amphitheater, see discussion in Chapter Two. On the distribution of amphitheaters throughout the Empire, see Jean-Claude Golvin, *L'amphithéâtre romain: essai sur la theorization de sa forme et des functions*, 2 vols. (Paris: Diffusion de Boccard, 1988), vol. 1, 275 and Jean-Claude Golvin and Christian Landes, *Amphithéâtres & Gladiateurs* (Paris: Les Presses du CNRS, 1990), 8–9.

[118] Compare also structures at Bosra, Neapolis, and Gerasa (Weiss, "Adopting," 23 and "Buildings," 78), and Tyre (John H. Humphrey, *Roman Circuses: Arenas for Chariot Racing* [London: B. T. Batsford, 1986], 461–477). Weiss notes literary references to examples at Gaza and Ashkelon (Weiss, "Adopting," 23 and "Buildings," 78). On circuses and hippodromes in the eastern Mediterranean, see Humphrey, *Roman Circuses*, 438–539, esp. 442.

may have hosted occasional contests.[119] Similarly, with no amphitheaters, most Galileans would have had only a vague familiarity
with Roman animal shows, gladiator fights, and other combat
sports.[120] Galilee's cities are conspicuously absent from the few
extant inscriptions listing cities in Palestine where such contests
were held.[121] Though several early rabbinic sayings reflect awareness
of the competitions,[122] none specifically refers to such activities in
Galilee itself or suggests that people regularly traveled outside of
Galilee to see fights.

SPONSORSHIP, LABOR, AND ROMAN IMPERIAL ARCHITECTURE

The timing of the construction of Roman urban architecture in
Galilee in the second and third centuries is hardly coincidental. It
corresponds to the increased presence of Roman troops and the
growing integration of the area into the Roman Empire. In this
respect, the extensive building activity in Galilee is typical: such
construction was widespread in the southern Levant as Rome annexed the former Herodian and Nabatean client kingdoms and
shifted a higher number of troops into the region.

One reason for the correlation between the increase in the Roman
military presence and the more widespread appearance of imperial
architecture is obvious: Roman soldiers did much of the building.[123]
Because earlier examples of monumental architecture like bathhouses and theaters were relatively few in the region, indigenous

---

[119] Weiss collects evidence for various athletic events (races, discus–throwing, javelin-tossing)
at Ashkelon, Scythopolis, Gerasa, and Caesarea Philippi, but notes none for Galilee
("Adopting," 38).

[120] Goodman, *State and Society*, 83. Whether a wall painting in the catacombs at Beth
She'arim depicts gladiators is unclear, in my opinion (*Beth She'arim*, vol. 1, 183–184); cf.
the lamp there with gladiatorial imagery (214 and fig. 22 no. 4).

[121] Second- and third-century CE contests are attested at Ashkelon, Damascus, Caesarea
Maritima, Neapolis, Scythopolis, Gaza, Philadelphia, and Caesarea Philippi (Weiss,
"Adopting," 38).

[122] Weiss notes references to the sale of animals (*m. Avodah Zarah* 1:7), bulls in a stadium (*m.
Bava Qamma* 4:4), and gladiators (*b. Gittin* 47a) ("Adopting"). See also Jacobs, "Theatres
and Performances."

[123] On this same pattern elsewhere, see the studies of Romanization cited in my Introduction.

architects and workers would have had little familiarity with how to draft the plans or implement their construction, especially in the early decades of the building boom. The Roman army, in contrast, was a source not only of military might, but also of surveyors, architects, and engineers, not to mention laborers. The use of soldiers in construction projects throughout the empire is well-documented, and in this regard, too, Galilee and the rest of Palestine were probably typical.[124] Inscriptions on the aqueduct at Caesarea Maritima, for example, record the work of soldiers from multiple legions.[125]

Roman soldiers also brought with them something else of key importance: money. The stationing of thousands of Roman troops in the area in the late first and early second centuries could not help but have a massive economic impact. The army is usually thought of as an agent of taxation – a function it certainly fulfilled – but its salaries, paid in silver, introduced large amounts of high denomination currency into local economies. In provinces on the empire's periphery, like Judea and Arabia, it is likely that they added more silver than they extracted, as Keith Hopkins as argued.[126] The overall increase of silver in the region's money supply eventually made more funds available for construction projects, regardless of who sponsored them. It also created a need for smaller change, bronzes of various denominations, which may be one reason for the flourishing of eastern civic mints in the second and third centuries.[127]

Acknowledging the role of Romans in construction activities does not, of course, preclude recognition of the important role that local workers also played. A Mishnaic tradition, for example, attests to Jewish participation in the building of basilicas and stadiums. It disapproved, probably because pagan prayers and ceremonies took

---

[124] Ramsey MacMullen, "Roman Imperial Building in the Provinces," *HSCP* 64 (1959): 207–236; MacMullen, *Soldier and Civilian*, 32–48; Mitchell, "Imperial Building"; G. R. Watson, *The Roman Soldier* (Ithaca: Cornell University Press, 1969), 143–145; Roy W. Davies, *Service in the Roman Army* (New York: Columbia University Press, 1989), 63–65; Isaac, *Limits*, 352–359; Futrell, *Blood*, 147–152; Nigel Pollard, *Soldiers, Cities, and Civilians in Roman Syria* (Ann Arbor: University of Michigan Press, 2000), 242–250.

[125] *GLI*, 12–14, 71–77, no. 45–54.

[126] Keith Hopkins, "Taxes and Trade in the Roman Empire (200 BC–AD 400)," *JRS* 70 (1980): 101–125; cf. Safrai, *Economy*, 339–349.

[127] Compare Harl, *Civic Coins*, 19.

place in those institutions. On the other hand, it regarded Jewish work on bathhouses as acceptable – at least until construction had progressed to the point when niches were created for statues.[128]

Who sponsored the construction of these new buildings? A dearth of euergetistic inscriptions in Sepphoris, Tiberias, and, in fact, most cities in the region makes this a surprisingly difficult question to answer.[129] When discussing particular buildings in Galilee, in most cases we do not know who initiated their construction or who paid the expenses. We can only speculate on such details, though a few generalizations are probably safe to make.

The emperor himself may have played a role.[130] Coins of Sepphoris from the early second century bear legends reading "Trajan gave," commemorating some type of benefaction to the city.[131] We have no idea what Trajan donated, though the date of the aqueduct's construction makes it a likely candidate.[132] At Caesarea Maritima, inscriptions on the aqueduct explicitly credit Hadrian as its donor.[133] Hadrian was particularly well known for his munificence, personally paying for dozens of projects (especially bathhouses, aqueducts, temples, and theaters). The bulk of evidence for his benefactions lies in Asia Minor and the west, however, not the Levant.[134] His successor, Antoninus Pius likewise lavished gifts upon many communities in the Empire. After him, however, imperial sponsorship of civic buildings seems to have dwindled.[135] That the flourishing of Roman architecture in Galilee and nearby areas

---

[128] *M. Avodah Zarah* 1:7. As always with rabbinic materials, whether this tradition presents a realistic depiction of Jewish activities or an idealized vision is debatable.

[129] See discussion in Chapter Five.

[130] On the role of the emperor and other officials in Romanization, see C. R. Whittaker, "Imperialism and Culture: The Roman Initiative," in Mattingly, *Dialogues*, 143–163.

[131] See discussion in Chapter Six.

[132] If this suggestion is correct, then it strengthens the argument that Roman soldiers had arrived in Galilee by 117 CE. Cf. Harl's suggestion that the inscription refers either to the right to mint coins or to some major gift (*Civic Coins*, 24).

[133] *GLI*, 12–14, 71–77, nos. 45–54.

[134] Inscriptions do not identify Hadrian as the builder of any structures in Palestine other than the Caesarea aqueduct (*Hadrian*, 108–143; Millar, *Roman Near East*, 105–107; Isaac, *Limits*, 352–359, 369–371), though they do record construction that occurred during his reign and dedications to him (e.g., for Gerasa, see Welles, "Inscriptions," 390–391 no. 30 and 424–425 nos. 143–145).

[135] Mitchell, "Imperial Building."

corresponds to the reigns of these emperors suggests that they might be at least partly responsible.[136] Roman governors were also often concerned with building and maintaining civic facilities, as the letters of Pliny and Trajan demonstrate,[137] and the army might sometimes construct facilities for their own use. It is telling, for example, that amphitheaters are mostly limited to cities with a known Roman military presence.[138] At least some bathhouses are likely to be the fruit of Roman labor, such as the one at Tel Shalem, with its army base.[139] The army is also known to have occasionally provided its service to projects sponsored by other parties.[140] Nevertheless, the mid-second century CE rabbi Shimon bar Yohai is said to have commented, "Everything that the Romans have built, they have built for themselves: market places, to house prostitutes, baths to pamper themselves and bridges to take tolls on them."[141]

It is difficult to imagine that civic elites and the local councils they controlled did not also sponsor at least some of this construction, in accordance with widespread Roman custom.[142] Initiating and supporting such projects allowed elites to advertise their own status and to participate in the culture of the wider empire; it provided them with an opportunity to construct and promote their own identities as wealthy Roman subjects. At cities with a high Roman presence, military officers, whether active or retired, might also make individual donations.[143] For Galilee's cities, however,

---

[136] Richard Duncan-Jones makes the intriguing suggestion that Hadrian's generous financial policies, such as the empire-wide remission of unpaid taxes, sparked a century of prosperity and construction in many provinces (*Structure and Scale in the Roman Economy* [Cambridge: Cambridge University Press, 1990], 59–67, followed by Birley, *Hadrian*, 97–98 and Boatwright, *Hadrian*, 10–11); cf. *Historia Augusta: Hadrian* 7.6 and Cassius Dio 69.8.1, 72.32.2.

[137] Pliny, *Epistles* 10.17b, 39, 41, 61. For evidence of the involvement of governors at Gerasa, see Gatier, "Governeurs"; *SEG* 27.1009.

[138] See the sources cited on amphitheaters earlier in the chapter.

[139] Laughlin suggests that Romans are responsible for the Capernaum bathhouse, noting its similarity to one at Ein Gedi, home to a Roman garrison ("Capernaum"); cf. Benjamin Mazar and Dan Barag, "En-Gedi," *NEAEHL*, vol. 2, 399–409.

[140] See the sources cited above on the role of the military in building.

[141] B. *Shabbat* 33b.

[142] For evidence at Gerasa, see Kraeling, "History," 61; *SEG* 27.1008; 39.1646, 1648, 1650; and 46.2060–2061 (discussed in Gatier, "Governeurs").

[143] For example, a Roman decurion donated to the southern theater at Gerasa (Welles, "Inscriptions," 399 no. 52; see other examples mentioned in Kraeling, "History," 61. Cf.

epigraphic commemoration of such contributions is lacking, raising the question of how enthusiastically Galilean elites embraced the practice of Roman euergetism.

CONCLUSION

The second and third centuries saw the widespread dissemination of Roman-style buildings in the southern Levant and elsewhere in the empire, and Galilee was no exception. The very ubiquity of such architecture in urban environments served a propagandistic function by creating an empire-wide network of physical symbols of Roman culture.[144] The new name of Sepphoris, Diocaesarea, likewise symbolized the empire's domination of the region.

Yet while it is important to recognize the ways in which the cityscapes of Galilee changed, it is equally important to keep those changes in perspective. Architecturally, Sepphoris and Tiberias exhibited more characteristics of the Greco-Roman city in this period than they had in the early first century. In terms of the amount and variety of Roman architecture, however, neither compared to larger cities like Gerasa,[145] Scythopolis,[146] and Caesarea Maritima.[147]

Though the exact architectural inspiration for the synagogue remains a point of considerable scholarly discussion, that debate should not hinder us from recognizing the obvious: in a general sense, synagogue designs also reflect the strong influence of Greco-Roman culture. Viewed from this perspective, the synagogue was,

---

two dedicatory inscriptions at Caesarea Paneas (Wilson, *Caesarea Philippi*, 40) and one at Gadara (*SEG* 39.1624).

[144] Compare Arthur Segal, "Imperial Architecture in the Roman East: The Local and the Unique," *Assaph (B)* 8 (2001): 31–48.

[145] Kraeling, *Gerasa*; Richardson, *City*, 78–102; David Kennedy, "The Identity of Roman Gerasa: An Archaeological Approach," *Mediterranean Archaeology* 11 (1998): 36–39; Jean-Pierre Braun et al., "The Town Plan of Gerasa in AD 2000: A Revised Edition," *ADAJ* 45 (2001): 433–436; and the sources cited in Chancey, *Myth*, 134–137.

[146] Yoram Tsafrir and Gideon Foerster, "Urbanism at Scythopolis-Beth Shean in the Fourth–Seventh Century," *Dumbarton Oaks Papers* 51 (1997): 85–146, esp. 88–99; Gideon Foerster, "Beth-Shean at the Foot of the Mound," *NEAEHL*, vol. 1, 223–235, esp. 223–228; Mazar and Bar-Hathan, "Beth She'an;" and the sources cited in Chancey, *Myth*, 140–143.

[147] *GLI*; Raban and Holum, *Caesarea Maritima*; Kenneth G. Holum, A. Raban, and J. Patrick, eds., *Caesarea Papers 2* (Portsmouth, R. I.: Journal of Roman Archaeology, 1999); Porat, "Caesarea"; Richardson, *City*, 104–128; and the sources cited in Chancey, *Myth*, 144–148.

ironically, the form of Greco-Roman public architecture that was most numerous and geographically widespread in Galilee. The number of synagogues in the region is greater than that of municipal basilicas, sports architecture, and bathhouses, and unlike those buildings, synagogues were more likely to be built in villages and smaller towns. Synagogue architecture thus provides us with an excellent example of one way in which an indigenous people might respond to the imposition of imperial architecture: by taking certain features of that architecture (in this case, the basic basilical shape and the use of columns) and incorporating them into a new style of structure that provided a communal expression of local religious and ethnic identity.

CHAPTER 5

The use of Greek in Jesus' Galilee

A key component of the view that Galilee was thoroughly Hellenized is the belief that Greek was widely spoken. Proponents of this
position cite several arguments for support: centuries of exposure to
Hellenism; the growing urbanization of the area from Antipas
onwards; the rabbis' use of Greek; the occurrence of Greek names;
and, most importantly, epigraphic evidence. At times, the logic of
these discussions appears circular: we know Galilee was Hellenized
because Greek was spoken there; we know Greek was often spoken
because Galilee was extensively Hellenized.[1]

The idea that many Galileans knew Greek is hardly new. Adolf
van Harnack and Shirley Jackson Case held it decades ago,[2] and a
long series of essays in *The Expository Times*, many titled "Did Jesus
Speak Greek?", sparred over the issue in the 1950s.[3] What is new,
however, is the extent to which the case is believed to have been
settled. We can now be confident, it is sometimes claimed, that
Greek was used frequently, not only among the elites but also

---

[1] On the languages of Palestine as a whole, see John P. Meier, *A Marginal Jew* (New York:
Doubleday, 1991), vol. 1, 255–268; James Barr, "Hebrew, Aramaic and Greek in the
Hellenistic Age," in *CHJ*, vol. 2, 79–114; Alan R. Millard, *Reading and Writing at the
Time of Jesus* (New York: New York University Press, 2000), esp. 84–131; Joseph A.
Fitzmyer, "The Languages of Palestine in the First Century AD," in *The Semitic
Background of the New Testament* (Grand Rapids, Mich. and Cambridge: William B.
Eerdmans; Livonia, Mich.: Dove Booksellers, 1997), 29–56; J. C. Greenfield, "The
Languages of Palestine, 200 BCE–200 CE," in Herbert H. Paper, ed., *Jewish Languages:
Themes and Variations* (Cambridge, Mass.: Association for Jewish Studies, 1978), 143–154;
Schürer, *History*, vol. 2, 52–80; Meyers and Strange, *Archaeology*, 62–91.

[2] Adolf van Harnack, *What is Christianity?*, trans. Thomas Bailey Saunders (repr., Philadelphia: Fortress, 1986; originally published in 1900), 33; Shirley Jackson Case, *Jesus: A
New Biography* (Chicago: University of Chicago Press, 1927), 200–212.

[3] Meier collects the bibliographical data for these articles in *Marginal Jew*, vol. 1, 287 n. 2.

among many of the common people, not only in the cities but also in the countryside. Jesus himself, in this view, may have been fairly conversant in Greek, introducing the possibility that the occasional gospel passage preserves his actual words, rather than a translation from the Aramaic.[4]

This confidence is all the more surprising given that we have no extant first-century texts of proven Galilean provenance. Efforts to locate the composition of gospels, especially Mark,[5] and the Q source[6] there remain largely speculative. The earliest rabbinic text, the Mishnah, was not compiled until the early third century, and it was written in Hebrew, not Greek. As for Josephus, though he was active in Galilee during the revolt, he composed none of his works there. He wrote in Rome, and even there he remained ambivalent towards the use of Greek.[7] We do know of at least one lost work from the end of the first century, the Greek account of the Jewish revolt by Justus of Tiberias,[8] but this single book is hardly the basis for generalizations about the Galilean population as a whole.

Literary evidence for Greek is thus lacking, but what about other types of data, such as inscriptions and names? If those categories of evidence show that Greek was well-known in Galilee in Jesus' day, then that would be one aspect of culture we could deem thoroughly Hellenized. Conversely, if such evidence is lacking, then languages

---

[4] On the languages of Jesus, see W. Argyle, "Greek among the Jews of Palestine in New Testament Times," *NTS* 20 (1973): 87–89; Ch. Rabin, "Hebrew and Aramaic in the First Century," in S. Safrai, M. Stern, D. Flusser, and W. C. van Unnik, eds., The *Jewish People in the First Century* (Assen/Amsterdam: Van Gorcum, 1976), vol. 1, 1007–1039; Stanley E. Porter, "Jesus and the Use of Greek in Galilee," in Bruce Chilton and Craig A. Evans, eds., *Studying the Historical Jesus: Evaluations of the State of Current Research* (Leiden: E. J. Brill, 1994), 123–154; Joseph A. Fitzmyer, "Did Jesus Speak Greek?" *BAR* 18:5 (1992): 58–63, 76–77; Robert H. Gundry, "The Language Milieu of First-Century Palestine: Its Bearing on the Authenticity of the Gospel Tradition," *JBL* 83 (1964): 404–408; Sevenster, *Do You Know?*; Matthew Black, *An Aramaic Approach to the Gospels and Acts* (Oxford: Clarendon Press, 1946); Gustaf Dalman, *The Words of Jesus*, trans. D. M. Kay (Edinburgh: T & T Clark, 1909).

[5] Willi Marxsen, *Mark the Evangelist*, trans. James Boyce et al. (Nashville, Abingdon, 1969); Werner Kelber, *The Kingdom in Mark: A New Place and a New Time* (Philadelphia; Fortress Press, 1974); and works discussed in Chancey, *Myth*, 13.

[6] Kloppenborg Verbin, *Excavating Q*; Mack, *Q: The Lost Gospel.*

[7] See *Ant.* 20.262–265; Sevenster, *Do You Know?* 61–76; Tessa Rajak, *Josephus: The Historian and his Society* (2nd ed., London: Duckworth, 2002), 46–64.

[8] Rajak, "Justus."

would be one more issue where a gap exists between oft-heard arguments and the actual published archaeological findings.

While few, if any, scholars would argue that Greek was spoken nowhere in Galilee, a thorough investigation reveals that there is little reason to believe that it was widespread.[9] On this issue, as on others relating to Hellenistic and Roman culture in Galilee, the quantity of our evidence has at times been exaggerated and its interpretation over-simplified. In this chapter, I provide a review of scholarship that reveals a now-familiar set of problems:[10] the use of finds from all over Palestine to draw conclusions about Galilee and the lumping together of artifacts from a range of centuries to shed light on the first century. I then provide a chronological overview of Galilee's inscriptions, analyzing them through the lens of the region's "epigraphic habit" and comparing them to those of the surrounding areas. Lastly, I consider the extent of Greek and Roman names among Galileans.

CHRONOLOGY, GEOGRAPHY, AND THE INTERPRETATION OF EVIDENCE

Even the staunchest advocates of the view that Galilee was highly Hellenized acknowledge that Aramaic remained the dominant language there, as it did elsewhere in the Jewish parts of Palestine.[11] Several factors make clear the continuity of its usage across a span of centuries stretching from long before Jesus to long after: its presence since the Persian period;[12] the seventeen Aramaic words of Jesus preserved in the Gospels, such as the *talitha cum* of Mark 5:41 and

---

[9] For reviews of the evidence, see Freyne, *Galilee from Alexander*, 139–145; Freyne, *Galilee, Jesus, and the Gospels*, 171–172; and Horsley, *Archaeology*, 154–175.

[10] The discussions of methodological issues by Meier (*Marginal Jew*, vol. 1, 255–268) and Horsley (*Archaeology*, 154–175) are among the best available. As the following discussion demonstrates, I share many of their perspectives.

[11] Compare Hengel, 'Hellenization', 8.

[12] On the development of Aramaic, see Joseph A. Fitzmyer and Daniel J. Harrington, *A Manual of Palestinian Aramaic Texts (Second Century BC–Second Century AD)* (Rome: Biblical Institute Press, 1978); Jonas C. Greenfield, "Aramaic and its Dialects," in Herbert H. Paper, eds., *Jewish Languages: Themes and Variations* (Cambridge, Mass.: Association for Jewish Studies, 1978), 29–43; Edward M. Cook, "Aramaic Language and Literature," in *OEANE*, vol. 1, 178–184.

the *ephphatha* of Mark 7:34;[13] inscriptions (mostly from later centuries); and post-Mishnaic rabbinic texts, especially the targumim.[14] Hebrew was probably used in Galilee, too, though to a much lesser extent. By the time of Jesus, Greek had definitely made some inroads there.[15] As for Latin, no one seriously suggests that it was used much; even those scholars who believe (erroneously, as I have tried to show) that Romans were numerous in first-century Galilee acknowledge that many of the soldiers would have spoken Greek themselves.

Earlier scholarship on the languages of Palestine often emphasized the importance of rabbinic materials. Those texts themselves are, of course, in Hebrew and Aramaic, but they sometimes refer to other languages, especially Greek, and they contain Latin and Greek loanwords.[16] Rabbinic works provide little help for the scholar investigating the use of Greek in the early first century, however. They were written after the two Revolts – indeed, most are much later – and thus reflect very different political, social, and, in many cases, geographical settings than early first-century CE Galilee.[17] In light of their later dates, it should be no surprise that they reflect knowledge of Greek. Some might preserve earlier traditions, but sifting out this early material is notoriously difficult. While some of the texts were written or edited in Palestine, others were put together

---

[13] Joachim Jeremias, *New Testament Theology: The Proclamation of Jesus* (New York: Charles Scribner's Sons, 1971), 3–8; the count would be eighteen if a text variant at Matt. 6:11 were included. Jeremias also notes eight Aramaic words attributed to Jesus in *b. Shabb.* 116b, though this late report is of dubious veracity.

[14] Roger Le Déaut, "The Targumim," in *CHJ*, vol. 2, 563–590; Avigdor Shinan, "The Aramaic Targum as a Mirror of Galilean Jewry," in Levine, *Galilee*, 241–247; Steven D. Fraade, "Rabbinic Views on the Practice of Targum, and Multilingualism in the Jewish Galilee of the Third–Sixth Centuries," in Levine, *Galilee*, 253–286.

[15] Sevenster, *Do You Know?*; Saul Lieberman, *Greek in Jewish Palestine: Studies in the Life and Manners of Jewish Palestine in the II–IV Centuries CE* (New York: Jewish Theological Seminary of America, 1942); G. Mussies, "Greek in Palestine and the Diaspora," in Safrai et al., *Jewish People*, vol. 1, 1040–1064; Gundry, "Language Milieu"; Argyle, "Greek"; Laurence H. Kant, "Jewish Inscriptions in Greek and Latin," *ANRW* II.20.2, 671–713; Hengel, *Judaism and Hellenism*, vol. 1, 58–64; Porter, "Jesus"; Pieter W. Van der Horst, "Greek in Jewish Palestine in Light of Jewish Epigraphy," in Collins and Sterling, *Hellenism*, 154–174.

[16] On loanwords in Jewish sources, see Hengel, *Judaism and Hellenism*, vol. 1, 60–61; Mussies, "Greek," 1050–1051; Schürer, *History*, vol. 2, 53–55, 60, 62, 70–80.

[17] On the difficulty of using the rabbinic materials to understand earlier centuries, cf. Barr, "Hebrew, Aramaic, and Greek," 110–111.

in Babylon. Some passages are associated with non-Galilean locations, and one can draw few conclusions about Galilee from material that originated in Jerusalem or Caesarea Maritima and even fewer from the sayings of rabbis in Babylon. Other traditions are impossible to associate with any specific locale. Furthermore, the historical accuracy of many stories and sayings is questionable; there is much legendary material mixed in among the factual. So, it is possible that even a quote attributed to an early first-century CE Galilean rabbi (and there are few such rabbis mentioned in the texts) might not shed any actual light on first-century Galilee.

A few classic examples illustrate these issues. *Mishnah Sotah* 9:14 says that at the time of the first revolt, "they" (presumably, the rabbis) forbade fathers to teach Greek to their sons. This claim raises obvious questions. It suggests that at least some people were studying and speaking Greek – but who, how many, where, and for what reasons? It also presupposes that some fathers taught their sons Greek, but was this typical or rare? Since Judea seems to have been the primary locale of the pre-revolt rabbis, does the saying tell us anything at all about Galilee? Since the saying is in a document that post-dates the revolt by over a century, is it historically reliable? If a rabbi or group of rabbis did issue such a prohibition, was it observed and respected by anyone outside rabbinic circles? The fact that it is not attributed to a named individual only exacerbates these issues.

An extravagant claim in the opposite direction is made in *b. Sotah* 49b, in which Rabbi Simeon ben Gamaliel (mid-second century CE) speaks of a thousand students in his father's house, five hundred studying Torah and another five hundred studying "Greek wisdom," with the latter phrase usually interpreted as including the language. The numbers here are clearly exaggerations, and the reliability of the tradition is extremely doubtful, especially given its late date. All that can safely be deduced from it is that Gamaliel was viewed as a highly respected rabbi and teacher who was well-versed not only in Torah but in Greek culture as well.[18] This and similar stories suggest that rabbis who were especially fluent in Greek were notable and worthy of special respect, not typical. Furthermore,

---

[18] See Sevenster's thorough discussion of this passage (*Do You Know?* 51–55).

such passages imply that learning Greek was somewhat unusual and required special study. It was often done for a particular purpose: to enable community leaders to communicate better with the governing Roman authorities.[19]

Other sayings refer to the use of Greek in legal documents. *Mishnah Gittin* 9:6 and 9:8, for example, allow for divorce certificates and the signatures of witnesses to be written in either Greek or Hebrew. From this we learn that scribes drawing up documents and witnesses might employ either language, but we do not learn what the norm was for different classes, different geographical areas, and different times.[20]

Largely on the basis of loanwords in rabbinic sources, Saul Lieberman claimed in his classic study that Greek was widespread among Jews in the second through fourth centuries CE. While the Greek of the common people, he argued, might have been "poor and vulgar . . . that of the learned Rabbis was far superior and of higher taste."[21] Yet many have contested his position. Everyone agrees that the number of Greek and Latin loanwords is high, but no one agrees on just what that number is. The most famous attempt to tabulate them, by Samuel Krauss at the end of the nineteenth century, produced as many questions as it did answers.[22] Krauss claimed to have found well over two thousand Greek and Latin loanwords,[23] but his sources, rabbinic writings from the third to the tenth centuries, covered such a large chronological and geographical canvas that it is difficult to draw too many conclusions about a given area or time period. Krauss's work was poorly received from the very start. Over a third of his identifications were challenged within the two covers of his own book in comments by his assistant Immanuel Löw. The retrospective critique of Haiim B. Rosén is

---

[19] Sevenster, *Do You Know?* 49.

[20] On Jewish legal documents, see Catherine Hezser, *Jewish Literacy in Roman Palestine* (Tübingen: Mohr Siebeck, 2001), 297–327.

[21] Lieberman, *Greek*, 37; on the rabbis and Greek culture in general, see Saul Lieberman, "How Much Greek in Jewish Palestine?" in Alexander Altmann, ed., *Biblical and Other Studies* (Cambridge: Harvard University Press, 1963), 123–141; and more recently, Levine, *Judaism*, 96–138.

[22] Samuel Krauss, *Griechische und lateinische Lehnwörter im Talmud, Midrasch und Targum*, 2 vols. (Berlin, 1898; reprint, Hildesheim: Georg Olms, 1964).

[23] Mussies, "Greek," 1050–1051.

typical. He argued that Krauss's study was characterized by "far fetched similarities, twisted meanings, omitting, adding and changing letters at . . . whim, invoking sound laws that hardly ever existed" – though it was still useful as a starting place for research.[24]

Eight decades later, Daniel Sperber took up Krauss's mantle, proceeding far more carefully.[25] A perusal of his work confirms the impression that many of the loanwords are administrative and governmental terms, an understandable phenomenon in light of the political situation in Palestine after the revolts, when contact with Greek- and Latin-speaking authorities would not have been unusual.[26] An influx of Greek loanwords, in particular, is typical of Aramaic dialects throughout the Near East in the third through seventh centuries CE,[27] after the increased Roman presence there. In short, though Greek and Latin loanwords in rabbinic writings reflect the rabbis' contact with speakers of those languages, they are not a reliable indicator of how widely or frequently the rabbis themselves used those languages. Use of Greek loanwords does not necessarily indicate the use of Greek sentences.[28]

Clearly, though, the rabbinic texts show that at least some rabbis spoke some Greek,[29] and we can infer the same about Jews outside of rabbinic circles. As J. N. Sevenster concluded, however, it is not clear exactly who spoke Greek, in what contexts and how fluently they spoke it, or how great the chronological variations in its usage were.[30] If we must be so guarded in drawing conclusions from rabbinic sources about the second and later centuries, then we

---

[24] Haiim B. Rosén, "Palestinian KOINH in Rabbinic Illustration," *JSS* 8 (1963): 56–73, quote from 57; cf. Sevenster, *Do You Know?* 39–41. Alexander puts the number of loanwords (not counting personal and geographical names and Roman administrative terms) at approximately 1,100, only 17 of them verbs ("Hellenism," 75–77).

[25] Daniel Sperber, *A Dictionary of Greek & Latin Legal Terms in Rabbinic Literature* (Ramat-Gan: Bar-Ilan University Press, 1982); cf. Daniel Sperber, *Essays on Greek and Latin in the Mishna, Talmud and Midrashic Literature* (Jerusalem: Makor Publishing, 1982).

[26] Compare Greenfield, "Languages," 153.

[27] Joseph A. Fitzmyer, "Phases of the Aramaic Language," in *A Wandering Aramean: Collected Aramaic Essays* (Chico, Cal: Scholars Press, 1979), 57–84.

[28] As Sevenster pointed out, no one argues on the basis of Latin loanwords that many rabbis were fluent in Latin (*Do You Know?* 41). Compare R. Katzoff, "Sperber's *Dictionary of Greek and Latin Legal Terms in Rabbinic Literature* – a Review Essay," *JSJ* 20 (1989): 195–206.

[29] For additional pertinent passages, see Hezser, *Jewish Literacy*, 247–250.

[30] Sevenster, *Do You Know?* 38–61, esp. 59; cf. Mussies, "Greek," 1059.

should be all the more cautious in using them to understand the early first century.

The same problems – the mixing together of materials from different geographical and chronological contexts – are evident in the use of archaeological data, the focus of more recent scholarship. Hengel once again provides a helpful starting place for discussion. He amassed a considerable list of evidence for the use of Greek among Palestinian Jews, including Greek personal names, loan-words, papyri, Greek texts among the Dead Sea Scrolls, ostraca, numismatic legends, and other types of inscriptions.[31] He draws attention to finds from a variety of areas, citing, for example, the third–second century BCE tomb inscriptions of Marisa; coins and inscriptions from coastal cities, Shechem, and the Decapolis; the ample epigraphic finds from the vicinity of Jerusalem, such as ossuaries, the Theodotus synagogue inscription, and the temple warning sign (all from the first century CE); and the correspondence, legal documents, book-length texts, and ostraca of the Judean desert.

In Hengel's view, if all Judaism was Hellenistic Judaism, then it followed naturally that many Galileans spoke Greek. Fishermen, tradesmen, and craftsmen would have needed Greek just to make a living.[32] One would have been especially likely to encounter Greek in Sepphoris and Tiberias, both of which (according to Hengel) had Greek schools that provided elementary training in rhetoric. Given Nazareth's proximity to Sepphoris, Jesus himself would surely have known some Greek, and the stories of his communicating with gentiles (the centurion at Capernaum, the Syro-Phoenician woman, Pontius Pilate) and traveling in non-Jewish areas like the Decapolis strongly suggest that he could converse in it.[33] Even some of Jesus' disciples – Philip, Andrew, and perhaps Thaddaeus and Bartholomew – had Greek names. What is notable about Hengel's argument, however, is just how short his list of Galilean archaeological evidence is: the Dionysos mosaic at Sepphoris; the inscriptions at the cemetery in Beth She'arim; the coins of Antipas. On the basis of

---

[31] Hengel, *Judaism and Hellenism*, vol. I, 58–65; *'Hellenization'*, 7–18.

[32] Compare Argyle, "Greek"; Porter, "Jesus," 136.

[33] Hengel, *'Hellenization'*, 17. Compare Argyle ("Greek") and Sevenster (*Do You Know?* 27).

archaeological finds, his case for Greek is much stronger for the "Greek cities" of Palestine and cosmopolitan Jerusalem than for Galilee.

Other scholars also point to the epigraphic corpus of Palestine as a whole as proof of the thoroughgoing use of Greek. Pieter W. Van der Horst, for example, writes, "The burden of proof is on the shoulders of those scholars who want to maintain that Greek was not the lingua franca of many Palestinian Jews in the Hellenistic-Roman-Byzantine period" since 50–65 percent of the public inscriptions are in Greek.[34] He thus lumps together finds from all over Palestine from a time span of a thousand years.

The importance of attention to geography is made clear when we consider ossuaries, sarcophagi that held the bones of the dead. Ossuaries constitute the bulk of our epigraphic evidence from first-century CE Palestine.[35] Hengel rightly pointed out that of the ones found around Jerusalem, approximately 39 percent had Greek, or, in a very few cases, Latin inscriptions.[36] Finds and publications subsequent to Hengel's study have been consistent with his statistic. L. Y. Rahmani's catalogue of 897 ossuaries from the late first century BCE to the third century CE included 227 with inscriptions, approximately a third of which were Greek. How many of these *inscribed* ossuaries were from Galilee, however? Only one, a sarcophagus with a Greek inscription found in a tomb with first and second century CE pottery at Qiryat Tiv'on.[37] Another ossuary with a Greek inscription, from the early second century CE at the latest, was found nearby at Kefar Barukh, in the Jezreel Valley. In short,

---

[34] Van der Horst, "Greek," 166; cf. Kee, "Early Christianity," 20–22.

[35] Hezser, *Jewish Literacy*, 364–373.

[36] Hengel, *'Hellenization'*, 10–11. James F. Strange once claimed, on the basis of the smaller body of evidence available at the time, that almost two thirds of ossuary inscriptions were in Greek ("Archaeology and the Religion of Judaism in Palestine," *ANRW* 2.19.1, 646–685, esp. 661). Strange's calculation was apparently derived from Fitzmyer, "Languages of Palestine," which he cites (cf. Fitzmyer, 51 n. 47).

[37] L. Y. Rahmani, *A Catalogue of Jewish Ossuaries in the Collections of the State of Israel* (Jerusalem: Israel Antiquities Authority, Israel Academy of Science and Humanities, 1994), 11–13, 172 no. 423 and 114 no. 145. Rahmani dates the Qiryat Tiv'on ossuary to the post-70 CE period, though whether he does so on the basis of ceramic finds or because of his theory that the practice of secondary burial spread to Galilee after the revolt is unclear. See Hengel's discussion of Rahmani's material in "Judaism and Hellenism Revisited," 27.

ossuaries tell us about the languages chosen for secondary burial inscriptions in and near Jerusalem, but our body of evidence from Galilee is too small for us to draw conclusions.[38]

The Dead Sea Scrolls, found far to the south of Galilee in the Judean desert, provide yet another example of finds deserving a more nuanced treatment than they sometimes receive. It is true that the scrolls include Greek manuscripts. One might argue that the fact that even a conservative Jewish sect like that at Qumran had Greek documents illustrates just how influential the language was. The evidence lends itself just as easily to another interpretation, however. The Greek texts at Qumran constitute only a small percentage of the total, about 25 manuscripts out of approximately 850, or 3 percent,[39] and in the remaining Hebrew and Aramaic manuscripts, Greek loanwords are quite rare.[40] So, one could just as easily argue that here, only a few miles from the most Hellenistic Jewish city in Palestine, Jerusalem, Greek barely makes an appearance.

Methodological problems multiply when other documents from the Judean desert are pulled into this discussion. Aside from the Dead Sea Scrolls and Greek ostraca and papyri at Masada (a minority of the writings discovered there[41]), almost all of our Greek finds from the Judean desert are from after the first revolt. The Babatha archives (93–132 CE) and the Bar Kochba letters post-date the destruction of the temple and after the stationing of a Roman

[38] A similar point can be made about appeals to literary texts written in Jerusalem as evidence for the languages used in Galilee. For example, the fact that the historian Eupolemus, a member of the Hasmonean inner circle in Jerusalem, wrote in Greek tells us about the interest of Jerusalem elites in Hellenistic culture, but not about Galileans (or, for that matter, about most commoners in Jerusalem). See Gruen, *Heritage and Hellenism*, 138–146; Hengel, *Judaism and Hellenism*, vol. 1, 92–95; Nikolaus Walter, "Jewish-Greek Literature of the Greek Period," in *CHJ*, vol. 1, 385–408, esp. 397–400.

[39] See James C. Vanderkam, "Greek at Qumran," in Collins and Sterling, ed., *Hellenism*, 175–181.

[40] This holds true even for the Copper Scroll (Florentino García Martínez, "Greek Loanwords in the Copper Scroll," in Florentino García Martínez and Gerard P. Luttikhuizen, eds., *Jerusalem, Alexander, Rome: Studies in Ancient Cultural Interaction in Honour of A. Hilhorst* [Leiden and Boston: Brill, 2003], 119–145).

[41] Yigael Yadin, Joseph Naveh and Ya'akov Meshorer, *Masada I: The Yigael Yadin Excavations 1963–1964 Final Reports* (Jerusalem: Israel Exploration Society, The Hebrew University, 1989); Hannah M. Cotton and Joseph Geiger, *Masada II: The Latin and Greek Documents* (Jerusalem: Israel Exploration Society, The Hebrew University, 1989), 9–10.

legion in Judea.[42] Yet despite the growth of Hellenistic influence in the decades since Jesus, the Semitic texts in these collections greatly outnumber the Greek ones. Using these texts to understand the linguistic environment of second-century Judea is complicated enough; using them to understand that of first-century Galilee is almost impossible.

Some Historical Jesus scholars, though, suggest that epigraphic finds have been abundant in Galilee. The Jesus Seminar's depiction of this issue in *The Five Gospels* is typical: since "recent archaeological excavations in Galilee indicate that Greek influence was widespread there in the first-century of our era," it is likely that Jesus knew Greek.[43] The comments of Marcus Borg (a member of the Seminar) are similar: "Recent archaeological finds suggest that the use of Greek was much more widespread than we thought, and this creates the very real possibility that Jesus, and perhaps the disciples, were bilingual."[44] Stanley Porter argues that "evidence is increasing that it [Galilee] was the Palestinian area most heavily influenced by Greek language and culture . . ."[45] and claims that the epigraphic evidence "clearly points to the presumption that Jesus' productive bilingual capacity included the ability to speak in Greek."[46]

But too often discussions purporting to concentrate specifically on Galilee are still characterized by the sorts of problems noted above, as Porter's study illustrates. Porter, characteristically, has done a remarkable amount of research. With its lengthy catalogue

---

[42] Naphtali Lewis, Yigael Yadin, and Jonas C. Greenfield, *The Documents from the Bar Kokhba Period in the Cave of Letters: Greek Papyri, Aramaic and Nabatean Signatures and Subscriptions* (Jerusalem: Israel Exploration Society, Hebrew University of Jerusalem, Shrine of the Book, 1989); Pierre Benoit, J. T. Milik, and Roland de Vaux, *Les Grottes de Murabba'at* (Oxford: Clarendon Press, 1961). As Millar points out (*RNE*, 364), the sole pre-Bar Kokhba letter from the Wadi Murabba'at caves, dating to 55/56 CE, is in Aramaic, not Greek. On other Near Eastern papyri, see H. M. Cotton, W. E. H. Cockle, and F. G. B. Millar, "The Papyrology of the Roman Near East: A Survey," *JRS* 85 (1995): 214–235.

[43] Funk, Hoover, et al., *The Five Gospels*, 28. Compare Funk's comments in *Honest*, 34, 79, and *Credible Jesus*, 5.

[44] Marcus J. Borg, "The Palestinian Background for a Life of Jesus," in Hershel Shanks, ed., *The Search for Jesus* (Washington, D. C.: Biblical Archaeology Society, 1994), 37–58, esp. 46–47.

[45] Porter, "Jesus," 134–136.   [46] Porter, "Jesus," 128–129.

of Greek inscriptions and thorough bibliographical information, his study is among the very best places to start when investigating this topic. Porter's suggestion that Galilee was the most Hellenized area in Palestine is largely supported by a list of inscriptions from elsewhere in Palestine (though often from nearby sites like Scythopolis and Mount Hermon). From Galilee itself, he can point to only numismatic inscriptions, the imperial prohibition of tomb robbing, a dedicatory inscription on a column from Capernaum, and the burial complex at Beth She'arim. The tomb-robbing inscription, as we have already seen, probably post-dates the beginning of direct Roman administration in 44 CE.[47] Porter dates the column inscription from Capernaum to the first or second century CE, but here he relies on out-dated scholarship. The synagogue from which that column came is now securely dated to the fourth or fifth century at the earliest – post-Constantinian coins mixed in with the mortar make the date indisputable.[48] As for the Beth She'arim inscriptions, Porter notes that approximately 80 percent are in Greek and states that "the earliest catacombs (first and second centuries AD) are *all* [emphasis in original] in Greek." The overwhelming majority of Beth She'arim's tombs, however, were constructed and used in the late second through the fourth centuries, and all of the complex's inscriptions are from this period. Not a single one dates to the first century.[49]

GALILEE'S INSCRIPTIONS

The lack of a standard compendium of Galilee's inscriptions has contributed to the confusion about their quantity and nature.[50] Yet

---

[47] See discussion in Chapter Two.

[48] S. Loffreda, "Coins from the Synagogue of Capharnaum," *LA* 47 (1997): 223–244; Stanislao Loffreda, "The Late Chronology of the Synagogue of Capernaum," in Levine, *Ancient Synagogues Revealed*, 52–56; Stanislao Loffreda, "Capernaum," *NEAEHL*, vol. 1, 291–295, esp. 294.

[49] Porter, "Jesus," 147; Porter here relies on E. Meyers and Strange, *Archaeology*, 84–85, but those scholars' wording was more reserved than Porter's. They stated that catacombs 6 and 11, which have Greek inscriptions, *may* (emphasis mine) be late first- or early second-century. In the excavation report itself, the sole inscription in Catacomb 6 is undated, and those in Catacomb 11 are dated to the third century (*Beth She'arim*, vol. 2, 87, 111).

[50] Jean-Baptiste Frey's classic work, *Corpus Inscriptionum Iudaicarum*, vol. 2 (Rome: Pontificio Instituto di Archeologia Cristiana, 1952), is over half a century old and full of

if we are to understand Galilee's linguistic milieu, a more detailed treatment of the evidence is needed than those currently available.[51] When the myriads of archaeological publications are sifted and their inscriptions presented in roughly chronological order, from the Hellenistic period up to the early fourth century CE, a very different picture emerges than the claims found in much recent New Testament scholarship. Inscriptions are far less numerous than one might think.[52]

As for the Hellenistic period (323–63 BCE), there is no abundance of inscriptions, of any type. Handles from imported amphorae (mostly from Rhodes) bearing Greek inscriptions have been found in both Galilee and surrounding sites, such as Ptolemais, Beth Yerah, Scythopolis, and Tel Anafa, particularly in Ptolemaic- and Seleucid-period contexts.[53] Coins with Greek legends circulated in Galilee, though none were minted in the region itself. Instead, they were struck by other parties – the Ptolemies, the Seleucids, the coastal cities, and a few cities of the Decapolis. From the time of Alexander Jannaeus (103–76 BCE) onwards, Hasmonean coins bore Greek inscriptions. Though produced in Jerusalem, they are frequent finds in Galilee, not only in first-century BCE contexts but also in later strata.

Coins and amphora handles aside, only a few other Hellenistic-era inscriptions, of any language, have been published from the

---

questionable datings. Catherine Hezser's recent and impressive collection of writings from Jewish Palestine does not focus specifically on Galilee (Hezser, *Jewish Literacy*, 356–421).

[51] Sources consulted to find inscriptions include the bibliographical references in *ABD*, *NEAEHL*, and *OEANE*; Tsafrir, Di Segni, and Green, *Tabula Imperii Romani*; excavation volumes; archaeological journals; and epigraphic compendia, especially *SEG*. On inscriptions in general, see B. H. McLean, *An Introduction to Greek Epigraphy of the Hellenistic and Roman Periods from Alexander the Great down to the Reign of Constantine (323 BC–AD 337)* (Ann Arbor: University of Michigan Press, 2002) and John Bodel, ed., *Epigraphic Evidence: Ancient History from Inscriptions* (London: Routledge, 2001).

[52] My survey thus omits Byzantine-era inscriptions, which are more numerous.

[53] Mordechai Aviam, "First Century Jewish Galilee: An Archaeological Perspective," in Edwards, *Religion and Society*, 7–27, esp. 12; Aviam, "Hellenistic Fortifications"; Gerald Finkielsztejn, "Amphoras and Stamped Handles from 'Akko," *Atiqot* 39 (2000): 135–153; Donald T. Ariel, "Stamped Amphora Handles," 154–163 in Frankel et al., *Settlement Dynamics*; Donald T. Ariel, "Two Rhodian Amphoras," *IEJ* 38 (1988): 31–35; Yohanan Landau and Vassilios Tzaferis, "Tel Istabah, Beth Shean: The Excavations and Hellenistic Jar Handles," *IEJ* 29 (1979): 152–157; Donald T. Ariel and Gerald Finkielsztejn, "Stamped Amphora Handles," in Herbert, *Tel Anafa I, i*, 183–240. Several have been found at Yoqne'am (Rosenthal-Heginbottom, "Stamped Jar Handles").

interior of Galilee.[54] A situla with Phoenician and Egyptian inscriptions from the pagan temple at Mizpeh Yamim dates to the Persian period but appears to have been in use until the temple's destruction in the second century BCE.[55] A gaming die found in southwestern Galilee from the Ptolemaic or Seleucid era bears in Greek the name of the god of fortune, Hermes.[56] A base for an Apis figurine at Beersheba has three inscriptions, one in hieroglyphic, one that is unreadable but perhaps Greek, and one that is Aramaic – קרב.[57] An ostracon from Sepphoris dated to the second century BCE has seven Semitic letters, אפמלסלש, the first five of which may reflect a Greek loan word, *epimeletes*.[58] At Kedesh, twenty-two sealings have been found, with Greek, Phoenician, and bilingual inscriptions, dating to the first half of the second century BCE.[59]

Similarly, we have very, very few Galilean inscriptions from the Early Roman period. In the first century CE, almost all are numismatic, from old Hasmonean currency, Herodian issues, or coins minted in nearby cities, especially Tyre. The *only* extant inscriptions definitely produced within Galilee during the first part of that century, the lifetime of Jesus, are the bronze coins of Herod Antipas and a lead market weight from Tiberias from 29/30 CE naming its *agoranomos*, Gaius Julius.[60]

Expanding the chronological parameters of our inquiry to include the decades between Antipas's reign and the end of the first century enlarges our epigraphic corpus only slightly. A mosaic at Magdala/Taricheae depicting a ship and *kantharos* includes the words KAI ΣΥ ("and you"), probably an apotropaic warning directed to visitors, returning their wishes, ill or good, back to them; its exact date is unclear.[61] A pre-67 CE ostracon from Yodefat bears Semitic

[54] On inscriptions found in nearby areas, see discussion below.
[55] Map coordinates 193/260; Frankel and Ventura, "Mispeh Yamim Bronzes."
[56] Rosa Last, "Inscribed Astragalus from Sha'ar Ha'amaqim," *ZPE* 130 (2000): 248.
[57] Map coordinates 189/259; Aviam, "First Century," 8–9.
[58] E. Meyers, "Sepphoris on the Eve," 130–131; Naveh, "Jar Fragment"; Naveh, "Epigraphic Miscellanea"; Joseph Naveh, "Jar Fragment with Inscription in Hebrew," in Nagy et al., *Sepphoris*, 170. See discussion in Chapter One.
[59] Ariel and Naveh, "Selected Inscribed Sealings."
[60] Qedar, "Two Lead Weights"; *SEG* 42.1473, 43.1076. On coins, see Chapter Five.
[61] Avner Raban, "The boat from Migdal Nunia and the anchorages of the Sea of Galilee from the time of Jesus," *International Journal of Nautical Archaeology and Underwater Exploration*

letters.[62] The remaining inscriptions, all Greek, are associated with government authorities: the imperial edict prohibiting tomb robbing;[63] several denominations of coins issued c. 53/54 CE by Tiberias, with Greek inscriptions; a coin issued by Agrippa II with Greek inscriptions, including the name of Tiberias;[64] and two coins minted by Sepphoris c. 68 CE with Greek inscriptions. In addition, one of the Sepphoris coins has a Latin inscription of the letters *SC* (the abbreviation for *senatus consulto*).[65] A market weight naming a city's *agoranomoi*, probably from Tiberias, apparently dates to the late first century; another weight may also have originated at one of those cities.[66]

Other inscriptions possibly date to the first century, though they could be later. A cooking pot found at Khirbet Qana was apparently inscribed with the alphabet, as demonstrated by a sherd inscribed with three Semitic letters (בגד).[67] A fragment from an ointment vase at Gush Halav is inscribed with the Greek letters ΑΡΙΣΤ; though it was found in a pre-fourth century CE context, the pottery style appears to be much earlier.[68] The date of an imported amphora

---

17 (1988): 311–329. The *kai su* inscription is apparently the only one found thus far in Israel, though it appears several times at Antioch. On its function, see Christine Kondoleon, *Domestic and Divine: Roman Mosaics in the House of Dionysos* (Ithaca and London: Cornell University Press, 1995), 19, 106 and Doro Levi, "The Evil Eye and the Unlucky Hunchback," in Richard Stilwell, ed., *Antioch-on-the-Orontes* (Princeton: Princeton University Press, 1941), vol. 3, 220–232, esp. 225–226.

[62] Adan-Bayewitz and Aviam, "Iotapata."

[63] See discussion in Chapter Two.

[64] *Treasury*, 106, 177–178.

[65] See Chancey, "Cultural Milieu," 132; Meshorer, "Coins of Sepphoris" and "Sepphoris and Rome." The presence of Latin on Sepphoris's coins makes them contrast all the more starkly with the nearest other revolt-era coinage, that of Gamla, which bore a paleo-Hebrew inscription referring to Jerusalem.

[66] One weight is dated to "year 43 of the great king Agrippa," which can only be Agrippa II. The weight was found at Magdala, but Qedar thinks it is from Tiberias ("Two Lead Weights"). On the date, see Kushnir-Stein, "Two Inscribed Lead Weights." Kushnir-Stein describes the second weight mentioned above, which was discovered in a museum collection.

[67] Esther Eshel and Douglas R. Edwards, "Language and Writing in Early Roman Galilee: Social Location of a Potter's Abecedary from Khirbet Qana," in Edwards, *Religion and Society*, 49–55.

[68] E. Meyers, C. Meyers, and Strange, *Gush Halav*, 126; cf. Eric M. Meyers, James F. Strange, Carol L. Meyers, Richard S. Hanson, "Preliminary Report on the 1977 and 1978 Seasons at Gush Halav (El Jish)," *BASOR* 233 (1979), 33–58, esp. 56.

handle with a Latin stamp is uncertain but in any case tells us little about the languages used at its find spot in northern Upper Galilee.[69] Other inscriptions that date to either the first or second century include: the Greek ossuary inscription at Qiryat Tiv'on;[70] graffiti (two letters, νθ – the number 59?) in a cave at Gush Halav,[71] and an unpublished fragmentary Latin inscription of just a few letters, found at Sepphoris.[72] The range of dates for these inscriptions is significant, especially when considering their value for understanding the linguistic milieu of first-century Galilee. There is a tremendous difference between Galilee in 50 CE and Galilee in 150 CE. The Latin inscription from Sepphoris, for example, probably post-dates the stationing there of Roman troops in the Revolt or the arrival of the legion in the second century.

Even inscriptions from later centuries of the Roman era are not as numerous as one might think. Many are from just two sites, Sepphoris and Tiberias. Both cities sporadically minted bronze coins with Greek inscriptions in the second and early third centuries.[73] At Sepphoris, a mid-second-century market weight identifies the *agoranomoi*, Simon son of Aianos, and Justus.[74] The basilical building there contains a mosaic inscription reading "Good Luck;" its date is uncertain, but it must be before the building's mid-fourth century destruction.[75] Some of the city's lavish mosaics also have Greek inscriptions. The early third-century triclinium mosaic with Dionysiac scenes has explanatory labels for each panel, and a mosaic in a nearby room reads *hygei*.[76] The more recently discovered

---

[69] Ariel, "Stamped Amphora Handles," 161 no. 34.

[70] Fanny Vitto, "Qiryat Tiv'on," *IEJ* 24 (1974): 279; "Kiriat Tiv'on," *RB* 9 (1972): 574–576; cf. Rahmani, *Catalogue*, 172 no. 423.

[71] Raqui Milman Baron, "A Survey of Inscriptions found in Israel, and published in 1992–1993," *SCI* 13 (1994): 142–161, esp. 143 no. 2.

[72] Strange commented on this unpublished inscription in his conference presentation, "Josephus on Galilee and Sepphoris," at the Josephus Seminar of the National Society of Biblical Literature Meeting, Denver, Col., November, 2001.

[73] See Chapter Six.

[74] Justus's father was probably also originally named, but that part of the inscription is lost. Meshorer, "Market Weight"; cf. his earlier reading in "Lead Weight."

[75] Strange, "Eastern Basilical Building."

[76] Talgam and Weiss, *Mosaics*, 47–73 and 19–20; Carol L. Meyers, Eric M. Meyers, Ehud Netzer, and Ze'ev Weiss, "The Dionysos Mosaic," in Nagy, *Sepphoris*, 111–116; E. Meyers, Netzer, and C. Meyers, *Sepphoris*, 34–35, 38–59.

Orpheus mosaic from the end of the third or early fourth century CE also has a Greek inscription, though the inscription may date to a later fourth-century restoration; likewise, an inscription on a later maritime mosaic in the same building probably also dates to later in the fourth century.[77] Yet another mosaic inscription was found in a nearby shop.[78] An amphora from the second or third century has red Greek letters on it,[79] and a Late Roman mortarium has a name, probably Eutychos, on its rim.[80] A tombstone with an Aramaic inscription and carved menorah is either Roman or Byzantine period.[81] Inscriptions may have adorned the city's theater in antiquity, though they are long since gone.

Most of the inscriptions found at Tiberias have been burial inscriptions. One, in Greek, originally marked the grave of a certain Julianus, son of Crispus; another, that of a Yosephus son of Eleasaros; yet another, that of Simon bar Semia.[82] Four inscriptions, two in Greek and two in Latin, are from the tombs of Roman soldiers and administrators.[83] Other Greek inscriptions include a marble plaque commissioned by a manumitted slave in honor of his former master[84] and a now lost dedication, perhaps of a statue (if so, it was a rare Galilean example of a statue-related inscription).[85]

---

[77] Ze'ev Weiss and Ehud Netzer, "Zippori – 1994–1995," *ESI* 18 (1998): 22–27; Ze'ev Weiss, "Zippori – 1997," *HA* 109 (1999): 16–18.

[78] Weiss, "Zippori 1999"; Weiss, "Zippori 2000."

[79] E. Meyers, Netzer, and C. Meyers, *Sepphoris*, 22.

[80] The inscription's first letters are lost; the ones still on the rim are τυχος. See B. Lifshitz, "Notes d'épigraphique Grecque," *RB* 77 (1970): 76–83, no. 14; cf. L. Y. Rahmani, "Miscellanea – Roman to Medieval," *Atiqot* 14 (1980): 103–113, esp. 104.

[81] Ze'ev Weiss, "Tombstone with Menorah and Inscription," in Nagy, *Sepphoris*, 185.

[82] That of Julianus is probably from the second century CE (Yossi Stepanski and Emanuel Damati, "Greek Funerary Inscriptions from Eastern Galilee," *ESI* 9 [1989/1990]: 79; Emanuel Damati, "Three Greek Inscriptions from Eastern Galilee," *Atiqot* 35 [1998]: 151–155). The inscription of Yosephos is probably late second- or early third-century (Emanuel Damati, "A Greek Inscription from a Mausoleum in Tiberias," *Atiqot* 38 [1999]: 227–228 [English Summary]). For that of Simon, see A. Ovadiah, "A Jewish Sarcophagus at Tiberias," *IEJ* 22 (1972): 229–232.

[83] For the Greek inscriptions, see Cagnat and LaFaye, *Inscriptiones Graecae*, vol. 3, no. 1204 and Leah Di Segni, "Ketuvot Teveryah," in Yizhar Hirschfeld, ed., *Teveryah* (Jerusalem: Yad Yitzhak Ben Zvi, 1988) (Hebrew), 70–95, esp. 90–91 no. 27. For the two Latin inscriptions, see Avi-Yonah, "Newly Discovered," 88–91 nos. 5 and 7. Other inscriptions (e.g., *CIJ* 2.984–986) in the vicinity of Tiberias could be from either Roman- or Byzantine-period.

[84] Di Segni, "Ketuvot," 76–77 no. 8.

[85] Di Segni, "Ketuvot," 86 no. 19; cf. Schwartz, *Imperialism*, 153.

Galilee's epigraphic record from the second and third centuries strongly reflects the impact of the Romans' arrival c. 120. Milestones on the roads connecting Sepphoris to Ptolemais and Tiberias and on the roads jutting out from Scythopolis in all directions had Latin inscriptions, according to normal Roman military conventions.[86] Many were also engraved with distances to nearby cities in Greek, presumably to make them at least somewhat more useful to a wider audience of travelers.[87] Roof tiles often bore the stamp of the VI Ferrata legion.[88] The graves of soldiers and administrators who died in service or after permanently settling in Galilee sometimes bore Latin inscriptions, as demonstrated by inscriptions at Tiberias, Gabara,[89] and Kefar Kanna.[90]

The treasure trove of Galilean inscriptions – approximately 280 inscriptions – is at the burial complex of Beth She'arim.[91] The overwhelming majority – roughly 80 percent – are in Greek. Some 16 percent in Hebrew, and the rest are in Aramaic or Palmyrene.[92] Despite the frequency with which these inscriptions are cited in discussions of first-century Galilee, all are later. While some scattered tombs date to the first century, those with inscriptions are from the late second to the early fourth century.

The other published Roman-era evidence can be quickly summarized. The Greek honorific inscription to Septimius Severus at Qazyon in Upper Galilee dates to c. 197 CE.[93] In western Upper Galilee, at Horvat Asaf, the Greek inscription on the tombstone of a woman named Marona has been dated to the second or third century CE.[94] Two ostraca, one, Greek and the other, Hebrew,

---

[86] See discussion in Chapter Two.
[87] See, for example, the milestone on the Sepphoris–Legio route (Isaac and Roll, "Judaea"), several on the Scythopolis–Legio road (Isaac and Roll, *Roman Roads*, nos. 3, 5, 8, 10–12, 15–19, 22) and a milestone on the Scythopolis–Pella road (*SEG* 39.1637). Cities may have occasionally erected or tended milestones (Isaac and Roll, *Roman Roads*, nos. 10–12).
[88] For example, at Horvath Hazon (map coordinates 187/257) (Bahat, "Roof Tile") and Kefar Hananya (Adan-Bayewitz, "Kefar Hananya").
[89] Map coordinates 182/250.
[90] Avi-Yonah, "Newly Discovered," 91 no. 7 and 88 no. 4; Mordechai Aviam will soon publish the one from Kefar Kanna (personal communication).
[91] *Beth She'arim*, vols. 2 and 3.
[92] Statistics from Lee I. Levine, "Beth She'arim," *OEANE*, vol. 2, 309–311.
[93] See discussion in Chapter Four.
[94] Map coordinates 205/269; Stepanski and Damati, "Greek Funerary Inscriptions," 79; Damati, "Three Greek Inscriptions."

from the third and fourth centuries CE, were found in the store-room of a large residence at Meiron.[95] At Horvat Hesheq, a pagan altar of unknown date with a Latin inscription was found reused in a church.[96] In Lower Galilee, a Semitic inscription on the "chair of Moses" from the synagogue at Chorazin dates to the fourth century at the earliest.[97] Two column inscriptions from Capernaum, one (previously mentioned) Greek and the other, Hebrew, date to the fourth century or perhaps even the fifth.[98] A Greek column inscription from the second century was reused in the Church of the Annunciation in Nazareth.[99] From the mid-fourth century on, inscriptions become more and more common in Galilee, especially in synagogues. And, of course, there are many inscriptions for which the dates are unclear, but which are probably from the Roman period.[100]

The chronological dimension of this epigraphic corpus is undeniable. Simply put, there is not much evidence from the first century CE, especially the earliest decades. Claims that there are numerous inscriptions from the time of Jesus are thus misleading, and the very meager number of first-century Greek inscriptions is an insufficient basis from which to generalize that Greek was widely spoken.

Most of the published inscriptions are from the Middle and Late Roman eras, and they probably do suggest a more widespread use of Greek in those later periods. They date to a very different point in Galilee's history than that of Jesus, and assuming they reflect the society of his day is extremely problematic. Since Jesus' time, Sepphoris and Tiberias had prospered and grown. Refugees from Judea, many presumably from Jerusalem, where Greek appears to have been more common, had come to Galilee following the revolts.[101]

---

[95] *Meiron,* 66; cf. critique of Gideon Foerster, "Excavations at Ancient Meron (Review Article)," *IEJ* 37 (1987): 262–269.

[96] Map coordinates 175/261; Mordechai Aviam, "Horvat Hesheq – A Unique Church in Upper Galilee," in *Jews,* 205–240.

[97] Yeivin, *Synagogue,* 29–31; Ze'ev Yeivin, "Chorazin," *NEAEHL,* vol. 1, 301–304.

[98] *CIJ,* vol. 2, 982–983. See discussion earlier in this chapter.

[99] Bellarmino Bagatti, *Excavations at Nazareth,* trans. E. Hoade (Jerusalem: Franciscan Printing Press, 1969), 316.

[100] Note the inscribed ring at Gush Halav (*Gush Halav,* 125) and an inscribed sarcophagus from Selame (map coordinates 185/254) (Sh. Applebaum, B. Isaac, and Y. Landau, "Varia Epigraphica," *SCI* 6 [1981/1982]: 98–118; 99 no. 2).

[101] Chancey, *Myth,* 60–61.

Most importantly, Rome's presence had increased dramatically. John P. Meier has suggested that 70 CE was a linguistic watershed for Palestine, after which Greek became more frequently spoken.[102] While this is probably true for Jerusalem and Judea, the watershed date for Galilee was more likely c. 120 CE, when the legion arrived. The problem of determining how much Greek was spoken in Galilee is more complex than counting and dating inscriptions, however. The published epigraphic findings have another surprising aspect: not only are Greek inscriptions rare in the first century, so are Semitic inscriptions. If Aramaic was the dominant spoken language in Galilee, as most scholars acknowledge, then why does it make such a poor showing in the region's epigraphic corpus? To answer this question, we must consider more carefully the complex relationship between the epigraphic and the oral uses of languages.

THE "EPIGRAPHIC HABIT"

Looking at inscriptions through the lens of a region's "epigraphic habit" (to use Ramsay MacMullen's famous phrase) might prevent us from interpreting them too facilely.[103] The "epigraphic habit" refers to an area's customs relating to inscriptions, i.e., the types of inscriptions engraved; the languages chosen for those inscriptions; the events, facts, and ideas recorded epigraphically; the chronological variations in the frequency of inscriptions; the parties that commissioned and erected inscriptions; and the parties reflected in inscriptions. Attention to the concept of the "epigraphic habit" should make us leery of making too many assumptions about the languages of the masses on the basis of inscriptions alone.

The chronological aspect of Galilee's epigraphic habit – few inscriptions in the first century, more in later ones – is clear. Though some scholars might be tempted to dismiss this pattern as the result of accidents of survival and discovery, a look at other regions reveals otherwise. The increase in the number of inscriptions

---

[102] Meier, *Marginal Jew*, vol. 1, 291 n. 27.
[103] Ramsay MacMullen, "The Epigraphic Habit in the Roman Empire," *American Journal of Philology* 103 (1982): 233–246; John Bodel, "Epigraphy and the Ancient Historian," in Bodel, *Epigraphic Evidence*, 1–56, esp. 6–15; Hezser, *Jewish Literacy*, 357–364.

in the second and later centuries CE conforms to an empire-wide pattern: after Roman troops and administrators are introduced into a region, considerably more inscriptions are produced. This is true not only of governmental inscriptions and publicly-displayed inscriptions of individuals and groups, but also of private inscriptions such as those associated with burials.[104] The Romans did not introduce inscriptions to Palestine, but they do seem to have introduced the custom of engraving more of them for a greater variety of purposes.

In a very real sense, then, the quantity of inscriptions itself reflects the effects of Romanization, though obviously other factors (such as economic) also affect the frequency. The fact that Galilee seems to have avoided the "Augustan boom" in inscriptions that Rome and other parts of the Mediterranean world experienced is explained,[105] at least partly, by the fact that the processes of Romanization were in only their nascent stages under Herod the Great and Antipas. Before the physical presence of Romans, inscriptions were a less significant part of Galilean life.[106]

Sensitivity to Galilee's epigraphic habit helps to explain the conspicuous absence of Aramaic among early inscriptions. The reality is that a region's inscriptions do not provide a full picture of the languages used. Instead, they usually reflect the values of the elites and the authorities.[107] In the inscriptions of the Roman world, local languages are often under-represented and Greek and Latin over-represented, a fact pointed out by Fergus Millar, Ramsay MacMullen, and others.[108] Because early Galilean inscriptions were

---

[104] MacMullen, "Epigraphic Habit"; MacMullen, "Frequency of Inscriptions in Roman Lydia," *ZPE* 65 (1986): 237–238.

[105] Greg Woolf, "Monumental Writing and the Expansion of Roman Society in the Early Empire," *JRS* 85 (1995): 214–235, esp. 37; Bodel, "Epigraphy," 8–10; Géza Alföldy, "Augustus und die Inschriften: Tradition und Innovation," *Gymnasium* 98 (1991): 289–324.

[106] The advent of the Romans also typically caused an increase in other types of writings, such as ostraca and papyri (MacMullen, "Epigraphic Habit," 237–240; Woolf, "Monumental Writing"; William V. Harris, *Ancient Literacy* [Cambridge and London: Harvard University Press, 1989], 141–143, 276–280, 283, 325; and Cotton, Cockle, and Millar, "Papyrology").

[107] Lapin, "Palestinian Inscriptions," 245–258.

[108] Ramsay MacMullen, "Provincial Languages in the Roman Empire," in *Changes in the Roman Empire: Essays in the Ordinary* (Princeton: Princeton University Press, 1990), 32–40; Fergus Millar, "Local Cultures in the Roman Empire: Libyan, Punic and Latin in Roman

mostly governmental, they were in the language typically used for official inscriptions in the Levant since the Ptolemies and the Seleucids, Greek. When the Romans arrived, they often deferred to the dominance of Greek, as the coins of the Judean procurators[109] and some issues from the imperial mints at Antioch and Alexandria demonstrate.[110]

Can we conclude from government-issued inscriptions, whether civic, Herodian, or Roman, that the Galileans who saw them knew Greek? When considering this question, we sometimes make what is probably a mistake: we imagine that most people were actually reading the inscriptions.[111] We too rarely ask an important question: if literacy rates were as low as we think – William V. Harris's comprehensive study suggests 10 percent for the empire, perhaps higher in the cities[112] – then who read these inscriptions? There is little reason to suppose that literacy was more common in Galilee than elsewhere in the Roman world; given that the region was mostly rural, it may have even been less common.[113] If most people were not literate anyway, can we assume that the language chosen for "official" inscriptions reflects in any way what was spoken by the majority of the population?[114] Greek letters engraved for governmental purposes tell us very little about what the masses spoke.[115] Instead, they tell us about the region's epigraphic habit and the cultural orientations of those commissioning the inscriptions and ordering the posting of edicts, the creation of market weights, the minting of currency.

Africa," *JRS* 58 (1965): 126–134; Ball, *Rome*, 3–4, 447; Harris, *Ancient Literacy*, 176–177, 187; Maryline Parca, "Local Languages and Native Cultures," in Bodel, *Epigraphic Evidence*, 57–72; Horsley, *Archaeology*, 155–159, 168.

[109] *Treasury*, 167–176.

[110] *RPC*, vol. 1, 606–630, 688–713.

[111] For examples of this reasoning, see Millard's discussion of Greek legends on Hasmonean coins (*Reading*, 107; cf. 167–168) and Sevenster's comments on the tomb-robbing edict (*Do You Know?* 120).

[112] Harris, *Ancient Literacy*, 22; cf. Mary Beard et al., *Literacy in the Roman World* (Ann Arbor, Mich.; Journal of Roman Archaeology, 1991) and Hezser, *Jewish Literacy*, 18–26, 34–36, 170–176.

[113] Hezser suggests that the literacy rate in Jewish Palestine was lower than in many other parts of the empire (*Jewish Literacy*, 496–504).

[114] On this point, see especially Meier, *Marginal Jew*, vol. 1, 255–257.

[115] *Contra* Sevenster, *Do You Know?* 120.

Coins provide the most obvious example of this point. It is clear from his money that Antipas, like the other Herods, wanted his currency to look like – and thus compare favorably with – other coinage emanating out of the eastern Mediterranean. His Greek numismatic legends attest to his Hellenizing and Romanizing aspirations. Similarly, Greek on the coins of Sepphoris and Tiberias reflects the civic elites' desire to have coinage like that of other Levant cities.[116]

Departing from convention by choosing a language other than Greek made a statement. This is seen clearly when one considers the Nabateans. Their early coins had Greek inscriptions, but after Rome's entrance into the area in the 60s BCE, they began minting coins with Nabatean legends, a statement of Nabatean distinctiveness in the face of growing Greco-Roman influence.[117] When Sepphoris put the Latin letters SC on a coin during the first revolt, those letters made the city's pro-Roman position unmistakable. The Herodian king Agrippa II went even further in expressing his Romanophile tendencies, minting coins in 85/86 and 86/87 CE that were copies of coins issued at Rome, down to their Latin inscriptions.[118]

Governmental inscriptions would not have needed to be read to convey their points. They carried symbolic and propagandistic messages that were perhaps more important than their literal meanings.[119] A few of Antipas's subjects could read the Greek legends on his coins, but probably not many. They did not have to, however, to understand what those legends communicated: that he was a tetrarch, ruling at the whim of the Romans, and that his new city Tiberias honored the emperor. Latin inscriptions at Paneas indicate that some of Agrippa's subjects knew Latin, but it is hard to imagine that most did. They also probably had little way of knowing that some of his coins were copies of Roman originals, but that did not

---

[116] On numismatic designs as a reflection of the values of civic elites, see Kenneth W. Harl, *Civic Coins and Civic Politics in the Roman East AD 180–275* (Berkeley: University of California Press, 1987), 31.

[117] Ya'akov Meshorer, *Nabatean Coins* (Jerusalem: Hebrew University, 1975).

[118] See *Treasury*, 111–112.

[119] Meier, *Marginal Jew*, vol. 1, 256–257; Horsley, *Archaeology*, 155–157; and Chancey, "City Coins."

prevent them from understanding his coins' message of alliance with the Romans. Similarly, not too many Greek-readers in Lower Galilee would have been needed to disseminate the message from the first-century imperial edict that grave robbing was a crime,[120] but fewer still would have been needed to spread the more important information, that Galilee was now directly subject to the emperor, not a mere client king. Likewise, second-century Galileans did not have to read the Latin milestones to understand the significance of the new paved roads that so physically marked their territory as under Roman occupation.[121]

After the late second century, as people engraved or commissioned other types of inscriptions, such as mosaic labels and burial epitaphs, they, too, usually conformed to the conventions typical of the Roman Near East by employing Greek. But even with this wider, private use of Greek, it is still difficult to determine precisely the particulars of Galilee's linguistic situation. Clearly, some people knew Greek, probably more than in the first century – but who, and how many?

A consideration of burial inscriptions, the largest single category of inscriptions here as in most of the Roman Empire,[122] sheds further light on Galilee's epigraphic habit. We have insufficient evidence to draw many conclusions about the first century, especially given the lack of inscribed ossuaries. Even in the third and fourth centuries, we have far fewer funerary inscriptions than might be expected, given how common such inscriptions were in other parts of the Mediterranean.[123]

What we do have, fortunately, is the remarkable catacomb complex at Beth She'arim. Though some people interred there were from other parts of Palestine and a few may have hailed from various parts of the eastern Diaspora, especially Palmyra, most were probably Galileans. The complex apparently was not intended for the masses; burial in its thirty-one catacombs probably reflects that the interred and/or their families had considerable financial resources. Thus, at Beth She'arim we see the burial practices of the elites, not commoners.

[120] See discussion in Chapter Two.
[121] Hezser argues similarly (*Jewish Literacy*, 362–363).
[122] Bodel, "Epigraphy," 30–41.   [123] Hezser, *Jewish Literacy*, 373–374.

Greek overwhelmingly dominates the approximately 280 inscriptions there, though Palmyrene, Aramaic, and Hebrew are also found. The Palmyrene inscriptions are easily enough explained; they reflect the origins of the interred. As for Aramaic, it is surprisingly rare. This is an important observation; despite being the commonly spoken language in Galilee, it was not the language typically chosen for burial inscriptions by the elites. Aside from isolated words here and there, it appears in only three inscriptions, all in one catacomb, and all with the same purpose: warning tomb robbers or other visitors to the complex not to tamper with graves. One of these Aramaic inscriptions is accompanied by a similar admonition in Greek.[124]

Departures from the preference for Greek often reveal something about the social location of the interred and/or those who sponsored their burial. Thus, while Hebrew inscriptions are scattered throughout the complex, they are especially prevalent in caves 14 and 20,[125] tombs that belonged to the families of rabbis.[126] The choice of Hebrew in these tombs reflects the rabbis' respect for the sacred language as well as an interest in differentiating their tombs from those of non-rabbinic families.

Inscriptions are found throughout the complex, on the walls of halls, the sides of individual arcosolia, ceilings, doors, lintels, sealing stones, and sarcophagus lids.[127] They had various functions: demonstrating ownership, identifying the occupants of specific graves, providing directions for visitors.[128] In a third-century burial hall, for example, three inscriptions point the way to the grave of Julianus Gemellus, one on the entrance to the hall; another, on an arch connecting two rooms; the third, on the wall of the arcosolium itself.[129] The Hebrew "shalom" is not uncommon in the complex, serving partly as consolation and partly as a social marker of Jewish identity.[130]

---

[124] *Beth She'arim*, vol. 3, 233–235. Similar Greek warnings are found elsewhere in the catacombs.

[125] Avigad, "The Excavations," 230–258.

[126] Weiss, "Social Aspects," 367.

[127] *Beth She'arim*, vol. 1, 193.

[128] *Beth She'arim*, vol. 1, 193; Weiss, "Social Aspects," 358.

[129] *Beth She'arim*, vol. 2, 8–9, nos. 13–15 and discussion on 193, 219.

[130] On this point, see Lapin, "Palestinian Inscriptions," 260–261.

Does the presence of these various inscriptions indicate that those who commissioned them, presumably the relatives of the deceased, could read them? This was undoubtedly sometimes the case – but can we assume that it was always so? Obviously, inscriptions that provided directions to specific graves reflect the assumption that someone would read them (or at least recognize and remember them), as do, perhaps, warnings against tomb robbing, but not all inscriptions are so obviously functional. Again, low literacy rates must be taken into consideration.[131] Inscriptions might sometimes be explained merely as convention. If so, they would reflect the mason's ability to carve such inscriptions, not necessarily the linguistic abilities of the deceased or the deceased's family.[132] Many are not of the highest quality; they are crude, with grammatical errors and poorly shaped letters. Overall, they provide little evidence for a high level of proficiency in reading Greek.[133]

Precisely because they are so different from the other inscriptions, two epitaphs are worthy of special mention. One marks the burial spot of Justus, son of Leontios and Sappho, the other that of Karteria. Both are considerably longer than most inscriptions in the complex, and both are written in meter, reflecting Hellenistic poetic conventions. The epitaph of Justus says that he has gone to Hades, in accordance with Fate (*Moira*) – providing the only references to those Greek concepts at Beth She'arim.[134] The dates of these inscriptions (third century) corresponds to what we see in the cities of Arabia. There, metrical inscriptions had first appeared in the second century after the area became a Roman province, but they were becoming more common in the third and fourth centuries.[135]

On the whole, the Beth She'arim evidence shows us that Galilean Jewish elites preferred Greek for burial inscriptions.[136] What

[131] On epitaphs and literacy, see Harris, *Ancient Literacy*, 221–222.

[132] Mussies, "Greek," 1041.

[133] *Beth She'arim*, vol. 1, 220.

[134] *Beth She'arim*, vol. 2, 97 no. 127 and 157 no. 183; cf. van der Horst, "Greek," 96.

[135] Pierre-Louis Gatier, "Répartition des inscriptions grecques de Jordanie. L'exemple des inscriptions métriques aux époques romaine et byzantine," in *Studies in the History and Archaeology of Jordan* (Ammon: Dept. of Antiquities, 1992), vol. 4, 291–294.

[136] As Hezser points out, however, these inscriptions are shorter and less elaborate than typical Roman inscriptions (*Jewish Literacy*, 396–397).

proportion of those elites could actually read or speak Greek remains open to debate – some, yes, but how many?[137] Whether burial inscriptions of the elites attest to a widespread, high-level competence in Greek among local Jews of all social classes is even more debatable.[138]

Synagogue inscriptions provide an additional example of the complexity of the "epigraphic habit," though almost all post-date our time period. With a few possible exceptions (e.g., Beth She'arim and Horvat 'Ammudim), synagogue inscriptions in Galilee are from the fourth century or later.[139] The same is true of most synagogue inscriptions elsewhere in Palestine,[140] though rabbinic sources attest to earlier inscriptions.[141] Aramaic, Greek, and Hebrew occur, with Aramaic the most common and Hebrew the least. The heightened visibility (literally) of Aramaic and Hebrew probably reflects the growing self-identity of "Jewishness" in late antiquity, a self-consciousness brought about not only by foreign domination but also by increasing Christian influence.[142] Different languages are

---

[137] *Contra* Sevenster, *Do You Know?* 181–182; Vanderkam, "Greek," 163.

[138] Strange ("Archaeology and the Religion," 661) and van der Horst ("Greek," 163) have made the opposite argument.

[139] Inscriptions from the synagogue at Beth She'arim are from either the third or fourth century (*Beth She'arim*, vol. 2, 189–198). The Aramaic inscriptions at Horvat 'Ammudim (one on a stone slab, one in a mosaic) are probably early fourth-century, though they could possibly be from the late third; see Levine, "'Ammudim, Horvat"; Levine, "Excavations;" and Chen, "Ancient Synagogue." Dothan suggested that the fresco of the early third-century stratum of the Hammath Tiberias synagogue was decorated with Greek writing, but it is difficult to identify any characters in the photograph he provides (*Hammath Tiberias*, 22 and plates 23:1–2 and 36:3). The Greek, Aramaic and Hebrew inscriptions from that synagogue's zodiac mosaic are from the fourth century.

[140] The most notable exception is the Theodotus inscription from Jerusalem (Levine, *Ancient Synagogue*, 54–56). See also this chapter's earlier discussion of the Capernaum inscriptions, which are still often cited (erroneously) as second century evidence.

[141] The standard collections of inscriptions are Joseph Naveh, *On Mosaic and Stone: The Aramaic and Hebrew Inscriptions from Ancient Synagogues* (Jerusalem: Carta and Israel Exploration Society, 1978) (Hebrew), updated in J. Naveh, "The Aramaic and Hebrew Inscriptions from Ancient Synagogues," *Eretz Israel* 20 (1989) 302–310 (Hebrew); Lea Roth-Gerson, *Greek Inscriptions from the Synagogues in Eretz Israel* (Jerusalem: Ben Zvi Institute, 1987) (Hebrew); see also Levine, *Ancient Synagogue*, 347–350; Steven Fine, "Synagogue Inscriptions," *OEANE*, vol. 5, 114–118; and Hezser, *Jewish Literacy*, 397–413. Several synagogue inscriptions once dated to the second through fourth centuries, such as *CIJ*, vol. 2, 974, 979, 987, must now be dated to the fourth century or later, in light of advances in our knowledge about the synagogue's development.

[142] Lapin, "Palestinian Inscriptions"; Seth Schwartz, "Language, Power and Identity in Ancient Palestine," *Past and Present* 148 (1995): 3–47, esp. 44.

associated with different functions. Hebrew is used in scripture quotations and allusions; labels of biblical scenes; and, in zodiac mosaics, to identify astrological symbols.[143] Greek and Aramaic are used for inscriptions that honor donors to the synagogue, the majority of inscriptions.

Who chose the languages for these inscriptions? The synagogue elders? The donors? The artisans? Regardless, they are expressions of beneficence, wealth, influence, and prestige by the elites.[144] Thus, one cannot necessarily conclude on the basis of the proportion of each language among a given synagogue's inscriptions what the majority of worshippers there spoke. The geographical distribution of the languages is also significant. Greek inscriptions are more common in larger communities, such as Sepphoris, than in smaller villages. Because Galilee's largest communities were in Lower Galilee, Greek inscriptions are more common there than in Upper Galilee.[145] Going beyond these most basic generalizations is difficult. Despite this abundance of evidence, our understanding of Galilee's linguistic situation in the fourth–seventh centuries remains partial.

The geographical dimension of Galilee's epigraphic habit highlighted by Byzantine-period synagogue inscriptions is reflected in the Roman-period evidence as well. Inscriptions from Lower Galilee outnumber those from Upper Galilee. The difference is probably due, at least in part, to the absence of major cities in the north. Upper Galilee's slower development of a tendency to create inscriptions may also be because of its greater distance from the bases of the Roman army.

An additional aspect of Galilee's epigraphic habit in the Roman period is the low number of certain types of inscriptions.[146] Pagan inscriptions – whether from altars, statues, votive objects, or

---

[143] Zodiac mosaics with Hebrew inscriptions have been found at Hammath Tiberias, Sepphoris, Na'aran (near Jericho), and Beth Alpha.

[144] Lapin, "Palestinian Inscriptions."

[145] Naveh, *On Mosaic and Stone*, v, 13 and Roth-Gerson, *Greek Inscriptions*, 9–10, 14; cf. discussion in Fine, "Synagogue Inscriptions"; Lee I. Levine, "Synagogues," *NEAEHL*, vol. 4, 1421–1427; Hachlili, *Ancient Jewish Art*, 225–227.

[146] On the distinctive epigraphic habits of other regions in the Empire, see Millett, *Romanization*, 81–82 and Greg Woolf, "Beyond Romans and Natives," *WA* 28 (1997): 339–350.

temples – are rare. Given the predominantly Jewish population, this is perhaps not surprising, but one might have expected to find the worship of Roman soldiers recorded epigraphically more often. Because statues do not appear to have been common, related inscriptions (i.e., identification of the person portrayed or of the donor) are lacking, with the exception of one inscription from Tiberias. Indeed, honorific inscriptions of all types are lacking. We find only one inscription to the emperor, at Qazyon, and none to civic elites or provincial officials. Inscriptions identifying the sponsors of buildings are conspicuously absent, though they become common in the Byzantine period, as synagogue inscriptions demonstrate. What makes the absence of these various types of inscriptions so striking is that one would have encountered them regularly in some cities, such as Gerasa. The lack of euergetistic inscriptions, in particular, raises the question of whether Galileans largely rejected this aspect of Roman culture.

THE NEIGHBORING AREAS

If one should insist that the "accidents of survival and discovery" are the only reason for the relatively small number of inscriptions from Galilee, the evidence from adjacent areas, most of it in Greek, stands as counter-testimony. Pre-Roman examples at many sites go beyond amphora handles and coins. Inscriptions from the vicinity of Scythopolis include at least four second-century BCE examples: the stele with orders from Seleucid kings and officials[147] two lead weights with the names of *agoranomoi*[148] and what is probably a list of priests of Zeus Olympios.[149] Two pagan dedicatory inscriptions from the mid-second century BCE were found near Ptolemais, one to Atargatis by a Didotous Neoptolemy,[150] the other to Zeus Soter by the Seleucid governor.[151] Excavations at Ptolemais also

---

[147] Landau, "Greek Inscription Found Near Hefzibah."
[148] *SEG* 27.1451; no author, *Inscriptions Reveal*, 110 no. 224; Kushnir-Stein, "New Hellenistic Lead Weights."
[149] *SEG* 8.33.
[150] M. Avi-Yonah, "Syrian Gods at Ptolemais-Accho," *IEJ* 9 (1959): 1–12.
[151] Landau, "Greek Inscription from Acre"; cf. J. Schwartz, "Note complémentaire."

revealed a second-century BCE epitaph memorializing a Cretan soldier.[152] At Gadara, a Greek building inscription probably dates to 85/84 BCE.[153] Mt. Hermon's long history as a site for temples resulted in a number of Hellenistic- and Roman-era pagan inscriptions there.[154] At the mid-second-century BCE Iturean site of Khirbet Zemel, five *pithoi* were inscribed with Greek names.[155]

As in Galilee, the number of inscriptions in the surrounding areas increases in the Roman period. They include the expected occasional ostraca, like the Aramaic example found at Jalame, southwest of Galilee.[156] They also include numerous burial inscriptions, like the probably third-century CE example at Kedesh reused by modern villages as a doorjamb,[157] the inscribed sarcophagus found near the coast at el Makr,[158] and the inscribed ossuary in the Jezreel at Kefar Barukh[159] (all three in Greek). Many are governmental, like

---

[152] Moshe Dothan, "Akko: Interim Excavation Report: First Season 1973/4," *BASOR* 224 (1976): 1–48, esp. 39–40. Note also the two other inscriptions mentioned in Mordechai Aviam, "Regionalism of Tombs and Burial Customs in the Galilee during the Hellenistic, Roman, and Byzantine Periods," in *Jews,* 257–313, specifically 262.

[153] *SEG* 50.1479.

[154] Shimon Dar, "The Greek Inscriptions from Senaim on Mount Hermon," *PEQ* 120 (1988): 26–44; Avraham Biran, "To the God who is in Dan," in Avraham Biran, ed., *Temples and High Places in Biblical Times* (Jerusalem: Nelson Glueck School of Biblical Archaeology of Hebrew Union College – Jewish Institute of Religion, 1981), 142–151.

[155] Map coordinates 229/289; Moshe Hartel, "Excavations at Khirbet Zemel, Northern Golan: An Ituraean Settlement Site," in Gal, *Eretz Zafon,* 75–117.

[156] On the second-century or later eight-character Aramaic inscription on a jar handle, see Joseph Naveh and G. D. Weinberg, "Appendix: Inscriptions," in Gladys Davidson Weinberg, ed., *Excavations at Jalame: Site of a Glass Factory in Late Roman Palestine* (Columbia: University of Missouri Press, 1988), 255–256.

[157] Chester C. McCown, "Epigraphic Gleanings," *AASOR* 2–3 (1921–1922): 109–115, esp. 114–115. This burial inscription is dated to year 393; my proposed third-century date reflects the assumption that it uses the era of Tyre, which began in 126/125 BCE. Other burial inscriptions include: two sarcophagi, one (early third-century) with a painted Greek inscription and another (late second-century) with a Hebrew inscription, found at Kefar Gil'adi, west of Paneas (J. Kaplan, "Kfar Gil'adi," *IEJ* 12 [1962]: 154–155; J. Kaplan, "Kfar Gil'adi," *IEJ* 8 [1958]: 274); a Greek epitaph (date unknown) from Yoqne'am (Applebaum, Isaac, and Landau, "Varia Epigraphica," 100 no. 4). At Belvoir (map coordinates 200/223), a second third-century Greek epitaph was recovered (*SEG* 50.1465). Further north, at Sidon, sixty-two Roman period epitaphs are in Greek (*SEG* 50.1400–1461). Gadara has recently yielded a third- or fourth-century CE Greek epitaph on a basalt rock (*SEG* 50.1516).

[158] Aviam, "Regionalism," 272.

[159] Rahmani, *Catalogue of Jewish Ossuaries,* 114 no. 145.

the inscribed market weights from Paneas[160] and Gaba.[161] A few inscriptions are honorific, like one at Gaba naming a citizen "first of the city and its founder."[162] The Roman colony at Ptolemais marked its boundary with a Latin inscription,[163] and along with the villages of Nea Come and Gedru, it honored Nero with a Latin inscription.[164] At the end of the third and in the early fourth century, Roman officials used Greek inscriptions to mark boundaries (apparently for taxation purposes) for many villages in the Huleh Valley and Golan.[165]

Unlike Galilee's inscriptions, many of those from the neighboring regions are explicitly pagan. At Qeren Naftali, a Tyrian village on the northern fringe of geographical Galilee, two dedicatory inscriptions, one to Athena (c. 50–150 CE), the other to the Heliopolitan Zeus (third century CE) were found.[166] Five inscriptions are associated with the early second-century CE temple at Kedesh, also in Tyrian territory.[167] Further north still, pagan worshippers left behind other inscriptions.[168] At Paneas, numerous pagan inscriptions from the second through fourth centuries have been found.[169] Other examples in the region are plenteous.[170]

[160] Alla Kushnir-Stein, "Two Inscribed Weights from Banias," *IEJ* 45 (1995): 48–51. Both are post-first century CE.

[161] Ayriel Siegelmann, "The Identification of Gaba Hippeon," *PEQ* 116 (1984–1985): 89–93.

[162] Z. Safrai and M. Lin, "Mishmar Ha'Emeq," *ESI* 6 (1987–1988): 111; Benjamin Isaac, "Two Greek Inscriptions from Tell Abu-Shusha," in Isaac, *Near East*, 31–33.

[163] Avi-Yonah, "Newly Discovered," 85–86 no. 2.

[164] Avi-Yonah, "Newly Discovered," 85–86 nos. 2–3.

[165] Danny Syon and Moshe Hartal note forty such stones in "A New Tetrarchic Boundary Stone," *SCI* 22 (2003): 233–239; cf. Millar, *RNE*, 194–195, 535–544.

[166] E. W. G. Masterman, "Two Greek Inscriptions from Khurbet Harrawi," *PEQ* 20 (1908): 155–157; cf. the conjectural readings offered in F. Abel, "Tell el-Harraouy," *RB* 17 (1908): 574–578 and J. Gabalda, "Bulletin," *RB* 18 (1909): 492–495. Dating is provided in Mordechai Aviam, "The Hellenistic and Hasmonaean Fortress and Herodian Siege Complex at Qeren Naftali," in *Jews*, 59–88.

[167] Four inscriptions are described in Fischer, Ovadiah, and Roll, "Epigraphic Finds." An unpublished additional inscription is mentioned in Aviam, "Borders."

[168] Mordechai Aviam, "Galilee," in *NEAEHL*, vol. 2, 453–454; Aviam, "Borders."

[169] Vassilios Tzaferis, "Cults and Deities Worshipped at Caesarea Philippi-Banias," in Eugene Ulrich et al., eds., *Priests, Prophets, and Scribes* (Sheffield: Sheffield Academic Press, 1992): 190–204; Zvi Ma'oz, "Banias, Temple of Pan – 1990," *ESI* 10 (1991): 59–61; Zvi Ma'oz, "Banias, Temple of Pan – 1993," *ESI* 15 (1996): 1–5; Robert C. Gregg and Dan Urman, *Jews, Pagans, and Christians in the Golan Heights* (Atlanta: Scholars Press, 1996), 280–283.

[170] Roman soldiers left behind Latin dedicatory inscriptions (Eck and Tepper, "Dedication"; Avi-Yonah, "Newly Discovered," 89–91 no. 6). Note the Greek reference to an *archiereus*

Focusing on the epigraphic finds from three nearby cities helps to reveal the distinctiveness of Galilee's epigraphic habit. The number of inscriptions at Scythopolis also increases after the wave of development that swept over the city in the second century CE. Most are Greek,[171] though a few are Latin.[172] At Caesarea Maritima, excavators have found over 400 Latin and Greek inscriptions, many from the Byzantine period, but a considerable number from the first three centuries CE.[173] Gerasa, furthest removed from Galilee of these cities, seems to provide an unending supply of new inscriptions. The 271 pre-Constantinian inscriptions in Kraeling's classic excavation volume[174] are constantly being supplemented with new ones,[175] usually in Greek but often in Latin. At these cities,[176] we find more than epitaphs; we also find inscriptions recording participation in pagan cults,[177] dedication of statues,[178] the honoring of

at Gaba (Safrai and Lin, "Mishmar Ha'Emeq"; Isaac, "Two Greek Inscriptions"). A fragmentary Greek inscription (date unknown) on a limestone block at Tel Jezreel possibly mentions the deity Leukothea (Pinhas Porat, "A Fragmentary Greek Inscription from Tel Jezreel," *TA* 24 [(1997]: 167–168). At Omrit, a Greek inscription names Aphrodite (Overman, Olive, and Nelson, "Discovering," 45).

[171] In addition to the inscriptions mentioned in subsequent notes, see *SEG* 8.32, 20.457, 20.458, 20.546, 37.1530, 47.2057.

[172] Last and Stein, "Ala Antiana"; Baron, "Survey," 148 no. 13 and 156 no. 28; two mentioned in Gatier, "Governeurs."

[173] *GLI.* Because most of the inscriptions are undated, providing an exact proportion of those from the Roman period is impossible.

[174] Welles, "Inscriptions" (in Kraeling, "Gerasa").

[175] In addition to the inscriptions cited below, see *SEG* 14.831, 32.1539, 35.1568, 35.1572–1573, 39.1453, 39.1651, 44.1400, 45.1997, 46.2057–2058, 46.2062, 46.2064, 47.2066–2067.

[176] In this and the following notes, categories overlap. For example, an inscription from an honorific statue is noted both as statue-related and as honorific, and an inscription recording euergetism for a pagan temple is listed as both pagan and construction-related. The examples cited here are illustrative; the full lists of inscriptions are too lengthy to include.

[177] At Scythopolis: *SEG* 20.456 (138–139 CE), 27.1446 (Severan period), 37.1529 (second century?), 41.1575 (144/145 CE), Leah Di Segni, "A Dated Inscription from Beth Shean and the Cult of Dionysos Ktistes in Roman Scythopolis," *SCI* 16 (1997): 139–161 (141/142 CE). At Caesarea: *GLI,* 67–70 no. 43, 118–124 nos. 119–128. At Gerasa: Welles, "Inscriptions," 373–395 nos. 2–44 and 445–446 nos. 195–198 (nos. 2–9, 17–18, 29 are first-century; the rest are mostly second- and third-century); *SEG* 35.1569 (27/28 CE), 27.1009–1010 (90–91 CE), 37.1550/45.1998 (date unknown), 39.1647–47 and 1649–1650 (mid-second century), 39.1655–1658 (early third century).

[178] At Scythopolis: 37.1531/40.1509 (second–third century), 46.2048 (second–third century portrait bust), possibly 27.1446. At Caesarea: *GLI,* 35–37 nos. 2–3, 132 no. 145. At Gerasa: Welles, "Inscriptions," 424–442 nos. 141–191 (mostly second–third century); *SEG* 14.831

dignitaries,[179] and donations for construction projects (often columns), whether temples, theaters, or other public buildings[180] – the very types of inscriptions that are largely lacking in Galilee's cities.[181]

The greater frequency of Greek inscriptions in these other cities may reflect a greater use of spoken Greek, but the complex set of issues revolving around oral and written languages must be kept in mind with them, as with Galilee. At Caesarea Maritima, for example, Latin inscriptions outnumber Greek inscriptions 2.5:1 in the pre-Constantinian period.[182] This is due to the city's self-identity as an island of Romanism in the Hellenistic East. Undoubtedly, more Latin was heard at Caesarea Maritima than at most places – but one suspects that more Greek was spoken than the 2.5:1 Latin: Greek ratio implies.

Dialects of Aramaic continued to be spoken in the Greek cities, though we will never know to what extent. Eusebius provides a glimpse of this phenomenon, though, recording a tradition that Christians worshipping in Scythopolis during the reign of Diocletian (284–305 CE) needed to have Greek scriptures translated into Aramaic.[183] One imagines that Aramaic was even more commonly heard in rural areas and small villages, though our lack of sources prevents us from knowing how much.[184]

(143 CE); 32.1537 (184 CE), 39.1646–47 and 1649–1650 (mid-second century), 46.2061 (late second century); Friedland, "Roman Marble Sculptures."

[179] In addition to inscriptions already mentioned, note at Gerasa: *SEG* 7.813 (early second century), 27.1008 (early second century), 39.1653 (first century), 39.1651 (mid-second century), 46.2057 (late first century CE), 46.2058 (130–135 CE); Caesarea: *GLI*, 35–64 nos. 2–24, 27–38 (mostly second–third century). References to the emperor are particularly frequent.

[180] At Scythopolis: Last and Stein, "Ala Antiana" (two columns); SEG 20.455/43.1073 (early fourth century?). At Caesarea: *GLI*, 37–54 nos. 4–38, 67–71 nos. 43–44. At Gerasa: in addition to inscriptions noted above, see Welles, "Inscriptions," 395–417 nos. 45–115 (nos. 45–52 are first century; the remainder are mostly second–third century), *SEG* 27.1009–1010 (theater); 39.1647–47 and 1649–1651 (brackets for temple of Artemis), 46.2059 (mid-second century, column).

[181] Similar inscriptions occur also at smaller cities; see, for example, John Dennis Wineland, *Ancient Abila: An Archaeological History* (Oxford: BAR, 2001), 70–76.

[182] *GLI*, 23.

[183] Schürer, *History*, vol. 2, 75 n. 252.

[184] Compare MacMullen, "Provincial Languages," 34.

Two aspects of this comparison stand out. First, we see the same chronological pattern with the surrounding cities, especially Caesarea Maritima, Scythopolis, and Gerasa, that we saw for Galilee, with a huge quantitative leap following the arrival of Roman troops in the region – though it is important to note that we also have a considerable number of first-century inscriptions for some of these cities, too. Second, we have a significant discrepancy between the number of inscriptions in some of these cities and the number in Sepphoris and Tiberias. This discrepancy is due to several aspects of the non-Galilean cities: their size; a more extended period of excavation, at least for Gerasa and Caesarea Maritima; perhaps greater prosperity; and longer established histories. But it is hard to avoid the conclusion that the higher number of inscriptions in some cities also reflects a greater receptivity to this aspect of Greco-Roman culture than offered in the Galilean cities.

GREEK AND LATIN NAMES IN FIRST-CENTURY GALILEE

Much has been made of the fact that some Palestinian Jews had Greek and Latin names. Such names are often cited as indicators that these languages were spoken, though this argument seems to be made more often regarding Greek than Latin. Yet the problematic nature of such reasoning is obvious. A number of factors go into picking a name, such as what names are currently in vogue, the symbolic or cultural value given to particular names, and cultural orientations and/or social aspirations.[185] Furthermore, these considerations reflect not the name bearers, but the name givers – typically, the parents. Greek and Latin names reflect Greco-Roman influence, but they are not sufficient evidence to theorize about what languages either the name-bearers or name-givers actually spoke.

Some scholars, like Schürer, have given the impression that such names were widespread: "The use of Greek and Latin personal names was . . . very frequent, even among the common people and the Pharisees and the rabbis."[186] Generalizations like this mask

---

[185] Compare MacMullen, "Provincial Languages."
[186] Schürer, *History*, vol. 2, 73. Schürer nonetheless acknowledges Aramaic as the predominant language.

the complexity of the issue. Because some names were perennially popular while the popularity of others varied over time, synchronic descriptions are extremely problematic.[187] Furthermore, this topic, like others, has often been treated with insufficient attention to chronology, geography, gender, and class. For example, Hengel's oft-quoted list of Greek names in the Maccabean and Hasmonean periods is drawn mostly from the elite classes of Jerusalem and its vicinity.[188] Rabbis with Greek and Latin names are typically from either the post-Bar Kokhba period or, if earlier, from Judea.[189] Similarly, the Greek names in many of the papyri from the Judean Desert date to the Bar Kokhba period.[190]

The most famous first-century examples of Galileans with Greek names are two of Jesus' disciples, the brothers Philip and Andrew.[191] The occurrence of the name Philip might have a geographical explanation. If the brothers were natives of Bethsaida, as John 1:44 reports, then they were from the territory of Herod Philip.[192] It is possible that Philip's parents chose that name because of its raised profile under the tetrarch or even in honor of him, though because we do not know the year of the disciple's birth we cannot determine this.[193] The name Andrew is more unusual among first-century CE Palestinian Jews, with only two known parallels.[194] Hengel plausibly suggests that Thaddaeus and Bartholomew were also Greek names, Thaddaeus a deformation of Theodotus[195] and Bartholomew

---

[187] N. Cohen, "The Jewish Names as Cultural Indicators in Antiquity," *JSJ* 7 (1976): 97–128; Williams, "Palestinian Jewish Personal Names," 108. On the chronological variation of names elsewhere in the Roman world, see MacMullen's comments on Egypt in "Provincial Languages," 36–37.

[188] Hengel, *Judaism and Hellenism*, vol. 1, 64.

[189] Schürer, *History*, vol. 2, 73; Krauss, *Griechische*, vol. 2, 647–650.

[190] Schürer, *History*, vol. 2, 74 n. 249.

[191] On Palestinian names in the New Testament, see Evans, *Jesus*, 67–89.

[192] Mark 1:29, however, cites Capernaum as the hometown of Andrew.

[193] There are two other first-century CE Philips from this general area, one, an officer of Agrippa II, whose father was from Gamla (also in the territory associated with Herod Philip) (*Life* 46, 179; *War* 2.421, 556; 4.81), and one from the Galilean village of Ruma (*War* 3.233). The fact that the name does not occur at Beth She'arim suggests that it enjoyed only a temporary popularity (*Beth She'arim*, vol. 2, 227–228).

[194] Both are in ossuary inscriptions (Tal Ilan, *Lexicon of Jewish Names in Late Antiquity: Part I Palestine 330 BCE–200 CE* [Tübingen: Mohr Siebeck, 2002], 262).

[195] Compare Ilan, *Lexicon*, 283–284.

derived from "Bar Ptolemy."[196] At least one follower of Jesus had a Latin name or nickname, if Acts 1:23 is trusted: Joseph called Barsabbas, also known as Justus.

At times, even Semitic names could reflect the influence of Hellenistic culture, as is conceivably the case with another name found among Jesus' disciples, Simon. The biblical name Shimon was quite similar to the common Greek name Simon and so was very easily Graecized. N. Cohen has pointed out that the name Shimon was used much more often in the Roman East than in the less Hellenized Jewish community in Babylonia.[197] The name's popularity in Palestine may also be due to its association with Simon the Maccabee.[198]

Despite such examples, Greek and Latin names seem to have been relatively uncommon in the Jewish parts of first-century CE Palestine, occurring much less often than in Diaspora Jewish communities.[199] Tal Ilan's impressively comprehensive study finds that only 14.5 percent of the known named Palestinian Jews from 330 BCE to 200 CE had Greek names, and only 3 percent had Latin names.[200] As Ilan points out, when considering these numbers we must take into account that our pool of known individuals is heavily weighted towards the elites. Thus, it is possible that these statistics are misleadingly high, and that an even smaller proportion of people had Greek and Latin names.

Most of the names from Palestine we know of are those of males, for several reasons.[201] Josephus's emphasis on politics results in a focus on men, and many of the women he does mention are connected somehow with political figures – wives, mothers, and daughters. Ossuaries, our primary source of inscriptions from this period, usually don't bear women's names.[202] Even in later

---

[196] Ilan agrees with both identifications (*Lexicon*, 283–284 and 304). Williams argues that Bartholomew comes from בר תלמי ("Palestinian Jewish Personal Names," 94 and 99–100), but Ilan lists no attestations of תלמי.

[197] N. Cohen, "Jewish Names," 112–117.

[198] Hengel, *Judaism and Hellenism*, vol. 1, 64; Ilan, *Lexicon*, 6–8; Markus Bockmuehl, "Simon Peter's Name in Jewish Sources," *JJS* 55 (2004): 58–80.

[199] Williams, "Palestinian Jewish Personal Names," 106.

[200] Ilan, *Lexicon*, 10, 13.

[201] Ilan, *Lexicon*, 3; Tal Ilan, "Notes on the Distribution of Jewish Women's Names in Palestine in the Second Temple and Mishnaic Periods," *JJS* 40 (1989): 186–200.

[202] Yifat Peleg, "Gender and Ossuaries," *BASOR* 325 (2002): 65–73; cf. Ilan, *Lexicon*, 43.

synagogue and burial inscriptions, female names are less common than men's, and those women who are named are usually mentioned in conjunction with a male relative.[203] The Mishnah is primarily concerned with halakhic matters and rarely mentions individual females by name.

Despite such challenges, we have enough evidence to know that most Jewish women in late Second Temple Palestine, like most men, had Hebrew and Aramaic names. Ilan's survey demonstrates this beyond doubt. She found that of the 247 women named in our sources, 145 had Hebrew names and 42 had Aramaic names. Only 45 bore Greek names, and only 10, Latin.[204] Many of the women with non-Semitic names were from Hasmonean and Herodian circles; one suspects that such names were even rarer amongst the masses.

One of Ilan's most surprising discoveries was that the 145 women with Hebrew names shared only eleven different names. Nearly half were called Salome, its longer version, Salomezion, Mariamme, or its shortened form, Maria – all Hasmonean names.[205] The fact that Hasmonean names are also remarkably common among males (31.5 percent)[206] suggests, perhaps, a celebration of that dynasty, a celebration turned into commemoration in Herodian times. In light of this trend, the abundance of women called Mary in the Gospels – Mary, mother of Jesus; Mary Magdalene; Mary, sister of Martha; Mary, mother of the disciple James; Mary wife of Clopas[207] – is more understandable, and it is no shock to find a Galilean named Salome at the foot of the cross.[208]

In first-century Galilee, the overwhelming majority of known names – and we have a sizable sample – are Semitic.[209] In addition to Mary and Salome, many of the other names in the Gospels – Jesus, James (Jacobus), Judas, Levi, John, Simon – are also typical of Palestinian Jews, being well-attested in Josephus, later rabbinic sources and epigraphic evidence. Only at Tiberias do we find

---

[203] Ilan, "Notes"; Peleg, "Gender"; Lapin, "Palestinian Inscriptions," 249–250.

[204] Of the remaining names, four are Persian and one is Nabatean (Ilan, "Notes," 31).

[205] A greater variety of names were found among the 45 women with Greek names (Ilan, "Notes," 31; cf. Ilan, *Lexicon*, 9).

[206] Ilan, *Lexicon*, 6–8, 56.

[207] Mark 6:3; Luke 8:2; 10:39; 24:10; John 19:25.

[208] Mark 15:40.   [209] See Appendix I.

a clustering of non-Semitic names. As early as the reign of Antipas an *agoranomos* had a Latin name, Gaius Julius.[210] A weight from the reign of Agrippa II from either Tiberias or Magdala/ Taricheae identifies the *agoranomoi* as Aianimos (or Animos; the reading is unclear), son of Monimos and Iaesaias, son of Mathias.[211] The first two names appear to be Greek;[212] the latter two, Semitic. A similar weight from Agrippa's reign, perhaps also from the same city, noted two *agoranomoi* with Latin names, Rufus and Julius.[213] At the time of the revolt, several prominent Tiberians had Greek and Roman names. Justus, son of Pistus, the critic to whom Josephus responds in his *Life*, led a pro-rebellion group. A pro-Roman and pro-Agrippan party was led by Julius Capellus, Compsos son of Compsos, Herod son of Miarus, and Herod son of Gamalus.[214] Justus, Pistus, Herod, Julius, Capellus, Compsos – all are Latin names.[215] Given the city's traditional association with the Herodian dynasty – not only was it founded by Antipas but at the time of the revolt was ruled by Agrippa II – the occurrence of the name Herod among royalist supporters is expected.[216] Some of these names – Compsos son of Compsos and Justus son of Pistus – reflect a pattern typical of the Roman East, in which Latin names are accompanied by the individuals' fathers' names, reflecting the Greek patronymic custom.[217] Other residents had more traditional Semitic names, such as Jesus, son of Sapphias, the leader of a pro-war group that Josephus characterizes as

---

[210] Qedar ("Two Lead Weights") identifies the *agoranomos* as a Roman because of this name, but since the weight pre-dates the arrival of significant numbers of Romans, Gaius Julius was more likely a local Galilean with a Roman name.

[211] Qedar, "Two Lead Weights"; Alla Kushnir-Stein, "Two Inscribed Lead Weights of Agrippa II," *ZPE* 141 (2002): 295–300.

[212] Ilan, *Lexicon*, 257, 297.

[213] Kushnir-Stein, "Two Inscribed Lead Weights of Agrippa."

[214] *Life* 34.

[215] N. Cohen, "Jewish Names," 120–121. The fact that Justus is equivalent in meaning to the Hebrew name Zaddok may explain its popularity (Mussies, "Jewish Personal Names," 245; Williams, "Palestinian Jewish Personal Names," 104–105).

[216] Williams, "Palestinian Jewish Personal Names," 98.

[217] On this phenomenon elsewhere in the Roman Empire, see the studies in D. Rizakis, ed., *Roman Onomastics in the Greek East: Social and Political Aspects: Proceedings of the International Colloquium on Roman Onomastics Athens, 7–9 September, 1993* (Athens: Research Centre for Greek and Roman Antiquity, National Hellenic Research Foundation 1996).

"composed of the most insignificant persons."[218] One wishes we knew of more names at Sepphoris, to see if they, too include as many non-Semitic examples among the upper classes. Josephus identifies no first-century Sepphoreans by name, but rabbinic sources refer to a Sepphorean priest named Joseph ben Elim (a Semitic name).[219]

Though Greco-Roman names appear to have been more common in later centuries, Semitic names still probably predominated. Beth She'arim provides our best example, though, again, we must realize that its sample is weighted towards the elites. Michael L. Peppard's analysis shows that 44 percent of the names were Semitic in origin (most of them biblical), 30 percent were Greek and 13 percent were Latin, with the remaining 13 percent difficult to categorize.[220] Greek and Latin names, though not rare,[221] are not as common here as they are in many Diaspora contexts.[222] The inscriptions also show that members of a single family might have names from different languages. Leonard V. Rutgers notes that one inscription refers to a mother with a Greek name (Eumatheia), a son with a Semitic name (Jacob), and another son with a Latin name (Justus).[223]

Some Greek and Latin names at Beth She'arim are the equivalents of Semitic names, such as Simon for Shimon and Leontios for Judah, but whether such names were selected because of these similarities or simply because they were popular cannot be determined.[224] A few Greek names are theophoric, but rather than referring to El or Yahweh, they allude to pagan deities – a custom wholly unattested for first-century Galilee. The names Diodora and Zenobia refer to Zeus, Dionysia refers to the god of wine, and Eisas

[218] *Life* 36, 66.

[219] *T. Yoma* 1:4 and elsewhere; see Miller, *Studies*, 63–88. Josephus does not identify this priest as a Sepphorean (*Ant.* 17.165ff).

[220] Michael L. Peppard, "Personal Names and Ethnicity in Late Ancient Galilee: The Data from Beth She'arim," in H. W, Attridge, D. B. Martin, and J. Zangenberg, eds., *Religion, Ethnicity, and Identity in Ancient Galilee* (Tübingen: Mohr Siebeek) (in press).

[221] *Beth She'arim*, vol. 2, 207–212 and vol. 3, 230–231.

[222] Leonard Victor Rutgers, *The Jews in Late Ancient Rome: Evidence of Cultural Interaction in the Roman Diaspora* (Leiden: E. J. Brill, 1995), 153–155.

[223] Rutgers, *Jews*, 153–155, using an example from *Beth She'arim*, vol. 2, page 95 no. 125. Rutgers demonstrates that within a single family, names might shift from one language of origin to another across the generations (see in particular his tables 6a and 6b).

[224] The same point can be made regarding Latin names with Semitic equivalents; cf. Ilan, *Lexicon*, 11 and Rutgers, *Jews*, 143–144.

is probably an abbreviation of Isidoros.[225] Graecized Latin names include Justus and the related feminine form Justa, as well as Agrippas, Germanus, and Julianus.

Full Roman names – a *praenomen, nomen,* and *cognomen,* or, at the least, *nomen* and *cognomen* – are wholly absent at Beth She'arim.[226] This was characteristic of the larger region; complete Roman names with the full *tria nomina* were uncommon throughout Syria and Arabia. They became slightly more frequent after the granting of universal Roman citizenship in 212 CE,[227] but this increase was eventually offset by an empire-wide trend of using only two names, or, by late antiquity, only one.[228]

CONCLUSION

Many of the standard claims about how extensively Greek was spoken in Galilee rely on evidence from a variety of areas and a wide range of centuries. Such generalizations are useful for understanding broad linguistic trends in a sizable geographical area across a large span of time, but they do little to help us understand a particular sub-region in a particular period. To understand Galilee, we must give priority to specifically Galilean evidence. Likewise, to understand the first century, we must give priority to first-century evidence.

When we do so, we see that enthusiastic claims about the high number of Galileans proficient in Greek are difficult to support.

---

[225] Mussies, however, argues that Dio ("Zeus") was sometimes associated with the Jewish god ("Jewish Personal Names," 249). The names of Muses were given to two women, Ourania, a Galilean also named Rachel, and Kalliope, from the coastal city of Byblos.

[226] On Roman names, see McClean, *Introduction*, 112–127; Olli Salomies, "Names and Identities: Onomastics and Prosopography," in Bodel, *Epigraphic Evidence*, 73–86, esp. 83–87; and Rutgers, *Jews*, 158–159.

[227] Maurice Sartre, "Les Progres de la citoyennete romaine dans les provinces romaines de Syrie et d'Arabie sous le haut-Empire," in Rizakis, *Roman Onomastics*, 239–250. A glance at the epigraphic corpus of the Decapolis city Gerasa is instructive: Roman names are more common, but they seem to be almost entirely associated with Roman soldiers and administrators or their descendents (whose ancestry is easily traced through the names themselves) (Pierre-Louis Gatier, "Onomastique et présence Romaine a Gérasa," in Rizakis, *Roman Onomastics*, 251–259). MacMullen argues that the frequency of Roman names in the provinces was probably lower than inscriptions suggest ("Provincial Languages").

[228] Rutgers, *Jews*, 159.

The number of first-century CE inscriptions is very low. This point is worth emphasizing: from the time of Jesus – the first thirty years of the century – a market weight from Tiberias and Antipas's coins constitute the full body of our published evidence.[229] There are not many inscriptions from Galilee from the rest of the first century, either. Most of Galilee's epigraphic corpus post-dates Jesus not only by decades, but centuries. That evidence probably does correspond to a greater use of Greek in the second century and afterwards, though we must always keep in mind that inscriptions often reflect epigraphic conventions as much as or even more than the languages typically spoken and read.

In first-century CE Galilee, who spoke Greek, how much did they speak, and in what contexts did they speak it? Even after reviewing all of the published evidence, these questions remain difficult to answer, though we can hazard a few observations. Obviously, at least some Herodian administrators and supporters did. The use of Greek on Herodian coins shows that officials could speak and/or read it (different skills, it must be remembered). This association of Greek with the elites means that it was probably more often encountered in the cities and thus in Lower Galilee than in Upper Galilee.[230] At least some elites in Sepphoris and Tiberias had facility in Greek. It is worth pointing out again, however, that neither city has been the source of many first-century inscriptions. After Galilee was put under direct Roman administration in 44 CE, there would have been greater impetus for members of the upper class who wanted to communicate with the Roman authorities to learn Greek, though there is little reason to assume that Romans were especially numerous until after c. 120 CE.

The extent of the non-administrative use of Greek, especially in the first century, remains in question. It is easy to demonstrate that Greek was the language of the governmental sphere. It is much harder to demonstrate that it was the primary conversational language, whether public or private, even among those elites who knew it. The fact that official inscriptions were made in Greek does not

---

[229] I refer here to inscriptions produced within Galilee, not those found in Galilee but originating elsewhere.

[230] Compare the studies by Eric M. Meyers cited in the Introduction.

mean that even the ones commissioning those inscriptions regarded Greek as their primary language. The association of Greek with government probably also means that there may have been a strong gender dimension to competence in it, since government was primarily the arena of men. If we are correct in assuming that some elites knew Greek, then obviously they were learning it from somewhere. Even so, there is no reason to suppose that Greek education, if available at all, was widespread. Though Hengel claims that Sepphoris and Tiberias had schools providing a Greek education,[231] there is no reference to them in our sources.

If we are unsure about the extent of Greek even amongst those connected with governments, we are all the more in the dark for everyone else.[232] Some scholars have claimed that Galileans of all classes would have needed to know Greek for various reasons – to trade with or travel in other regions; to converse with neighbors in the border areas; to sell fish, pottery, and other wares; to import and export various products. Such statements reflect the assumption that the epigraphic data from surrounding regions conveys the whole linguistic picture for them. It is true that Greek inscriptions were more common, even in the first century CE, in some nearby cities and areas, but it is also likely that local languages – dialects of Aramaic – continued to be spoken, even if they are not represented in the epigraphic record. So, while Greek may have been used more in some of the surrounding communities, especially those with longer established identities as Greek cities, it is likely that Galileans who needed to communicate with people from those areas could get by without an advanced, or perhaps even basic, knowledge of Greek. While some Galilean commoners – again, how many is impossible to determine – probably knew some Greek, to generalize that many had considerable competence in it is to go far beyond the evidence. As for Jesus, how much Greek he knew will never be clear, but he most likely would not have needed it to be a carpenter, to teach the Galilean crowds, to travel around the lake, or to venture into the villages associated with Tyre, Caesarea Philippi, and the Decapolis cities. The probable association of Greek with urban elites also renders problematic reconstructions of Q that simultaneously argue

---

[231] Hengel, 'Hellenization', 17.   [232] Compare Hezser, *Jewish Literacy*, 243.

for a Galilean provenance, a mid-first-century date for the earliest stratum, and a social context of poor, wandering charismatics. It is unlikely that literacy would have been widespread among such a group and unclear why the rare literate member would have chosen to compose such a text in Greek rather than Aramaic.[233]

It is possible that Greek was more widely spoken than our evidence suggests – but how could we ever tell? Because of our general ignorance about who used Greek, how often, and in what circumstances, it is extremely difficult to apply socio-linguistic models such as multilingualism (speaking multiple languages) and multiglossia (using different languages in different social contexts) to the first century.[234]

Consider a hypothetical Jewish male who was an elite of Tiberias in the mid-first century CE. That he spoke Aramaic, we can be fairly certain. Whether he spoke Hebrew is more difficult to determine, since our knowledge of how that language was used is so limited. If he did, then it would be appropriate to characterize him as bilingual. He probably rarely encountered Latin. But what of Greek? Was he multilingual, shifting comfortably back and forth between Aramaic and Greek, using both languages in a variety of settings: in his home, at social occasions, for business purposes? Or is the model of multiglossia more helpful for understanding him? Did he know how to speak Greek, but use it (for example) only when civic business required him to converse with Roman provincial officials, otherwise almost always opting for Aramaic? Or, as an elite, did he have rudimentary reading ability in Greek, enough to make him the rare citizen who could actually decipher what local coins and market weights said, but have little capacity for oral communication in it? Or was he wholly lacking in the language? We have no way to adjudicate between these possibilities, and if we are unable to do so

---

[233] For example, Vaage, *Galilean Upstarts.* Kloppenborg's reconstruction of Q addresses these issues by rejecting the itinerancy thesis and postulating a scribal authorship (Kloppenborg Verbin, *Excavating Q*).

[234] For attempts to apply such models, see Hezser, *Jewish Literacy*, 243–247; Rabin, "Hebrew," 1007–1009, followed by Horsley, *Archaeology*, 158–162; Porter, "Jesus," 132–133; and Stanley E. Porter, ed., *Diglossia and Other Topics in New Testament Linguistics* (Sheffield: Sheffield Academic Press, 2000). Note Schwartz's reservations about these models in "Language," 17–18.

for our hypothetical civic elite, then we are all the more unable to do so for common Galileans, both in the cities as well as in the villages scattered across the region.

If our understanding of the extent of Greek is incomplete, at least we can safely observe that the most important factor for measuring its epigraphic use is chronology. Antipas's reign marked the beginning of a process in which Greek would be used more and more in inscriptions, but it was a process that took time. After the Romans arrived in large numbers in the second century, the number of Greek inscriptions increased noticeably. Even then, however, Aramaic probably remained the most commonly-spoken language. Understanding Galilee's *linguistic* development requires us to be attentive to where Galilee was in its *historical* development – and to retroject data from the second or third century into the early first is to misunderstand the Galilee of Jesus.

CHAPTER 6

The coinage of Galilee

Coins provide us with a vivid example of how Hellenistic, Roman, and local tastes might be combined. The placement of a portrait on the obverse and a symbol on the reverse and the use of inscriptions to identify the minting authority had been widespread under the Greeks.[1] The Romans and their subject peoples refashioned Hellenistic numismatic customs to suit their own needs. They used busts to propagate the emperor's image and legends to advertise his honorific titles. The designs of coins reflected the values and tastes of their minting authorities, whether imperial officials, the staffs of client kings, or civic elites.[2] Coins thus offer us insight into the ideologies and preferences of the upper classes, and they might sometimes reflect deference to the values of the masses. Though we can rarely discern what commoners thought of these designs, we can understand, at least in a general sense, some of the messages to which they were exposed.[3]

In Galilee, coins were quite likely the primary source of most people's exposure to writing, the portrait of the emperor, and explicit pagan imagery. In this chapter, I will provide an overview of Galilee's coinage, both the coins struck in the region and those minted elsewhere.[4] Because coins often remained in circulation for a

[1] Christopher Howgego, *Ancient History from Coins* (London and New York: Routledge, 1995), 1–12.
[2] See Harl, *Civic Coins* and Chancey, "City Coins."
[3] On the use of coins to convey messages, however vague or general, see Chancey, "City Coins," 103–104.
[4] For overviews, see Rappaport, "Numismatics," 25–29 and C. H. V. Sutherland, "The Pattern of Monetary Development in Phoenicia and Palestine during the Early Empire," in Arie Kindler, ed., *The Patterns of Monetary Development in Phoenicia and Palestine during Antiquity* (Tel Aviv: Schocken, 1967), 88–105.

long time and sometimes traveled far from their places of origin, many Galileans would have been aware of changes in numismatic trends over time and of features that made locally-minted coins similar to and different from those produced elsewhere. They would have had some cognizance of the cultural and political stances reflected in the choice of language, the presence or absence of a bust, and the use of a plant symbol versus that of a deity or a temple. Galileans in the early first century CE would have recognized how Hasmonean coins differed from those of the coastal cities, and how newer Herodian issues represented something of a middle ground. Those living a century and a half later would have known that the middle ground had disappeared as Galilee's coins became virtually indistinguishable from those minted elsewhere in the Roman East.

THE COINAGE OF HELLENISTIC GALILEE

Though no coins were minted in Galilee until the early first century CE, coins produced elsewhere had entered the region long before. Persian-period pieces, usually struck at either Jerusalem or one of the coastal cities, typically Tyre or Sidon, occasionally turn up in excavations, and a few Early Hellenistic-period hoards have been found.[5] More commonly discovered are coins of the Ptolemies and Seleucids.[6] Both kingdoms struck coins at Tyre, Sidon, Ptolemais,

---

[5] *Treasury*, 1–18; *City-Coins*, 12; Rappaport, "Numismatics," 25–29. Persian-period coins (mostly Tyrian and/or Sidonian) have been found at Moshav Dalton in Upper Galilee, and, to the west, Tel Abu Hawam (map coordinates 152/245) (Stern, *Archaeology*, 561 and *Material Culture*, 12–13). The quantities of Persian coins from Meiron and the Franciscan excavations at Capernaum are more typical: two and one, respectively (Joyce Raynor, Ya'akov Meshorer, with Richard Simon Hanson, *The Coins of Ancient Meiron* [Winona Lake, Ind: ASOR, Eisenbrauns, 1988], 84). Early Hellenistic hoards have been recovered at Beth Yerah (J. Baramki, "Coin Hoards from Palestine, II," *QDAP* 11 [1945]: 86–90) and Tarshiha (map coordinates 175/268) (Arnold Spaer, "A Hoard of Alexander Tetradrachms from Galilee," *INJ* 3 [1965–1966]: 1–7).

[6] See the chart of finds at several sites in Raynor and Meshorer, *Coins*, 84. At et-Tell (Bethsaida?), a mostly Hellenistic site, 26 Ptolemaic and 64 Seleucid coins were found (a 1996 tally) (Arie Kindler, "The Coin Finds at the Excavations of Bethsaida," in Arav and Freund, *Bethsaida*, vol. 2, 250–268). Finds at nearby Gamla included several hundred Seleucid coins, but only a few Ptolemaic issues (Danny Syon, "The Coins from Gamala: Interim Report," *INJ* 12 [1992–1993]: 34–55; Syon and Yavor, "Gamla 1997–2000." See also Danny Syon, "Coins from the Excavations at Khirbet esh-Shuhara," in

and other cities, with Alexandria being the most important mint of the Ptolemies and Antioch serving that function for the Seleucids.[7] The currencies of the two kingdoms provide good examples of the variations found in the Hellenistic period. Ptolemaic coinage was based on the Phoenician standard, with the shekel as the standard numismatic unit. Obverses of silver coins bore portraits of the Ptolemaic ruler and sometimes his queen; those of bronze coins, Zeus.[8] Reverses of both types typically depicted an eagle. Their inscriptions were usually in Greek, though a few coins found in Palestine have Hebrew inscriptions. In contrast, Seleucid coins were based on the standard of Athens, with denominations based on the drachm. Antioch, the mint nearest Palestine, struck coins with the ruler's bust on their obverses and usually a deity (often a seated Zeus or Apollo) on the reverses.[9]

After the Hasmonean conquest of Galilee, the influx of Seleucid currency into the region ceased, replaced with coins minted in Jerusalem by John Hyrcanus I, Aristobulus (most likely Aristobulus I), Alexander Jannaeus, Hyrcanus II (perhaps), and Mattathias Antigonus.[10] These coins, the very first in history to be struck by an independent Jewish government, are found often throughout Israel. Those of Alexander Jannaeus, who struck coins in large numbers, are especially common.[11]

The Hasmoneans' coins provide a good example of how the dynasty adopted and adapted some aspects of Greek culture. Like the Seleucids, they apparently minted coins according to the Attic standard.[12] Unlike both the Seleucids and the Ptolemies, they placed no animals, deities, or royal busts on their coins. This choice

---

Gal, *Eretz Zafon*, 181; Donald T. Ariel, "The Coins from Khirbet Zemel," in Gal, *Eretz Zafon*, 119–124; and Y. Meshorer, "Coins 1968–1986," in Herbert, ed., *Tel Anafa I, i,* 241–260.

[7] On coins minted in Jerusalem in the time of Antiochus VII, see *Treasury,* 30–31.

[8] Ptolemaic gold coins are rare (R. A. Hazzard, *Ptolemaic Coins: An Introduction for Collectors* [Toronto: Kirk & Bentley, 1995]).

[9] Edward T. Newell, *The Seleucid Mint of Antioch* (Chicago: Obol International, 1978).

[10] Determining which Hasmonean ruler struck specific coins is notoriously difficult because of the repeated use of names (i.e., John, Judah, Jonathan) within the dynasty (*Treasury,* 23).

[11] Shachar, "Historical and Numismatic Significance."

[12] For example, the smallest denomination of Hyrcanus I (identified by Meshorer as a half-prutah) was roughly the weight of the smallest Seleucid unit, the lepton. The smallest coin

presumably reflects deference to the Jewish prohibition of "graven images."[13]

We should not characterize the coins of the Hasmoneans as "aniconic," however, because such a term obscures the fact that images do appear on them. Wreaths often encircled inscriptions – a common numismatic design in both the Hellenistic and Roman eras. The most prevalent symbol was that of double cornucopiae, with the addition of a pomegranate between the horns differentiating it from the cornucopiae found on Seleucid and other Hellenistic coins.[14] Ya'akov Meshorer, the premier authority on ancient Jewish numismatics, has argued that most Hasmonean symbols had distinctively Jewish meanings. The lily, for example, was commonly depicted in Jewish art and appeared in the decoration of the temple, and the palm branch may have been intended to recall the festival of Sukkot.[15] Whether many Jews would have made such associations cannot be determined. Only on the coins of the last Hasmonean king, Mattathias Antigonus, do we find what we can truly consider a Jewish symbol: the earliest known artistic depiction of a menorah.[16] Aside from it, most of these designs (or at least similar ones) also appeared on other Mediterranean coins as well, and so their use reflects the Hasmoneans' comfort with such standard Hellenistic motifs.

Another feature that differentiated Hasmonean coins was their limited use of Greek. Greek characters and monograms, their meanings unclear, are found on certain coins of Hyrcanus I.[17] Most of his money, however, uses a script of Hebrew already ancient by his reign; the choice of script thus symbolically connected the Hasmonean dynasty to earlier Jewish history. The inscriptions included Hyrcanus's name and a title legitimizing his authority as

of Mattathias Antigonus (a prutah, according to Meshorer) was probably equivalent to a dilepton (*Treasury*, 23–33, 39, 54).

[13] See discussion in Chapter Seven.

[14] Other symbols include single and double cornucopiae without the pomegranate, a wreath, an anchor, a star, a star within a diadem, and a crested helmet (*Treasury*, 33–38).

[15] *Treasury*, 8–10, 35.

[16] *Treasury*, 54–57. Another symbol on his coins might also have special Jewish significance; Meshorer regards it as the table for the shewbread in the temple, but Rappaport ("Numismatics," 40) interprets it as a four-candle menorah.

[17] *Treasury*, 42–43.

ruler and high priest: "Yehohanan the High Priest and the Council of the Jews."[18] Hyrcanus's son Aristobulus followed his example, also using paleo-Hebrew.

The coins issued by Alexander Jannaeus reflect a very different choice. While some have only paleo-Hebrew inscriptions, others are bilingual, with Greek on one side and paleo-Hebrew or Aramaic on the other. We thus see Alexander Jannaeus combining Hyrcanus's symbolic appeal to Israel's past with his own openness to Greek as the standard numismatic language. In addition, his coins identify him by his Greek name and demonstrate that he proclaimed himself "king," the first Hasmonean to do so.[19] The last of the Hasmonean kings, Mattathias Antigonus, also put both Greek and paleo-Hebrew on his coins.

Hasmonean coins circulated long after the end of the dynasty itself, often appearing in Roman-period contexts.[20] For first-century CE Jews, they would have been numismatic reminders of an era before the Herods and the Romans, the old Semitic inscriptions all the more in contrast with the Greek found on the coins minted in their own day.

THE COINAGE OF THE ROMAN PERIOD

A remarkable mixture of currency was used in Roman Palestine. Coins issued by the Herodian rulers joined older Hasmonean ones, and an occasional Nabatean piece probably made its way north. In addition, the number of Levant cities striking coins grew, so that

---

[18] Some coins added *rosh* to the inscription, reading "Yehohanan the High Priest and the Head of the Council of the Jews" (*Treasury*, 201, 207).

[19] *Treasury*, 209–210.

[20] The proportion of Hasmonean coins found at Yodefat, for example, is 41.2 percent (81 out of 221) (Adan-Bayewitz and Aviam, "Iotapata," 155–159); at Meiron and Khirbet Shema, approximately 10 percent (108/1003 and 42–54/517, respectively) are Hasmonean. At all three sites, most Hasmonean coins are issues of Alexander Jannaeus. The numbers of Hasmonean coins at Gush Halav and Nabratein are considerably lower (both sites had fewer Hellenistic and Early Roman remains in general) (Raynor and Meshorer, *Coins*, 84; Richard S. Hanson and Michael L. Bates, "Numismatic Report," in *Khirbet Shema'*, 146–169; Joyce Raynor, "Numismatics," in *Gush Halav*, 230–245). For Sepphoris, see Catharine S. Bunnell, "Catalogue of the Coins," in Waterman, *Preliminary Report*, 35–86 and Meyers, "Sepphoris on the Eve," 110. Nearly two thirds of Gamla's over 6,300 coins are Hasmonean (Syon, "Coins from Gamala"; Syon and Yavor, "Gamla").

practically every city of any stature issued coins at some point. Roman imperial coinage grew increasingly common as the centuries progressed. Of the civic mints, Tyre had special importance, supplying much of Palestine's coinage.[21] Tyre's coins are especially common in Galilee because of its proximity.[22] Earlier research interpreted high numbers of Tyrian coins at Galilean (particularly Upper Galilean) sites as evidence of extensive trade between the city and those specific communities.[23] While there was indeed considerable exchange between Tyre and Galilee,[24] the primary reason so much Tyrian coinage is found is because so much of it was struck. That is to say, the presence of a large number of Tyrian coins at a particular site might or might not be the result of direct trade with the city; it might simply reflect how widely used Tyre's mass-produced coins were.[25]

The main imperial mints, both near and far, added considerably to the diversity.[26] Their coins were a primary means of spreading Roman propaganda, particularly in their widespread dissemination of the emperor's image.[27] Antioch was an especially important source of currency for much of the eastern Mediterranean, and its coins are fairly common in Galilee.[28] The number of imperial coins in Galilee increased considerably in the third and fourth centuries.

---

[21] Tyrian coins make up 15 percent of the 3,000 city coins held by the Eretz Israel Museum in Tel Aviv (Ze'ev Safrai, *The Economy of Roman Palestine* [London and New York: Routledge, 1994], 401).

[22] Dan Barag, "Tyrian Currency in Galilee," *INJ* 6/7 (1982–1983): 7–13; Freyne, "Galileans, Itureans and Phoenicians," 200–203; Richard S. Hanson, *Tyrian Influence in the Upper Galilee* (Cambridge, Mass.: ASOR, 1980). At Magdala, for example, a hoard of 188 bronze coins from 74–222 CE was 40 percent Tyrian, and at Meiron over 10 percent of the coins came from Tyre (Ya'akov Meshorer, "A Hoard of Coins from Migdal," *Atiqot* 11 [1976]: 54–71; Raynor and Meshorer, *Coins*, 79). At Gamla, approximately 14 percent of the coins are either Tyrian or Sidonian (Syon, "Coins from Gamala"; Syon and Yavor, "Gamla"). In contrast, at Yodefat, Seleucid coins minted at Tyre have been found, but not later Tyrian civic coins (Adan-Bayewitz and Aviam, "Iotapata," 160).

[23] Hanson, *Tyrian Influence.*

[24] Chancey, *Myth*, 156, 162.

[25] Barag, "Tyrian Currency."

[26] On imperial mints, see Harold Mattingly et al., eds., *The Roman Imperial Coinage*, 10 vols. (London: Spinks, 1923–1994) and *RPC*.

[27] Clifford Ando, *Imperial Ideology and Provincial Loyalty in the Roman Empire* (Berkeley: University of California Press, 2000), 8–9, 215–228.

[28] *RPC*, vol. 1, 606–630.

Antioch continued to predominate, but coins of Alexandria, Rome, Caesarea of Cappadocia, Constantinople, and other mints were also numerous.[29] Other parties sometimes issued coins. Between 6 and 62 CE, several of the Roman governors of Judea did so, though few of these pieces (typically referred to as "procuratorial coinage") have turned up in Galilee.[30] During the two Jewish revolts, rebels issued coins from Jerusalem, in the first case, minting new ones, in the latter, overstriking on older ones.[31] Their circulation does not seem to have extended very far north; only a few from the first revolt have been found in Galilee, and none from the Bar Kokhba revolt. Likewise, coins struck by Vespasian and Titus at Caesarea Maritima celebrating their victory over the Jews with Greek inscriptions of "Judea captured" made little headway into the region.[32]

Almost all of the coins struck in Palestine itself were bronze. More valuable coins of gold and silver were produced elsewhere. Coins made of these precious metals were less likely to be accidentally dropped (and thus preserved) and more likely to be melted down at some point than those made of bronze and other copper alloys. The result is that finds of gold coins are extraordinarily rare in Galilee.[33] Even silver is fairly uncommon, though enough has been found to allow general observations about its usage.

---

[29] At Meiron twelve different Late Roman imperial mints were represented (Raynor and Meshorer, *Coins*, 89). At nearby Jalame, imperial coins form the majority (Gloria S. Merker, "The Coins," 103–115, esp. 103, in Weinberg, *Excavations*); note also coins at Hurfeish (map coordinates 182/269) (Danny Syon, "The Coins from Burial Caves D and E at Hurfeish," in Gal, *Eretz Zafon*, 167–175) and Hanita (map coordinates 166/277) (Dan Barag, "Hanita, Tomb XV: A Tomb of the Third and Early Fourth Century CE," *Atiqot* 13 [1978]: 1–60).

[30] On procuratorial coins, see *Treasury*, 167–176. For rare Galilean examples, see Raynor and Meshorer, *Coins*, 84; Raynor, "Numismatics," 231; John F. Wilson, "The Bronze and Silver Coins," in Vassilios Tzaferis, ed., *Excavations at Capernaum: Volume I: 1978–1982* (Winona Lake, Ind.: Eisenbrauns, 1989), 139–143, esp. 140 no. 1; Adan-Bayewitz and Aviam, "Iotapata," 155–160; Syon, "Coins," 239; Syon and Yavor, "Gamla."

[31] *Treasury*, 115–165; Mildenburg, *Coinage*; Boaz Zissu and Hanan Eshel, "The Geographical Distribution of Coins from the Bar Kokhba War," *INJ* 14 (2000–2002): 157–167.

[32] *RPC*, vol. 2, 317–318. Similar "Judea Capta" coins, albeit with inscriptions in Latin rather than Greek, were struck elsewhere in the empire (*Treasury*, 185–191).

[33] I could find reference to only one such coin, southwest of Galilee at Jalame (Merker, "Coins," 103).

Most of Palestine's silver was produced at Tyre until the mid-60s CE, when the city began producing bronze alone.[34] Its shekels and half-shekels were exceptionally pure (95 percent silver), a fact that, along with the sheer number minted, helps account for their widespread popularity.[35] This unparalleled level of quality may be why the Jerusalem temple required that the half-shekel temple tax be paid in Tyrian currency,[36] despite the pagan imagery of the city's chief deity Melqart-Hercules on its obverse and an eagle on its reverse. Alternatively, Tyrian coinage may have been the required form of payment because it was the most prevalent form of silver currency available, both when the tax was instituted during the Hasmonean era[37] and in the first century CE. The continuing requirement that the tax be paid in it even after silver tetradrachms and (to a lesser extent) denarii had entered the region might reflect deference to longstanding custom, or, perhaps, a rejection of Roman coins as symbols of imperial domination.

Tyre was not the sole producer of silver coins in the southern Levant, however. Sidon minted shekels until 30/29 BCE and half-shekels, though only on a few occasions, until 43/44 CE.[38] The Nabatean kings also struck silver, as did Jewish rebels in Jerusalem in the first revolt.[39] From 55 CE on, the imperial mint at Antioch struck silver coins, usually tetradrachms but occasionally denarii, the silver denomination widely used in the Roman West, and other types.[40]

---

[34] The exact date of the cessation of Tyre's silver is unclear (*RPC*, vol. 1, 655–656; *Treasury*, 78; Hanson, *Tyrian Influence*). Andrew Burnett, Michel Amandry, and Pere Paul Ripollès (*RPC*, vol. 1, 655–656) successfully argue against Meshorer's proposal (*Treasury*, 78) that after 20 BCE, "Tyrian" shekels were produced in Jerusalem to provide the temple with high-quality currency.

[35] *RPC*, vol. 1, 655.

[36] *Treasury*, 74. *M. Shekalim* 2:4 preserves a memory of this tradition, and *t. Ketubot* 13:20 declares that any time silver is specified in the Pentateuch, it should be understood as Tyrian silver. See also *m. Bekhorot* 8:7 (references are drawn from *Treasury*). On the temple tax in general, see Sanders, *Judaism*, 156–157 and *Jewish Law from Jesus to the Mishnah* (London: SCM Press, Philadelphia: Trinity Press International, 1990), 49–51.

[37] On the invention of the custom in the Hasmonean era, see Albert I. Baumgarten, "Invented Traditions of the Maccabean Era," in Hubert Cancik, Hermann Lichtenberger, and Peter Schäfer, eds., *Geschichte, Tradition, Reflexion: Festschrift für Martin Hengel zum 70. Geburtstag* (Tübingen: J. C. B. Mohr [Paul Siebeck], 1996), vol. 1, 197–210.

[38] *RPC*, vol. 1, 651.

[39] Meshorer, *Nabatean Coins* and *Treasury*, 115–134.

[40] Antioch produced denarii in the reign of Vespasian, for example (*RPC*, vol. 2, 270–273).

For the remainder of the Roman period, it and other imperial mints provided most of Palestine's silver, though several cities were allowed to mint tetradrachms during the reigns of Caracalla, Macrinus, and Diadumenian.[41] Of the various silver denominations, tetradrachms were dominant in Galilee, if hoards at Tiberias[42] and Gush Halav[43] are representative. Denarii are less frequently found, especially in early contexts.

If all of Palestine's coins had been made according to the Roman system, determining their values would be a simpler task. In the Augustan period, for example, we know that 1 gold aureus was worth 25 silver denarii, and, in turn, that 1 denarius = 4 sestertii = 8 dupondii = 16 asses = 64 quadrantes. Instead, as we have already seen, we find a bewildering mixture of coins of different sizes and weights, minted by different authorities, and struck on different standards – Roman, Phoenician, and Greek.[44] The fact that very few coins have inscriptions specifying their values complicates the matter further, as does the difficulty in associating particular coins with the denominations mentioned in literary sources. Changes over the centuries, such as the disappearance and addition of denominations and the devaluing and debasing of silver muddy the situation even more.[45] Ancient people may have understood the system, but we probably never will, at least not completely – though not for lack of scholarly efforts.[46]

---

[41] For example, Ptolemais, Caesarea, Gaza, Aelia Capitolina, Neapolis, and Gadara (*City-Coins*, 12–13 no. 5; 20–21 nos. 27–28; 30–31 no. 61; 62–63 no. 173; 50 no. 135; 82 no. 222; Sutherland, "Pattern," 96). Other silver denominations issued at various times by imperial mints included antoniniani, quinarii, cistophori, drachms, and didrachms.

[42] H. Hamburger, "A Hoard of Syrian Tetradrachms from Tiberias," *Atiqot* 2 (1959): 133–145. The 218 tetradrachms are dated from 59/60 CE–119 CE.

[43] The third-century hoard held 180 tetradrachms but only 22 denarii (H. Hamburger, "A Hoard of Syrian Tetradrachms and Tyrian Bronze Coins from Gush Halav," *IEJ* 4 [1954]: 201–226). Nonetheless, the denarius does appear to have been in use (however limited) in Palestine. Sperber counts approximately 220 occurrences of the Hebrew word *denar* in Tannaitic sources; in later traditions, however, the word came to refer to gold, rather than silver pieces (*Roman Palestine*, 31–34).

[44] On denominations and standards, see David L. Vagi, *Coinage and History of the Roman Empire, c. 82 B. C.–A. D. 480* (Chicago: Fitzroy Dearborn, 1999), 77–116 and David R. Sear, *Greek Coins and Their Values* (London: Seaby, 1951), vol. 1, xxix–xxxiv.

[45] Compare Michael Crawford, "Finance, Coinage and Money from the Severans to Constantine," *ANRW* II.2, 560–593.

[46] See *RPC*, vol. 1, 26–37 and 585–590, vol. 2, 20–29 and 301–303; Kenneth W. Harl, *Coinage in the Roman Economy, 300 BC to AD 700* (Baltimore and London: The Johns

The complexity of the situation is reflected in the disparate monetary references in the gospels.[47] The denarius, for example, is mentioned numerous times – this, despite the fact that the coin, produced at distant mints, appears to have had only limited circulation in Palestine at the time of Jesus.[48] References to it might reflect the dating and provenance of the gospels more than the historical setting of Jesus.[49] The famous saying about taxes illustrates the problem. According to Mark 12:13–17, the Pharisees and Herodians approached Jesus on his visit to Jerusalem and asked him whether it was lawful to pay the census tax to the Romans.[50] Jesus requested that they bring him a denarius and then asked whose image and inscription were found upon it. When they answered " 'Caesar's,' " Jesus enigmatically replied that they should "render unto Caesar the things of Caesar, and unto God the things that are God's." Even putting aside questions of historicity, it is difficult to know what to make of this numismatic reference. Asking for a Tyrian shekel would not have allowed Jesus to make his point, since it bore no imperial portrait. On the other hand, one might have expected him to ask for a tetradrachm, which was much more common than the denarius. Perhaps Jesus' request for a denarius heightens the political edge of his comment, since it was even more distinctively Roman than a tetradrachm. Or perhaps the reference to the denarius reflects the setting of Mark, not of Jesus.

The story of Peter and the fish in Matthew 17:24-27 raises similar issues. After Peter is asked whether Jesus pays the didrachm tax

---

Hopkins University Press, 1996). On the use of rabbinic sources to understand the third- and fourth-century currency and economy, see Daniel Sperber, *Roman Palestine 200–400: Money and Prices* (Ramat-Gan: Bar-Ilan University, 1974). Rachel Barkay provides an excellent treatment of civic denominations and rabbinic terms in *The Coinage of Nysa-Scythopolis (Beth-Shean)* (Jerusalem: Israel Numismatic Society, 2003), 171–184.

[47] On coins mentioned in the gospels and Josephus, see Sutherland, "Pattern," 91–93. On coins and the New Testament, see Larry J. Kreitzer, *Striking New Images: Roman Imperial Coinage and the New Testament World* (Sheffield: Sheffield Academic Press, 1996).

[48] Burnett et al. provide an overview of the denarius's use in *RPC*, vol. 1, 26–30, 36–37.

[49] For example, Mark 6:37; 12:15; 14:5; Matt. 18:28; 20:2, 9, 10, 13, 19; 22:19 (= Mark 12:15); Luke 7:41; 10:35; 20:24 (= Mark 12:15); John 6:7 and 12:5 (which are curiously similar to Mark 6:37 and 14:5).

[50] Compare parallels in Matthew 22:15–22 and Luke 20:20–26.

(apparently the temple tax), Jesus tells him to cast a hook into the Sea of Galilee, pull up the first fish he catches, and open its mouth to find a stater, presumably a silver coin.[51] In this pericope, Matthew refers to a denomination of the widely used Attic standard (didrachm) rather than to the half-shekel of the Phoenician standard that was actually required for the tax.[52]

Other passages include a mixture of numismatic references. In the story of the "widow's mite," Mark 12:42 notes that two lepta are equivalent to a quadrans, thus explaining how the Greek denomination relates to a Roman one. The parallel passage, Luke 21:2, retains the reference to two lepta but omits mention of the quadrans, while Matthew leaves out the story altogether. In reporting that Jesus said that one should settle his differences with his opponent before going to court, lest he lose his last coin, Luke 12:59 again opts for a Greek term, lepton, while Matthew 5:26 specifies a quadrans. To complicate matters further, we also find references to larger and older units of measurement such as the talent (Matt. 18:24) and the mina (Luke 19:12–27).[53]

As even this brief survey suggests, a full description of the different types of coins used in Galilee during the time of Jesus and the following centuries is impractical. Concentrating on the relatively small number of coins actually struck there by Herodian client kings and the region's two cities, however, is quite illuminating. An examination of these coins within their larger regional and political contexts illustrates the region's changing cultural climate.

---

[51] The exact meaning of stater in this passage is unclear; the term was used variously to refer to gold, silver, or electrum coins.

[52] Warren Carter suggests that the reference reflects the post-70 situation, when the Romans changed the tax to the didrachm amount and directed it to the temple of Jupiter Capitolinus (*Matthew and Empire: Initial Explorations* [Harrisburg: Trinity Press International, 2001], 130–144).

[53] We find another reference to a drachm in Luke 15:8–9 and a reference to an assarion (a Roman as?) in Luke 12:6/Matt. 10:29. The other well-known references to money occur in Matthew's story of the betrayal of Jesus. The writer gives us no clue what he has in mind when he specifies Judas's reward as thirty pieces of silver (26:15, 27:3–10); his wording is seemingly intended to echo Zech. 11:12–13.

HERODIAN COINS

Bronze coins of all members of the Herodian dynasty circulated in Galilee, though apparently not in great numbers.[54] At Yodefat, only a handful of the 221 identifiable coins are from the Herodian kings; at Meiron, 19 of 1003; from the 1931 excavations at Sepphoris, 2 of 390. Nearby Gamla has yielded an unusually large number of coins, but the proportion of Herodian issues is low: only 245 of over 6,300 coins, compared to over 3,900 Hasmonean pieces. Finds at other sites are similarly limited.[55] Herodian coins are modest in number because relatively few were made and most were struck outside the region. Only Antipas, Agrippa I (perhaps), and Agrippa II minted any in Galilee itself. For the two Agrippas, production within the region was extremely limited; both produced almost all of their coinage elsewhere.[56]

Simply by issuing coins, the Herodian kings signaled that they still had considerable autonomy. When Antipas and Philip struck coins, for example, they demonstrated to their subjects (and perhaps also to the Roman officials at Caesarea and Jerusalem) that they remained in power, unlike their brother Archelaus, who had been deposed in 6 CE.[57] The designs on the Herods' coins also conveyed political messages. Commoners looking through a handful of coins would have recognized the importance of at least some of their details: whether the obverses were decorated with busts, and, if so, of whom; what symbols were chosen for the reverses; the royal or imperial titles found upon them; and the languages of such inscriptions

---

[54] The Herods struck no silver, unlike the neighboring Nabatean rulers (Meshorer, *Nabatean Coins*) and some more distant kings (*RPC*, vol. 1, 26).

[55] Adan-Bayewitz and Aviam, "Iotapata"; Raynor and Meshorer, *Coins*, 84; Syon, "Coins from Gamala"; Syon and Yavor, "Gamla"; cf. Freyne, "Itureans." McCollough and Edwards note the discovery of a coin of Archelaus at Sepphoris ("Transformations," 138). Other Herodian dynasty coins have been found at Nabratein (one) and Gush Halav (one) (Raynor, "Numismatics," 237); Capernaum (one out of 617 at the Franciscan excavations) (Raynor and Meshorer, *Coins*, 84 and Augusto Spijkerman, *Cafarnao: Catalogo delle Monete della Città* [Jerusalem: Franciscan Printing Press, 1975], no. 122); et-Tell (eight out of approximately 220) (Kindler, "Coin Finds").

[56] Because none of Herod the Great's money was minted in Galilee, his coins are not numerous there.

[57] Strickert suggests that Antipas and Philip issued coins at approximately the same time as Pilate to demonstrate their independence from the prefect ("Coins," 170–171).

(regardless of whether they could actually read them). Given the diversity of currencies in the region, they would also have had some sense of the similarities and differences between coins of the Herods and those of other authorities, and thus some sense of the ways in which the kings were adapting certain Greco-Roman norms while rejecting others.

The single most notable feature was probably the presence or absence of a bust. Coins without one would have stood out from many, though not all, of the coins produced in the surrounding areas. If a bust was present, it typically was that of the client king, the emperor, or one of their family members.[58] Portraying himself or a relative was a way for a ruler to express his own authority and relative independence.[59] Depicting the emperor or his family members was, on some level, a statement of Roman identity, an assurance of loyalty, a propagation of imperial ideology, and a sign of respect for numismatic norms. Similarly, a mixture of royal and imperial busts on an individual king's coins implicitly illustrated his subordinate status, since anyone holding coins that included busts of both rulers would have no trouble determining who was more powerful. The same can be said of someone holding the coins issued by Philip that had his bust on one side and emperor's on the other.[60]

The coins of a client king often reflected his ambiguous status in other ways. They might proclaim him *basileus*, ethnarch, or tetrarch, but, whatever the title, it had been bestowed by the emperor and could be changed or removed at his whim. The choice of language also had cultural and political significance. The use of Greek on the Herods' coins made them comparable to most other money

---

[58] Deities were extremely rare on the Herods' coins, though Tyche appears on a coin of Agrippa I minted at Caesarea (*Treasury*, 232 no. 122).

[59] Compare coins from Bosporus, Armenia Minor, and Cilicia (*RPC*, vol. 1, 330–334, 570, 575).

[60] In any case, variations in portraiture are not unusual on client king coinage. Possibilities include: portraits of figures other than rulers (e.g., deities on Galatian coins [*RPC*, vol. 1, 536–537]); fluctuations between members of both the royal and imperial families (coins of the Nabateans [Meshorer, *Nabataean Coins*, 9–12, 17–18]; Paphlagonia, Pontus, Commagene [*RPC*, vol. 1, 536–537, 567–569, 571–574], and Armenia [Paul Z. Bedoukian, *Coinage of the Artaxiads of Armenia* {London: Royal Numismatic Society, 1978}]); imperial portraits alone (e.g., coins of Thrace [*RPC*, vol. 1, 312–315]).

circulating in the region.[61] It clearly differentiated their coins from those of the nearest other client kings, the Nabateans, who had switched from Greek to Nabatean after Pompey.[62] It would also have distinguished them from the still circulating Hasmonean coins, with their Semitic inscriptions. On a few coins, Agrippa II utilized Latin, a decision that emphasized his staunchly pro-Roman loyalties.

When Antipas issued coins, the very first ever to be struck in Galilee, he apparently modeled them after those of his father.[63] Herod the Great had avoided anthropomorphic and zoomorphic imagery almost entirely,[64] choosing symbols that apparently were acceptable to most Jews.[65] Both Antipas and his brother Archelaus did the same.[66] In an important respect, however, Antipas differed from Herod. Antipas's coins were apparently based on Roman standards rather than the Hellenistic standards used by his father and the Hasmoneans before him. His brothers and the later Herodian rulers followed suit, issuing coins that appear to have been most compatible with Roman denominations.[67]

---

[61] Outside the East, Latin was the norm, though with some variation; cf. the mixture of Neo-Punic, Greek, and Latin on client king coins in Mauretania and Numidia until the early first century CE (Jean Mazard, *Corpus Nummorum Numidiae Mauretaniaeque* [Paris: Arts et Métiers Graphiques, 1955]).

[62] Meshorer, *Nabatean Coins.* After the Roman annexation of Nabatean territory in 106 CE, city coins there used Greek (e.g., Petra's coins in *City-Coins,* 120).

[63] *Treasury,* 81–85; *RPC,* vol. 1, 679–680.

[64] *Treasury,* 61–78. The exception was an eagle, which Meshorer associates with the Roman eagle as well with the golden eagle Herod placed over the temple (Josephus, *War* 1.648–655 and *Antiquities* 17.150–152; *Treasury,* 67–69; cf. Fine, *Art*). The eagle was a common numismatic symbol (e.g., coins minted at Rome 29–27 BCE in C. H. V. Sutherland and R. A. G. Carson, eds., *The Roman Imperial Coinage,* vol. 1.1 [London: Spink and Son, 1984], 61) and at Tyre, Sidon and Ascalon in *RPC,* vol. 1 part 2, 800).

[65] Meshorer (*Treasury,* 65–71) differentiates between symbols on Herod's undated coins (e.g., tripod, apex, winged caduceus, aphlastone, laurel branch), which he plausibly argues were minted in Samaria, and those on his dated coins (a table, diadem, wreath, palm branches, vine, anchor, double cornucopiae with caduceus, single cornucopia, galley, and eagle), which were probably struck in Jerusalem. He argues that these latter symbols are all associated with Jewish art and the temple. While this may be true, similar symbols show up elsewhere on Mediterranean coins.

[66] *Treasury,* 78–81.

[67] *Treasury,* 71–72, 80, 84–85, 90; Strickert, "Coins," esp. 173–178. Though Archelaus initially minted coins compatible with Greek denominations, his later issues were heavier, following the Roman system.

The first of Antipas's coins appears to have been minted in year four of his reign (c. 1 CE).[68] The coin was presumably struck at Sepphoris, the only sizable city in the region at the time. Its legend is the earliest Greek inscription from Sepphoris and one of the earliest from all of Galilee. Though not all of the letters on its obverse are legible, they apparently read "Herod Tetrarch." One side of the coin bears an image of a grain of barley or wheat, the other, that of a seven-branched palm tree.

The subsequent coins of Antipas all appear to have been struck at Tiberias. He released multiple denominations in 20 CE, presumably in conjunction with the foundation of the city, and in 29, 30, 33 and 39 CE. The reverses of all but the last series have inscriptions with the name of Tiberias (often abbreviated) encircled by a wreath, reflecting the ruler's pride in his new city as well as his flattery of the emperor.

Like the coin from Sepphoris, Antipas's later coins were inscribed with the ruler's name and title, "Herod Tetrarch," as well as a date according to the year of his reign.[69] The obverses of those struck in 20 CE depicted a reed, a symbol presumably chosen because of the plant's presence at the Sea of Galilee.[70] Other coins were decorated with imagery associated with palm trees. Coins of 29, 30, and 33 CE bore a solitary palm, while those issued in 39 CE varied by denomination, the largest depicting a palm tree with clusters of dates; the middle, a palm branch; and the smallest, dates.

It is probably no coincidence that Antipas's last coins bore no references to Tiberias, since the emperor for whom it was named had died in 37 CE. The coins of 39 CE had a new element, however: inscriptions of the emperor's name and titles. This addition probably reflects the tetrarch's attempt to flatter Caligula as he unsuccessfully sought the more prestigious title of *basileus*.[71]

---

[68] David Hendin, "A New Coin Type of Herod Antipas," *INJ 15* (in press).

[69] Unlike the earlier coin, where the name and title apparently were in the nominative case, in later issues, they were in the genitive case. In this chapter, I do not distinguish between inscriptions that occur in the genitive and those in the nominative, since the case is unimportant for my central points.

[70] The symbol apparently has no parallels among contemporary coinage (index in *RPC*, vol. 1, 793).

[71] *Treasury*, 82–83; *Ant.* 18.230–256.

It has been suggested that Antipas struck coins to help shift Galilee from a barter economy to a monetized economy. William E. Arnal hypothesizes that the tetrarch minted coins to address a regional shortage. By increasing the money supply, he hoped to facilitate more efficient collection of taxes and to enable the masses to descend into debt more easily. Arnal suggests that although the efforts of Antipas were not entirely successful, they did hasten the pace of monetization. In this view, Antipas's introduction of local coins created a socio-economic crisis that is reflected in the earliest stratum of Q.[72]

This proposal is problematic. The tetrarch's coins were all bronze and thus relatively small change; it is unlikely that their main purpose was to make taxation and the transfer of wealth easier, since silver would have been preferable for both purposes. Furthermore, the theory assumes that the primary reason a client king issued currency was economic. Such coins were often intended primarily as propaganda, however, serving to express cultural, political, and ideological values. Antipas does not seem to have minted very many coins, probably because a considerable amount of Hasmonean currency was still in circulation as well as money from nearby cities like Tyre.[73] While the overall trajectory of the Roman period was toward further monetization,[74] the relatively small amount of money issued under Antipas probably did little to hinder or hasten the process.

The conservative nature of the designs on Antipas's coins is clear when we compare them to those of his brother Philip.[75] Philip's bore portraits, the first coins issued by a Jewish king to do so.

---

[72] Arnal, *Jesus*, 134–146.

[73] Compare *Treasury*, 85. The site that has yielded the most coins of Antipas is nearby Gamla, where 55 were found (Syon, "Coins from Gamala"). Other find spots include Yodefat, Gush Halav, and nearby et-Tell (one coin at each site; Adan-Bayewitz and Aviam, "Iotapata"; Kindler, "Coin Finds"; Raynor, "Numismatics," 237) and Meiron (three coins, Raynor and Meshorer, *Coins*, 84). Meshorer notes that coins of Antipas are often found in excavations of later synagogues (e.g., Hammath Tiberias, Meiron, Gush Halav, Nabratein, Arbel, Capernaum; *AJC*, vol. 2, 41, 205n. 27–28), showing that people sometimes held on to them for centuries, despite their low value.

[74] By the Late Roman era, significantly more coins circulated throughout Palestine (Safrai, *Economy*, 302, 404–414, 427–428).

[75] *Treasury*, 85–90; Strickert, "Coins."

Perhaps he felt comfortable departing from Jewish numismatic custom since most of his subjects were gentiles. On some he placed images of the emperor, on others, of himself. On the largest of his earliest series, for example, he put Augustus on the obverse and himself on the reverse; on a later coin he put jugate heads of Augustus and his wife Livia. His inscriptions typically named both himself and the emperor.[76] Philip was also the first Jewish king to depict a pagan temple on his coins, a tetrastyle building, perhaps the temple to Augustus built by Herod the Great.

The coins of Agrippa I made even more extensive use of imperial and royal images,[77] as demonstrated by a series minted c. 40/41 CE (perhaps at Tiberias, since they are most common in its vicinity). The largest denomination, clearly a copy of a coin issued at Rome,[78] had Caligula on its obverse and a man riding a quadriga on its reverse.[79] The next smallest had a bust of Caligula's wife Caesonia on its obverse and his favorite sister (and purported lover) Drusilla on the reverse, standing and holding a Nike figure. The third size was decorated with Agrippa's portrait and, on the back, a depiction of his wife Cypros. The smallest coin showed the king's son, Agrippa II, with double cornucopiae on the reverse. Thus, as the coins decreased in size, the statures of those portrayed decreased, with the largest coin depicting the emperor and the smallest the client king's heir.[80]

Many of Agrippa's other coins, minted at Paneas, Jerusalem, and Caesarea Maritima, display similar receptiveness to Greco-Roman customs, with busts on their obverses and anthropomorphic imagery or temples on their reverses. Two make the stature of client kings

---

[76] In addition, Strickert argues that a coin depicting Livia found at et-Tell was probably minted by Philip, though it has no inscription naming him ("Coins," 172).

[77] *Treasury,* 90–114.

[78] *Treasury,* 91–93. Earlier coins of Agrippa had also been modeled after those at Rome, such as two from 37/38 CE (A. Burnett, "The Coinage of King Agrippa I of Judaea and a New Coin of King Herod of Chalcis," in H. Huvelin, M. Christol, and G. Gautier, eds., *Mélanges de Numismatique: Offerts à Pierre Bastien à l'occasion of de son 75e anniversaire* [Wettern, Belgium: Editions NR, 1987], 28–39, esp. 27–28).

[79] On the Roman coin, the rider was Caligula's father Germanicus, but whether the rider on Agrippa's coin was intended or perceived as Germanicus (as suggested in *Treasury,* 93–95) or as Agrippa himself is impossible to determine. Cf. Burnett, "Coinage" and Meshorer's earlier comments in *AJC,* vol. 2, 53–54.

[80] Compare a series with similar images minted in 39 CE, probably at Paneas.

relative to that of the emperor especially clear. The first depicts Agrippa and Herod of Chalcis crowning the emperor Claudius, with an inscription naming the three figures. Its reverse depicts two clasped hands, a Roman sign for a treaty, and the inscription "Sworn treaty of the great king Agrippa to Augustus Caesar, the Senate and the Roman People: his friendship and alliance." The coin probably refers to an agreement in 41 CE that enlarged Agrippa's kingdom.[81] The second coin depicts Claudius on its obverse and a temple with four figures on its reverse, Claudius, Agrippa, and two unidentifiable people. The image may refer to the consecration of the aforementioned treaty at Rome.[82] The reverse image is surrounded by the inscription "Great King Agrippa Philocaesar." The last word, also found on a smaller coin of the same series, is a title that rarely appeared on mid-first-century client king coinage[83] though it is occasionally found in other inscriptions.[84]

At least one coin of Agrippa II was probably minted in Galilee, as reflected by the wreath-encircled Greek "Tiberias" on its reverse. An image of a palm branch and the inscription ΒΑ ΑΓΡΙΠΑ ΝΙΚ ΣΕΒ, "King Agrippa, Victory of the Emperor" are found on the obverse, as well as the date, "Year 15." The coin is clearly a celebration of the Roman victory in the Jewish revolt.[85]

---

[81] Burnett, "Coinage," 31–35; on the treaty, see Josephus, *Antiquities* 19.275 and *War* 2.216; Suetonius, *Claudius*, 25.5. Meshorer accepts this interpretation in *Treasury*, 100–101; it differs considerably from his earlier position in *AJC*, vol. 2, 55–57. Herod of Chalcis minted an almost identical coin c. 42/43 CE. A similar image can be seen on a coin issued by King Artaxis of Armenia, but with the positions reversed: the king is being crowned by Tiberius's son Germanicus, rather than the emperor being crowned by a king (Bedoukian, *Coinage*, 77, no. 168).

[82] Burnett, "Coinage," 35–37; cf. Meshorer's reservations in *Treasury*, 98–99.

[83] A similar title, *philoclaudius*, is found on coins of Herod of Chalcis from 43 CE (*Treasury*, 263 nos. 362–364). For discussion of such titles (i.e., *philoromaios, philosebastos,* and *philogermanicus*), see Braund, *Rome*, 105–107. In the first century CE, they are more often found on civic coins in reference to local officials, especially in the province of Asia; cf. the appearance of *philocaesar* at several cities (*RPC*, vol. 1, 443, 493, 496, 496), the use of *philantoniou* in Cilicia in 39–31 BCE (*RPC*, vol. 1, 575), and the later occurrence of such titles at Edessa (*philoromaios* c. 166 CE) and Lower Cilbiani (*philosebastos*, under Caracalla) (Barclay V. Head et al., *Historia Numorum: A Manual of Greek Numismatics*, rev. ed. [Chicago: Argonaut, 1963], 814, 649–650).

[84] Richardson, *Herod*, 204–208 nos. 2a-b and 6–8, 210.

[85] *Treasury*, 106–107. *NIK SEB*, an unparalleled inscription, is apparently the abbreviated Greek equivalent for the Latin *Victoria Augusti*, a common numismatic inscription in the west.

Agrippa's other coins were mostly struck in Paneas.[86] Their designs showed that he, even more than his predecessors, fully joined the numismatic mainstream of the Roman world. Missing entirely are portraits of himself or his wife, replaced instead with busts of the emperor. Perhaps Agrippa's reluctance to depict himself reflects an additional measure of deference to the emperor in the wake of the first revolt. Deities – Tyche, Nike, Moneta, and, because of the importance of the cultic site at Paneas, Pan – are frequently shown on the reverses, though on smaller denominations other symbols sometimes appear (e.g., an anchor, single and double cornucopiae, a palm tree, and corn).[87] His inscriptions honor the emperor as well as himself, sometimes adding a date based on the year of his reign. Coins minted in the mid-80s CE, some of them copies of coins of Rome, had Latin inscriptions, the first and only Herodian coins to do so. Latin was unusual enough on the region's coins that his subjects must have recognized its use as an emphatic statement of Roman identity.[88]

Agrippa was the last of the Herodian client kings. After his death in the 90s,[89] the Romans annexed his territory. With the end of his dynasty and that of the Nabateans in 106 CE came the end of royal coinage in the area and, with it, the end of numismatic expressions of nominal independence from Rome.

CIVIC COINS

Sepphoris and Tiberias struck no civic coins until after Jesus' lifetime.[90] When they began doing so, they joined the dozens of cities in Syria, Palestine, and the Transjordan and the hundreds of cities

---

[86] *Treasury*, 102–114, 233–240; note that Meshorer mistakenly attributes the wartime coins of Sepphoris to Agrippa II.

[87] Tyche and Pan would later appear on Paneas's civic coinage (Ya'akov Meshorer, "The Coins of Caesarea Paneas," *INJ* 8 [1984–1985]: 37–58).

[88] *Treasury*, 111–112. Other coins with Latin inscriptions may also be from Agrippa II (*RPC*, vol. 1, nos. 4845–4846).

[89] See discussion in Chapter Two.

[90] There is no one compendium that includes all of the civic coins of Sepphoris and Tiberias; one must consult multiple works. For Sepphoris, see Meshorer's works ("Coins of Sepphoris," "Sepphoris and Rome," *City-Coins*, 36–37 and "Hoard of Coins from Migdal," nos. 145–148) and M. Rosenberger, *City-Coins of Palestine*, 3 vols. (Jerusalem: 1972–1977), vol. 3, 60–63. For Tiberias, see Meshorer, *City-Coins*, 34–35, "Hoard of Coins

elsewhere in the Roman East that also produced currency.[91] This proliferation of civic mints is all the more notable since the exact opposite phenomenon happened in the western empire, where civic minting ended by the mid-first century CE.[92] Cities issued coins for a variety of purposes, which Rachel Barkay succinctly describes: to "supply local currency, produce revenue, finance special projects (whether civil or military), express the city's pride in itself, commemorate extraordinary events . . . or [for] a combination of several of these reasons" – goals she sums up as "profits, prestige, and publicity."[93] The changes in coin designs over the decades reflect the growing openness of civic elites to Greco-Roman numismatic customs.

As would be expected, the coins of both Sepphoris and Tiberias utilized Greek. The use of indigenous languages on civic coins was rare throughout the Empire.[94] In the east, most cities opted for Greek, except those with the status of Roman colony, which usually chose Latin. Thus, during the Jewish revolt, Ptolemais, recently declared a colony, departed from its four centuries of tradition and switched from Greek to Latin. After Vespasian declared Caesarea Maritima a colony, it did likewise.[95] Other cities that later received colonial status followed the same pattern.[96]

The first Galilean civic coins were a series of three denominations minted at Tiberias c. 53 CE.[97] The designs of all three are identical,

from Migdal," nos. 129–130; *Treasury* 177–178 (see discussion below); Kindler, *Coins*; and Rosenberger, *City-Coins*, vol. 3, 63–67.

[91] On the city coins of Palestine and the Transjordan, see Barkay, *Coinage*, 185–196; *City-Coins*; Spijkerman, *Coins*; Rosenberger, *City-Coins*; Arie Kindler and Alla Stein, *A Bibliography of the City Coinage of Palestine: From the 2nd Century BC to the 3rd Century AD* (Oxford: BAR, 1987); Chancey, "City Coins."

[92] *RPC*, vol. 1, 18–19; Howgego, *Ancient History*, 58.

[93] Barkay, *Coinage*, 27–30, quote from 29.

[94] Compare the unusual use of Phoenician alongside Greek on some Tyrian coins (*RPC*, vol. 1, nos. 4704–4739) and the letter *mem* on coins of Gaza (nos. 4894–4896).

[95] *RPC*, vol. 1, nos. 4749–4751; *RPC*, vol. 2, no. 2231; *City-Coins*, 110–111. Cf. also Beirut (*RPC*, vol. 1, 648–651).

[96] *City-Coins*, 114–116, 119, 120; Kindler, "Status." Though Meshorer proposed that a coin of Tiberias attests to colonial status (*City-Coins*, 35, 113 no. 86), Joshua Ezra Burns's recent first-hand inspection of the coin found no evidence to support Meshorer's reading (personal communication).

[97] Meshorer earlier suggested that these coins were minted under Agrippa II (*AJC*, vol. 2, 166–167, 279), but in *Treasury* (177–178, 261) he suggests they were issued by the Roman

with a palm branch, the date ("year 13"), and the name of the emperor (Claudius Caesar) on the obverse and a wreath surrounding the city's name on the reverse. The avoidance of figural art and the use of the palm branch reflect continuity with the earlier coins struck at the city by Antipas.

No other Galilean civic currency was issued until Sepphoris released two coins c. 68 CE, during the first revolt.[98] Its coins served as political propaganda, making the stance of the city (or at least its leadership) clear to its own citizens, the roman forces, nearby King Agrippa, and other Galileans. The obverse of each bore an inscription within a wreath, LΔI/ NEPΩNO /KΛAYΔIOY/ KAICAPO/ C ("Year 14, of Nero Claudius Caesar"). The reverses read EΠI OYECΠACIANOY EIPHNOΠOΛIC NEPΩNIA CEΠΦΩ ("Under Vespasian, Eirenopolis-Neronias-Sepphoris"), showing that the city renamed itself in honor of Nero and proclaimed itself "Eirenopolis," that is, the "City of Peace." While the exact meaning of the phrase *epi Vespasian* is unclear – it could be a dating formula, purely honorific, or an indication that he authorized the city to mint coins[99] – it clearly shows respect to the general. In addition, one reverse was decorated with the Latin abbreviation *SC*, the only Latin ever to appear on Sepphoris's coins. The two letters are a widely used abbreviation for *senatus consulto* and thus a strong pro-Roman statement. Rather than representing an actual decision of the Roman Senate, they probably reflect flattery of the Romans, an honorific gesture toward the Senate, and an intentional mimicking of imperial coins minted at Antioch.[100] The other coin's reverse

---

administration, thus agreeing with Kindler (*Coins*, 17). Nothing about the coins themselves suggests they are procuratorial issues, however, and there is little reason for the Roman authorities to have issued coins at Tiberias. I am now convinced that they are civic coins (cf. my earlier uncertainty in *Myth*, 92).

[98] See Meshorer, "Coins of Sepphoris"; Meshorer, "Sepphoris and Rome"; Henri Seyrig, "Irenopolis-Neronias-Sepphoris," *Numismatic Chronicle* 10 (1950): 284–289 and "Ireno-polis-Neronias-Sepphoris: An Additional Note," *Numismatic Chronicle* 15 (1955): 157–159. Meshorer mistakenly attributes these coins to Agrippa II in *Treasury* 103–106; cf. H. Hamburger, "The Coin Issues of the Roman Administration from the Mint of Caesarea Maritima," *IEJ* 20 (1970): 81–91, who attributes them to Vespasian. For earlier discussions, see Chancey and Meyers, "How Jewish"; Chancey, "Cultural Milieu"; Chancey, *Myth*, 81–82.

[99] *RPC*, vol. 1, 1–5.   [100] *RPC*, vol. 1, nos. 4297–4298.

displayed a symbol used on both non-Jewish and Jewish coinage, a caduceus between two cornucopiae.[101] Sepphoris was far from alone in using coins to make a political statement during the war. Ptolemais and Caesarea both issued coins that displayed legionary standards, and those of Ptolemais expressed pride in the city's elevation to colony, showing Nero ceremonially determining its boundaries by plowing with an ox.[102] Other wartime coins reflected the opposite end of the political spectrum. Silver and bronze coins produced by rebels in Jerusalem eschewed Greek inscriptions, using archaic Hebrew letters instead, a robust statement of distinctive Jewish identity in a time of crisis. "Holy Jerusalem" appeared on some; "Freedom of Zion" or "of the redemption of Zion" on others. The dating system was equally political, noting the year of the revolt ("Year One," "Year Two"). The coins were based on the Phoenician, rather than the Roman or Attic, standard, and, in another departure from normal practice, inscriptions specified each one's value (a shekel, half-shekel, or quarter-shekel). Their symbols were all associated with the Jerusalem Temple, depicting either vessels (e.g., chalice, amphora), decorations (a branch with three pomegranates, a vine), or items used in the festival of Sukkot (*lulav* bundles, a date palm).[103] Gamla also issued a revolt coin that depicted a chalice and bore paleo-Hebrew inscriptions, with "of the redemption" on one side and "Holy Jerusalem" on the other. Gamla's coins were struck not out of a need for additional bronze currency but as a statement of solidarity with the rebels and opposition to Rome and its client, Agrippa II, in whose territory they were located.[104]

Against this backdrop, the pro-Roman message conveyed by the coins of Sepphoris is even clearer. Yet even with their desire to make an unambiguous statement, the leadership of Sepphoris chose not to cross the line of Jewish tradition by placing the emperor's bust on these coins. This decision clearly distinguished them from most civic

---

[101] The same symbol appears on revolt-era coins issued at Paneas by Agrippa II; that city, like Sepphoris, renamed itself in honor of Nero (*Treasury*, 233 no. 132).

[102] *City-Coins*, 12 no. 2 and 20 no. 32; a coin with plowing emperor image was issued by Caesarea under Septimius Severus (20 no. 26).

[103] *Treasury*, 115–134.   [104] *Treasury*, 130–131; Syon, "Coins from Gamala."

coins struck in the region during the war, which did depict the emperor.[105]

When the next Galilean coins were issued, under Emperor Trajan (98–117 C. E.), a shift in sensibilities was evident. For the first time, both cities' coins bore the emperor's portrait. The willingness of both cities to place a human image on their coins reflects the growing influence of Greco-Roman culture and a desire to symbolize their loyalty to the governing authorities.

The four coins of Sepphoris had an inscription around Trajan's bust, ΤΡΑΙΑΝΟΣ ΑΥΤΟΚΡΑΤΩΡ ΕΔΩΚΕΝ or "Emperor Trajan gave." Each reverse bore the city's ethnic label, ΣΕΠΦΩΡΗΝΩΝ, and one of four symbols: a laurel wreath, caduceus, two ears of grain or corn, and a palm tree.[106] Meshorer has argued that these symbols are all Jewish and that the reference to Trajan's gift (a unique inscription on Roman coinage) reflects his granting permission to the city to mint distinctively Jewish coinage.[107] Yet, there is little that is unique about the coins. The symbols on the reverses do appear on earlier Jewish coins, but they were also found on coins of pagan cities. Thus, the phrase "Emperor Trajan gave" probably refers not to special permission to strike special Jewish coins, but, some other gift to the city.[108]

The coins of Tiberias had a more typical inscription around their imperial busts: ΑΥΤ ΚΑΙ ΝΕΡ ΤΡΑΙΑΝΟΣ ΣΕΒ ΓΕΡ, or "Autocrator Caesar Nero Trajan Sebastos Germanicus."[109] Their reverses had dates, calculated in years from the city's foundation[110] and

---

[105] For example Ascalon, Hippos, Gadara, Gerasa, Scythopolis (*RPC,* vol. 1, nos. 4889–4892, 4807–4808, 4822–4824, 4839–4841, 4834–4835).

[106] Meshorer, "Sepphoris and Rome," 163–164; "Coins of Sepphoris."

[107] Meshorer, "Sepphoris and Rome," 163–164; "Coins of Sepphoris." As Meshorer observes, the coins are similar to those of Neapolis under Domitian ("Sepphoris and Rome," 164 n. 24).

[108] Compare Harl, *Civic Coins,* 24 and plate 27 and discussion in my Chapter Four. Noting that no other coins were struck at Sepphoris until the time of Antoninus Pius, Meshorer speculates that the city was punished for its support of the Diaspora Jewish revolt in 115–117 CE (*City-Coins,* 36; "Sepphoris and Rome," 165). There is no evidence to suggest that the city was sympathetic to that revolt, however, and civic currency was often issued sporadically rather than at regular intervals. There is thus no reason to think that the absence of coins under Hadrian reflected his punishment.

[109] Kindler, *Coins,* 55–57 nos. 3–6; *City-Coins,* 112–113 nos. 77–80.

[110] This technique of dating was typical, though it stands out when juxtaposed with the more Romano-centric dates on the coins of many older cities in the region, which were based on

"Tiberias Claudiopolis," the name that would appear on most subsequent coinage. The two smallest coins had conservative symbols on their reverses, both surrounded with circular borders of dots: one, an anchor, and the other, a palm branch between two cornucopiae. The largest coin was decorated with an image of Tyche, the city-goddess, holding a rudder and cornucopiae and standing upon the prow of a ship, a clear reference (like the anchor) to the city's lakeside location. The second largest denomination depicted the goddess of health, Hygieia, a deity undoubtedly chosen because of the hot baths at Hammath Tiberias. She sits on a rock from which water flows, holding a snake that eats from a phial in her other hand. These coins were the first minted in Galilee to have images of gods.

For the duration of their minting activity, Tiberias and Sepphoris produced coins that were strikingly similar to those of other cities. Their adoption of the imagery of deities, temples, and emperors indicated their elites' full-scale participation in this aspect of the civic culture of the eastern Roman Empire. Three of Tiberias's coins, the earliest dating to Hadrian, depicted the ancient image of a seated Zeus within a tetrastyle temple.[111] A later coin had a Hygieia motif and another showed Hygieia and Asclepius, the god of healing, holding serpents and facing each other. Others depicted deities associated with water and shipping – Tyche, holding a bust, with her right foot on the prow of a galley, and Poseidon, likewise standing with his foot on a galley, holding a dolphin.

The coins of Sepphoris were similar. One depicted a seated Zeus within a tetrastyle temple, an appropriate image for a city named Diocaesarea, while another showed the Capitoline Triad, Jupiter, Juno, and Minerva, within a tetrastyle temple, an image probably intended as a pro-Roman statement.[112] Other deities also appear:

Pompey's arrival in 63 BCE (Chancey, "City Coins," 105–106 and discussion in Chapter Two).

[111] Meshorer (*City-Coins*, 34) has plausibly suggested that the building might be the shrine to Hadrian mentioned in Epiphanius (*Adv. Haereses* 30.12.1.), since the emperor was often associated with that deity. He also suggests that these coins were made when Hadrian visited Palestine, though there is no explicit evidence that the emperor came to Galilee.

[112] *City-Coins*, 60 no. 163. The trio is rare on coins from Palestine and Jordan, though they are found on a Hadrianic coin of Aelia Capitolina (Meshorer, *Coinage of Aelia Capitolina,*

one coin has a bust of a goddess, perhaps Hera, while the other shows a goddess with helmet, spear, and shield, sometimes identified as Athena.

From Antoninus Pius on, the coins of Sepphoris bear its new name, Diocaesarea, often accompanied by a traditional civic title, "the Holy, City of Asylum, Autonomous" (or, in one case, just "Holy and Autonomous").[113] Titles like these had a long history in the Mediterranean, going back to at least the second century BCE, but they appear to have become especially popular in the second and third centuries CE.[114] They were largely honorific; the days of truly autonomous cities were long over by the Roman period. Rachel Barkay suggests that titles like these were used in the Roman period to affirm a city's sense of a Greek identity.[115]

During the reigns of Caracalla and Elagabalus, Sepphoris minted coins with reverse designs that consisted solely of wreaths surrounding inscriptions proclaiming faithfulness to Rome. Because of the use of abbreviations, their exact wording remains open to debate. One minted under Caracalla read ΔΙΟΚΑΙΣΑΡ ΙΕΡΑΣΑΥΤ ΠΙΣΦΙΛΣΥΜ ΜΑΧ ΡΩΜΑΙ or "Diocaesarea the Holy, City of Shelter [asylum], Autonomous, Faithful Friend and Ally of the Romans."[116] There are variations among the abbreviations on other coins of the same series; some refer also to the ΣΚΔΡΩ, presumably the Greek equivalent for the Latin SPQR, "Senate and the Roman

27–28, 70 no. 1). Schwartz suggests that the image reflects the city's payment of the required Jewish tax to the Capitoline Jupiter (*Imperialism*, 139).

[113] A coin under Antoninus Pius read ΔΙΟΚΑΙ ΙΕΡ ΑΣ Υ ΑΥΤΟ; that of Julia, ΔΙΟΚΑΙ ΙΕΡ ΑΣ Υ.

[114] Tyre's coins had borne them since at least 126 BCE; Sidon's, since 82/81 BCE; Ptolemais since 39/38 BCE (Kindler, "Status"). For Hippos, Gadara and other Decapolis cities, see Spijkerman, *Coins*, 300–303; for Paneas and other east Mediterranean cities, see Head, *Historia Numorum*, lxxx and 927.

[115] Barkay, *Coinage*, 160–165. Scythopolis went further than other cities in the region, adding the title "Greek city" (ΕΛ ΠΟ) to its coins of 175/176 CE; this title is also attested in an inscription (Foerster and Tsafrir, "Nysa-Scythopolis"). Note the inscription on a limestone block at Gerasa from 130 CE referring to the city as "Holy, Inviolate, and Autonomous," with the Greek terms transliterated, rather than translated, into Latin (Welles, "Inscriptions," 390–391 no. 30).

[116] ΔΙΟΚΑΙΣΑΡΙΑΣ ΙΕΡΑΣ ΑΣΥΛΟΥ ΑΥΤΟΝΟΜΟΥ ΠΙΣΤΟΣ ΦΙΛΟΣ ΣΥΜΜΑΧΟΣ ΡΩΜΑΙΩΝ, following Harl's reading (*Civic Coins*, 81; cf. C. M. McCray, "Jewish Friends and Allies of Rome," *American Numismatic Society Museum Notes* 25 [1980]: 53–57), rather than Meshorer's ("Sepphoris and Rome," 168).

People," while others refer just to the "Roman People" (ΔP).[117] A coin minted under Elagabalus had a similar inscription.[118] Such references to the "Roman People" may have been especially appropriate after Caracalla's broad grant of citizenship in 212 CE to all free people. Declarations of fidelity to Rome were common on city coins of the third century, a particularly difficult time for the Empire because of economic troubles and the Parthian threat. Perhaps the inscriptions of Sepphoris's coins indicate, as Harl has suggested, that the city sent money, supplies, or some other type of support to Elagabalus during his military expeditions, as other cities did.[119] One wonders if the armed goddess mentioned earlier who graces a smaller coin minted under Elagabalus should be identified as Roma, rather than Athena, in a similar display of patriotic sentiment.[120]

Civic minting reached its peak under the Antonines and Elagabalus, with large amounts of currency struck throughout the eastern empire.[121] This spurt of activity turned out to be the last, however, as the debasement of silver currency and the resulting inflation made bronze civic coinage impractical and prohibitively costly. The coins of Sepphoris and Tiberias struck under Elagabalus were the final coins minted in Roman Galilee. One by one, cities in Palestine stopped issuing new coins until Ptolemais, one of the last active civic mints in the Empire, ceased production in 268 CE. From this point on, imperial mints would be the sole source of new currency.[122]

---

[117] Meshorer reconstructs ΣΚΔΡΩ as ΣΥΓΚΛΗΤΟΥ ΚΑΙ ΔΗΜΟΥ ΡΩΜΑΙΩΝ.

[118] Meshorer, "Sepphoris and Rome," 168 no. 4.

[119] Harl, *Civic Coins*, 81–82. In light of similar inscriptions on other cities' coins, there appears to be little reason to accept Meshorer's argument that these coins reflect an alliance between the rabbinic Sanhedrin and Rome or confirmation of rabbinic traditions that Caracalla and Judah ha-Nasi shared a special friendship ("Sepphoris and Rome," 166–171, citing *b. Avodah Zarah* 10a–b).

[120] Similar images on other coins might also be interpreted as Roma. Such symbols might be intended to evoke both deities, rather than one or the other. See Rosenberger, *City-Coins*, vol. 3, 63 no. 17; cf. images Spijkerman identifies as Roma on the slightly later (244–249 CE) coins of Philippopolis (*Coins*, plate 58). On numismatic depictions of Roma in general, see Harl, *Civic Coins*, 73.

[121] Harl, *Civic Coins*, 107; Crawford, "Finance," 572–575; Barkay, *Coinage*, 30; cf. finds in the Franciscan excavations at Capernaum, where coins from Elagabalus greatly outnumber those of other emperors (Raynor and Meshorer, *Coins*, 87).

[122] Barkay, *Coinage*, 31–32, 193–195; Sperber, *Roman Palestine*, 133–135, 143–144; Harl, *Civic Coins*, 9; Howgego, *Ancient History*, 138–140.

CONCLUSION

Overall, Galilee's coinage attests to a comfort level with the numismatic conventions of the Greco-Roman world that increased over time. In the early Hellenistic period, the Ptolemies, Seleucids and coastal cities provided its coins, which had Greek legends, human portraits, and images of animals or deities. After the Hasmonean annexation of Galilee, Jewish coins minted in Jerusalem became an important source of currency, their lack of anthropomorphic and zoomorphic imagery and their use of Semitic inscriptions (sometimes instead of Greek, sometimes alongside it) notably contrasting with other regional coinage.

By the early first century CE, a variety of coinages were in use in Galilee. Coins struck by Antipas reflect a selective adaptation of Greco-Roman numismatic practices – the consistent use of Greek and the selection of plant motifs, but the continuing avoidance of figural art. The series produced under Agrippa I c. 40/41 CE at Tiberias depicted members of both the imperial and royal families. These coins were much more like those struck in other areas than the coins of Agrippa's predecessor Antipas – a difference apparent to any Galilean who encountered them. Coins produced later in the century by Sepphoris and Tiberias returned to the more reserved course charted by Antipas.

In contrast, coins minted in Galilee in the second and third centuries reflect a wholesale adoption of Greco-Roman numismatic customs. This development is exemplified by the coins with the emperor's bust, deities, and a tetrastyle temple that Tiberias issued c. 119/120 CE – the same approximate time that the VI Ferrata legion arrived in the region. Within a few decades, Sepphoris had struck similar bronzes.

After the mid-third century, all new currency came from the emperor's mints. Coins might employ Greek for their inscriptions or be nominally based on the old Attic standard, but they still were designed according to primarily Roman, not local, tastes and values. In this respect, the Romanization of coinage, not only of Galilee but of the entire eastern Mediterranean, was complete.

CHAPTER 7

Greco-Roman art and the shifting limits of acceptability

In the first century CE, Galileans seem to have had a conservative attitude towards Greco-Roman art, particularly in regard to figural representations – that is, depictions of animals, humans, deities, and mythological figures.[1] As we have seen, such images were absent even from coins struck in Galilee, despite the fact that Galileans encountered them frequently on coins minted outside the region. In the early second century, however, they began appearing on Galilean coins, and by the late second and the third centuries, they were found on a variety of media, such as sarcophagi, mosaics, and lamps. The timing of this trend strongly suggests that it, too, should be considered within the context of Romanization. This chapter will explore the development of Greco-Roman art in Galilee, paying special attention to the shifting boundaries of acceptability regarding anthropomorphic and zoomorphic imagery.

JEWISH ART AND FIGURAL REPRESENTATION IN THE FIRST CENTURY CE

The most significant difference between the art of first-century CE Jews in Palestine and the art of most (though not all) other areas of the Roman world was the avoidance of figural art.[2] For Jews, this

---

[1] Hellenistic-era examples of such figural art are rare. There is little in the interior of Galilee to compare with the mythological and anthropomorphic imagery on the sealings of the Hellenistic archive from the Tyrian village of Kedesh, for example (Ariel and Naveh, "Selected Inscribed Sealings"). Note, however, the possibly Hellenistic-period life-sized anthropomorphic relief carving in northwest Upper Galilee (Frankel et al., *Settlement Dynamics*, 109) and the figurines mentioned below.

[2] Compare the rarity of animal and human images in Britain before the Roman conquest (Catherine Johns, "Art, Romanisation, and Competence," in Scott and Webster, *Roman Imperialism*, 9–23).

avoidance was grounded in the Torah's prohibitions of "graven images" (Exodus 20:4–6, Deuteronomy 4:15–18), a category interpreted broadly in this period to include representation in a variety of media – mosaics, frescoes, reliefs, statues, and figurines.[3] This attitude comes across clearly in Josephus's descriptions of Herodian and first-century Palestine, as Steven Fine points out.[4] Josephus reports Jewish hostility to the golden eagle Herod the Great erected over the gate of the Jerusalem temple and anxiety over the trophies he placed in his theater.[5] He notes in passing that Jews were forbidden to honor statues and sculptures,[6] and he describes in detail how the emperor Caligula's attempt to install a statue of himself in the Jerusalem temple brought the province's Jews to the brink of revolt (c. 40 CE).[7] His report of an incident that occurred in Tiberias early in the revolt suggests, however, that there were class-based variations in Jewish attitudes towards figural representations. The Romanophile Antipas had built a palace in the city that was decorated with images of animals. The building had probably been steadily used by other Herodian and Roman administrators in the three decades since Antipas. Josephus claims that he himself was sent to Tiberias by the revolt leadership in Jerusalem to destroy the palace. Its art was thus exceptional enough to be famous even several days' journey to the south. As Josephus portrays the situation, the elites of Tiberias, led by a man with the Latin name Capella (a possible indicator of high social status), saw no need to burn it down. This reluctance did not stop other parties from doing so. Josephus identifies those who razed the structure as Tiberians and Galileans and denigrates them as "sailors and [the] destitute class." In contrast to the elites, they were led by a man with a Semitic name, Jesus. Even allowing for the pejorative nature of Josephus's

---

[3] Fine, *Art*; Lee I. Levine, "Archaeology and the Religious Ethos of Pre-70 Palestine," in James H. Charlesworth and Loren L. Johns, eds., *Hillel and Jesus: Comparative Studies of Two Major Religious Leaders* (Minneapolis: Fortress, 1997), 110–120; Rachel Hachlili, "Synagogues in the Land of Israel: The Art and Architecture of Late Antique Synagogues," in Fine, *Sacred Realm*, 96–129, esp. 112–115; Hachlili, *Ancient Jewish Art*, 79–82.

[4] Fine discusses the pertinent passages (*Art*); cf. Richardson, *Building Jewish*, 225–239, 332–336.

[5] *War* 1.648–654; *Ant.* 15.272–279.

[6] *War* 1.650; *Ant.* 17.328–329.   [7] *War* 2.192–203; *Ant.* 19.261–309.

description of them, it seems probable that their actions reflected sentiments of at least some of the Galilean masses.[8] Archaeological evidence also reveals diversity in Jewish attitudes towards figural art. Excavations in Jerusalem, mostly in the domestic quarters of temple elites, have revealed representations of birds, fish, and other animals in frescoes, stucco moldings, and reliefs on table tops – all this, despite Deuteronomy's explicit prohibition of likenesses of any living things.[9] Steven Fine has persuasively argued that these finds, especially when considered in conjunction with images of inanimate objects, such as vines and flowers, demonstrate that characterizations of Jewish art as "aniconic" are inadequate, failing to reflect that certain images, even of animals, were acceptable to at least some Jews in particular contexts. Images that could be interpreted as idols were clearly prohibited, but those occurring in "safe" contexts, such as private domestic space, might be acceptable to some parties. Fine suggests that a term like "anti-idolic" better captures the nuances of Jewish attitudes towards art.[10] It is important to emphasize that these images were found in residences of the upper class, not the commoners, and that images of animals appear to have been the exception, not the norm. Most decorations consisted only of geometric and floral patterns.

FRESCOES AND MOSAICS

Frescoes and mosaic art had entered Palestine in the Hellenistic period,[11] but it was under the influence of Roman culture that they gained popularity. Herod the Great's palaces (none of them in

---

[8] *Life* 65–67. Josephus refers to "Herod the tetrarch," a title that can only refer to Antipas, since Agrippa I and II both received the title "king."

[9] Fine collects references to the Jerusalem material in *Art.*

[10] Fine, *Art*; cf. Meyers, "Jewish Art and Architecture" and "Jewish Art in the Greco-Roman Period."

[11] The walls of the pagan tombs at Maresha were covered with paintings of animals (Amos Kloner, "Mareshah," *OEANE*, vol. 3, 412–413), the luxurious building at Tel Anafa was painted in Greek-style (Herbert, "Introduction," 17), and some of the houses at Beth Yerah were decorated with colored plaster (Hestrin, "Beth Yerah"). An early example (second century BCE?) of a colorful mosaic was found at Dor, depicting what seems to be a comedic theatrical mask (no author, "Victory on the Harbor: Greek Remains Found at Dor," *BAR* 27:4 [2001]: 17). Hasmonean palaces also had frescoes (Berlin, "Between Large

Galilee) were extensively decorated in Italian styles, with frescoed walls and mosaics that reflected awareness of trends from the Italian peninsula – with the notable difference that Herod's decorations were free of figural representations. By the first century CE, both frescoes and mosaics were occasionally found throughout Palestine, including Galilee, where they adorned the interiors of at least some public buildings and elite residences. At Sepphoris, for example, fragments of painted plaster were found inside the remains of a house on the western side of the acropolis. The walls had been decorated at least twice. Unfortunately, the pieces of plaster were too small to allow reconstruction of the overall pattern, but it appears to have consisted of blocks of color broken up by basic lines and dots.[12] As for Galilee's mosaics, those from the first century show a strong preference for geometric and floral patterns and motifs.[13]

The use of such art forms in the domestic space of Galilean elites reflects their openness to these aspects of Roman culture, both in terms of the media themselves and the styles of decoration. Yet, the difference between their manifestations in Galilee and those found on the Italian peninsula is striking. Unlike the frescoes at the most famous site in Italy, Pompeii, Galilee's frescoes have no human images, whether of elites or of people holding everyday occupations, such as a baker; no still-life scenes of fruit or animals, no fantastic depictions of architecture or columns, and no mythological motifs.[14] Galilee's frescoes show how its elites mediated between two different

Forces," 34–35, 42; Netzer, *Hasmonean and Herodian Palaces*, vol. 1, 1–7). On the likelihood that the Hasmonean kings themselves were open to figural art, see Meyers, "Jewish Art in the Greco-Roman Period" and Fine, *Art*.

[12] This description of the fresco is based on my participation in the excavation of Area 85.1 of the Duke University excavations; see also Reed, *Archaeology*, 126. Similar pieces of fresco have been found in houses at Yodefat (Adan-Bayewitz and Aviam, "Iotapata," 165; Aviam, "First Century," 17), Cana (Richardson, *Building Jewish*, 104), Kh. et-Taiyiba (map coordinates 169/243) (M. Peleg, "Horvat 'Ofrat [Kh. et-Taiyiba]," *ESI* 4 [1985]: 88–89), and Gamla (Andrea Rotloff, "Gamla – Das Masada des Nordens?" in Faßbeck et al., *Leben am See Gennesaret*, 110–117, esp. the photo on 111).

[13] For example, the first-century CE building with eight pools at Sepphoris (Strange, "Six Campaigns"). We see a similar restraint even at a pagan site like Hellenistic-period Tel Anafa, where thousands of tesserae have been found (Herbert, "Occupational History," 64–65). R. and A. Ovadiah, however, suggest that one mosaic there may have once depicted humans (*MPI*, no. 234).

[14] August May, *Pompeii: Its Life and Art*, trans. Francis W. Kelsey (New Rochelle, N. Y.: Caratzas Brothers, 1982), 471–485; L. Richardson, Jr., *Pompeii: An Architectural History* (Baltimore and London: The Johns Hopkins University Press, 1988), 96–104.

values: the desire to participate in the artistic culture of the larger Roman world and the desire to observe the Jewish prohibition of "graven images."

As we saw with the elite residences in Jerusalem, however, the boundaries of acceptability were flexible. This is shown quite clearly by a mosaic from Magdala,[15] one of the few sizable, mostly intact mosaics recovered thus far from first-century CE Galilee.[16] Because its images are not limited to the standard motifs, it provides a striking contrast to other mosaics. Several objects, such as a *kantharos* and a plate, are depicted, but the image that has received by far the most attention is a boat, because of the rough similarity between it and an actual boat recovered from the mud of the Sea of Galilee in 1986.[17] What differentiates this mosaic most, however, is another image, a fish, the only example of figural representation published thus far from Galilee's first-century mosaics.

This mosaic includes a Greek inscription – also a rarity in first-century Galilee – the apotropaic phrase *kai su*.[18] The presence of these words suggests an awareness on the part of the owner or the artisans of trends in mosaic design from elsewhere in the Roman East, since no other inscriptions of this sort have yet been discovered in Palestine. Whether that familiarity was gained by first-hand viewing of such mosaics or by looking through mosaic pattern books cannot be determined.[19]

The house containing this work was sizable, suggesting that it belonged to someone of wealth and status. Was the owner a member of the area's gentile minority, for whom such images would presumably have been uncontroversial? Or was he or she a Jew who was not offended by depictions of living things? Were the artisans local Galileans? If not, from where did they come?

---

[15] Raban, "Boat"; cf. also Virgilio Corbo, "Piazza e villa urbana a Magdala," *LA* 28 (1978): 232–240 and J. Richard Steffy and Shelley Wachsmann, "The Migdal Boat Mosaic," *Atiqot* 19 (1990): 115–118.

[16] The rarity of such mosaics is demonstrated by the fact that none from the first century is cited in the comprehensive *MPI*.

[17] For the other objects depicted, see Raban, "Boat" and R. Reich, "A Note on the Roman Mosaic at Magdala on the Sea of Galilee," *LA* 41 (1991): 455–458.

[18] See discussion in Chapter Five.

[19] On mosaic pattern books, see Hachlili, *Ancient Jewish Art*, 391–395.

Compared to later Galilean mosaics, however, the image of the fish is reserved. Soon, the region's mosaics would reflect the dramatic shift in its cultural climate that followed the arrival of the Romans. This change is nowhere more evident than in the early third-century peristyle residence on the acropolis at Sepphoris. The triclinium mosaic in the largest room shows none of the shying away from figural representations that earlier ones did; it depicts not only humans, but also deities and other mythological figures. In both its subject matter and the high level of its craftsmanship, it is unparalleled in Roman-period Galilee.[20] With twenty-three different colors of tesserae, the smallest only two or three millimeters wide, this mosaic is every bit the artistic equal of the finest in neighboring Syria.[21]

The rectangular mosaic (9 meters by 7 meters) is arranged lengthwise from north to south. A female portrait is found at each of its shorter ends, in the center of the border that surrounds its fifteen interior panels. Very little of the southern portrait has survived the centuries, but the northern one is fairly well-preserved, depicting a woman whom excavators have evocatively dubbed the "Mona Lisa of the Galilee."[22]

Striking as this human image is, it is less startling than the dominant theme of the mosaic, the deity Dionysos. The central and largest of the mosaic's panels depicts Dionysos and Heracles, with a Greek inscription identifying the scene as a "symposium." Heracles tips back a cup of wine while Dionysos holds his aloft upside down, revealing that he has already emptied it. The two are surrounded by Dionysos's followers, maenads and satyrs. The fourteen panels surrounding the "symposium" contain typical Dionysiac

---

[20] For detailed descriptions, see Talgam and Weiss, *Mosaics*, 47–113; Eric M. Meyers, Ehud Netzer, and Carol L. Meyers, "Artistry in Stone: The Mosaics of Ancient Sepphoris," *BA* 50 (1987): 223–231; and C. Meyers, E. Meyers, Netzer, and Weiss, "Dionysos Mosaic."

[21] E. Meyers, Netzer, and C. Meyers, *Sepphoris*, 42; Katherine M. D. Dunbabin, *The Mosaics of the Greek and Roman World* (Cambridge: Cambridge University Press, 1999), 188; Talgam and Weiss, *Mosaics*, 1–16. Asher Ovadiah and Y. Turnheim suggest that the artisans were from Antioch, since the mosaic is so unusual for Palestine ("The Female Figure in the Dionysiac Mosaic at Sepphoris," in Ovadiah, *Art and Archaeology*, 349–373).

[22] Ovadiah and Turnheim suggest that this face represents some idealized value, such as happiness or moderation ("Female Figure").

scenes, each with an explanatory Greek inscription, such as the "bathing of Dionysus" (ΔΙΟΝΥΣΟΥ ΛΟΥΤΡΑ) by nymphs; "gift-bearers" (ΔΩΡΟΦΟΡΟΙ), including a centaur; the "procession" (ΠΟΜΠΗ) of Dionysos, riding in a chariot holding his thyrsos, preceded by two satyrs; and the "wedding" (ΥΜΕΝΑΙΟΣ) of Dionysos and Ariadne. Two of these panels show the predictable outcome of a drinking bout in which one of the participants is the god of wine. The first has Dionysos surrounded by his entourage, leaning back and holding up his cup. The other shows Heracles who, in contrast, needs to be physically supported by two attendants, one of whom holds a bowl for him. Does the bowl hold wine or water, or is it a container in which he may get sick? Both panels are labeled "drunkenness" (ΜΕΘΗ).

In addition to the two female portraits, the border framing the fifteen interior panels is filled with medallions of acanthus leaves, wildlife scenes, and pictures of *erotes* hunting birds. Additional panels form a "U" around the mosaic's southern end and reveal another Dionysiac scene: a processional of people, some on foot and others riding animals, bearing what appear to be gifts. One carries a duck; another walks with a chest or box upon her head; another has a stick across his shoulder with a basket of fruit attached to each end. Surrounding this section are smaller panels that alternate fish or birds with images of what are either faces or theatrical masks. At some point, a portion of this section of the mosaic was replaced with a Nile river scene.[23]

As surprising as the appearance of such motifs in Galilee is, they are appropriate, in some respects, for this specific location. It is not hard to imagine the wining and dining that must have occurred around this mosaic. Dionysiac imagery was also a very appropriate choice for a house located so near the theater, given the deity's traditional association with the theatrical arts. Perhaps one of the city's gentile minority lived in the house and commissioned the mosaic. Alternatively, perhaps it belonged to a member of the city's

---

[23] A more complete Nilotic scene is found in a fifth-century CE building at Sepphoris. For discussion of such scenes, see Yehudit Turnheim, "Nilotic Motifs and the Exotic in Roman and Early Byzantine Eretz Israel," *Assaph (B)* 7 (2002): 17–40.

Jewish elite who was comfortable disregarding earlier Jewish understandings of the prohibition of graven images, at least in private domestic space.[24]

Dionysiac motifs are found on mosaics and frescoes throughout the Mediterranean, and so we see in the Sepphoris mosaic the work of artisans fully in touch with the artistic currents of the larger Greco-Roman world.[25] There were not many such mosaics in Palestine, however. One might expect to find similar art at Nysa-Scythopolis, given its association with Dionysos, but thus far no mosaic depictions of him have been discovered there, though statues and relief carvings have.[26] The (geographically) nearest parallel is at Gerasa: the second- or third-century CE Mosaic of the Muses and the Poets, with its Dionysiac procession, Heracles, and other mythological characters.[27] Other Dionysiac mosaics are found in Syria at Antioch and Seleucia; two of these, roughly contemporary with that of Sepphoris, also depict the god drinking with Heracles.[28] Noting the similarity in dates of these mosaics, Sean Freyne has raised the possibility that their appearance reflects the association of Dionysos and Heracles as the patronal gods of Septimius Severus and Caracalla. If Freyne is correct, then the

---

[24] On attempts to identify the owner of the house, see Talgam and Weiss, *Mosaics*, 27–131. The *mikveh* mentioned in E. Meyers, Netzer, and C. Meyers, *Sepphoris*, 36, apparently dates to an earlier phase of use (Talgam and Weiss, *Mosaics*, 27–28).

[25] Such motifs are especially common in North Africa (Hédi Slin, "Dionysus," in Michèle Blanchard-Lemée, ed., *Mosaics of Roman Africa: Floor Mosaics from Tunisia* [New York: George Braziller, 1996], 87–119; Katherine M. D. Dunbabin, *The Mosaics of Roman North Africa: Studies in Iconography and Patronage* [Oxford: Clarendon Press, 1978], 173–187). See also Shelley Hales, "The Houses of Antioch: A Study of the Domestic Sphere in the Imperial Near East," in Scott and Webster, *Roman Imperialism*, 171–191; Bowersock, *Hellenism*, 41–53; and Caroline Houser, ed., *Dionysos and His Circle: Ancient through Modern* (Cambridge, Mass.: Fogg Art Museum, Harvard University, 1979).

[26] Nysa was the legendary burial place of Dionysos's nursemaid. See Asher Ovadiah and Y. Turnheim, "Dionysos in Beth Shean," in Ovadiah, *Art and Archaeology*, 203–226; Belayche, *Iudaea-Palaestina*, 262–267.

[27] Michele Piccirillo, *The Mosaics of Jordan* (Ammon: American Center of Oriental Research, 1993), 20, 283.

[28] Four Dionysiac mosaics are found at Antioch (Sheila Campbell, *The Mosaics of Antioch* [Toronto: Pontifical Institute of Mediaeval Studies, 1988], 16–17, 63–64, 73, 20–21) and one at Seleucia (Roger Ling, *Ancient Mosaics* [Princeton: Princeton University Press, 1998], 53). Dionysos and other mythological figures appear in the Byzantine-period mosaics at the non-Galilean sites Sheikh Zeweid and Erez (*MPI*, nos. 69 and 77).

Dionysos mosaics at Sepphoris and elsewhere were reflecting the political ideology of their day.[29] The rarity of mosaic depictions of Dionysos is matched by the rarity of those of other deities, not only in Galilee but throughout Roman-period Palestine and the Transjordan.[30] The central panel of another, less well-published triclinium mosaic at Sepphoris, from a house on the eastern plateau, shows the god Orpheus playing a stringed instrument (late third or the fourth century) and scenes of everyday life; a later mosaic in the same building had maritime imagery.[31] For the most part, though, with one additional striking exception, one must go elsewhere in the Roman East to find such mosaics.

That exception is the synagogue at Hammath Tiberias, where renovations added several mosaics that reflect no hesitancy at all about figural representation.[32] Parts of these mosaics seem to date to the early fourth century, though other portions may be later. Several in the eastern part of the building bear images of circles, squares, lines, flowers, scales, diamonds, and similar designs, along with an Aramaic and a Greek inscription. It is in the western part of the synagogue, however, that we find the more daring designs. Three panels form a north–south rectangle, with the central panel dominated by a zodiac circle. This zodiac is the first of several that would later appear in Galilean synagogues. In this case, the twelve astrological signs are each represented by their symbol (e.g., a lion for Leo, a woman for Virgo, etc.) and a Hebrew inscription identifying them. At the center of the circle is a depiction of the sun god, Helios, driving his solar chariot. Depictions of the Four Seasons, represented by human busts with accompanying Hebrew inscriptions, adjoin the

[29] Sean Freyne, "Dionysos and Herakles in Galilee: The Sepphoris Mosaic in Context," in Edwards, *Religion and Society*, 56–69.
[30] Other examples include a pavement at Neapolis showing Achilles and other figures (third century CE); an unidentified scene at Antipatris (third century CE) (R. Ovadiah and A. Ovadiah, nos. 217 and 233; cf. discussion on 175); and a mosaic showing marine deities at En Ya'el (Edelstein, "En Ya'el").
[31] Ze'ev Weiss in several articles: "Zippori 1997;" "Zippori 1998," *HA* 110 (1999): 20–23; "Zippori 1999;" "Zippori 2000;" also Weiss and Netzer, "Zippori – 1994–1995." On Orpheus mosaics, see Asher Ovadiah and S. Mucznik, "Orpheus Mosaics in the Roman and Early Byzantine Periods," in Ovadiah, *Art and Archaeology*, 528–548.
[32] Dothan, *Hammath Tiberias*, 33–52.

outside of the circle to fill out the panel's rectangular shape. All of these symbols are paralleled to varying degrees elsewhere in Roman art. Here we see the full-scale appropriation of Greco-Roman motifs, Judaized by their Hebrew labels and their placement within Jewish sacred space. Here, figural art is clearly no hindrance to worship and may even be an aid. A later renovation of the synagogue might reflect a different attitude, since it placed a wall through the center of the circle.[33]

Other symbols are found in the panels atop and below the zodiac, each of which is surrounded by a multi-colored guilloche pattern. The panel to the north shows two lions flanking Greek inscriptions identifying the synagogue's founders and donors.[34] That to the south depicts a Torah shrine with a triangular gable, flanked on each side by a large menorah and several smaller Jewish symbols – a *shofar*, an incense shovel, and a *lulav*, the latter grouped with an *ethrog* and myrtle and willow branches – that were associated with Jewish festivals and temple rituals. The mosaic thus provides early examples of symbols that would become even more common in later synagogue art. It also shows us how Jews adapted the Roman medium of mosaics to express Jewish identity by depicting distinctly Jewish symbols.

The elaborate mosaic at Hammath Tiberias and a less well-preserved fourth-century zodiac mosaic at Japhia's synagogue are forward-looking in this respect, having more in common with Byzantine-period designs than with those from the Roman period.[35] Other Galilean mosaics were simpler, though they were decorated with motifs drawn from the standard Greco-Roman repertoire, sometimes depicting living things, sometimes not. The basilical

---

[33] The specific functions or meanings of zodiac circles in synagogue art are a matter of debate; see Fine, *Art*; Hachlili, *Ancient Jewish Art*, 301–309; Levine, *Ancient Synagogue*, 572–578.

[34] For the inscriptions, see Dothan, *Hammath Tiberias*, 55–60.

[35] Note, for example, the third-century phase of the mosaic at Hammath Tiberias, or the late third- or early fourth-century phase at Horvat 'Ammudim (Dothan, *Hammath Tiberias*, 24; Levine, "'Ammudim, Horvat"). On Japhia, see Dan Barag, "Japhia," *NEAEHL*, vol. 2, 659–660. For an overview of synagogue art, see Hachlili, "Synagogues," 116–127 and *Ancient Jewish Art*, 221–223, 287–289; Fine, *Art*; Levine, *Ancient Synagogue*, 561–579; Levine, *Judaism and Hellenism*, 149–160.

building at Sepphoris, for example, contains several mosaics (probably third-century), the largest of which shows birds, fish, and various sea creatures.[36] The "House of Orpheus" contained several additional mosaics besides that depicting the deity, one of which also depicted maritime life, and other mosaics were found in nearby shops and in another peristyle house.[37] The floors of the multiple rooms of the fourth-century bathhouse at Tiberias portrayed birds, fish, donkeys, panthers, and an elephant.[38] In addition, lines and floral and geometric motifs are found on other mosaics scattered across Galilee.[39] In this context, the reference in a fragment of *y. Avodah Zarah* 3:3, 42d to "images on mosaics" and "images on the walls" in third-century Tiberias make perfect sense as a reflection of the growing popularity of these art forms.[40] Mosaics would become even more common in the Byzantine period, and Jewish aversion to figural representation even more relaxed.[41]

It is more difficult to get a sense of the designs found in Middle and Late Roman fresco and other forms of interior painting, because so much of the pertinent evidence is in the form of small pieces. It is clear, however, that by then, some wall decorations included depictions of animals. James F. Strange has provided a helpful description of the paint found on the walls and columns of the basilical building at Sepphoris. Noting that the structure's interior had been plastered four different times, he points out that

[36] Such motifs were increasingly common in Palestine in the second and third century; see Lucille A. Roussin, "The Birds and Fishes Mosaic," in Nagy, *Sepphoris*, 123–125 and Strange, "Eastern Basilical Building."

[37] Weiss, "Zippori 1997" and "Zippori 1999."

[38] Hirschfeld, "Tiberias," *NEAEHL*; cf. the animals in a mosaic in Judea at Lod/Diospolis (Asher Ovadiah and Sonia Mucznik, "Classical Heritage and Anti-Classical Trends in the Mosaic Pavement of Lydda [Lod]," *Assaph (B)* 3 (1998): 1–15.

[39] On the bathhouse at Rama, see Tzaferis, "Roman Bath," 68–69; on a third-century public building at Tiberias, see Hirschfeld, "Tiberias," *NEAEHL* and *Guide*, 30. On eleven mosaics at Beth She'arim, all either Late Roman or Byzantine, see Fanny Vitto, "Byzantine Mosaics at Bet She'arim: New Evidence for the History of the Site," *Atiqot* 28 (1996): 115–146. On the fourth–fifth century CE mosaic at nearby Beth Yerah, see Hestrin, "Beth Yerah."

[40] See discussion in Fine, *Art*, from which the reference above is taken.

[41] The explosion in the number of mosaic pavements in Israel is reflected in a 1980 survey that noted less than a dozen from the Roman period but 335 from the fourth–sixth centuries (Claudine Dauphin, "Mosaic Pavements as an Index of Prosperity and Fashion," *Levant* 12 [1980]: 125–134).

the second and fourth layers featured not only several colors and patterns, but also images of birds, in styles typical of the third and fourth centuries – and probably typical of frescoes from other public buildings.[42]

STATUES

Statues were a ubiquitous feature in much of the Roman world, particularly in the cities, where they were prominently displayed in the forum or agora and in bathhouses, theaters, amphitheaters, hippodromes, stadiums, and municipal buildings. For the Romans, statues of the emperor were a primary means of propagating imperial ideology,[43] and city councils and leading citizens often honored him by placing his statue in public spaces. He was not the only person so honored; so were provincial officials, civic leaders and local citizens, often as thanks for sponsoring the construction of a building or for some other act of benefaction. Statues of deities were found in similar contexts, and, of course, in temples, which held images of the deities worshiped there and of other gods, often donated by grateful worshipers. Private homes might contain the busts of ancestors, and gardens of the elites might be decorated with portraits of philosophers. Statues were not limited to cities; they have also been recovered from smaller communities, although with less frequency.

None of this was the case in Galilee. Statues were one form of Greco-Roman art that apparently never became widespread there. One suspects that encountering statues would have been just as jarring to Jesus as not encountering them would have been to a traveler familiar with the statuary of the Italian peninsula or western Asia Minor. If any stood in the Galilee of his day, they were few in number. That, at least, is the impression left by the meager archaeological evidence for statues, all of it post-first-century. At Sepphoris,

---

[42] Strange, "Eastern Basilical Building," 118–119. For another example, note the painted stucco found in a house at Jalame (275–350 CE) (Saul S. Weinberg, "The Buildings and Installations," in G. Weinberg, *Excavations*, 5–23, esp. 8).

[43] Ando, *Imperial Ideology*, 228–245.

only a few marble fragments have been found.[44] Second-century coins of both Sepphoris and Tiberias depict cult statues standing within temples, and others have freestanding images of deities that may correspond to cult statues.[45] As noted earlier, however, whether numismatic images always reflect actual temples and indicate specific gods worshiped is unclear, at least in regard to predominantly Jewish cities. A sixth-century CE inscription at Sepphoris shows that at some unknown point, a column that served as a pedestal for "divine statues" was erected there.[46] A (now lost) Greek inscription from Tiberias reflects the dedication of a statue of a goddess in the mid to late second century,[47] and fragments of statues have been found at Nazareth and at Arav el-Khilf.[48]

Rabbinic references convey the same basic impression: while statues may have been present in second- and third-century Galilee (especially Tiberias), they were neither especially numerous nor were they popular among Jews. Most such references are general in nature, lacking geographical specificity.[49] *M. Avodah Zarah*, a tractate on avoiding idolatry, provides examples of rabbinic treatments of the subject; it is especially pertinent, since the Mishnah was compiled in early third-century Galilee.[50] The tractate usually does not refer explicitly to statues, typically using the standard rabbinic

---

[44] Ze'ev Weiss, "Greco-Roman Influences on the Art and Architecture of the Jewish City in Roman Palestine," in Hayim Lapin, ed., *Religious and Ethnic Communities in Late Roman Palestine* (Baltimore: University Press of Maryland, 1998), 219–246, esp. 245. Weiss does not date the objects, but the rarity of marble in Palestine before the second century makes it a likely *terminus post quem*.

[45] Kindler, *Coins*, 57 no. 7; 59 no. 11; 60 no. 13; *City-Coins*, 37 nos. 91–93.

[46] Because the inscription specifies that the column stood before a Christian basilica, M. Avi-Yonah speculates that the statues may have been of emperors rather than of classical deities ("A Sixth Century Inscription from Sepphoris," *IEJ* 11 [1961]: 184–187).

[47] Schwartz, *Imperialism*, 153.

[48] At Nazareth, two votive feet were found in a cistern below the Church of the Annunciation; their place and date of origin are not known (Bagatti, *Excavations*, 316). In addition, a fragment of a white stone statue was discovered in either the Jezreel or in Lower Galilee (A. Berman, "Lower Galilee and Jezreel Valley – Reports," *ESI* 7–8 [1988–1989]: 200).

[49] On rabbinic references to statues, see Yaron Z. Eliav, "Viewing the Sculptural Environment: Shaping the Second Commandment," in Schäfer, *Talmud Yerushalmi*, vol. 3, 411–433.

[50] When discussing the tractate, we must keep in mind that not all of the sayings recorded in it necessarily originated in Galilee, that their level of historical accuracy varies widely (and often cannot be judged one way or the other with confidence), and that the rabbis' judgments do not appear to have been universally accepted by their contemporaries.

phrase for idolatry, *avodah zarah*, though a few sayings refer explicitly to "images" (*tselemim*).[51] Regardless of the terms used, many of its references to idolatry include statues within their purview. The legal topics addressed include whether Jews could build bathhouses (yes, until supports for idols are set up),[52] whether they could make jewelry for an idol (opinions differed),[53] whether they could rent a house or bathhouse to a gentile who might bring idols into it (no),[54] whether all images were prohibited to Jews (opinions varied),[55] whether one could keep sherds of broken images (not if they were pieces of the hand or foot),[56] whether the wall of a house that had fallen on an idol could be rebuilt (no),[57] how a Jew might nullify an idol (by cutting off the tip of its ear, nose, finger),[58] and whether pedestals for statues of kings could be set up (yes).[59] These discussions appear hypothetical, but they reflect contexts in which it was imaginable that Jews might encounter idols.

At no point, however, do they identify any Galilean communities as having idols. Indeed, the tractate assumes that while some cities in Palestine had idols, others did not.[60] When the rabbis discussed whether a Jew could do business with a shop displaying idols, the example they cited was not Sepphoris or Tiberias but Beth Shean.[61] Likewise, a story in which Rabban Gamaliel is asked why he felt comfortable bathing in a bathhouse with a statue of Aphrodite is set not in Galilee but in Ptolemais. Gamaliel replied that the statue was ornamental in that context, and not an object of worship, thus revealing how some rabbis found ways to differentiate pagan art from pagan cultic practices.[62]

The later commentary in the *Palestinian Talmud*, in contrast, preserves traditions about statues in Tiberias. One passage records the instruction of R. Yohanan, a third-century rabbi there, to Bar Derosai to destroy the idols in the city's bathhouse; Bar Derosai

---

[51] For example, 3:1, 2.   [52] 1:7.   [53] 1:8.
[54] 1:9.   [55] 3:1.   [56] 3:2.   [57] 3:6.
[58] 4:4–5.   [59] 4:6.   [60] 1:4.   [61] 1:4.
[62] 3:4; see Fine, *Art*; Seth Schwartz, *Imperialism*, 167–171 and "The Rabbi in Aphrodite's Bath: Palestinian Society and Jewish Identity in the High Roman Empire," in Simon Goldhill, ed., *Being Greek under Rome: Cultural Identity, the Second Sophistic and the Development of Empire* (Cambridge: Cambridge University Press, 2001), 335–361.

broke all of them but one.[63] Another summarizes events that purportedly occurred at the deaths of several prominent third-century rabbis, claiming that "when R. Nahum bar Simai died, they covered the *eikonia* with mats. . . . When R. Hanan died, the statues bent over. . . . When R. Yohanan died, the *eikonia* bent over – they said it was because no *eikonion* was as beautiful as he."[64] Obviously, these descriptions are metaphorical or legendary, but they nonetheless provide evidence of sculptures and other images in the city.

A quick glimpse at certain other parts of Palestine shows that archaeological evidence for statues is abundant in comparison with Galilee. As is the case for the Levant as a whole, most statues discovered thus far are from the second century or later, a date that reflects when Palestine and other parts of the Levant became integrated into the Roman Empire's marble trade.[65] Not all statues were made of marble, however; some were sculpted from local materials, limestone and basalt.[66] Little evidence for statues made of easily-melted bronze has survived the centuries, as is typically the case throughout the empire.

The largest corpuses of marble sculptures in the entire Levant have come from Caesarea Maritima and Paneas, each of which has yielded numerous fragments of various sizes as well as related inscriptions.[67] At Caesarea Maritima, a lengthy list of deities were represented,[68] as were several emperors from Hadrian onwards,[69]

---

[63] *Y. Avodah Zarah* 4, 43d; Eliav, "Roman Bath," 434–435.

[64] *Y. Avodah Zarah* 3:1, 42c. The exact meaning of *eikonia* here is unclear; see Schwartz, *Imperialism*, 145–148 (from which the translation above is drawn) and Schwartz, "Rabbi," 342.

[65] Hellenistic-period evidence is very rare, although Dor, Ptolemais, and Scythopolis have provided examples (Andrew Stewart, "Marble Sculpture," in Stern, *Excavations at Dor*, vol. 1, 457–459; Mordechai Aviam, "A Hellenistic Marble Statue from a *Favissa* at 'Akko-Ptolemais," in Mordechai Aviam, *Jews*, 36–40; Fischer, *Marble Studies*, 38). We know statues existed in the first century in non-Jewish areas, such as Sebaste and Caesarea Maritima (*War* 1.413–414; *Ant.* 15.339, 19.357). On Palestine and the marble trade, see Fischer, *Marble Studies*, 40–41, 233.

[66] Basalt statues were particularly common in the Golan (Gregg and Urman, *Jews, Pagans and Christians*, 50–52, 131–132, 183, 269, 284).

[67] In addition to the sources cited below, see Fischer, *Marble Studies*, 140–150, 157–158.

[68] Moshe Fischer, "Marble, Urbanism, and Ideology in Roman Palestine: The Caesarea Example," in Raban and Holum, *Caesarea Maritima*, 251–261, esp. 258; Rivka Gersht, "Representations of Deities and the Cults of Caesarea," in Raban and Holum, *Caesarea Maritima*, 305–324.

[69] Fischer, "Marble," 256–259, 260.

Hadrian's lover Antinoos,[70] the philosopher Olympiodoros, a Roman official, and an unidentified woman.[71] Inscriptions on statue pedestals preserve information about sculptures that are themselves long lost. One records that a friend of Titus Flavius Callistus, a freedman of Augustus, honored him with a statue; another shows that the city dedicated a statue to Marcus Flavius Agrippa, "priest, *duovir*, orator of Caesarea, the first colony of Flavius Augustus."[72] At Paneas, excavators have found nearly 250 marble fragments from at least 28 sculptures of deities and mythological figures. Most of these statues were associated with the temples outside the city. The cliff wall behind those temples is dotted with niches, some with inscriptions identifying the statues that once stood within them.[73]

Similar discoveries, such as whole statues, busts, fragments, and inscriptions from statue bases, have been made at numerous other nearby sites,[74] including Tyre,[75] Mt. Carmel,[76] Beth Yerah,[77] Gadara,[78] and Abila.[79] At Scythopolis, a major importer of marble, finds include portions of statues of deities (e.g., Athena, a young Dionysos, Tyche) and of a cuirassed Roman official, as well as a pedestal inscription referring to a statue of Marcus Aurelius. Excavators also discovered over 150 limestone funerary busts, an especially unusual find for Palestine. Just as surprising as the busts themselves

---

[70] Birley, *Hadrian*, 259.

[71] Rivka Gersht, "Three Greek and Roman Portrait Statues from Caesarea Maritima," *Atiqot* 28 (1996): 99–113; cf. *GLI*, 35 no. 1.

[72] *GLI*, 35–37 nos. 2–3.

[73] E. Friedland, "Graeco-Roman Sculpture in the Levant: The Marble from the Sanctuary of Pan at Caesarea Philippi (Banias)," in Humphrey, *Roman and Byzantine Near East*, vol. 2, 7–22; Tzaferis, "Cults"; Zvi Ma'oz, "Banias," *NEAEHL*, vol. 1, 136–143, esp. 140–141. Note also the discovery of a statue of Aphrodite near Tel Dan that may be pre-Roman (Biran, "To the God," 147).

[74] For other sites, see Friedland, "Graeco-Roman Sculpture," 8; Thomas Weber, "A Survey of Roman Sculptures in the Decapolis: Preliminary Report," *ADAJ* 34 (1990): 351–352; and Fischer, *Marble Studies*, 133–203.

[75] Nina Jidejian, *Tyre through the Ages* (Beirut: Dar el-Mashreq Publishers, 1969), 110.

[76] Fischer, *Marble Studies*, 150–151.

[77] Sukenik, "Ancient City"; Fischer, *Marble Studies*, 158.

[78] Peter Cornelius Bol et al., "Gadara in der Dekapolis," *Archäologischer Anzeiger* (1990): 193–266; Thomas Weber, *Umm Qeis, Gadara of the Decapolis* (Amman, 1989), 20, 27; Ilona Skupinska-Løvset, *Funerary Portraiture of Roman Palestine: An Analysis of the Production in its Culture-Historical Context* (Gothenburg: Paul Åströms, 1983), 99.

[79] W. Harold Mare, "The Artemis Statue Excavated at Abila of the Decapolis in 1994," *ADAJ* 41 (1997): 277–281; Wineland, *Ancient Abila*, 42–43, 108.

are depictions of the deceased, who are shown wearing clothing, jewelry, and hair styles typical of the Roman world.[80] Not far away, at the Roman army camp at Tel Shalem, a cuirassed bronze statue of Hadrian in splendid condition[81] and a bronze head of a youth[82] were recovered.

Elise Friedland has drawn attention to the significance of imported marble statues as a reflection of Romanization, using third-century CE statues and inscriptions from Gerasa as an example.[83] Within the basilical hall of the city's eastern bathhouse stood statues of mythological figures, local elites, the governor of the province, and the emperor. Inscriptions, all in Greek, record that the city had dedicated several of these statues. Two statues of local figures depict them clad not in *himation* and tunic, the garb shown on most eastern statuary, but in the Roman attire of the toga.[84] Here, in one of the most Roman of rooms, a basilical hall, in one of the most Roman of buildings, a bathhouse, we find one of the most Roman of customs, the donation of statues by the city to honor prominent people. Together, the statues and inscriptions demonstrate how Gerasa's civic elites participated in Roman euergetistic customs and showed loyalty to Roman authorities. Commoners using these facilities may or may not have shared such sentiments, but they would have had no doubt about the feelings of their city's leaders.

---

[80] Fischer, *Marble Studies*, 160–162; Fanny Vitto, "Two Marble Heads of Goddesses from Tel Naharon-Scythopolis," *Atiqot* 20 (1991): 33–45; Gideon Foerster and Yoram Tsafrir, "A Statue of Dionysos as a Youth Recently Discovered in Beth Shean," *Qadmoniot* 23 (1990): 52–54 (Hebrew); Tsafrir and Foerster, "Urbanism," 90–96; Ilona Skupinska-Løvset, "Funerary Busts from Tell El-Hammam," *Atiqot* 29 (1996): 35–41; Skupinska-Løvset, *Funerary Portraiture*, 120–140. In addition, a marble head of a young woman may be from Scythopolis (Ilona Skupinska-Løvset, *Portraiture in Roman Syria: A Study in Social and Regional Differentiation within the Art of Portraiture* [Lodz: Wydawnictwo Uniwersytetu Lodzkiego, 1999], 81).

[81] Foerster, "Cuirassed Bronze Statue"; Skupinska-Løvset, *Portraiture in Roman Syria*, 60–63. Richard A. Gergel suggests that Hadrian's bust has been combined with an earlier Hellenistic-period cuirassed statue ("The Tel Shalem Hadrian Reconsidered," *AJA* 95 [1994]: 231–251).

[82] Skupinska-Løvset, *Portraiture in Roman Syria*, 117.

[83] Friedland, "Roman Marble Sculptures"; cf. Friedland, "Graeco-Roman Sculpture," 8.

[84] Compare R. R. R. Smith, "Cultural Choice and Political Identity in Honorific Portrait Statues in the Greek East in the Second Century AD," *JRS* 88 (1988): 56–93, esp. 63–70.

But for Galilee, we have almost none of this – just a few statue fragments, the numismatic images, one sixth-century inscription, and the mostly vague rabbinic references. Statues appear to have been rare there not only in the early phases of the region's Romanization, but for the entire Roman era. The lack of evidence for statues of gods is not that surprising, since the region remained predominantly Jewish. Statues and busts of the emperor, if they existed at all, also appear to have been uncommon, probably for the same reason, especially given their association with the imperial cult. More unexpected, perhaps, is the lack of portraits of Roman officials and prominent citizens, statues that clearly would not have been understood as divine images. Perhaps this fact is related to the avoidance of imperial portraits – how could someone honor a provincial or civic official with sculpture if it was unacceptable to honor the emperor in the same way? The lack of such statues might also be interpreted as a rejection of this aspect of Roman euergetistic culture.

OTHER FORMS OF FIGURAL REPRESENTATION

The decorations on Galilee's lamps exemplify the region's changing cultural atmosphere. Prior to 70 CE, most lamps in Palestine had been made by spinning clay on a pottery wheel and then paring the resulting lamp with a knife. After the revolt, though, more and more lamps were cast from molds, as was typical elsewhere in the Mediterranean region. This form of manufacturing made decoration easier.[85] In addition, round disk-shaped lamps, also common in the Roman world, began appearing in Palestine in the late first century CE and were widely used for the rest of the Roman period, becoming particularly common in the third century. Some were locally made, but many were imports.[86] Their central disks provided

---

[85] Before the Roman period, lamps with figural representation were quite rare, though Aviam notes two Hellenistic-period lamps with images of Eros at Yodefat ("Hasmonaean Dynasty's Activities," 47–48; cf. "First Century," 13–14). At Qeren Naftali, in northern Upper Galilee, several lamps with figural depictions date to either the first century BCE or the first century CE (Aviam, "Hellenistic and Hasmonaean Fortress," 82–83).

[86] Anna Manzoni MacDonnell, "The Terracotta Lamps," in Weinberg, *Excavations,* 116–136, esp. 117–120. On the increase in the use of discus lamps, see Varda Sussman, "Caesarea Illuminated by its Lamps," in Raban and Holum, *Caesarea Maritima,* 346–358.

space for more complex images. These two developments encouraged the use of a greater variety of motifs on lamps from the late first through the early fourth centuries throughout Galilee: gladiators,[87] a lion,[88] erotic scenes,[89] a Medusa, Helios, a man's head,[90] a dolphin,[91] a female head, a winged figure,[92] a male figure, a horse, and other animals.[93] The menorah also entered the decorative repertoire, especially in the fourth century, as finds at Sepphoris and Jalame show. An *aedicula* found on a lamp at Sepphoris might also be a Jewish symbol, since it closely resembles ancient depictions of a Torah shrine, though it could also be interpreted as a niche for statues.[94] In the first half of the fourth century, as the Christian presence in Palestine grew, an occasional lamp was decorated with the Greek monogram *chi rho*, an abbreviation for *Christos*.[95] Many lamps of various shapes, styles, and sizes, including those both with and without figural representation, were decorated with ovolo patterns, leafs, and similar designs.[96] Perhaps the low cost of lamps allowed them to become "popular art" – that is, art for the masses who could not afford mosaics for their floors or sarcophagi for their loved ones. The range of motifs found on them allowed the purchaser some choice and thus some self-expression – though we are not able to determine what options were available at any given place or time.

Funerary art from the second through fourth centuries also reflects Greco-Roman culture. Spectacular examples of decorated sarcophagi were found at Beth She'arim in catacomb 20. Many of the more than 125 limestone sarcophagi there were decorated in

---

[87] *Beth She'arim*, vol. 1, 213–218, esp. fig. 22 no. 4.

[88] *Beth She'arim*, vol. 3, 184 no. 2.

[89] Avigad, *Beth She'arim*, vol. 3, 184–185 nos. 3–3a; Eric C. Lapp, "Clay Oil Lamps," in Nagy, *Sepphoris*, 217–224, esp. 220–221 no. 114.

[90] The Medusa at Sepphoris, the Helios at Nabratein, and the man's head at a Galilean tomb; see Lapp, "Clay Oil Lamps," 220 no. 113, 221 no. 115, and 220 no. 111.

[91] At Dishon and Jalame: Lapp, "Clay Oil Lamps," 219 no. 110; MacDonnell, "Terracotta Lamps," 124 no. 19.

[92] *Meiron*, 152.

[93] At Jalame: MacDonnell, "Terracotta Lamps," 117–120, 124 no. 19, 125 no. 27, 126 nos. 36–37.

[94] See Lapp, "Clay Oil Lamps," 221–222 no. 116; MacDonnell, "Terracotta Lamps," 120.

[95] *Beth She'arim*, vol. 3, 188 no. 23.

[96] See the lamps from Gush Halav, Jalame, and Beth She'arim (*Gush Halav*, 158–161; MacDonnell, "Terracotta Lamps," 120; *Beth She'arim*, vol. 3, 185–190 nos. 4–33).

Roman style with garlands, rosettes, and geometric and floral patterns and, in some cases, figural designs – e.g., animals, winged figures, a bearded male face. Numerous fragments of marble sarcophagi in the same catacomb also displayed images typical of contemporary Roman sarcophagi, including humans in togas, the goddess Nike, the battle between the Amazons and the Greeks, the rape of Leda by a swan-like Zeus, and other mythological scenes.[97] These sarcophagi were imports, like all marble items in Palestine, and many had been decorated in their places of origin.[98] What makes the sarcophagi of Catacomb 20 all the more surprising is that it was the place of interment for many rabbis and their families. The use of these sarcophagi shows that many rabbis were quite open toward figural art. It also reminds us once again that at Beth She'arim we see expressions of the values of elites, not of the masses.[99]

In graves outside the catacombs, excavators found five lead coffins, a form of burial introduced to the region in the third century CE.[100] The decorations on one of them are representative of what is found on the others. On its lid, vines run down each of the long edges. Intertwined with the vines are vases, clusters of grapes, heads of women, and birds. Between the vines, running down the lid's center, are intersecting lines that form a diamond

[97] *Beth She'arim*, vol. 3, 164–173; Fischer, *Marble Studies*, 206–207; on the Leda and the Swan sarcophagus, see Michael Avi-Yonah's study, "The Leda Sarcophagus from Beth She'arim," in *Art in Ancient Palestine* (Jerusalem: Magnes Press, 1981), 257–269. For similar designs elsewhere in the Roman world, see Diana E. E. Kleiner, *Roman Sculpture* (New Haven and London: Yale University Press, 1992), 256–259, 304–305, 350–351.

[98] Many of them, particularly those with the garland design, probably originated at Proconnesus and entered Palestine through the port at Caesarea. Similar sarcophagi have been found at Samaria, Neapolis, Gadara, and Tyre (*GLI*, 24–25; Byron R. McCane, "Sarcophagus," *OEANE*, vol. 4, 481–482). On the importing of carved sarcophagi, see Rivka Gersht, "Imported Marble Sarcophagi from Caesarea," *Assaph (B)* 2 (1996): 13–26.

[99] Vitto suggests that the marble sarcophagi were brought to Beth She'arim during the Byzantine period to be melted down for glass ("Byzantine Mosaics," 141), but there seems little reason to pose such a theory, since similar designs are found in other media in Late Roman Jewish contexts.

[100] *Beth She'arim*, vol. 3, 137, 173–182; the coffin described above is no. 1; cf. L. Y. Rahmani, *A Catalogue of Roman and Byzantine Lead Coffins from Israel* (Jerusalem: Israel Antiquities Authority, 1999), nos. 1, 3–6. In addition, a fragment of a lead coffin decorated with the image of Dionysos was found in Catacomb 20 (*Beth She'arim*, vol. 3, 177 and Rahmani, *Catalogue of Roman and Early Byzantine Lead Coffins*, no. 90).

pattern, with flowers and menorahs in the diamonds. The patterns on the long sides of the coffin are similar to that on its top. Only one of the short sides is decorated, with an image of a menorah in an arch. Lead coffins were made on the Phoenician coast in the third and fourth centuries,[101] and the excavator suggests that these were brought to Beth She'arim for the interment of Phoenician Jews, several of whom were buried there.

Beth She'arim is highly unusual, however. Elsewhere in Galilean burial art, figural representations appear to have been relatively uncommon even after the first century. Tombs at Hanita and Kh. el-Humsin were painted with floral designs and, in the case of the former site, birds.[102] A few decorated lead coffins have been found in and near Galilee, with stamped images of grape clusters, vines, columns, deities, animals, and humans (often nude).[103] Ossuaries at Daburriya, Kabul, Mashhad, and Sepphoris bore carvings of wreaths, columns, and the facades of buildings, but not animal images.[104] Decorated limestone sarcophagi in western Galilee often bore rosettes, garlands, and circles, while many in the Sea of Galilee area often had a *tabula ansata* between two discs, and architectural façades on the edges.[105] Clay sarcophagi from various sites in Galilee, many of them imported from Cyprus and the southern coast of Asia Minor, were likewise usually decorated with only simple carvings, or occasionally paint.[106] In contrast, at the northern pagan site, Kedesh, a funerary stele with portraits of the

---

[101] Rahmani, *Catalogue of Roman and Early Byzantine Lead Coffins*, 4–7.
[102] Map coordinates 166/277 and 163/272; Aviam, "Regionalism," 296.
[103] At K. Gil'adi and K. Yuval (west of Dan), el Makr and el–Bi'na (both east of Akko), Kibbutz Mesillot (southwest of Beth She'arim), Yagur (northwest of Beth She'arim), and at a now unknown location (Rahmani, *Catalogue of Roman and Early Byzantine Lead Coffins*, nos. 10–15, 84–88).
[104] For example, at Daburriya (185/233), Kabul (170/252), Mashhad, and Sepphoris. See Aviam, "Regionalism," 277 and the following articles in the English summary section of Gal, *Eretz Zafon*: Mordechai Aviam, "Finds from a Burial Cave at Daburriya," 181; Mordechai Aviam, "A Burial Cave at Kabul," 182; Zvi Gal, Butrus Hana and Mordechai Aviam, "A Burial Cave at Zippori," 182.
[105] Aviam, "Regionalism."
[106] Anastasia Shapiro, "Petrographic Analysis of Roman Clay Sarcophagi from Northwestern Israel and Cyprus," *Atiqot* 33 (1997): 1–5; Mordechai Aviam and Edna J. Stern, "Burial in Clay Sarcophagi in Galilee during the Roman Period," *Atiqot* 33 (1997): 19.

deceased was found, as were elaborately decorated sarcophagi like those at Beth She'arim.[107] The limited amount of monumental and public architecture in first-century Galilee, most of it in the cities, would have resulted in a correspondingly limited amount of relief art and other carved decorations. Where such art was present, it probably consisted of standard non-figural designs like those found both in Palestine and elsewhere in the Roman world. In subsequent centuries, relief art became more common in both interior and exterior contexts. Beth She'arim again provides one of the best examples. The outside entrances of two of its caves are framed by carved arches,[108] and scattered throughout the complex are reliefs, carvings, and paintings. Geometrical patterns predominate, but one also finds architectural motifs (e.g., columns and arches), depictions of animals and humans, and Jewish symbols (incense shovels, Torah arks, *lulavs*, *ethrogs*, *shofars*, and, especially, menorahs).[109] Carved decorations are also found at synagogues, though almost entirely in Byzantine, rather than Roman contexts. At the synagogue at Nabratein, the limestone pediment of a Torah shrine from the building's third-century phase is decorated with carvings of two lions flanking a triangular gable.[110] Carvings of animals (lions and eagles) and menorahs at other synagogues (Horvat 'Ammudim, Hammath Tiberias, Japhia) may also date to the Late Roman period, though they are probably later.[111] Even in Byzantine-period synagogues, most decorative carvings were of the standard floral and geometric patterns, not of animal or anthropomorphic designs.[112]

---

[107] The stele is probably late first-century CE. Another such stele, probably from the early second century CE, was found at Scythopolis. Funerary steles are rare throughout Palestine, though they are found in Syria (Skupinska-Løvset, *Portraiture in Roman Syria*, 231–232). On the sarcophagi, see Aviam, "Regionalism," 278–284.

[108] *Beth She'arim*, vol. 3, 88.

[109] *Beth She'arim*, vols. 1 and 3; Nahman Avigad and Benjamin Mazar, "Beth She'arim," *NEAEHL*, vol. 1, 236–248.

[110] This Torah shrine is the earliest discovered thus far; see Carol L. Meyers, "Replica of a Limestone Ark Fragment," in Nagy, *Sepphoris*, 181–182.

[111] Levine, "'Ammudim, Horvat"; Levine, "Excavations"; Chen, "Ancient Synagogue"; Dothan, "Hammath Tiberias"; Barag, "Japhia."

[112] Notable exceptions include decorations at Chorazin (the carvings are probably fifth century, though the synagogue was built in the fourth) and Bar'am (fifth-century) (Natalie Naomi May, "The Décor of the Korazim Synagogue Reliefs [Summary]," in Yeivin,

Figurines appear to have been rare in Galilee.[113] Early Roman finds include the curly-haired female head from et-Tell and a first- or second-century CE bone carving of a female from Tiberias.[114] A small (6cm high) eagle figurine at Tiberias probably dates to the Middle or Late Roman periods.[115] A few other figurines have been found in later contexts at Sepphoris. Two from the second or third century, one of Prometheus and the other perhaps of Pan, were found in a cistern.[116] Were they cultic objects, or could they have served some decorative purpose? They may have belonged to one of the city's gentile minority or to a Jew with syncretistic religious practices or who was especially receptive to Greco-Roman art. In contrast, the tiny bronze bull, incense altar, and bowl, all from the fill of a cistern sealed in the mid-fourth century, were clearly intended for cultic use.[117] The function of a third- or fourth-century bone carving of a Roman soldier found elsewhere on the site is difficult to determine.[118]

Synagogue, 51–54; Ruth Jacoby, *The Synagogues of Bar'am*; *Jerusalem Ossuaries* [Jerusalem: Israel Academy of Sciences and Humanities; the Masto Grust, Hebrew University, 1987]; Aviam, "Ancient Synagogues").

[113] Figurines from earlier periods include three Iron Age examples and one Persian at et-Tell (Arav, "Bethsaida Preliminary Report, 1987–1993," 18; Arav, "Bethsaida Preliminary Report, 1994–1996," 92, 95, 104), two Persian-era and one Hellenistic terracotta figurines at Yoqne'am (Rosenthal-Heginbottom, "Stamped Jar Handles," 65), the Persian-period figurines at Mizpeh Yamim (map coordinates 193/260) (Frankel and Ventura, "Mispe Yamim Bronzes"), a small fragment of a man (Hercules?) holding a snake at Meiron from between 200 and 50 BCE (*Meiron*, 152), three Hellenistic-period figurines (Apis, Aphrodite, and Horus) at Beersheba (map coordinates 189/259) (Aviam, "First Century," 8–12; Aviam, "Hellenistic Fortifications," 28–29); Hellenistic figurines at Ptolemais (Natalie Messika, "Excavation of the Courthouse Site at 'Akko: The Hellenistic Terracotta Figurines from Areas TB and TC," *Atiqot* 31 [1997]: 121–128); Hellenistic-period figurines of Greek mythological figures (one of Pan, another perhaps of Demeter) at Tel Anafa (Herbert, "Tel Anafa, 1980," *Muse* 14 (1980): 24–30; Weinberg, "Tel Anafa").

[114] On the figurine at et-Tell, see the discussion in previous chapter; on the Tiberias figurine, see Yizhar Hirschfeld, "Tiberias," *ESI* 9 (1989/1990): 107–109.

[115] Yizhar Hirschfeld, "Tiberias," *ESI* 16 (1997): 35–42, esp. 40–41.

[116] C. Meyers and E. Meyers, "Sepphoris"; Sarah H. Cormack, "Figurine of Pan (?) or a Satyr," and "Figurine of Prometheus," in Nagy, *Sepphoris*, 171–172.

[117] Strange, "Six Campaigns," 345 and "Some Implications," 40; Dennis H. Groh, "Figurine of the Head and Forelegs of a Bull" and Thomas R. W. Longstaff, "Miniature Altar," both in Nagy, *Sepphoris*, 173.

[118] Renato Rosenthal, "Late Roman and Byzantine Bone Carvings from Palestine," *IEJ* 26 (1976): 96–103, esp. 99. In addition to the figurines noted above, mention should be made of the small head of an Athena figurine found just outside Galilee at Gaba (Raphael Giveon, "Geva, a New Fortress City: From Tuthmosis to Herod," *Bulletin of the Anglo-Israel Archaeology Society* 3 [1983–1984]: 45–46).

A few examples of anthropomorphic and animal imagery appear in other media.[119] A handful or sites have yielded gems and jewelry engraved with such designs, like the red carnelian gem with a depiction of a helmeted goddess – Athena or Roma? – found in fourth-century CE fill at Khirbet Shema'.[120] A Late Roman ceramic fragment at Gush Halav was stamped with an image that resembles a hare.[121] At Hanita, in northern Upper Galilee, a Late Roman stone weight was inscribed with a human face.[122] At Sepphoris, a bronze plaque showing a winged figure seated on a goat, standing in front of what is perhaps an altar, was found in an early context (first century BCE or CE).[123] Such an image apparently was highly unusual for Early Roman Galilee.

CONCLUSION

In Jesus' time, some Galileans were indeed using, albeit in a relatively limited way, forms of art, decorative patterns, and motifs that

---

[119] In addition to the other examples discussed in this paragraph, note the ring decorated with an image of a lion found at Iksal; whether it is Roman or Byzantine is unclear (Abdalla Mokary, "Iksal," *HA* 115 [2003]: 27). Note also the small stone slab from Yodefat (c. 67 CE) with a carving of a column, trees, and an image that Mordechai Aviam identifies as a crab ("The Archaeology of the Battle at Yodefat," in Mordechai Aviam, *Jews, Pagans and Christians*, 110–122, esp. 120).

[120] The deity is compared to Athena in *Khirbet Shema'*, 250–253, but Roma and Athena were often portrayed very similarly (see Cornelius C. Vermeule, *The Goddess Roma in the Art of the Roman Empire* [Cambridge: Spink and Son, 1959]); cf. gems found at Gadara with images that have been identified with Roma (Martin Henig and Mary Whiting, *Engraved Gems from Gadara in Jordan: The Sa'd Collection of Intaglios and Cameos* [Oxford: Oxford University Committee for Archeology, 1987], nos. 161–164). Large numbers of gems have been found at Gadara (423 gems) and Caesarea Maritima (165 gems; Anit Hamburger, "Gems from Caesarea Maritima," *Atiqot* 8 [1968]: 1–38); note also the discovery of twelve at Jerusalem (Orit Peleg, "Roman Intaglio Gemstones from Aelia Capitolina," *PEQ* 135 [2003]: 54–69). Several sites in and near Galilee have each yielded a third- or fourth-century engraved gem: a tomb at H. Kenes (map coordinates 178/258) (Leea Porat, "Quarry and Burial Caves at H. Kenes [Karmiel]," *Atiqot* 33 [1997]: 15); Asherat (map coordinates 165/264) (Howard Smithline, "Three Burial Caves from the Roman Period in Asherat," *Atiqot* 33 [1997]: 11–12); Hanita, midway between Ptolemais and Tyre (Barag, "Hanita," 43); Giv'at Yasaf (map coordinates 159/263) (Hana Abu Uqsa, "A Burial Cave from the Roman Period East of Giv'at Yasaf," *Atiqot* 33 [1997]: 10–11).

[121] *Gush Halav*, 126.

[122] Map coordinates 166/277; Rahmani, "Miscellanea," 106–107.

[123] Ellen Reeder, "Relief Plaque with Figural Scene," in Nagy, *Sepphoris*, 174.

reflect Greco-Roman cultural influence. They did so, however, in ways that reflected the traditional Jewish abhorrence of "graven images." Avoidance of depictions of living creatures appears to have been the norm. There were exceptions, though, as demonstrated by the images of animals reported at Antipas's palace at Tiberias and by the fish in the Magdala mosaic. Both examples reflect the desires of elites to decorate their homes in ways that resembled residences elsewhere in the Roman world. Without knowing more about Antipas's palace, we cannot know whether the controversial images were in areas accessible to citizens and official visitors, or whether they were in more private rooms. With the Magdala mosaic, we know that it was in domestic space, open only to those whom the household invited in.

Greco-Roman styles of art and decoration became more common in the second and third centuries. The most obvious difference from the first century (especially the pre-70 period) was the growing acceptance of figural art. Mosaics clearly reflect changes in the region's artistic tastes. At Sepphoris, we find panels depicting a full-blown mythological narrative; at Hammath Tiberias, a mosaic depicting a pagan deity, astrological symbols, and objects associated with the Jewish temple, all on a synagogue floor. Other Galilean mosaics contain a variety of motifs: a few have images of deities; several, images of animals; and several more, the standard geometric and floral patterns and symbols. Other forms of decoration also reflect a willingness to display images that would once have been considered off-limits by most Jews. Some sarcophagi and lead coffins were decorated with anthropomorphic and animal designs; others, with rosettes, garlands, and other motifs typical of Roman art. A wide range of designs appears on lamps.

When interpreting this evidence, we must keep in mind the importance of social class. Because most mosaics are in residences of the upper classes or in public buildings, which also reflect the values of the elites, it is difficult to determine what commoners thought of them, though they would probably have encountered them often, especially in the cities. Our sample of burial containers is also heavily weighted towards the elites. Many of the coffins of the lower classes were presumably made of wood and have thus decayed over the centuries, leaving us with little idea how, if at all, they were decorated. In contrast, the decorated sarcophagi that have survived the centuries, whether of marble, clay, or lead, were used by people of high social status.

The limitations of those forms of evidence highlight the importance of lamps. From the late first century CE on, a broad cross-section of Galilean society was willing to purchase and use lamps decorated with animal and anthropomorphic designs. Perhaps such lamps were first imported to Palestine for Roman soldiers and administrators or for other pagans; we do not yet have enough information to trace their spread through the region. In any case, they quickly made their way into Jewish contexts. This was one form of Greco-Roman decoration with which many Jews apparently had little problem. Fine's concept of "anti-idolic" is helpful for understanding their popularity; even when they depicted pagan deities, they were clearly not objects of worship.

Decorated lamps are also exceptional in that they appear in a variety of geographical contexts – both urban and rural, in both Lower and Upper Galilee. Other forms of art also appear throughout Galilee, but at a higher frequency in larger communities than smaller ones and in the south than in the north (mosaics are the clearest example). We thus find the same regional and urban-rural distinctions that we observed with architecture and inscriptions.

Galilean art in the Middle and Late Roman periods also reflects another important development, the growing usage of Jewish symbols, such as *lulavs, ethrogs, shofars*, and incense shovels.[124] The most common of these is the menorah, which appears in the Beth She'arim graffiti, on lead coffins discovered nearby, on lamps from several sites, and in the synagogue mosaic at Hammath Tiberias. The symbol itself was not new,[125] but its frequent depiction on a variety of objects was. Such symbols would become even more common in the Byzantine period. Their increasingly widespread usage reflects Jewish appropriation of Greco-Roman art forms to express Jewish identity. It can hardly be a coincidence that

---

[124] For discussion of individual symbols, see Hachlili, *Ancient Jewish Art*, 234–285.
[125] See Fine's discussion of the menorah in *Art*.

the proliferation of Jewish symbols begins at the same time that Hellenistic images become more common, at the same time that Jews struggled to interpret and adapt to the destruction of one of their chief institutions, the temple, and at the same time that they dealt with the harsh reality of a long-term foreign military presence. One way Jews responded to these challenges was to increase their own use of symbols to construct and assert their distinctive identity.[126]

Synagogue art from the third and fourth centuries brings all the strands of this chapter's discussion together. Reliefs, other carvings, frescoes, mosaics – all demonstrate how Jews accepted the art forms of their Roman dominators while simultaneously using them to express their Jewishness.[127] The mosaic at Hammath Tiberias illustrates the extent to which Jews could adapt that medium for their own needs. The zodiac and Helios show the adaptation of astrological signs to Jewish usage, even though we do not fully understand their function. The temple-related symbols and the Torah ark make a robust statement of Jewish identity. These latter images might also be interpreted as commentary on Roman rule, pointing backward to the Roman destruction of the temple, and forward to its eschatological restoration, when the Romans would no longer be able to obstruct the sacrificial cult.

The willingness to tolerate and perhaps even appreciate mythological, animal, and human images in some media apparently did not extend to statues. We have little sign of their presence in first-century Galilee. We have slightly more evidence in later centuries, but not nearly as much as we have for some nearby pagan cities. Some Jews might learn to live with statues in certain contexts – witness Gamaliel's willingness to enter the bathhouse in neighboring Ptolemais – but for the most part, statues do not appear to have gained the same level of acceptability in Galilee as did other forms of representation. The same can be said of figurines, which never became commonplace.

---

[126] Jewish symbols became even more common in the Byzantine period, as Jews responded to an increased Christian presence in Palestine.
[127] Compare Fine, *Art*.

In the early first century CE, Greco-Roman art was making inroads in Galilean culture, especially in elite circles. But Jewish acceptance of such art had its limits. Animal representations stretched them and anthropomorphic representations were beyond them. In this regard, Galilean art was like that of other Jewish areas of Palestine. Galilean attitudes towards art were not monolithic. The boundaries dividing acceptable from unacceptable varied within and between artistic media, social classes, and different geographical areas. The most important variable, however, was chronology.

Conclusion

The image of Greco-Roman culture in the Galilee of Jesus suggested by this investigation is a complex one. By Jesus' time, the region's encounter with Hellenism was over three centuries old. Despite occasional scholarly claims to the contrary, however, the penetration of Greek culture does not seem to have been especially deep, at least in respect to the spheres of culture we have considered. Greek inscriptions appeared on the region's Hellenistic-period coinage (all of it minted elsewhere), but otherwise inscriptions appear to have been uncommon. So, too, were examples of Hellenistic architecture and Hellenistic art. Other aspects of Hellenism may well have affected the lives of many Galileans – one thinks, for example, of the administrative changes that would have marked shifts of power – but describing those effects in detail remains a challenge.

Antipas's rise to the throne, which occurred at approximately the same time as Jesus' birth, brought with it significant changes. The rebuilding of Sepphoris and establishment of Tiberias allowed the client king to demonstrate his enthusiasm for the mingling of Greek, Roman, and local cultures that was taking place throughout the Levant. Both cities exhibited some of the characteristics of the typical Greco-Roman city. From early in the first century, for example, at least some of Sepphoris's streets were arranged on a grid. Evidence from the mid-century shows that the civic government of Tiberias was organized along Hellenistic lines, and presumably that of Sepphoris was structured similarly. Antipas issued the first coins ever struck within the region, and most of them advertised the foundation of his new lakeside city. At some point, Sepphoris built a basilica and by the time of the revolt, Tiberias had acquired a stadium. Other

Greco-Roman buildings appeared elsewhere in Galilee, such as the basilica at Beth She'arim and the hippodrome at Magdala. As important as these developments are, they must be kept in perspective. Antipas inherited his father's passion for construction, but apparently not his father's financial resources. Sepphoris and Tiberias were modest in comparison to Caesarea; neither had the extensive array of monumental architecture found there. Greco-Roman urban architecture was now more a part of the cultural and physical landscape of Galilee (especially Lower Galilee) than it had ever been before, but it is not as if such buildings were evenly distributed throughout the region. Aside from coins, inscriptions – in any language – still appear to have been uncommon. Though Greek had made inroads as a language of government and probably (to some extent) of the civic and cultural elites, it is difficult to demonstrate that it was widely spoken. Admittedly, our understanding of the language's role in first-century Galilean society is incomplete, but it seems safe to say that arguments for its extensive use have sometimes been oversimplified and that the amount of epigraphic evidence for it has often been overstated. Greco-Roman art was becoming more common in first-century Galilee, as demonstrated, for example, by the increasing production of mosaics, but the biblical prohibition of figural representations was a line that most Galileans did not yet feel comfortable crossing. It is difficult to imagine that Jesus and other first-century Galilean Jews were totally ignorant of Greek mythology, but with few if any statues or other portrayals of deities and heroes, no temples except those on the region's fringes, no pagan festivals or pageants, and no evidence for widespread Greek education, there is little reason to assume thorough familiarity with it, either. Coins minted outside the region would have been the main sources of exposure to images of Greek and local deities and demigods. The beliefs, images, stories, and rituals in which those figures played a role would have been associated with pagan cities, not Galilee's own. Some of those cities, however, stood only a very few miles away, such as Scythopolis and Hippos, and many Galileans would have known something of the pagan rituals that took place there.

Clifford Ando describes a universal symbolic language in the Roman Empire, a language comprised of statues of the emperor, coins with imperial portraits and other Roman symbols, Roman milestones, Roman military standards and the soldiers who carried them, and Roman architecture, all combining to propagate imperial ideology.[1] Yet it is notable that these symbols are mostly absent from the Galilee of Jesus, not appearing for decades. Even numismatic portraits of the emperor, though present, were less common there in the early first century than in most of the Empire, since they were not found on Hasmonean, Tyrian, and much Herodian coinage.

Other symbols, though, would have been more familiar to most Galileans, by oral report if not by first-hand experience. These were the new cities planted by Antipas and named in honor of the ruler of Rome. The rebuilt Zippori-Sepphoris became Autocratoris, and Tiberias was named eponymously from its foundation. Every spoken reference to Sepphoris was accompanied by a decision to utilize either the traditional name or the honorific one, and every reference to Tiberias was also a reference to the emperor. The Romans may not have been physically present on a regular basis in early first-century Galilee, but these two cities reminded Galileans of Roman domination. Galileans would also have known of the auxiliary troops in Judea, especially in Jerusalem, where they overlooked Judaism's most sacred spot, the temple. Later, those troops were replaced by the X Fretensis legion, which watched over the temple's ruins.

By 120 CE, a Roman legion had arrived in northern Palestine, supplementing the legion to the south. Whereas Roman troops had previously traversed or briefly campaigned in Galilee, the VI Ferrata came to stay. Its main base was in the Jezreel Valley, but various detachments were stationed within Galilee itself, especially Lower Galilee. Its deployment was part of a larger reorganization of Roman forces. Previously, Rome's might in the East had been concentrated primarily in northern Syria, but now two legions occupied Palestine and a third, the III Cyrenaica, was stationed in adjacent Arabia.

The changes in the material culture of Palestine and the Transjordan that followed in the wake of this influx of Roman soldiers were dramatic. In most of the region, Greco-Roman influence is far more visible in the remains of the second and third centuries CE

---

[1] Ando, *Imperial Ideology*, 8–9, 206–273.

than in the strata of the first and earlier centuries, and the chrono-logical differences are significant enough to problematize efforts to draw conclusions about the first century from this later data. Newly paved Roman roads, marked by Roman milestones, connected prominent towns with the region's major routes. Monumental architecture became more common in many cities – especially Roman-style theaters and baths but occasionally stadiums, hippodromes, *nymphaea,* and, in a few cases, amphitheaters. The use of inscriptions increased and the number of civic mints multiplied. The mosaics that decorated public buildings and elite residences became more lavish and more numerous.

Developments in Galilee, particularly in its two cities, were a part of this larger pattern. Monumental architecture was more common in these centuries than it had been in the first. Inscriptions became more frequent. More Galileans grew comfortable with images of animals, men, even gods. The coins of Sepphoris and Tiberias grew indistinguishable from those of other cities. Once again, however, maintaining perspective is key: Galilee's cities were more Hellenized and Romanized than its villages; they were not as Hellenized and Romanized as the larger cities in Judea, Arabia, and Syria. Galilean communities had some characteristics common to Greco-Roman cities; they did not have others. In this respect, too, Galilee was typical, for such variety was common among the cities of the Roman East.

Some may object that to emphasize the differences between the evidence from the second and third centuries CE and that of earlier centuries is to ignore the haphazard nature of archaeological discovery, the randomness of survival, and the obliteration of earlier buildings by later construction – factors that all suggest that there was considerably more evidence for Greco-Roman culture in the first century CE than what we have now. There is some legitimacy to this objection. First-century Galilee had buildings, inscriptions, and other artifacts that exemplified Hellenistic and/or Roman culture that were destroyed long ago or have not yet been found. We must always remain mindful that we do not have the full picture.

Nonetheless, we must base our historical reconstructions on what we have, not on what we do not have. We cannot let our under-standing of antiquity be based on speculation about what has been lost – especially if that speculation is marked by the erroneous assumption that Greco-Roman culture was thoroughly uniform across centuries and regions. Instead, we should acknowledge the implications of the evidence that we are fortunate enough to possess. Galilee will yield more buildings, inscriptions, coins, mosaics, and other artifacts. Those future finds, however, are likely to conform to the patterns we have already discovered: some evidence from the earlier centuries, but more from the later; some evidence, occasionally, from smaller settlements, but more from the cities; some evidence from Galilean communities, but more from the larger cities of the region. Those patterns are consistent enough that they most likely reflect ancient social realities, not accidents of survival and discovery.

All Judaism was Hellenistic Judaism, but not all Judaism was affected by Hellenism in the same ways or to the same extent. In making this point, I am not trying to turn back the clock to the pre-Hengel period. As Hengel rightly demonstrated, the idea that we can dichotomize Judaism into Diaspora/Hellenistic Judaism and Palestinian/non-Hellenistic Judaism is clearly wrong. Nonetheless, to replace that simplistic dichotomy with a view that levels out the differences in how Hellenism and local culture interacted, as some readers of Hengel have done, is to replace one erroneous view with another. The reality is that when considering Hellenism, issues of geography, chronology, and class matter a great deal. Some sectors of Palestine were, indeed, less Hellenized than parts of the Diaspora. Hellenism in Galilee may have had points of contact with Hellenism in northern Syria, the various subregions of Asia Minor, or the Greek peninsula, but it was not identical to them. Furthermore, the interactions of Hellenistic and local culture in each of those areas also had distinctive characteristics. At an earlier point in scholarship, the aim seemed to be to demonstrate that Galilee was just as Hellenized as "everywhere else." The reality, of course, is that no place was just like everywhere else.

Much of what scholarship has designated as "Hellenization" occurred not under Alexander or the Diadochoi but under the Romans. In the East, the processes of Hellenization and Romanization were inextricably intertwined. It was under the Romans, not the Greeks, that urban architecture, figural art, and Greek inscriptions became more common. Galileans would have been aware of the newness of such developments, and they probably associated them with heightened Roman influence.

What parties were responsible for the dissemination of Roman culture in Galilee? The question is more complicated than it first appears, and though we are sometimes able to speak definitively, we must often think in terms of possibility and probability. Such is the nature of our evidence.

Antipas played a key role. His efforts at Sepphoris and Tiberias were a strong and intentional statement of his Romanness. The tetrarch's administrators, supporters, and clients, probably concentrated in the cities, may have enthusiastically embraced his Romanizing agenda. Antipas's works paled in comparison to what would follow after the arrival of Roman troops in the second century, however, when large public columned buildings, aqueducts, bathhouses, and other structures became more common. Indeed, it appears that in Galilee as throughout the southern Levant, the single most influential agent of Romanization was the Roman military. At least some Roman urban architecture was probably imposed upon local culture by the Romans themselves. Once soldiers made such buildings more common, local builders may have mimicked them.

A fuller understanding of the variegated processes of Romanization eludes us. Our lack of building inscriptions keeps us from determining how extensive a role civic councils and wealthy individuals played in sponsoring the construction of distinctively Roman buildings. Nor do we have enough information to identify who frequented Roman bathhouses and theaters. The use of Roman motifs on civic coinage tells us that elites chose to conform to the norms of the Empire in this regard, but we have no way of determining how other Galileans responded to such coinage – how many regarded Roman designs as something of which to be proud and how many saw it as a cause for regret. The same can be said for certain forms of Greco-Roman art, such as mosaics, the more elaborate of which only the wealthy could afford. The appearance of figural representations on second- and third-century lamps, however, demonstrates that some Galileans, commoners and elites alike, had few problems with such decorations.

When trying to comprehend this complicated picture, we see again that the sometimes very different insights produced by various studies of Romanization can each prove useful.[2] F. Haverfield was partly right: the Romans sometimes deliberately spread aspects of their culture, and the elites sometimes embraced it. So, too, was Martin Millett: the elites sometimes emulated the Romans, and the commoners sometimes emulated the elites. But all too often we can speak only of *sometimes*, not of *always*, and the further down the social ladder we examine, the more difficult it becomes to say anything at all.

Recent studies on Romanization elsewhere in the Empire by Jane Webster and others have emphasized that indigenous peoples developed strategies of resistance to imperial power. It is easy to recognize overt resistance – in the case of Galilee, the participation of some villages in the first revolt against Rome – but harder to recognize subtler forms, largely because of methodological difficulties.[3] How does one determine, for example, if Galilee's seeming avoidance of the Roman custom of euergetism reflects resistance to imperial culture or merely a slow rate of acculturation? The same question can be posed regarding Galilee's gradual acceptance of figural art. Can slow rates of acculturation ever be "mere," or do they always have political implications as well?

Consider again the social and political implications of trends in personal names. Jesus bore the name of a biblical hero, Joshua, who had successfully led Israel against its enemies. That name pointed beyond Joshua himself, however, with its literal meaning of "Yahweh saves." The name Joshua is attested several times in first-century Galilee,[4] and it continued to be widespread among Palestinian Jews into the rabbinic period. Does its frequent usage reflect, on some level, personal or corporate hopes for Yahweh's deliverance of Israel again – or merely a long-lasting trend? Similarly, by giving their children Hasmonean names (like Mary) long

---

[2] See discussion in the Introduction.
[3] Compare Douglas Edwards and Peter Richardson, "Jesus and Palestinian Social Protest: Archaeological and Literary Perspectives," in Anthony J. Blasi, Jean Duhaime, and Paul-André Turcotte, eds., *Handbook of Early Christianity: Social Science Approaches* (Walnut Creek, Cal.: AltaMira, 2002), 247–266.
[4] See Appendix I.

after that dynasty had faded, were Galileans and other Jews celebrating the memory of the independence that preceded Roman domination? Interestingly, though Greek and Latin names seem to have grown more common over the centuries, they never displaced the popularity of indigenous Semitic names.

Webster has noted that strategies of resistance sometimes resulted in the creation of artifacts that hybridized aspects of local and imperial cultures. We can identify multiple instances in Galilee's material record of what we might consider resistant adaptation:

- the striking of coins in the first century that utilized common numismatic motifs but avoided anthropomorphic or zoomorphic imagery
- the more frequent creation of inscriptions but the occasional use of local languages, rather than Greek
- the growing repertoire of Jewish symbols, such as the menorah
- the use of those symbols on round discus lamps of the post-70 CE era, in contrast with the mythological figures, animals, and sexual poses found on other discus lamps
- the creation of architecturally distinct synagogues that put Greco-Roman building styles to use for the construction of Jewish identity
- the "iconographic silence" of the earliest of those synagogues.[5]

But are such phenomena properly categorized as resistance? The fact that our methodology for identifying resistance is in need of further refinement should not stop us from acknowledging the legitimacy of the question and its importance for how we reconstruct and write history. Indeed, many of the developments that are typically understood as – depending on one's terminological and methodological preferences – examples of fidelity to Judaism or efforts to construct a distinctive Jewish ethnic and/or religious identity should also be understood within the context of a local people adjusting to and at times resisting imperial rule.[6] The survival of Jewish monotheism meant the rejection of Rome's gods and Rome's rituals, and the emphasis on halakhah resulted in the

---

[5] The phrase "iconographic silence" comes from James F. Strange, "Some Implications," 39–40.
[6] Compare Schwartz, *Imperialism.*

creation of counterculture(s) to the ways of Romans and of other pagans. These efforts to maintain distinctiveness were particularly Jewish, but other peoples in other parts of the Empire also made their choices about which aspects of Roman culture to embrace, which ones to adapt, and which ones to reject.

In general, we scholars have been quicker to recognize the diversity in the *Judaism* of Hellenistic Judaism than in the *Hellenism* of Hellenistic Judaism. Likewise, we have not always emphasized sufficiently the significance of the *Roman* in Greco-Roman. Much of Galilee's encounter with Hellenistic culture occurred in the context of its encounter with Roman imperial culture.

The extent of that Greco-Roman culture in Galilee during the lifetime of Jesus has often been greatly exaggerated. Many of the characteristics that are routinely ascribed to early first-century Galilee more properly apply to Galilee in the second and third centuries. In the Galilee of Jesus, the Galilee of the Roman client king Antipas, we see hints of what was later to come. It was a time of transition, a fact of which many Galileans themselves were probably fully aware. The Romans did not occupy Galilee, but Jesus, growing up a few miles from Autocratoris, traveling extensively around what would become known as the Sea of Tiberias,[7] would have had daily reminders of Rome nonetheless. Recent scholarship has rightly emphasized that his proclamation of an alternative kingdom, the Kingdom of God, must be understood within the context of a people aware that the imperial shadow that had already fallen on Judea would one day likely cover Galilee as well.

---

[7] John 6:1.

Appendix: Galilean names in the first century CE[1]

Jesus and his Family (Mark 6:3/Matt. 13:55)

Jesus of Nazareth
Mary, mother
Joseph, father
James, brother (cf. Acts 12:17)
Joses, brother
Judas, brother
Simon, brother

Disciples (Mark 3:14–19/Matt. 10:1–4/Luke 6:12–16, Acts 1:13, John 1:35–50)[3]

Andrew
Bartholomew
Boarneges, surname of James and John
James, son of Alphaeus
James, son of Zebedee
John, son of Zebedee
Judas Iscariot

---

[1] For additional information about a given name, see Ilan, *Lexicon*.
[2] Though some New Testament characters may be fictional, I include them for the sake of thoroughness. Because names in non-canonical gospels are, in my opinion, even less likely to refer to historical personages or to reflect first-century Galilee, I have not included them. On particular names, see Ilan, *Lexicon* and Evans, *Jesus*, 67–89.
[3] I make no attempt to here to address historical questions about the number of disciples or the differences between the gospels' lists of names.

Judas, son of James
Levi
Matthew
Matthias, appointed after the resurrection (Acts 1:23)
Nathanael
Philip
Simon (Peter)[4]
Simon (the Canaanaean/Zealot)[5]
Thaddaeus[6]
Thomas

Parents of disciples

Alphaeus, father of Levi (Mark 2:14)
Alphaeus, father of James (Mark 3:18, Acts 1:13)
James, father of Judas (Luke 6:16, Acts 1:13)
Jonah, father of Simon (Matt. 16:17)[7]
Mary, mother of James (Luke 24:10)[8]
Simon Iscariot, father of Judas (John 6:71)
Zebedee, father of James and John (Mark 3:17/Matt. 10:1–4)

Members of the Herodian family

Herod (Antipas)
Herodias (wife of Herod Philip and Herod Antipas) (Mark 6:17/Matt. 14:3; Luke 3:19)

Other Galileans

Chuza, steward of Herod (Luke 8:3)
Clopas, husband of Mary (John 19:25)[9]
Jairus, *archisynagoge* (Mark 5:22/ Luke 8:41)

---

[4] See discussion in Bockmuehl, "Simon Peter's Name."
[5] On the possibility that κανανάιος is related to the Semitic name קן, see Ilan, *Lexicon*, 409.
[6] Note the text critical problems in Matthew 10:3, where some manuscripts have Lebbaeus or Lebbaeus called Thaddaeus.
[7] See discussion in Bockmuehl, "Simon Peter's Name."
[8] Presumably the James here is Jesus' disciple, though this is debatable.
[9] See note below on Mary, wife of Clopas.

Joanna, wife of Chuza (Luke 8:3, 24:10)
Joseph called Barsabbas, also called Justus (candidate for disciple) (Acts 1:23)
Martha, sister of Mary (Luke 10:38)[10]
Mary from Magdala (Taricheae) (Mark 15:40/Matt. 27:56/Luke 24:10, Luke 8:2, John 19:25)
Mary, mother of James and Joseph/Joses (Mark 15:40/Matt. 27:56)[11]
Mary, sister of Martha (Luke 10:39)
Mary, wife of Clopas (John 19:25)[12]
Simon (Luke 7:40, 44)
Salome (Mark 15:40)
Susanna (Luke 8:3)

NAMES FROM JOSEPHUS

Annaeus/Jannaeus, son of Levi (Taricheae) (*War* 2.597, *Life* 131)
Antyllus, father of Capella (Tiberias) (*Life* 69)
Capella, son of Antyllus (Tiberias) (*Life* 69)
Cleitus (Tiberias) (*Life* 170; *War* 2.642)
Compsos, son of Compsos (Tiberias) (*Life* 33)
Compsos, father of Crispus and Compsos (Tiberias) (*Life* 33)
Crispus, son of Compsos (Tiberias) (*Life* 33, 382, 388, 393)
Dassion (Taricheae) (*Life* 131)
Eleazar, converter of Izates (*Ant.* 20.43–47)
Eleazar, son of Sameas (from Saba, at Jotapata) (*War* 3.229)
Gamalas, father of Jesus (see Jesus, son of Gamalas)[13]
Gamalus, father of Herod (Tiberias) (*Life* 33)
Gephtaios/Tephthaios (from Garis) (*War* 5.474)
Herod Antipas
Herod of Tiberias (*Life* 96)
Herod, son of Gamalus (Tiberias) (*Life* 33)

---

[10] Luke places these sisters in an unspecified village through which Jesus passes while en route to Jerusalem; theoretically, he could have intended a village in southern Galilee. John 11:1, however, places Mary and Martha in Bethany, near Jerusalem.

[11] This Mary may well be Jesus' mother, noted on the previous list, though this is impossible to determine with certainty.

[12] John does not specify that Mary, wife of Clopas, was a Galilean, but it is possible that she was the same person as Jesus' mother's sister (also mentioned in 19:25), who was presumably a Galilean.

[13] Ilan understands Gamalus as the equivalent of the Semitic name Gamaliel (*Lexicon*, 282, "Herod," no. 9).

Herod, son of Miarus (Tiberias) (*Life* 33)[14]
Jacobus, bodyguard of Josephus (*Life* 96, 240)
Jeremiah, military leader (*Life* 240, 399)
Jesus the Galilean, military leader (*Life* 105, 200)
Jesus, son of Gamalas (*War* 4.160, 238, 270, 283, 316, 322, 325; *Life* 193, 204)
Jesus, son of Sapphias, chief magistrate at Tiberias (*War* 2.599; 3.450, 452, 457, 467, 498; *Life* 66, 67, 134, 178, 186, 246, 271, 278, 279, 294, 295, 300, 301)
John of Gischala (*Life* 43 and elsewhere)
Jonathan, son of Sisenna (*Life* 186)
Judas, father of Simon (*Ant.* 20.102)
Julius Capellus (Tiberias) (*Life* 32, 36, 67, 69, 296)
Justus, son of Pistus (Justus of Tiberias) (*Life* 36, 42, and elsewhere)
Levi, father of Annaeus/Jannaeus (*Life* 131)
Levi, father of John of Gischala (*War* 2.575, 585, 4.85; *Life* 43, 122, 189)
Levi, associated with Josephus (*War* 2.642; *Life* 171, 319)
Manaemos, son of Judas the Galilean (*War* 2.433, 437, 440, 442, 446, 447, 448, 449; *Life* 21, 46)
Miaros, father of Herod (Tiberias) (*Life* 33)
Netiras (from Ruma, at Jotapata) (*War* 3.233)
Philip (from Ruma, at Jotapata) (*War* 3.233)
Sameas, father of Elezar (see Eleazar)
Sapphias, father of Jesus of Tiberias (see Jesus, son of Sapphias)
Simon (Gabara) (*Life* 124)
Simon, brother of John of Gischala (*Life* 186)
Simon, son of Judas (*Ant.* 20.102)
Sisennas, father of Jonathan (Gischala) (*Life* 190)

Note also the following individuals, associated with nearby Gamla:
Chares, kinsman of Philip (*War* 4.18, 68; *Life* 177, 186)
Jacimus, father of Philip (*War* 2.421, 556; 4.81; *Life* 46, 179)
Jacobus, son of Judas the Galilean (*Ant.* 20.102)
Jesus, kinsman of Chares (*Life* 186)
Joseph (*War* 4.56, 66; *Life* 185)
Judas the Galilean (*War* 2.118, 433; 7.253; *Ant.* 18.4, 23; 20.102)
Philip, son of Jacimus (officer of Agrippa II) (*War* 2.421, 556; 4.81; *Life* 46, 179)
Simon, son of Judas the Galilean (*Ant.* 20.102)

---

[14] Ilan understands Miarus as the equivalent of the Semitic name Meir (*Lexicon*, 282, "Herod," no. 10).

NAMES FROM INSCRIPTIONS

Gaius Julius (market weight, Tiberias)[15]
Aianimos (or Animos), son of Monimos (market weight, Tiberias or Magdala)
Iaesaias, son of Mathias (market weight, Tiberias or Magdala)[16]
R [. . .] Rufus (market weight, possibly Magdala or Tiberias)
Julius [. .]bo [. .]os (market weight, possibly Magdala or Tiberias)[17]
Maria, daughter of Saulos (grave inscription, Qiryat Tiv'on)[18]
Salome (possibly identified as "the Galilean" on an ostracon at Masada)[19]

NAMES FROM RABBINIC SOURCES[20]

Elisha ben Avuyah (Ginnosar, Tiberias)[21]
Halafta (Sepphoris) (*t. Shabbat* 13:2)[22]
Hanina ben Dosa (Arav) (*b. Berakhot* 34b)[23]
Hanina ben Teradyon (Sikhnin) (*b. Sanhedrin* 32b)
Ishamel (*t. Bava Qamma* 8.14; the name is Shimon Shezuri in the Vienna manuscript)[24]

---

[15] Qedar, "Two Lead Weights."
[16] For this and the previous name, see Qedar, "Two Lead Weights" and Kushnir-Stein, "Two Inscribed Lead Weights of Agrippa." Kushnir-Stein argues that a similar weight from Agrippa's reign, now in a private collection, also originated in Galilee; it notes two *agoranomoi* with Latin names, Rufus and Julius.
[17] For the weight with this and the previous name, see Kushnir-Stein, "Two Inscribed Lead Weights of Agrippa."
[18] Rahmani, *Catalogue*, 172 no. 423.
[19] Ilan, *Lexicon*, 251, "Salome" no. 61.
[20] As the brevity of this list suggests, there are few rabbis that we can confidently associate with first-century Galilee. The number goes up in the second century, particularly in the post-Bar Kochbah period. Günter Stemberger discusses individual rabbis in *Introduction to the Talmud and Midrash*, trans. Markus Bockmuehl, 2nd edn. (London: T & T Clark, 1996), and Shmuel Safrai provides a helpful overview of first-century Galilean rabbis in "The Jewish Cultural Nature of Galilee in the First Century," *Immanuel* 24/25 (1990): 147–186, esp. 149–165. Safrai includes a few names not listed here (mostly because of concerns about dates).
[21] See Safrai, "Jewish Cultural Nature," 158–159 for discussion of possible references.
[22] *T. Shabbat* 13:2 refers to him traveling to Tiberias, thus suggesting he lived in Lower Galilee, and a late commentary on the Mishnah makes his presence in Sepphoris explicit (Safrai, "Jewish Cultural Nature," 152–154).
[23] See discussion in Stemberger, *Introduction*, 68.
[24] This tradition notes that the father of Ishmael/Shimon was from Galilee; whether we should regard the son as Galilean, too, is open to debate; see discussion in Goodman, "Galilean Judaism," 606.

Jose ha-Galili (Galil?)[25]
Joseph ben Elim (Sepphoris) (*t. Yoma* 1:4)
Nehemiah (Shihin) (pre-135 CE)[26] (*y. Sotah* 2:5)
Nittai/Mattai (Arbel) (*m. Abot* 1:6, *m. Hagigah* 2.2)[27]
Yohanan ben Zakkai (Arav) (*m. Shabbat* 17:7, 22:3; *y. Shabbat* 16.15d)[28]
Yose Holiqopri (Tiv'on) (*m. Makhshirin* 1:3)
Zaddok (Tiv'on) (*t. Niddah* 4:3–4)

---

[25] The name could mean "the Galilean," or it could designate Jose as being from Galil. See Safrai, "Jewish Cultural Nature," 163–164 and Stemberger, *Introduction*, 73 for discussion of possible references.

[26] Ilan, *Lexicon*, 197.

[27] See discussion in Stemberger, *Introduction*, 64.

[28] On Yohanan ben Zakkai 's activity in Galilee, see Goodman, "Galilean Judaism," 603 and Safrai, "Jewish Cultural Nature," 149–152.

Select bibliography

This bibliography comprises the key texts referred to in the book. The publication details of all other references cited in the footnotes are given in full, at first mention in the notes.

Adam, Jean-Pierre. *Roman Building: Materials and Techniques.* Trans. by Anthony Matthews. Bloomington and Indianapolis: Indiana University Press, 1994.

Adan-Bayewitz, David. "Kefar Hananya 1986." *IEJ* 37 (1987): 178–179.

Adan-Bayewitz, David and Mordechai Aviam. "Iotapata, Josephus, and the Siege of 67: Preliminary Report on the 1992–1994 Seasons." *JRA* 10 (1997): 131–165.

Alcock, Susan E., ed. *The Early Roman Empire in the East.* Oxford: Oxbow Books, 1997.

Alexander, Philip S. "Hellenism and Hellenization as Problematic Historiographical Categories." In Troels Engberg-Pedersen, ed., *Paul Beyond the Judaism/Hellenism Divide,* 63–80. Louisville, Ken.: Westminster John Knox Press, 2001.

Alföldy, Géza. "Augustus und die Inschriften: Tradition und Innovation." *Gymnasium* 98 (1991): 289–324.

Amit, David, Joseph Patrich, and Yizhar Hirschfeld, eds. *The Aqueducts of Israel.* Portsmouth, R. I.: Journal of Roman Archaeology, 2002.

Ando, Clifford. *Imperial Ideology and Provincial Loyalty in the Roman Empire.* Berkeley: University of California Press, 2000.

Applebaum, Shimon. "The Roman Colony of Ptolemais-'Ake and its Territory." In *Judaea in Hellenistic and Roman Times: Historical and Archaeological Essays,* 70–96. London: E. J. Brill, 1989.

"Syria-Palaestina as a Province of the Severan Empire." In *Judaea in Hellenistic and Roman Times: Historical and Archaeological Essays,* 143–154. London: E. J. Brill, 1989.

Applebaum, Shimon, B. Isaac, and Y. Landau. "Varia Epigraphica." *SCI* 6 (1981/1982): 98–118.

Arav, Rami. "Bethsaida Excavations: Preliminary Report, 1987–1993." In Rami Arav and Richard A. Freund, eds., *Bethsaida: A City by the North Shore of the Sea of Galilee*, vol. 1, 3–64. Kirksville, Mo.: Thomas Jefferson University Press, 1995.

"Bethsaida Excavations: Preliminary Report, 1994–1996." In Rami Arav and Richard A. Freund, eds., *Bethsaida: A City by the North Shore of the Sea of Galilee*, vol. 2, 3–113. Kirksville, Mo.: Truman State University Press, 1999.

Hellenistic Palestine: Settlement Patterns and City Planning, 337–31 BCE. Oxford: BAR, 1989.

Arav, Rami, Richard A. Freund, and John F. Shroder, Jr. "Bethsaida Rediscovered." *BAR* 26:1 (2000): 44–56.

Argyle, W. "Greek among the Jews of Palestine in New Testament Times." *NTS* 20 (1973): 87–89.

Ariel, Donald T. "The Coins from Khirbet Zemel." In Zvi Gal, ed., *Eretz Zafon: Studies in Galilean Archaeology*, 119–124. Jerusalem: Israel Antiquities Authority, 2002.

"Stamped Amphora Handles." In Rafael Frankel, Nimrod Getzov, Mordechai Aviam, and Avi Degani, *Settlement Dynamics and Regional Diversity in Ancient Upper Galilee: Archaeological Survey of Upper Galilee*, 154–163. Jerusalem: Israel Antiquities Authority, 2001.

Ariel, Donald, T. and Gerald Finkielsztejn. "Stamped Amphora Handles." In Sharon Herbert, ed., *Tel Anafa I, i: Final Report on Ten Years of Excavation at a Hellenistic and Roman Settlement in Northern Israel*, 183–240. Ann Arbor, Mich: Journal of Roman Archaeology, 1994.

Ariel, Donald T. and Joseph Naveh. "Selected Inscribed Sealings from Kedesh in the Upper Galilee." *BASOR* 329 (2003): 61–80.

Arnal, William E. *Jesus and the Village Scribes*. Minneapolis: Fortress Press, 2001.

Aune, David E. "Jesus and the Romans in Galilee: Jews and Gentiles in the Decapolis." In Adela Yarbro Collins, ed., *Ancient and Modern Perspectives on the Bible and Culture: Essays in Honor of Hans Dieter Betz*, 230–251. Atlanta: Scholars Press, 1998.

Aviam, Mordechai. "The Ancient Synagogues at Bar'am." In Mordechai Aviam, *Jews, Pagans and Christians in the Galilee*, 147–169. Rochester: University of Rochester Press; Woodbridge, Suffolk: Boydell & Brewer, 2004.

"Borders between Jews and Gentiles in the Galilee." In Mordechai Aviam, *Jews, Pagans and Christians in the Galilee*, 9–21. Rochester: University of Rochester Press; Woodbridge, Suffolk: Boydell & Brewer, 2004.

"First Century Jewish Galilee: An Archaeological Perspective." In Douglas R. Edwards, ed., *Religion and Society in Roman Palestine*, 7–27. New York and London: Routledge, 2004.

"The Hasmonaean Dynasty's Activities in the Galilee." In Mordechai Aviam, *Jews, Pagans and Christians in the Galilee*, 41–50. Rochester: University of Rochester Press; Woodbridge, Suffolk: Boydell & Brewer, 2004.

"The Hellenistic and Hasmonaean Fortress and Herodian Siege Complex at Qeren Naftali." In Mordechai Aviam, *Jews, Pagans and Christians in the Galilee*, 59–88. Rochester: University of Rochester Press; Woodridge, Suffolk: Boydell & Brewer, 2004.

"Hellenistic Fortifications in the 'Hinterland' of 'Akko-Ptolemais." In Mordechai Aviam, *Jews, Pagans and Christians in the Galilee*, 22–30. Rochester: University of Rochester Press; Woodbridge, Suffolk: Boydell & Brewer, 2004.

"Regionalism of Tombs and Burial Customs in the Galilee during the Hellenistic, Roman, and Byzantine Periods." In Mordechai Aviam, *Jews, Pagans and Christians in the Galilee*, 257–313. Rochester: University of Rochester Press; Woodbridge, Suffolk: Boydell & Brewer, 2004.

"Some Notes on the Roman Temple at Kedesh." In Mordechai Aviam, *Jews, Pagans, and Christians in the Galilee*, 139–146. Rochester: University of Rochester Press; Woodbridge, Suffolk: Boydell & Brewer, 2004.

"Two Roman Roads in the Galilee." In Mordechai Aviam, *Jews, Pagans, and Christians in the Galilee*, 133–138. Rochester: University of Rochester Press; Woodbridge, Suffolk: Boydell & Brewer, 2004.

Aviam, Mordechai and Peter Richardson. "Josephus' Galilee in Archaeological Perspective." In Steve Mason, ed., *Flavius Josephus: Translation and Commentary*, vol. 9, 177–209. Leiden: Brill, 2001.

Avigad, Nahman. *Beth She'arim*, vol. 3, *The Excavations 1953–1958*. New Brunswick: Rutgers University Press, 1976.

Avi-Yonah, Michael. "The Foundation of Tiberias." *IEJ* 1 (1950–1951): 160–169.

"The Leda Sarcophagus from Beth She'arim." In *Art in Ancient Palestine*, 257–269. Jerusalem: Magnes Press, 1981.

"Newly Discovered Latin and Greek Inscriptions." *QDAP* 12 (1946): 84–102.

"A Sixth Century Inscription from Sepphoris." *IEJ* 11 (1961): 184–187.

"Syrian Gods at Ptolemais-Accho." *IEJ* 9 (1959): 1–12.

Bagatti, Bellarmino. *Excavations at Nazareth*. Trans. E. Hoade. Jerusalem: Franciscan Printing Press, 1969.

Bahat, D. "A Roof Tile of the Legio VI Ferrata and Pottery Vessels from Horvat Hazon." *IEJ* 24 (1974): 160–169.

Ball, Warwick. *Rome in the East: The Transformation of an Empire.* London and New York: Routledge, 2001.

Barag, Dan. "Hanita, Tomb XV: A Tomb of the Third and Early Fourth Century CE." *Atiqot* 13 (1978): 1–60.

"Tyrian Currency in Galilee." *INJ* 6/7 (1982–1983): 7–13.

Baramki, J. "Coin Hoards from Palestine, II." *QDAP* 11 (1945): 86–90.

Barclay, John M. G. *Jews in the Mediterranean Diaspora: From Alexander to Trajan (323 BCE–117 CE).* Berkeley: University of California Press, 1996.

Barkay, Rachel. *The Coinage of Nysa-Scythopolis (Beth-Shean).* Jerusalem: Israel Numismatic Society, 2003.

"Coins of Roman Governors issued by Nysa-Scythopolis in the Late Republican Period." *INJ* 13 (1994–1999): 54–62.

"A New Coin Type of Dionysos from Canatha." *INJ* 11 (1990–1991): 72–76.

Bar-Kochva, Bezalel. *Judas Maccabeus: The Jewish Struggle against the Seleucids.* Cambridge: Cambridge University Press, 1989.

Baron, Raqui Milman. "A Survey of Inscriptions found in Israel, and published in 1992–1993." *SCI* 13 (1994): 142–161.

Barr, James. "Hebrew, Aramaic and Greek in the Hellenistic Age." In *CHJ*, vol. 2, 79–114.

Bartel, Brad "Colonialism and Cultural Responses: Problems Related to Roman Provincial Analysis." *WA* 12 (1980): 11–26.

Batey, Richard A. "'Is Not This the Carpenter?'" *NTS* 30 (1984): 249–258.

Jesus and the Forgotten City: New Light on Sepphoris and the Urban World of Jesus. Grand Rapids, Mich.: Baker Book House, 1991.

"Jesus and the Theatre." *NTS* 30 (1984): 563–574.

"Sepphoris: An Urban Portrait of Jesus." *BAR* 18:3 (1992): 50–63.

Baumgarten, Albert I. "Invented Traditions of the Maccabean Era." In Hubert Cancik, Hermann Lichtenberger, and Peter Schäfer, eds., *Geschichte, Tradition, Reflexion: Festschrift für Martin Hengel zum 70. Geburtstag*, vol. 1, 197–210. Tübingen: J. C. B. Mohr (Paul Siebeck), 1996.

Beacham, Richard C. *The Roman Theatre and its Audience.* Cambridge: Harvard University Press, 1992.

Beard, Mary et al., eds. *Literacy in the Roman World.* Ann Arbor, Mich.: Journal of Roman Archaeology, 1991.

Belayche, Nicole. *Iudaea-Palaestina: The Pagan Cults in Roman Palestine (Second to Fourth Centuries).* Tübingen: J. C. B. Mohr Siebeck, 2001.

Bénabou, Marcel. *La résistance africaine à la romanisation.* Paris: François Maspero, 1976.

Ben-Tor, Amnon, Yuval Portugali, and Miriam Anissar. "The Third and Fourth Seasons of Excavations at Tel Yoqne'am, 1979 and 1981." *IEJ* 33 (1983): 30–53.

Berlin, Andrea M. "Between Large Forces: Palestine in the Hellenistic Period." *BA* 60:1 (1997): 2–57.

"From Monarchy to Markets: The Phoenicians in Hellenistic Palestine." *BASOR* 306 (1997): 75–88.

"The Plain Wares." In Sharon Herbert, ed., *Tel Anafa, II: Final Report on Ten Years of Excavation at a Hellenistic and Roman Settlement in Northern Israel,* ix–246. Ann Arbor, Mich.: Kelsey Museum, 1997.

"Power and its Afterlife: Tombs in Hellenistic Palestine." *NEA* 65:2 (2002): 138–148.

"Romanization and anti-Romanization in pre-Revolt Galilee." In Andrea M. Berlin and J. Andrew Overman, eds., *The First Jewish Revolt: Archaeology, History, and Ideology,* 57–73. London and New York: Routledge, 2002.

Bernett, Monika. "Der Kaiserkult als teil der Politischen Geschichte Iudeas unter den Herodianern und Roemern (30 v. – 66 n. Chr.)." Habilitationsschrift, Munich 2002.

Bickerman, Elias J. *God of the Maccabees: Studies on the Origin and Meaning of the Maccabean Revolt.* Trans. Horst R. Moehring. Leiden: E. J. Brill, 1979.

Bieber, Margaret. *The History of the Greek and Roman Theater,* 2nd edn. Princeton: Princeton University Press, London: Oxford University Press, 1961.

Binder, Donald T. *Into the Temple Courts: The Place of the Synagogues in the Second Temple Period.* Atlanta: Society of Biblical Literature, 1999.

Biran, Avraham. "To the God who is in Dan." In Avraham Biran, ed., *Temples and High Places in Biblical Times,* 142–151. Jerusalem: Nelson Glueck School of Biblical Archaeology of Hebrew Union College – Jewish Institute of Religion, 1981.

Birley, Anthony R. *Hadrian: The Restless Emperor.* London and New York: Routledge, 1997.

Blagg, Thomas and Martin Millett, eds. *The Early Roman Empire in the West.* Oxford: Oxbow Books, 1990.

Boatwright, Mary T. *Hadrian and the Cities of the Roman Empire.* Princeton: Princeton University Press, 2000.

"Theaters in the Roman Empire." *BA* 53 (1990): 184–192.

Bockmuehl, Markus. "Simon Peter's Name in Jewish Sources." *JJS* 55 (2004): 58–80.

Bodel, John. "Epigraphy and the Ancient Historian." In John Bodel, ed., *Epigraphic Evidence: Ancient History from Inscriptions,* 1–56. London: Routledge, 2001.

Bol, Peter Cornelius et al. "Gadara in der Dekapolis." *Archäologischer Anzeiger* (1990): 193–266.

Borg, Marcus J. *Meeting Jesus Again for the First Time: The Historical Jesus & the Heart of Contemporary Faith.* San Francisco: HarperSanFrancisco, 1994.

"The Palestinian Background for a Life of Jesus." In Hershel Shanks, ed., *The Search for Jesus*, 37–58. Washington, D.C.: Biblical Archaeology Society, 1994.

Bösen, Willibald. *Galiläa als Lebensraum und Wirkungsfeld Jesu.* Basel and Vienna: Herder Freiburg, 1985.

Bowersock, G. W. "The Annexation and Initial Garrison of Arabia." *ZPE* 5 (1970): 37–47.

Hellenism in Late Antiquity. Ann Arbor: University of Michigan Press, 1990.

Roman Arabia. Cambridge, Mass. and London: Harvard University Press, 1983.

"The Tel Shalem Arch and P. Nahal Hever/ Seiyal 8." In Peter Schäfer, ed., *The Bar Kokhba War Reconsidered: New Perspectives on the Second Jewish Revolt against Rome*, 171–180. Tübingen: Mohr Siebeck, 2003.

Bowsher, Julian M. C. "Civic Organisation within the Decapolis." *ARAM* 4:1 & 2 (1992): 265–281.

Brandt, Roel and Jan Slofstra, eds. *Roman and Native in the Low Countries: Spheres of Interaction.* Oxford: BAR, 1983.

Braun, Jean-Pierre et al. "The Town Plan of Gerasa in AD 2000: A Revised Edition." *ADAJ* 45 (2001): 433–436.

Braund, David. *Rome and the Friendly King: The Character of the Client Kingship.* London and Canberra: Croom Helm; New York: St. Martin's Press, 1984.

Brown, Frank E. "Violation of Sepulture in Palestine." *American Journal of Philology* 52 (1931): 1–29.

Bruce, F. F. *New Testament History.* New York: Doubleday, 1969.

Bunnell, Catharine S. "Catalogue of the Coins." In Leroy Waterman, *Preliminary Report of the University of Michigan Excavations at Sepphoris, Palestine, in 1931*, 35–86. Ann Arbor: University of Michigan Press, 1937.

Burnett, A. "The Coinage of King Agrippa I of Judaea and a New Coin of King Herod of Chalcis." In H. Huvelin, M. Christol, and G. Gautier, eds., *Mélanges de Numismatique: Offerts à Pierre Bastien à l'occasion of de son 75e anniversaire*, 28–39. Wettern, Belgium: Editions NR, 1987.

Burnett, Andrew, Michel Amandry, and Ian Carradice, eds. *Roman Provincial Coinage*, vol. 2. London: British Museum Press; Paris: Bibliothèque Nationale, 1999.

Burnett, Andrew, Michel Amandry, and Pere Paul Ripollès, eds. *Roman Provincial Coinage*, vol. 1. London: British Museum Press, Paris: Bibliothèque Nationale, 1992.

Burrell, Barbara. "Palace to Praetorium: The Romanization of Caesarea." In Avner Raban and Kenneth G. Holum, eds., *Caesarea Maritima: A Retrospective after Two Millenia*, 228–250. Leiden: E. J. Brill, 1996.

Cagnat, R. and G. LaFaye, eds. *Inscriptiones Graecae ad Res Romanas Pertinenetes*, vol. 3. Paris: Académie des inscriptions et belles-lettres, 1906.

Case, Shirley Jackson. *Jesus: A New Biography*. Chicago: University of Chicago Press, 1927.

"Jesus and Sepphoris." *JBL* 45 (1926): 14–22.

Chancey, Mark A. "Archaeology, Ethnicity, and First-Century CE Galilee: The Limits of Evidence." In Margaret Daly-Denton, Brian McGing, Anne Fitzpatrick McKinley, and Zuleika Rodgers, eds., forthcoming.

"City Coins and Roman Power in Palestine: From Pompey to the Great Revolt." In Douglas R. Edwards, ed., *Religion and Society in Roman Palestine*, 103–112. New York and London: Routledge, 2004.

"The Cultural Milieu of Ancient Sepphoris." *NTS* 47:2 (2001): 127–145.

"Galilee and Greco-Roman Culture in the Time of Jesus: The Neglected Significance of Chronology." In *SBLSP 2003*, 173–188. Atlanta: Scholars Press, 2003.

The Myth of a Gentile Galilee. Cambridge: Cambridge University Press, 2002.

Chancey, Mark and Eric M. Meyers. "How Jewish was Sepphoris in Jesus' Time?" *BAR* 26:4 (2000): 18–33, 61.

Chancey, Mark and Adam Porter. "The Archaeology of Roman Palestine," *NEA* 64 (2001): 164–203.

Chen, Doron. "The Ancient Synagogue at Horvat 'Ammudim: Design and Chronology." *PEQ* 118 (1986): 135–137.

Cohen, Getzel M. *The Hellenistic Settlements in Europe, the Islands, and Asia Minor*. Berkeley: University of California Press, 1995.

Cohen, N. "The Jewish Names as Cultural Indicators in Antiquity." *JSJ* 7 (1976): 97–128.

Colledge, Malcolm. "Greek and non-Greek Interaction in the Art and Architecture of the Hellenistic East." In Amélie Kuhrt and Susan Sherwin-White, eds., *Hellenism in the East*, 134–162. Berkeley and Los Angeles: University of California Press, 1987.

Corbo, Virgilio C. "Piazza e villa urbana a Magdala." *LA* 28 (1978): 232–240.

"Scavi archeologici Magdala, 1971–1973." *LA* 24 (1974): 19–37.

Cotton, H. M., W. E. H. Cockle, and F. G. B. Millar. "The Papyrology of the Roman Near East: A Survey." *JRS* 85 (1995): 214–235.

Cotton, Hannah M. "*Legio VI Ferrata.*" In Yann Le Bohec, ed., *Les Légions de Rome sous le Haut–Empire*, 351–357. Lyon: Diffusion de Boccard, 2000.

Crossan, John Dominic. *The Birth of Christianity*. San Francisco: HarperSanFrancisco, 1998.

The Historical Jesus: The Life of a Mediterranean Jewish Peasant. San Francisco: HarperSanFrancisco, 1991.

"Itinerants and Householders in the Earliest Jesus Movement." In William E. Arnal and Michel Desjardins, eds., *Whose Historical Jesus?*, 7–24. Waterloo, Ont.: Wilfrid Laurier University Press, 1997.

Jesus: A Revolutionary Biography. San Francisco: HarperSanFrancisco, 1994.

Crossan, John Dominic and Jonathan L. Reed. *Excavating Jesus: Beneath the Stones, Behind the Texts*. San Francisco: HarperSanFrancisco, 2001.

Cumont, Franz. "Un rescrit imperial sur la violation de sepulture." *Revue Historique* 163 (1930): 241–266.

Dabrowa, Edward. "The Frontier in Syria in the First Century AD." In Philip Freeman and David Kennedy, eds., *The Defence of the Roman and Byzantine East*, vol. 1, 93–108. Oxford: BAR, 1986.

"*Legio X Fretensis*." In Yann Le Bohec, ed., *Les Légions de Rome sous le Haut-Empire*, 317–325. Lyon: Diffusion de Boccard, 2000.

Dalman, Gustaf. *The Words of Jesus*. Trans. D. M. Kay. Edinburgh: T & T Clark, 1909.

Damati, Emanuel. "A Greek Inscription from a Mausoleum in Tiberias." *Atiqot* 38 (1999): 227–228 (English summary section).

"Three Greek Inscriptions from Eastern Galilee." *Atiqot* 35 (1998): 151–155.

Dar, Shimon. "The Greek Inscriptions from Senaim on Mount Hermon." *PEQ* 120 (1988): 26–44.

Dauphin, Claudine. "Mosaic Pavements as an Index of Prosperity and Fashion." *Levant* 12 (1980): 125–134.

de Zulueta, F. "Violation of Sepulture in Palestine at the Beginning of the Christian Era." *JRS* 22 (1932): 184–197.

Di Segni, Leah. "A Dated Inscription from Beth Shean and the Cult of Dionysos Ktistes in Roman Scythopolis." *SCI* 16 (1997): 139–161.

"Ketuvot Teveryah." In Yizhar Hirschfeld, ed., *Teveryah*, 70–95. Jerusalem: Yad Yitzhak Ben Zvi, 1988. (Hebrew)

Dodge, Hazel. "Amusing the Masses: Buildings for Entertainment and Leisure in The Roman World." In D. S. Potter and D. J. Mattingly, eds., *Life, Death and Entertainment in the Roman Empire*, 205–255. Ann Arbor: University of Michigan Press, 1999.

"The Architectural Impact of Rome in the East." In Martin Henig, ed., *Architecture and Architectural Sculpture in the Roman Empire*, 108–120. Oxford: Oxford University Committee for Archaeology, 1990.

Dothan, Moshe. "Akko: Interim Excavation Report: First Season 1973/4." *BASOR* 224 (1976): 1–48.
  Hammath Tiberias: Early Synagogues and the Hellenistic and Roman Remains. Jerusalem: Israel Exploration Society, 1983.
Downing, F. Gerald. *Christ and the Cynics.* Sheffield: JSOT, 1988.
  Cynics and Christian Origins. Edinburgh: T & T Clark, 1992.
  Jesus and the Threat of Freedom, London: SCM, 1987.
Dunbabin, Katherine M. D. *The Mosaics of the Greek and Roman World.* Cambridge: Cambridge University Press, 1999.
Durand, Xavier. *Des Grecs en Palestine au IIIe Siècle avant Jésus–Christ: Le Dossier Syrien des Archives de Zénon de Caunos (261–252).* Paris: J. Gabalda, 1997.
Eck, Werner and Gideon Foerster. "Ein Triumphbogen im Tal von Beth Shean bei Tel Shalem." *JRA* 12 (1999): 294–313.
Eck, Werner and Yotam Tepper. "A Dedication to Silvanus near the Camp of the Legio VI Ferrata near Lajjun." *SCI* 20 (2001): 85–88.
Edwards, Douglas R. "First-Century Urban/Rural Relations in Lower Galilee: Exploring the Archaeological and Literary Evidence." In J. David Lull, ed., *SBLSP 1988,* 169–182. Atlanta: Scholars Press, 1988.
  "The Socio-Economic and Cultural Ethos of the Lower Galilee in the First Century: Implications of the Nascent Jesus Movement." In Lee I. Levine, ed., *The Galilee in Late Antiquity,* 39–52. New York and Jerusalem: The Jewish Theological Seminary of America, 1992.
Eliav, Yaron Z. "The Roman Bath as a Jewish Institution: Another Look at the Encounter between Judaism and the Greco–Roman Culture." *JSJ* 31 (2000): 416–454.
Engberg-Pedersen, Troels, ed. Paul *Beyond the Judaism/Hellenism Divide.* Louisville, Ken.: Westminster John Knox Press, 2001.
Eshel, Esther and Douglas R. Edwards. "Language and Writing in Early Roman Galilee: Social Location of a Potter's Abecedary from Khirbet Qana." In Douglas R. Edwards, ed., *Religion and Society in Roman Palestine,* 49–55. New York and London: Routledge, 2004.
Evans, Craig. *Jesus and the Ossuaries.* Waco: Baylor University Press, 2003.
Feldman, Louis H. "Hengel's *Judaism and Hellenism* in Retrospect." *JBL* 96 (1977): 371–382.
  "How Much Hellenism in Jewish Palestine?" *HUCA* (1986): 83–111.
Fine, Steven. *Art and Judaism in the Greco-Roman World: Toward a New Jewish Archaeology.* Cambridge: Cambridge University Press, 2005.
Fine, Steven, ed. *Sacred Realm: The Emergence of the Synagogue in the Ancient World.* New York and Oxford: Yeshiva University Museum and Oxford University Press, 1996.

Finkielsztejn, Gerald. "Amphoras and Stamped Handles from 'Akko." *Atiqot* 39 (2000): 135–153.

Fischer, Moshe L. *Marble Studies: Roman Palestine and the Marble Trade.* Konstanz: Universitätsverlag Konstanz, 1998.

"Marble, Urbanism, and Ideology in Roman Palestine: The Caesarea Example." In Avner Raban and Kenneth G. Holum, eds., *Caesarea Maritima: A Retrospective after Two Millenia,* 251–261. Leiden: E. J. Brill, 1996.

Fischer, Mosche, Benjamin Isaac, and Israel Roll. *Roman Roads in Judaea II: The Jaffa–Jerusalem Roads.* Oxford: BAR, 1996.

Fischer, Moshe, Asher Ovadiah, and Israel Roll. "The Epigraphic Finds from the Roman Temple at Kedesh in the Upper Galilee." *TA* 13 (1986): 60–66.

"The Roman Temple at Kedesh, Upper Galilee: A Preliminary Study." *TA* 11 (1984): 146–172.

Fischer, Thomas. "Palestine, Administration of (Seleucid)." Trans. Frederick H. Cryer. *ABD*, vol. 5, 92–96.

Fisher, Clarence Stanley. "Architectural Remains." In George Andrew Reisner, Clarence Stanley Fisher, and David Gordon Lyon, *Harvard Excavations at Samaria: 1908–1910.* Cambridge: Harvard University Press, 1924, vol. 1, 91–223.

Fitzmyer, Joseph A. "Did Jesus Speak Greek?" *BAR* 18:5 (1992): 58–63, 76–77.

"The Languages of Palestine in the First Century AD." In *The Semitic Background of the New Testament,* 29–56. Grand Rapids, Mich. and Cambridge: William B. Eerdmans; Livonia, Mich.: Dove Booksellers, 1997.

"The Phases of the Aramaic Language." In *A Wandering Aramean: Collected Aramaic Essays,* 57–84. Society of Biblical Literature Monograph Series no. 25. Chico, Cal: Scholars Press, 1979.

Fitzmyer, Joseph A. and Daniel J. Harrington. *A Manual of Palestinian Aramaic Texts (Second Century BC–Second Century AD).* Rome: Biblical Institute Press, 1978.

Foerster, Gideon. "Architectural Models of the Greco–Roman Period and the Origin of the 'Galilean Synagogue.'" In Lee I. Levine, ed., *Ancient Synagogues Revealed,* 45–48. Jerusalem: Israel Exploration Society; Detroit: Wayne State University Press, 1982.

"A Cuirassed Bronze Statue of Hadrian." *Atiqot* 17 (1985): 139–157.

Foerster, Gideon and Yoram Tsafrir. "Nysa-Scythopolis – A New Inscription and the Titles of the City on its Coins." *INJ* 9 (1986–1987): 53–58.

"A Statue of Dionysos as a Youth Recently Discovered in Beth Shean." *Qadmoniot* 23 (1990): 52–54. (Hebrew)

Fraade, Steven D. "Rabbinic Views on the Practice of Targum, and Multilingualism in the Jewish Galilee of the Third–Sixth Centuries." In Lee I. Levine, ed., *The Galilee in Late Antiquity*, 253–286. New York and Jerusalem: The Jewish Theological Seminary in America, 1992.

Frankel, Rafael and Raphael Ventura. "The Mispe Yamim Bronzes." *BASOR* 311 (1998): 39–55.

Frankel, Rafael, Nimrod Getzov, Mordechai Aviam, and Avi Degani. *Settlement Dynamics and Regional Diversity in Ancient Upper Galilee: Archaeological Survey of Upper Galilee.* Jerusalem: Israel Antiquities Authority, 2001.

Freund, Richard A. "The Incense Shovel of Bethsaida and Synagogue Iconography in Late Antiquity." In Rami Arav and Richard A. Freund, eds., *Bethsaida: A City by the North Shore of the Sea of Galilee*, vol. 2, 413–460. Kirksville, Mo.: Truman State University Press, 1999.

Frey, Jean-Baptiste. *Corpus Inscriptionum Iudaicarum*, vol. 2. Rome: Pontificio Instituto di Archeologia Cristiana, 1952.

Freyne, Sean. "Dionysos and Herakles in Galilee: The Sepphoris Mosaic in Context." In Douglas R. Edwards, ed., *Religion and Society in Roman Palestine*, 56–69. New York and London: Routledge, 2004.

"Galileans, Itureans, and Phoenicians: A Study of Regional Contrasts in the Hellenistic Age." In John J. Collins and Gregory E. Sterling, eds., *Hellenism in the Land of Israel*, 184–215. Notre Dame, Ind.: University of Notre Dame Press, 2001.

Galilee and Gospel. Boston and Leiden: Brill Academic Publishers, 2002.

Galilee from Alexander the Great to Hadrian: 323 BCE to 135 CE. Wilmington, Del.: Michael Glazier; Notre Dame, Ind.: University of Notre Press, 1980; reprint, Edinburgh: T & T Clark, 1998.

Galilee, Jesus, and the Gospels. Philadelphia: Fortress Press, 1988.

Friedland, Elise. "Graeco-Roman Sculpture in the Levant: The Marble from the Sanctuary of Pan at Caesarea Philippi (Banias)." In J. H. Humphrey, ed., *Roman and Byzantine Near East*, vol. 2, 7–22. Portsmouth, R. I.: Journal of Roman Archaeology, 1999.

"The Roman Marble Sculptures from the North Hall of the East Baths at Gerasa." *AJA* 107 (2003): 413–448.

Funk, Robert W. *A Credible Jesus: Fragments of a Vision.* Santa Rosa: Polebridge Press, 2002.

Honest to Jesus: Jesus for a New Millennium. San Francisco: HarperSanFranciso, 1996.

Funk, Robert W., Roy W. Hoover, and the Jesus Seminar. *The Five Gospels: The Search for the Authentic Words of Jesus.* New York: Macmillan, 1993.

Futrell, Allison. *Blood in the Arena: The Spectacle of Roman Power.* Austin: University of Texas Press, 1997.

Gal, Zvi. *Lower Galilee during the Iron Age.* Winona Lake, Ind.: Eisenbrauns, 1992.

Gal, Zvi, ed. *Eretz Zafon: Studies in Galilean Archaeology.* Jerusalem: Israel Antiquities Authority, 2002.

Gale, Aaron M. "Tradition in Transition, or Antioch versus Sepphoris: Rethinking the Matthean Community's Location." In *SBLSP 2003*, 141–156. Atlanta: Scholars Press, 2003.

Galor, Katharina. "Domestic Architecture in Roman and Byzantine Galilee and Golan." *NEA* 66:1–2 (2003): 44–57.

Gatier, Pierre-Lois. "Governeurs et Procurateurs à Gérasa." *Syria* 73 (1996): 47–56.

"Rèpartition des inscriptions grecques de Jordanie. L'exemple des inscriptions métriques aux époques romaine et byzantine." In *Studies in the History and Archaeology of Jordan*, vol. 4, 291–294. Ammon: Dept. of Antiquities, 1992.

Gergel, Richard A. "The Tel Shalem Hadrian Reconsidered." *AJA* 95 (1994): 231–251.

Gersht, Rivka. "Imported Marble Sarcophagi from Caesarea." *Assaph (B)* 2 (1996): 13–26.

"Representations of Deities and the Cults of Caesarea." In Avner Raban and Kenneth G. Holum, eds., *Caesarea Maritima: A Retrospective after Two Millenia*, 305–324. Leiden: E. J. Brill, 1996.

"Three Greek and Roman Portrait Statues from Caesarea Maritima." *Atiqot* 28 (1996): 99–113.

Gilliam, J. F. "Romanization of the Greek East: The Role of the Army." In J. F. Gilliam, *Roman Army Papers*, 281–287. Amsterdam: J. C. Gieben, 1986.

Giovannini, Adalberto and Marguerite Hirot. "L'inscription de Nazareth: Nouvelle Interpétation." *ZPE* 124 (1999): 107–132.

Giveon, Raphael. "Geva, a New Fortress City: From Tuthmosis to Herod." *Bulletin of the Anglo-Israel Archaeology Society* 3 (1983–1984): 45–46.

Gleason, Kathryn Louise. "Rule and Spectacle: The Promontory Palace." In Avner Raban and Kenneth G. Holum, eds., *Caesarea Maritima: A Retrospective after Two Millenia*, 208–227. Leiden: E. J. Brill, 1996.

Goldstein, Jonathan A. "The Hasmonean Revolt and the Hasmonean Dynasty." In *CHJ*, vol. 2, 292–351.

Goodchild, R. G. "The Coast Road of Phoenicia and its Roman Milestones." *Berytus* 9 (1949): 91–127.

Goodman, Martin. "Galilean Judaism and Judaean Judaism." In *CHJ*, vol. 3, 596–617.

State and Society in Roman Galilee, AD 132–212. Totowa, N. J.: Rowman and Allanheld, 1983.

Grabbe, Lester L. "Hellenistic Judaism." In Jacob Neusner, ed., *Judaism in Late Antiquity*, part 2, 53–83. Leiden: E. J. Brill, 1995.

Judaism from Cyrus to Hadrian, 2 vols. Minneapolis: Fortress, 1992.

Gracey, M. H. "The Armies of the Judaean Client Kings." In Philip Freeman and David Kennedy, eds., *The Defence of the Roman and Byzantine East: Proceedings of a colloquium held at the University of Sheffield in April 1986*, vol. 1, 311–323. Oxford: BAR, 1986.

Grainger, John D. "'Village Government' in Roman Syria and Arabia." *Levant* 27 (1995): 179–195.

Greene, John T. "The Honorific Naming of Bethsaida-Julias." In Rami Arav and Richard A. Freund, eds., *Bethsaida: A City by the North Shore of the Sea of Galilee*, vol. 2, 333–346. Kirksville, Mo.: Truman State University Press, 1999.

Greenfield, Jonas C. "Aramaic and its Dialects." In Herbert H. Paper, ed., *Jewish Languages: Themes and Variations*, 29–43. Cambridge, Mass.: Association for Jewish Studies, 1978.

"The Languages of Palestine, 200 BCE–200 CE." In Herbert H. Paper, ed., *Jewish Languages: Themes and Variations*, 143–154. Cambridge, Mass: Association for Jewish Studies, 1978.

Gregg, Robert C. and Dan Urman. *Jews, Pagans, and Christians in the Golan Heights.* Atlanta: Scholars Press, 1996.

Gruen, Erich S. *Heritage and Hellenism: The Reinvention of Jewish Tradition.* Berkeley: University of California Press, 1998.

Grzybek, Erhard and Marta Sordi. "L'édit de Nazareth et la politique de Néron à l'égard des chrétiens." *ZPE* 120 (1998): 279–291.

Guenther, Heinz O. "Greek: The Home of Primitive Christianity." *TJT* 5 (1989): 247–279.

Gundry, Robert H. "The Language Milieu of First-Century Palestine: Its Bearing on the Authenticity of the Gospel Tradition." *JBL* 83 (1964): 404–408.

Hachlili, Rachel. *Ancient Jewish Art and Archaeology in the Land of Israel.* Leiden: E. J. Brill, 1988.

"Synagogues in the Land of Israel: The Art and Architecture of Late Antique Synagogues." In Steven Fine, ed., *Sacred Realm: The Emergence of the Synagogue in the Ancient World*, 96–129. New York and Oxford: Yeshiva University Museum and Oxford University Press, 1996.

Halpern-Zylberstein, Marie-Christine. "The Archeology of Hellenistic Palestine." In *CHJ*, vol. 2, 1–34.

Hamburger, Anit. "Gems from Caesarea Maritima." *Atiqot* 8 (1968): 1–38.

Hamburger, H. "The Coin Issues of the Roman Administration from the Mint of Caesarea Maritima." *IEJ* 20 (1970): 81–91.

"A Hoard of Syrian Tetradrachms and Tyrian Bronze Coins from Gush Halav." *IEJ* 4 (1954): 201–226.

"A Hoard of Syrian Tetradrachms from Tiberias." *Atiqot* 2 (1959): 133–145.

Hänlein-Schäfer, Heidi. *Veneratio Augusti: Eine Studie zu den Tempeln des ersten römischen Kaisers*. Rome: Giorgio Bretschneider Editore, 1985.

Hanson, Richard Simon. *Tyrian Influence in the Upper Galilee*. Cambridge, Mass.: American Schools of Oriental Research, 1980.

Hanson, Richard Simon and Michael L. Bates. "Numismatic Report." In Eric M. Meyers, A. Thomas Kraabel and James F. Strange, *Ancient Synagogue Excavations at Khirbet Shema' Upper Galilee, Israel, 1970–1972*, 146–169. Durham, N. C.: Duke University Press, 1976.

Harl, Kenneth W. *Civic Coins and Civic Politics in the Roman East AD 180–275*. Berkeley: University of California Press, 1987.

Coinage in the Roman Economy, 300 BC to AD 700. Baltimore and London: The Johns Hopkins University Press, 1996.

Harris, William V. *Ancient Literacy*. Cambridge, Mass. and London: Harvard University Press, 1989.

Haverfield, F. *The Romanization of Great Britain*, 4th edn., Oxford: Clarendon Press, 1923 (1st edn., 1906).

Hendin, David. "A New Coin Type of Herod Antipas." *INJ* 15 (in press).

Hengel, Martin. *The 'Hellenization' of Judaea in the First Century after Christ*. Trans. John Bowden. London: SCM Press, Philadelphia: Trinity Press International, 1989.

Jews, Greeks and Barbarians: Aspects of the Hellenization of Judaism in the Pre-Christian Period. Trans. John Bowden. Philadelphia: Fortress, 1980.

Judaism and Hellenism. Studies in their Encounter in Palestine during the Early Hellenistic Period. Trans. John Bowden, 2 vols. Philadelphia: Fortress, 1974.

"Judaism and Hellenism Revisited." In John J. Collins and Gregory E. Sterling, eds., *Hellenism in the Land of Israel*, 6–37. Notre Dame, Ind.: University of Notre Dame Press, 2001.

Henig, Martin and Mary Whiting. *Engraved Gems from Gadara in Jordan: The Sa'd Collection of Intaglios and Cameos*. Oxford: Oxford University Committee for Archeology, 1987.

Herbert, Sharon C. "Introduction." In Sharon Herbert, ed., *Tel Anafa, I, i: Final Report on Ten Years of Excavation at a Hellenistic and Roman Settlement in Northern Israel*, 1–25. Ann Arbor: Mich.: Kelsey Museum, 1994.

"Occupational History and Stratigraphy." In Sharon C. Herbert, ed., *Tel Anafa, I: Final Report on Ten Years of Excavation at a Hellenistic and Roman Settlement in Northern Israel,* vol. 1, 26–182. Ann Arbor: Mich.: Kelsey Museum, 1994.

Herbert, Sharon C. ed. *Tel Anafa, I: Final Report on Ten Years of Excavation at a Hellenistic and Roman Settlement in Northern Israel,* 2 vols. Ann Arbor: Mich.: Kelsey Museum, 1994.

Tel Anafa II, i: The Hellenistic and Roman Pottery. Ann Arbor, Mich.: Kelsey Museum; Columbia, Mo.: Museum of Art and Archaeology of the University of Missouri, 1997.

Herbert, Sharon C. and Andrea M. Berlin. "A New Administrative Center for Persian and Hellenistic Galilee: Preliminary Report of the University of Michigan/University of Minnesota Excavations at Kedesh." *BASOR* 329 (2003): 13–59.

Hestrin, Ruth. "Beth Yerah." *NEAEHL,* vol. 1, 255–259.

Heszer, Catherine. *Jewish Literacy in Roman Palestine.* Tübingen: Mohr Siebeck, 2001.

Hill, George Frances. *Catalogue of the Greek Coins of Palestine (Galilee, Samaria and Judaea).* London: British Museum, 1914.

Hingley, Richard. "The 'Legacy' of Rome: The Rise, Decline, and Fall of the Theory of Romanization." In Jane Webster and Nicholas J. Cooper, eds., *Roman Imperialism: Post-Colonial Perspectives,* 35–48. Leicester Archaeology Monographs No. 3, Leicester: University of Leicester, 1996.

Hirschfeld, Yizhar. "Architecture and Stratigraphy." In Yizhar Hirschfeld et al., eds., *Ramat Hanadiv Excavations,* 235–327. Jerusalem: Israel Exploration Society, 2000.

"General Discussion: Ramat Hanadiv in Context." In Yizhar Hirschfeld et al., eds., *Ramat Hanadiv Excavations,* 679–735. Jerusalem: Israel Exploration Society, 2000.

A Guide to Antiquity Sites in Tiberias. Jerusalem: Israel Antiquities Authority, 1992.

The Palestinian Dwelling in the Roman-Byzantine Period. Jerusalem: Franciscan Printing Press and Israel Exploration Society, 1995.

The Roman Baths of Hammat Gader. Jerusalem: Israel Exploration Society, 1997.

Holder, Paul A. *Studies in the Auxilia of the Roman Army from Augustus to Trajan.* Oxford: BAR, 1980.

Holum, Kenneth G., A. Raban, and J. Patrick, eds. *Caesarea Papers 2.* Portsmouth, R. I.: Journal of Roman Archaeology, 1999.

Horsley, Richard A. *Archaeology, History and Society in Galilee: The Social Context of Jesus and the Rabbis.* Valley Forge, Penn.: Trinity Press International, 1996.

Galilee: History, Politics, People. Valley Forge, Penn.: Trinity Press International, 1995.

Houser, Caroline, ed. *Dionysos and His Circle: Ancient through Modern.* Cambridge, Mass.: Fogg Art Museum, Harvard University, 1979.

Howgego, Christopher. *Ancient History from Coins.* London and New York: Routledge, 1995.

Ilan, Tal. *Lexicon of Jewish Names in Late Antiquity: Part I Palestine 330 BCE–200 CE.* Tübingen: Mohr Siebeck, 2002.

"Notes on the Distribution of Jewish Women's Names in Palestine in the Second Temple and Mishnaic Periods." *JJS* 40 (1989): 186–200.

Iliffe, J. H. "Greek and Latin Inscriptions in the Museum." *QDAP* 2 (1933): 120–126.

Inscriptions Reveal: Documents from the Time of the Bible, the Mishna and the Talmud. Jerusalem: Israel Museum, 1972.

Isaac, Benjamin. "The Decapolis in Syria: A Neglected Inscription." In Benjamin Isaac, *The Near East under Roman Rule,* 313–321. Leiden: E. J. Brill, 1998.

The Limits of Empire: The Roman Army in the East, rev. edn. Oxford: Clarendon Press, 1990.

"Roman Colonies in Judaea: The Foundation of Aelia Capitolina." In Benjamin Isaac, *The Near East under Roman Rule,* 87–108. Leiden: E. J. Brill, 1998.

"Two Greek Inscriptions from Tell Abu-Shusha." In Benjamin Isaac, *The Near East under Roman Rule,* 31–33. Leiden: E. J. Brill, 1998.

Isaac, Benjamin and Israel Roll. "Judaea in the Early Years of Hadrian's Reign." In Benjamin Isaac, *The Near East under Roman Rule,* 182–197. Leiden: E. J. Brill, 1998.

"Legio II Traiana in Judaea." In Benjamin Isaac, *The Near East under Roman Rule,* 198–205. Leiden: E. J. Brill, 1998.

"Legio II Traiana in Judaea – A Reply." In Benjamin Isaac, *The Near East under Roman Rule,* 208–210. Leiden: E. J. Brill, 1998.

"A Milestone of AD 69 from Judaea: The Elder Trajan and Vespasian." In Benjamin Isaac, *The Near East under Roman Rule,* 36–45. Leiden: E. J. Brill, 1998.

Roman Roads in Judaea I: The Legio–Scythopolis Road. Oxford: BAR, 1982.

Jacobs, Martin. "Römische Thermenkultur im Spiegel des Talmud Yerushalmi." In Peter Schäfer and Catherine Heszer, eds., *The Talmud Yerushalmi and Graeco-Roman Culture,* vol. 1, 219–311. Tübingen: Mohr Siebeck, 1998.

"Theatres and Performances as Reflected in the Talmud Yerusahlmi." In Peter Schäfer, ed., *The Talmud Yerushalmi and Graeco-Roman Culture,* vol. 1, 327–347. Tübingen: Mohr Siebeck, 1998.

Jacobson, David M. "Three Roman Client Kings: Herod of Judaea, Archelaus of Cappadocia and Juba of Mauretania." *PEQ* 133 (2001): 22–38.

Jacoby, Ruth. *The Synagogues of Bar'am; Jerusalem Ossuaries.* Jerusalem: Israel Academy of Sciences and Humanities; The Masto Grust, Hebrew University, 1987.

Jennings, Jr., Theodore W. and Tat-Siong Benny Liew. "Mistaken Identities but Model Faith: Rereading the Centurion, the Chap, and the Christ in Matthew 8:5–13." *JBL* 123 (2004): 267–294.

Jensen, Morten Hørning. "Josephus and Antipas: A Case Study on Josephus' Narratives on Herod Antipas." In Zuleika Rodgers, ed., *Making History: Josephus and Historical Method.* Leiden: E. J. Brill, 2005.

Jeremias, Joachim. *New Testament Theology: The Proclamation of Jesus.* New York: Charles Scribner's Sons, 1971.

Jidejian, Nina. *Tyre through the Ages.* Beirut: Dar el-Mashreq Publishers, 1969.

Johns, Catherine. "Art, Romanisation, and Competence." In Sarah Scott and Jane Webster, eds., 9–23. *Roman Imperialism and Provincial Art.* Cambridge: Cambridge University Press, 2003.

Jones, A. H. M. *The Cities of the Eastern Roman Provinces,* 2nd edn. Oxford: Oxford University Press, 1971.

"The Urbanization of Palestine." *JRS* 21 (1931) 78–85.

Kahn, Lisa C. "King Herod's Temple of Roma and Augustus at Caesarea Maritima." In Avner Raban and Kenneth G. Holum, eds., *Caesarea Maritima: A Retrospective after Two Millenia,* 130–145. Leiden: E. J. Brill, 1996.

Kant, Laurence H. "Jewish Inscriptions in Greek and Latin." *ANRW* II.20.2, 671–713.

Kasher, Aryeh. *Jews and Hellenistic Cities in Eretz-Israel.* Tübingen: J. C. B. Mohr (Paul Siebeck), 1990.

Kee, Howard Clark. "Early Christianity in the Galilee: Reassessing the Evidence from the Gospels." In Lee I. Levine, ed., *The Galilee in Late Antiquity,* 3–22. New York and Jerusalem: The Jewish Theological Seminary of America, 1992.

Jesus in History: An Approach to the Study in the Gospels, 3rd edn. Orlando, Fla.: Harcourt Brace & Company, 1996.

Kelber, Werner. *The Kingdom in Mark: A New Place and a New Time.* Philadelphia: Fortress Press, 1974.

Kennedy, David. "Greek, Roman, and Native Cultures in the Roman Near East." In J. H. Humphrey, ed., *The Roman and Byzantine Near East,* vol., 2, 76–106. Portsmouth, R. I.: Journal of Roman Archaeology, 1999.

"The Identity of Roman Gerasa: An Archaeological Approach." *Mediterranean Archaeology* 11 (1998): 36–39.

"*Legio VI Ferrata:* The Annexation and Early Garrison of Arabia."
HSCP 84 (1980): 283–309.

The Roman Army in Jordan. London: Council for British Research in
the Levant, 2000.

Keppie, Lawrence. "The Army and the Navy." In Alan K. Bowman,
Edward Champlin, and Andrew Lintott, eds., *The Cambridge Ancient
History,* vol. 10, 371–396. Cambridge: Cambridge University Press,
1996.

"The History and Disappearance of the Legion XXII Deiotariana."
In Lawrence Keppie, *Legions and Veterans: Roman Army Papers
1971–2000,* 225–232. Stuttgart: Franz Steiner Verlag, 2000.

"The Legionary Garrison of Judaea under Hadrian." *Latomus* 32 (1973):
859–864.

"Legions in the East from Augustus to Trajan." In Philip Freeman &
David Kennedy, eds., *The Defence of the Roman & Byzantine East,*
vol. 2, 411–429. Oxford: BAR, 1986.

The Making of the Roman Army: From Republic to Empire. Totowa,
N. J.: Barnes and Noble Books, 1984.

Kindler, Arie. "The Coin Finds at the Excavations of Bethsaida." In Rami
Arav and Richard A. Freund, eds., *Bethsaida: A City by the North
Shore of the Sea of Galilee,* vol. 2, 250–268. Kirksville, Mo.: Truman
State University Press, 1999.

The Coins of Tiberias. Tiberias: Hamei Tiberia, 1961.

"The Status of Cities in the Syro-Palestinian Area as Reflected by their
Coins." *INJ* 6–7 (1982–1983): 79–87.

Kindler, Arie and Alla Stein. *A Bibliography of the City Coinage of Palestine:
From the 2nd Century BC to the 3rd Century AD.* Oxford: BAR, 1987.

Klein, Samuel. *Beiträge zur Geographie und Geschichte Galiläas.* Leipzig:
Verlag von Rudolf Haupt, 1906.

Kleiner, Diana E. E. *Roman Sculpture.* New Haven and London: Yale
University Press, 1992.

Kloner, Amos. "The Roman Amphitheatre at Beth Guvrin Preliminary
Report." *IEJ* 38 (1988): 15–24.

Kloppenborg, John S. "The Sayings Gospel Q: Recent Opinion on the
People Behind the Document." *CRBS* 1 (1993): 9–34.

Kloppenborg Verbin, John S. *Excavating Q: The History and Setting of the
Sayings Gospel.* Minneapolis: Fortress Press, 2000.

Kokkinos, Nikos. *The Herodian Dynasty: Origins, Role in Society and
Eclipse.* Sheffield: Sheffield Academic Press, 1998.

Kraeling, Carl H. "The History of Gerasa." In Carl H. Kraeling, ed.,
Gerasa: City of the Decapolis, 27–72. New Haven: American Schools
of Oriental Research, 1938.

Krauss, Samuel. *Griechische und lateinische Lehnwörter im Talmud, Midrasch und Targum*, 2 vols. Berlin, 1898. Reprint. Hildesheim: Georg Olms, 1964.

Kushnir-Stein, Alla. "New Hellenistic Lead Weights from Palestine and Phoenicia." *IEJ* 52 (2002): 225–230.

"Two Inscribed Lead Weights of Agrippa II." *ZPE* 141 (2002): 295–300.

"Two Inscribed Weights from Banias." *IEJ* 45 (1995): 48–51.

Landau, Yohanan H. "A Greek Inscription Found Near Hefzibah." *IEJ* 16 (1966): 54–70.

"A Greek Inscription from Acre." *IEJ* 11 (1961): 118–126.

Landau, Yohanan H. and Vassilios Tzaferis. "Tel Istabah, Beth Shean: The Excavations and Hellenistic Jar Handles." *IEJ* 29 (1979): 152–157.

Lapin, Hayim. "Palestinian Inscriptions and Jewish Ethnicity." In Eric M. Meyers, *Galilee through the Centuries: Confluence of Cultures*, 239–268. Winona Lake, Ind.: Eisenbrauns, 1999.

Last, Rosa and Alla Stein. "Ala Antiana in Scythopolis: A New Inscription from Beth-Shean." *ZPE* 81 (1990): 224–228.

Laughlin, John C. H. "Capernaum: From Jesus' Time and After." *BAR* 19:5 (1993): 54–61.

Le Déaut, Roger. "The Targumim." In *CHJ*, vol. 2, 563–590.

Lehmann, Clayton Miles and Kenneth G. Holum. *The Greek and Latin Inscriptions of Caesarea Maritima*. Boston, Mass.: The American Schools of Oriental Research, 2000.

Levine, Lee I. *The Ancient Synagogue: The First Thousand Years*. New Haven and London: Yale University Press, 2000.

"Archaeology and the Religious Ethos of Pre-70 Palestine." In James H. Charlesworth and Loren L. Johns, eds., *Hillel and Jesus: Comparative Studies of Two Major Religious Leaders*, 110–120. Minneapolis: Fortress, 1997.

"Excavations at the Synagogue of Horvat 'Ammudim." *IEJ* 32 (1982): 1–12.

Jerusalem: Portrait of the City in the Second Temple Period (538 BCE–70 CE). Philadelphia: Jewish Publication Society and Jewish Theological Seminary of America, 2002.

Judaism and Hellenism in Antiquity: Conflict or Confluence? Peabody, Mass.: Hendrickson Publishers, 1998.

The Rabbinic Class of Roman Palestine in Late Antiquity. Jerusalem: Yad Izhak Ben-Zvi; New York: Jewish Theological Seminary of America, 1989.

Lieberman, Saul. *Greek in Jewish Palestine: Studies in the Life and Manners of Jewish Palestine in the II–IV Centuries CE*. New York: Jewish Theological Seminary of America, 1942.

Hellenism in Jewish Palestine: Studies in the Literary Transmission, Beliefs and Manners of Palestine in the I Century B.C.E.–IV

Century C.E. New York: Jewish Theological Seminary of America, 1950.

"How Much Greek in Jewish Palestine?" In Alexander Altmann, ed., *Biblical and Other Studies*, 123–141. Cambridge, Mass.: Harvard University Press, 1963.

Lifshitz, Baruch. "Légions romaines en Palestine." In Jacqueline Bibauw, ed., *Hommages á Marcel Renard*, 458–469. Brussels: Latomus, 1969.

"Notes d'épigraphique Grecque." *Revue Biblique* 77 (1970): 76–83.

"Sur la date du transfert de la legio VI Ferrata en Palestine." *Latomus* 19 (1960): 109–111.

Loffreda, S. "Coins from the Synagogue of Capharnaum." *LA* 47 (1997): 223–244.

"The Late Chronology of the Synagogue of Capernaum." In Lee I. Levine, ed., *Ancient Synagogues Revealed*, 52–56. Jerusalem: Israel Exploration Society; Detroit: Wayne State University Press, 1982.

Recovering Capharnaum. Jerusalem: Franciscan Printing Press, 1993.

MacDonnell, Anna Manzoni. "The Terracotta Lamps." In Gladys Davidson Weinberg, ed., *Excavations at Jalame: Site of a Glass Factory in Late Roman Palestine*, 116–136. Columbia: University of Missouri Press, 1988.

Mack, Burton L. *The Lost Gospel: The Book of Q and Gospel Origins.* San Francisco: HarperSanFrancisco, 1993.

A Myth of Innocence: Mark and Christian Origins. Philadelphia: Fortress Press, 1988.

"Q and a Cynic-Like Jesus." In William E. Arnal and Michel Desjardins, eds., *Whose Historical Jesus?*, 25–36. Waterloo, Ont.: Wilfrid Laurier University Press, 1997.

MacMullen, Ramsay. "The Epigraphic Habit in the Roman Empire." *American Journal of Philology* 103 (1982): 233–246.

"Frequency of Inscriptions in Roman Lydia." *ZPE* 65 (1986): 237–238.

"Provincial Languages in the Roman Empire." In *Changes in the Roman Empire: Essays in the Ordinary*, 32–40. Princeton: Princeton University Press, 1990.

Romanization in the Time of Augustus. New Haven and London: Yale University Press, 2000.

Soldier and Civilian in the Later Roman Empire. Cambridge: Harvard University Press, 1963.

Magness, Jodi. "The Question of the Synagogue: The Problem of Typology." In Alan J. Avery-Peck and Jacob Neusner, eds., *Judaism in Late Antiquity: part 3, vol. 4: The Special Problem of the Synagogue*, 1–48. Leiden: Brill, 2001.

"A Response to Eric M. Meyers and James F. Strange." In Alan J. Avery-Peck and Jacob Neusner, eds., *Judaism in Late Antiquity:*

part 3, vol. 4: The Special Problem of the Synagogue, 79–91. Leiden: Brill, 2001.

"Synagogue Typology and Earthquake Chronology at Khirbet Shema' in Israel." In *Journal of Field Archaeology* 24 (1997): 211–220.

Maisler, B., M. Stekelis, and M. Avi-Yonah. "The Excavations at Beth Yerah (Khirbet el-Kerak) 1944–1946." *IEJ* 2 (1952): 165–173, 218–229.

Manns, Frederic. *Some Weights of the Hellenistic, Roman and Byzantine Periods.* Trans. by Godfrey Kloetzli. Jerusalem: Franciscan Printing Press, 1984.

Mare, W. Harold. "The Artemis Statue Excavated at Abila of the Decapolis in 1994." *ADAJ* 41 (1997): 277–281.

Martin, Dale B. "Paul and the Judaism/Hellenism Dichotomy: Toward a Social History of the Question." In Troels Engberg-Pedersen, ed., *Paul Beyond the Judaism/Hellenism Divide*, 29–61. Louisville, Ken.: Westminster John Knox Press, 2001.

Martínez, Florentino García. "Greek Loanwords in the Copper Scroll." In Florentino García Martínez and Gerard P. Luttikhuizen, eds., *Jerusalem, Alexander, Rome: Studies in Ancient Cultural Interaction in Honour of A. Hilhorst*, 119–145. Leiden and Boston: Brill, 2003.

Marxsen, Willi. *Mark the Evangelist.* Trans. James Boyce et al. Nashville, Abingdon, 1969.

Masterman, E. W. G. "Two Greek Inscriptions from Khurbet Harrawi." *PEQ* 20 (1908): 155–157.

Mattingly, David J. "Being Roman: expressing identity in a provincial setting." *JRA* 17 (2004): 5–25.

"From One Colonialism to Another: Imperialism and the Maghreb." In Jane Webster and Nicholas J. Cooper, eds., *Roman Imperialism: Post-Colonial Perspectives*, 49–69. Leicester: University of Leicester, 1996.

Mattingly, David J. ed. *Dialogues in Roman Imperialism: Power, Discourse, and Discrepant Experience in the Roman Empire.* Portsmouth, R. I.: Journal of Roman Archaeology, 1997.

May, Natalie Naomi. "The Décor of the Korazim Synagogue Reliefs (Summary)." In Ze'ev Yeivin, *The Synagogue at Korazim: The 1962–1964, 1980–1987 Excavations*, 51–54. Jerusalem: Israel Antiquities Authority, 2000.

Mazar, Benjamin. *Beth She'arim*, vol. 1, *The Catacombs 1–4.* New Brunswick: Rutgers University Press, 1973.

Mazar, Gaby and Rachel Bar-Hathan. "The Beth She'an Excavation Project, 1992–1994." *ESI* 17 (1998): 7–38.

McCane, Byron R. *Roll Back the Stone: Death and Burial in the World of Jesus.* Harrisburg: Trinity Press International, 2003.

McLean, B. H. *An Introduction to Greek Epigraphy of the Hellenistic and Roman Periods from Alexander the Great down to the Reign of Constantine (323 BC–AD 337)*. Ann Arbor: The University of Michigan Press, 2002.

McCollough, C. Thomas. "The Roman Theater at Sepphoris: Monumental Statement of Polis at Play." Unpublished paper presented at the ASOR/AAR/SBL Southeastern Regional Meeting, Knoxville, Tenn., March 1998.

McCollough, C. Thomas and Douglas R. Edwards. "Transformations of Space: The Roman Road at Sepphoris." In Douglas R. Edwards and C. Thomas McCollough, eds., *Archaeology and the Galilee: Texts and Contexts in the Graeco-Roman and Byzantine Periods*, 135–142. Atlanta: Scholars Press, 1997.

McCray, C. M. "Jewish Friends and Allies of Rome." *American Numismatic Society Museum Notes* 25 (1980): 53–57.

Meadows, Karen, Chris Lemke and Jo Heron, eds. *TRAC 96: Proceedings of the Sixth Annual Theoretical Roman Archaeology Conference*. Oxford: Oxbow Books, 1997.

Meeks, Wayne A. "Judaism, Hellenism, and the Birth of Christianity." In Troels Engberg-Pedersen, ed., *Paul Beyond the Judaism/Hellenism Divide*, 17–27. Louisville, Ken.: Westminster John Knox Press, 2001.

Meier, John P. *A Marginal Jew*, vol. 1. New York: Doubleday, 1991.

Merker, Gloria S. "The Coins." In Gladys Davidson Weinberg, ed., *Excavations at Jalame: Site of a Glass Factory in Late Roman Palestine*, 103–115. Columbia: University of Missouri Press, 1988.

Meshorer, Ya'akov. *Ancient Jewish Coinage*, 2 vols. Dix Hills, N. Y.: Amphora Books, 1982.

City-Coins of Eretz-Israel and the Decapolis in the Roman Period. Jerusalem: Israel Museum, 1985.

The Coinage of Aelia Capitolina. Jerusalem: Israel Museum, 1989.

"Coins 1968–1986." In Sharon Herbert, ed., *Tel Anafa, I, i: Final Report on Ten Years of Excavation at a Hellenistic and Roman Settlement in Northern Israel*, 241–260. Ann Arbor, Mich.: Kelsey Museum, 1994.

"The Coins of Caesarea Paneas." *INJ* 8 (1984–1985): 37–58.

"Coins of Sepphoris." In Rebecca Martin Nagy, Carol L. Meyers, Eric M. Meyers, and Ze'ev Weiss, eds. *Sepphoris in Galilee: Crosscurrents of Culture*, 195–198. Winona Lake, Ind.: Eisenbrauns, 1996.

"A Hoard of Coins from Migdal." *Atiqot* 11 (1976): 54–71.

"The Lead Weight: Preliminary Report." *BA* 49 (1986): 16–17.

"Market Weight." In Rebecca Martin Nagy, Carol L. Meyers, Eric M. Meyers, and Ze'ev Weiss, eds., *Sepphoris in Galilee: Crosscurrents of Culture*, 201. Winona Lake, Ind.: Eisenbrauns, 1966.

Nabatean Coins. Jerusalem: Hebrew University, 1975.

"Sepphoris and Rome." In O. Mørkholm and N. M. Waggoner, eds. *Greek Numismatics and Archaeology: Essays in Honor of Margaret Thompson*, 159–171. Belgium: Cultura Press, 1979.

A Treasury of Jewish Coins. Jerusalem: Yad Ben Zvi Press; Nyack, N. Y.: Amphora Books, 2001.

Messika, Natalie. "Excavation of the Courthouse Site at 'Akko: The Hellenistic Terracotta Figurines from Areas TB and TC." *Atiqot* 31 (1997): 121–128.

Metzger, Bruce. "The Nazareth Inscription Once Again." In E. E. Ellis and E. Grässer, eds., *Jesus und Paulus: Festschrift für Werner Georg Kümmel zum 70. Geburtstag*, 221–238. Göttingen: Vandenhoeck & Ruprecht, 1975.

Meyers, Carol L., Eric M. Meyers, Ehud Netzer, and Ze'ev Weiss. "The Dionysos Mosaic." In Rebecca Martin Nagy, Carol L. Meyers, Eric M. Meyers, and Ze'ev Weiss, eds., *Sepphoris in Galilee: Crosscurrents of Culture*, 111–116. Winona Lake, Ind.: Eisenbrauns, 1996.

Meyers, Eric M. "Ancient Synagogues: An Archaeological Introduction." In Steven Fine, ed., *Sacred Realm: The Emergence of the Synagogue in the Ancient World*, 3–20. New York and Oxford: Yeshiva University Museum and Oxford University Press, 1996.

"Aspects of Everyday Life in Roman Palestine with Special Reference to Private Domiciles and Ritual Baths." In John R. Bartlett, ed., *Jews in the Hellenistic and Roman Cities*, 193–220. London and New York: Routledge, 2002.

"The Challenge of Hellenism for Early Judaism and Christianity." *BA* 55 (1992): 84–91.

"The Cultural Setting of Galilee: The Case of Regionalism and Early Judaism." In *ANRW* 2.19.1, 686–702.

"The Dating of the Gush Halav Synagogue: A Response to Jodi Magness." In Alan J. Avery-Peck and Jacob Neusner, eds., *Judaism in Late Antiquity: part 3, vol. 4: The Special Problem of the Synagogue*, 49–70. Leiden: Brill, 2001.

"Galilean Regionalism as a Factor in Historical Reconstruction." *BASOR* 221 (1976): 93–101.

"Galilean Regionalism: A Reappraisal." In W. S. Green, ed., *Approaches to Ancient Judaism*, vol. 5, 115–131. Missoula, Mont.: Scholars Press for Brown University, 1978.

"Jesus and his Galilean Context." In Douglas R. Edwards and C. Thomas McCollough, eds., *Archaeology and the Galilee: Texts and Contexts in the Graeco-Roman and Byzantine Periods*, 57–66. Atlanta: Scholars Press, 1997.

"Jewish Art and Architecture in Ancient Palestine (70–235 CE)." In *CHJ*, vol. 4 (in press).
"Jewish Art in the Greco-Roman Period: Were the Hasmonean and Herodian eras Aniconic?" (in press).
"Roman Sepphoris in Light of New Archaeological Evidence and Recent Research." In Lee I. Levine, ed., *The Galilee in Late Antiquity*, 321–338. New York and Jerusalem: The Jewish Theological Seminary of America, 1992.
"Second Temple Studies in the Light of Recent Archaeology: Part I: The Persian and Hellenistic Periods." *CRBS* 2 (1994): 25–42.
"Sepphoris on the Eve of the Great Revolt (67–68 CE): Archaeology and Josephus." In Eric M. Meyers, ed., *Galilee through the Centuries: Confluence of Cultures*, 109–122. Winona Lake, Ind.: Eisenbrauns, 1999.
Meyers, Eric M., A. Thomas Kraabel and James F. Strange. *Ancient Synagogue Excavations at Khirbet Shema' Upper Galilee, Israel, 1970–1972*. Durham, N. C.: Duke University Press, 1976.
Meyers, Eric M., Carol L. Meyers, and James F. Strange, eds. *Excavations at the Ancient Synagogue of Gush Halav: Meiron Excavation Project Reports*, vol. 5. Winona Lake, Ind.: Eisenbrauns, 1990.
Meyers, Eric M., Ehud Netzer, and Carol L. Meyers. "Artistry in Stone: The Mosaics of Ancient Sepphoris." *BA* 50 (1987): 223–231.
Sepphoris. Winona Lake: Eisenbrauns, 1992.
"Sepphoris: Ornament of all Galilee." *BA* 49 (1989): 4–19.
Meyers, Eric M. and James F. Strange. *Archaeology, the Rabbis, and Early Christianity*. Nashville: Abingdon, 1981.
Meyers, Eric M., James F. Strange, and Dennis E. Groh. "The Meiron Excavation Project: Archeological Survey in Galilee and Golan, 1976." *BASOR* 230 (1978): 1–24.
Meyers, Eric M., James F. Strange, and Carol L. Meyers. *Excavations at Ancient Meiron, Upper Galilee, Israel 1971–1972, 1974–1975, 1977*. Cambridge, Mass.: The American Schools of Oriental Research, 1981.
"Preliminary Report on the 1980 Excavations at en-Nabratein, Israel." *BASOR* 244 (1981): 1–25.
"Second Preliminary Report on the 1981 Excavations at en–Nabratein, Israel." *BASOR* 246 (1982): 35–54.
Meyers, Eric M., James F. Strange, Carol L. Meyers, and Richard S. Hanson. "Preliminary Report on the 1977 and 1978 Seasons at Gush Halav (El Jish)." *BASOR* 233 (1979): 33–58.
Mildenberg, Leo. *The Coinage of the Bar Kokhba War*. Aarau: Verlag Sauerländer, 1984.

Millar, Fergus. "Local Cultures in the Roman Empire: Libyan, Punic and Latin in Roman Africa." *JRS* 58 (1965): 126–134.

"The Problem of Hellenistic Syria." In Amélie Kuhrt and Susan Sherwin-White, eds., *Hellenism in the East*, 110–133. Berkeley and Los Angeles: University of California Press, 1987.

"The Roman *Coloniae* of the Near East: A Study of Cultural Relations." In Heikki Solin and Mika Kajava, eds., *Roman Eastern Policy and Other Studies in Roman History*, 7–58. Helsinki: Societas Scientiarum Fennica, 1990.

The Roman Near East: 31 BC–337 CE. Cambridge, Mass. and London: Harvard University Press, 1993.

Millard, Alan R. *Reading and Writing at the Time of Jesus.* New York: New York University Press, 2000.

Miller, Stuart S. *Studies in the History and Traditions of Sepphoris.* Leiden: E. J. Brill, 1984.

Millett, Martin. "Romanization: Historical Issues and Archaeological Interpretation." In Thomas Blagg and Martin Millett, eds., *The Early Roman Empire in the West*, 35–41. Oxford: Oxbow Books, 1990.

The Romanization of Britain: An Essay in Archaeological Interpretation. Cambridge: Cambridge University Press, 1990.

Mitchell, Stephen. "Imperial Building in the Eastern Roman Provinces." *HSCP* 91 (1987): 333–365.

Mor, Menahem. "The Geographical Scope of the Bar Kokhba Revolt." In Peter Schäfer, ed., *The Bar Kokhba War Reconsidered: New Perspectives on the Second Jewish Revolt against Rome*, 107–131. Tübingen: Mohr Siebeck, 2003.

"The Roman Army in Eretz-Israel in the Years AD 70–132." In Philip Freeman & David Kennedy, eds., *The Defence of the Roman & Byzantine East*, vol. 2, 575–602. Oxford: BAR, 1986.

Moxnes, Halvor. "The Construction of Galilee as a Place for the Historical Jesus – Part I." *BTB* 31 (2001): 26–37.

"The Construction of Galilee as a Place for the Historical Jesus – Part II." *BTB* 31 (2001): 64–77.

Mussies, G. "Greek in Palestine and the Diaspora." In S. Safrai and M. Stern with D. Flusser and W. C. van Unnik, eds., *The Jewish People in the First Century*, vol. 1, 1040–1064. Assen/Amsterdam: Van Gorcum, 1976.

"Jewish Personal Names in Some Non-Literary Sources." In Jan Willem van Henten and Pieter Willem van der Horst, eds., *Studies in Early Jewish Epigraphy*, 242–276. Leiden: E. J. Brill, 1994.

Nagy, Rebecca Martin, Carol L. Meyers, Eric M. Meyers, and Ze'ev Weiss, eds. *Sepphoris in Galilee: Crosscurrents of Culture.* Winona Lake, Ind.: Eisenbrauns, 1996.

Naveh, Joseph. "The Aramaic and Hebrew Inscriptions from Ancient Synagogues." *Eretz Israel* 20 (1989): 302–310. (Hebrew)

"Epigraphic Miscellanea." *IEJ* 52 (2002): 240–253.

On Mosaic and Stone: The Aramaic and Hebrew Inscriptions from Ancient Synagogues. Jerusalem: Carta and Israel Exploration Society, 1978. (Hebrew)

Naveh, Joseph and G. D. Weinberg. "Appendix: Inscriptions." In Gladys Davidson Weinberg, ed., *Excavations at Jalame: Site of a Glass Factory in Late Roman Palestine*, 255–256. Columbia: University of Missouri Press, 1988.

Netzer, Ehud. "Architecture in Palaestina Prior to and During the Days of Herod the Great." In Edmund Buchner et al., eds., *Akten des XIII internationalen Kongresses für klassische Archäologie: Berlin 1988*, 37–50. Mainz: Verlag Philipp von Zabern, 1990.

Hasmonean and Herodian Palaces at Jericho: Final Reports of the 1973–1987 Excavations, vol. 1. Jerusalem: Israel Exploration Society and Institute of Archaeology, 2001.

"Herodian bath-houses." In J. De Laine and D. E. Mohnston, eds., *Roman Baths and Bathing*, 45–55. Portsmouth, R. I.: Journal of Roman Archaeology, 1999.

"The Herodian Triclinia – A Prototype for the 'Galilean-Type' Synagogue." In Lee. I. Levine, ed., *Ancient Synagogues Revealed*, 49–51. Jerusalem: Israel Exploration Society; Detroit: Wayne State University Press, 1982.

The Palaces of the Hasmoneans and Herod the Great. Jerusalem: Yad Ben-Zvi Press, Israel Exploration Society, 2001.

"The Synagogues from the Second Temple Period according to Archaeological Finds and in Light of the Literary Sources." In G. Claudio Bottini, Leah Di Segni and L. Daniel Chrupcala, eds., *One Land – Many Cultures: Archaeological Studies in Honour of Stanislao Loffreda*, 277–285. Jerusalem: Franciscan Printing Press, 2003.

Newby, Zaphra. "Art and Identity in Asia Minor." In Sarah Scott and Jane Webster, eds., *Roman Imperialism and Provincial Art*, 192–213. Cambridge: Cambridge University Press, 2003.

Nielsen, Inge. "Early Provincial Baths and their Relations to Early Italic Baths." In J. De Laine and D. E. Mohnston, eds., *Roman Baths and Bathing*, 35–43. Portsmouth, R. I.: Journal of Roman Archaeology, 1999.

Thermae et Balnea: The Architecture and Cultural History of Roman Public Baths, 2 vols. Aarhus: Aarhus University Press, 1993.

Oleson, John Peter et al. *The Harbours of Caesarea Maritima*, 2 vols. Oxford: BAR, 1989, 1994.

Oppenheimer, Aharon. "Roman Rule and the Cities of the Galilee in Talmudic Literature." In Lee I. Levine, ed., *The Galilee in Late*

Antiquity, 115–139. New York and Jerusalem: The Jewish Theological Seminary of America, 1992.

Ovadiah, Asher. "A Jewish Sarcophagus at Tiberias." *IEJ* 22 (1972): 229–232.

"Observations on the Origin of the Architectural Plan of Ancient Synagogues." In Asher Ovadiah, *Art and Archaeology in Israel and Neighbouring Countries*, 77–86. London: Pindar Press, 2002.

Ovadiah, Asher and Sonia Mucznik. "Classical Heritage and Anti-Classical Trends in the Mosaic Pavement of Lydda (Lod)." *Assaph (B)* 3 (1998): 1–15.

"Orpheus Mosaics in the Roman and Early Byzantine Periods." In Asher Ovadiah, *Art and Archaeology in Israel and Neighbouring Countries*, 528–548. London: Pindar Press, 2002.

Ovadiah, Asher, and Y. Turnheim. "Dionysos in Beth Shean." In Asher Ovadiah, *Art and Archaeology in Israel and Neighbouring Countries*, 203–226. London: Pindar Press, 2002.

"The Female Figure in the Dionysiac Mosaic at Sepphoris." In Asher Ovadiah, *Art and Archaeology in Israel and Neighbouring Countries*, 349–373. London: Pindar Press, 2002.

Ovadiah, Ruth and Asher Ovadiah. *Hellenistic, Roman, and Early Byzantine Mosaic Pavements in Israel*. Rome: Lerva di Bretschneider, 1987.

Overman, J. Andrew. "Recent Advances in the Archaeology of the Galilee in the Roman Period." *CRBS* 1 (1993): 35–57.

"Who Were the First Urban Christians? Urbanization in Galilee in the First Century." In J. David Lull, ed., *SBLSP 1988*, 160–168. Atlanta: Scholars Press, 1988.

Overman, J. Andrew, Jack Olive, and Michael Nelson. "Discovering Herod's Shrine to Augustus: Mystery Temple Found at Omrit." *BAR* 29:2 (2003): 40–49, 67–68.

Parca, Maryline. "Local Languages and Native Cultures." In John Bodel, ed., *Epigraphic Evidence: Ancient History from Inscriptions*, 57–72. London: Routledge, 2001.

Parker, H. M. D. *The Roman Legions*. Oxford: Clarendon Press, 1928.

Peleg, Yifat. "Gender and Ossuaries." *BASOR* 325 (2002): 65–73.

Peppard, Michael L. "Personal Names and Ethnicity in Late Ancient Galilee: The Data from Beth She'arim." In H. W. Attridge, D. B. Martin, and J. Zangenberg, eds., *Religion, Ethnicity, and Identity in Ancient Galilee*. Tübingen: Mohr Siebeck (in press).

Pestman, P. W. et al. *A Guide to the Zenon Archive*, 2 vols. Leiden: E. J. Brill, 1981.

Piccirillo, Michele. *The Mosaics of Jordan*. Ammon: American Center of Oriental Research, 1993.

Porat, Pinhas. "A Fragmentary Greek Inscription from Tel Jezreel." *TA* 24 (1997): 167–168.

Porath, Y. "Herod's 'Amphitheatre' at Caesarea: a Multipurpose Entertainment Building." In J. H. Humphrey, *The Roman and Byzantine Near East: Some Recent Archaeological Research*), 15–27. Ann Arbor, Mich.: Journal of Roman Archaeology, 1995.

Porter, Adam. "Amathus: Gabinius' Capital in Peraea?" *JJS* 50 (1999): 223–229.

"Transjordanian Jews in the Greco-Roman Period: A Literary-Historical Examination of Jewish Habitation East of the Jordan River from its Biblical Roots through the Bar-Kochba Revolt." Ph. D. Dissertation, Duke University, 1999.

Porter, Stanley E., ed. *Diglossia and Other Topics in New Testament Linguistics*. Sheffield: Sheffield Academic Press, 2000.

"Jesus and the Use of Greek in Galilee." In Bruce Chilton and Craig A. Evans, eds., *Studying the Historical Jesus: Evaluations of the State of Current Research*, 123–154. Leiden: E. J. Brill, 1994.

Qedar, Shraga. "The Coins of Marisa: A New Mint." *INJ* 12 (1993): 27–33.

"Two Lead Weights of Herod Antipas and Agrippa II and the Early History of Tiberias." *INJ* 9 (1986–1987): 29–35.

Raban, Avner. "The Boat from Migdal Nunia and the Anchorages of the Sea of Galilee from the Time of Jesus." *International Journal of Nautical Archaeology and Underwater Exploration* 17 (1988): 311–329.

Raban, Avner and Kenneth G. Holum, eds. *Caesarea Maritima: A Retrospective after Two Millenia*. Leiden: E. J. Brill, 1996.

Rabin, Ch. "Hebrew and Aramaic in the First Century." In S. Safrai et al., eds., *The Jewish People in the First Century*, vol. 1, 1007–1039. Assen/Amsterdam: Van Gorcum, 1976.

Rahmani, L. Y. *A Catalogue of Jewish Ossuaries in the Collections of the State of Israel*. Jerusalem: Israel Antiquities Authority, Israel Academy of Science and Humanities, 1994.

A Catalogue of Roman and Byzantine Lead Coffins from Israel. Jerusalem: Israel Antiquities Authority, 1999.

"Miscellanea – Roman to Medieval." *Atiqot* 14 (1980): 103–113.

Rajak, Tessa. "Hasmonean Kingship and the Invention of Tradition." In Per Bilde, Troels Engberg-Pedersen, Lise Hannestad, and Jan Zahle, eds., *Aspects of Hellenistic Kingship*, 99–115. Aarhus, Denmark: Aarhus University Press, 1996.

"The Hasmoneans and the Uses of Hellenism." In Philip R. Davies and Richard T. White, eds., *A Tribute to Geza Vermes: Essays on Jewish and Christian Literature and History*, 261–280. JSOT Supplement Series 100, Sheffield: JSOT Press, 1990.

"Judaism and Hellenism Revisited." In *The Jewish Dialogue with Greece and Rome: Studies in Cultural and Social Interaction*, 1–11. Leiden: Brill, 2001.

"Justus of Tiberias." *Classical Quarterly* 23 (1973): 345–368.

Rappaport, Uriel. "Numismatics." In *CHJ*, vol. 1, 25–59.

Raynor, Joyce. "Numismatics." In Eric M. Meyers, Carol L. Meyers, and James F. Strange, *Excavations at the Ancient Synagogue of Gush Halav*, 230–245. Winona Lake, Ind.: Eisenbrauns, 1990.

Raynor, Joyce and Ya'akov Meshorer, with Richard Simon Hanson. *The Coins of Ancient Meiron*. Winona Lake, Ind: ASOR, Eisenbrauns, 1988.

Rea, J. R. "The Legio II Traiana in Judaea?" *ZPE* 38 (1980): 220–221.

Reed, Jonathan L. *Archaeology and the Galilean Jesus: A Re-Examination of the Evidence*. Harrisburg, Penn.: Trinity Press International, 2000.

"The Social Map of Q." In John S. Kloppenborg, ed., *Conflict and Invention: Literary, Rhetorical, and Social Studies on the Sayings Gospel Q*, 17–36. Valley Forge: Trinity Press International, 1995.

"Stone Vessels and Gospel Texts: Purity and Socio-Economics in John 2." In Jürgen Zangenberg and Stefan Alkier, eds., *Zeichen aus Text und Stein: Studien auf den Weg zu einer Archäologie des Neuen Testaments*, 381–401. Tübingen and Basel: A. Francke Verlag, 2003.

Reich, Ronny. "The Bet Yerah 'Synagogue' Reconsidered." *Atiqot* 22 (1993): 137–144.

"The Hot Bath-House (*balneum*), the Miqweh, and the Jewish Community in the Second Temple Period." *JJS* 39 (1988): 102–107.

"A Note on the Roman Mosaic at Magdala on the Sea of Galilee." *LA* 41 (1991): 455–458.

Retzleff, Alexandra. "Near Eastern Theatres in Late Antiquity." *Phoenix* 57 (2003): 115–138.

Reynolds, Joyce. "Cities." In David Braund, ed., *The Administration of the Roman Empire: 241 BC–AD 193*, 15–51. Exeter: University of Exeter, 1988.

Richardson, Peter. *Building Jewish in the Roman East*. Waco: Baylor University Press, 2004.

City and Sanctuary: Religion and Architecture in the Roman Near East. London: SCM Press, 2002.

Herod: King of the Jews and Friend of the Romans. Columbia: University of South Carolina Press, 1996.

"Towards a Typology of Levantine/Palestinian Houses." *JSNT* 27 (2004): 47–68.

Rizakis, D., ed. *Roman Onomastics in the Greek East: Social and Political Aspects: Proceedings of the International Colloquium on Roman Onomastics, Athens, 7–9 September, 1993*. Athens: Research Centre for Greek and Roman Antiquity, National Hellenic Research Foundation, 1996.

Robinson, James M. "History of Q Research." In James M. Robinson, Paul Hoffmann, and John S. Kloppenborg, eds., *The Critical Edition of Q*, xix–lxxi. Minneapolis: Fortress Press; Leuven: Peeters Publishers, 2000.

Roller, Duane W. *The Building Program of Herod the Great.* Berkeley: University of California Press, 1998.

Rosén, Haiim B. "Palestinian KOINH in Rabbinic Illustration." *JSS* 8 (1963): 56–73.

Rosenberger, M. *City-Coins of Palestine*, 3 vols. Jerusalem, 1972–1977.

Rosenthal, Renate. "Late Roman and Byzantine Bone Carvings from Palestine." *IEJ* 26 (1976): 96–103.

Rosenthal-Heginbottom, Renate. "Stamped Jar Handles and Terracotta Fragments." In A. Ben-Tor, M. Avissar, Y. Portugali, et al., *Yoqne'am I: The Late Periods*, 60–65. Jerusalem: Israel Exploration Society, 1996.

Roth-Gerson, Lea. *Greek Inscriptions from the Synagogues in Eretz Israel.* Jerusalem: Ben Zvi Institute, 1987. (Hebrew)

Rotloff, Andrea. "Gamla – Das Masada des Nordens?" In Gabriele Faßbeck, Sandra Fortner, Andrea Rottloff, and Jürgen Zangenberg, eds., *Leben am See Gennesaret*, 110–117. Mainz am Rhein: Phillip von Zabern, 2003.

Roussin, Lucille A. "The Birds and Fishes Mosaic." In Rebecca Martin Nagy, Carol L. Meyers, Eric M. Meyers, and Zeev Weiss, eds., *Sepphoris in Galilee: Crosscurrents of Culture*, 123–125. Winona Lake, Ind.: Eisenbrauns, 1996.

Rowe, Alan. *The Topography and History of Beth-Shan.* Philadelphia: University of Pennsylvania Press, 1930.

Rutgers, Leonard Victor. "Incense Shovels at Sepphoris." In Eric M. Meyers, ed., *Galilee through the Centuries: Confluence of Cultures*, 177–198. Winona Lake, Ind.: Eisenbrauns, 1999.

The Jews in Late Ancient Rome: Evidence of Cultural Interaction in the Roman Diaspora. Leiden: E. J. Brill, 1995.

"Recent Trends in the Study of Ancient Diaspora Judaism." In *The Hidden Heritage of Diaspora Judaism*, 15–44. 2nd edn. Leuven: Peeters, 1998.

Saddington, D. B. "The Development of the Roman Military and Administrative Personnel in the New Testament." In *ANRW* 2.26.3, 2409–2435.

The Development of the Roman Auxiliary Forces from Caesar to Vespasian (49 BC–AD 79). Harare: University of Zimbabwe, 1982.

Safrai, Ze'ev. *The Economy of Roman Palestine.* London and New York: Routledge, 1994.

"The Roman Army in the Galilee." In Lee I. Levine, ed., *The Galilee in Late Antiquity*, 103–114. New York and Jerusalem: The Jewish Theological Seminary of America, 1992.

Saldarini, Anthony J. "The Gospel of Matthew and Jewish-Christian Conflict in the Galilee." In Lee I. Levine, ed., *The Galilee in Late Antiquity*, 23–38. New York and Jerusalem: The Jewish Theological Seminary of America, 1992.

Salomies, Olli. "Names and Identities: Onomastics and Prosopography." In John Bodel, ed., *Epigraphic Evidence: Ancient History from Inscriptions*, 73–86. London: Routledge, 2001.

Sanders, E. P. *The Historical Figure of Jesus*. London: Allen Lane, Penguin Press, 1993.

"Jesus in Historical Context." *Theology Today* 50 (1993): 429–448.

"Jesus' Galilee." In Ismo Dundergerg, Kari Syreeni, and Christopher Tuckett, eds., *Fair Play: Diversity and Conflicts in Early Christianity: Essays in Honour of Heikki Räisänen*, 3–41. Leiden: Brill, 2002.

Jewish Law from Jesus to the Mishnah. London: SCM Press, Philadelphia: Trinity Press International, 1990.

Judaism: Practice and Belief: 63 BCE – 66 CE. London: SCM Press; Philadelphia: Trinity Press International, 1992.

Sandmel, Samuel. "Palestinian and Hellenistic Judaism and Christianity: The Question of the Comfortable Theory." *HUCA* 50 (1979): 137–148.

Sartre, Maurice. "Les Progres de la citoyennete romaine dans les provinces romaines de Syrie et d'Arabie sous le haut–Empire." In D. Rizakis ed., *Roman Onomastics in the Greek East: Social and Political Aspects: Proceedings of the International Colloquium on Roman Onomastics, Athens, 7–9 September, 1993*, 239–250. Athens: Research Centre for Greek and Roman Antiquity, National Hellenic Research Foundation, 1996.

Sawicki, Marianne. *Crossing Galilee: Architectures of Contact in the Occupied Land of Jesus*. Harrisburg, Penn.: Trinity Press International, 2000.

Schäfer, Peter, ed. *The Talmud Yerushalmi and Graeco-Roman Culture*, 3 vols. Tübingen: Mohr Siebeck, 1998–2002.

Schumacher, G. *Tell El Mutesellim*, 2 vols. Leipzig, 1908.

Schürer, Emil. *The History of the Jewish People in the Age of Jesus Christ*. Rev. and ed. by Geza Vermes, Fergus Millar and Matthew Black, 3 vols. Edinburgh: T & T Clark, 1973–1987.

Schwabe, Moshe and Baruch Lifshitz. *Beth She'arim*, vol. 2, *The Greek Inscriptions*. New Brunswick: Rutgers University Press, 1974.

Schwartz, Joshua J. "Archeology and the City." In Daniel Sperber, *The City in Roman Palestine*, 149–187. New York and Oxford: Oxford University Press, 1998.

Schwartz, Seth. *Imperialism and Jewish Society, 200 BCE to 640 CE*. Princeton and Oxford: Princeton University Press, 2001.

"Language, Power and Identity in Ancient Palestine." *Past and Present* 148 (1995): 3–47.

"The Rabbi in Aphrodite's Bath: Palestinian Society and Jewish Identity in the High Roman Empire." In Simon Goldhill, ed., *Being Greek under Rome: Cultural Identity, the Second Sophistic and the Development of Empire*, 335–361. Cambridge: Cambridge University Press, 2001.

Scott, Sarah and Jane Webster, eds. *Roman Imperialism and Provincial Art.* Cambridge: Cambridge University Press, 2003.

Seagar, Robin. *Pompey the Great: A Political Biography*, 2nd edn., 53–62. Oxford: Blackwell, 2002.

Segal, Arthur. "Imperial Architecture in the Roman East: The Local and the Unique." *Assaph (B)* 8 (2001): 31–48.

From Function to Monument. Oxford: Oxbow Press, 1997.

"Theaters." *OEANE*, vol. 5, 199–203.

Theatres in Roman Palestine and Provincia Arabia. Leiden: E. J. Brill, 1995.

Sevenster, J. N. *Do You Know Greek? How Much Greek Could the First Jewish Christians Have Known?* Leiden: E. J. Brill, 1968.

Seyrig, Henri. "Irenopolis-Neronias-Sepphoris." *Numismatic Chronicle* 10 (1950): 284–289.

"Irenopolis-Neronias-Sepphoris: An Additional Note." *Numismatic Chronicle* 15 (1955): 157–159.

"Le monnayage de Ptolémaïs en Phénicie." *Revue Numismatique* [1962]: 25–50.

Shachar, Ilan. "The Historical and Numismatic Significance of Alexander Jannaeus's Later Coinage as found in Archaeological Excavations." *PEQ* 136 (2004): 5–33.

Shahar, Yuval. "The Underground Hideouts in Galilee and their Historical Meaning." In Peter Schäfer, ed., *The Bar Kokhba War Reconsidered: New Perspectives on the Second Jewish Revolt against Rome*, 217–240. Tübingen: Mohr Siebeck, 2003.

Shatzman, Israel. *The Armies of the Hasmonaeans and Herod: From Hellenistic to Roman Frameworks.* Tübingen: J. C. B. Mohr (Paul Siebeck), 1991.

Sherwin-White, A. N. *Roman Foreign Policy in the East, 168 BC to AD 1.* Norman: University of Oklahoma Press, 1983.

Shinan, Avigdor. "The Aramaic Targum as a Mirror of Galilean Jewry." In Lee I. Levine, ed., *The Galilee in Late Antiquity*, 241–247. New York and Jerusalem: The Jewish Theological Seminary of America, 1992.

Shroder, Jr., John F. and Moshe Inbar. "Geological and Geographic Background to the Bethsaida Excavations." In Rami Arav and Richard A. Freund, eds., *Bethsaida: A City by the North Shore of the*

Sea of Galilee, vol. 1, 65–98. Kirksville, Mo.: Thomas Jefferson University Press, 1995.

Siegelmann, Ayriel. "The Identification of Gaba Hippeon." *PEQ* 116 (1984–1985): 89–93.

Skupinska-Løvset, Ilona. "Funerary Busts from Tell El-Hammam." *Atiqot* 29 (1996): 35–41.

Funerary Portraiture of Roman Palestine: An Analysis of the Production in its Culture-Historical Context. Gothenburg: Paul Åströms, 1983.

Portraiture in Roman Syria: A Study in Social and Regional Differentiation within the Art of Portraiture. Lodz: Wydawnictwo Uniwersytetu Lodzkiego, 1999.

Slane, Kathleen Warner. "The Fine Wares." In Sharon Herbert, ed., *Tel Anafa II, i: The Hellenistic and Roman Pottery*, 247–418. Ann Arbor, Mich.: Kelsey Museum; Columbia, Mo.: Museum of Art and Archaeology of the University of Missouri, 1997.

Slin, Hédi. "Dionysus." In Michèle Blanchard-Lemée, ed., *Mosaics of Roman Africa: Floor Mosaics from Tunisia*, 87–119. New York: George Braziller, 1996.

Slofstra, Jan. "An Anthropological Approach to the Study of Romanization." In Roel Brandt and Jan Slofstra, eds., *Roman and Native in the Low Countries: Spheres of Interaction*, 71–104. Oxford: B. A. R., 1983.

Smallwood, E. Mary. *The Jews under Roman Rule.* Leiden: E. J. Brill, 1976.

Smith, Mark D. "A Tale of Two Julias: Julia, Julias, and Josephus." In Rami Arav and Richard A. Freund, eds., *Bethsaida: A City by the North Shore of the Sea of Galilee*, vol. 2, 333–346. Kirksville, Mo.: Truman State University Press, 1999.

Smith, Robert Houston. *Pella of the Decapolis*, 2 vols. Wooster, Ohio: The College of Wooster, 1973.

Smith, Robert H. and Anthony W. McNicoll. "The 1982 and 1983 Seasons at Pella of the Decapolis." *BASOR Supplement* 24 (1985): 21–50.

Smith, R. R. R. "Cultural Choice and Political Identity in Honorific Portrait Statues in the Greek East in the Second Century AD." *JRS* 88 (1988): 56–93.

Spaer, Arnold. "A Hoard of Alexander Tetradrachms from Galilee." *INJ* 3 (1965–1966): 1–7.

Speidel, Michael P. "The Roman Army in Arabia." In *ANRW* 2.8, 687–730.

"The Roman Army in Judaea under the Procurators: The Italian and the Augustan Cohort in the Acts of the Apostles." *Ancient Society* 13–14 (1982–1983): 233–240.

Sperber, Daniel. *The City in Roman Palestine.* New York and Oxford: Oxford University Press, 1998.

A Dictionary of Greek & Latin Legal Terms in Rabbinic Literature. Ramat-Gan: Bar-Ilan University Press, 1982.

Essays on Greek and Latin in the Mishna, Talmud and Midrashic Literature. Jerusalem: Makor Publishing, 1982.

Roman Palestine 200–400: Money and Prices. Ramat-Gan: Bar-Ilan University, 1974.

Spijkerman, Augustus. *Cafarnao: Catalogo delle Monete della Città.* Jerusalem: Franciscan Printing Press, 1975.

The Coins of the Decapolis and Provincia Arabia. Jerusalem: Franciscan Printing Press, 1978.

Steffy, J. Richard and Shelley Wachsmann. "The Migdal Boat Mosaic." *Atiqot* 19 (1990): 115–118.

Stepanski, Yossi and Emanuel Damati. "Greek Funerary Inscriptions from Eastern Galilee." *ESI* 9 (1989/1990): 79.

Stern, Ephraim. *Archaeology of the Land of the Bible*, vol. 2, *The Assyrian, Babylonian, and Persian Periods, 732–332 BCE.* New York: Doubleday, 2001.

"Between Persia and Greece: Trade, Administration and Warfare in the Persian and Hellenistic Periods (539–63 BCE)." In Thomas E. Levy, ed., *The Archaeology of Society in the Holy Land*, 432–445. New York: Facts on File, 1995.

Material Culture of the Land of the Bible in the Persian Period, 538–332 BC. Warminster: Aris & Phillips; Jerusalem: Israel Exploration Society, 1982.

Strange, James F. "Archaeology and the Religion of Judaism in Palestine." *ANRW* 2.19.1, 646–685.

"The Eastern Basilical Building." In Rebecca Martin Nagy, Carol L. Meyers, Eric M. Meyers, and Ze'ev Weiss, eds., *Sepphoris in Galilee: Crosscurrents of Culture*, 117–121. Winona Lake, Ind.: Eisenbrauns, 1996.

"First-Century Galilee from Archaeology and from the Texts." In Eugene H. Lovering, Jr., ed., *SBLSP 1994*, 81–90. Atlanta: Scholars Press, 1994.

"Josephus on Galilee and Sepphoris." Paper delivered at the Josephus Seminar of the National Society for Biblical Literature Meeting, Denver, Col., November, 2001.

"Six Campaigns at Sepphoris: The University of South Florida Excavations, 1983–1989." In Lee I. Levine, ed., *The Galilee in Late Antiquity*, 339–356. New York and Jerusalem: The Jewish Theological Seminary of America, 1992.

"Some Implications of Archaeology for New Testament Studies." In James H. Charlesworth and Walter P. Weaver, eds., *What has*

Archaeology to do with Faith?, 23–59. Philadelphia: Trinity Press International, 1992.

"Synagogue Typology and Khirbet Shema': A Response to Jodi Magness." In Alan J. Avery-Peck and Jacob Neusner, eds., *Judaism in Late Antiquity: part 3, vol. 4: The Special Problem of the Synagogue*, 71–78. Leiden: Brill, 2001.

Strickert, Fred. *Bethsaida: Home of the Apostles.* Collegeville, Minn: Liturgical Press, 1989.

"The Coins of Philip." In Rami Arav and Richard A. Freund, eds., *Bethsaida: A City by the North Shore of the Sea of Galilee*, vol. 1, 165–189. Kirksville, Mo.: Thomas Jefferson University Press, 1995.

Sukenik, L. "The Ancient City of Philoteria (Beth Yerah)." *JPOS* 2 (1922): 101–107.

Sussman, Varda. "Caesarea Illuminated by its Lamps." In Avner Raban and Kenneth G. Holum, eds., *Caesarea Maritima: A Retrospective after Two Millenia*, 346–358. Leiden: E. J. Brill, 1996.

Sutherland, C. H. V. "The Pattern of Monetary Development in Phoenicia and Palestine during the Early Empire." In Arie Kindler, ed., *The Patterns of Monetary Development in Phoenicia and Palestine during Antiquity*, 88–105. Tel Aviv: Schocken, 1967.

Syon, Danny. "The Coins from Burial Caves D and E at Hurfeish." In Zvi Gal, *Eretz Zafon: Studies in Galilean Archaeology*, 167–175. Jerusalem: Israel Antiquities Authority, 2002.

"The Coins from Gamala: Interim Report." *INJ* 12 (1992–1993): 34–55.

"Coins from the Excavations at Khirbet esh-Shuhara." In Zvi Gal, *Eretz Zafon: Studies in Galilean Archaeology*, 181. Jerusalem: Israel Antiquities Authority, 2002.

Syon, Danny and Moshe Hartal. "A New Tetrarchic Boundary Stone." *SCI* 22 (2003): 233–239.

Syon, Danny and Zvi Yavor. "Gamla 1997–2000." *HA* 114 (2002): 2–4.

Talgam, R., and Z. Weiss. *The Mosaics of the House of Dionysos at Sepphoris: Excavated by E. M. Meyers, E. Netzer, and C. L. Meyers.* Jerusalem: Hebrew University, 2004.

Tcherikover, Victor. *Hellenistic Civilization and the Jews.* Philadelphia and Jerusalem: Jewish Publication Society of America, 1959. Reprint, Peabody, Mass.: Hendrickson, 1999.

Tsafrir, Yoram. "Numismatics and the Foundation of Aelia Capitolina: A Critical Review." In Peter Schäfer, ed., *The Bar Kokhba War Reconsidered: New Perspectives on the Second Jewish Revolt against Rome*, 31–36. Tübingen: Mohr Siebeck, 2003.

Tsafrir, Yoram, Leah Di Segni, and Judith Green. *Tabula Imperii Romani: Iudaea, Palaestina: Eretz Israel in the Hellenistic, Roman, and*

Byzantine Periods. Jerusalem: Israel Academy of Sciences and Humanities, 1994.

Tsafrir, Yoram and Gideon Foerster. "Urbanism at Scythopolis-Beth Shean in the Fourth–Seventh Century." *Dumbarton Oaks Papers* 51 (1997): 85–146.

Tsuk, Tsvika. "An Aqueduct to Legio." In David Amit, Joseph Patrich, and Yizhar Hirschfeld, eds., *The Aqueducts of Israel,* 409–411. Portsmouth, R. I.: Journal of Roman Archaeology, 2002.

"The Aqueduct to Legio and the Location of the Camp of the VIth Roman Legion." *TA* 15–16 (1988–1989): 92–97.

"The Aqueducts to Sepphoris." In David Amit, Joseph Patrich, and Yizhar Hirschfeld, eds., *The Aqueducts of Israel,* 279–294. Portsmouth, R. I.: Journal of Roman Archaeology, 2002.

Tuckett, Christopher M. *Q and the History of Early Christianity.* Edinburgh: T & T Clark, 1996.

Turnheim, Yehudit. "Nilotic Motifs and the Exotic in Roman and Early Byzantine Eretz Israel." *Assaph (B)* 7 (2002): 17–40.

Tzaferis, Vassilios. "Cults and Deities Worshiped at Caesarea Philippi-Banias." In Eugene Ulrich et al., eds., *Priests, Prophets, and Scribes,* 190–204. Sheffield: Sheffield Academic Press, 1992.

"A Roman Bath at Rama." *Atiqot* 14 (1980): 66–75.

Tzori, N. "An Inscription of the Legio VI Ferrata from the Northern Jordan Valley." *IEJ* 21 (1971): 554.

Vaage, Leif E. *Galilean Upstarts: Jesus' First Followers According to Q.* Valley Forge: Trinity Press International, 1994.

Van der Horst, Pieter W. "Greek in Jewish Palestine in Light of Jewish Epigraphy." In John J. Collins and Gregory E. Sterling, eds., *Hellenism in the Land of Israel,* 154–174. Notre Dame, Ind.: University of Notre Dame Press, 2001.

van Dommelen, Peter. "Colonial Constructs: Colonialism and Archaeology in the Mediterranean." *WA* 28:3 (1997): 305–323.

Vanderkam, James C. "Greek at Qumran." In John J. Collins and Gregory E. Sterling, eds., *Hellenism in the Land of Israel,* 175–181. Notre Dame, Ind.: University of Notre Dame Press, 2001.

Vermes, Geza. *Jesus the Jew.* Philadelphia: Fortress Press, 1975.

Vitto, Fanny. "Byzantine Mosaics at Bet She'arim: New Evidence for the History of the Site." *Atiqot* 28 (1996): 115–146.

"Two Marble Heads of Goddesses from Tel Naharon-Scythopolis." *Atiqot* 20 (1991): 33–45.

Ward-Perkins, J. B. *Roman Imperial Architecture.* Middlesex: Penguin, 1981.

Waterman, Leroy. *Preliminary Report of the University of Michigan Excavations at Sepphoris, Palestine, in 1931.* Ann Arbor: University of Michigan Press, 1937.

272   *Select bibliography*

Weber, Thomas. "A Survey of Roman Sculptures in the Decapolis: Preliminary Report." *ADAJ* 34 (1990): 351–352.
    Umm Qeis, Gadara of the Decapolis. Amman: Al Kutba, 1990.
Webster, Jane. "Art as Resistance and Negotiation." In Sarah Scott and Jane Webster, eds., *Roman Imperialism and Provincial Art*, 24–52. Cambridge: Cambridge University Press, 2003.
    "Creolizing the Roman Provinces." *AJA* 105 (2001): 209–225.
    "Necessary Comparisons: A Post-Colonial Approach to Religious Syncretism in the Roman Provinces." *WA* 28:3 (1997): 324–338.
    "Roman Imperialism and the 'Post Imperial Age.'" In Jane Webster and Nicholas J. Cooper, eds., *Roman Imperialism: Post–Colonial Perspectives*, 1–17. Leicester Archaeology Monographs No. 3, Leicester: University of Leicester, 1996.
Weinberg, Gladys Davidson, ed. *Excavations at Jalame: Site of a Glass Factory in Late Roman Palestine.* Columbia: University of Missouri Press, 1988.
Weinberg, Saul S. "The Buildings and Installations." In Gladys Davidson Weinberg, ed. *Excavations at Jalame: Site of a Glass Factory in Late Roman Palestine*, 5–23. Columbia: University of Missouri Press, 1988.
    "Tel Anafa: The Hellenistic Town." *IEJ* 21 (1971): 86–109.
Weiss, Ze'ev. "Adopting a Novelty: The Jews and the Roman Games in Palestine." In J. H. Humphrey, ed., *The Roman and Byzantine Near East*, vol. 2, 23–50. Portsmouth, R. I.: Journal of Roman Archaeology, 1999.
    "Buildings for Entertainment." In Daniel Sperber, *The City in Roman Palestine*, 77–91. New York and Oxford: Oxford University Press, 1998.
    "Greco-Roman Influences on the Art and Architecture of the Jewish City in Roman Palestine." In Hayim Lapin, ed., *Religious and Ethnic Communities in Late Roman Palestine*, 219–246. Baltimore: University Press of Maryland, 1998.
    "Social Aspects of Burial in Beth She'arim: Archaeological Finds and Talmudic Sources." In Lee I. Levine, ed., *The Galilee in Late Antiquity*, 357–372. New York and Jerusalem: The Jewish Theological Seminary of America, 1992.
    "Zippori – 1997." *HA* 109 (1999): 16–18.
    "Zippori 1999." *HA* 112 (2000): 21–23.
    "Zippori 2000." *HA* 113 (2001): 25–27.
    "Zippori 2001." *HA* 114 (2002): 23–24.
Weiss, Ze'ev and Ehud Netzer. "Architectural Development of Sepphoris during the Roman and Byzantine Periods." In Douglas R. Edwards

and C. Thomas McCollough, eds., *Archaeology and the Galilee: Texts and Contexts in the Graeco–Roman and Byzantine Periods*, 117–130. Atlanta: Scholars Press, 1997.

"Hellenistic and Roman Sepphoris: The Archaeological Evidence." In Rebecca Martin Nagy, Carol L. Meyers, Eric M. Meyers, and Ze'ev Weiss, eds., *Sepphoris in Galilee: Crosscurrents of Culture*, 29–37. Winona Lake, Ind.: Eisenbrauns, 1996.

"Zippori – 1994–1995." *ESI* 18 (1998): 22–27.

Welles, C. B. "The Inscriptions." In Carl H. Kraeling, ed., *Gerasa: City of the Decapolis*, 355–496. New Haven: American Schools of Oriental Research, 1938.

Westermann, William Linn, Clinton Walker Keyes, and Herbert Liebesny. *Zenon Papyri: Business Papers of the Third Century BC Dealing with Palestine and Egypt*. New York: Columbia University Press, 1940.

Whittaker, C. R. "Imperialism and Culture: The Roman Initiative." In D. J. Mattingly, ed., *Dialogues in Roman Imperialism: Power, Discourse, and Discrepant Experience in the Roman Empire*, 143–163. Portsmouth, R. I.: Journal of Roman Archaeology, 1997.

Wiedemann, Thomas. *Emperors and Gladiators*. London and New York: Routledge, 1992.

Williams, Margaret H. "Palestinian Jewish Personal Names in 'Acts'." In Richard Bauckham, ed., *The Book of Acts in its Palestinian Setting*, 79–113. Grand Rapids, Mich.: Eerdmans, 1995.

Wilson, John F. "The Bronze and Silver Coins." In Vassilios Tzaferis, ed., *Excavations at Capernaum: Volume I: 1978–1982*, 139–143. Winona Lake, Ind.: Eisenbrauns, 1989.

Caesarea Philippi: Banias, The Lost City of Pan. London and New York: I. B. Tauris, 2004.

Wilson, John F. and Vassilios Tzaferis. "Banias Dig Reveals King's Palace." *BAR* 24:1 (1998): 54–61, 85.

Wineland, John Dennis. *Ancient Abila: An Archaeological History*. Oxford: BAR, 2001.

Winogradov, Zalmon S. "The Aqueduct of Tiberias." In David Amit, Joseph Patrich, and Yizhar Hirschfeld, eds., *The Aqueducts of Israel*, 295–304. Portsmouth, R. I.: Journal of Roman Archaeology, 2002.

Woolf, Greg. *Becoming Roman: The Origins of Provincial Civilization in Gaul*. Cambridge: Cambridge University Press, 1998.

"Beyond Romans and Natives." *WA* 28 (1997): 339–350.

"Monumental Writing and the Expansion of Roman Society in the Early Empire." *JRS* 85 (1995): 214–235.

Yegül, Fikret. *Baths and Bathing in Classical Antiquity*. New York: Architectural History Foundation; Cambridge and London: MIT Press, 1992.

Yeivin, S. "Historical and Archaeological Notes." In Leroy Waterman, *Preliminary Report of the University of Michigan Excavations at Sepphoris, Palestine, in 1931*, 17–34. Ann Arbor: University of Michigan Press, 1937.

Yeivin, Ze'ev. *The Synagogue at Korazim: The 1962–1964, 1980–1987 Excavations*. Jerusalem: Israel Antiquities Authority, 2000.

Zangenberg, Jürgen. "Magdala – Reich an Fisch und reich durch Fisch." In Gabriele Faßbeck, Sandra Fortner, Andrea Rottloff, and Jürgen Zangenberg, eds., *Leben am See Gennesaret*, 93–98. Mainz am Rhein: Phillip von Zabern, 2003.

Zissu, Boaz and Hanan Eshel. "The Geographical Distribution of Coins from the Bar Kokhba War." *INJ* 14 (2000–2002): 157–167.

Index of passages

RABBINIC SOURCES

M. ABOT

M. AVODAH ZARAH

M. BAVA QAMMA

M. BEKHOROT

M. GITTIN

M. HAGIGAH

M. MAKHSHIRIN

M. SHABBAT

Selective index of places

Index of people and topics

DATE DUE

HIGHSMITH #45230

Printed
in USA